Delaware & New Jersey

D1510836

Published by AAA Publishing
1000 AAA Drive, Heathrow, FL 32746-5063
Copyright AAA 2015, All rights reserved

The publisher has made every effort to provide accurate, up-to-date information but accepts no responsibility for loss or injury sustained by any person using this book. TourBook® guides are published for the exclusive use of AAA members. Not for sale.

Advertising Rate and Circulation Information: (407) 444-8280

Printed in the USA by Quad/Graphics

This book is printed on paper certified by third-party standards for sustainably managed forestry and production.

 Printed on recyclable paper.
Please recycle whenever possible.

Stock #4670

CONTENTS

Attractions, hotels, restaurants and other travel experience information are all grouped under the alphabetical listing of the city in which those experiences are physically located—or the nearest recognized city.

Delaware

New Jersey

■ Atlantic City 72-86

Featured Information

Make the Most of Your Travels

Great vacations start long before you leave home, and
they last long after you return. Savor every moment with
TourBook resources that bring travel to life.

Dream
Picture the possibilities with
visual references that inspire.

Plan
Navigate your way with
vibrant maps you can trust.

Experience
Explore your destination with
expert picks and itineraries.

*Turn the page to
begin your journey.*

A to Z City Listings

Cities and places are listed alphabetically within each state or province. Attractions, hotels and restaurants are listed once — under the city in which they are physically located.

Cities that are considered part of a larger destination city or area have an expanded city header. The header identifies the larger region and cross-references pages that contain shared trip planning resources:

- Destination map – outline map of the cities that comprise a destination city or area
- Attraction spotting map – regional street map marked with attraction locations
- Hotel/restaurant spotting map and index – regional street map numbered with hotel and restaurant locations identified in an accompanying index

Cities that are not considered part of a larger destination city or area but have a significant number of listings may have these resources within the individual city section:

- Attraction spotting map
- Hotel/restaurant spotting map and index

Location Abbreviations

Directions are from the center of town unless otherwise specified, using these highway abbreviations:

Bus. Rte.=business route
CR=county road
FM=farm to market
FR=forest road
Hwy.=Canadian highway
I=interstate highway
LR=legislative route
R.R.=rural route
SR/PR=state or provincial route
US=federal highway

Maps

Use the navigable road maps and accompanying legend in the Atlas Section for route planning. Check the destination maps for general location reference. In select cities only, refer to the mass transit overview maps to cross-reference station names and numbers. For attraction and hotel/restaurant spotting maps, see the legend below to identify symbols and color coding.

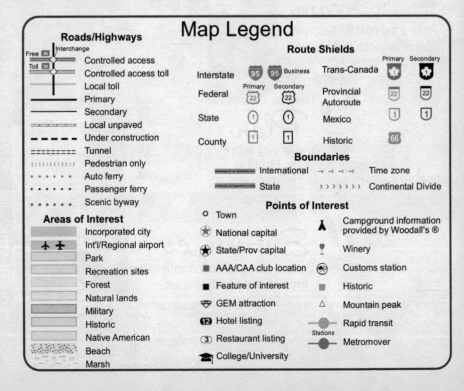

Map Legend

Roads/Highways

Free — Interchange
Toll —
Controlled access
Controlled access toll
Local toll
Primary
Secondary
Local unpaved
Under construction
Tunnel
Pedestrian only
Auto ferry
Passenger ferry
Scenic byway

Areas of Interest

Incorporated city
Int'l/Regional airport
Park
Recreation sites
Forest
Natural lands
Military
Historic
Native American
Beach
Marsh

Route Shields

Interstate · 95 · 95 Business
Federal · Primary 22 · Secondary 22
State · Primary 1 · Secondary 1
County · 1 · 1

Trans-Canada · Primary · Secondary
Provincial Autoroute · 22 · 22
Mexico · 1 · 1
Historic · 66

Boundaries

International
State
Time zone
Continental Divide

Points of Interest

○ Town
⊛ National capital
★ State/Prov capital
■ AAA/CAA club location
■ Feature of interest
GEM attraction
12 Hotel listing
3 Restaurant listing
College/University

X Campground information provided by Woodall's ®
Winery
Customs station
Historic
△ Mountain peak
Rapid transit
Stations
Metromover

About Listed Establishments

AAA/CAA Approved attractions, hotels and restaurants are listed on the basis of merit alone after careful evaluation and approval by full-time, professionally trained AAA/CAA inspectors. An establishment's decision to advertise in the TourBook guide has no bearing on its evaluation or rating; nor does inclusion of advertising imply AAA endorsement of products and services.

Information in this guide was believed accurate at the time of publication. However, since changes inevitably occur between annual editions, please contact your AAA travel professional or visit AAA.com or download the AAA mobile app to confirm prices and schedules.

Attraction Listings

<table>
<tr><td>GEM SAVE ATTRACTION NAME, 3 mi. n.
off SR 20A (Main Ave.), consists of 250 acres with Olmsted-designed gardens, a 205-foot marble and coquina bell tower and a Mediterranean-style mansion. One of the state's oldest attractions, the tower and gardens were dedicated to the American people in 1929 by President Calvin Coolidge on behalf of their founder, a Dutch immigrant.
  Hours: Gardens daily 8-6. Last admission 1 hour before closing. Visitor center daily 9-5. Estate tours are given at noon and 2. Carillon concerts are given at 1 and 3. Phone ahead to confirm schedule. Cost: $10; $3 (ages 5-12). Gardens and estate $16; $8 (ages 5-12). Phone: (555) 555-5555.
  EV GT ⅋ ⚘ 🚇 Dupont Circle,13</td></tr>
</table>

GEM AAA/CAA travel experts may designate an attraction of exceptional interest and quality as a AAA GEM — a *Great Experience for Members®. See GEM Attraction Index (listed on CONTENTS page) for a complete list of locations.*

Consult the online travel guides at AAA.com or visit AAA Mobile for additional things to do if you have time.

Cost

Prices are quoted without sales tax in the local currency (U.S. or Canadian dollars). Children under the lowest age specified are admitted free when accompanied by an adult. Most establishments accept credit cards, but a small number require cash, so please call ahead to verify.

Adventure Travel

Activities such as air tours, hiking, skiing and white-water rafting are listed to provide member information and do not imply AAA/CAA endorsement. For your safety, be aware of inherent risks and adhere to all safety instructions.

Icons

SAVE AAA Discounts & Rewards℠ member discount

EV Electric vehicle charging station on premises. Domestic station information provided by the U.S. Department of Energy. Canadian station information provided by Plug'n Drive Ontario.

GT Guided Tours available

🏕 Camping facilities

🍴 Food on premises

🎯 Recreational activities

🐾 Pets on leash allowed

⛱ Picnicking allowed

In select cities only:

🚇 Mass transit station within 1 mile. Icon is followed by station name and AAA/CAA designated station number within listing.

Information-Only Attraction Listings

Bulleted listings, which include the following categories, are listed for informational purposes as a service to members:

- **Gambling establishments** (even if located in a AAA/CAA Approved hotel)
- **Guided food tours**
- **Participatory recreational activities** (those requiring physical exertion or special skills)
- **Wineries that offer tours and tastings**

Mobile Tags

Scan QR codes throughout the TourBook guide to see online offers, menus, videos and more on your smartphone or tablet. If you need a QR scanner app, download one for free from your app store.

If you see a non-QR code in an ad, check the nearby text for details on which app you'll need to scan it.

Hotel and Restaurant Listings

1 **Diamond Rating** – AAA/CAA Approved hotels and restaurants are assigned a rating of one to five Diamonds. Red Diamonds distinguish establishments that participate in the AAA/CAA logo licensing program. For details, see p. 11 or AAA.com/Diamonds.

fyi indicates hotels and restaurants that are not AAA/CAA Approved and/or Diamond Rated but are listed to provide additional choices for members:

- **Hotels** may be unrated if they are too new to rate, under construction, under major renovation or not evaluated; or if they do not meet all AAA requirements. Hotels that do not meet all AAA requirements may be included if they offer member value or are the only option; details are noted in the listing.
- **Restaurants** may be unrated if they have not yet been evaluated by AAA.

2 **Classification or Cuisine Type** – Noted after the Diamond Rating.

- **Hotel Classifications** indicate the style of operation, overall concept and service level. Subclassifications may also be added. (See p. 12 list.)
- **Restaurant Cuisine Types** identify the food concept from more than 100 categories. If applicable, a classification may also be added. (See p. 13 list.)

3 **Dollar Amounts** – Quoted without sales tax in the local currency (U.S. or Canadian dollars), rounded up to the nearest dollar. Most establishments accept credit cards, but a small number require cash, so please call ahead to verify.

- **Hotel Rates** indicate the publicly available two-person rate or rate range for a standard room, applicable all year.
- **Restaurant Prices** represent the minimum and maximum entrée cost per person. Exceptions may include one-of-a-kind or special market priced items.

4 **Spotting Symbol** – Ovals containing numbers correspond with numbered location markings on hotel and restaurant spotting maps.

5 **Parking** – Unless otherwise noted, parking is free, on-site self parking.

6 **Hotel Value Nationwide** – Blue boxes highlight member benefits available at AAA/CAA Approved locations across a hotel chain. (See Just For Members section for details.)

7 **Hotel Unit Limited Availability** – Unit types, amenities and room features preceded by "some" are available on a limited basis, potentially as few as one.

8 **Hotel Terms** – Cancellation and minimum stay policies are listed. Unless otherwise noted, most properties offer a full deposit refund with cancellations received at least 48 hours before standard check-in. Properties that require advance payment may not refund the difference for early departures. "Resort fee" indicates a charge may apply above and beyond the quoted room rate.

9 **Hotel Check-in/Check-out** – Unless otherwise noted, check-in is after 3 p.m. and check-out is before 10 a.m.

10 **Restaurant Dress Code** – Unless otherwise noted, dress is casual or dressy casual.

11 **Restaurant Menu** – Where indicated, menus may be viewed in a secure online environment at AAA.com or, if a mobile tag is provided, via the restaurant's website.

12 **Hotel Icons** – May be preceded by CALL and/or SOME UNITS.

Member Information:

SAVE Rate guarantee: discounted standard room rate or lowest public rate available at time of booking for dates of stay.

ECO Eco-certified by government or private organization. Visit AAA.com/eco for details.

Electric vehicle charging station on premises. Domestic station information provided by the U.S. Department of Energy. Canadian station information provided by Plug'n Drive Ontario.

Smoke-free premises

In select cities only:

Mass transit station within 1 mile. Icon is followed by station name and AAA/CAA designated station number within listing.

Services:

Airport transportation

Pets allowed (Call property for restrictions.)

Pets allowed (Call property for restrictions and fees.)

Restaurant on premises

Restaurant off premises

Room service for 2 or more meals

Full bar

HOTEL LISTING

RESTAURANT LISTING

⊞ Child care

BIZ Business area

🕭M Accessible features (Call property for available services and amenities.)

Activities:

🎲 Full-service casino

🌊 Pool

💪 Health club on premises

In-Room Amenities:

HS High-speed Internet service

sHS High-speed Internet service (Call property for fees.)

📶 Wireless Internet service

📶 Wireless Internet service (Call property for fees.)

📶 No wireless Internet service

🎬 Pay movies

🗄 Refrigerator

📟 Microwave

💻 Coffee maker

🌡 No air conditioning

📺 No TV

☎ No telephones

---

13 Restaurant Icons

SAVE AAA Discounts & Rewards[SM] member discount

ECO Eco-certified by government or private organization. Visit AAA.com/eco for details.

⚡ Electric vehicle charging station on premises. Domestic station information provided by the U.S. Department of Energy. Canadian station information provided by Plug'n Drive Ontario.

🌡 No air conditioning

🕭M Accessible features (Call property for available services and amenities.)

🚭 Designated smoking section

B Breakfast

L Lunch

D Dinner

24 Open 24 hours

LATE Open after 11 p.m.

🐾 Pet-friendly (Call property for restrictions.)

In select cities only:

🚇 Mass transit station within 1 mile. Icon is followed by station name and AAA/CAA designated station number within listing.

Just For Members

Understanding the Diamond Ratings

Hotel and restaurant evaluations are unscheduled to ensure our professionally trained inspectors encounter the same experience members do.

- When an establishment is Diamond Rated, it means members can expect a good fit with their needs. The inspector assigns a rating that indicates the type of experience to expect.
- While establishments at high levels must offer increasingly complex personalized services, establishments at every level are subject to the same basic requirements for cleanliness, comfort and hospitality. Learn more at AAA.com/Diamonds.

Hotels

Budget-oriented, offering basic comfort and hospitality.

Affordable, with modestly enhanced facilities, décor and amenities.

Distinguished, multifaceted with enhanced physical attributes, amenities and guest comforts.

Refined, stylish with upscale physical attributes, extensive amenities and high degree of hospitality, service and attention to detail.

Ultimate luxury, sophistication and comfort with extraordinary physical attributes, meticulous personalized service, extensive amenities and impeccable standards of excellence.

Restaurants

Simple, familiar specialty food at an economical price. Often self-service, basic surroundings.

Familiar, family-oriented experience. Home-style foods and family favorites, often cooked to order, modestly enhanced and reasonably priced. Relaxed service, casual surroundings.

Fine dining, often adult-oriented. Latest cooking trends and/or traditional cuisine, expanded beverage offerings. Professional service staff and comfortable, well-coordinated ambience.

Distinctive fine-dining, typically expensive. Highly creative chefs, imaginative presentations and fresh, top-quality ingredients. Proficient service staff, upscale surroundings. Wine steward may offer menu-specific knowledge.

Luxurious and consistently world-class. Highly acclaimed chefs, artistic and imaginative menu selections using the finest ingredients. Maitre d' and unobtrusive, expert service staff.

What's the difference?

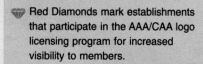 Red Diamonds mark establishments that participate in the AAA/CAA logo licensing program for increased visibility to members.

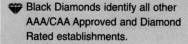 Black Diamonds identify all other AAA/CAA Approved and Diamond Rated establishments.

Hotel Classifications

Quality and comfort are usually consistent across each Diamond Rating level, but décor, facilities and service levels vary by classification.

Berry Manor Inn, Rockland, ME

Bed & Breakfast — Typically owner-operated with a high degree of personal touches. Guests are encouraged to interact during evening and breakfast hours. A continental or full, hot breakfast is included in the room rate.

Killarney Lodge, Algonquin Provincial Park, ON

Cabin — Often located in wooded, rural or waterfront locations. Freestanding units are typically rustic and of basic design. As a rule, essential cleaning supplies, kitchen utensils and complete bed and bath linens are supplied.

Hyatt Regency Clearwater Beach Resort & Spa, Clearwater Beach, FL

Condominium — Apartment-style accommodations of varying design or décor, units often contain one or more bedrooms, a living room, full kitchen and an eating area. As a rule, essential cleaning supplies, kitchen utensils and complete bed and bath linens are supplied.

Montpelier Plantation and Beach, St. Kitts and Nevis

Cottage — Often located in wooded, rural, or waterfront locations. Freestanding units are typically home-style in design and décor. As a rule, essential cleaning supplies, kitchen utensils and complete bed and bath linens are supplied.

Nottoway Plantation & Resort, White Castle, LA

Country Inn — Although similar in definition to a bed and breakfast, country inns are usually larger in scale with spacious public areas and offer a dining facility that serves breakfast and dinner.

The Shores Resort & Spa, Daytona Beach Shores, FL

Hotel — Typically a multistory property with interior room entrances and a variety of guest unit styles. The magnitude of the public areas is determined by the overall theme, location and service level, but may include a variety of facilities such as a restaurant, shops, a fitness center, a spa, a business center and meeting rooms.

Alexander Holiday Homes, Kissimmee, FL

House — Freestanding units of varying home-style design. Typically larger scale, often containing two or more bedrooms, a living room, a full kitchen, a dining room and multiple bathrooms. As a rule, essential cleaning supplies, kitchen utensils and complete bed and bath linens are supplied.

Bryce View Lodge, Bryce Canyon City, UT

Motel — A one- or two-story roadside property with exterior room entrances and drive up parking. Public areas and facilities are often limited in size and/or availability.

Ranch — Typically a working ranch featuring an obvious rustic, Western theme, equestrian-related activities and a variety of guest unit styles.

Vista Verde Guest Ranch, Clark, CO

Hotel Subclassifications

These additional descriptives may be added to the classification for more information:

- **Boutique** — Often thematic, typically informal yet highly personalized; may have a luxurious or quirky style that is fashionable or unique.

- **Casino** — Extensive gambling facilities are available, such as blackjack, craps, keno and slot machines.

- **Classic** — Renowned and landmark properties, older than 50 years, well known for their unique style and ambience.

- **Contemporary** — Overall theme reflects characteristics of present mainstream trends.

- **Extended Stay** — Offers a predominance of long-term accommodations with a designated full-service kitchen area within each unit.

- **Historic** — More than 75 years old with one of the following documented historical features: Maintains the integrity of the historical nature, listed on the National Register of Historic Places, designated a National Historic Landmark or located in a National Register Historic District.

- **Resort** — Extensive recreational facilities and programs may include golf, tennis, skiing, fishing, water sports, spa treatments or professionally guided activities.

- **Retro** — Overall theme reflects a contemporary design that reinterprets styles from a past era.

- **Vacation Rental** — Typically houses, condos, cottages or cabins; these properties are "home away from home" self-catering accommodations.

- **Vintage** — Overall theme reflects upon and maintains the authentic traits and experience of a past era.

Service Animals

Under the Americans with Disabilities Act (ADA), U.S. businesses that serve the public must allow people with disabilities to bring their service animals into all areas of the facility where customers are normally allowed to go.

Businesses may ask if an animal is a service animal and what tasks the animal has been trained to perform. Businesses may not ask about the person's disability, require special identification for the animal or request removal of the animal from the premises except in limited cases that require alternate assistance. Businesses may not charge extra fees for service animals, including standard pet fees, but may charge for damage caused by service animals if guests are normally charged for damage they cause.

Call the U.S. Department of Justice ADA Information Line: (800) 514-0301 or TTY (800) 514-0383, or visit ada.gov. Regulations may differ in Canada.

Restaurant Classifications

If applicable, in addition to the cuisine type noted under the Diamond Rating, restaurant listings may also include one or both classifications:

- **Classic** — Renowned and landmark operation in business for 25 plus years; unique style and ambience.

- **Historic** — Meets one of the following: Listed on National Register of Historic Places, designated a National Historic Landmark or located in a National Register Historic District.

AAA/CAA Approved Hotels

For members, AAA/CAA Approved means quality assured.

- Only properties that meet basic requirements for cleanliness, comfort and hospitality pass inspection.
- Approved hotels receive a Diamond Rating that tells members the type of experience to expect.

Guest Safety

Inspectors view a sampling of rooms during evaluations and, therefore, AAA/CAA cannot guarantee the presence of working locks and operational fire safety equipment in every guest unit.

Member Rates

AAA/CAA members can generally expect to pay no more than the maximum TourBook listed rate for a standard room. Member discounts apply to rates quoted within the rate range and are applicable at the time of booking. Listed rates are usually based on last standard room availability. Within the range, rates may vary by season and room type. Obtain current AAA/CAA member rates and make reservations at AAA.com.

Exceptions

- Rates for properties operating as concessionaires for the U.S. National Park Service are not guaranteed due to governing regulations.
- Special advertised rates and short-term promotional rates below the rate range are not subject to additional member discounts.
- During special events, hotels may temporarily increase room rates, not recognize discounts or modify pricing policies. Special events may include Mardi Gras, the Kentucky Derby (including pre-Derby events), college football games, holidays, holiday periods and state fairs. Although some special events are listed in the TourBook guides and on AAA.com, it's always wise to check in advance with AAA travel professionals for specific dates.

If you are charged more than the maximum TourBook listed rate, question the additional charge. If an exception is not in effect and management refuses to adhere to the published rate, pay for the room and contact AAA/CAA. The amount paid above the stated maximum will be refunded if our investigation indicates an unjustified charge.

Reservations and Cancellations

When making your reservation, identify yourself as a AAA/CAA member and request written confirmation of your room type, rate, dates of stay, and cancellation and refund policies. At registration, show your membership card.

To cancel, contact the hotel, your AAA/CAA club office or AAA.com, depending on how you booked your reservation. Request a cancellation number or proof of cancellation.

If your room is not as specified and you have written confirmation of your reservation for a specific room type, you should be given the option of choosing a different room or receiving a refund. If management refuses to issue a refund, contact AAA/CAA.

Contacting AAA/CAA About Approved Properties

If your visit to a AAA/CAA Approved attraction, hotel or restaurant doesn't meet your expectations, please tell us about it — **during your visit or within 30 days**. Be sure to save your receipts and other documentation for reference.

Use the easy online form at AAA.com/TourBookComments to send us the details.

Alternatively, you can email your comments to: memberrelations@national.aaa.com or submit them via postal mail to: AAA Member Comments, 1000 AAA Dr., Box 61, Heathrow, FL 32746.

AAA/CAA Preferred Hotels

All AAA/CAA Approved hotels are committed to providing quality, value and member service. In addition, those designated as AAA/CAA Preferred Hotels also offer these extra values at Approved locations nationwide. Valid AAA/CAA membership required.

- **Best AAA/CAA member rates for your dates of stay.**
- **Seasonal promotions and special member offers.** Visit AAA.com to view current offers.
- **Member benefit.** See the blue boxes in hotel listings for the chains shown in the right-hand column below to find values offered at AAA/CAA Approved locations nationwide, subject to availability. Details valid at the time of publication and may change without notice.

- **Total satisfaction guarantee.** If you book your stay with AAA/CAA Travel and your stay fails to meet your expectations, you can apply for a full refund. Bring the complaint to the hotel's attention during the stay and request resolution; if the complaint is not resolved by the hotel, ask your AAA/CAA travel agent to request resolution through the AAA/CAA Assured Stay program.

	Best Western, Best Western Plus and Best Western Premier
HILTON WORLDWIDE	Hilton Hotels & Resorts, Waldorf Astoria Hotels & Resorts, Conrad Hotels & Resorts, Curio - A Collection by Hilton, DoubleTree, Embassy Suites Hotels, Hilton Garden Inn, Hampton Hotels, Homewood Suites, Home2 Suites and Hilton Grand Vacations
	Park Hyatt, Andaz, Grand Hyatt, Hyatt Regency, Hyatt, Hyatt Place and Hyatt House
	The Ritz-Carlton, Gaylord Hotels, JW Marriott Hotels, EDITION, Autograph Collection Hotels, Renaissance Hotels, AC Hotels, Marriott Hotels & Resorts, Courtyard, SpringHill Suites, Fairfield Inn & Suites, Residence Inn, and TownePlace Suites
	Aloft, Element, Four Points, Le Meridien, Sheraton, St. Regis, Westin, W Hotels and The Luxury Collection

Member Discounts

Visit AAA.com/searchfordiscounts to find locations and available member discounts. Your AAA/CAA club may offer even greater discounts on theme park tickets. Amtrak and theme park discounts may be used for up to six tickets; restaurant savings may be used for up to six patrons. Other restrictions may apply. All offers subject to change. For complete restrictions, visit your AAA office or AAA.com/restrictions.

ATTRACTIONS

SeaWorld, Busch Gardens, Sesame Place

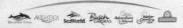

- Save on admission at the gate, participating AAA/CAA offices or AAA.com/SeaWorld.
- Save 10% on up-close dining; visit Guest Relations for details.

Six Flags

- Save on admission at the gate, participating AAA/CAA offices or AAA.com/SixFlags.
- Save 10% on merchandise of $15 or more at in-park stores.

Universal Orlando Resort and Universal Studios Hollywood

- Save on tickets at select AAA/CAA offices or AAA.com/Universal. In-park savings available in FL.
- Save on Blue Man Group tickets and at select food and merchandise venues at Universal CityWalk®.

DINING

Hard Rock Cafe

- Save 10% on food, nonalcoholic beverages and merchandise at all locations in the U.S. and Canada and select international locations.

Landry's Seafood House, The Crab House, Chart House, Oceanaire, Saltgrass Steak House, Muer Seafood Restaurants and Aquarium Restaurants

- Save 10% on food and nonalcoholic beverages at all of the above restaurants.
- Save 10% on merchandise at Aquarium, Downtown Aquarium and Rainforest Cafe restaurants.

SHOPPING

Banana Republic Factory Store

- Save 10% on all purchases, including sale merchandise.

BANANA REPUBLIC
FACTORY STORE

Gap Outlet/Gap Factory Store

- Save 10% on all purchases, including sale merchandise.

Reebok/Rockport Outlet

- Save 20% on the entire purchase.

Tanger Outlet Centers

- Receive a free coupon book with discounts up to 20% at select merchants.

Tanger Outlets

TRANSPORTATION

Amtrak

- Save 10% on rail fare booked at least three days in advance of travel date at AAA.com/Amtrak.

AMTRAK

El Monte RV

- Save up to 10% on nightly rates booked at least 24 hours in advance of pickup at AAA.com/ElMonteRV or (800) 337-2156.

EL MONTE RV
RENTALS • SALES

Hertz

- Save on daily, weekend, weekly and monthly rentals at AAA.com/Hertz or (800) 654-3080.

RACK UP THE REWARDS

Make membership an even more rewarding experience.

Here at AAA, we believe that financial rewards and benefits are what our members have come to expect. The AAA Member Rewards Visa® credit card lets you earn reward points on all of your purchases. Open an account today and let the rewards start rolling in!

✓ Earn 1 point for every $1 in purchases with your AAA Member Rewards Visa® card!*

✓ Earn double points for gas, grocery and drug store purchases!

✓ Earn triple points on qualifying AAA and travel purchases!

✓ Redeem for a AAA Voucher that gives you up to 40% more value than cash back!**

✓ Exclusive rewards to make you smile!

VISIT AAA.com/creditcard   **STOP BY** any AAA branch

Warm colors reflect in Lums Pond, Bear

One way to acquaint yourself with Delaware is to rely on its oldest "residents." Restored houses and taverns, abandoned mills, groomed village greens and meticulous gardens sprinkle the state, silently declaring their chapter in history.

Gingerbread does not go stale in Laurel; about 800 colorful Victorian houses appear much as they did in the 18th and 19th centuries.

Erected in 1638, the first log cabin sits proudly in Wilmington.

The granite, pentagon-shaped fortress of Fort Delaware looms on Pea Patch Island. Woodburn, the Dover governor's mansion since 1965, was reputed to have been a station on the Underground Railroad. And the Amish way of life is alive and well near Dover—the clop of horses' hooves echoes along modern, blacktop roads.

Fort Delaware State Park, Delaware City

Delaware

Ghosts of noteworthy residents are omnipresent. Thomas McKean, a delegate to the Continental Congress of 1774, practiced law in New Castle. John Dickinson, the Penman of the American Revolution who wrote the Articles of Confederation and documents protesting British rule, lived in Dover. And the Robinson House in Wilmington served as a home for George Washington during the Revolutionary War.

In New Castle, cobblestone roads dating from Colonial days serve as a path to the past. Dwellings that line the streets bear diverse architectural styles, mirroring the melting pot of cultures that has called the town home. The colors of Great Britain, the Netherlands, Sweden and the United States flap in the breeze over the Georgian-style courthouse, representing four changes in ownership.

Which George is it?

History oozes out of every blade of grass on The Green in Dover. The square is a spitting image of its original platting in 1722. During the Revolutionary War, the tract served as a meeting place for Delaware's Continental Regiment; they mustered here in 1775 and set out on a march to join Washington's army in the fight for independence. Blue hen chickens, noted for their pugnacious nature, waddled along to fight with the men.

One year later: The Declaration of Independence is read aloud to crowds gathered on The Green. Their enthusiasm shows in the shouts of "Freedom!" and the torching of King George III's portrait. Near The Green, a tavern now known as the Kent County Court House upheld the same independent spirit—locals maintain that it sported a sign showing the shoulders of the "Old George" and a face painted over with the likeness of the "New George."

And overlooking the square was the Golden Fleece Tavern, where, on a chilly December day in 1787, delegates to Delaware's Constitutional Congress took a deep breath and voted to ratify the Constitution, making Delaware the first state to do so. A bronze plaque commemorates the site.

Going Dutch

Coined the "first town in the first state," the harbor port of Lewes was settled by the Dutch in 1631. To commemorate its 300th anniversary, residents erected the Zwaanendael building; the elaborate stonework and ornamental gable are copies of similar features adorning a town hall in Holland.

Among brightly painted Victorian homes in Lewes stands one near-casualty of war, the cedar-shingled Cannonball House. Why the name? You guessed it—during a British bombardment in the War of 1812, a cannonball was fired at the house and lodged into the wall, becoming a permanent part of the structure. Fortunately, the naval attack resulted only in the death of a chicken and the wounding of a pig.

Through careful preservation of original architecture and landscaping, Delaware history and culture remain vital. The physical appearance of many sites, coupled with the tradition they embrace, makes for a fascinating story.

Recreation

About 25 miles of coastline add up to excitement. Colorful windsurfing sails dot the shallow bays at Delaware Seashore State Park in Rehoboth Beach. Salty breezes cater to sailing, and boaters can explore numerous coves. Delaware Bay is another great place where first mates can cast off.

Picture yourself casually paddling amid wildflowers, lily pads and stands of bald cypress trees. It isn't paradise, just the designated wilderness canoe trail at Trap Pond State Park. If a wilder ride is more your style, tube down Brandywine Creek in Wilmington.

The lure of the rod and reel is difficult to resist in Delaware. Fishing in Killens Pond State Park hooks bluegill, catfish, carp, crappie, largemouth bass, perch and pickerel. Brandywine Creek and Trap Pond state parks also attract anglers. Two piers make for pleasant casting at Lums Pond, where ice fishing is an option in winter.

Make some new winged acquaintances while bird-watching. Grab your binoculars and climb to the top of the refurbished World War II observation tower at Cape Henlopen State Park in Rehoboth Beach for a 360-degree bird's-eye view; at Gordon's Pond, bird lovers can see osprey, as well as the endangered piping plover and American bald eagle. The dunes at Fenwick Island State Park also are home to several species of endangered seabirds.

Follow the trails on Burton's Island in Delaware Seashore State Park for a peek at noisy gulls and terns nesting in the salt marshes. Also be sure to check out the Bombay Hook National Wildlife Refuge in Smyrna; it's a habitat for migrating and wintering ducks and northbound migrating geese. The marshes of Fort Delaware State Park provide a summer home for nine species of egrets, herons and ibis.

Bombay Hook National Wildlife Refuge, Smyrna

Historic Timeline

1609	Henry Hudson claims the territory for the Dutch; he finds the area inhabited by Lenni Lenape Indians.
1631	Inhabitants of the first European settlement are massacred by Indians.
1638	Swedes establish New Sweden colony, the Delaware Valley's first permanent settlement, under Dutchman Peter Minuit's leadership.
1664	Delaware falls under British rule.
1682	William Penn arrives in New Castle and takes possession of Delaware.
1776	Delaware's Caesar Rodney casts the deciding vote for the Declaration of Independence.
1777	John Dickinson, Penman of the American Revolution, drafts the Articles of Confederation.
1787	Delaware becomes the first state to ratify the U.S. Constitution.
1986	Salvagers retrieve the hull of the sunken HMS *DeBraak* off the coast of Lewes.
2001	Ruth Ann Minner takes office as Delaware's first female governor.
2009	Joseph Biden, a six-term U.S. senator from Delaware, is sworn in as vice president of the United States.

What To Pack

Temperature Averages
Maximum/Minimum

	JANUARY	FEBRUARY	MARCH	APRIL	MAY	JUNE	JULY	AUGUST	SEPTEMBER	OCTOBER	NOVEMBER	DECEMBER
Dover	44/27	47/29	55/36	65/44	75/54	83/63	87/68	85/67	80/60	69/48	59/40	48/31
Harrington	42/24	44/24	54/33	63/41	73/51	81/60	86/66	84/64	77/56	67/45	57/36	47/28
Lewes	45/28	47/30	55/36	65/44	74/54	82/63	86/68	85/67	79/62	69/50	59/41	50/33
New Castle	39/24	43/26	52/33	63/42	72/52	81/62	86/67	84/66	77/58	66/46	55/37	44/28
Odessa	41/24	45/26	55/33	65/42	75/52	83/61	87/65	86/64	80/57	68/45	57/37	46/29
Wilmington	41/24	45/26	55/33	65/42	75/52	83/61	87/65	86/64	80/57	68/45	57/37	46/29

From the records of The Weather Channel Interactive, Inc.

Good Facts To Know

ABOUT THE STATE

POPULATION: 897,934.

AREA: 1,982 square miles; ranks 49th.

CAPITAL: Dover.

HIGHEST POINT: 448 ft., near Ebright Road, Brandywine.

LOWEST POINT: Sea level, Atlantic Ocean.

TIME ZONE(S): Eastern. DST.

GAMBLING

MINIMUM AGE FOR GAMBLING: 21.

REGULATIONS

TEEN DRIVING LAWS: No more than one unrelated passenger is permitted. Driving is not permitted 10 p.m.-6 a.m. (exceptions for work and school-related activities). The minimum age for an unrestricted driver's license is 17. Phone (302) 744-2500 for more information about Delaware driver's license regulations.

SEAT BELT/CHILD RESTRAINT LAWS: Seat belts are required for driver and all passengers 16 and older. Children ages 8-16 or over 65 pounds are required to be in a child restraint or seat belt; child restraints are required for children under age 8 and 65 pounds or less.

CELL PHONE RESTRICTIONS: Text messaging and the use of handheld cell phones are banned. Teenage drivers operating with a learner's permit or an intermediate license may not use a cell phone (even if it is hands-free) while driving.

HELMETS FOR MOTORCYCLISTS: Required for riders under 19.

RADAR DETECTORS: Permitted.

MOVE OVER LAW: Driver is required to slow down and vacate the lane nearest stopped police, fire and rescue vehicles as well as tow trucks when those vehicles are using audible or flashing signals.

FIREARMS LAWS: Contact the Delaware State Police, Ordnance Section, 391 Clark Farm Rd. Smyrna, DE 19977; phone (302) 659-6020.

HOLIDAYS

HOLIDAYS: Jan. 1 ▪ Martin Luther King Jr. Day, Jan. (3rd Mon.) ▪ Good Friday ▪ Memorial Day, May (last Mon.) ▪ July 4 ▪ Labor Day, Sept. (1st Mon.) ▪ Veterans Day, Nov. 11 ▪ Election Day, Nov. (1st Tues. following 1st Mon.) ▪ Thanksgiving, Nov. (4th Thurs.) ▪ day after Thanksgiving, Nov. (4th Fri.) ▪ Christmas, Dec. 25.

MONEY

TAXES: Delaware does not have a statewide sales tax, but there is an 8 percent hotel occupancy tax (10 percent in the city of Wilmington).

VISITOR INFORMATION

INFORMATION CENTERS: State welcome centers that provide details about state attractions, accommodations, historic sites, parks and events are on I-95 between exit 1 and exit 3 on the edge of Newark, phone (302) 737-4059 ▪ and at the junction of US 13 and SR 1 north of Smyrna, exit 19A, phone (302) 653-8910. The I-95 center is open daily 8-8 (closed Christmas). The US 13 center is open Mon.-Fri. 7-5, Fri.-Sun. 7-7, Memorial Day-Labor Day, and daily 7-5, rest of year.

FURTHER INFORMATION FOR VISITORS:
Delaware Tourism Office
99 Kings Hwy.
Dover, DE 19901
(866) 284-7483

FISHING AND HUNTING REGULATIONS:
Delaware Division of Fish and Wildlife
89 Kings Hwy.
Dover, DE 19901
(302) 739-9910

RECREATION INFORMATION:
Delaware Division of Parks and Recreation
89 Kings Hwy.
Dover, DE 19901
(302) 739-9220

Access trusted AAA/CAA services on the go with the AAA and CAA Mobile apps

Delaware Annual Events

Please call ahead to confirm event details.

JANUARY

- Yuletide at Winterthur
  Winterthur
  302-888-4600
- Leo Brady Exercise Like the
  Eskimos / Bethany Beach
  302-539-2100
- MLK Day of Celebration
  Seaford
  302-628-1908

FEBRUARY

- Victorine's Valentine's Day
  Wilmington
  302-658-2400
- Polar Bear Plunge
  Rehoboth Beach
  302-831-4653
- African-American History
  Month / Dover
  302-739-3277

MARCH

- Chocolate Festival
  Rehoboth Beach
  302-227-2772
- St. Patrick's Day Parade
  Dover
  302-678-2940
- Wilmington Winter
  Bluegrass / Claymont
  302-792-2700

APRIL

- Tulip Festival / Lewes
  302-645-8073
- Colonists' Day / Wilmington
  302-420-0464
- Ag Day / Newark
  302-831-2501

MAY

- Horseshoe Crab and
  Shorebird Festival / Milton
  302-684-1101
- Dover Days Festival / Dover
  302-734-1736
- A Day in Old New Castle
  New Castle
  302-322-5774

JUNE

- Clifford Brown Jazz
  Festival / Wilmington
  302-576-2139
- Kids Fest / Harrington
  302-422-4453
- St. Anthony of Padua
  Italian Festival / Wilmington
  302-421-3790

JULY

- Liberty Day Celebration
  Newark
  302-366-7060
- Delaware State Fair
  Harrington
  302-398-3269
- Nanticoke Riverfest
  Seaford
  302-629-9173

AUGUST

- Riverfront Blues Festival
  Wilmington
  302-576-2139
- Bargains on the Broadkill
  and the Great Duck Race
  Milton
  302-684-1101
- Lewes Antiques Show
  Lewes
  302-645-7670

SEPTEMBER

- Oktoberfest / Newark
  302-366-9454
- Brandywine Festival of the
  Arts / Wilmington
  302-690-5555
- Nanticoke Indian Powwow
  Millsboro
  302-945-3400

OCTOBER

- Sea Witch Festival
  Rehoboth Beach
  800-441-1329
- Rehoboth Beach Jazz
  Festival / Rehoboth Beach
  302-856-1818
- Boast the Coast Maritime
  Festival / Lewes
  302-645-8073

NOVEMBER

- Christmas at Hagley
  Wilmington
  302-658-2400
- World Championship
  Punkin' Chunkin'
  Bridgeville
  302-684-8196
- Holiday Tree Lighting and
  Hometown Sing-a-Long
  Rehoboth Beach
  302-227-2772

DECEMBER

- Christmas Parade / Lewes
  302-645-8073
- Victorian Christmas at
  Ross Mansion / Seaford
  302-628-9828
- Sankta Lucia Celebration
  Wilmington
  302-652-5629

Delaware state quarter

Explore Dutch history at Zwaanendael Museum, Lewes

World War II observation tower, Cape Henlopen State Park

Legislative Hall, Dover

A couple enjoy the sunrise, Bethany Beach

Index: Great Experience for Members

AAA editor's picks of exceptional note

 Biggs Museum of American Art

 Hagley Museum and Library

 Nemours Mansion and Gardens

 Winterthur Museum, Garden & Library

See Orientation map on p. 28 for corresponding grid coordinates, if applicable.

Dover (D-2)
Biggs Museum of American Art *(See p. 33.)*

Wilmington (B-2)
Hagley Museum and Library *(See p. 50.)*

Nemours Mansion and Gardens
(See p. 51.)

Winterthur Museum, Garden & Library
(See p. 51.)

Take Your Imagination to New Destinations

Use AAA Travel Guides online to explore the possibilities.

 Go to AAA.com/travelguide today.

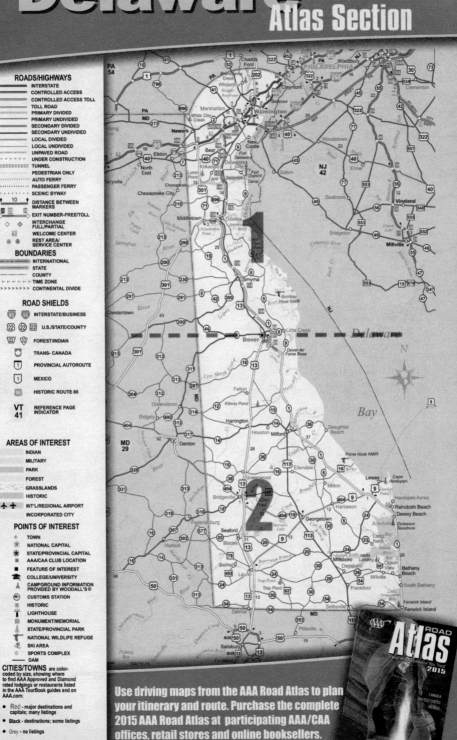

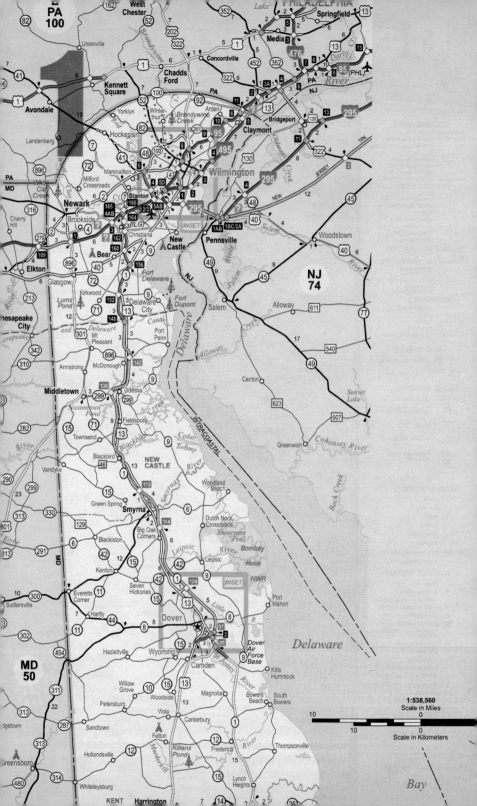

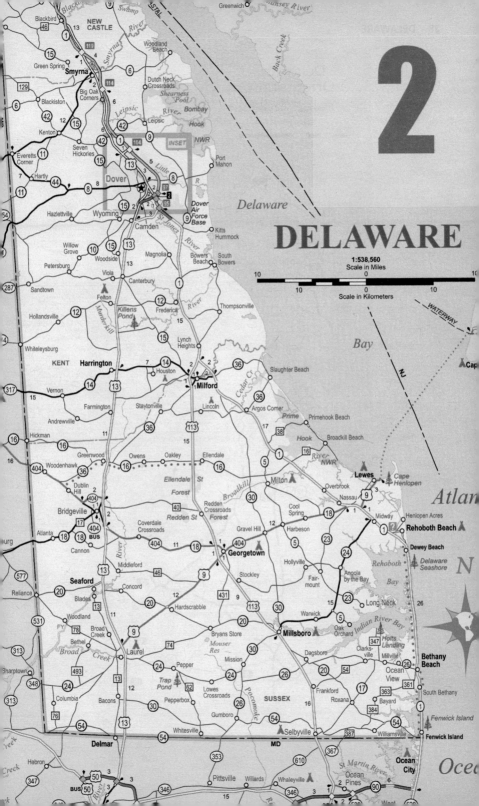

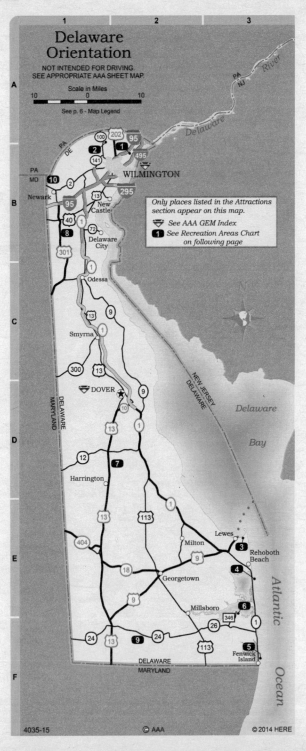

Delaware
Orientation

NOT INTENDED FOR DRIVING.
SEE APPROPRIATE AAA SHEET MAP.

Scale in Miles

See p. 6 - Map Legend

Only places listed in the Attractions
section appear on this map.
See AAA GEM Index
See Recreation Areas Chart
on following page

WILMINGTON

Newark

New
Castle

Delaware
City

Odessa

Smyrna

DOVER

Harrington

Milton

Lewes

Rehoboth
Beach

Georgetown

Millsboro

Fenwick
Island

DELAWARE
MARYLAND

PA
DE

PA
MD

DELAWARE
MARYLAND

NEW JERSEY
DELAWARE

Delaware River

Delaware

Bay

Atlantic

Ocean

4035-15   © AAA   © 2014 HERE

Recreation Areas Chart

The map location numerals in column 2 show an area's location on the preceding map.

	MAP LOCATION	CAMPING	PICNICKING	HIKING TRAILS	BOATING	BOAT RAMP	BOAT RENTAL	FISHING	SWIMMING	PETS ON LEASH	BICYCLE TRAILS	WINTER SPORTS	VISITOR CENTER	LODGE/CABINS	FOOD SERVICE
STATE															
Bellevue (B-2) 329 acres 4 mi. n.e. of Wilmington off I-95. Historic. Tennis; fitness track, horse trails.	1		•	•				•		•	•	•			
Brandywine Creek (B-1) 1,010 acres 9 mi. n.w. of Wilmington at jct. SRs 92 and 100 and Adams Dam Rd. Canoeing, hunting; horse trails. Non-motorized boats only.	2		•	•	•			•		•	•	•	•		
Cape Henlopen (E-3) 6,000 acres 1 mi. e. of Lewes on SR 9. Historic. Hunting, disc golf (18 holes); bathhouse, nature trails. *(See Rehoboth Beach p. 44.)*	3	•	•	•				•	•	•	•		•	•	•
Delaware Seashore (E-3) 2,799 acres 5 mi. from Dewey Beach to Indian River Inlet off SR 1. Hunting, sailing, windsurfing; bathhouse, horse trails, marina. *(See Rehoboth Beach p. 44)*	4	•	•	•	•	•	•	•	•	•			•	•	•
Fenwick Island (F-3) 442 acres extending from South Bethany Beach to Fenwick Island off SR 1. Surfing; bathhouse.	5		•					•	•	•	•				
Holts Landing (E-3) 203 acres 9 mi. n.e. of Dagsboro off SR 26 on the s. shore of the Indian River Bay. Hunting; horse trails.	6	•	•	•	•			•		•					
Killens Pond (D-2) 1,098 acres 12 mi. s. of Dover off US 13. Historic. Canoeing, disc golf (18 holes); game courts, nature trails.	7	•	•	•	•	•	•	•	•	•	•			•	
Lums Pond (B-1) 2,091 acres 10 mi. s. of Newark off SR 71. Historic. Hunting; game courts, horse trails, nature trails.	8	•	•	•	•	•		•	•	•	•	•	•		
Trap Pond (F-2) 2,689 acres 6 mi. s.e. of Laurel off SR 24. Bird-watching, hunting, kayaking; horse trails, nature trails.	9	•	•	•	•	•	•	•		•	•		•	•	
White Clay Creek (B-1) 3,600 acres 3 mi. n. of Newark via SR 896. Historic. Disc golf, hunting; fitness trails.	10		•	•				•		•	•	•			

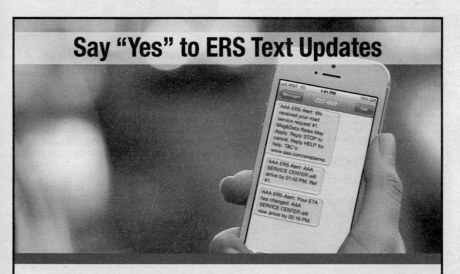

BEAR   pop. 19,371

BEST WESTERN PLUS NEWARK/CHRISTIANA INN
(302)326-2500

Hotel
$110-$160

AAA Benefit:
Members save up to 20%!

Address: 875 Pulaski Hwy 19701 **Location:** I-95 exit 4, 3.3 mi se on SR 1 exit 160, then just e on US 40. **Facility:** 75 units. 3 stories, interior corridors. **Amenities:** safes. **Pool(s):** heated indoor. **Activities:** hot tub, exercise room. **Guest Services:** valet and coin laundry.

/ SOME UNITS

BETHANY BEACH   pop. 1,060

HOLIDAY INN EXPRESS BETHANY BEACH
302/541-9200

Hotel. Rates not provided. **Address:** 39642 Jefferson Bridge Rd 19930 **Location:** On SR 1, 0.5 mi s of jct SR 26. **Facility:** 100 units. 4 stories, interior corridors. **Pool(s):** outdoor. **Activities:** exercise room. **Guest Services:** coin laundry.

WHERE TO EAT

BETHANY BLUES BBQ   302/537-1500

Barbecue. Casual Dining. $10-$30 **AAA Inspector Notes:** For those at the beach and in the mood for barbecue, this spot has it all. A family-friendly setting and consistently good service make this a popular spot with both locals and tourists. Barbecue is the specialty, with St. Louis and baby back ribs, chicken, pulled pork, sausage and beef brisket. In addition to the barbecue selections, steaks and seafood dishes are also available. **Features:** full bar. **Address:** 6 N Pennsylvania Ave 19930 **Location:** Jct SR 1 and 26, just e. **Parking:** street only. D

BLUE COAST SEAFOOD GRILL   302/539-7111

Seafood. Casual Dining. $21-$32 **AAA Inspector Notes:** The specialty here is fresh fish. The setting is natural with water views from the comfortable dining room. The kitchen uses fresh ingredients, local when available, in preparing simple yet flavorful dishes. **Features:** full bar, patio dining. **Address:** 1111 Hwy One 19930 **Location:** On SR 1, 1.4 mi n of jct SR 26. D CALL

THE COTTAGE CAFE RESTAURANT & PUB   302/539-8710

American. Casual Dining. $6-$29 **AAA Inspector Notes:** Traditional American cuisine is served in a casual, comfortable dining ambience. The staff is friendly and helpful, the atmosphere is suitable for families and the menu includes chicken, beef, seafood and pasta. In the summer months a buffet is served on weekends. **Features:** full bar, patio dining, Sunday brunch, happy hour. **Address:** 33034 Coastal Hwy 19930 **Location:** On SR 1, 0.7 mi s of jct SR 26. L D

SEDONA   302/539-1200

American Fine Dining $24-$36

AAA Inspector Notes: At this stylish little restaurant, creative American cuisine is exemplified by tapas specialties and full-size entrées. The owner is warm, welcoming and seems to know almost everyone. Reservations are highly recommended. Phone for off-season hours. **Features:** full bar. **Reservations:** suggested. **Address:** 26 Pennsylvania Ave 19930 **Location:** Just e of jct SR 1 and Garfield Ave. **Parking:** street only. *Menu on AAA.com* D

CLAYMONT   pop. 8,253

CROWNE PLAZA WILMINGTON NORTH
302/792-2700

Hotel
Rates not provided

Address: 630 Naamans Rd 19703 **Location:** I-95 exit 11, just w on SR 92; I-495 exit 6 (Naamans Rd). **Facility:** 189 units. 8 stories, interior corridors. **Pool(s):** outdoor. **Activities:** exercise room. **Guest Services:** valet and coin laundry, area transportation.

/ SOME UNITS

DELAWARE CITY   (B-1) pop. 1,695, elev. 4'

A river wharf occupied the site of Delaware City for the quarter century following 1800. In 1814 the Department of the Navy allowed the construction of a battery and fortifications on the Delaware River at what was then called Newbold's Point. Around 1825 streets were laid out at the junction of the Delaware River and the Chesapeake and Delaware Canal, which was being dug across the peninsula.

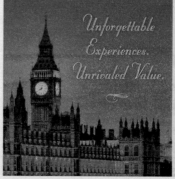

BAHA MAR

WELCOME TO THE NEW RIVIERA

THE BAHAMIAN RIVIERA AWAITS. Introducing a glamorous new playground with the world's most celebrated hotels, including the dazzling debut of the Baha Mar Casino & Hotel. Get ready for the rendezvous of the century in Nassau, The Bahamas. For an exclusive preview, visit BahaMar.com | 844.800.BAHA

BAHA MAR CASINO & HOTEL | ROSEWOOD | SLS LUX | GRAND HYATT

By the time the canal opened in 1829, however, railroads were handling most of the freight the canal had been built to ship. Delaware City's wide streets and grand name thus became reminders of a boom that never came.

The fortifications are gone from Newbold's Point, but Battery Park remains, offering a view of the river, Pea Patch Island and the New Jersey shoreline from the foot of Clinton Street. In the park is a restored Chesapeake and Delaware Canal lock built in 1829.

FORT DELAWARE STATE PARK is on Pea Patch Island. The park is accessible only by a ferry that departs from 45 Clinton St. The 288-acre park features an 1859 fort, costumed interpreters portraying 19th-century island soldiers and residents, nature trails and an observation tower that provides views of nesting spots for egrets, herons and other wading birds.

Private boats are not permitted in the park. Picnic tables and grills are available. **Time:** Allow 4 hours minimum. **Hours:** Wed.-Sun. and holidays 9:30-6, mid-June through Labor Day; Sat. 9:30-6 in May. Ferries depart at 10, 11, 11:30, noon, 1, 1:30, 2 and 3 (also at 3:30, 4 and 5 on Sat., Sun. and holidays). Phone ahead to confirm schedule. **Cost:** (includes ferry fare) $11; $10 (ages 62+ and military with ID); $6 (ages 2-12). **Phone:** (302) 834-7941.

DEWEY BEACH pop. 341

BEACH HOUSE DEWEY   302/227-4000
Motel. Rates not provided. **Address:** 1710 Hwy 1 19971 **Location:** Jct SR 1 and Dagsworthy St; center. **Facility:** 47 units. 3 stories (no elevator), exterior corridors. **Pool(s):** outdoor. **Activities:** beach access.

BEST WESTERN GOLD LEAF   (302)226-1100

Hotel
$85-$330

AAA Benefit: Members save up to 20%!

Address: 1400 Coastal Hwy 19971 **Location:** Jct SR 1 and Rodney St; center. **Facility:** 76 units. 4 stories, interior corridors. **Terms:** check-in 4 pm, 2 night minimum stay - seasonal, 7 day cancellation notice. **Amenities:** safes. **Pool(s):** outdoor. **Activities:** beach access, exercise room. **Guest Services:** coin laundry.

HYATT PLACE DEWEY BEACH   (302)864-9100

Hotel
$99-$359

HYATT PLACE

AAA Benefit: Members save 10%!

Address: 1301 Coastal Hwy 19971 **Location:** On SR 1; center. **Facility:** 108 units. 3 stories, interior corridors. **Amenities:** safes. **Pool(s):** heated indoor. **Activities:** beach access, exercise room. **Guest Services:** coin laundry. **Featured Amenity:** breakfast buffet. *(See ad this page.)*

/ SOME UNITS

THE SURF CLUB HOTEL   302/227-7059
Extended Stay Hotel $69-$269 **Address:** 1 Read St 19971 **Location:** Oceanfront. Just e of SR 1; center. **Facility:** 49 efficiencies, some houses. 4 stories (no elevator), exterior corridors. **Terms:** 2-3 night minimum stay - seasonal and/or weekends, 7 day cancellation notice-fee imposed. **Pool(s):** outdoor. **Activities:** sauna, hot tub. **Guest Services:** coin laundry.

▼ *See AAA listing this page* ▼

WHERE TO EAT

NALU SURF BAR & GRILLE   302/227-1449

♦♦ ♦♦ Hawaiian. Casual Dining. $6-$23 **AAA Inspector Notes:** Although popular for its generous early-afternoon happy hour and weekend DJs, the restaurant also is a great source for inexpensive eats. Casual fare including burgers, tacos and dogs is prepared with a Hawaiian twist. (Spam is available as a topping on almost any dish.) Kitschy tiki posts and a bamboo thatched bar lend to the mood. **Features:** full bar. **Address:** 1308 Coastal Hwy 19971 **Location:** Jct Dickinson Ave. **Parking:** on-site (fee). L D LATE CALL 🅼

PORT   302/227-0669

♦♦ ♦♦ Seafood. Casual Dining. $17-$27 **AAA Inspector Notes:** This small spot has a casual atmosphere and a great menu featuring local seafood. Specialties include beloved pad thai, étouffée, seared ahi tuna, lobster and lemon grass soup and, of course, local crab cakes. **Features:** full bar. **Address:** 1205 Coastal Hwy 19971 **Location:** On SR 1, between Vandyke and Collins aves; center.

 D

DOVER (D-2) pop. 36,047, elev. 37'
• Hotels p. 34 • Restaurants p. 35

Although one early missionary feared the prevalent "bugs and mascatoes," Dover was established in 1683 as the seat of Kent County and adopted as the state capital in 1777 after British forces invaded New Castle, forcing statesmen to flee south. Delaware's deciding vote for independence from British rule had been cast in Philadelphia a year earlier by Continental Congress delegate Caesar Rodney, whose historic 80-mile ride from Dover brought him to Independence Hall just minutes before the debate closed.

The city grew quickly in the early 18th century, with stately houses built around an attractive green designed by William Penn. It was at the Golden Fleece Tavern on The Green that Delawareans voted in 1787 to ratify the Constitution, making Delaware the first of the 13 states to do so.

Dover residents were divided about the slavery issue, but many prominent families helped runaway slaves escape to the North by means of the Underground Railroad. One such station may have been Woodburn, now the governor's residence, on King's Highway south of Division Street. Free tours of the home and gardens are available upon request; phone (302) 739-5656.

Dover claims as its favorite daughter astronomer Annie Jump Cannon, who developed a prismatic technique of telescopic photography that enabled her to classify more than 400,000 stars. Her work at the Harvard Observatory during the first half of the 20th century contributed greatly to the Henry Draper Catalog, which is still used by astronomers.

Although Legislative Hall has been in use only since 1933, its 18th-century style handmade brick exterior and interior woodwork give it the same appearance as much of historic Dover. Visitors may view the governor's reception area and portraits of Delaware's governors and World War II heroes. The building is on Legislative Avenue between Martin Luther King, Jr. Blvd. and William Penn St.; for guided tours phone (302) 739-9194.

Fine 18th- and 19th-century houses remain concentrated around The Green and north and south State Street. Many examples of Victorian architecture line S. State and S. Bradford streets, and 19th-century commercial structures still stand along Loockerman Street.

The Old Dover Historic District includes Christ Church, The Green, the Richardson and Robbins Complex, Wesley College and Woodburn, birthplace of Annie Jump Cannon.

Live harness racing takes place at Dover Downs on US 13 late October to mid-April; phone (302) 674-4600 or (800) 711-5882.

Note: Policies vary concerning admittance of children to pari-mutuel betting facilities. Phone for information.

Dover International Speedway at Dover Downs hosts two weekends of NASCAR racing in June and September, including the AAA 400; phone (302) 883-6500 or (800) 441-7223.

Central Delaware Chamber of Commerce: 435 N. DuPont Hwy. (US 13), Dover, DE 19901. **Phone:** (302) 734-7513.

Self-guiding tours: Brochures outlining tours to many of the city's most interesting buildings and attractions are available at the First State Heritage Park Visitor Center, 121 Martin Luther King, Jr. Blvd.; phone (302) 744-5055.

AIR MOBILITY COMMAND MUSEUM is off SR 1/US 113 exit 91, then .7 mi e., following signs. Vintage airplanes and military aviation artifacts are displayed in a restored World War II hangar on Dover Air Force Base. The museum is home to the behemoth C-5A Galaxy, the largest airlifter in the Air Force; the VC-9C, which transported America's presidents, vice presidents and first ladies from 1975-2011; a B-17G (Flying Fortress); a C-47 airlift aircraft; and C-124A and C-133B transports as well as jet fighters and trainers. Visitors are also able to fly free flight simulators, sit in a real jet cockpit, climb the control tower to watch airfield operations and learn from interactive exhibits. **Time:** Allow 1 hour, 30 minutes minimum. **Hours:** Tues.-Sun. 9-4. Closed major holidays. **Cost:** Free. **Phone:** (302) 677-5938.

BIGGS MUSEUM OF AMERICAN ART is w. on Court St., then n. to jct. of Martin Luther King, Jr. Blvd. and Federal St. The museum contains Sewell C. Biggs' personal art and antiques collection, which was in the making for more than half a century. It is in the 1858 former Kent County government building, one of the state's first fireproof buildings.

Works spanning nearly 300 years survey major periods in American art. Exhibits feature the paintings of regional artists and celebrated masters: Albert Bierstadt, William Merritt Chase, Childe Hassam, George Inness, Charles Willson Peale, Frank Schoonover and Gilbert Stuart. The collection also includes pastels, drawings, modern art and sculpture.

Biggs' assemblage of fine furniture and silver represents the work of some of the best Delaware and Philadelphia craftsmen of the Colonial and Federal periods. **Time:** Allow 1 hour minimum. **Hours:** Tues.-Sat. 9-4:30, Sun. 1:30-4:30. Closed Jan. 1, Thanksgiving, Christmas Eve and Christmas. **Cost:** Free. **Phone:** (302) 674-2111. GT

 DELAWARE AGRICULTURAL MUSEUM AND VILLAGE, 2 mi. n. to 866 N. DuPont Hwy. (US 13) at jct. US 13 Alt., illustrates agricultural heritage and rural life. The exhibition hall houses tractors, horse-drawn equipment and farming implements dating from 1670 through the 1950s. Buildings dating from the Civil War era to about 1900 include a one-room schoolhouse, sawmill, barbershop, train station, farmhouse, general store, country church and blacksmith and wheelwright shops.

Time: Allow 1 hour, 30 minutes minimum. **Hours:** Tues.-Sat. 10-3. Closed major holidays. **Cost:** $6; $4 (ages 65+); $3 (ages 4-17). **Phone:** (302) 734-1618.

DELAWARE'S STATE HOUSE is on the e. side of The Green at S. State St. The restored 1791 building contains period furnishings, building artifacts and historical photographs and documents. Programs about state history and the Underground Railroad are offered. **Time:** Allow 30 minutes minimum. **Hours:** Mon.-Sat. and some state holidays 9-4:30, Sun. 1:30-4:30. Closed Jan. 1, Easter, Thanksgiving and Christmas. Phone ahead to confirm schedule. **Cost:** Free. **Phone:** (302) 739-2438. GT

DELAWARE STATE POLICE MUSEUM, 1425 N. DuPont Hwy., features uniforms, weapons, vehicles and equipment used in law enforcement. Other exhibits include an interactive mock crime scene and a police memorial. Visitors can sit at an emergency call center console. **Time:** Allow 30 minutes minimum. **Hours:** Mon.-Fri. 9-3, third Sat. of the month 11-3. Closed major holidays. **Cost:** Free. **Phone:** (302) 739-7700.

JOHN DICKINSON PLANTATION, 6 mi. s. on US 113, then .1 mi. e. to 340 Kitts Hummock Rd., was the boyhood home of John Dickinson, known as the Penman of the American Revolution and attributed with drafting the Articles of Confederation in 1778. Dickinson's 1740s brick house and reconstructed farm complex exemplify area 18th-century plantation architecture. **Time:** Allow 1 hour, 30 minutes minimum. **Hours:** Wed.-Sat. 10-3:30. Last tour begins 30 minutes before closing. Closed major holidays. **Cost:** Donations. **Phone:** (302) 739-3277. GT

GAMBLING ESTABLISHMENTS

- **Dover Downs Hotel & Casino** is at 1131 N. DuPont Hwy. **Hours:** Daily 24 hours. Closed Easter and Christmas. **Phone:** (302) 674-4600 or (800) 711-5882.

BEST WESTERN GALAXY INN (302)735-4700

Motel
$70-$95

AAA Benefit: Members save up to 20%!

Address: 1700 E Lebanon Rd 19901 **Location:** SR 1 exit 95, just w on SR 10. Located near Dover Air Force Base. **Facility:** 63 units. 2 stories (no elevator), interior corridors. **Pool(s):** outdoor. **Activities:** exercise room. **Guest Services:** coin laundry.

COMFORT INN & SUITES (302)677-0505

Hotel $80-$229 **Address:** 764 Leipsic Rd 19901 **Location:** SR 1 exit 104, 2.5 mi s on US 13. Located in a commercial area, near Dover International Speedway. **Facility:** 89 units. 4 stories, interior corridors. **Pool(s):** heated indoor. **Activities:** hot tub, exercise room. **Guest Services:** valet and coin laundry.

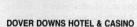

DAYS INN DOVER (302)674-8002

Motel
$62-$275

Address: 272 N DuPont Hwy 19901 **Location:** SR 1 exit 104, 2.8 mi s on US 13. Located in a commercial area. **Facility:** 79 units. 1 story, exterior corridors. **Terms:** cancellation fee imposed. **Amenities:** safes. **Activities:** exercise room. **Guest Services:** coin laundry. **Featured Amenity:** continental breakfast.

DOVER DOWNS HOTEL & CASINO (302)674-4600

Hotel
$139-$299

Address: 1131 N DuPont Hwy 19903 **Location:** SR 1 exit 104, 1.9 mi s on US 13. Adjacent to Dover Downs Race Track. **Facility:** This full-service hotel offers handsome, comfortable guest rooms and inviting public spaces. Many rooms have a view of the adjacent racetrack. Check-in is at 5 pm on Sundays. 500 units. 10 stories, interior corridors. **Parking:** on-site and valet. **Terms:** check-in 4 pm, cancellation fee imposed, resort fee. **Amenities:** safes. **Dining:** 5 restaurants, also, Doc Magrogan's Oyster House, Michele's, see separate listings, entertainment. **Pool(s):** heated indoor. **Activities:** hot tub, exercise room, spa. **Guest Services:** valet laundry.

FAIRFIELD INN & SUITES BY MARRIOTT-DOVER
(302)677-0900

AAA Benefit: Members save 5% or more!

Address: 655 N DuPont Hwy 19901 **Location:** SR 1 exit 104, 2.7 mi s on US 13. Located in a commercial area, near Dover International Speedway. **Facility:** 77 units. 4 stories, interior corridors. **Pool(s):** heated indoor. **Activities:** hot tub, exercise room. **Guest Services:** valet and coin laundry. **Featured Amenity: full hot breakfast.**

HAMPTON INN-DOVER
(302)736-3500

Hotel $89-$370 **Address:** 1568 N DuPont Hwy 19901 **Location:** SR 1 exit 104, 1 mi s. Located in a commercial area. **Facility:** 81 units. 4 stories, interior corridors. **Terms:** 1-7 night minimum stay, cancellation fee imposed. **Pool(s):** outdoor. **Activities:** exercise room. **Guest Services:** valet and coin laundry.

AAA Benefit: Members save 5% or more!

HILTON GARDEN INN DOVER
(302)674-3784

Hilton Garden Inn

AAA Benefit: Members save 5% or more!

Address: 1706 N DuPont Hwy 19901 **Location:** SR 1 exit 104, just s. **Facility:** 95 units. 4 stories, interior corridors. **Terms:** 1-7 night minimum stay, cancellation fee imposed. **Pool(s):** heated indoor. **Activities:** hot tub, exercise room. **Guest Services:** valet and coin laundry.

HOLIDAY INN EXPRESS HOTEL & SUITES DOVER
302/678-0600

Hotel. Rates not provided. **Address:** 1780 N DuPont Hwy 19901 **Location:** SR 1 exit 104, just s on US 13. Located in a commercial area. **Facility:** 81 units. 5 stories, interior corridors. **Pool(s):** outdoor. **Activities:** exercise room. **Guest Services:** coin laundry.

MAINSTAY SUITES DOVER
(302)678-8383

Extended Stay Hotel $60-$319 **Address:** 201 Stover Blvd 19901 **Location:** SR 1 exit 95 northbound, just n on Bay Rd; exit 95 southbound, 1.5 mi n on Bay Rd; 0.7 mi s of jct US 13. **Facility:** 92 units, some efficiencies. 4 stories, interior corridors. **Terms:** check-in 4 pm. **Amenities:** safes. **Pool(s):** heated indoor. **Activities:** exercise room. **Guest Services:** coin laundry.

MICROTEL INN & SUITES BY WYNDHAM DOVER
(302)674-3800

Hotel $80-$249

Address: 1703 Lebanon Rd 19901 **Location:** SR 1 exit 95, just w on SR 10. Located near Dover Air Force Base. **Facility:** 71 units. 3 stories, interior corridors. **Terms:** cancellation fee imposed. **Amenities:** safes. **Activities:** exercise room. **Guest Services:** coin laundry. **Featured Amenity: continental breakfast.**

RESIDENCE INN BY MARRIOTT-DOVER
(302)677-0777

Extended Stay Hotel $97-$189 **Address:** 600 Jefferic Blvd 19901 **Location:** SR 1 exit 104, 2.7 mi s on US 13. Located in a commercial area, near Dover International Speedway. **Facility:** 98 units, some two bedrooms, efficiencies and kitchens. 4 stories, interior corridors. **Pool(s):** heated indoor. **Activities:** hot tub, exercise room. **Guest Services:** valet and coin laundry.

AAA Benefit: Members save 5% or more!

SLEEP INN & SUITES DOVER
(302)735-7770

Hotel $80-$350 **Address:** 1784 N DuPont Hwy 19901 **Location:** SR 1 exit 104, just s on US 13. **Facility:** 62 units. 3 stories, interior corridors. **Amenities:** safes. **Pool(s):** outdoor. **Activities:** exercise room. **Guest Services:** coin laundry.

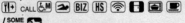

WHERE TO EAT

DOC MAGROGAN'S OYSTER HOUSE
302/857-3223

Seafood. Casual Dining. $7-$26 **AAA Inspector Notes:** This haven on the casino floor serves fresh seafood that's flown in daily. Ask the staff about the preparation method—Cajun, Old Bay steamed or pan-seared—that will best bring out the flavor of your fish. You also might consider nightly food and drink specials, not to mention special entertainment. If you like oysters, visit on buck-a-shuck Mondays. **Features:** full bar, happy hour. **Address:** 1131 N DuPont Hwy 19901 **Location:** SR 1 exit 104, 1.9 mi s on US 13; in Dover Downs Hotel & Casino. **Parking:** on-site and valet.

HIBACHI JAPANESE STEAKHOUSE
302/734-5900

Japanese. Casual Dining. $14-$50 **AAA Inspector Notes:** Fresh meat, seafood and vegetable dishes are prepared during a tableside show that's popular with local families. A full sushi menu also is available. During select days and times, the restaurant offers a self-serve, all-you-can-eat option. **Features:** full bar, early bird specials. **Address:** 691 N DuPont Hwy 19901 **Location:** SR 1 exit 104, 2.1 mi s.

MICHELE'S
302/857-2120

American. Fine Dining. $28-$54 **AAA Inspector Notes:** Sleek, modern and sexy, this restaurant employs an attentive staff. An extensive wine list complements the kitchens creations. While offering choices for a wide range of tastes, steak and seafood are the specialties. **Features:** full bar, Sunday brunch. **Reservations:** suggested. **Address:** 1131 N DuPont Hwy 19901 **Location:** SR 1 exit 104, 1.9 mi s on US 13; in Dover Downs Hotel & Casino. **Parking:** on-site and valet.

Enjoy peace of mind with AAA/CAA Insurance products

SHUCKER'S PIER 13   302/674-1190

▼▼ Seafood. Casual Dining. $8-$44 **AAA Inspector Notes:** This casual restaurant has been a favorite spot with the locals for their excellent variety of fresh seafood, pasta and meat dishes. Ravioli with Maryland blue claw crabmeat and twin 4-ounce filet mignon medallions are among the more popular items. **Features:** full bar. **Address:** 889 N DuPont Hwy 19901 **Location:** SR 1 exit 104, 2.8 mi s on US 13. ⓛ Ⓓ

WHERE PIGS FLY   302/678-0586

▼▼ Barbecue. Casual Dining. $8-$18 **AAA Inspector Notes:** For those who like barbecue, this is the place to feast. The hickory-smoked, pulled-pork sandwich is a local favorite, though the ribs and chicken are worth checking out. The homemade barbecue sauce is tasty. **Features:** beer only. **Address:** 617 Loockerman St 19901 **Location:** SR 1 exit 95, 2 mi n on Bay Rd, then 0.3 mi n on US 13. ⓛ Ⓓ

FENWICK ISLAND (F-3) pop. 379, elev. 10'

DISCOVERSEA SHIPWRECK MUSEUM is at 708 Coastal Hwy. on the 2nd floor of the Sea Shell City store. The museum consists of one of the Mid-Atlantic's largest exhibits of shipwreck and recovered artifacts. The rotating collection's some 10,000 articles represent wreck sites from various locations throughout the world and include such objects as coins, weapons, jewelry and dishes. **Time:** Allow 30 minutes minimum. **Hours:** Daily 11-7, Memorial Day-Labor Day; Sat.-Sun. 11-3, weekend after Labor Day-Dec. 31 and Apr. 1-day before Memorial Day. Phone ahead to confirm schedule. **Cost:** Free. **Phone:** (302) 539-9366 or (888) 743-5524.

ATLANTIC COAST INN   302/539-7673

▼▼ Motel. Rates not provided. **Address:** 37558 Lighthouse Rd 19944 **Location:** Jct SR 1 and 54. **Facility:** 54 units, some two bedrooms, efficiencies and kitchens. 2 stories (no elevator), exterior corridors. **Pool(s):** outdoor. **Activities:** beach access. **Guest Services:** coin laundry.

🍴 🏊 📶 ✕ 🔌 🖥 📺 💻

WHERE TO EAT

JUST HOOKED   302/581-0098

▼▼▼ American. Casual Dining. $9-$25 **AAA Inspector Notes:** This spot features a farm to table focus using local products almost exclusively, so of course the menu changes often. The cooking style mixes rustic and sophisticated elements to create unique dishes such as fresh fish with citrus yogurt, truffled asparagus salad, roasted corn and jalapeño crab bisque, and spice-encrusted tuna. You'll also find modern interpretations of such favorites as crab cakes and shrimp & grits. **Features:** full bar. **Address:** 1500 Coastal Hwy 19944 **Location:** 1 mi n of SR 1; in Sunshine Plaza.

ⓛ Ⓓ CALL 🔄M

NANTUCKETS   302/539-2607

▼▼▼ American. Fine Dining. $24-$34 **AAA Inspector Notes:** In a restored clapboard cottage, this restaurant has many cozy rooms eclectically decorated with knick-knacks, antiques and artwork. Favorites on the New England-inspired menu include chowder, bouillabaisse, lobster shepherd's pie, duck, and blue cheese-encrusted filet mignon. **Features:** full bar, early bird specials, happy hour. **Reservations:** suggested. **Address:** 601 Coastal Hwy 19944 **Location:** On SR 1, just n of jct W SR 54. **Parking:** on-site and street. Ⓓ

Get AAA/CAA travel information in the digital and printed formats you prefer

---

SMITTY MCGEE'S   302/436-4716

▼▼ American. Casual Dining. $8-$12 **AAA Inspector Notes:** Diners should come hungry, as this sports bar serves up huge plates of pub grub including burgers, pizzas and a wide variety of tasty sandwiches. Those who dare to try the hot wings should start out slowly, as even the mild ones have a spicy bite. Parking and boat slips are ample, but bathrooms are not. **Features:** full bar. **Address:** 37234 Lighthouse Rd (SR 54) 19975 **Location:** Jct SR 1, 2.3 mi w. ⓛ Ⓓ ⟦LATE⟧

GEORGETOWN (E-2) pop. 6,422

ELSIE WILLIAMS DOLL COLLECTION is at 21199 College Drive (Seashore Hwy.) w. of SR 113, in the library on the Delaware Technical and Community College campus. The diverse collection includes more than 600 dolls by such makers as Bru, Madame Alexander and Peggy Nisbet. Many of the dolls were originally owned by the wife of the late U.S. Sen. John Williams.

Time: Allow 30 minutes minimum. **Hours:** Mon.-Thurs. 8 a.m.-10 p.m., Fri. 8-4:30, Sat. 8-1. Closed major holidays. Phone ahead to confirm schedule. **Cost:** Free. **Phone:** (302) 856-9033.

TREASURES OF THE SEA EXHIBIT, on SR 18 (Seashore Hwy.) w. of SR 113, in the library building on the Delaware Technical and Community College campus, displays jewels, gold and silver ingots and coins, bronze cannons and gold chains recovered from the ill-fated Spanish galleon *Nuestra Señora de Atocha*. Carrying an estimated $400 million in treasure, the ship sank in a 1622 hurricane. Videotapes chronicle the discovery of the galleon; visitors also may listen to a recording about the finding of the cannons.

Time: Allow 1 hour minimum. **Hours:** Mon.-Tues. 10-4, Fri. noon-4, Sat. 9-1; closed major holidays and late Dec.-early Jan. Phone ahead to confirm schedule. **Cost:** $3; $2.50 (ages 65+); $1 (students with ID); free (ages 0-4). **Phone:** (302) 856-5700. ⟦GT⟧

THE BRICK HOTEL ON THE CIRCLE   302/855-5800

▼▼▼▼
Historic
Country Inn
$110-$175

Address: 18 The Circle 19947 **Location:** Jct US 113, 0.8 mi w on US 9/SR 404, just right at The Circle. **Facility:** Built in 1836, the inn has also serves as a courthouse, bank and a post office and sits in the center of town overlooking the circle park-site for many festivals. 14 units. 2-3 stories, interior corridors. *Bath:* shower only. **Terms:** 2 night minimum stay - seasonal and/or weekends, 10 day cancellation notice-fee imposed. **Dining:** The Brick Restaurant & Tavern, see separate listing. **Guest Services:** valet laundry. **Featured Amenity:** continental breakfast.

 🍴 🍸 ⟦BIZ⟧ 📶 ✕ ✉

COMFORT INN & SUITES-GEORGETOWN   302/854-9400

▼▼ Hotel. Rates not provided. **Address:** 20530 DuPont Blvd 19947 **Location:** On US 113, 0.5 mi n of jct SR 404. **Facility:** 71 units. 2 stories (no elevator), interior corridors. **Pool(s):** outdoor. **Guest Services:** coin laundry.

🏊 ⟦BIZ⟧ 📶 🔌 🖥 💻 / SOME UNITS

WHERE TO EAT

THE BRICK RESTAURANT & TAVERN   302/856-1836

▼▼▼ American. Fine Dining. $10-$26 **AAA Inspector Notes:** *Historic.* Set in a lovingly restored hotel in the center of town, they feature a menu of traditional specialties such as cream of crab soup, oyster, veggie or chicken pot pie, steaks, fresh local fish and various nightly specials. If you wish to indulge in an afternoon tea with all the accompaniments, you will need to make a reservation as it is served on Thursdays at 2 pm. **Features:** full bar, Sunday brunch. **Address:** 18 The Circle 19947 **Location:** Jct US 113, 0.8 mi w on US 9/SR 404, just right at The Circle; in The Brick Hotel On The Circle.

B L D CALL ᴄ̗M

HARRINGTON (D-1) pop. 3,562, elev. 63'

In central Delaware's agricultural region, Harrington is home to the Delaware State Fair. The fairgrounds complex on US 13 features Quillen Arena and an ice rink for public skating and hockey matches.

Harrington Raceway, at the fairgrounds, offers spring and fall harness racing sessions; phone (302) 398-7223.

Note: Policies vary concerning admittance of children to pari-mutuel betting facilities. Phone for information.

MESSICK AGRICULTURAL MUSEUM, 1.2 mi. w. of jct. US 13 and SR 14W on Walt Messick Rd., houses an extensive collection of early 1900s farm implements. Horse-drawn plows and vehicles, including a covered wagon, represent farm life in the 19th century. An early 20th-century kitchen and smokehouse are furnished in period. The museum has a collection of classic automobiles and trucks spanning several decades. **Time:** Allow 1 hour minimum. **Hours:** Mon.-Fri. 8-4. Closed major holidays. **Cost:** Free. **Phone:** (302) 398-3729.

GAMBLING ESTABLISHMENTS

- **Harrington Raceway & Casino** is at Delaware State Fairgrounds off US 13. **Hours:** Daily 24 hours. Closed Easter and Christmas. **Phone:** (888) 887-5687.

BAYMONT INN & SUITES HARRINGTON   (302)398-3900

▼▼ ▼▼ Hotel $65-$89 **Address:** 1259 Corn Crib Rd 19952 **Location:** On US 13, 0.6 mi s of jct SR 14. Across from Delaware State Fairgrounds. **Facility:** 70 units. 2 stories, interior corridors. **Amenities:** safes. **Pool(s):** heated indoor. **Activities:** hot tub, limited exercise equipment. **Guest Services:** coin laundry.

CALL ᴄ̗M   / SOME UNITS ⓢ

**HOLIDAY INN EXPRESS HOTEL &
SUITES-HARRINGTON (DOVER AREA)**   (302)398-8800

▼▼▼
Hotel
$119-$269

Address: 17271 S DuPont Hwy 19952 **Location:** On US 13; jct SR 14. **Facility:** 86 units. 3 stories, interior corridors. **Terms:** cancellation fee imposed, resort fee. **Pool(s):** heated outdoor. **Activities:** exercise room. **Featured Amenity:** continental breakfast.

SAVE CALL ᴄ̗M BIZ 🛜 🅗

LEWES (E-3) pop. 2,747, elev. 17'
• Hotels p. 38 • Restaurants p. 38

West of Cape Henlopen, Lewes (LOO-is) was founded in 1631 by a group of settlers from Hoorn, Holland. Originally called *Zwaanendael,* Valley of the Swans, the little colony intended to establish an agricultural and whaling industry, but the Siconese Indians destroyed it within a year. The interruption was brief, however. Promptly rebuilt, the town flourished, surviving pirate attacks, British bombardment in the War of 1812 and the profusion of summer vacationers to its beaches.

The DeVries Monument on Pilottown Road commemorates the 1631 Dutch settlement. Constructed before the exact position of the Dutch fort was determined, the monument later was discovered to be on the site of the fortification's north bastion.

Lewes is the traditional home of the pilots who guide ships up Delaware Bay. This maritime orientation also makes the town a natural site for the College of Earth, Ocean and Environment at the University of Delaware.

Ferries connect Lewes with Cape May, N.J., daily. The 17-mile trip takes 85 minutes. For information write Cape May-Lewes Ferry, Cape May Terminal, 1200 Lincoln Blvd., Cape May, NJ 08204; phone (302) 644-6030 or (800) 643-3779. Cape May-Lewes ferry information also is available at AAA Mid-Atlantic, 55 Greentree Dr., in Dover; phone (302) 674-8020.

Lewes Chamber of Commerce and Visitor's Bureau: 120 Kings Hwy., Lewes, DE 19958. **Phone:** (302) 645-8073 or (877) 465-3937.

Self-guiding tours: Brochures and maps, including a self-guiding maritime trail covering 12 sites, are available from the chamber of commerce and visitor bureau.

FISHERMAN'S WHARF CRUISES, 3 mi. e. of SR 1 on SR 9 Bus. Rte. (Anglers Rd.), just beside the drawbridge, offers dolphin- and whale-watching cruises. Sunset cruises and fishing excursions are also available.

Hours: Two-hour dolphin cruises depart daily at 9:30, early June-early Sept. (weather permitting). Three-hour dolphin and whale-watching cruises depart daily at 1:30, late May-early Sept. (weather permitting). Sunset cruises depart daily at 7 p.m., early June-July; at 6:30 p.m. early Aug.-early Sept. (weather permitting). **Cost:** Dolphin cruise $29; $15 (ages 0-12); Dolphin and whale-watching cruise $35; $20 (ages 0-12). Sunset cruise $20; $10 (ages 0-12). Hours and fares may vary; phone ahead. Reservations are recommended. **Phone:** (302) 645-8862.

FISHER-MARTIN HOUSE is at Kings Hwy. and Savannah Rd. The restored early 18th-century structure presents changing art exhibits and houses the Lewes Chamber of Commerce and Visitor's Bureau. **Time:** Allow 30 minutes minimum. **Hours:** Mon.-Fri.

10-4, Sat. 9-3, Sun. 10-2, Memorial Day weekend-Sept. 30; Mon.-Fri. 10-4, rest of year. Closed major holidays. **Cost:** Free. **Phone:** (302) 645-8073.

LEWES HISTORICAL SOCIETY, at Shipcarpenter and Third sts., encompasses 12 historic structures. Among the buildings are Thompson Country Store, a furnished 19th-century store moved from a site near Milford; Plank House, a tiny one-room log cabin built before 1700; and the 1789 Burton-Ingraham House, furnished with Chippendale and Empire antiques. Ryves Holt House, at Second and Mulberry streets, contains the visitor center.

Time: Allow 1 hour, 30 minutes minimum. **Hours:** Guided tours Tues., Wed., Sat.-Sun. at 2, mid-June to mid-Aug. (also Fri. at 2 in Sept.) . Phone ahead to confirm schedule. **Cost:** $10 (includes all sites); free (ages 0-12). **Phone:** (302) 645-7670.

LIGHTSHIP OVERFALLS is at jct. Pilottown Rd. and Shipcarpenter St. With a 1,000-watt flashing electric lantern, a foghorn with a 5-mile range and a radio beacon capable of transmitting 25 miles, this floating lighthouse served as a navigation aid along the East Coast, first in Long Island Sound, then in Boston Harbor. Built in 1938, it was decommissioned in 1972. A tour includes the interior and exterior of the ship.

Time: Allow 1 hour minimum. **Hours:** Mon. and Thurs.-Sat. 10-4, Sun. noon-4, Memorial Day weekend-Columbus Day. **Cost:** $5, free (ages 0-14). **Phone:** (302) 644-8050.

SEASIDE NATURE CENTER, 1 mi. e. on US 9 past Cape May-Lewes Ferry to Cape Henlopen State Park, has several large fish aquariums, touch tanks, live snakes and turtles, and an exhibit about the park's natural habitats. The Seaside Interpretive Trail, a self-guiding tour of the natural and human history of Cape Henlopen, leads from the center to Delaware Bay. Naturalist-led programs are offered, and guided kayak tours and rentals are available during summer months. Historic Fort Miles features guided battery tours and programs, a gun park, observation tower and several buildings.

Grills and tables are available for picnicking. **Time:** Allow 30 minutes minimum. **Hours:** Daily 9-5, mid-June through Labor Day; 9-4, rest of year. **Cost:** Park entrance fee Mar.-Nov. $8 (per private out-of-state vehicle); $4 (per private in-state vehicle); free (rest of year). Center free. Tour fees vary according to type of tour. **Phone:** (302) 645-6852. GT 🏕

ZWAANENDAEL MUSEUM is at Savannah Rd. and Kings Hwy. Built in 1931 to commemorate the 300th anniversary of Delaware's first European settlement, the museum features interactive activities. It also showcases objects recovered from a local shipwreck as well as exhibits describing Delaware Bay maritime history and the War of 1812. **Time:** Allow 30 minutes minimum. **Hours:** Tues.-Sat. 10-4:30, Sun. 1:30-4:30, Apr.-Oct.; Tues.-Sat. 10-4:30, rest of year. Closed state holidays. **Cost:** Free. **Phone:** (302) 645-1148.

WINERIES

- **Nassau Valley Vineyards Winery and Visitors Center,** 2 mi. w. on US 9 to jct. US 404 and SR 1, then .5 mi. n. on SR 1 to overpass, then w. onto CR 14B, following signs to 33 Nassau Commons. **Hours:** Mon.-Sat. 11-5, Sun. noon-5. Closed Jan. 1, Easter, Thanksgiving and Christmas. **Phone:** (302) 645-9463. GT

HOTEL BLUE   302/645-4880

▼▼▼▼ **Boutique Hotel.** Rates not provided. **Address:** 110 Anglers Rd, Suite 107 19958 **Location:** Over US 9 bridge, just e; in historic Lewes. **Facility:** This boutique hotel features beautifully appointed rooms, all featuring a balcony or patio, plush bedding and a gas fireplace. The large bathrooms include sinks lit in neon blue. 16 units. 3 stories, interior corridors. **Amenities:** safes. **Pool(s):** outdoor. **Activities:** exercise room.

🍽 🏊 🛜 ✕ 🔒 🖥 💻

THE INN AT CANAL SQUARE   302/644-3377

▼▼▼ Diamond
. Hotel
$105-$310

Address: 122 Market St 19958 **Location:** Waterfront. Just nw of jct Savannah Rd (US 9 business route). **Facility:** 25 units, some two bedrooms and kitchens. 4 stories, interior corridors. **Terms:** 2 night minimum stay - weekends, 7 day cancellation notice-fee imposed. **Activities:** exercise room, massage. **Guest Services:** valet laundry, area transportation. **Featured Amenity: continental breakfast.**

SAVE 🍽 CALL ⓜ BIZ 🛜 ✕

🔒 💻 / SOME UNITS 🐕 🖥

SLEEP INN & SUITES   (302)645-6464

▼▼ **Hotel** $70-$380 **Address:** 18451 Coastal Hwy 19958 **Location:** On SR 1, 1.5 mi s. Located in a commercial area. **Facility:** 81 units. 4 stories, interior corridors. **Amenities:** safes. **Pool(s):** heated outdoor. **Activities:** exercise room. **Guest Services:** valet and coin laundry.

🍽 🏊 BIZ 🛜 ✕ 🔒 🖥 💻 / SOME UNITS 🍴

WHERE TO EAT

THE BUTTERY   302/645-7755

▼▼▼ American. Fine Dining. $12-$38 **AAA Inspector Notes:** In the heart of the historic shopping and gallery district, this quaint, converted residence offers a charming setting for casual lunches and more formal dinners. The kitchen is skilled in preparing veal, grilled duck breast and jumbo lump crab cakes. The staff is friendly and professional. **Features:** full bar, patio dining, Sunday brunch, happy hour. **Reservations:** suggested. **Address:** 102 2nd St 19958 **Location:** Jct 2nd St and Savannah Rd (US 9 business route). **Parking:** street only. L D 🐕

NECTAR CAFE AND JUICE BAR   302/645-5842

▼▼ Breakfast Vegetarian. Casual Dining. $7-$12 **AAA Inspector Notes:** Eat healthy (or not) at this charming spot that exudes vintage charm. Breakfast specialties include pecan French toast, green eggs and ham, omelets and blueberry pancakes. Lunch offers big salads, BLTs, black bean burgers, a tomato soup and grilled cheese combo, and even classic cheeseburgers. **Features:** full bar. **Address:** 111 Neil's 19958 **Location:** Just w of US 9/Savannah Rd (US 9 business route); between Front and 2nd sts; downtown. **Parking:** street only. B L

STRIPER BITES   302/645-4657

▼▼ Seafood. Casual Dining. $9-$29 **AAA Inspector Notes:** This nautical-style bistro serves up a variety of classic seafood dishes along with steaks, sandwiches and pasta. Rowboats and anchors hanging from the ceiling are the centerpieces of the shore-inspired decor. Expect excellent happy hour prices on food and drink from 4-6 pm Monday through Friday. A large patio overlooks the street. **Features:** full bar, happy hour. **Address:** 107 Savannah Rd 19958 **Location:** Jct Front St, just w. **Parking:** on-site and street.

[L] [D] CALL [&M]

SURFING CRAB   302/644-4448

▼▼ Seafood. Casual Dining. $11-$39 **AAA Inspector Notes:** Guests won't be disappointed with this crab house. Locals and tourists alike have made this one of their favorites. The atmosphere is simple and casual, as one would expect, with cement floors, brown paper over the tables and painted cinder block walls. The house specialty is hard-shell blue crabs. The menu also offers a fresh fish selection, crab cakes, fried jumbo shrimp, fish and chips and blackened chicken breast. Open weekdays at 4 p.m. and Friday through Sunday at noon. **Features:** full bar. **Address:** 16723 Coastal Hwy 19958 **Location:** On SR 1, 1.4 mi n of jct SR 404 and US 9. [D]

HALF FULL   302/645-8877

[fyi] Not evaluated. Thin-crust gourmet pizzas, beer and wine make up the menu at this small downtown eatery. **Address:** 113 Market St 19958 **Location:** Jct Front St, just s; downtown.

MIDDLETOWN pop. 18,871

HAMPTON INN MIDDLETOWN   (302)378-5656

▼▼▼ Hotel $109-$299 **Address:** 117 Sand Hill Dr 19709 **Location:** SR 1 exit 136, 2.8 mi w on SR 299, then just n on SR 15. **Facility:** 72 units. 4 stories. interior corridors. **Terms:** 1-7 night minimum stay, cancellation fee imposed. **Pool(s):** heated indoor. **Activities:** hot tub, exercise room. **Guest Services:** valet and coin laundry.

AAA Benefit: Members save 5% or more!

[📶] CALL [&M] [�̲] [BIZ] [📶] [🖥] / SOME UNITS [🛏] [HS] [🅱]

MILFORD pop. 9,559

DAYS INN & SUITES MILFORD   (302)839-5000

▼▼ Hotel $51-$102 **Address:** 699 N DuPont Blvd 19963 **Location:** SR 1, s to US 113 S. **Facility:** 57 units, some efficiencies. 3 stories, interior corridors. **Amenities:** safes. **Pool(s):** heated indoor. **Activities:** hot tub, exercise room. **Guest Services:** coin laundry.

[📶] CALL [&M] [🚲] [BIZ] [HS] [📶] [🅱] [🖥] [🖥]

MILLSBORO (E-2) pop. 3,877, elev. 26'

NANTICOKE INDIAN MUSEUM, at jct. SRs 24 (John J. Williams Hwy.) and 5, is in a restored community schoolhouse. Exhibits interpret the history and development of the Nanticoke Indians, Delaware's first residents and its only state-recognized American Indian tribe. Highlights include basketwork, ceremonial dress, pottery, arrowheads and stone implements. Other collections include tribal dolls and kachinas and a reference library. **Time:** Allow 30 minutes minimum. **Hours:** Tues.-Sat. 10-4, Sun. noon-4, Apr.-Dec.; Thurs.-Sat. 10-4, Sun. noon-4, rest of year. **Cost:** $3; $1 (children). **Phone:** (302) 945-7022.

ATLANTIC INN-MILLSBORO   302/934-6711

▼▼ Motel. Rates not provided. **Address:** 28534 DuPont Blvd 19966 **Location:** US 113, just s of SR 24. **Facility:** 82 units. 2 stories (no elevator), exterior corridors. **Pool(s):** outdoor. **Activities:** limited exercise equipment. **Guest Services:** coin laundry.

[📶] [🚲] [📶] [X] / SOME UNITS [🛏] [🅱] [🖥]

BLUE WATER GRILL   302/934-5160

▼▼ American. Casual Dining. $7-$25 **AAA Inspector Notes:** This casual spot is the perfect place for a friendly lunch or family dinner, with its menu of homemade sandwiches, appetizers, seafood and desserts. Charming staffers are as quick with their service as they are with a smile. **Features:** full bar, happy hour. **Address:** 226 Main St 19966 **Location:** 0.5 mi e of jct US 113. **Parking:** street only. [L] [D]

THE GEORGIA HOUSE   302/422-6763

▼▼ Southern. Casual Dining. $8-$24 **AAA Inspector Notes:** This casual spot is set in a restored, turn-of-the-20th-century storefront and features a menu of Eastern Shore favorites. They are especially known for their wonderful she-crab soup. Other favorites include meatloaf, chicken-fried steak, pot roast, and fried shrimp. Don't miss the great Southern-style, country side dishes. **Features:** full bar, patio dining. **Address:** 18 S Walnut St 19963 **Location:** Jct NE Front and SE Front sts; downtown. [L] [D] CALL [&M]

MILTON (E-2) pop. 2,576, elev. 13'

PRIME HOOK NATIONAL WILDLIFE REFUGE is 8 mi. n. via SR 1, then 1 mi. e. on Broadkill Beach Rd. (SR 16). Black and wood ducks, mallards, pintails and shorebirds such as red knots and ruddy turnstones congregate spring and fall at this 10,000-acre marsh habitat primarily for migratory birds. Indigenous mammals include red and gray foxes, white-tailed deer and the endangered Delmarva fox squirrel. A half-mile boardwalk and more than 7 miles of canoe trails are available.

Time: Allow 1 hour, 30 minutes minimum. **Hours:** Refuge open daily 30 minutes before dawn to 30 minutes after dusk. Refuge headquarters Mon.-Fri. 7:30-4, Visitor center Sat.-Sun. 10-4, Apr.-Nov. Closed major holidays. Phone ahead to confirm schedule. **Cost:** Free. **Phone:** (302) 684-8419.

MONTCHANIN

THE INN AT MONTCHANIN VILLAGE & SPA   302/888-2133

▼▼▼ Historic Country Inn. Rates not provided. **Address:** 528 Montchanin Rd 19710 **Location:** I-95 exit 8A/B, 1.1 mi n on US 202 (Concord Pike), 0.3 mi w on Powder Mill Rd, 2 mi s on SR 141 (Powder Mill Rd/Barley Mill Rd), then 1 mi n on SR 100 (Powder Mill Rd). **Facility:** Eleven buildings dotted throughout this former 1800s hamlet of the Winterthur estate house a variety of spacious, well-appointed guest rooms. 28 units, some two bedrooms. 1-2 stories (no elevator), exterior corridors. **Amenities:** safes. **Dining:** Krazy Kat's, see separate listing. **Activities:** exercise room, spa. **Guest Services:** valet laundry.

[📶] [🚲] [BIZ] [📶] [X] [🅱] [🖥] [🖥]

KRAZY KAT'S   302/888-4200

▼▼▼ Continental. Fine Dining. $10-$34 **AAA Inspector Notes:** Fresh cuisine, with a highlight on seafood and a quaffable wine list, make this the destination for a special occasion dinner, a night out with friends or a leisurely Sunday brunch. Whimsical décor, featuring portraits of dogs and cats in military regalia, lightens the mood. **Features:** full bar, Sunday brunch. **Reservations:** suggested. **Address:** 528 Montchanin Rd 19710 **Location:** I-95 exit 8A/B, 1.1 mi n on US 202 (Concord Pike), 0.3 mi w on Powder Mill Rd, 2 mi s on SR 141 (Powder Mill Rd/Barley Mill Rd), then 1 mi n on SR 100 (Montchanin Rd); in The Inn at Montchanin Village & Spa.

[B] [L] [D]

NEWARK (B-1) pop. 31,454, elev. 137'

Newark originated as the crossroads of two Lenni Lenape Indian trails spanning the peninsula between the Chesapeake Bay and the Delaware River. The intersection gradually matured into a village, and brickyards, mills and tanneries developed in the vicinity.

Legend maintains that in 1777 Betsy Ross' flag was flown for the first time at nearby Cooch's Bridge, the site of Delaware's only Revolutionary War battle. The Battle of Cooch's Bridge took place west off SR 896 via Welsh Tract Road or Old Baltimore Pike.

IRON HILL MUSEUM, I-95 to SR 896, then 1 mi. s. to 1355 Old Baltimore Pike, is housed in a former one-room schoolhouse built by the du Pont family in 1923. Collections include rocks, minerals, floral and faunal specimens, archeological and historical displays, mounted birds and iron exhibits. Hiking trails pass old iron ore mining pits. Picnic tables are available. Guided tours are available by reservation. **Time:** Allow 1 hour, 30 minutes minimum. **Hours:** Tues.-Fri. 10-3, Sat. noon-4. Closed major holidays. **Cost:** $2; free (ages 0-5). **Phone:** (302) 368-5703.

UNIVERSITY OF DELAWARE visitor center is at 210 S. College Ave. The nearly 22,000-student campus is noted for the elm-lined mall (The Green) extending from Old College to Laurel Hall. **Time:** Allow 2 hours minimum. **Hours:** Guided 2.5-hour tours are given Mon. and Fri. at 10 and 2; Tues.-Thurs. at noon; and on select Sat. at 10 and noon. Tours are not available holidays and during final exams. **Cost:** Free. Reservations are required. **Phone:** (302) 831-8123. Newark, 178

Mineralogical Museum is at 255 Academy St. in Penny Hall. The small museum houses mineral displays from its 6,000-specimen collection illustrating specific themes including gemstones from exhausted mines or mines that no longer exist, minerals from caves and the geometry of crystalline shapes. **Time:** Allow 30 minutes minimum. **Hours:** Wed.-Sun. noon-5 (also Thurs. 5-8). Closed between exhibitions and during university holidays. Phone ahead to confirm schedule. **Cost:** Free. **Phone:** (302) 831-4940, or (302) 831-8037 for current hours. Newark, 178

COMFORT INN & SUITES
302/737-3900
Hotel. Rates not provided. **Address:** 3 Concord Ln 19713 **Location:** I-95 exit 3 southbound; exit 3B northbound, 0.5 mi w on SR 273. **Facility:** 112 units. 4 stories, interior corridors. **Amenities:** video games. **Pool(s):** outdoor. **Activities:** exercise room. **Guest Services:** valet and coin laundry.

COURTYARD BY MARRIOTT-NEWARK AT THE UNIVERSITY OF DELAWARE (302)737-0900

Hotel $132-$229

COURTYARD Marriott

AAA Benefit: Members save 5% or more!

Address: 400 David Hollowell Dr 19716 **Location:** I-95 exit 1B southbound; exit 1 northbound, 3 mi n on SR 896. On the campus of University of Delaware, adjacent to Clayton Hall Conference Center. **Facility:** 126 units. 4 stories, interior corridors. **Pool(s):** heated indoor. **Activities:** hot tub, exercise room. **Guest Services:** valet and coin laundry, area transportation.

COURTYARD BY MARRIOTT-WILMINGTON NEWARK/CHRISTIANA MALL (302)456-3800

Hotel $153-$252 **Address:** 48 Geoffrey Dr 19713 **Location:** I-95 exit 4B, 0.3 mi n on SR 7 exit 166, then just e on SR 58 (Churchmans Rd). Adjacent to shopping complex. **Facility:** 152 units.

AAA Benefit: Members save 5% or more!

4 stories, interior corridors. **Pool(s):** heated indoor. **Activities:** hot tub, exercise room. **Guest Services:** valet and coin laundry, boarding pass kiosk.

EMBASSY SUITES NEWARK/WILMINGTON SOUTH (302)368-8000

Hotel $119-$189 **Address:** 654 S College Ave 19713 **Location:** I-95 exit 1B southbound; exit 1 northbound, 0.8 mi n on SR 896. Opposite University of Delaware Stadium. Newark, 178.

AAA Benefit: Members save 5% or more!

Facility: 154 units. 6 stories, interior corridors. **Terms:** 1-7 night minimum stay, cancellation fee imposed. **Amenities:** safes. **Pool(s):** heated indoor. **Activities:** hot tub, exercise room. **Guest Services:** valet and coin laundry, area transportation.

EXTENDED STAY AMERICA NEWARK/CHRISTIANA
302/283-0800
Extended Stay Hotel. Rates not provided. **Address:** 333 Continental Dr 19713 **Location:** I-95 exit 4B, 0.3 mi n on SR 7 exit 166, then 0.4 mi w on SR 58 (Churchmans Rd). Located at rear of Christiana Executive Campus. Churchmans Crossing, 177. **Facility:** 142 efficiencies. 3 stories, interior corridors. **Guest Services:** coin laundry.

HILTON WILMINGTON/CHRISTIANA (302)454-1500

Hotel $119-$199

Hilton
HOTELS & RESORTS

AAA Benefit: Members save 5% or more!

Address: 100 Continental Dr 19713 **Location:** I-95 exit 4B, 0.3 mi n on SR 7 exit 166, then 0.4 mi w on SR 58 (Churchmans Rd). Located in a business park area. Churchmans Crossing, 177. **Facility:** 266 units. 4 stories, interior corridors. **Terms:** 1-7 night minimum stay, cancellation fee imposed. **Amenities:** safes. **Pool(s):** outdoor. **Activities:** hot tub, exercise room. **Guest Services:** valet and coin laundry, area transportation.

HOLIDAY INN EXPRESS & SUITES HOTEL WILMINGTON-NEWARK
(302)737-2700

ΨΨΨ **Hotel** $150-$225 **Address:** 1201 Christiana Rd 19713 **Location:** I-95 exit 3 southbound; exit 3B northbound, 0.5 mi w on SR 273. **Facility:** 120 units. 4 stories, interior corridors. **Pool(s):** heated indoor. **Activities:** hot tub, exercise room. **Guest Services:** valet and coin laundry.

CALL

HOMEWOOD SUITES BY HILTON NEWARK/WILMINGTON SOUTH
(302)453-9700

ΨΨΨ **Extended Stay Hotel** $109-$179 **Address:** 640 S College Ave 19713 **Location:** I-95 exit 1B southbound; exit 1 northbound, 0.8 mi n on SR 896. Opposite the Bob Carpenter Center.

AAA Benefit: Members save 5% or more!

🅱 Newark, 178. **Facility:** 91 efficiencies, some two bedrooms. 6 stories, interior corridors. **Terms:** 1-7 night minimum stay, cancellation fee imposed. **Amenities:** safes. **Pool(s):** heated indoor. **Activities:** exercise room. **Guest Services:** valet and coin laundry, area transportation.

QUALITY INN WILMINGTON-NEWARK/CHRISTIANA MALL
(302)292-1500

ΨΨ
Motel
$89-$299

Address: 65 Geoffrey Dr 19713 **Location:** I-95 exit 4B, 0.3 mi n on SR 7 exit 166, then just e on SR 58 (Churchmans Rd). Located in a shopping complex. **Facility:** 133 units. 3 stories, interior/exterior corridors. **Pool(s):** heated outdoor. **Activities:** exercise room. **Guest Services:** valet laundry. **Featured Amenity:** continental breakfast.

RAMADA NEWARK/WILMINGTON
(302)738-3400

ΨΨ ΨΨ
Hotel
$79-$129

Address: 260 Chapman Rd 19702 **Location:** I-95 exit 3 southbound; exit 3A northbound, 0.3 mi e on SR 273 E, then just s. **Facility:** 96 units. 2 stories (no elevator), interior corridors. **Pool(s):** outdoor. **Activities:** exercise room. **Guest Services:** valet and coin laundry. **Featured Amenity:** full hot breakfast.

RED ROOF PLUS WILMINGTON - NEWARK
302/292-2870

ΨΨ
Motel
Rates not provided

Address: 415 Stanton Christiana Rd 19713 **Location:** I-95 exit 4B, 0.5 mi n on SR 7. **Facility:** 119 units. 3 stories, exterior corridors. **Amenities:** safes.

RESIDENCE INN BY MARRIOTT WILMINGTON/NEWARK/CHRISTIANA
(302)453-9200

ΨΨΨ **Extended Stay Hotel** $174-$286 **Address:** 240 Chapman Rd 19702 **Location:** I-95 exit 3 southbound; exit 3A northbound, 0.3 mi e on SR 273 E, then 0.5 mi s. **Facility:** 120 units, some two bedrooms, efficiencies and kitchens. 2 stories (no elevator), exterior corridors. **Activities:** exercise room. **Guest Services:** valet and coin laundry, area transportation.

AAA Benefit: Members save 5% or more!

STAYBRIDGE SUITES-NEWARK/WILMINGTON
302/366-8097

ΨΨΨ **Extended Stay Hotel.** Rates not provided. **Address:** 270 Chapman Rd 19702 **Location:** I-95 exit 3 southbound; exit 3A northbound, 0.3 mi e on SR 273 E, then just s. **Facility:** 73 efficiencies, some two bedrooms. 4 stories, interior corridors. **Pool(s):** outdoor. **Activities:** exercise room. **Guest Services:** valet and coin laundry, boarding pass kiosk.

TOWNEPLACE SUITES BY MARRIOTT-WILMINGTON/CHRISTIANA/NEWARK
(302)369-6212

ΨΨΨ **Extended Stay Hotel** $122-$200 **Address:** 410 Eagle Run Rd 19702 **Location:** I-95 exit 3 southbound; exit 3A northbound, just e. **Facility:** 72 efficiencies. 4 stories, interior corridors. **Pool(s):** outdoor. **Activities:** exercise room. **Guest Services:** valet and coin laundry.

AAA Benefit: Members save 5% or more!

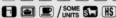

WHERE TO EAT

ALI BABA RESTAURANT
302/738-1111

ΨΨ Middle Eastern. Casual Dining. $11-$18 **AAA Inspector Notes:** Here you can sample Middle Eastern cuisine prepared from Moroccan and Lebanese recipes. The Moroccan atmosphere incorporates tapestries and sofa seating in the back room, and traditional seating in the front. Lunch service is available Thursday and Friday from 11 am. **Features:** full bar. **Reservations:** suggested, weekends. **Address:** 175 E Main St 19711 **Location:** I-95 exit 1B, 2.5 mi n on SR 896, 0.5 mi e on E Delaware Ave, then just w; downtown. **Parking:** street only. D

CAFFE GELATO RESTAURANT
302/738-5811

ΨΨ Italian. Casual Dining. $6-$32 **AAA Inspector Notes:** On bustling Main Street, near the University of Delaware, this intimate café prepares Mediterranean cuisine with a Northern Italian influence. The kitchen creates a wide range of daily specials in addition to the regular menu items. The lunch menu is available until 5 pm and offers salads, soups, panini and pasta dishes. Save room for gelato; it's homemade and a rainbow of flavors are offered. **Features:** full bar, patio dining, Sunday brunch, happy hour. **Reservations:** suggested. **Address:** 90 E Main St 19711 **Location:** I-95 exit 1B, 2.5 mi n on SR 896, 0.5 mi e on E Delaware Ave, then just w; downtown. 🅱 Newark, 178. L D

IRON HILL BREWERY & RESTAURANT
302/266-9000

ΨΨ American. Gastropub. $10-$28 **AAA Inspector Notes:** Hand-crafted beers made on the premises match with the innovative American cuisine. The downtown dining room is casual, comfortable and friendly. Lighter fare is available throughout the day, and the dinner menu begins at 5 pm. **Features:** full bar, patio dining, Sunday brunch, happy hour. **Address:** 147 E Main St 19711 **Location:** I-95 exit 1B, 2.5 mi n on SR 896, 0.5 mi e on E Delaware Ave, then just w; downtown. **Parking:** street only. L D LATE

LA CASA PASTA RESTAURANT   302/738-9935
WWW Italian. Casual Dining. $8-$33 **AAA Inspector Notes:**
For more than 30 years, this friendly, unpretentious restaurant has
served delicious, fresh seafood, veal and homemade pasta dishes.
The chef/owner specializes in Northern and Southern Italian cooking.
A lunch buffet is available Monday through Friday. **Features:** full bar,
happy hour. **Reservations:** suggested. **Address:** 120 Four Seasons
Pkwy 19702 **Location:** I-95 exit 1A southbound; exit 1 northbound,
1.5 mi s on SR 896. [L] [D]

MAD MAC'S   302/737-4800
WW WW American. Casual Dining. $10-$25 **AAA Inspector Notes:**
Located within minutes of the University of Delaware campus, the
restaurant features a casual dining room and a popular bar. The
menu offers an extensive selection of macaroni and cheese dishes,
such as lobster mac, pizza mac, Cajun shrimp-and-crab mac, and the
list goes on. Not in the mood for mac? You'll also find burgers, sandwiches and full entrées on the menu. **Features:** full bar, Sunday
brunch. **Address:** 801 S College Ave 19713 **Location:** I-95 exit 1B
southbound; exit 1 northbound, 0.5 mi n on SR 896.
[L] [D]

MICHAEL'S FAMILY RESTAURANT & PUB   302/368-4230
WW WW American. Casual Dining. $8-$28 **AAA Inspector Notes:**
Buffet choices in this restaurant include prime rib, huge mussels and
snow crab legs. The regular menu offers sandwiches, burgers, pasta,
beef and seafood selections. Save room for the popular bananas
Foster or the ice cream sundae bar. Only closed on Christmas Day.
Features: full bar, early bird specials, Sunday brunch, happy hour.
Address: 1000 Churchmans Rd 19713 **Location:** I-95 exit 4B, 0.3
mi n on SR 7 exit 166, then 0.4 mi w. 🅼 Churchmans Crossing,
177. [B] [L] [D] [🍴]

MORELIA MEXICAN RESTAURANT & BAR   302/369-6888
WW WW Mexican. Casual Dining. $7-$16 **AAA Inspector Notes:** In
a shopping plaza, this casual restaurant offers a comfortable setting,
efficient service and a nice selection of Mexican items, ranging from
tacos and burritos to steak and shrimp dishes. **Features:** full bar. **Address:** 4617 Stanton Ogletown Rd 19713 **Location:** I-95 exit 4B, 0.3
mi n on SR 7 exit 166, 0.8 mi w on SR 58 (Churchmans Rd), then 0.7
mi s on SR 4; in The Omega Shop. 🅼 Churchmans Crossing, 177.
[L] [D] [🍴]

NEW CASTLE (B-1) pop. 5,285, elev. 17'

William Penn first set foot in North America near
what is now the corner of Strand and Delaware
streets. The town prospered under Penn's Quaker
administration, producing two signers of the Declaration of Independence—George Read and Thomas
McKean.

New Castle was a trade center until 1824 when a
fire leveled the business district. Although the New
Castle-Frenchtown Railroad gave New Castle new
life in 1832, in the mid-19th century the main railroad
lines were rerouted through Wilmington, isolating
the town. New Castle's resulting seclusion has had
one desirable effect: Much of its Colonial and Federal architecture remains unaltered.

The Old Library Museum, housed in a restored
1892 Victorian library designed by Philadelphia architect Frank Furness and featuring a cupola, skylight and leaded-glass doors, presents changing
historic exhibits; phone (302) 322-2794.

New Castle's inhabitants own a 700-acre tract of
land dating from the earliest days of Dutch settlement. Administered by the Trustees of New Castle
Common instead of the municipal government, its
many uses yield considerable revenue for the
common good of the community.

Self-guiding tours: Brochures for the New Castle
Heritage Trail walking tour are available at the New
Castle Court House Museum *(see attraction listing)*
and the city administration building at the corner of
Third and Delaware streets across from The Green.
The tour covers historic areas and buildings dating
from the mid-17th century.

AMSTEL HOUSE, 2 E. Fourth St., is an example of
18th-century Georgian architecture. The 1730s
house, once the home of Governor Nicholas Van
Dyke Sr., interprets life in the Colonial period
through furnishings, an open-hearth kitchen and
household equipment. **Time:** Allow 30 minutes
minimum. **Hours:** Guided tours depart Wed.-Sat. at
10, noon and 2, Sun. at noon and 2, Apr.-Dec; by
appointment rest of year. Closed major holidays.
Cost: $6; $2 (ages 6-12). Combination ticket with
Dutch House $10; $3 (ages 6-12). **Phone:** (302)
322-2794.

DUTCH HOUSE, 32 E. Third St., was built in the
late 17th century and is one of the oldest brick
houses in the state. The structure contains decorative arts and historical artifacts, plus 17th- and 18th-
century Colonial Dutch furnishings characteristic of
a settler's house. **Time:** Allow 30 minutes minimum.
Hours: Guided tours depart Wed.-Sat. at 11, 1 and
3, Sun. at 1 and 3, Apr.-Dec.; by appointment rest of
year. Closed major holidays. **Cost:** $6; $2 (ages
6-12). Combination ticket with Amstel House $10; $3
(ages 6-12). **Phone:** (302) 322-2794.

THE GREEN, on Delaware St. between Third and
Market sts., was laid out by Peter Stuyvesant in
1655. The Green and adjacent Market Square were
the sites of fairs and weekly markets until the early
19th century. An 1809 U.S. arsenal and the 1798
New Castle Academy are on The Green. **Phone:**
(302) 323-4453.

NEW CASTLE COURT HOUSE MUSEUM is at 211
Delaware St. between Market and Third sts. Built in
1732, the courthouse was occupied by the Colonial
Assembly until 1776; was the site of the adoption of
Delaware's first constitution on Sept. 20, 1776; and
served as the state's first capitol until 1777. It has
been restored to its Colonial appearance and contains portraits, artifacts and furnishings relating to
Delaware history. **Time:** Allow 30 minutes minimum.
Hours: Wed.-Sat. 10-3:30, Sun. 1:30-4:30. Closed
major holidays. **Cost:** Free. **Phone:** (302) 323-4453.

NEW CASTLE PRESBYTERIAN CHURCH, 25 E.
Second St., is believed to have been the direct suc-
cessor of the original Dutch Reformed Church of
1657. Built in 1707, it was one of several churches
forming the first presbytery in America. The cemetery contains marked graves dating from the early
1700s. **Hours:** Daily 8:30-12:30. **Cost:** Free.
Phone: (302) 328-3279.

ORIGINAL TICKET OFFICE, at the Battery on the s. side of Delaware St., was part of the now defunct New Castle and Frenchtown Railway. One of the first in the nation, the 1832 office marked the eastern terminus of the line. It was moved to its present site in the 1950s. Nearby is a section of reconstructed track with wooden rails pegged to stone sleepers, the forerunner of wooden railroad ties. The interior of the structure is not accessible. **Cost:** Free. **Phone:** (302) 322-2794.

READ HOUSE AND GARDENS, 42 The Strand, was built in 1801-03 by the son of George Read, one of the signers of the Declaration of Independence. A fine example of Federal architecture, the 22-room mansion is furnished in period and features carved woodwork, relief plasterwork and gilded fanlights. Tours highlight the lifestyles of three resident families. A 1.5-acre formal Victorian garden graces the grounds.

Time: Allow 30 minutes minimum. **Hours:** Wed.-Fri. and Sun. 11-4, Sat. 10-4, Apr.-Dec.; by appointment rest of year. The house is open only by guided 35- to 45-minute tours; departure times vary. Last tour departs at 3:30. Closed major holidays. **Cost:** Gardens free. House tours $7; $6 (ages 10-21, ages 65+ and military with ID); free (ages 0-9). **Phone:** (302) 322-8411. GT

THE STRAND, near the river, is a block-long street bordered by shady brick walks and brick gutters. A number of townhouses dating from the 18th century survived the great fire that swept the street in 1824. The law office of Thomas McKean, a delegate to the Continental Congress of 1774, was at 22 The Strand. Packet Alley runs from The Strand to the river. **Phone:** (302) 322-2794.

CLARION HOTEL-THE BELLE (302)428-1000
▼▼▼ **Hotel** $109-$189 **Address:** 1612 N DuPont Hwy 19720 **Location:** Jct I-295, just n on US 13. Next to Graceland Memorial Park Cemetery. **Facility:** 125 units. 2 stories, interior corridors. **Amenities:** safes. **Pool(s):** outdoor. **Activities:** exercise room. **Guest Services:** valet laundry, area transportation.

SHERATON WILMINGTON SOUTH NEW CASTLE
(302)328-6200
▼▼▼▼
Hotel
$99-$239

AAA Benefit: Members save up to 15%, plus Starwood Preferred Guest® benefits!

Address: 365 Airport Rd 19720 **Location:** I-95 exit 5A (SR 141 S). **Facility:** 192 units. 6 stories, interior corridors. **Parking:** on-site and valet. **Terms:** cancellation fee imposed. **Amenities:** safes. **Pool(s):** heated indoor. **Activities:** hot tub, exercise room. **Guest Services:** valet laundry, area transportation.

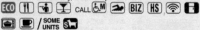
WHERE TO EAT

JESSOP'S TAVERN & COLONIAL RESTAURANT 302/322-6111
▼▼ American. Casual Dining. $10-$25 **AAA Inspector Notes:** *Historic.* American and English pub fare is served in hearty portions in the atmosphere of a 1724 Colonial brick home. The popular crab chowder, chicken pot pie and fish and chips pair with a variety of local and United Kingdom beers. Both Swedish and Dutch culinary influences reflect New Castle's early heritage. **Features:** full bar. **Address:** 114 Delaware St 19720 **Location:** In downtown historic district. **Parking:** street only. L D

ODESSA (C-1) pop. 364, elev. 52'

With its emergence in the early 19th century as one of the area's most important grain shipping ports, the name of the town known as Cantwell's Bridge was changed to Odessa, after Russia's seaport. Farmers brought their produce to town, where it was shipped down Appoquinimink Creek to the Delaware River, then to domestic and foreign ports.

The significance of the port was eclipsed in the mid-1800s with the coming of the railroad. The railroad bypassed the city on its way through the Delmarva Peninsula and the Midwest became the nation's major grain producing region. Odessa was a primary station of the Underground Railroad prior to the outbreak of the Civil War. Well-preserved examples of 18th- and 19th-century architecture line Odessa's shaded streets.

HISTORIC HOUSES OF ODESSA, on Main and Second sts., is a cluster of 18th-century historic structures, including fine houses furnished in period. Admission is by 90-minute guided tour that departs from the visitor center in the Historic Odessa Bank, designed by Philadelphia architect Samuel Sloane and built in 1853. Brochures for self-guiding walking tours are available. **Hours:** Guided tours are given as needed Tues.-Sat. 10-4:30, Sun. 1-4:30, Mar.-Dec. Last tour begins 1 hour before closing. Other times by reservation. Closed Easter, July 4, Thanksgiving, Christmas Eve and Christmas. **Cost:** $10; $8 (ages 5-17 and 60+). **Phone:** (302) 378-4119.

Collins-Sharp House, on Second and High sts., dates to around 1700, making it one of Delaware's oldest houses. The English gambrel-roof house was moved from Collins Beach on the Delaware River to its present location in 1962. **Hours:** Guided tours are given as needed Tues.-Sat. 10-4:30, Sun. 1-4:30, Mar.-Dec. Last tour begins 1 hour before closing. Other times by reservation. Closed Easter, July 4, Thanksgiving, Christmas Eve and Christmas. **Cost:** (includes all the Historic Houses of Odessa) $10; $8 (ages 5-17 and 60+). **Phone:** (302) 378-4119.

Corbit-Sharp House, on the s. side of Main St. at Second St., is a 22-room brick Georgian house. Built in 1774 by William Corbit, a Quaker and local tanner, the home stayed in the Corbit family for more than 150 years. Period furniture and local handicrafts decorate the late 18th-century house; Colonial revival-style gardens adorn the grounds. Changing exhibits are featured.

Hours: Guided tours are given as needed Tues.-Sat. 10-4:30, Sun. 1-4:30, Mar.-Dec. Last tour begins 1 hour before closing. Other times by reservation. Closed Easter, July 4, Thanksgiving, Christmas Eve and Christmas. **Cost:** (includes all the Historic Houses of Odessa) $10; $8 (ages 5-17 and 60+). **Phone:** (302) 378-4119.

Wilson-Warner House, next to the Corbit-Sharp House, was built by a local merchant in 1769. Fine paneling and 18th- and 19th-century furniture reflecting items recorded in the Wilson family bankruptcy sale in 1829 grace the interior. The 13-room brick Georgian house was purchased by family descendent Mary Corbit Warner and later became one of Delaware's first house museums upon her death in 1923. **Hours:** Guided tours are given as needed Tues.-Sat. 10-4:30, Sun. 1-4:30, Mar.-Dec. Last tour begins 1 hour before closing. Other times by reservation. Closed Easter, July 4, Thanksgiving, Christmas Eve and Christmas. **Cost:** (includes all the Historic Houses of Odessa) $10; $8 (ages 5-17 and 60+). **Phone:** (302) 378-4119.

REHOBOTH BEACH (E-3) pop. 1,327
• Restaurants p. 46

Rehoboth is a biblical term meaning "room enough." Its remote location kept the beach area almost untouched until 1872 when the Rehoboth Beach Camp Meeting Association of the Methodist Episcopal Church purchased land along the sea and platted a town. Made accessible by a railroad line extended from Lewes in 1878, the town was the site of revival camp meetings until the 1880s.

When the highway replaced the railroad in the 1920s, Rehoboth Beach was well on its way to becoming a popular resort. The nearest ocean resort to the nation's capital, the town is deluged every summer by humidity-weary Washingtonians. Natives of Delaware seem scarce by comparison in the summer capital.

Clamming, crabbing, nature cruises, deep-sea and freshwater fishing, golfing, birding, sailing and swimming are some of the recreational pursuits available to visitors. In late October, the town hosts the 🧙 Sea Witch Halloween and Fiddler's Festival, during which fiddlers compete in banjo, fiddle and bluegrass categories; a parade, craft show and costume contest round out the festivities.

Camping is available at Delaware Seashore State Park *(see Recreation Areas Chart)* on a 7-mile strip of land between the Atlantic Ocean and the Rehoboth and Indian River bays. Cape Henlopen State Park *(see Recreation Chart)* offers camping, nature trails, bathhouses, surf fishing and swimming areas where Delaware Bay meets the Atlantic Ocean.

Rehoboth Beach-Dewey Beach Chamber of Commerce and Visitor Center: Rehoboth Railroad Station, 501 Rehoboth Ave., P.O. Box 216, Rehoboth Beach, DE 19971-0216. **Phone:** (302) 227-2233 or (800) 441-1329.

Shopping areas: [SAVE] Tanger Outlets on SR 1 has more than 130 outlet stores, including Ann Taylor, Corningware, Izod, Michael Kors, Polo Ralph Lauren, Reebok and Van Heusen.

ADMIRAL ON BALTIMORE (302)227-1300

🚩🚩 **Motel** $69-$589 **Address:** 2 Baltimore Ave 19971 **Location:** Just off the boardwalk. **Facility:** 73 units. 5 stories, exterior corridors. **Terms:** closed 11/12-3/14, 2 night minimum stay - seasonal and/or weekends, 7 day cancellation notice-fee imposed. **Pool(s):** heated indoor. **Activities:** beach access.

AMERICINN LODGE & SUITES OF REHOBOTH BEACH
(302)226-0700

🚩🚩 **Hotel** $89-$359 **Address:** 36012 Airport Rd 19971 **Location:** Just w of SR 1; just w on Miller Rd, just s. **Facility:** 49 units. 2 stories (no elevator), interior corridors. **Terms:** 2 night minimum stay - seasonal and/or weekends, 3 day cancellation notice-fee imposed, resort fee. **Amenities:** safes. **Pool(s):** heated indoor. **Activities:** hot tub. **Guest Services:** coin laundry.

THE ATLANTIS INN 302/227-9446

🚩🚩 **Motel.** Rates not provided. **Address:** 154 Rehoboth Ave 19971 **Location:** At Rehoboth Ave and 2nd St; downtown. **Facility:** 94 units, some kitchens. 4 stories, exterior corridors. **Pool(s):** outdoor. **Guest Services:** coin laundry.

BOARDWALK PLAZA HOTEL (302)227-7169

🚩🚩🚩 🚩🚩🚩 Hotel $129-$649 **Address:** 2 Olive Ave 19971 **Location:** Oceanfront. Just n of Rehoboth Ave. Located on the boardwalk. **Facility:** This small hotel features a romantic Victorian theme complete with fine antiques throughout. Some guest rooms and suites offer balconies overlooking the boardwalk and beach. 83 units, some two bedrooms, efficiencies and kitchens. 4 stories, interior corridors. **Parking:** on-site and valet. **Terms:** 3 night minimum stay - seasonal and/or weekends, 3 day cancellation notice. **Amenities:** safes. **Dining:** Victoria's, see separate listing. **Activities:** hot tub, exercise room. **Guest Services:** valet laundry. *(See ad p. 45.)*

COMFORT INN REHOBOTH BEACH   (302)226-1515

Hotel
$75-$350

Address: 19210 Coastal Hwy 19971 **Location:** On SR 1, 1.5 mi n. Located in outlet mall area. **Facility:** 96 units. 3 stories, interior corridors. **Terms:** check-in 4 pm. **Pool(s):** outdoor. **Activities:** exercise room. **Guest Services:** coin laundry. **Featured Amenity:** breakfast buffet.

FAIRFIELD INN & SUITES REHOBOTH BEACH   (302)645-7766

fyi Hotel $129-$219 Too new to rate, opening scheduled for March 2015. **Address:** 19113 Coastal Hwy 19971 **Location:** SR 1. **Amenities:** 94 units, coffeemakers, microwaves, refrigerators, pool, exercise facility.

AAA Benefit: Members save 5% or more!

HAMPTON INN REHOBOTH BEACH/LEWES
(302)645-8003

Hotel
$89-$329

AAA Benefit: Members save 5% or more!

Address: 18826 Coastal Hwy 19971 **Location:** On SR 1, 2 mi n. Located in outlet mall area. **Facility:** 85 units. 4 stories, interior corridors. **Terms:** 1-7 night minimum stay, cancellation fee imposed. **Pool(s):** heated indoor. **Activities:** exercise room. **Guest Services:** valet and coin laundry.

HENLOPEN HOTEL   302/227-2551

Hotel. Rates not provided. **Address:** 511 N Boardwalk 19971 **Location:** Oceanfront. 0.5 mi n on 1st St from Rehoboth Ave. **Facility:** 93 units, some kitchens. 7 stories, exterior corridors. **Terms:** check-in 4 pm.

HOLIDAY INN EXPRESS-REHOBOTH BEACH   302/227-4030

Hotel. Rates not provided. **Address:** 19953 Shuttle Rd 19971 **Location:** On SR 1, just n. Located in outlet mall area. **Facility:** 81 units. 4 stories, interior corridors. **Pool(s):** outdoor. **Activities:** exercise room. **Guest Services:** coin laundry.

THE OCEANUS MOTEL   302/227-8200

Motel. Rates not provided. **Address:** 6 2nd St 19971 **Location:** Just s of Rehoboth Ave. **Facility:** 38 units. 3 stories (no elevator), exterior corridors. **Pool(s):** outdoor. **Guest Services:** coin laundry.

Recommend places
you'd like us to inspect at
AAA.com/TourBookComments

▼ See AAA listing p. 44 ▼

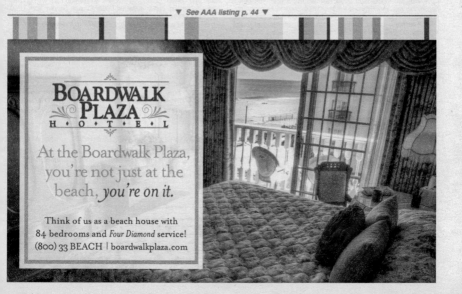

WHERE TO EAT

1776 STEAKHOUSE
302/645-9355

▼▼▼▼ Steak. Fine Dining. $8-$45 **AAA Inspector Notes:** Dry-aged steaks are the house specialty, but the extensive seafood offerings shouldn't be overlooked. The good food and friendly, professional service have garnered a strong local following. And though the atmosphere is comfortable, it can get a little loud. **Features:** full bar. **Reservations:** suggested. **Address:** 18585 Coastal Hwy, Suite 6 19971 **Location:** On SR 1, 2.5 mi n; in Midway Shopping Center. L D

ADRIATICO RISTORANTE & SEAFOOD CAFE
302/227-9255

▼▼▼ Italian. Casual Dining. $10-$32 **AAA Inspector Notes:** In the heart of downtown, the cozy Italian restaurant specializes in veal, seafood, chicken and pasta. Seasonal patio seating is available. **Features:** full bar. **Address:** 30 Baltimore Ave 19971 **Location:** Corner of 1st St and Baltimore Ave; center. **Parking:** street only. D

A(MUSE.)
302/227-7107

▼▼▼ New American. Fine Dining. $24-$35 **AAA Inspector Notes:** This chic, modern spot features a farm-to-table theme utilizing the freshest and best ingredients from a 200-mile radius. Menu items change seasonally but favorites include blue crab toasties, potted chicken and creative interpretations of local seafood. The design mixes modern and vintage elements like the wall covered with pages from the "Joy of Cooking." A small patio is lit by twinkling lights and lined in driftwood. **Features:** full bar, happy hour. **Reservations:** required. **Address:** 44 Baltimore Ave 19971 **Location:** Just n of Rehoboth Ave; between 1st and 2nd sts. **Parking:** street only. D

BIG FISH GRILL
302/227-3474

▼▼ Seafood. Casual Dining. $10-$30 **AAA Inspector Notes:** The main attraction is fresh seafood, including raw bar items, sandwiches and local crab cakes. The casual, loud and comfortable restaurant is popular with locals and tourists alike. In summer, it's not uncommon to experience an hour-long wait for a table. **Features:** full bar. **Address:** 20298 Coastal Hwy 19971 **Location:** Just s on SR 1. L D CALL 🅜

BLUE MOON RESTAURANT
302/227-6515

▼▼▼▼ American. Fine Dining. $24-$49 **AAA Inspector Notes:** Less than two blocks from the ocean and inside a striking beach house, this restaurant specializes in creative, modern American cuisine with international influences. Friendly and efficient service is offered. **Features:** full bar, Sunday brunch. **Reservations:** suggested. **Address:** 35 Baltimore Ave 19971 **Location:** Between 1st and 2nd sts. **Parking:** street only. D

BRAMBLE & BRINE
302/227-7702

▼▼▼▼ New American. Fine Dining. $23-$42 **AAA Inspector Notes:** Set in a lovingly restored cottage chock-full of antiques and collectibles, this new restaurant manages to feel modern and vintage simultaneously. The owner/chef has an impressive resume of working in famous kitchens and the evidence is clear in his creatively delicious dishes. The menu changes daily, but he is known for his skills in preparing duck and the Berkshire pork chop, though the accoutrements change seasonally to best highlight the freshest local produce. **Features:** full bar. **Reservations:** suggested. **Address:** 315 Rehoboth Ave 19971 **Location:** On SR 1A, between State Rd and Scarborough Ave. **Parking:** street only. D

THE CULTURED PEARL
302/227-8493

▼▼ Asian. Fine Dining. $17-$32 **AAA Inspector Notes:** This longtime popular spot offers a lengthy menu of great Asian specialties, including creative sushi options, stir-fry dishes, seafood and even a cream of crab soup. When the weather agrees, the rooftop patio can't be beat for serenity. The spa-like setting offers a bird's-eye view of town and koi ponds from tables draped in flowing white fabric and twinkling lights. **Features:** full bar, happy hour. **Reservations:** suggested. **Address:** 301 Rehoboth Ave 19971 **Location:** Jct 4th St and Lake Ave. **Parking:** street only. D

DOGFISH HEAD BREWINGS & EATS
302/226-2739

▼▼ American. Gastropub. $7-$23 **AAA Inspector Notes:** This is the famed spot where it all started for this brewer and distiller. The pub menu features American favorites, often with beer as an ingredient. Specialties include pizzas, sandwiches, crab cakes, pretzel bites, burgers and meatloaf. Don't miss their off-centered beers and spirits; some seasonal varieties are only available here. For the ultimate indulgence try the bacon-beer blue-cheesecake. **Features:** full bar, patio dining. **Address:** 320 Rehoboth Ave 19971 **Location:** On SR 1A, between State Rd and Scarborough Ave. **Parking:** on-site and street. L D

EDEN
302/227-3330

▼▼▼ New American. Fine Dining. $22-$34 **AAA Inspector Notes:** This romantic spot in a beach-chic setting serves contemporary dishes with bold, fresh flavors. Many herbs, vegetables and fruits from the garden are used to prepare seasonal and traditional dishes. Specialty items include the lobster and crab tower appetizer with mango salsa, wasabi-crusted tuna, and a variety of seafood and steak entrées. The elegantly decorated dining room has booths that mimic draped beach cabanas. An extensive wine list has more than 100 choices by the bottle. **Features:** full bar, patio dining, happy hour. **Reservations:** suggested. **Address:** 23 Baltimore Ave 19971 **Location:** Just n of Rehoboth Ave. **Parking:** street only. D

ESPUMA
302/227-4199

▼▼▼ New Mediterranean. Fine Dining. $18-$39 **AAA Inspector Notes:** Spanish for "foam," this restaurant delivers traditional dishes prepared with modern techniques. The seasonal menu includes a vegan sweet corn soup that is poured tableside with rich figs. The three-day roasted pork is served with a freshly made organic zucchini cake. Other favorites include paella with mussels and chorizo, pasta, and a variety of seafood dishes. Don't skip dessert, as the house-made ice cream sliders will be a hit with everyone. Live entertainment is offered. **Features:** full bar, happy hour. **Reservations:** required. **Address:** 28 Wilmington Ave 19971 **Location:** Just s of jct Rehoboth Ave. **Parking:** street only. D CALL 🅜

FINS FISH HOUSE & RAW BAR
302/226-3467

▼▼ Seafood. Casual Dining. $9-$27 **AAA Inspector Notes:** When locals are looking for great seafood and company, they head straight to this spot for happy hour, when oysters are a buck each and drink specials abound. Fresh seafood is prepared every which way, from clams casino and seafood potato skins to basil-shrimp scampi and lobster rolls. Casual and comfortable, this place also whips up beef and chicken dishes. Vegetarians will have to stick with grazing the salad menu. Lunch is served Friday through Sunday from 11:30 am. **Features:** full bar, happy hour. **Address:** 243 Rehoboth Ave 19971 **Location:** Just e of jct 2nd St. **Parking:** street only. D

JAKE'S SEAFOOD HOUSE
302/227-6237

▼▼ Seafood. Family Dining. $10-$50 **AAA Inspector Notes:** The casual downtown restaurant prepares seafood with an Old Baltimore taste. **Features:** full bar. **Address:** 29 Baltimore Ave 19971 **Location:** Corner of 1st St and Baltimore Ave; center. **Parking:** street only. L D

JAKE'S SEAFOOD HOUSE RESTAURANT
302/644-7711

▼▼ Seafood. Casual Dining. $11-$47 **AAA Inspector Notes:** The fun, upbeat restaurant prepares a variety of seafood in the Old Baltimore style. **Features:** full bar. **Address:** 19178 Coastal Hwy 19971 **Location:** On SR 1, 1.5 mi n. L D

JUST IN THYME RESTAURANT
302/227-3100

▼▼▼ American. Fine Dining. $19-$28 **AAA Inspector Notes:** This comfortable, homey atmosphere is suitable for any occasion. Dishes prepared by the chef/owner blend a Continental influence with American style. A notable local favorite is carpetbagger steak, a black Angus filet mignon stuffed with Saga blue cheese and lump crab meat. Fresh fish always is available. **Features:** full bar, early bird specials, happy hour. **Reservations:** suggested. **Address:** 38163 Robinsons Dr 19971 **Location:** 1.1 mi s on SR 1. D

MARIACHI RESTAURANT 302/227-0115

♦♦ ♦♦ Latin American. Casual Dining. $10-$23 **AAA Inspector Notes:** Within walking distance of the oceanside boardwalk, this spacious restaurant offers a cool respite from the action on the beach. Delicious Latin American and Spanish dishes are served by a welcoming, knowledgeable staff. Ask about the daily specials. The second-floor dining room and balcony offer ocean views. **Features:** full bar, patio dining, Sunday brunch, happy hour. **Reservations:** suggested. **Address:** 14 Wilmington Ave 19971 **Location:** Just w of the boardwalk. **Parking:** on-site and street. [L] [D]

NAGE BISTRO & WINE BAR 302/226-2037

♦♦♦♦ New American. Fine Dining. $12-$33 **AAA Inspector Notes:** Creative food without the 'tude is the motto that this place definitely lives up to. A meal can be made up of the small plate offerings, which include truffle oil macaroni and cheese, pop rock shrimp and ricotta gnocchi. The seafood a la Nage is packed with shrimp, scallops, mussels and clams in a tomato-saffron broth. Desserts are made in-house and any choice is top-notch. **Features:** full bar, Sunday brunch, happy hour. **Reservations:** suggested. **Address:** 19730 Coastal Hwy 19971 **Location:** On SR 1, just n. [L] [D]

THE PIG + FISH RESTAURANT COMPANY 302/227-7770

♦♦ ♦♦ American. Gastropub. $10-$28 **AAA Inspector Notes:** This popular spot has the catch phrase "eat like a pig, and drink like a fish." The menu will satisfy your cravings for comfort foods, with a twist. Try the Tabasco-smoked pork tenderloin topped with a savory sage honey glaze, pork "wings," lobster mac 'n' cheese, and flatbread pizzas. An expansive beer and wine list includes many regional choices. Lunch is served Friday through Sunday. **Features:** full bar, happy hour. **Address:** 236 Rehoboth Ave 19971 **Location:** Between Scarborough Ave and 2nd St. **Parking:** street only. [D]

RISTORANTE ZEBRA 302/226-1160

♦♦♦♦ Northern Italian. Fine Dining. $16-$36 **AAA Inspector Notes:** This restaurant has a strong local following due to its consistent Italian cooking. The skilled kitchen uses only fresh ingredients in preparing its seasonally changing menu, which lists a nice selection of homemade pasta, veal, beef, chicken, seafood and homemade desserts. The atmosphere is casual with upscale air. Efficient, attentive service is offered. **Features:** full bar. **Reservations:** required, weekends in summer. **Address:** 32 Lake Ave 19971 **Location:** Jct Rehoboth Ave, just ne. **Parking:** street only. [D]

ROOT GOURMET 302/727-5664

♦ Natural/Organic Deli. Quick Serve. $9-$12 **AAA Inspector Notes:** This spot offers great healthy food in a quick-serve environment. Organic and local produce and meats can be found in salads, soups, entrées, and wood-fired flatbreads. Also pantry items and great dips are served alongside artisan breads and fabulous desserts. **Features:** patio dining. **Address:** 19724 Coastal Hwy 19971 **Location:** On SR 1, just n. [L] [D] CALL ⌂M

SAKETUMI 302/645-2818

♦♦♦ Asian. Casual Dining. $9-$36 **AAA Inspector Notes:** Japanese, Thai and Chinese cuisine come together beautifully in a hip, sexy atmosphere. Guests can order specialty cocktails or glasses of wine from the equally diverse drink menu. Portions are ample. **Features:** full bar. **Address:** 18814 Coastal Hwy 19971 **Location:** On SR 1, 2 mi n. [L] [D]

SHOREBREAK LODGE 302/227-1007

♦♦ ♦♦ American. Casual Dining. $10-$30 **AAA Inspector Notes:** Just a short stroll from the boardwalk, this casual restaurant offers a nice selection of American dishes creatively prepared by the chef/owner. The menu changes regularly, as it is driven by the availability of fresh ingredients, local when available. Selections may include grilled beer-braised pork sirloin steak with Gorgonzola grits, scallops and short ribs with Parmesan risotto or maybe grilled Kansas City veal chop with charred romaine and roasted criminis. **Features:** full bar. **Reservations:** suggested, in summer. **Address:** 10 Wilmington Ave 19971 **Location:** Between the boardwalk and 1st St. **Parking:** street only. [D]

SUMMER HOUSE RESTAURANT 302/227-3895

♦♦ ♦♦ American. Casual Dining. $10-$32 **AAA Inspector Notes:** A few blocks north of the boardwalk, guests can easily stroll in to enjoy their seafood specialties. The standard menu may be short, but the daily specials are often varied and feature seasonal ingredients. The space is comfortable, ideal for lingering to enjoy a drink at the bar before heading back to the beach. **Features:** full bar, Sunday brunch, happy hour. **Address:** 228 Rehoboth Ave 19971 **Location:** Between Scarborough Ave and 2nd St. **Parking:** street only. [L] [D]

TOUCH OF ITALY 302/703-3090

♦♦ ♦♦ Italian. Casual Dining. $10-$24 **AAA Inspector Notes:** If you can't find something delicious here, I don't know where you will. This spacious spot has a huge menu of antipasti, cheeses, salamis, pastas, pastries, sandwiches, pizzas and entrées. The choices extend far beyond red sauce with more imaginative pasta dishes--some freshly made in house. Other specialties are roasted in their wood-fired oven. This is a convivial spot to enjoy a meal, however many people opt for to-go meals from the deli counter. **Features:** full bar. **Reservations:** suggested. **Address:** 19724 Coastal Hwy 19971 **Location:** On SR 1, just n. [L] [D] CALL ⌂M [AC]

VICTORIA'S 302/227-0615

♦♦♦♦
American Fine Dining $10-$36

AAA Inspector Notes: Antiques and floral prints set a Victorian theme at this spot overlooking the boardwalk and sea. The traditional menu features local favorites, including lots of crab, naturally. Other offerings are fried green tomatoes, Virginia oysters, braised short ribs, and steak. On pleasant days, the seating on the boardwalk, enclosed by iron gates and arches, can't be beat. **Features:** full bar, early bird specials, Sunday brunch. **Reservations:** suggested. **Address:** 2 Olive Ave 19971 **Location:** Just n of Rehoboth Ave; in Boardwalk Plaza Hotel. **Parking:** on-site (fee).

[B] [L] [D] 🛒

NICOLA PIZZA 302/227-6211

[fyi] Not evaluated. This local pizza joint has been a favorite of beachgoers since the 1970s when the owners opened their first spot around the corner. Now with this larger spot open, too, more can come in and enjoy great pizza, sandwiches, beach fries, pastas, and, of course, the famed Nic-o-boli. **Address:** 71 Rehoboth Ave 19971 **Location:** Between 1st St and N Boardwalk.

SEAFORD pop. 6,928
• Restaurants p. 48

DAYS INN & SUITES (302)629-4300

♦♦ Hotel $60-$102 **Address:** 23450 Sussex Hwy 19973 **Location:** On US 13, just n of jct SR 20. **Facility:** 61 units. 2 stories, interior corridors. **Pool(s):** heated outdoor. **Activities:** limited exercise equipment. **Guest Services:** coin laundry.

[¶↑+] 🛄 [BIZ] [HS] 📶 🖥 🖨 🖵

HAMPTON INN SEAFORD (302)629-4500

♦♦♦ Hotel $109-$219 **Address:** 22871 Sussex Hwy 19973 **Location:** 1.5 mi n on US 13 from SR 20; in Sussex Plaza. **Facility:** 66 units. 3 stories, interior corridors. **Terms:** 1-7 night minimum stay, cancellation fee imposed. **Pool(s):** heated indoor. **Activities:** hot tub, exercise room. **Guest Services:** valet and coin laundry.

AAA Benefit: Members save 5% or more!

[¶↑+] CALL ⌂M 🛄 [BIZ] [HS] 📶 🖥 🖨 🖵

HOLIDAY INN EXPRESS-SEAFORD   (302)629-2000

WWWW **Hotel** $89-$200 **Address:** 24058 N Sussex Hwy 19973 **Location:** On US 13, just s of SR 20 W. **Facility:** 81 units. 4 stories, interior corridors. **Terms:** 3 day cancellation notice. **Pool(s):** outdoor. **Activities:** exercise room. **Guest Services:** valet and coin laundry.

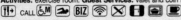
WHERE TO EAT

BON APPETIT RESTAURANT   302/629-3700

WWWW **AAA Inspector Notes:** This classic French restaurant is a local institution
French   where the owner walks the elegant room
Fine Dining   lined with Parisian prints and seems to
$10-$27   know everyone. The menu is equally classic with specialties such as poached mussels, escargot, pâté, duck apricot, and steak with Bearnaise butter. **Features:** full bar. **Reservations:** suggested. **Address:** 312 High St 19973 **Location:** 1.2 mi w on Middleford Rd from jct US 13; downtown. **Parking:** street only. L D

SMYRNA (C-1) pop. 10,023, elev. 33'

BOMBAY HOOK NATIONAL WILDLIFE REFUGE is s. on US 13, e. on SR 12, s. on SR 9, then about 2.5 mi. e. on Whitehall Neck Rd. Although the refuge primarily protects migrating ducks, geese and other seasonal birds, wildlife can be seen year-round. Five walking trails and a 12-mile round-trip driving route offer opportunities to explore the 15,978-acre refuge, and three observation towers provide a panorama of the area.

Picnic tables are available near the visitors center. **Hours:** Refuge open daily dawn-dusk. Visitor center open Mon.-Fri. 8-4, Sat.-Sun. 9-5, Mar.-May and Sept. 1 to mid-Dec.; Mon.-Fri. 8-4, rest of year. **Cost:** $4 (per private vehicle); $2 (for persons arriving by bicycle or on foot). **Phone:** (302) 653-6872.

BEST WESTERN SMYRNA INN   (302)659-3635

WW WW
Hotel
$85-$299

 AAA Benefit:
Members save up to 20%!

Address: 190 Stadium St 19977 **Location:** SR 1 exit 114, just s on DuPont Blvd; in Gateway North Shopping Center. **Facility:** 72 units. 3 stories, interior corridors. **Terms:** cancellation fee imposed. **Pool(s):** outdoor. **Activities:** exercise room. **Guest Services:** coin laundry.

STANTON

LA TONALTECA   302/636-9484

WW WW Mexican. Casual Dining. $6-$25 **AAA Inspector Notes:** Popular with locals, this restaurant offers a wide variety of Mexican dishes in a colorful, friendly atmosphere. Service is efficient and ingredients are fresh; the guacamole is not to be missed. **Features:** full bar. **Address:** 1724 W Newport Pike 19804 **Location:** I-95 exit 4B, 1.8 mi n on SR 7, then 1 mi e on SR 4; in First State Plaza. L D

WILMINGTON (B-2) pop. 70,851, elev. 134'
• Hotels p. 51 • Restaurants p. 52
• Attractions map p. 49

Quakers laid out Wilmington in 1731. The settlement grew into an important market and shipping center. Industrial growth followed, stimulated by Wilmington's accessibility to other eastern ports and by the abundant water power in the Brandywine River Valley.

In the early 19th century Wilmington attracted Éleuthère Irénée du Pont and his two sons, who intended to finance a colony based on Utopian ideas. Seeing a need for high-quality gunpowder, however, the du Ponts abandoned their original plan, and in 1803 their new Eleutherian Mills produced the first barrel of Du Pont powder. The du Pont influence was instrumental in shaping Delaware's largest city into an industrial, financial and shipping hub.

A highlight of Wilmington's downtown renewal effort is the 1871 Grand Opera House, 818 N. Market St., with its ornate cast-iron facade. Free tours are available by reservation; phone (302) 658-7897. The Custom House, Sixth and King streets, was Wilmington's first federal building. Built in 1855, it is noted for its simple but bold exterior lines and impressive interior.

The Quaker Hill Historic District, downtown between Jefferson and Tatnall streets and Second and Eighth streets, was Wilmington's first neighborhood. It contains residences built 1745-1890, 19th-century churches and an 1816 Quaker meeting hall with a large cemetery.

The 18th-century John Chads House, built by a local innkeeper and ferry operator, is open for tours, which include a beehive oven baking demonstration.

Riverwalk is a mile-long landscaped path along the Christina River with scenic overlooks and parks as well as access to several cafes.

The Wilmington and Western Railroad offers 1- and 2-hour scenic rides through the Red Clay Valley area on weekends as well as seasonal specialty rides March through December. For schedule and fare information phone (302) 998-1930.

Greater Wilmington Convention and Visitors Bureau: 100 W. 10th St., Suite 20, Wilmington, DE 19801. **Phone:** (302) 295-2210 or (800) 489-6664.

Self-guiding tours: Maps for a self-guiding walking tour of the Quaker Hill Historic District are available from the Quaker Hill Historic Preservation Foundation at 521 N. West St.; phone (302) 655-2500.

Shopping areas: Vendors at Riverfront Market, a European-style marketplace in a historic warehouse, sell fresh produce, meat, fish and gourmet food items.

BRANDYWINE PARK AND ZOO is at 1001 N. Park Dr. along the Brandywine River between Augustine and Market sts. The 180-acre park was designed by the creator of New York City's Central Park, Frederick Law Olmstead, and features the Josephine

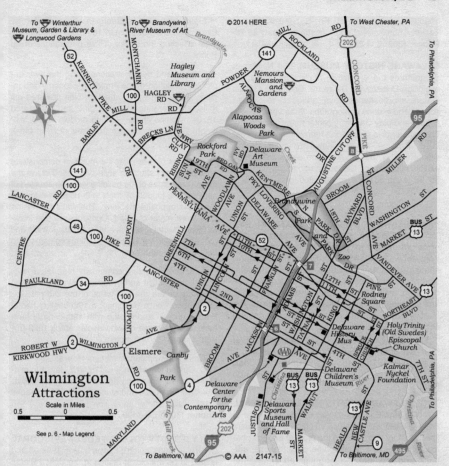

To Winterthur Museum, Garden & Library & Longwood Gardens

To Brandywine River Museum of Art

©2014 HERE

To West Chester, PA

Wilmington Attractions

Scale in Miles
0.5   0   0.5

See p. 6 - Map Legend

Garden, which has 118 Japanese cherry trees. The zoo houses a Florida bobcat, Amur tiger, small mammals and a variety of North and South American reptiles and birds.

Time: Allow 2 hours minimum. **Hours:** Park daily dawn-dusk. Zoo daily 10-4. **Cost:** Park free. Zoo admission May-Sept. $7; $5 (ages 3-17 and 62+). Admission rest of year $5; $4 (ages 62+); $3 (ages 3-17). **Phone:** (302) 571-7747.

DELAWARE ART MUSEUM, 2301 Kentmere Pkwy., contains a renowned collection of American paintings and illustrations by 19th-, 20th- and 21st-century artists and one of the largest collections of pre-Raphaelite art outside the United Kingdom. A 9-acre sculpture park, changing exhibits and an art research library provide further enrichment. A children's gallery features hands-on activities designed to stimulate creativity.

Time: Allow 1 hour minimum. **Hours:** Wed.-Sat. 10-4, Sun. noon-4. Library available by appointment. Closed Jan. 1, July 4, Thanksgiving and Christmas.

Cost: $12; $10 (ages 60+); $6 (ages 7-18 and college students with ID); free (on Sun.). **Phone:** (302) 571-9590 or (866) 232-3714.

DELAWARE CENTER FOR THE CONTEMPORARY ARTS is at 200 S. Madison St. Seven galleries feature curated exhibits by nationally- and internationally-known artists. The facility also contains 26 artist studios. **Time:** Allow 1 hour minimum. **Hours:** Tues. and Thurs.-Sat. 10-5, Wed. and Sun. noon-5. Closed major holidays. **Cost:** Free. **Phone:** (302) 656-6466. Wilmington, 176

DELAWARE CHILDREN'S MUSEUM is at 550 Justison St. The museum helps children learn through play in a fun, stimulating environment. Interactive exhibits highlight money management, the human body and other subjects, with trains and cars for the very young to explore. Examples include the Stratosphere, a climbing structure; the Power of Me, a biology and nutrition exhibit; Econnect, focusing on nature; and Bank on It, which explores math. **Time:** Allow 1 hour, 30 minutes minimum. **Hours:** Tues.-Thurs. and Sun. 10-3 (also some holiday Mondays 10-3); Fri.-Sat. 10-8. Closed Easter, Thanksgiving and Christmas. **Cost:** $8.75. **Phone:** (302) 654-2340. 🍴 ♿ Wilmington, 176

DELAWARE HISTORY MUSEUM, 504 N. Market St., features the interactive, multimedia permanent exhibition Distinctively Delaware. Changing exhibits feature art, costumes, toys, antiques, re-created scenes and historic photographs. Grandma's Attic is a learn-and-play discovery center for children. **Note:** The museum is closed for renovations until Feb. 2016. **Time:** Allow 30 minutes minimum. **Hours:** Wed.-Fri. 11-4, Sat. 10-4. Phone ahead for current exhibit information. Closed major holidays. **Cost:** $6; $5 (ages 65+ and college students and military with ID); $4 (ages 3-18). **Phone:** (302) 656-0637. ♿ Wilmington, 176

SAVE **DELAWARE MUSEUM OF NATURAL HISTORY,** 5 mi. n.w. on SR 52, contains a variety of natural history exhibits in naturalistic settings, from native flora and fauna to specimens representing Africa and the Great Barrier Reef. Noteworthy are an extensive shell collection, life-size dinosaurs and a full-scale model of a giant squid, and mounted African animals and extinct birds. The Nature Nook features hands-on exhibits and activities.

Time: Allow 1 hour, 30 minutes minimum. **Hours:** Mon.-Sat. 9:30-4:30, Sun. noon-4:30. Closed Jan. 1, Easter, July 4, Thanksgiving and Christmas. **Cost:** $9; $8 (ages 60+); $7 (ages 3-17). **Phone:** (302) 658-9111.

SAVE **DELAWARE SPORTS MUSEUM AND HALL OF FAME** is off I-95 exit 6, following signs to Frawley Stadium. The museum chronicles Delaware sports history from 1860 to the present through photographs, audio- and videotape presentations, artifacts and memorabilia. Highlighted among the sports notables that represent more than 30 sports are Olympic athletes, professional players, coaches, journalists and sportscasters. A 12-minute videotape provides an overview. **Time:** Allow 30 minutes minimum. **Hours:** Tues.-Sat. noon-5, Apr.-Oct. Guided tours are available by reservation year-round from 10-4. **Cost:** $4; $3 (ages 50+); $2 (ages 13-19). **Phone:** (302) 425-3263.
♿ Wilmington, 176

GEM **HAGLEY MUSEUM AND LIBRARY** is 3 mi. n. on SR 52 and .5 mi. n. on SR 141, then s. to Old Barley Mill Rd., following signs. The museum occupies 235 acres on the site of the original du Pont gunpowder mills, estate and gardens. Many restored mills show the development of water power on the Brandywine River.

The visitor center is in an old stone cotton-spinning mill that houses interactive science exhibits tracing DuPont Co. history, from explosives manufacturing to the development of chemical products that changed the world. Highlights include a reproduction of Jeff Gordon's #24 DuPont NASCAR race car and a space suit made of DuPont materials.

Eleutherian Mills, a Georgian house erected by Éleuthère Irénée du Pont in 1803, contains furnishings reflecting the tastes of five generations of du Ponts.

Exhibits and demonstrations along the river depict the evolution of the American economy and include a wooden water wheel, turbine powered roll mills, an operating steam engine and a restored 1870s machine shop. Working models in the Millwright Shop demonstrate the production of black powder.

The ruins of mills near the museum demonstrate an unusual construction style once used along the river. Three sides of the building were constructed of heavy stone topped by roofs with ridges set toward the walls opposite the river. The walls facing the river were made of wood. Consequently, the inevitable accidental explosions blew the back walls and roof sections toward the river, minimizing damage to both buildings and workers.

A restored workers' community features a one-room schoolhouse and a worker's dwelling. Also on the grounds are the first office of the DuPont Co., Lammot du Pont's workshop, a 19th-century formal French garden and a barn with 19th-century farm tools, antique horse-drawn vehicles and a 1928 DuPont Motors Co. automobile.

Time: Allow 3 hours minimum. **Hours:** Daily 9:30-4:30. Guided tours Mon.-Fri. 11 and 2, Jan. 1 to mid-Mar. Closed Thanksgiving and Christmas. **Cost:** $14; $10 (ages 62+ and students with ID); $5 (ages 6-14). Visitor center admission $6; $2 (ages 6-14). **Phone:** (302) 658-2400.

HOLY TRINITY (OLD SWEDES) EPISCOPAL CHURCH, 606 Church St., was built in 1698-99 and is said to be the oldest church in the United States standing as originally built and still in use as a house of worship. It was erected by descendants of the Swedish colonists who crossed the Atlantic aboard the *Kalmar Nyckel* in 1638. **Time:** Allow 30 minutes minimum. **Hours:** Guided tours are given Wed.-Sat. 10-4, Apr.-Dec.; Wed.-Fri. 1-4, Sat. 10-4, in Mar.; by appointment rest of year. Closed Jan.1, July 4, Thanksgiving, day after Thanksgiving, Christmas Eve and Christmas. **Cost:** $4 (includes the Hendrickson House); $2 (ages 6-12). Reservations are recommended. **Phone:** (302) 652-5629.
♿ Wilmington, 176

Hendrickson House, on Church St., is a Swedish colonial home erected in Pennsylvania in 1690. After more than 250 years in its original location, the house was dismantled, moved to the site of Old Swedes Church, and now houses the library, museum and office of Old Swedes Foundation. **Hours:** Guided tours are given Wed.-Sat. 10-4, Apr.-Dec.; Wed.-Fri. 1-4, Sat. 10-4, in Mar.; by appointment rest of year. **Cost:** $4 (included with Holy Trinity (Old Swedes) Episcopal Church); $2 (ages 6-12). **Phone:** (302) 652-5629. ♿ Wilmington, 176

SAVE **KALMAR NYCKEL FOUNDATION** is at 1124 E. Seventh St., adjacent to Fort Christina Park. The *Kalmar Nyckel* is a re-creation of the ship that brought the first European settlers to the Delaware Valley in 1638. The ship is usually in the shipyard for maintenance November through April. During sailing season, it rotates between the shipyard and docks at *Kalmar Nyckel* Shipyard and Dravo Plaza in Wilmington, Del., as well as docks at Lewes, Del., and other ports along the East Coast.

Time: Allow 30 minutes minimum. **Hours:** Phone ahead for the ship docking schedule; sailings occur mid-Apr. through Oct. 31. Closed major holidays. **Cost:** Sailing fee $35; $20 (ages 0-17). **Phone:** (302) 429-7447 or (866) 659-7447.

Wilmington, 176

NEMOURS MANSION AND GARDENS is 3.5 mi. n.w. to Alapocas Dr. and SR 141 S. (Powder Mill Rd.). This modified Louis XVI chateau was built in 1909-10 by Alfred I. du Pont. The 47,000-square-foot mansion contains European antiques, tapestries, Oriental rugs and paintings as well as several of A.I. du Pont's innovations.

The 222-acre estate is a fine example of formal French gardens. Admission, by guided tour only, includes rooms on three of the mansion's floors as well as a bus tour through the estate's gardens.

Note: Tour includes several stairways. **Time:** Allow 3 hours minimum. **Hours:** Tours are given Tues.-Sat. at 9, noon and 3, Sun. at noon and 3, May-Dec. Visitors should arrive at least 15 minutes before tour departs. Closed Thanksgiving and Christmas. **Cost:** $15. Reservations are required. **Phone:** (302) 651-6912 or (800) 651-6912.

ROCKWOOD MUSEUM, off I-95 exit 9 (Marsh Rd.) at 610 Shipley Rd. Museum entrance is off Washington Street extension. A rare example of Rural Gothic architecture, the 72-acre estate contains an 1851 manor house furnished as it was in 1892. Also on the grounds are a conservatory, the gardener's cottage, the carriage house, a lighted walking trail and six acres of gardens that exemplify fine landscape design. Guided tours of the grounds are available.

Time: Allow 2 hours minimum. **Hours:** Grounds daily 6 a.m.-10 p.m. House tours are given on the hour Wed.-Sat. 10-3, Sun. noon-3. Closed major holidays. **Cost:** Grounds free. House tours $10; $4 (ages 2-12). **Phone:** (302) 761-4340.

RODNEY SQUARE, bounded by Market, King, 10th and 11th sts., contains an equestrian statue of Caesar Rodney. This Delaware statesman made a hurried night ride from Dover to Philadelphia on July 2, 1776, to sway a tie vote to the side of independence. **Hours:** Dawn to dusk. **Phone:** (302) 655-7161. Wilmington, 176

WINTERTHUR MUSEUM, GARDEN & LIBRARY is 6 mi. n.w. off I-95 exit 7 (Pennsylvania Ave.) on SR 52. The former home of Henry Francis du Pont was designed in the style of an English country estate and holds one of the richest collections of American decorative arts, reflecting both early America and the du Pont family's life at this glorious estate. Guided tours of the 175-room house are available and special exhibitions in the galleries include the Campbell Collection of Soup Tureens.

The 1,000-acre estate reflects du Pont's mastery of horticulture and includes a 60-acre naturalistic garden considered a masterpiece of color and design. Narrated tram tours and guided garden walks are available. Enchanted Woods is a unique three-acre children's garden at Winterthur canopied by majestic oak trees and transformed into a place of mystery and discovery. Yuletide at Winterthur, featuring the house bedecked in holiday finery, is held mid-November to early January.

Time: Allow 2 hours minimum. **Hours:** Tues.-Sun. 10-5. Last tour ticket sold at 3:15. Library hours are Mon.-Fri. 8:30-4:30. Closed Thanksgiving and Christmas. **Cost:** General admission $20; $18 (ages 62+ and students with ID); $5 (ages 2-11). Guided 1-hour tour (includes general admission) $30; $28 (ages 62+ and students with ID); $17 (ages 8-11). Guided 2-hour tour (includes general admission) $40; $38 (ages 62+ and students with ID); $27 (ages 8-11). Reservations are recommended for tours in May and Dec. **Phone:** (302) 888-4600, (800) 448-3883 or TTY (302) 888-4907.

GAMBLING ESTABLISHMENTS

• **Delaware Park** is at 777 Delaware Park Blvd. **Hours:** Daily 24 hours. Closed Easter and Christmas. **Phone:** (800) 417-5687.

COURTYARD BY MARRIOTT-WILMINGTON DOWNTOWN
(302)429-7600

Hotel
$167-$275

COURTYARD Marriott

AAA Benefit: Members save 5% or more!

Address: 1102 West St 19801 **Location:** I-95 exit 7 northbound; exit 7A southbound, 0.3 mi e; between 11th and 12th sts; downtown. Wilmington, 176. **Facility:** 126 units. 10 stories, interior corridors. **Parking:** on-site (fee). **Activities:** exercise room. **Guest Services:** valet and coin laundry.

DOUBLETREE BY HILTON HOTEL DOWNTOWN WILMINGTON-LEGAL DISTRICT
(302)655-0400

Hotel $119-$169 **Address:** 700 N King St 19801 **Location:** Between 7th and 8th sts; downtown. Wilmington, 176. **Facility:** 217 units. 9 stories, interior corridors. **Parking:** on-site (fee). **Terms:** 1-7 night minimum stay, cancellation fee imposed. **Amenities:** safes. **Pool(s):** heated indoor. **Activities:** exercise room. **Guest Services:** valet laundry, area transportation.

AAA Benefit: Members save 5% or more!

DOUBLETREE BY HILTON HOTEL WILMINGTON
(302)478-6000

Hotel $109-$199 **Address:** 4727 Concord Pike (Rt 202) 19803 **Location:** I-95 exit 8, 3.8 mi n on US 202. Adjacent to Concord Shopping Mall. **Facility:** 244 units. 5-7 stories, interior corridors. **Terms:** check-in 4 pm, 1-7 night minimum stay, cancellation fee imposed. **Activities:** hot tub, exercise room. **Guest Services:** valet laundry, rental car service, area transportation.

AAA Benefit: Members save 5% or more!

HOMEWOOD SUITES BY HILTON BRANDYWINE VALLEY
(302)479-2000

Extended Stay Hotel $129-$339 **Address:** 350 Rocky Run Pkwy 19803 **Location:** I-95 exit 8, 3.8 mi n; just off US 202. Located in a commercial area. **Facility:** 113 efficiencies, some two bedrooms. 4 stories, interior corridors. **Terms:** 1-7 night minimum stay, cancellation fee imposed. **Amenities:** video games, safes. **Pool(s):** heated outdoor. **Activities:** valet and coin laundry, area transportation.

AAA Benefit: Members save 5% or more!

HOTEL DU PONT
302/594-3100

Historic Hotel
Rates not provided

Address: 11th & Market Streets 19801 **Location:** I-95 exit 7, 0.5 mi se; at 11th St; downtown. Wilmington, 176. **Facility:** Set in the heart of downtown, this historic luxury 1913 hotel is a city landmark. An on-site Victorian-style theater offers Broadway productions. 217 units, some two bedrooms. 13 stories, interior corridors. **Parking:** on-site (fee) and valet. **Amenities:** video games, safes. **Dining:** The Green Room, see separate listing. **Activities:** sauna, exercise room, massage. **Guest Services:** valet laundry, area transportation. Affiliated with A Preferred Hotel.

INN AT WILMINGTON
302/479-7900

Hotel
Rates not provided

Address: 300 Rocky Run Pkwy 19803 **Location:** I-95 exit 8, 3.8 mi n; just off US 202. Located in a commercial area. **Facility:** 71 units, some efficiencies. 4 stories, interior corridors. **Amenities:** Some: safes. **Activities:** exercise room. **Guest Services:** valet laundry, area transportation. **Featured Amenity:** continental breakfast.

SHERATON SUITES WILMINGTON DOWNTOWN
(302)654-8300

Hotel
$89-$319

Sheraton

AAA Benefit: Members save up to 15%, plus Starwood Preferred Guest® benefits!

Address: 422 Delaware Ave 19801 **Location:** I-95 exit 7 northbound; exit 7A southbound, 0.3 mi e; downtown. Wilmington, 176. **Facility:** 223 units. 16 stories, interior corridors. **Parking:** on-site (fee). **Terms:** 2 night minimum stay - seasonal, cancellation fee imposed. **Amenities:** video games. **Pool(s):** heated indoor. **Activities:** exercise room. **Guest Services:** valet and coin laundry.

WESTIN WILMINGTON
(302)654-2900

Hotel
$149-$399

WESTIN HOTELS & RESORTS **AAA Benefit:** Members save up to 15%, plus Starwood Preferred Guest® benefits!

Address: 818 Shipyard Dr 19801 **Location:** I-95 exit 6, just w, then 0.5 mi s. Wilmington, 176. **Facility:** 180 units. 10 stories, interior corridors. **Terms:** cancellation fee imposed. **Amenities:** safes. **Pool(s):** heated indoor. **Activities:** exercise room. **Guest Services:** valet laundry, area transportation. **Featured Amenity:** full hot breakfast.

WHERE TO EAT

CAFE MEZZANOTTE
302/658-7050

Italian
Fine Dining
$9-$32

AAA Inspector Notes: In the heart of the downtown business district, this Italian restaurant has an upscale, relaxing atmosphere, as well as a popular martini bar. The menu offers a nice selection of homemade pasta, meat and seafood dishes. Everything—including sauces, soups, bread and desserts—is prepared fresh in the kitchen. **Features:** full bar, patio dining, happy hour. **Reservations:** suggested. **Address:** 1007 Orange St 19801 **Location:** Jct 11th and Tatnall sts. Wilmington, 176. **Parking:** no self-parking.

CIAO'S PIZZA
302/654-5331

Pizza. Quick Serve. $4-$15 **AAA Inspector Notes:** This popular spot in the heart of Trolley Square offers a delightful selection of calzones, stromboli, salads, baked specialty entrées and of course, gourmet pizzas. Whether you're looking for a quick slice from the counter or a longer lunch in the upstairs dining room, this joint has got it all. The variety of white pizza options come highly recommended. **Features:** patio dining. **Address:** 1600 Delaware Ave 19806 **Location:** I-95 exit 7, just n on SR 52 to Delaware Ave, then 0.4 mi n. **Parking:** street only. [L] [D]

CORNER BISTRO
302/477-1778

American. Casual Dining. $9-$22 **AAA Inspector Notes:** Set in a cozy, intimate setting, this casual café features modern furnishings and touches throughout and a marble-top, 8-chair bar. The menu provides hearty American dishes with some French influence including their homemade onion soup gratin and tarte flambé. **Features:** full bar, Sunday brunch. **Address:** 3604 Silverside Rd 19810 **Location:** I-95 exit 8, 3.1 mi n, then just e; just off US 202. [L] [D] CALL [M]

DEEP BLUE BAR & GRILL
302/777-2040

Seafood. Fine Dining. $8-$28 **AAA Inspector Notes:** If you're in the mood for seafood, this contemporary downtown bistro is just the place. The kitchen staff is skilled and innovative, which is evident in the taste of dishes such as seared tuna over wasabi mashed potatoes and truffle-crusted salmon. The raw bar comprises oysters from around the world. **Features:** full bar, happy hour. **Address:** 111 W 11th St 19801 **Location:** Jct 11th and Tatnall sts. Wilmington, 176. **Parking:** on-site (fee). [L] [D] CALL [M]

THE GREEN ROOM
302/594-3155

Continental
Fine Dining
$10-$40

AAA Inspector Notes: This formal dining room has large, ornately draped windows overlooking the bustling downtown scene. Beautiful dark wood wall columns and ceiling beams, masterful gold-leaf embellishments, massive chandeliers and a mezzanine piano balcony create a wonderful setting for a memorable dining experience. The glorious feast for the eyes matches the elegantly presented Continental dishes, including seafood, duck and beef selections. An a la carte lunch buffet is available weekdays. **Features:** full bar, Sunday brunch. **Reservations:** suggested. **Address:** 11th & Market Streets 19801 **Location:** I-95 exit 7, 0.5 mi se; at 11th St; downtown; in Hotel du Pont. Wilmington, 176. **Parking:** on-site (fee) and valet. [B] [L] [D] CALL [M]

HARRY'S SAVOY GRILL & BALLROOM
302/475-3000

Steak. Casual Dining. $12-$36 **AAA Inspector Notes:** Casual and fun, the bustling restaurant boasts a menu of such specialties as prime rib, horseradish-crusted salmon and crème brûlée. French posters, a vivid mural and cozy fireplaces add to the comfortable feel. Service is swift and friendly. **Features:** full bar, patio dining, Sunday brunch, happy hour. **Reservations:** suggested. **Address:** 2020 Naamans Rd 19810 **Location:** I-95 exit 11, 2.5 mi w on SR 92 (Naamans Rd). [L] [D]

HARRY'S SEAFOOD GRILL
302/777-1500

Seafood. Casual Dining. $12-$42 **AAA Inspector Notes:** On the riverfront, the restaurant has become a favorite with locals. Innovative American cuisine emphasizes fresh seafood, which is updated daily. The extensive wine selection includes 50 wines by the glass. The atmosphere is fun, and the staff friendly and attentive. When the weather is appropriate, the riverside patio is a popular seating option. **Features:** full bar, patio dining. **Reservations:** suggested. **Address:** 101 S Market St 19801 **Location:** I-95 exit 6, 0.7 mi to Riverfront Market. Wilmington, 176. [L] [D] CALL [M]

IRON HILL BREWERY & RESTAURANT
302/472-2739

American. Gastropub. $10-$28 **AAA Inspector Notes:** Hand-crafted beers made on the premises pair nicely with the innovative American cuisine. Along the riverfront, the setting is casual and comfortable. Seasonal outdoor seating is an option. **Features:** full bar, patio dining. **Address:** 620 Justison St 19801 **Location:** I-95 exit 6, just s. Wilmington, 176. [L] [D] CALL [M]

MIKIMOTOS
302/656-8638

Japanese. Casual Dining. $10-$25 **AAA Inspector Notes:** Step inside this sleek, modern dining room featuring a circular sushi bar at its center and intimate lighting throughout. The dark wood furnishings and attractively appointed bar area coordinate perfectly with the overall décor. The menu provides a variety of options including bento boxes, salads, teriyaki entrées and some Thai-influenced options. However, we recommend sticking with their perfectly made specialty sushi rolls. **Features:** full bar, happy hour. **Reservations:** suggested, weekends. **Address:** 1212 Washington St 19801 **Location:** Between 12th and 13th sts. Wilmington, 176. [L] [D] CALL [M]

PICCOLINA TOSCANA
302/654-8001

Northern Italian. Fine Dining. $8-$32 **AAA Inspector Notes:** Tuscan cooking is expertly prepared and complemented by an extensive wine selection. The casually upscale café is comfortable, and service is friendly and attentive. Patio seating is available when the weather cooperates. **Features:** full bar, patio dining, Sunday brunch, happy hour. **Address:** 1412 N DuPont St 19806 **Location:** I-95 exit 7, just n on SR 52 to Delaware Ave, 0.5 mi n, then just w. [L] [D]

WALTER'S STEAKHOUSE
302/652-6780

Steak. Casual Dining. $20-$32 **AAA Inspector Notes:** Pleasant, efficient servers bring out preparations of aged certified Angus beef, in addition to veal and lamb dishes and two of the most popular seafood-oriented house specials: crab imperial and Norwegian salmon. You'll feel at home in the casually upscale steakhouse's cozy atmosphere. **Features:** full bar. **Reservations:** suggested. **Address:** 802 N Union St 19805 **Location:** I-95 exit 7, 0.8 mi n on SR 52, then just w. [D]

WASHINGTON STREET ALE HOUSE
302/658-2537

American. Casual Dining. $9-$22 **AAA Inspector Notes:** This casual pub and restaurant is the perfect spot whether you're coming in to sample a few beers from the extensive list or to nosh on such hearty menu options as crab-crusted salmon and the always-popular Kobe beef burger. **Features:** full bar, Sunday brunch, happy hour. **Address:** 1206 N Washington St 19801 **Location:** Between 12th and 13th sts. Wilmington, 176. [L] [D] [🚆]

Keep your focus safely

on the road when driving

Barnegat Lighthouse State Park, Barnegat Light

New Jersey

Grand estates. Ethnic neighborhoods. Revolutionary War sites. Miles of beaches. Nostalgic Atlantic City. The Garden State abounds with cultural, historical and natural treasures.

Flowering trees, shrubs and botanical displays brighten Chatfield Garden in Elizabeth, Duke Farms in Hillsborough, Ecogardens at Leaming's Run in Cape May Court House, Leonard J. Buck Garden in Far Hills, New Jersey Botanical Garden in Ringwood and Rutgers Gardens in New Brunswick.

The Kittatinny Mountains, although unsuitable for large-scale agriculture, carve a notch in terms of geologic diversity. Millions of years of evolution—flood, uplift, glaciation and erosion—molded the terrain. Dairy farms are tucked amid the ash, maple and oak forests lining the mountains.

Salt marshes, swamps, cranberry bogs and stands of cedar, oak and pine characterize

Canoeing in the Pine Barrens

the Pine Barrens. And New Jersey's extensive preservation efforts—in the Great Swamp, Basking Ridge and the Hackensack Meadows, among other places—guarantee habitats for birds and other native wildlife.

Vital to National History

And, since it's the third oldest state, New Jersey has historical significance as well.

Museums house Native American relics that tell about the state's first inhabitants.

The beach resort of Long Branch was a favorite summer getaway for presidents Ulysses Grant, Rutherford Hayes, James Garfield, Chester Arthur, Benjamin Harrison, William McKinley and Woodrow Wilson. Another president, Grover Cleveland, was a Caldwell native.

But Washington had the state's highest presidential profile. During the Revolutionary War he tracked through Fort Lee, Freehold, Hackensack, Morristown and Somerville.

Washington Crossing State Park in Titusville commemorates the general's crossing of the Delaware River before surprising and defeating British forces at Trenton; the Old Barracks Museum has exhibits about this pivotal skirmish.

And Washington did, indeed, sleep here. During his military occupation, the general lived and worked at the Dey and Ford mansions and the Wallace House.

Jump a few years ahead to discover why New Jersey has so many ethnicities: Ellis

Island was the entry point for millions of newcomers.

Today's visitors, though, prefer different accommodations: Atlantic City's casino hotels. The gambling center offers baccarat, blackjack, craps, roulette and most games in between. The boardwalk also is a big draw; experience it from a rolling chair that an attendant pushes up and down the pier.

Ingenious as the chairs may be, they can't hold a candle—or rather, a light bulb—to the inventions of Thomas Alva Edison. The imagination of the "Wizard of Menlo Park" gave rise to the phonograph, movie camera and automatic telegraph.

Thriving in the Great Swamp

The Great Swamp, which was once Lake Passaic, is a vital wetland near Basking Ridge. The marshy woodland habitat nurtures muskrats, foxes, fish and birds.

The Pine Barrens weave scrub, pitch pine, river, swamps and bogs into an area suitable for cranberry and blueberry production and recreational escapes. Among the oddities of this southern-region woodland: stunted pygmy pines; ventriloquist tree frogs; and the "Jersey Devil," a mythical winged creature who in January 1909 supposedly noshed on trash in Burlington, fended off a ferocious broom beating in Camden and circled above Clementon trolley riders until the drivers felt it necessary to bear arms for protection.

Water surrounds the state, except for 48 miles bordering New York. Ocean cruises depart from Cape May and Wildwood. A sea view is also possible from Barnegat Lighthouse in Barnegat Light or the north tower at Twin Lights State Historic Site in Highlands.

Recreation

Many long stretches of sand are set aside as public beaches. Enjoy swimming in such seaside towns as Avalon, Brigantine, Point Pleasant Beach and Sea Bright. Barnegat Bay is good for windsurfing and kayaking.

Canoe inland waterways such as the canal in Delaware & Raritan Canal Park in Somerset or raft down the placid Delaware River. Parasail in Beach Haven or Neptune, or scuba dive or snorkel in Belmar, Manasquan, Somers Point and Strathmere.

Saltwater fishing yields marlin, tuna and sea bass. Deep-sea charters are based in Atlantic City, Belmar, Cape May and the Wildwoods. Muskellunge, pike, shad, bass, perch and walleye dwell in Delaware Water Gap National Recreation Area's fresh water. And the south branch of the Raritan River in Hunterdon County is a hub for fly-fishing.

Bird-watchers can spot more than 435 species here along the Atlantic Flyway. Warblers, ospreys and great horned owls visit the Sandy Hook Unit of Gateway National Recreation Area, and the Edwin B. Forsythe National Wildlife Refuge welcomes egrets, Canada and snow geese and golden eagles.

Hiking takes you to spectacular gorges and waterfalls in Delaware Water Gap National Recreation Area. From Wharton State Forest north of Batsto, pick up the Batona (short for back to nature) Trail for the best views of the Pine Barrens. New Jersey's part of the Appalachian Trail traces the Kittatinny Ridge to High Point.

Bicycle and horseback riders use the wooded trails at Middletown's Hartshorne Woods Park or Andover's Kittatinny Valley State Park. And spectacular scenery makes Jenny Jump State Forest in Hope a favorite camping destination.

Cold-weather activity peaks in the Skylands in northwest New Jersey. Mountain Creek in Vernon is the premier downhill skiing resort. Herrontown Woods in Princeton, High Point State Park in Sussex and Holmdel Park in Holmdel offer cross-country skiing. Snowmobiling and sledding areas blanket Belleplain State Forest, near Woodbine.

Cranberry harvest, Batsto

Historic Timeline

1524	Giovanni da Verrazano makes landfall in the region.
1609	Henry Hudson claims the region for the Netherlands.
1664	England seizes control of New Netherland, renaming it for the island of Jersey that lies in the English Channel.
1776	Gen. George Washington crosses the Delaware to defeat the British at Trenton.
1787	New Jersey becomes the third state to ratify the U.S. Constitution.
1838	Samuel Morse demonstrates the telegraph in Morristown.
1870	The boardwalk is invented in Atlantic City; casino gambling there is legalized about a century later.
1876	Thomas Alva Edison builds his laboratory at Menlo Park.
1937	The airship *Hindenburg* crashes at Lakehurst.
1998	The U.S. Supreme Court rules that most of Ellis Island is in New Jersey.
2012	Sandy, a hurricane turned post-tropical cyclone, makes landfall near Atlantic City.

What To Pack

Temperature Averages Maximum/Minimum	JANUARY	FEBRUARY	MARCH	APRIL	MAY	JUNE	JULY	AUGUST	SEPTEMBER	OCTOBER	NOVEMBER	DECEMBER
Atlantic City	41/23	44/25	52/32	61/40	71/50	80/59	85/65	83/64	77/56	66/44	56/36	46/27
Cape May	42/27	43/28	51/35	60/43	69/53	78/62	84/67	83/66	77/60	66/49	56/40	47/31
Newark	38/24	41/27	50/34	61/44	71/54	80/64	85/69	83/68	76/60	65/48	54/39	43/30
Salem	39/24	43/26	52/33	63/42	72/52	81/62	86/67	84/66	77/58	66/46	55/37	44/28
Trenton	39/21	41/24	50/31	61/39	72/49	80/58	85/63	83/62	76/54	65/42	54/35	43/27
Vernon	34/14	38/16	47/25	59/35	70/45	78/54	83/59	82/57	74/49	63/37	51/30	39/21

From the records of The Weather Channel Interactive, Inc.

Good Facts To Know

ABOUT THE STATE

POPULATION: 8,791,894.

AREA: 8,723 square miles; ranks 47th.

CAPITAL: Trenton.

HIGHEST POINT: 1,803 ft., High Point.

LOWEST POINT: Sea level, Atlantic Ocean.

TIME ZONE(S): Eastern. DST.

GAMBLING

MINIMUM AGE FOR GAMBLING: 21.

REGULATIONS

TEEN DRIVING LAWS: Driving is not permitted 11 p.m.-5 a.m. No more than one unrelated passenger is permitted. The minimum age for an unrestricted driver's license is 18. Phone (609) 292-6500.

SEAT BELT/CHILD RESTRAINT LAWS: Seat belts required for driver and all passengers age 8 and older. Child restraints required for under age 8 and under 80 pounds and must be in the rear seat if possible. AAA recommends the use of seat belts and appropriate child restraints for the driver and all passengers.

CELLPHONE RESTRICTIONS: Drivers are prohibited from using hand-held cellphones and text messaging while driving. Special learner's permit, examination permit and probationary license holders are subject to a complete ban on cellphone use.

HELMETS FOR MOTORCYCLISTS: Required for all riders.

RADAR DETECTORS: Permitted.

MOVE OVER LAW: Driver is required to slow and vacate the lane nearest stopped police, fire and rescue vehicles using audible or flashing signals. The law also applies to recovery vehicles such as tow trucks.

FIREARMS LAWS: Contact the New Jersey State Police Division Headquarters, Firearms Investigation Unit, P.O. Box 7068, West Trenton, NJ 08628-0068; phone (609) 882-2000, ext. 2060.

SPECIAL REGULATIONS: Motorists are not permitted to pump their own gas at service stations.

HOLIDAYS

HOLIDAYS: Jan. 1 ■ Martin Luther King Jr. Day, Jan. (3rd Mon.) ■ Washington's Birthday/Presidents Day, Feb. (3rd Mon.) ■ Memorial Day, May (last Mon.) ■ July 4 ■ Labor Day, Sept. (1st Mon.) ■ Columbus Day, Oct. (2nd Mon.) ■ Election Day, Nov. (1st Tues. following 1st Mon.) ■ Veterans Day, Nov. 11 ■ Thanksgiving, Nov. (4th Thurs.) ■ Christmas, Dec. 25.

MONEY

TAXES: New Jersey's state sales tax is 7 percent. Localities may impose an Occupancy Tax of up to 5 percent. Atlantic City has a 3-percent alcoholic beverage tax and a 9-percent lodgings and related services tax. Combined state and city taxes may be subject to different maximum percentages.

VISITOR INFORMATION

INFORMATION CENTERS: State welcome centers are at Milepost 3.5 on the Atlantic City Expwy. in Atlantic City ■ Milepost 172N on the Garden State Pkwy. N. near Montvale ■ Milepost 18.3 on the Garden State Pkwy. S. near Ocean View ■ in Elizabeth at the Jersey Garden Outlet Mall at 651 Kapkowski Rd. ■ off I-195 exit 16 on Monmouth Rd. in the Jackson Premium Outlets in Jackson ■ I-295N exit 2B near Deepwater ■ off exit 14B in Liberty State Park in Jersey City ■ Milepost 100 on the Garden State Pkwy. near Belmar ■ in Piscataway at 100 Sutphen Rd. at Rutgers The State University of New Jersey ■ Milepost 71.9 on the New Jersey Turnpike S. near Cranbury ■ off the New Jersey Turnpike N. exit 13A or exit 14 in Newark Liberty International Airport, International Arrivals, Terminal B and Terminal C in Newark ■ in Flemington in the Liberty Village Premium Outlets on SR 12 ■ in Bridgewater at US 22 and Grove Street ■ and in Trenton at the corner of Lafayette and Barrack sts.

All centers except those at Trenton and Bridgewater are open daily year-round. All are closed Dec. 25. Hours vary according to the site, but generally are 8-4 or 9-5. Phone (609) 292-2470 for exact schedules.

FURTHER INFORMATION FOR VISITORS:
New Jersey Department of State
Division of Travel and Tourism
225 W. State St.
P.O. Box 460
Trenton, NJ 08625-0460
(800) 847-4865

FISHING AND HUNTING REGULATIONS:
Department of Environmental Protection
Division of Fish and Wildlife
501 E. State St., 3rd Floor
P.O. Box 402
Trenton, NJ 08625-0400
(609) 292-2965

RECREATION INFORMATION:
Division of Parks and Forestry, State Park Service
501 E. State St., 4th Floor
P.O. Box 420, Mail code 501-04
Trenton, NJ 08625-0420
(609) 292-2773

New Jersey Annual Events

Please call ahead to confirm event details.

JANUARY

- Garden State Outdoor Sportsmen's Show / Edison 800-248-7469
- Fire and Ice Festival Mount Holly 609-914-0811
- January Jazz Fest Hackettstown 908-979-0900

FEBRUARY

- Progressive Insurance Atlantic City Boat Show Atlantic City 212-984-7000
- Super Pet Expo / Edison 301-564-4050, ext. 101
- Maple Sugaring Demonstrations / Chatham 973-635-6629

MARCH

- Sugarloaf Crafts Festival Somerset 301-990-1400
- The Quilt Fest of New Jersey / Somerset 215-862-5828
- Belmar and Lake Como St. Patrick's Day Parade Belmar 732-280-2648

APRIL

- Shad Festival / Lambertville 609-397-0055
- Bayfest / Somers Point 609-927-2053, ext. 3101
- New Jersey Folk Festival New Brunswick 732-932-9174

MAY

- Cape May Spring Festival Cape May 609-884-5404
- Greek Festival / Piscataway 732-463-1642
- International Kite Festival Wildwood 732-822-4884

JUNE

- New Jersey Seafood Festival / Belmar 732-681-3700, ext. 214
- Italian-American Festival North Wildwood 609-780-2563
- Spring Fine Art and Crafts at Brookdale Park Bloomfield 908-874-5247

JULY

- New Jersey Festival of Ballooning / White House Station 973-882-5464
- New Jersey Sandcastle Contest / Belmar 718-273-4954
- Inn to Inn Tours Ocean City 609-399-1412

AUGUST

- Hermit Crab Races and Sand Sculpting Contest Ocean City 609-525-9300
- Westfield Street Fair and Craft Show / Westfield 908-654-1400
- New Jersey State Fair Sussex County Farm and Horse Show / Augusta 973-948-5500

SEPTEMBER

- Cape May Food and Wine Festival / Cape May 609-884-5404
- Antique and Classic Boat Show / Tuckerton 609-296-8868
- Fine Art and Crafts at Anderson Park Upper Montclair 908-874-5247

OCTOBER

- Indian Summer Weekend Ocean City 609-525-9300
- Victorian Weekend Cape May 609-884-5404
- Fall Fine Art and Crafts Show at Brookdale Park Bloomfield 908-874-5247

NOVEMBER

- Dickens Days / Clinton 908-735-4101
- Hoboken Artists Studio Tour Hoboken 201-420-2207
- Christmas Tree Lighting Princeton 609-921-2333

DECEMBER

- Gingerbread Wonderland Morristown 973-326-7601
- NJ Dutch-American Historical Holidays / Wayne 973-694-7192
- Christmas Candlelight House Tours / Cape May 609-884-5404

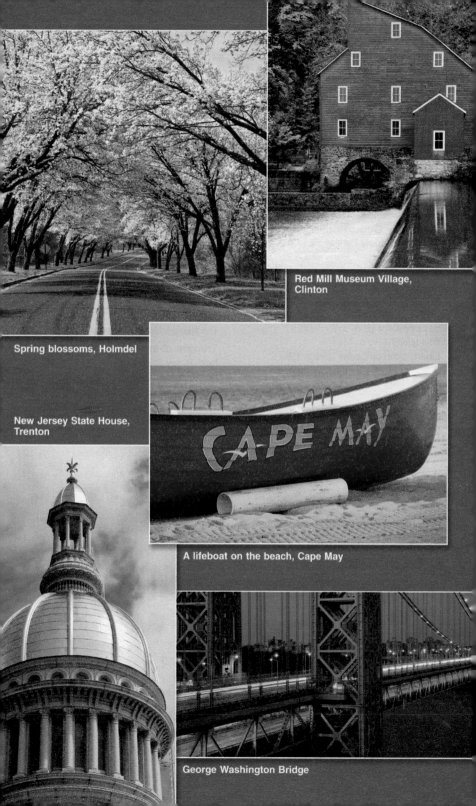

Spring blossoms, Holmdel

Red Mill Museum Village, Clinton

New Jersey State House, Trenton

A lifeboat on the beach, Cape May

CAPE MAY

George Washington Bridge

Index: Great Experience for Members

AAA editor's picks of exceptional note

Six Flags Great
Adventure & Safari

Morristown National
Historical Park

Old Barracks Museum

Liberty Science
Center

See Orientation map on p. 66 for corresponding grid coordinates, if applicable.

New Jersey
Atlas Section

ROADS/HIGHWAYS

	INTERSTATE
	CONTROLLED ACCESS
	CONTROLLED ACCESS TOLL
	TOLL ROAD
	PRIMARY DIVIDED
	PRIMARY UNDIVIDED
	SECONDARY DIVIDED
	SECONDARY UNDIVIDED
	LOCAL DIVIDED
	LOCAL UNDIVIDED
	UNPAVED ROAD
	UNDER CONSTRUCTION
	TUNNEL
	PEDESTRIAN ONLY
	AUTO FERRY
	PASSENGER FERRY
	SCENIC BYWAY
10	DISTANCE BETWEEN MARKERS
	EXIT NUMBER-FREE/TOLL
	INTERCHANGE FULL/PARTIAL
	WELCOME CENTER
	REST AREA/ SERVICE CENTER

BOUNDARIES

	INTERNATIONAL
	STATE
	COUNTY
	TIME ZONE
>>>>>>	CONTINENTAL DIVIDE

ROAD SHIELDS

95 95	INTERSTATE/BUSINESS
22 22 22	U.S./STATE/COUNTY
127 2	FOREST/INDIAN
	TRANS- CANADA
1	PROVINCIAL AUTOROUTE
1	MEXICO
66	HISTORIC ROUTE 66
VT 41	REFERENCE PAGE INDICATOR

AREAS OF INTEREST

	INDIAN
	MILITARY
	PARK
	FOREST
	GRASSLANDS
	HISTORIC
✈	INT'L/REGIONAL AIRPORT
	INCORPORATED CITY

POINTS OF INTEREST

○	TOWN
✴	NATIONAL CAPITAL
✷	STATE/PROVINCIAL CAPITAL
▲	AAA/CAA CLUB LOCATION
■	FEATURE OF INTEREST
🏛	COLLEGE/UNIVERSITY
⛺	CAMPGROUND INFORMATION PROVIDED BY WOODALL'S®
⊙	CUSTOMS STATION
	HISTORIC
	LIGHTHOUSE
	MONUMENT/MEMORIAL
	STATE/PROVINCIAL PARK
	NATIONAL WILDLIFE REFUGE
	SKI AREA
○	SPORTS COMPLEX
	DAM

CITIES/TOWNS are color-coded by size, showing where to find AAA Approved and Diamond rated lodgings or restaurants listed in the AAA TourBook guides and on AAA.com:

- ● Red - major destinations and capitals; many listings
- ● Black - destinations; some listings
- ● Grey - no listings

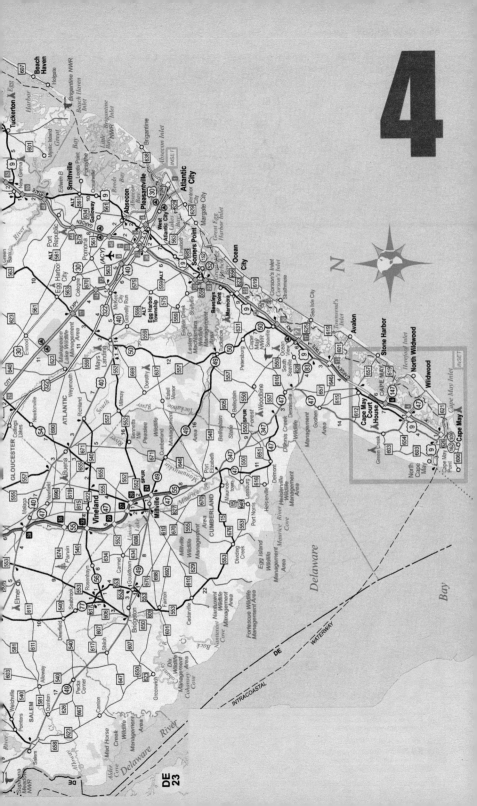

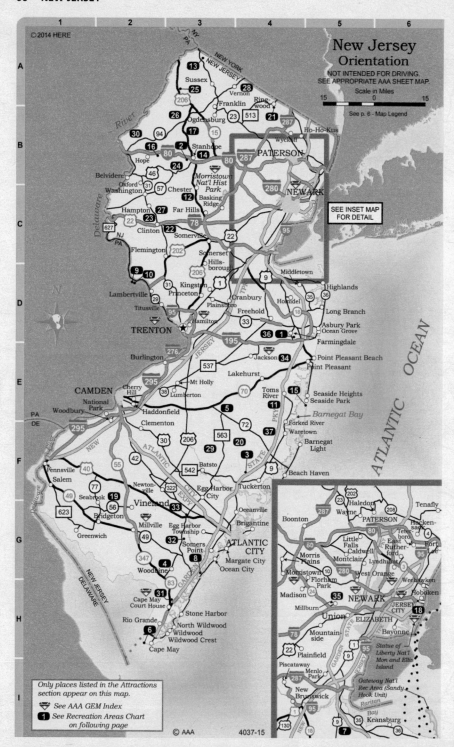

New Jersey
Orientation

NOT INTENDED FOR DRIVING.
SEE APPROPRIATE AAA SHEET MAP.

Scale in Miles
15   0   15

See p. 6 - Map Legend

SEE INSET MAP
FOR DETAIL

Only places listed in the Attractions
section appear on this map.

⏷ See AAA GEM Index
① See Recreation Areas Chart
on following page

© AAA   4037-15

Recreation Areas Chart

The map location numerals in column 2 show an area's location on the preceding map.

	MAP LOCATION	CAMPING	PICNICKING	HIKING TRAILS	BOATING	BOAT RAMP	BOAT RENTAL	FISHING	SWIMMING	PETS ON LEASH	BICYCLE TRAILS	WINTER SPORTS	VISITOR CENTER	LODGE/CABINS	FOOD SERVICE
NATIONAL RECREATION AREAS (See place listings.)															
Gateway (I-6) over 26,000 acres in the New York City metropolitan area with units in both New York and New Jersey.															
Breezy Point District (I-6) in Jamaica Bay Unit, Rockaway Peninsula, N.Y.			•	•				•	•		•	•	•		•
Jamaica Bay Unit (I-6) in Brooklyn and Queens, N.Y. Golf; horse rental, marina, sports facilities, wildlife refuge.		•	•	•	•	•		•	•	•	•		•		•
Sandy Hook Unit (I-6) off SR 36 at Highlands, N.J. 1,600 acres. Bird-watching; beach.			•	•				•	•	•	•		•		•
Staten Island Unit (I-6) in Staten Island, N.Y. Historic. Bird-watching; marina, model airplane field.			•	•	•			•	•	•	•		•		•
STATE															
Allaire (D-4) 3,199 acres 1.5 mi. w. of Garden State Pkwy. exit 98. Historic. Cross-country skiing; bridle trails, historic buildings, nature center, nature trails. (See Farmingdale p. 114.)	**1**	•	•	•				•		•	•	•	•	•	•
Allamuchy Mountain (B-3) 7,276 acres 2 mi. n. of Hackettstown on CR 517. Hunting, rock climbing.	**2**	•	•	•	•	•		•		•	•	•			
Bass River Forest (F-4) 27,635 acres 3 mi. w. of Tuckerton on CR 592. Nature programs. Bridle trails, cross-country skiing, hunting, snowmobiling.	**3**	•	•	•	•	•	•	•	•	•				•	•
Belleplain Forest (G-3) 21,320 acres on CR 550 at Belleplain. Bridle trails. Cross-country skiing, hunting, ice fishing, snowmobiling.	**4**	•	•	•	•	•	•	•	•	•	•	•	•		•
Brendan T. Byrne Forest (E-3) 36,647 acres s. of Fort Dix off SRs 70 and 72. Bridle trails. Cross-country skiing, hunting; playground.	**5**	•	•	•				•	•	•	•	•		•	
Cape May Point (H-2) 235 acres 1.2 mi. w. of Cape May via Sunset Blvd. (CR 606). Historic. Bird-watching; interpretive center; lighthouse tours, nature trails. (See Cape May p. 97.)	**6**		•	•				•		•		•			
Cheesequake (I-5) 1,569 acres 3 mi. w. of Matawan on SR 34. Canoeing, cross-country skiing, kayaking, sledding, snowshoeing; nature trails.	**7**	•	•	•				•	•	•	•	•			•
Corson's Inlet (G-3) 341 acres just n. of Strathmere on Ocean Dr. Crabbing; interpretive tours.	**8**		•	•	•	•		•		•					
Delaware and Raritan Canal (D-2) 5,379 acres 7 mi. w. of New Brunswick on CR 514. Bridle trails, canoeing, cross-country skiing; nature programs	**9**		•	•				•		•	•	•	•		
Bull's Island Section (D-2) 79 acres 3 mi. n. of Stockton on SR 29.	**10**	•	•	•	•	•		•		•			•		
Double Trouble (E-4) 7,881 acres 1 mi. w. of Garden State Pkwy. S. exit 77 in Berkeley. Canoeing, hunting, kayaking; bridle trails.	**11**		•	•				•		•	•	•			
Hacklebarney (C-3) 978 acres 3 mi. s.w. of Chester via US 206. Hunting. Playground. Interpretive programs.	**12**		•	•				•		•			•		
High Point (A-3) 14,193 acres 8 mi. n.w. of Sussex on SR 23. Scenic. Bridle trails, cross-country skiing, hunting, ice fishing, snowmobiling; nature trails.	**13**	•	•	•	•	•		•	•	•		•	•		•
Hopatcong (B-3) 159 acres 2 mi. n. of Landing off I-80. Canoeing, ice fishing, ice boating, ice-skating, sledding, snowmobiling; sports courts and fields; playground.	**14**		•		•	•		•	•	•		•			•
Island Beach (E-4) 3,003 acres 3 mi. s. of Seaside Park on SR 35. Bird-watching, Bridle trails, canoeing, kayaking, sailboarding, scuba diving, surfing; coastal dunes, interpretive tours, nature trails. (See Seaside Park p. 191.)	**15**		•	•				•	•			•		•		
Jenny Jump Forest (B-2) 4,288 acres 3 mi. e. of Hope off CR 519. Cross-country skiing, hunting, ice fishing. Astronomy observation point; playground.	**16**	•	•	•	•			•		•		•		•		
Kittatinny Valley (B-3) 3,641 acres 1 mi. n. of SR 206 off Goodale Rd. in Andover. Cross-country skiing, horseback riding, hunting, ice fishing, snowshoeing; nature trails.	**17**		•	•				•		•		•			

Recreation Areas Chart

The map location numerals in column 2 show an area's location on the preceding map.

	MAP LOCATION	CAMPING	PICNICKING	HIKING TRAILS	BOATING	BOAT RAMP	BOAT RENTAL	FISHING	SWIMMING	PETS ON LEASH	BICYCLE TRAILS	WINTER SPORTS	VISITOR CENTER	LODGE/CABINS	FOOD SERVICE
Liberty (H-6) 1,212 acres off New Jersey Tpke. exit 14B. Crabbing, kayaking. Interpretive center, marina, playground. *(See Jersey City p. 128.)*	18		•	•	•	•			•	•	•	•		•		•
Parvin (F-2) 1,952 acres 6 mi. w. of Vineland on CR 540. Canoeing, hunting; interpretive programs, nature trails.	19	•	•	•	•	•	•	•	•	•			•	•	•
Penn Forest (F-4) 3,366 acres 5 mi. s.e. of Chatsworth off CR 563. Canoeing, cross-country skiing, hunting.	20		•	•	•			•		•					
Ringwood (B-4) 6,199 acres 2.5 mi. n. of Ringwood via Skyline Dr., CR 511 and Sloatsburg Rd. Cross-country skiing, hunting, ice fishing, sledding, snowmobiling; bridle trails, historic buildings. *(See Ringwood p. 188.)*	21		•	•	•		•	•	•	•	•	•	•		
Ringwood Manor 895 acres. Historic.			•	•				•		•			•		
Shepherd Lake 1,220 acres. Canoeing, ice fishing, ice-skating.			•	•	•	•	•	•	•	•					•
Round Valley (C-3) 3,684 acres 2 mi. s. of Lebanon off US 22. Canoeing, cross-country skiing, horseback riding, ice fishing, ice-skating, scuba and skin diving, sledding, waterfowl hunting, wilderness camping.	22	•	•	•	•			•	•	•	•	•			
Spruce Run (C-2) 2,012 acres 3 mi. n. of Clinton on SR 31. Cross-country skiing, hunting, ice boating, ice fishing; playground.	23	•	•	•	•	•		•	•	•		•			•
Stephens (B-3) 805 acres 2 mi. e. of Hackettstown on CR 604. Cross-country skiing, hunting, rock climbing; bridle trails, interpretive programs, playground.	24	•	•	•				•		•	•	•			
Stokes Forest (A-3) 16,067 acres 3 mi. n. of Branchville on US 206. Canoeing, cross-country skiing, hunting, ice fishing, ice-skating, snowmobiling; bridle trails, nature trails.	25	•	•	•				•	•	•	•			•	•
Swartswood (B-3) 2,472 acres 5 mi. w. of Newton on CRs 622 and 619. Birding, horseback riding, hunting, ice fishing, ice-skating, inline skating, skateboarding, sledding, snowmobiling. Playground.	26	•	•	•	•	•	•	•	•	•	•	•			
Voorhees Park (C-2) 1,400 acres 2 mi. n. of High Bridge on CR 513. Cross-country skiing, hunting, sledding; exercise course, playground, sky-watching programs.	27	•	•	•				•		•		•			
Wawayanda (A-4) 34,350 acres 3 mi. e. of Vernon on CR 94. Canoeing, cross-country skiing, hunting, ice fishing, ice-skating, snowmobiling; bridle trails.	28	•	•	•	•			•	•	•		•			
Wharton Forest (F-3) 115,111 acres 35 mi. s. of Trenton off US 206. Nature programs. Bird-watching, canoeing, cross-country skiing, hunting, ice fishing, ice-skating; bridle trails. *(See Batsto p. 88.)*	29	•	•	•	•	•		•	•	•	•	•	•		
Worthington Forest (B-2) 6,584 acres 16 mi. n.e. of Blairstown on Millbrook Rd. Canoeing, cross-country skiing, hunting, snowmobiling; interpretive programs.	30	•	•	•	•			•		•		•			
OTHER															
Cape May County (H-2) 200 acres 2 mi. n. of Cape May Court House on US 9N. Disc golf, nature trails, zoo. *(See Cape May Court House p. 101.)*	31		•	•				•		•			•		•
Estell Manor County Park (G-3) 1,700 acres 3 mi. s. of Mays Landing on SR 50. Canoeing, cross-country skiing, hunting, kayaking; exercise trail, nature center, sports fields.	32	•	•	•				•		•	•	•	•		
Lake Lenape Park (G-3) 1,900 acres on Old Harding Hwy. in Mays Landing. Birding; playground.	33	•	•	•				•		•					
Ocean County (E-4) 325 acres in Lakewood on SR 88. Cross-country skiing; driving range, nature trails, sports fields, tennis, volleyball.	34		•	•			•	•				•			
South Mountain Reservation (H-5) 2,047 acres off I-280 exit 7, then 2 mi. s. on Pleasant Valley Way in West Orange. Cross-country skiing, indoor ice-skating; archery range, bridle trails, zoo.	35		•	•				•		•		•			
Turkey Swamp Park (D-4) 2,111 acres 4.5 mi. s. of Freehold via US 9, CR 524 and Georgia Rd. Ice-skating, horseback riding; archery range, nature trails. *(See Freehold p. 117.)*	36	•	•	•	•			•	•	•	•		•		

Recreation Areas Chart

The map location numerals in column 2 show an area's location on the preceding map.

	MAP LOCATION	CAMPING	PICNICKING	HIKING TRAILS	BOATING	BOAT RAMP	BOAT RENTAL	FISHING	SWIMMING	PETS ON LEASH	BICYCLE TRAILS	WINTER SPORTS	VISITOR CENTER	LODGE/CABINS	FOOD SERVICE
Wells Mills County Park (F-4) 910 acres 5 mi. w. of Waretown on Wells Mills Rd. (CR 532). Canoe rental, hiking trails, nature center, observation deck. *(See Waretown p. 205.)*	37	•	•	•		•	•			•	•	•		

ABSECON pop. 8,411
• Part of Atlantic City area — see map p. 73

BEST WESTERN GARDEN STATE INN   (609)645-0697

Motel
$60-$280

AAA Benefit: Members save up to 20%!

Address: 701 White Horse Pike (US 30) 08201 **Location:** Garden State Pkwy exit 40, 1 mi e. **Facility:** 62 units. 2 stories (no elevator), exterior corridors. **Pool(s):** heated outdoor.

 SAVE ▥ ⊠ HS 🛜 🖥 🍽 🖥

COMFORT INN ATLANTIC CITY NORTH   (609)641-7272
▼▼▼ Hotel $50-$90 **Address:** 539 E Absecon Blvd 08201 **Location:** Garden State Pkwy exit 40 southbound; exit northbound, U-turn through Atlantic City Service Plaza, exit 40, then 4.5 mi e on US 30. **Facility:** 205 units. 7 stories, interior corridors. **Amenities:** safes. **Activities:** exercise room.

BIZ 🛜 🖥 🍽 🖥

LET'S GET SOCIAL
Stay connected with #AAA

Visit with us on your favorite social media sites for the latest updates on hot discounts, cool destinations and handy automotive know-how:

• Plus.google.com/+AAAnews
• Facebook.com/AAAFanPage
• Twitter.com/AAA_Travel
• Pinterest.com/AAA
• YouTube.com/AAA

Talk with us!

HOLIDAY INN EXPRESS & SUITES   (609)383-9070
▼▼▼ Hotel $99-$299 **Address:** 655 White Horse Pike (US 30) 08201 **Location:** Garden State Pkwy exit 40, 1 mi e. **Facility:** 86 units, some two bedrooms. 3 stories, interior corridors. **Amenities:** safes. **Pool(s):** heated indoor. **Activities:** hot tub, exercise room. **Guest Services:** valet and coin laundry.

🔌 🛏 HS 🛜 ⊠ 🖥 🍽 / SOME UNITS 🖥

QUALITY INN & SUITES ATLANTIC CITY MARINA DISTRICT   (609)652-3300
▼▼ Hotel $45-$260 **Address:** 328 E White Horse Pike (US 30) 08205 **Location:** Garden State Pkwy exit 40 southbound; exit northbound, U-turn through Atlantic City Service Plaza, s to exit 40, then just e. **Facility:** 60 units. 1-2 stories (no elevator), exterior corridors. **Terms:** check-in 3:30 pm. **Pool(s):** heated outdoor.

▥ 🛏 🛜 🖥 🍽 🖥 / SOME UNITS 🅂

RED ROOF INN & SUITES ATLANTIC CITY   609/646-5000
▼▼ Hotel. Rates not provided. **Address:** 405 E Absecon Blvd 08201 **Location:** Garden State Pkwy exit 40 southbound; exit northbound, U-turn through Atlantic City Service Plaza, s to exit 40, then 3.3 mi e. **Facility:** 199 units. 6 stories, interior corridors. **Terms:** check-in 4 pm. **Amenities:** safes. **Pool(s):** outdoor. **Activities:** exercise room. **Guest Services:** coin laundry.

🛏 BIZ 🛜 ⊠ 🖥 🍽 / SOME UNITS 🐾 🖥 🖥

WHERE TO EAT

PHOENIX DINER   609/646-1958
▼▼▼ American. Casual Dining. $5-$24 **AAA Inspector Notes:** Here is another great Jersey diner wrapped in shiny chrome and marble. Tons of choices abound on the lengthy menu including classic favorites, great Greek selections and affordable daily three-course lunch specials. **Address:** 200 White Horse Pike (US 30) 08201 **Location:** Garden State Pkwy exit 40 southbound; exit northbound, U-turn through Atlantic City Service Plaza, s to exit 40, then 3 mi e. B L D CALL ♿M

SACK O' SUBS   609/646-6555
▼ Sandwiches. Quick Serve. $5-$15 **AAA Inspector Notes:** Operating since 1969, this family-owned business offers delicious hot and cold subs prepared fresh to diners' specifications. Guests can choose to eat in, pick up or call for delivery—the sub shop even overnights subs nationwide. **Address:** 784 White Horse Pike (US 30) 08201 **Location:** Garden State Pkwy exit 40, 1.5 mi e; in Absecon Center Plaza. L D

ALLAMUCHY pop. 78

MATTAR'S BISTRO   908/852-2300
▼▼▼ American. Casual Dining. $10-$28 **AAA Inspector Notes:** The updated décor at this long-time local favorite includes a comfortable lounge, a dining room with sweeping views and an outdoor patio. The menu features such entrées as cedar-planked salmon, lobster ravioli and a hefty double-cut pork chop. The live music and comedy shows on the weekend also are a popular draw here, so reservations are a good idea. **Features:** full bar, patio dining, happy hour. **Reservations:** suggested, weekends. **Address:** 1115 Rt 517 07820 **Location:** I-80 exit 19, 1.4 mi s. L D

ASBURY pop. 273

MOUNTAIN VIEW CHALET   908/735-4660
▼▼ American. Casual Dining. $11-$34 **AAA Inspector Notes:** Just minutes from downtown Phillipsburg and historic Clinton, the chalet serves upscale fare in a casual setting. This is the kind of place where regulars are known by name and newcomers leave as friends. The food, everything from steaks and seafood to veal and pasta, keeps the roadside restaurant a busy and popular place. **Features:** full bar. **Reservations:** suggested. **Address:** 154 SR 173 08802 **Location:** I-78 exit 11, just e. L D CALL ♿M

ASBURY PARK (D-5) pop. 16,116, elev. 21'

Asbury Park was established in 1871 as a summering spot for temperance advocates so that the nearby camp meeting center of Ocean Grove *(see place listing p. 174)* would have no unseemly neighbors. During the late 1930s and 1940s Asbury Park's mile-long boardwalk and its centerpiece, the restored Convention Hall, made the city a premier shore resort.

The city declined during the 1960s as newly constructed shopping centers drew people away. It gained new life, however, as a music center. Local blue-collar bars began nurturing their own brand of home-grown rock 'n' roll, which soon was made famous by such performers as Bruce Springsteen, Jon Bon Jovi and Southside Johnny.

Asbury Park Chamber of Commerce: Springwood Center, 1201 Springwood Ave., #104, P.O. Box 649, Asbury Park, NJ 07712. **Phone:** (732) 775-7676.

THE BERKELEY HOTEL   732/776-6700

fyi Not evaluated. **Address:** 1401 Ocean Ave 07712 **Location:** Jct Sunset Ave, just n. Facilities, services, and décor characterize a midscale property. This historic boutique hotel is located across the street from the boardwalk.

HOTEL TIDES   732/897-7744

fyi Not evaluated. **Address:** 408 Seventh Ave 07712 **Location:** Jct Main St, just e. Facilities, services, and décor characterize a midscale property.

BRICKWALL TAVERN & DINING ROOM   732/774-1264

American. Casual Dining. $7-$21 **AAA Inspector Notes:** Things get hopping at this casual pub-style dining spot, with locals and visitors alike enjoying live music, trivia and themed party nights. The large menu has salads, many sandwiches, finger foods and a few entrées including yellowfin tuna and St. Louis ribs. Wash it all down with one of the many fine beers on tap. **Features:** full bar, happy hour. **Address:** 522 Cookman Ave 07712 **Location:** Jct Main St, just e; downtown. **Parking:** street only.

L D LATE

MOONSTRUCK   732/988-0123

American. Fine Dining. $16-$32 **AAA Inspector Notes:** The upscale setting features wraparound dining porches and multiple levels housed in an updated Victorian home. The menu is a classic mix of American cuisine with preparations inspired by the Mediterranean region. For something decadent, try the walnut-crusted rack of lamb with pomegranate demi-glacé. For lighter options, choose the Mediterranean platter or grilled shrimp with pesto linguine. **Features:** full bar, happy hour. **Address:** 517 Lake Ave 07712 **Location:** Jct Main St and Lake Ave, just e. **Parking:** on-site and street.

D

STELLA MARINA BAR & RESTAURANT   732/775-7776

Italian. Casual Dining. $13-$33 **AAA Inspector Notes:** Located in a prime oceanfront spot overlooking the historic boardwalk, this fun and friendly bistro serves a wide variety of classic Italian meat, seafood, and vegetarian dishes, and they also have a raw bar and pizza oven. **Features:** full bar, patio dining. **Reservations:** suggested. **Address:** 800 Ocean Ave 07712 **Location:** On boardwalk. **Parking:** street only. L D

Atlantic City

Then & Now

Atlantic City has had its ups and downs, but like the Comeback Kid, the scrappy city keeps on swinging. The beach resort's heyday came during the 1920s and early '30s Prohibition era when liquor laws were flouted and mobsters and crime ruled. The decadence of those golden days is re-created in the HBO television series "Boardwalk Empire."

This early 1900s playground of the wealthy still bears some of the scars of the economic downturn that hit in the 1950s, when air travel inspired curious travelers to seek adventure farther from home. Like an aged beauty queen, Atlantic City lapsed into sad decline, with abandoned buildings, poverty, disrepair and empty streets taking the place of grand hotels and promenading tourists dressed to the nines. Once the first casino, Resorts International, entered the picture in the late 1970s, the feisty beach town entered another profitable period.

Soon entertainment entrepreneurs like Merv Griffin, Donald Trump and Steve Wynn were on the scene, spurring casino development and creating an East Coast gambling hub. By the 21st century, several casino hotels occupied the Boardwalk, and while business was bustling inside these mega establishments, something was still not quite right outside. The city itself continued to languish.

When the Borgata casino hotel opened in 2003 to much fanfare, the occasion marked another transitory winning streak in the direction of a revitalized city. First-rate shops and restaurants sprouted and slowly but surely started to glam up the Boardwalk and marina areas.

The potential almost seemed realized—until the Great Recession, Superstorm Sandy in 2012 and the advent of casinos in nearby areas took their toll on tourism dollars. In 2014, Atlantic Club Casino Hotel, Showboat—The Mardi Gras Casino, Trump Plaza Hotel & Casino, and even newly built Revel announced in quick succession that they were folding. Then there's Trump Taj Mahal Casino Hotel remaining in the hand after filing bankruptcy—meaning anything could happen.

So don't count out "America's Favorite Playground." Folks still come here for the challenge of mastering Lady Luck. They can also mingle at the latest martini or tequila bar and dance the night away in chic velvet-rope dance clubs reminiscent of Vegas.

With nighttime thrills aplenty, it's nice to know that you can also indulge in laid-back pursuits, such as luxuriating in a spa or embarking on a relaxing ocean cruise. *ARTLANTIC*, a public art project that beautifies Boardwalk-adjacent

Enjoy the amusement rides at Steel Pier

(Continued on p. 74.)

Destination Atlantic City

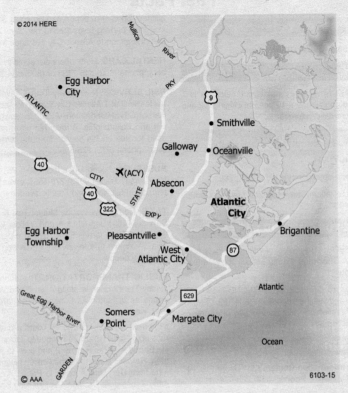

This map shows cities in the Atlantic City vicinity where you will find attractions, hotels and restaurants. Cities are listed alphabetically in this book on the following pages.

Fast Facts

ABOUT THE CITY

POP: 39,558 ▪ **ELEV:** 21 ft.

MONEY

SALES TAX: New Jersey's statewide sales tax is 7 percent; the county has a 10 percent lodging tax and $5 per day rental car surcharge.

WHOM TO CALL

EMERGENCY: 911

POLICE (non-emergency): (609) 347-5780

HOSPITALS: AtlantiCare Regional Medical Center, (609) 345-4000.

WHERE TO LOOK AND LISTEN

NEWSPAPERS: *The Press of Atlantic City* is published daily. Check the events section for entertainment offerings.

RADIO: Atlantic City radio station WOND (1400 AM) offers news and weather reports ▪ WNJN (89.7 FM), a member of National Public Radio, also offers news and weather reports.

VISITOR INFORMATION

Boardwalk Information Center: 2301 Boardwalk, Atlantic City, NJ 08401. **Phone:** (888) 228-4748.

Atlantic City Convention & Visitors Authority: 2314 Pacific Ave., Atlantic City, NJ 08401. **Phone:** (609) 348-7100 or (888) 228-4748.

TRANSPORTATION

AIR TRAVEL: Atlantic City International Airport (ACY), 12.5 miles west of Atlantic City, is served by several airlines. Short-term airport parking costs $1 per hour; long-term parking costs $9-$13 per day. Cab service from the airport to Atlantic City averages $35.

RENTAL CARS: Hertz offers discounts to AAA members; phone (609) 646-7733 or (800) 654-3080.

RAIL SERVICE: New Jersey Transit travels from the rail terminal at 1 Atlantic City Expwy. to Absecon, Egg Harbor City, Hammonton, Atco, Lindenwold, Cherry Hill and Philadelphia. A valid rail ticket also can be used for free shuttle service from the terminal to casinos; phone (973) 275-5555.

BUSES: Greyhound Lines Inc., (800) 231-2222, and New Jersey Transit, (973) 275-5555, operate from the terminal at Michigan and Atlantic avenues.

TAXIS: Companies include Mutual Taxi & Limousine Service, (609) 345-6111 ▪ and Yellow Cab, (609) 344-1221. Base fare is $3.40, plus 60c per one-tenth mile. Maximum fare to any city destination is $13 for up to five people.

PUBLIC TRANSPORTATION: The buses of New Jersey Transit operate along Atlantic and Ventnor avenues as far south as Longport. The fare is $1.50 each way.

Minibuses (jitneys) operate 24 hours a day. Route 1 runs from New Hampshire Avenue to Jackson Avenue via Pacific Avenue. Routes 2 and 3 go to the marina area, Harrah's Resort and the Golden Nugget; route 2 runs from Delaware Avenue to Pacific Avenue, and route 3 runs from Dr. Martin Luther King Boulevard to Inlet on Pacific Avenue. From 7 a.m. to 7 p.m. jitneys run on route 4 from Jackson Avenue to Indiana Avenue, with stops at the bus terminal, convention center and within two blocks of the rail terminal. Jitney fare is $2.25; 75c (ages 62+). Prepaid 10-ticket books are available for $20; $7.50 (ages 62+). Airport shuttles also are available with reservations. For more information phone (609) 344-8642.

(Continued from p. 72.)

areas, beckons as a daytime diversion. Beachcombers can sun themselves on a stretch of sand close to the hotels' tiki bars and live bands. The more active can join a friendly game of beach volleyball, escape to the jetties for saltwater fishing or consider a parasailing adventure. For some exercise along with a view, the ambitious tackle the 228 steps of the Absecon Lighthouse.

And what's more, Atlantic City is fun in a retro sort of way. Brimming with nostalgia, the Boardwalk lures casual strollers to "hit the boards" and take a trip down memory lane. You'll pass Boardwalk Hall, home of the Miss America Pageant, reminders of which also are reflected by memorabilia at the Atlantic City Historical Museum and by commemorative plaques cemented in Michigan Avenue's sidewalk. And the famous rolling chairs, which made their debut in the 1880s, can still whisk you to and fro on the Boardwalk—for a small fee, of course.

Despite redevelopment, some landmarks continue to withstand the test of time. Rediscover your inner kid by taking a roller coaster or Ferris wheel ride at Steel Pier, site of amusements and other diversions since 1898. Or amble over to White House Sub Shop, lauded for its uber-sandwiches sampled by the likes of the Beatles, Frank Sinatra and Elvis Presley. Before you leave, don't forget to pick up that iconic Atlantic City souvenir—some saltwater taffy from Fralinger's or James' Candy, both satiating generations of patrons with their sugary concoctions since the late 1800s.

Must Do: AAA Editor's Picks

- Stroll along the **Atlantic City Boardwalk** just like folks have been doing since 1870. You'll witness a real slice of beachside life as you amble along the iconic wooden structure in search of salt water taffy, food stands or souvenir shops. It's also a great place to watch passersby as they check out the scene. Don't feel like walking? Hail one of the famous rolling chairs, and an operator will push you to your destination.

- Create your own art tour by visiting the displays and green spaces adjacent to several Boardwalk landmarks. Meant to reclaim neglected spaces, *ARTLANTIC* resulted in three transitory art projects. One site—featuring undulating terraces, a rising pirate ship and, in season, a "red" garden—can be found around the Boardwalk by Martin Luther King Boulevard and Indiana Avenue. At Florida and Pacific avenues, a mural of a beach scene covers the West Hall of Boardwalk Hall. (Construction of new retail stores, however, caused California Avenue's "Étude Atlantis" to be more short-lived.)

- Climb to the top of the **Absecon Lighthouse.** The 1857 structure is one of the country's oldest of its kind and reputedly the tallest in New Jersey. Your reward for tackling the 228 steps will be expansive views of the coast and the Atlantic City skyline. You also can explore a small museum including a reproduced lightkeeper's dwelling and a Fresnel lens exhibit.

- Indulge in some **casino gambling.** With most casino hotels open around the clock—offering blackjack, craps, poker, roulette, slots and more—you're bound to find a good fit. If Lady Luck is on your side, spend your winnings in one of the hot nightlife venues, glitzy shops or pampering spas dotted throughout the casino hotels.

- Talk a walk on the **beach.** Atlantic City's stretch of sand has free access and runs from Jackson to Maine avenues, with the Boardwalk lining a 6-mile section. Calm waters (warm during summer) lure swimmers, while surfers head to the beaches at Delaware, New Hampshire and Raleigh avenues.

- Ride a **jitney.** These small 13-passenger buses are a great way to get around the city, stopping at tourist attractions, casino hotels, the NJ Transit Rail Terminal and other points of interest. Casino hoppers will be pleased to know that the jitneys run 24 hours a day for $2.25 per ride; 75c (ages 62+).

- Shop until you drop. Bargain hunters head to the **Tanger Outlets–The Walk,** an outdoor mall primarily situated on Michigan between Atlantic and Baltic avenues. All the usual chains are represented, and you can refuel at one of the restaurants within the complex. Nostalgic shoppers will appreciate the Miss America plaques embedded in the sidewalk along Michigan Avenue.

- Go **boating. Atlantic City Cruises** offers a dolphin-watching adventure as well as a morning skyline tour complemented by narration about area history. This and other sightseeing cruises depart from historic Gardner's Basin, a former fishing village that's also the spot to rent water sports equipment and bikes, hire a fishing charter or explore craft shops.

- **Entertain** yourself. The casino hotels host a vast array of enticing performances and events—magic and comedy acts, boxing matches and musical shows are typically part of the agenda. Boardwalk Hall serves as a key concert and sports venue.

- Plan a day trip to **Historic Smithville and Village Greene,** a re-creation of a 1700s village. Here, you can browse charming shops displaying such wares as lace, crafts, quilts, candles and other collectibles, or grab a bite in a quaint inn or tavern.

- Have fun at an **amusement pier.** Steel Pier is the place to be if you want to go for a spin on the Ferris wheel, ride the Crazy Mouse roller coaster, brave the bumper cars or try your hand at some carnival games. Central Pier features a game arcade along with a large go-cart track.

Absecon Lighthouse

Atlantic City 1-day Itinerary

AAA editors suggest these activities for a great short vacation experience.

Morning

- Jump-start your day by fueling up at a breakfast buffet in one of Atlantic City's casino hotels. Popular choices include the Sultan's Feast at **Trump Taj Mahal Casino Hotel**, the Borgata Buffet at **Borgata Hotel Casino & Spa** and the Waterfront Buffet (open 9 a.m. on weekends) at Harrah's Resort.

- If the weather is nice, consider reserving a spot on the morning skyline tour provided by **Atlantic City Cruises**, departing from Gardner's Basin. The narrated trip travels past the city's eclectic assortment of casino hotels, providing a good orientation to the various points of interest you'll no doubt visit later today. And you'll enjoy the coastal scenery and cooling ocean breezes, too.

- Those seeking a greater level of activity—perhaps to burn off that buffet breakfast—can climb the 228 steps leading to the top of **Absecon Lighthouse** at the Boardwalk's northern end. (A replicated lightkeeper's quarters will interest those who don't want to tackle the steps.) You can peer through the lighthouse's lens toward the south—you'll want to head in this direction so you can spend the afternoon exploring the Boardwalk, Atlantic City's pride and joy.

Afternoon

- Stroll along the Boardwalk (or have someone push you in a rolling chair), and you'll encounter several diverse amusements interspersed among the casino hotels. If you're traveling from the north end of the Boardwalk (near the lighthouse) to the south, you may want to stop off at the Garden Pier (at New Jersey Avenue), home of the **Atlantic City Historical Museum** and the **Atlantic City Art Center**. You'll be able to view such articles as the area's sports history and Miss America memorabilia at the museum, while the art center showcases a rotating collection of paintings, photography and sculpture. If you're in the mood for some good old-fashioned fun—complete with cotton candy and corn dogs—head to Steel Pier. Conjure up childhood memories or entertain the kids by engaging in midway games or braving the bumper cars, roller coaster and other rides.

- Continuing southward along the Boardwalk, be on the lookout for Fralinger's Salt Water Taffy, 1325 Boardwalk at Tennessee. You might want to pick up a box of these colorful concoctions for a souvenir—they're still using the original 1880s recipe. Near the junction of Park Place and the Boardwalk, you'll encounter the **New Jersey Korean War Veterans Memorial**; its granite wall is inscribed with the names of New Jerseyans who died in the conflict. As you approach the intersection of the Boardwalk and Arkansas

New Jersey Korean War Veterans Memorial

Avenue, you'll find yourself in prime shopping territory: The Pier Shops at Caesars is a high-end mall housing several luxury retailers.

- If you're looking for a great place to have a snack, head 3 blocks west at Boardwalk & Mississippi to arrive at the **White House Sub Shop**. You might want to split one of the enormous hoagies or cheese steaks, which you and a friend can savor while checking out the celebrity photos and other bric-a-brac displayed on the walls. Retrace your steps back to the Boardwalk, where you can pick up some literature at the Boardwalk Information Center (2301 Boardwalk). The center resides in Boardwalk Hall, famed for hosting the Miss America Pageant. Sneak a peek at the hall's pipe organ, said to be the world's largest.

Evening

- Atlantic City has plenty of dinner spots tucked into the casino hotels. [SAVE] **Hard Rock Cafe** in the Trump Taj Mahal is a popular spot for casual dining. You'll also find a number of restaurants dotting the Boardwalk—**Carmine's** is a good choice for classic Italian, while **The Palm Restaurant** serves up tender dry-aged steaks.

- You'll have no trouble entertaining yourself during Atlantic City evenings. If you're hoping to encounter Lady Luck, you need only wander the Boardwalk or hop on a shuttle bus (known as a jitney): Tropicana Casino, **Bally's Atlantic City** and Caesars Atlantic City are included in the lineup of casino gambling venues bordering the oceanside promenade.

Arriving
By Car

The city's principal gateway is the Atlantic City Expressway, a superhighway that connects with nearly all major mid-Atlantic highways. In the Philadelphia-Camden metropolitan area the expressway collects I-76 traffic from central Pennsylvania; I-95 from the Washington, D.C.-Baltimore-Wilmington corridor to the southwest and Newark-New York City to the northeast; I-295 between Wilmington and Trenton; and the New Jersey Turnpike.

A few miles west of Atlantic City the expressway intersects with the Garden State Parkway, a major coastal route linking Newark to the north and, via the Cape May-Lewes Ferry, Delaware and southern Maryland to the south. US 30 and US 40/322 also enter Atlantic City, arriving via Absecon Boulevard and Albany Avenue respectively. The Atlantic City Expressway is the preferred route.

Getting Around
Street System

As neatly gridlike as the Monopoly board on which some of its street names are perpetuated, Atlantic City's basic plan is easy to comprehend. Avenues parallel to the ocean are named for oceans or seas: Arctic, Mediterranean and Baltic. Some of these change names near the inlet or "downbeach"; for example, Baltic becomes Madison at its north end and Winchester at its south.

With a few exceptions, streets perpendicular to the ocean bear the names of states in an order roughly approximating the state's geographic position. New Hampshire and Vermont are at the northeast end of the island; Indiana and Illinois are about in the middle. Why Iowa Avenue is farther south than Texas and California avenues remains a mystery.

Numbers are in blocks of 100, increasing as they progress southward from Maine Avenue and inland from the Boardwalk. The few diagonal streets are mostly extensions of the roads that lead into the city.

Parking

Most businesses provide parking spaces near their premises, and most casino-hotels charge a state-mandated $3 fee for parking. That fee is valid at all Atlantic City casino-hotels for one day, with the proceeds earmarked for the revitalization of Atlantic City. Some casino-hotels may charge as much as $5 for parking, with the fee rising to $20 to park during special events.

Public parking lots are many and scattered throughout the city, and Boardwalk Hall at Mississippi Avenue and Boardwalk offers indoor parking. Daily rates—sometimes applied to any part of a 12-hour period—at privately owned lots range from $6 to $10 weekdays and from $10 to $20 weekends.

Shopping

As you might guess, Atlantic City's casino hotels lure their customers with numerous ways to spend their winnings, therefore providing the most lucrative hunting ground for shoppers. **The Pier Shops at Caesars** features a cornucopia of high-end boutiques showcasing designer clothes and baubles; the complex stretches along an expansive pier providing sweeping coastal views. Upscale restaurants housed on Level 3 complement the roster of luxury retailers that includes Burberry, Gucci, Louis Vuitton and Tiffany & Co.

The Quarter at Tropicana, a multi-level establishment with an Old Havana-inspired theme, also dazzles shoppers. An assortment of emporiums like Swarovski and White House/Black Market entices visitors, along with a collection of lively nightspots and restaurants ranging from casual to elegant. The Tropicana's **Marketplace** is a smaller, more family-friendly shopping alternative that includes a food court and spills out onto the Boardwalk.

The Waterfront at Harrah's presents a handful of shops touting shoes, jewelry and apparel in a marbled galleria, while the Borgata's contribution to retail bliss is **The Shoppes at the Water Club**, a small yet sleek assembly of fine merchants including Hugo Boss and Just Cavalli. In short, wherever there is a casino hotel you are bound to find spots worthy of a spending spree.

The glitter of the casinos has not diminished the Boardwalk's older charms: You'll have fun trolling for

Colorful salt-water taffy

Enjoy a night out in Atlantic City

Nightlife

Whether you're inclined to sip a margarita at a laid-back beachside hamlet, nurse a martini in a sleek lounge or dance the night away in a high-energy club, you've come to the right place: the casino hotels deliver all of this, and then some. Almost all the hotels present some type of entertainment, many with varied venues catering to the whims of their guests. Be sure to inquire in advance regarding operating hours, cover charges and dress codes.

The Borgata Hotel cultivates a lively scene that draws the younger set to its two standout clubs. **Mixx** welcomes a hip crowd when its doors open Saturday at 10 p.m. and Sunday at 11 p.m. The dance floor is a sea of constant motion, and a VIP bottle service paired with a plush setting assures some celebrity presence. The 20-somethings also gravitate to **mur.mur**, a cozy, colorfully lit hot spot frequented by in-demand DJs; in addition to being open Friday and Saturday at 10, the club also offers "mur.mur Monday," which tends to attract a more age-diverse clientele. Anyone who favors tequila will enjoy ordering a flight at the **Gypsy Bar**, but be forewarned—the rock music is loud. And the kind of audience you'll encounter at the **Music Box**, Borgata's venue for comedians and musicians, depends on who's performing.

Clubs at **The Quarter** is the Tropicana's answer to entertaining the masses—visitors can suit their fancy by choosing from a dozen or so thriving nightspots. At **Cuba Libre**, salsa dancers mesmerize all walks of life at the weekend Late Night Latin Floorshow, and the rum bar makes a mean mojito. Karaoke aficionados have tons of fun at **Planet Rose**, a smallish lounge with flashy décor and a medley of nightly drink specials. All ages appreciate the live acts at **The Comedy Stop**, one of the city's top venues for stand-up.

Bally's **Blue Martini** is a comfortable spot with a list of some 100 martinis (half-price during happy hour) to choose from; the bar's frosted ice rail keeps your drink cold. Those looking for a watering hole with 24-hour access can amble up to the Western-themed **Mountain Bar** at Bally's Wild West Casino, featuring nightly acts during summer.

Other casino hotels also have superb nightspots adding to the mix. **Dusk** at Caesars satisfies a youngish, well-heeled crowd on the hunt for a club with cutting-edge DJs, spinning lights and vibrant colors. Harrah's lures patrons to the circular **Xhibition Bar** and **The Pool After Dark**, complete with cabanas and bikini-clad waitresses.

A couple of worthy venues are removed from the hubbub of casino gambling. The Chelsea Hotel's fifth floor thrives with a range of nighttime opportunities sure to satisfy a variety of tastes. A DJ spins tunes amid lush greenery and poolside seating at

kitschy souvenirs, beachwear and T-shirts emblazoned while you wait. And like a kid in a candy store, you'll be tempted by an amazing variety of old-time treats, especially those colorful dollops of salt-water taffy. Fixtures like **Fralinger's Salt Water Taffy**, **James' Candy** and **Boardwalk Peanut Shoppe** satisfy cravings and supply great trip mementos.

[SAVE] **Tanger Outlets–The Walk**, a shopping, dining and entertainment complex concentrated around Atlantic, Arctic and Baltic avenues (between the Boardwalk and the convention center), captivates shoppers with its impressive medley of national chains. You'll encounter all the usual suspects—Adidas, Banana Republic, Eddie Bauer and Gap, to name a few—along with some higher-end designer outlets to round out the mix.

Locals usually hit the shops downtown at the north end of Atlantic Avenue—mainly strip malls and groceries—or venture to one of the suburban shopping malls. These include the **Central Square Shopping Centre** on US 9 in **Linwood**, with more than 70 specialty stores; **Hamilton Mall** in **Mays Landing** next to the Atlantic City Race Course, with some 150 shops; and **Harbor Square** at 6725 Black Horse Pike in **Egg Harbor Township**.

Historic Smithville and Village Greene, about a 25-minute drive, offers a family-oriented shopping experience in a re-creation of a 1700s coastal town with quaint cobblestone streets and a charming gazebo. Kids can ride the carousel and mini-train or play in the arcade while their parents peruse stores laden with handicrafts, antiques, Christmas ornaments and other treasures.

the Chelsea's open-air **Cabana Club**; the club's interior lounge, the Art Deco-inspired **C5**, is an edgy yet intimate nook perfect for a nightcap.

Big Events

Many shows and events take place in the **Atlantic City Convention Center**. Shows include the **Progressive Insurance Atlantic City Boat Show** and the **Atlantic City Classic Car Show** in February.

Bands, floats and performers proceed down the **Boardwalk** for the **St. Patrick's Day Parade,** which is in March. Then, the **Atlantic City Antiques Show** returns to the Atlantic City Convention Center in mid-April.

Thunder Over the Boardwalk (Atlantic City Airshow), a 1-day aviation extravaganza over the beach and the Boardwalk, lands in mid-August.

Sports & Rec

Before gambling came to this resort, it was the sun, ocean breezes and breakers washing the wide sand beach that made Atlantic City a leading playground. Popular as early as the 19th century, the beach is still a major attraction. Because there is less undertow than at other beach areas, **swimming** is particularly good. **Surfing** is permitted at Crystal Beach at New Hampshire Avenue; the Delaware Avenue beach; and the Downtown Beach at Raleigh Avenue. The beaches at South Carolina and Albany avenues have facilities that are accessible to the physically impaired. Lifeguards are on duty July 1-Labor Day (and at some beaches Memorial Day-June 30 and day after Labor Day- Sept. 30).

Fishing is as close as the ocean or inlet. Surf or pier fishing brings in striped bass, flounder, tautog and snapper blues; the inlet also yields croakers and crabs. Farther out, such fighters as marlin, tuna and bonito can be caught. In general, the summer months see the heaviest runs of most species.

Boating can be for fun as well as for fishing; the Thorofares—the network of waterways that separates Absecon and other islets from the mainland—provide a different perspective from which to view the city. Rental crafts ranging from one-person day sailers to six-person powerboats are available.

Bicycling is a popular pastime, particularly along the Boardwalk. Bicycle rentals, available from about 6 a.m. to 10 p.m., can be found along the length of the Great Wood Way.

Golf courses can be found all around the Atlantic City area. Public golf courses, all with 18 holes, include Atlantic City Country Club, 1 Leo Fraser Dr., Northfield; Blue Heron Pines Golf Club, 550 Country Club Dr., Egg Harbor City; Harbor Pines Golf Club, 500 Saint Andrews Dr., Egg Harbor Township; Links at Brigantine Beach, 1075 North Shore Dr., Brigantine; Seaview Golf Resort and Spa (both the Bay and Pines courses), 401 S. New York Rd., Absecon;

and Twisted Dune Golf Club, 2101 Ocean Heights Ave., Egg Harbor Township.

Some large hotels provide facilities for **racquetball, squash** or **tennis.** Public tennis courts are at 400 N. Jerome Ave. in Margate City and at S. Suffolk and Atlantic avenues in Ventnor.

Gambling

Gambling in Atlantic City is confined to the casino-hotels. To qualify for a casino operation, a hotel must have a minimum of 500 rooms and meet architectural requirements, not the least of which is approval of the design by the Atlantic City Planning Board and the New Jersey Casino Control Commission. Casinos are open daily 24 hours. The minimum age for participation is 21.

Baccarat, minibaccarat, big six wheel, blackjack, craps, poker, red dog, pai gow, sic bo, roulette, slots and keno are available, making the visitor who resists the temptation to gamble a rarity. It is recommended that those who accept the challenge to gamble first pick up one of the readily obtainable "how-to" books about gambling. While knowing something about the game won't alter the odds, which ultimately favor the house, it will increase the chances of breaking even or provide some understanding of why the bet was lost.

Some casinos will provide literature about the games; others even give classes for novice patrons. For first-time visitors, credit will be tight or nonexistent. Once credit has been established with further visits, it will be as easy to obtain $1,000 as $10.

Thunder Over the Boardwalk

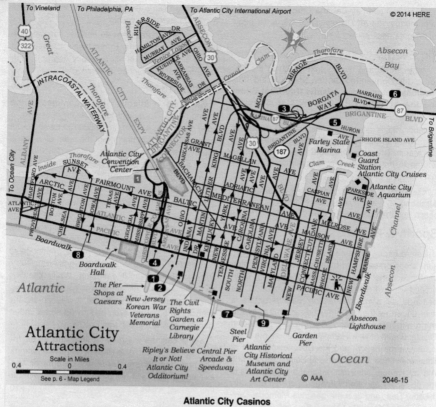

© 2014 HERE

Atlantic City Attractions

Scale in Miles

0.4   0   0.4

See p. 6 - Map Legend

© AAA   2046-15

Atlantic City Casinos

1. Bally's Atlantic City
2. Bally's Wild Wild West Casino
3. Borgata Hotel, Casino & Spa
4. Caesars Atlantic City
5. Golden Nugget
6. Harrah's Resort
7. Resorts Casino Hotel
8. Tropicana Casino and Resort
9. Trump Taj Mahal Casino Hotel

🚩 ATTRACTIONS

SAVE **ABSECON LIGHTHOUSE** is at jct. Pacific and Rhode Island aves. at 31 S. Rhode Island Ave. This restored 1857 lighthouse, the tallest beacon on the Jersey Shore and the third tallest in the country, still has its original Fresnel lens. Visitors can climb 228 steps to the top for a panorama of the Atlantic City skyline, nearby Brigantine and Absecon Inlet. The reconstructed Keeper's House contains a museum.

Time: Allow 1 hour minimum. **Hours:** Daily 10-5 (also Thurs. 5-8), July-Aug.; Thurs.-Mon. 11-4, rest of year. Last lighthouse access 30 minutes before closing. Closed Thanksgiving and 2 weeks for Christmas. **Cost:** Museum and exhibits free. Fee to climb to the top of the lighthouse $7; $5 (ages 65+); $4 (ages 4-12); free (military with ID). **Phone:** (609) 449-1360.

ATLANTIC CITY AQUARIUM is at 800 N. New Hampshire Ave. at Gardner's Basin. Visitors can regard the marine life of both local (Mullica River) and foreign (Australia) ecosystems. Highlights include living coral, jellyfish, moray eels and colorful tropical fish. Touch tanks for sharks and Cownose stingrays provide a hands-on experience. Other exhibits include a tropical rainforest exhibit, which houses turtles, iguanas and rays, as well as a piranha tank. **Hours:** Daily 10-5. Closed Jan. 1, Thanksgiving and Christmas. **Cost:** $8; $6 (ages 62+); $5 (ages 4-12). **Phone:** (609) 348-2880.

ATLANTIC CITY ART CENTER is on the Boardwalk at New Jersey Ave. on Garden Pier. It has three galleries that feature rotating displays of artwork by well-known contemporary artists and artisans. **Time:** Allow 30 minutes minimum. **Hours:** Mon.-Sat. 10-5; hours may be extended in summer. Closed major holidays. Phone ahead to confirm schedule. **Cost:** Free. **Phone:** (609) 347-5837.

ATLANTIC CITY HISTORICAL MUSEUM is on the Boardwalk at New Jersey Ave. on Garden Pier. Exhibits depict Atlantic City's reign as a vacation playground. One display salutes the Steel Pier's celebrated diving horse; another features Miss America memorabilia. A 35-minute film chronicles the city's history. **Time:** Allow 1 hour minimum. **Hours:** Daily 10-5. Closed Jan. 1, Election Day, Thanksgiving and Christmas. **Cost:** Free. **Phone:** (609) 347-5839.

THE CIVIL RIGHTS GARDEN AT CARNEGIE LIBRARY is at 39 S. Martin Luther King Blvd. at Pacific Ave. A symbolic tribute to the individuals and events leading up to and during the civil rights movement, it features 11 black granite columns inscribed with passages from contributors to the struggle for equality. The columns increase in height but are unfinished, signifying that full equality has not been reached. The landscaped area also includes a bronze bell and reflecting pool. **Time:** Allow 30 minutes minimum. **Hours:** Daily 8-5. Hours may be extended in summer; phone ahead. **Cost:** Free. **Phone:** (609) 347-2160.

NEW JERSEY KOREAN WAR VETERANS MEMORIAL is in Brighton Park at jct. Boardwalk and Park Pl. Etched in the memorial's granite wall are the names of the 890 New Jerseyans who died or were listed as missing in action in the Korean War. A bronze eternal flame rests atop the wall, and bronze statues depict such poignant scenes as soldiers in combat gear standing in pensive, reflective stances or assisting wounded comrades. A Medal of Honor Wall depicts five New Jerseyans who received the Medal of Honor.

Two video screens continuously play documentaries chronicling the 1950-53 conflict. **Time:** Allow 30 minutes minimum. **Hours:** Daily 24 hours. **Cost:** Free. **Phone:** (609) 530-7049.

RIPLEY'S BELIEVE IT OR NOT! ATLANTIC CITY ODDITORIUM! is on the Boardwalk at jct. New York Ave. More than 400 displays showcase the strange occurrences and unusual artifacts observed and collected by Robert Ripley throughout his travels around the world. Video presentations, illusions and interactive exhibits also are featured.

Time: Allow 1 hour minimum. **Hours:** Open daily. Hours vary by season. Phone ahead to confirm schedule. **Cost:** $16.99; $13.99 (ages 65+); $10.99 (ages 5-12). **Phone:** (609) 347-2001 or (877) 713-4231.

Sightseeing
Boardwalk Tours

Atlantic City's highlight is its Boardwalk, which can be explored on foot or by bicycle. Another way of seeing the Boardwalk is in the legendary rolling chair, which resembles a huge wicker chair on wheels. Pushed by an attendant, the chairs seat up to three people. The Royal Rolling Chairs company can be found at 114 S. New York Ave.

The chairs operate daily 8 a.m.-1 a.m. (also Fri.-Sat. 1-4 a.m.), weather permitting. The fare for up to two people is $5 for 5 blocks and fewer, $10 for 6 to 12 blocks, $15 for 13 to 21 blocks, $20 for 22 to 34 blocks, $25 per half-hour and $40 per hour; phone (609) 347-7500.

Boat Tours

ATLANTIC CITY CRUISES is at Historic Gardner's Basin at 800 N. New Hampshire Ave. Narrated 1-hour Morning Skyline and Afternoon Delight trips, hour-long Happy Hour cruises and 2-hour naturalist-narrated Dolphin Watching cruises are offered aboard the 130-passenger *Cruisn 1*.

Time: Allow 1 hour minimum. **Hours:** Afternoon Delight cruises depart daily at 4; Happy Hour cruises depart daily at 6; and Morning Skyline cruises depart Mon.-Sat. at 11, mid-June to mid-Sept. Dolphin Watching cruises depart daily at 1, June 1-late Sept.; Wed. and Sat.-Sun. at 1, in May and Oct. 1 through late Oct. Phone ahead to confirm schedule.

Cost: Morning Skyline, Afternoon Delight or Happy Hour cruise $18; $15 (ages 60+); $9 (ages 5-15). Happy Hour cruise with cocktails $35. Dolphin Watching cruise $35; $30 (ages 60+); $20 (ages 5-15). **Phone:** (609) 347-7600.

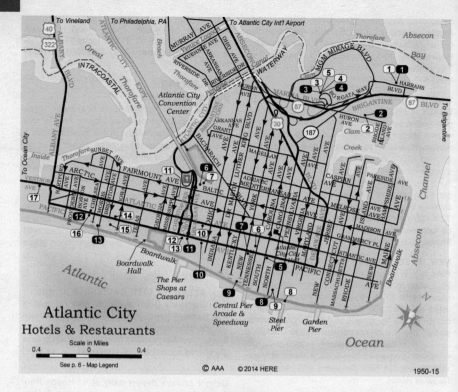

Atlantic City
Hotels & Restaurants

Scale in Miles
0.4   0   0.4

See p. 6 - Map Legend

© AAA   © 2014 HERE

1950-15

Atlantic City

This index helps you "spot" where approved hotels and restaurants are located on the corresponding detailed maps. Hotel daily rate range is for comparison only. Restaurant price range is a combination of lunch and/or dinner. Turn to the listing page for more detailed rate and price information and consult display ads for special promotions.

ATLANTIC CITY

Map Page	Hotels	Diamond Rated	Rate Range	Page
1 this page	Harrah's Resort Atlantic City	▽▽▽	Rates not provided	84
2 this page	**Golden Nugget Atlantic City**	▽▽▽▽	Rates not provided (SAVE)	84
3 this page	**Borgata Hotel Casino & Spa**	◇◇◇◇	$109-$699 (SAVE)	83
4 this page	**The Water Club by Borgata**	▽▽▽▽	$139-$699 (SAVE)	84
5 this page	Courtyard by Marriott Atlantic City	▽▽▽	$69-$148	84
6 this page	**Sheraton Atlantic City Convention Center Hotel**	▽▽▽	$79-$299 (SAVE)	84
7 this page	**BEST WESTERN Envoy Inn**	▽▽	$60-$400 (SAVE)	83
8 this page	Resorts Atlantic City	▽▽▽	$49-$399	84
9 this page	**Bluegreen Vacations at Atlantic Palace, an Ascend Resort Collection Member**	▽▽	Rates not provided (SAVE)	83
10 this page	Bally's Atlantic City	▽▽▽	Rates not provided	83
11 this page	**Caesars Atlantic City**	▽▽▽	Rates not provided (SAVE)	84
12 this page	Quality Inn Flamingo	▽▽	$50-$300	84
13 this page	Days Inn/Atlantic City-Oceanfront	▽▽	$100-$600	84

Map Page	Restaurants	Diamond Rated	Cuisine	Price Range	Page
① p. 82	Bill's Bar & Burger	◆◆	Burgers	$8-$14	84
② p. 82	Vic & Anthony's Steakhouse	◆◆◆	Steak	$25-$45	86
③ p. 82	Bobby Flay Steak	◆◆◆	Steak	$29-$125	85
④ p. 82	Old Homestead Steakhouse	◆◆◆	Steak	$32-$56	85
⑤ p. 82	Fornelletto Cucina & Wine Bar	◆◆◆	Italian	$15-$38	85
⑥ p. 82	Melaka Restaurant	◆◆	Asian	$6-$20	85
⑦ p. 82	Tun Tavern	◆◆	American	$9-$39	86
⑧ p. 82	Hard Rock Cafe	◆◆	American	$10-$29 SAVE	85
⑨ p. 82	Gallagher's	◆◆◆	Steak	$25-$45	85
⑩ p. 82	Los Amigos	◆◆	Mexican	$7-$29	85
⑪ p. 82	White House Sub Shop	◆	Deli	$7-$17	86
⑫ p. 82	The Continental	◆◆◆	International Small Plates	$10-$28	85
⑬ p. 82	Buddakan	◆◆◆	Asian	$9-$37	85
⑭ p. 82	The Palm Restaurant	◆◆◆	American	$24-$55	85
⑮ p. 82	P.F. Chang's China Bistro	◆◆◆	Chinese	$9-$26	86
⑯ p. 82	Girasole Ristorante & Bar	◆◆◆	Italian	$11-$29	85
⑰ p. 82	iPho AC	◆◆	Vietnamese	$8-$15	85

ATLANTIC CITY (G-4)

- **Restaurants p. 84**
- **Hotels & Restaurants map & index p. 82**

BALLY'S ATLANTIC CITY   609/340-2000 **10**

◆◆◆ **Hotel.** Rates not provided. **Address:** Park Pl & Boardwalk 08401 **Location:** Oceanfront. Between Ohio and Michigan aves. **Facility:** Room sizes and furnishings vary among the four towers at this large hotel. There are some restrictions at the pool regarding children during some periods. 1262 units, some two bedrooms. 3-30 stories, interior corridors. **Terms:** check-in 4 pm, valet. **Parking:** on-site (fee) and valet. **Amenities:** safes. **Dining:** 12 restaurants, entertainment. **Pool(s):** heated indoor. **Activities:** sauna, hot tub, steamroom, spa. **Guest Services:** valet laundry.

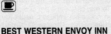

BEST WESTERN ENVOY INN   (609)344-7117 **7**

◆◆
Motel
$60-$400

AAA Benefit: Members save up to 20%!

Address: 1416 Pacific Ave 08401 **Location:** Jct Pacific and New York aves. **Facility:** 74 units. 4 stories, interior/exterior corridors. **Amenities:** safes. **Activities:** exercise room.

Discover a wealth of savings and offers on the AAA/CAA travel websites

BLUEGREEN VACATIONS AT ATLANTIC PALACE, AN ASCEND RESORT COLLECTION MEMBER
609/344-8800 **9**

Vacation Rental
Condominium
Rates not provided

Address: 1507 Boardwalk 08401 **Location:** Oceanfront. Jct New York Ave and Boardwalk. **Facility:** This nice high-rise adjacent to the boardwalk offers studios and one- to two-bedroom suites. 201 condominiums. 31 stories, interior corridors. **Parking:** on-site (fee). **Terms:** check-in 4 pm. **Amenities:** safes. **Pool(s):** outdoor. **Activities:** sauna, hot tub, steamroom, game room, exercise room. **Guest Services:** coin laundry.

BORGATA HOTEL CASINO & SPA   (609)317-1000 **3**

Hotel
$109-$699

Address: One Borgata Way 08401 **Location:** Atlantic City Expwy exit 1, 1.6 mi n. **Facility:** Polished marble, hand-crafted chandeliers and a stable of fine restaurants border the bustling casino. Some guest rooms overlook the water. 2002 units, some two bedrooms. 43 stories, interior corridors. **Parking:** on-site (fee) and valet. **Terms:** check-in 4 pm, 3 day cancellation notice-fee imposed, resort fee. **Amenities:** safes. **Dining:** 11 restaurants, also, Bobby Flay Steak, Fornelletto Cucina & Wine Bar, Old Homestead Steakhouse, see separate listings, nightclub, entertainment. **Pool(s):** heated indoor. **Activities:** sauna, hot tub, steamroom, spa. **Guest Services:** valet laundry, area transportation.

(See map & index p. 82.)

CAESARS ATLANTIC CITY
609/348-4411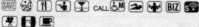

Resort Hotel
Rates not provided

Address: 2100 Pacific Ave 08401 **Location:** Oceanfront. At Arkansas Ave. **Facility:** This upscale resort offers spacious suites and a large shopping/dining complex on the pier. The location puts you right in the middle of the boardwalk action and a short walk to the convention center. 1141 units, some two bedrooms. 14 stories, interior corridors. **Parking:** valet and street only. **Terms:** check-in 4 pm. **Amenities:** video games, safes. **Dining:** 8 restaurants, also, Buddakan, The Continental, see separate listings, entertainment. **Pool(s):** heated outdoor. **Activities:** sauna, hot tub, steamroom, spa. **Guest Services:** valet laundry, area transportation.

COURTYARD BY MARRIOTT ATLANTIC CITY
(609)345-7070 **5**

Hotel $69-$148 **Address:** 1212 Pacific Ave 08401 **Location:** Corner of S Carolina and Pacific aves. **Facility:** 206 units. 17 stories, interior corridors. **Parking:** on-site (fee) and valet. **Terms:** check-in 4 pm. **Activities:** exercise room. **Guest Services:** valet and coin laundry.

AAA Benefit: Members save 5% or more!

DAYS INN/ATLANTIC CITY-OCEANFRONT
(609)344-6101 **13**

Hotel $100-$600 **Address:** Boardwalk & Morris Ave 08401 **Location:** Oceanfront. On the boardwalk. **Facility:** 107 units. 5 stories, interior corridors.

GOLDEN NUGGET ATLANTIC CITY
609/441-2000 **2**

Contemporary Hotel
Rates not provided

Address: Huron Ave & Brigantine Blvd 08401 **Location:** SR 87, 0.8 mi n of US 30; at Frank S Farley Marina. **Facility:** This stylish property offers the perfect outdoor pool lounge with a stone fire pit, private cabanas and large courtyard area with daily events. Rooms, many with great views, have a modern boutique style. 727 units, some two bedrooms. 14-27 stories, interior corridors. **Parking:** valet and street only. **Terms:** check-in 4 pm. **Amenities:** safes. **Dining:** 7 restaurants, also, Vic & Anthony's Steakhouse, see separate listing, nightclub, entertainment. **Pool(s):** heated outdoor. **Activities:** hot tub, steamroom, marina, spa. **Guest Services:** valet laundry.

HARRAH'S RESORT ATLANTIC CITY
609/441-5000 **1**

Hotel. Rates not provided. **Address:** 777 Harrah's Blvd 08401 **Location:** Waterfront. 0.9 mi n of US 30 on Brigantine Blvd. **Facility:** The sprawling public spaces here include great restaurants, shops and a very lively glass-domed year-round pool. Rooms vary a bit among the different towers but all are spacious and well appointed. 2590 units, some two bedrooms. 25-45 stories, interior corridors. **Parking:** on-site (fee) and valet. **Terms:** check-in 4 pm. **Amenities:** Some: safes. **Dining:** 7 restaurants, also, Bill's Bar & Burger, see separate listing, entertainment. **Pool(s):** heated indoor. **Activities:** sauna, hot tub, miniature golf, recreation programs, game room, exercise room, spa. **Guest Services:** valet laundry, area transportation.

QUALITY INN FLAMINGO
(609)431-4001 **12**

Hotel $50-$300 **Address:** 3101 Pacific Ave 08401 **Location:** Between S Chelsea and S Montpelier aves. **Facility:** 71 units. 3 stories (no elevator), exterior corridors. **Parking:** on-site (fee). **Amenities:** safes. **Activities:** exercise room.

RESORTS ATLANTIC CITY
(609)340-6000 **8**

Hotel $49-$399 **Address:** 1133 Boardwalk 08401 **Location:** Oceanfront. At east end of N Carolina Ave. **Facility:** This hotel's attractive marble-accented lobby has an Art Deco-inspired style and the rooms are bright and cheerful with upscale shore décor. 942 units, some two bedrooms. 14-24 stories, interior corridors. **Parking:** on-site (fee) and valet. **Terms:** check-in 4 pm, 3 day cancellation notice-fee imposed, resort fee. **Amenities:** safes. **Dining:** 7 restaurants, also, Gallagher's, see separate listing, nightclub, entertainment. **Pool(s):** heated outdoor, heated indoor. **Activities:** sauna, hot tub, steamroom, spa. **Guest Services:** valet laundry.

SHERATON ATLANTIC CITY CONVENTION CENTER HOTEL
(609)344-3535 **6**

Hotel
$79-$299

AAA Benefit: Members save up to 15%, plus Starwood Preferred Guest® benefits!

Address: 2 Convention Blvd 08401 **Location:** Garden State Pkwy exit 38 to Atlantic City Expwy to Arctic Ave, just e to Michigan Ave, then just n. **Facility:** 502 units. 16 stories, interior corridors. **Parking:** valet and street only. **Terms:** cancellation fee imposed. **Amenities:** video games, safes. **Dining:** Tun Tavern, see separate listing. **Pool(s):** heated indoor. **Activities:** hot tub, exercise room. **Guest Services:** valet laundry, boarding pass kiosk.

THE WATER CLUB BY BORGATA
(609)317-1000 **4**

Contemporary Hotel
$139-$699

Address: 1 Renaissance Way 08401 **Location:** Atlantic City Expwy exit 1, 1.6 mi n. **Facility:** Part of the upscale Borgata casino complex, this hotel ups the ante on luxury and has some of the finest accommodations in Atlantic City. With modern décor, rooms and bathrooms here are spacious. 800 units, some two bedrooms. 38 stories, interior corridors. **Parking:** on-site (fee) and valet. **Terms:** check-in 4 pm, 3 day cancellation notice-fee imposed, resort fee. **Amenities:** safes. **Dining:** 11 restaurants, entertainment. **Pool(s):** heated outdoor, heated indoor. **Activities:** hot tub, spa. **Guest Services:** valet laundry, area transportation.

WHERE TO EAT

BILL'S BAR & BURGER
609/441-5800 **1**

Burgers. Casual Dining. $8-$14 **AAA Inspector Notes:** The name says it all—burgers of all types are what they do here at this relaxed spot just off the casino floor. This is the Atlantic City outpost of the popular New York City burger chain. Night owls might hang out in the large bar and watch one of several TVs. **Features:** full bar. **Address:** 777 Harrah's Blvd 08401 **Location:** 0.9 mi n of US 30 on Brigantine Blvd; in Harrah's Resort Atlantic City. **Parking:** on-site (fee) and valet.

(See map & index p. 82.)

BOBBY FLAY STEAK
609/317-1000 ③

▼▼▼ Steak. Fine Dining. $29–$125 **AAA Inspector Notes:** Popular TV chef Bobby Flay adds his twist to the steakhouse with some interesting and flavorful steak toppings and sauces, and the menu also features a range of seafood and many lobster dishes from the lobster bar. The setting is casual and exciting in the David Rockwell-designed restaurant that is just off the casino floor. Note that children under 8 are not permitted in the casino and minors traveling on the assigned walkway paths must be accompanied by an adult. **Features:** full bar. **Reservations:** suggested. **Address:** One Borgata Way 08401 **Location:** Atlantic City Expwy exit 1, 1.6 mi n; in Borgata Hotel Casino & Spa. **Parking:** on-site (fee) and valet.

D CALL &M

BUDDAKAN
609/674-0100 ⑬

▼▼▼▼ Asian. Casual Dining. $9–$37 **AAA Inspector Notes:** The huge golden Buddha statue overlooking the main dining room is the most prominent feature of this heavily themed Chinese restaurant. The menu offers some familiar items including spring rolls, lo mein, fried rice and several seafood selections, but dishes are enhanced with some modern twists and upscale ingredients. The dishes here are best enjoyed family-style and it is a great place to go as a group for a fun and casual dinner. **Features:** full bar, happy hour. **Address:** One Atlantic Ocean 08401 **Location:** At Arkansas Ave; in Caesars Atlantic City. **Parking:** on-site (fee) and valet.

L D CALL &M

CARMINE'S
609/572-9300

▼▼ Southern Italian. Family Dining. $23–$43 **AAA Inspector Notes:** This Atlantic City outpost is a replica of the famed Broadway favorite. Wonderful Southern Italian food is served in abundant, family-style portions. Guests are hard-pressed to choose from favorites such as lush pasta ragu in tomato-based sauce loaded with pork braciole, beef chuck roast, meatballs and sausage, linguine with clam sauce, chicken Marsala and the hefty stuffed veal chop. Diners who succumb to the assorted temptations in the bread basket may regret it when the tiramisu arrives. **Features:** full bar, happy hour. **Reservations:** suggested. **Address:** 2801 Pacific Ave, Suite 103 08401 **Location:** At Pacific and Brighton aves; downtown; in The Quarter of the Tropicana Casino and Resort. **Parking:** on-site (fee) and valet.

L D CALL &M

THE CONTINENTAL
609/674-8300 ⑫

▼▼▼ International Small Plates. Casual Dining. $10–$28 **AAA Inspector Notes:** Fun and casual, this place serves a wide-ranging menu with tapas, entrées and a good selection of vegetarian items. The menu covers everything from Korean barbecue, Thai, Mexican and some tasty Kobe beef sliders. The restaurant and bar have a distinctive retro look including a 1960s era fire pit in one of the dining areas. **Features:** full bar, Sunday brunch, happy hour. **Address:** One Atlantic Ocean 08401 **Location:** At Arkansas Ave; in Caesars Atlantic City. **Parking:** on-site (fee) and valet. L D CALL &M

FORNELLETTO CUCINA & WINE BAR
609/317-1000 ⑤

▼▼▼▼ Italian. Casual Dining. $15–$38 **AAA Inspector Notes:** Descend the stairs (or elevator) to this casual wine cellar where excellent modern Italian cuisine is served. The menu offers a range of flavorful options with small plates, salads, pizza, pastas and such entrées as basil-crusted halibut and veal osso buco ravioli. **Features:** full bar. **Reservations:** suggested. **Address:** One Borgata Way 08401 **Location:** Atlantic City Expwy exit 1, 1.6 mi n; in Borgata Hotel Casino & Spa. **Parking:** on-site (fee) and valet. D CALL &M

GALLAGHER'S
609/340-6555 ⑨

▼▼▼ Steak. Fine Dining. $25–$45 **AAA Inspector Notes:** There is no mistaking the main attraction here as you walk past the glass meat locker at the entrance where USDA Prime steaks are dry aged for 21 days. This is an outpost of the classic New York steakhouse that is known as the first place to serve the New York strip steak. There also are some fresh seafood selections including Maine lobster. For a quicker, casual meal, there is also Gallagher's Burger Bar right next door with a menu of burgers and sandwiches. **Features:** full bar. **Address:** 1133 Boardwalk 08401 **Location:** At east end of N Carolina Ave; in Resorts Atlantic City. **Parking:** on-site (fee) and valet. D CALL &M

GIRASOLE RISTORANTE & BAR
609/345-5554 ⑯

▼▼▼ Italian. Fine Dining. $11–$29 **AAA Inspector Notes:** Frequented by trendsetters and Jersey bigwigs, this upscale restaurant offers chic surroundings that appear to have a designer's touch. The menu does not disappoint and provides fresh pasta, delicious brick-oven pizza and tasty seafood specialties. The variety of beef carpaccio appetizers are the perfect start to any meal. **Features:** full bar. **Reservations:** suggested. **Address:** 3108 Pacific Ave 08401 **Location:** Just n of jct Montpelier Ave; in Ocean Club Condominiums. **Parking:** valet and street only. L D

HARD ROCK CAFE
609/441-0007 ⑧

▼▼ American. Casual Dining. $10–$29 **AAA Inspector Notes:** Rock 'n' roll memorabilia decorates the walls of the popular theme restaurant. Live music on the weekends contributes to the bustling atmosphere. On the menu is a wide variety of American cuisine—from burgers and sandwiches to seafood, steaks and pasta. **Features:** full bar, happy hour. **Address:** 1000 Boardwalk at Virginia Ave 08401 **Location:** At Virginia Ave; in Trump Taj Mahal Casino Hotel. **Parking:** on-site (fee). SAVE L D LATE CALL &M

IPHO AC
609/340-0063 ⑰

▼▼ Vietnamese. Casual Dining. $8–$15 **AAA Inspector Notes:** This unassuming storefront is a casual spot for steaming bowls of fragrant, traditional noodle soups filled with fresh meats or fish. All are served with fresh cilantro, basil, lime and sprouts. Condiments are on the tables. The broken rice and vermicelli dishes of grilled meats and shrimp are a wonderful complement to the soups, and meals are richly satisfying. Servers help newcomers navigate the menu and may recommend the fried egg rolls. **Address:** 3808 Ventnor Ave 08401 **Location:** Just s of Trenton Ave. **Parking:** street only. L D

LOS AMIGOS
609/344-2293 ⑩

▼▼ Mexican. Casual Dining. $7–$29 **AAA Inspector Notes:** Every inch of this charming dining room has been colorfully and fancifully painted with animals and brilliant geometric designs, creating a festive atmosphere. The menu offers a hint of nouveau—such as Southwest spring rolls with avocado cream, spicy crab soup, wasabi-crusted grilled tuna and roast pork chimichangas with smoked chile barbecue sauce—but most seasonings are traditional. **Features:** full bar, happy hour. **Address:** 1926 Atlantic Ave 08401 **Location:** 2 blks from convention center. **Parking:** on-site and street. L D CALL &M

MELAKA RESTAURANT
609/344-8928 ⑥

▼▼ Asian. Casual Dining. $6–$20 **AAA Inspector Notes:** It is easy to pass by this unassuming storefront, but those who do will miss out on a world of flavors packed into savory, aromatic dishes with attractive garnishes. A helpful picture book showing many popular items accompanies the somewhat daunting menu. Friendly, gracious servers gladly assist in meal selections. **Address:** 28 S Tennessee Ave 08401 **Location:** Between Atlantic and Pacific aves. L D LATE

OLD HOMESTEAD STEAKHOUSE
609/317-1000 ④

▼▼▼ Steak. Fine Dining. $32–$56 **AAA Inspector Notes:** This is an outpost of the venerable Old Homestead Steakhouse in Manhattan, and you can get the same excellent Prime aged steaks such as the signature 34-ounce Gotham rib-eye. The menu has all the items one would expect at a classic, upscale steakhouse with oysters, crab, lobster and huge desserts. **Features:** full bar. **Reservations:** suggested. **Address:** One Borgata Way 08401 **Location:** Atlantic City Expwy exit 1, 1.6 mi n; in Borgata Hotel Casino & Spa. **Parking:** on-site (fee) and valet. D CALL &M

THE PALM RESTAURANT
609/344-7256 ⑭

▼▼▼▼ American. Fine Dining. $24–$55 **AAA Inspector Notes:** This bustling restaurant is noted for Prime, dry-aged steaks and Nova Scotia lobsters. The huge portions are delivered by an attentive staff in an atmosphere that is fun and lively. At the end of the meal, servers present tempting pastries tableside. Caricature-lined walls lend to the feeling that patrons are dining in an art gallery. Even if you bring a big appetite you still may leave with a doggy bag. **Features:** full bar, happy hour. **Reservations:** suggested. **Address:** 2801 Pacific Ave 08401 **Location:** At Pacific and Brighton aves; downtown; in The Quarter of the Tropicana Casino and Resort. **Parking:** valet only. D

(See map & index p. 82.)

P.F. CHANG'S CHINA BISTRO   609/348-4600   15
▼▼▼ Chinese. Fine Dining. $9-$26 **AAA Inspector Notes:** Trendy, upscale decor provides a pleasant backdrop for New Age Chinese dining. Appetizers, soups and salads are a meal by themselves. Vegetarian plates and sides, noodles, chow meins, chicken and meat dishes are created from exotic, fresh ingredients. **Features:** full bar, happy hour. **Address:** 2801 Pacific Ave 08401 **Location:** At Pacific and Brighton aves; downtown; in The Quarter of the Tropicana Casino and Resort. [L] [D]

TUN TAVERN   609/347-7800   7
▼▼ American. Casual Dining. $9-$39 **AAA Inspector Notes:** Atlantic City's only brewery serves a wide selection of microbrews, lagers, stouts and more. Dining consists of an upscale menu of American fare, from elaborate salads, hefty sandwiches and hearty burgers to seafood entrees, pasta and steaks. Behind the bar and visible through large glass panes, the brewery makes for quite the conversation piece, but it's the hand-crafted beers that really have everyone talking. **Features:** full bar, patio dining, happy hour. **Address:** 2 Convention Blvd 08401 **Location:** Garden State Pkwy exit 38 to Atlantic City Expwy to Arctic Ave, just e to Michigan Ave, then just n; in Sheraton Atlantic City Convention Center Hotel.
[L] [D] [LATE]

VIC & ANTHONY'S STEAKHOUSE   609/441-8355   2
▼▼▼▼ Steak. Fine Dining. $25-$45 **AAA Inspector Notes:** The setting is very upscale and refined at this new outpost of the original standout restaurant in Houston. The menu offers many of the usual upscale steakhouse items including USDA Prime beef, Maine lobster and king crab, as well as a few other extras like quail and local fish. **Features:** full bar, happy hour. **Reservations:** suggested. **Address:** Huron Ave & Brigantine Blvd 08401 **Location:** SR 87, 0.8 mi n of US 30; at Frank S Farley Marina; in Golden Nugget Atlantic City. **Parking:** on-site (fee) and valet. [D] CALL&M

WHITE HOUSE SUB SHOP   609/345-1564   11
▼ Deli. Quick Serve. $7-$17 **AAA Inspector Notes:** *Classic.* Since 1946, visitors have flocked from all over to taste what some consider to be the quintessential submarine sandwich. Frank Sinatra was known to visit when in town, and photographs on the walls document the steady stream of celebrities who have done the same. Do not expect much ambience—it is the hearty, satisfying subs that bring new hordes of fans through the door year after year. They accept cash only and seating is limited. **Address:** 2301 Arctic Ave 08401 **Location:** Jct Arctic and Mississippi aves. **Parking:** street only.
[L] [D]

AVALON pop. 1,334

TORTILLA FLATS   609/967-5658
▼▼ Mexican. Casual Dining. $7-$22 **AAA Inspector Notes:** Bright murals, piñatas and peppers add to the whimsy of this little restaurant, a favorite spot for traditional Mexican and Southwestern fare. Also here are bursts of originality, such as burritos stuffed with portobello mushrooms or sun-dried tomatoes. **Address:** 2540 Dune Dr 08202 **Location:** Garden State Pkwy exit 13, 3.5 mi se on CR 601, then 0.3 mi n. **Parking:** street only. [D]

AVENEL pop. 17,011
• Hotels & Restaurants map & index p. 152

COMFORT SUITES AT WOODBRIDGE
    (732)396-3000   107

▼▼▼
Hotel
$99-$159

Address: 1275 US 1 07001 **Location:** 1.8 mi n of jct SR 35. **Facility:** 101 units. 7 stories, interior corridors. **Activities:** exercise room. **Guest Services:** valet and coin laundry, area transportation. **Featured Amenity:** breakfast buffet.

FAIRFIELD INN & SUITES BY MARRIOTT WOODBRIDGE
    (732)396-9700   106
▼▼▼ Hotel. $111-$183 **Address:** 1295 US 1 S 07001 **Location:** 1.8 mi n of jct SR 35. **Facility:** 90 units. 6 stories, interior corridors. **Pool(s):** heated indoor. **Activities:** hot tub, exercise room. **Guest Services:** valet and coin laundry, area transportation.

> **AAA Benefit:** Members save 5% or more!

⊕ CALL &M ⊘ BIZ HS 🛜 ✕ ▭ / SOME UNITS 🛄 🖼

HOLIDAY INN EXPRESS-WOODBRIDGE   732/726-1900   108
▼▼▼ Hotel. Rates not provided. **Address:** 874 US Hwy 1 N 07001 **Location:** 0.5 mi n of jct SR 35. **Facility:** 78 units. 4 stories, interior corridors. **Terms:** check-in 4 pm. **Pool(s):** heated indoor. **Activities:** hot tub, exercise room. **Guest Services:** valet and coin laundry.
CALL &M ⊘ BIZ HS 🛜 ✕ 🛄 🖼 ▭

AVON-BY-THE-SEA pop. 1,901

ATLANTIC VIEW INN   732/774-8505
▼▼▼ Historic Bed & Breakfast. Rates not provided. **Address:** 20 Woodland Ave 07717 **Location:** Jct Ocean Ave, just w. **Facility:** Situated across the street from the beach, the inn offers an English country ambiance with cheerful floral fabrics and plush feather beds. 12 units, some two bedrooms. 3 stories (no elevator), interior corridors. **Activities:** bicycles.
⊕ 🛜 ✕ 📠 🛄

BARNEGAT LIGHT (F-4) pop. 574, elev. 10'

Barnegat Light, the northernmost community on Long Beach Island, was settled by Scandinavian fishermen; whalers first came to the isle in the early 18th century. Fishing, particularly for tuna, and summertime diversions sustain the town.

Because the area around Lovelladies Harbor has a scenic appeal likened to that of Cape Cod, the town, named for an 18th-century landowner, has become a well-known art colony. Long Beach Island is an 18-mile-long segment of the barrier isles that outline the New Jersey coast. Its width ranges from about 3 blocks to 1 mile. A long causeway carries SR 72 across Barnegat Bay to Ship Bottom.

BARNEGAT LIGHTHOUSE STATE PARK is n. on Long Beach Blvd. to Broadway. The 32-acre park surrounds "Old Barney," the historic Barnegat Lighthouse. A forest nature trail and fishing, crabbing and bird-watching opportunities are available. Fires are not permitted. **Hours:** Park open daily 8 a.m.-10 p.m., Memorial Day-Labor Day; 8-8, day after Labor Day-Sept. 29 and May 1-day before Memorial Day; 8-4, rest of year. Phone ahead to confirm schedule. **Cost:** Free. **Phone:** (609) 494-2016. 🎣

Barnegat Lighthouse is at the northern tip of Long Beach Island at jct. Broadway Ave. and Third St. Known as the "Grand Old Champion of the Tides," the lighthouse was rebuilt 1857-58 by Gen. George G. Meade after the original 1834 structure toppled into the sea. The tower rises 172 feet above the tides and marks Barnegat Shoals, the scene of more than 200 shipwrecks. Climb the 217 steps to the top for a fine view of the surrounding area. An interpretive center next to the lighthouse traces its history.

Hours: Daily 10-4:30, May-Oct.; Sat.-Sun. 9-3:30, rest of year. Closed Jan. 1, Thanksgiving and Christmas. **Cost:** Memorial Day-Labor Day $3; $1 (ages 6-11). Rest of year free. **Phone:** (609) 494-2016.

BASKING RIDGE (C-3) elev. 320'
• Hotels & Restaurants map & index p. 152

A hillside where animals from the surrounding swamplands could sun themselves inspired the name Basking Ridge. More than 10,000 years ago most of the region to the east was part of Lake Passaic, created when an accumulation of earth and stone carried by the Wisconsin Glacier blocked the Passaic River. A portion of the former lake, now a wetland, is known as the "Great Swamp" of New Jersey.

GREAT SWAMP NATIONAL WILDLIFE REFUGE is e. on Lee's Hill Rd. to 32 Pleasant Plains Rd. The land now occupied by this 7,768-acre refuge was going to be used for the construction of an airport before local residents intervened. Marsh and swamp woodland habitats are home to muskrats, foxes, fish, turtles and nearly 250 species of birds, including raptors, waterfowl and migrating birds.

A wildlife observation center features boardwalk trails and observation blinds. More than 8 miles of hiking trails wind through the habitats. **Hours:** Trails daily dawn-dusk. Visitor center open Thurs.-Fri. noon-4, Sat.-Sun. 10-4. **Cost:** Free. **Phone:** (973) 425-1222.

SOMERSET COUNTY PARK COMMISSION ENVIRONMENTAL EDUCATION CENTER is off I-287 exit 30A, 3 mi. s. on Maple Ave., then 1 mi. e. to 190 Lord Stirling Rd. The center is on a 450-acre tract of the Great Swamp Basin. The interpretive building, one of the country's first public buildings to be heated and cooled by solar power in the late 1970s, offers a library, exhibit areas and nature programs. The sanctuary has nature trails, boardwalks, observation towers and blinds that allow visitors to view native wildlife.

Note: Pets, horses, bicycles and motorized vehicles are prohibited on the nature trails. **Time:** Allow 2 hours minimum. **Hours:** Education center daily 9-5. Trails daily dawn-dusk. Closed most holidays; phone for schedule. **Cost:** Free. **Phone:** (908) 766-2489.

COURTYARD BY MARRIOTT BASKING RIDGE
(908)542-0300 **92**

Hotel
$207-$339

AAA Benefit: Members save 5% or more!

Address: 595 Martinsville Rd 07920 **Location:** I-78 exit 33, just n. **Facility:** 235 units. 4 stories, interior corridors. **Pool(s):** heated indoor. **Activities:** hot tub, exercise room. **Guest Services:** valet and coin laundry, boarding pass kiosk.

DOLCE BASKING RIDGE
908/953-3000 **91**

Hotel. Rates not provided. **Address:** 300 N Maple Ave 07920 **Location:** I-287 exit 30A, 0.3 mi e. **Facility:** A secluded setting and an attentive staff make for a relaxed and enjoyable stay at this conference hotel. Original art lends an air of quiet sophistication. 171 units. 3 stories, interior corridors. **Pool(s):** heated indoor. **Activities:** hot tub, tennis, exercise room. **Guest Services:** valet and coin laundry, area transportation.

HOTEL INDIGO BASKING RIDGE
908/580-1300 **93**

Hotel. Rates not provided. **Address:** 80 Allen Rd 07920 **Location:** I-78 exit 33, 0.3 mi n. on CR 525, then 0.3 mi w. **Facility:** 112 units. 4 stories, interior corridors. *Bath:* shower only. **Activities:** exercise room. **Guest Services:** valet laundry, area transportation.

THE OLDE MILL INN
908/221-1100 **90**

Hotel. Rates not provided. **Address:** 225 US 202 & N Maple Ave 07920 **Location:** I-287 exit 30B (2nd ramp), just w. **Facility:** 102 units. 2 stories, interior/exterior corridors. **Amenities:** safes. **Dining:** The Grain House at The Olde Mill Inn, see separate listing. **Activities:** exercise room. **Guest Services:** valet laundry, area transportation.

WHERE TO EAT

3 WEST
908/647-3000 **137**

American. Casual Dining. $10-$30 **AAA Inspector Notes:** This mission-style bar and restaurant derives its mood from a wood-burning fireplace, as well as accents of dark wood, leather, soft fabrics, brick, copper and warm earth tones. This is a popular meeting place for an evening out with friends. On the menu are such preparations as seared honey-spiced shrimp, warm mushroom tart, roasted duck breast, venison and varied meats grilled over hardwoods. **Features:** full bar, patio dining. **Reservations:** suggested. **Address:** 665 Martinsville Rd 07920 **Location:** I-78 exit 33, 0.3 mi n. L D CALL

THE GRAIN HOUSE AT THE OLDE MILL INN
908/221-1150 **135**

American. Casual Dining. $7-$29 **AAA Inspector Notes:** *Historic.* In a tree-covered area set back from the street, this converted 1768 barn has a quaint Colonial charm. Attractive fireplaces provide warmth in cooler weather. Examples of American country-inn comfort foods include crab cakes, steaks and French onion soup. The bar is a cozy place to meet friends. **Features:** full bar, Sunday brunch. **Reservations:** suggested. **Address:** 225 US 202 & N Maple Ave 07920 **Location:** I-287 exit 30B (2nd ramp), just w; in The Olde Mill Inn. L D

(See map & index p. 152.)

TRATTORIA BOLU   908/647-0033   138
▽▽ ▽▽ Italian. Casual Dining. $9-$25 **AAA Inspector Notes:** This is a great, casual spot for Italian food that leans more to the light and creative side with thin, crisp, brick-oven pizzas, handmade pastas and salads made with fresh, organic, local ingredients. There is also an antipasto bar that changes daily. The brick pizza oven is the focal point of the warm, welcoming décor, which is cozy with a touch of urban hipness. **Address:** 25 Mountainview Blvd 07920 **Location:** I-78 exit 33, just s.   L   D   CALL 🚶M

URBAN TABLE   908/647-6007   136
▽▽ ▽▽ American. Casual Dining. $11-$23 **AAA Inspector Notes:** This casual eatery has a fun urban theme and an interesting menu that includes great burgers, large entrée salads, a little sushi and also some healthy entrées like pan roasted mahi mahi with toasted farro, kale and Mediterranean salsa verde. **Features:** full bar, Sunday brunch. **Reservations:** suggested. **Address:** 665 Martinsville Rd 07920 **Location:** I-78 exit 33, 0.3 mi n.
B   L   D   CALL 🚶M

BATSTO (F-3) elev. 13'

Established in 1766, Batsto became a prominent iron foundry and was of great military importance to the Patriots' cause during the Revolution. The village's prosperity grew after the war, a time when ironworks, glassworks, a brickyard, a gristmill and a sawmill provided livelihoods for nearly 1,000 people.

Fortunes dwindled when competition from cheap Pennsylvania coal forced the town's more expensive charcoal-fired furnaces to close in 1855. An 1874 fire burned half of Batsto to the ground, but 2 years later wealthy Philadelphia financier Joseph Wharton purchased the town site and the surrounding 100,000 acres.

INSIDER INFO:
The Pine Barrens

If most people don't know about New Jersey's Pine Barrens, it could be because the 450,000 year-round residents of this national reserve that overlies more than a million acres of the state's bottom half, prefer to keep a good thing to themselves.

Wedged between the roar of traffic along the New Jersey Turnpike and the Garden State Parkway, this quiet wilderness shows little evidence of the human settlement and enterprise that have occurred. Yet the Pines are far from barren.

The area's heart is a tapestry of impenetrable scrub and pitch pine, rivers, swamps and bogs where rebelling Colonials mined iron to make cannonballs. Villages, foundries and glassworks churned out the region's products until the late 1800s, after which the forest resumed full reign.

Local residents, affectionately called the "Pineys," learned to "work the woods" by selling its seasonal gifts and tending its cranberry and blueberry crops. Cranberries have been commercially raised in the Pine Barrens since about 1835, while the first commercial blueberry planting was made in 1916. The Pine Barrens account for approximately 25 percent of the state's agricultural income.

Many recreational opportunities exist in the Pine Barrens. Boating, canoeing, swimming, fishing and hunting are popular activities. Hikers can enjoy the Batona Trail, a marked wilderness trail that traverses the Pine Barrens, or explore old abandoned towns and the restored Batsto Village. More than 1,000 known sites in the vicinity show that man lived in this area as early as 10,000 B.C.

Left undisturbed are the woodland's wonders: a confusing tangle of sand roads cut during Colonial times, 12,000 acres of stunted pygmy pines in an area called the Plains, insectivorous plants, exotic orchids, ventriloquist tree frogs found almost nowhere else and a legendary winged creature known as the "Jersey Devil."

The muck soil in the Pine Barrens produces monobactum, a microorganism expected to revolutionize the antibiotics industry. An aquifer inside the Pine's deep sand beds holds 17 trillion gallons of water with the purity of glacial ice. The water in this shallow aquifer usually is at or near the surface, producing bogs, marshes and swamps. A maze of serpentine streams fed by the aquifer, stained the color of tea by cedar sap, rises within the low dome of land on which the Pines exist.

With development encroaching on all sides, the Pines' uniqueness becomes more apparent each year—except to local residents, who have always known it.

BATSTO HISTORIC VILLAGE is off CR 542 on Batsto Rd. This restored 19th-century village within Wharton State Forest (see Recreation Areas Chart) grew up around the Batsto Iron Works. Buildings include an iron master's mansion, a sawmill, a church, a gristmill, a general store, an icehouse, a post office and workers' houses. The visitor center houses a museum with permanent and changing historical exhibits. Visitors can take a cell phone audio tour.

Time: Allow 2 hours minimum. **Hours:** Grounds daily dawn-dusk. Visitor center open daily 9-4. Mansion tours are given when staff is available. Closed Jan. 1, Thanksgiving, Christmas and state holidays. Phone ahead to confirm schedule. **Cost:** Grounds and visitor center free. Mansion tour $3; $1 (ages 6-11). **Parking:** Sat.-Sun. and holidays $5, Memorial Day-Labor Day. **Phone:** (609) 561-3262 or (609) 561-0024. 🏕

BAY HEAD pop. 968

THE GRENVILLE HOTEL   732/892-3100
♛ ♛ **Historic Hotel.** Rates not provided. **Address:** 345 Main Ave (SR 35) 08742 **Location:** SR 35 S; at Bridge Ave. **Facility:** This 1890-era inn offers easy access to the beach. The rooms feature somewhat modest comfort and are accented with a few antiques. 29 units. 4 stories, interior corridors. **Parking:** street only. **Dining:** The Grenville, see separate listing. **Activities:** beach access.

⊞ ⊞ 🛰 ⊠ ☎ / SOME UNITS 🔊 🔒

WHERE TO EAT

THE GRENVILLE   732/892-3100
♛ ♛ ♛ Continental. Casual Dining. $8-$40 **AAA Inspector Notes:** *Historic.* A charming dining room incorporates hints of the restaurant's stately past, especially with its fireplace lit in the winter. In warmer months, outside porch seating is an option. Creative Continental dishes exhibit a French flair, and wine selections come from the owner's vineyards. **Features:** wine only, patio dining, Sunday brunch. **Reservations:** suggested. **Address:** 345 Main Ave (SR 35) 08742 **Location:** SR 35 S; at Bridge Ave; in The Grenville Hotel. **Parking:** street only.   L   D

BAYONNE (H-6) pop. 63,024, elev. 39'

TEAR OF GRIEF MEMORIAL is off New Jersey Tpke. exit 14A, 1 mi. s. on SR 440S, then e. on Port Terminal Blvd. to Harbor View Park at Bayonne Harbor. Also known as "To the Struggle Against World Terrorism" and locally as The Teardrop, the monument pays homage to those who died in the Sept. 11, 2001, terrorist attacks in New York, Pennsylvania and Washington, D.C., as well as to the victims of the 1993 World Trade Center bombing.

The 100-foot-tall rectangular bronze monument, a gift from Russia designed by artist Zurab Tsereteli, has a fissure in its center in which a teardrop is suspended. The names of those who perished in the attacks are engraved on the memorial's base.

Note: The monument is in an isolated waterfront warehouse area. **Time:** Allow 15 minutes minimum. **Hours:** Harbor View Park open daily dawn-dusk. **Cost:** Free. **Phone:** (201) 858-6127 for the Bayonne Parks & Recreation Department, or (800) 542-7894 for Hudson County Tourism.

BEACH HAVEN (F-4) pop. 1,170, elev. 10'
• **Restaurants p. 90**

The Surflight Theatre, at the corner of Engleside and Beach avenues, presents a year-round schedule of plays, musicals, children's shows, ballet and concerts; for information and tickets phone (609) 492-9477.

FANTASY ISLAND AMUSEMENT PARK is 6.4 mi. s. of jct. SR 72 and Long Beach Blvd. at 320 W. 7th St. This Victorian-style amusement park includes a Ferris wheel, carousel, mini-coaster, virtual roller coaster, children's rides, a boardwalk arcade and evening entertainment.

Time: Allow 2 hours minimum. **Hours:** Rides operate daily 6-11 p.m., mid-June through Labor Day weekend; Sat.-Sun. 2-11:30 p.m., mid-May to mid-June. Arcade opens Sun.-Fri. at noon, Sat. at 10 a.m., July 4-Labor Day; daily at noon, early May-July 3 and day after Labor Day-Sept. 30; Sat.-Sun. at noon, rest of year. Closing times vary; phone ahead. **Cost:** Park and entertainment free. Ride tokens 95c; $38 (40 tokens); $19 (20 tokens). Individual rides require three to seven tokens. **Phone:** (609) 492-4000. ⊞

LONG BEACH ISLAND HISTORICAL MUSEUM is at Beach and Engleside aves. Focusing primarily on the area's tie to the water, displays include swimsuits, early fishing equipment, boats, Victorian clothing, marine life and storm photographs. An 1880 fisherman's cottage on the grounds is undergoing restoration. **Hours:** Daily 10-4 (also Wed. 7-9 p.m.), late June-Labor Day; Sat.-Sun. noon-4, Memorial Day-late June and day after Labor Day-early Oct. **Cost:** $3; free (ages 0-12). **Phone:** (609) 492-0700.

THUNDERING SURF WATER PARK is at 806 N. Bay Ave. Features include the Flowhouse, where visitors can indulge in simulated boogie boarding and flow boarding; eight waterslides; the Cowabunga Beach interactive water play area for younger children; the Lazy Crazy River, which has interactive play elements both in and out of the water; a toddler area with dancing and bubbling fountains and four kiddie slides; two observation decks; and a sun deck. Also on the grounds are two 18-hole "adventure" golf courses.

Time: Allow 2 hours minimum. **Hours:** Water park open daily 9:30-6, mid-June through Labor Day; daily 10-5, week after Labor Day; Sat.-Sun. 10-6, Memorial Day to mid-June (weather permitting). Adventure golf open daily 9 a.m.-11 p.m., mid-May through Labor Day; daily 11-8, week after Labor Day; Sat.-Sun. 11-9, Apr. 1-May 15 (weather permitting). Phone ahead to confirm schedule.

Cost: Two-hour park ticket $27.99; $23.99 (under 42 inches tall); $13.99 (ages 0-2 and 65+, expectant mothers and nonparticipants). Three-hour park ticket $32.99; $28.99 (under 42 inches tall); $18.99 (ages 0-2 and 65+, expectant mothers and nonparticipants). Discount offered to military with ID. Flowhouse $40 (1 hour); $25 (half-hour) Golf (18 holes) $10; $7.50 (ages 0-11). Golf (36 holes) $13; $10 (ages 0-11). **Phone:** (609) 492-0869.

RECREATIONAL ACTIVITIES
Parasailing
• **Beach Haven Parasail** departs from 2702 Long Beach Blvd. at Bay Haven Marina, next to the Buccaneer Motel. **Hours:** Daily 9 a.m.-dusk, mid-May through Labor Day. **Phone:** (609) 492-0375.

JOLLY ROGER MOTEL   609/492-6931
♛ **Motel.** Rates not provided. **Address:** 5416 S Bay Ave 08008 **Location:** SR 72 Cswy, 9 mi s on Long Beach Blvd (which becomes Bay Ave). **Facility:** 12 units. 3 stories (no elevator), interior/exterior corridors. **Bath:** shower only.

⊞ 🛰 ⊠ ☎ 🔒 ▭

SEA SPRAY MOTEL   609/492-4944

Motel
Rates not provided

Address: 2600 S Bay Ave 08008 **Location:** Jct SR 72 Cswy and Long Beach Blvd (which becomes Bay Ave), 8 mi s. **Facility:** 52 units, some two bedrooms, three bedrooms and kitchens. 2 stories (no elevator), exterior corridors. **Pool(s):** heated outdoor. **Activities:** game room.

SAVE 🈂 📶 ✕ 🛆 🖥 📺 📟

WHERE TO EAT

TUCKERS   609/492-2300

▼▼▼ American. Family Dining. $7-$30 **AAA Inspector Notes:** It is a good thing this place can accommodate large crowds. Hearty dishes range from burgers, pasta and sandwiches to steak, chops and fresh fish and seafood. A huge bar between the two dining areas is a favorite watering hole for islanders and vacationers. Servers are friendly though a bit hurried in executing their duties. **Features:** full bar, patio dining, Sunday brunch, happy hour. **Address:** 101 S West Ave 08008 **Location:** 6.9 mi s of SR 72 Cswy to Engleside Ave, just w. L D

BEDMINSTER
• Hotels & Restaurants map & index p. 152

PLUCKEMIN INN   908/658-9292 (147)

New
American
Fine Dining
$14-$38

AAA Inspector Notes: In the rolling Jersey hills of horse country, this amazing little treasure is among the Garden State's most attractive restaurants. Its reconstructed, Federal-style décor brings a touch of country charm to the table, and the 15-story, 15,000-bottle wine tower is bound to impress even the most jaded oenophile. Sophisticated and innovative fare, such as Wester Ross Scottish salmon paired with butter beans, Manila clams, calamari and crushed fennel is skillfully executed with style and finesse. **Features:** full bar, patio dining. **Reservations:** suggested. **Address:** 359 US 206 S & Pluckemin Way 07921 **Location:** I-287 exit 22A, 0.3 mi n to US 202/206, then just s. L D CALL 🖪M

BEESLEYS POINT

TUCKAHOE INN RESTAURANT & TAVERN   609/390-3322

▼▼ American. Family Dining. $7-$34 **AAA Inspector Notes:** Overlooking scenic Great Egg Harbor, this laid-back restaurant takes advantage of its location with a nice glass-enclosed porch and an outside deck along with an amazing view through the large picture window. The menu centers on the familiar with steak, burgers, sandwiches, and of course, fresh seafood dishes. **Features:** full bar. **Reservations:** suggested. **Address:** 1 Harbor Rd & US 9 08223 **Location:** On US 9; at southern terminus of Great Egg Harbor Beesleys Point Bridge. L D

BELLMAWR pop. 11,583

CLUB DINER   856/931-2880 (154)

▼▼ American. Family Dining. $6-$13 **AAA Inspector Notes:** This eatery offers patrons simple home-style cooking in a casual, friendly atmosphere. Breakfast provides all the traditional favorites from omelets to French toast, while dinner provides a variety of pasta, hot sandwiches, seafood specialties and large steak entrées. **Address:** 20 N Black Horse Pike 08031 **Location:** I-295 exit 28, 0.8 mi s; New Jersey Tpke exit 3, just n. B L D (24)

BELMAR pop. 5,794

THE INN AT THE SHORE BED & BREAKFAST   (732)681-3762

▼▼ **Historic Bed & Breakfast** $170-$305 **Address:** 301 4th Ave 07719 **Location:** Jct Ocean Ave, just w. **Facility:** This inn, which has a wraparound porch and a brick patio, features a fireplace in the common area as well as in some rooms. The décor is relaxed and homey. 11 units. 2 stories (no elevator), interior corridors. *Bath:* some shared. **Parking:** street only. **Terms:** 14 day cancellation notice. **Activities:** bicycles. HS 📶 ✕ / SOME UNITS 📺

BELVIDERE (B-2) pop. 2,681, elev. 259'

WINERIES
• **Four Sisters Winery at Matarazzo Farms** is at 783 CR 519. **Hours:** Thurs.-Tues. 10-6, May-Dec.; Thurs.-Mon. 10-5, rest of year. Closed Jan. 1, Easter, Thanksgiving and Christmas. **Phone:** (908) 475-3671. GT 🍴

HOTEL BELVIDERE   908/475-2006

▼▼▼ **Historic Hotel.** Rates not provided. **Address:** 430 Front St 07823 **Location:** Jct New and Morris sts; center. **Facility:** This hotel offers modern conveniences but is furnished with an eye to the past. 21 units. 3 stories (no elevator), interior corridors. *Bath:* shower only. HS 📶 ✕ 🛆 / SOME UNITS 🖥

BERKELEY HEIGHTS pop. 13,183
• Hotels & Restaurants map & index p. 152

TRAP ROCK RESTAURANT & BREWERY   908/665-1755 (123)

▼▼▼ American. Casual Dining. $12-$34 **AAA Inspector Notes:** This restaurant and brewery presents a menu of creative entrées and sandwiches made from fresh local ingredients. The attractive décor and comfortable ambience is the strong point here; a blend of Old World tavern and alpine lodge. The best bet is to visit for lunch or for drinks and appetizers. There is a good selection of house-brewed beers and wines by the glass. **Features:** full bar, patio dining. **Reservations:** suggested. **Address:** 279 Springfield Ave 07922 **Location:** Center. L D CALL 🖪M

BERLIN pop. 7,588

DAYS INN   (856)767-7711

▼▼ Hotel $70-$135 **Address:** 311 S Rt 73 08009 **Location:** Just e of US 73. **Facility:** 39 units. 2 stories (no elevator), interior corridors. 📶➕ CALL 🖪M BIZ 📶 🛆 🖥 📟

BERNARDSVILLE pop. 7,707
• Hotels & Restaurants map & index p. 152

THE BERNARDS INN   (908)766-0002 (81)

Historic
Country Inn
$167-$356

Address: 27 Mine Brook Rd 07924 **Location:** Jct US 202 and CR 525 (Mt Airy Rd), just s; downtown. **Facility:** Located in a charming town in the rolling hills of horse country, this beautiful inn displays a handsome Town and Country-style décor that is comfortably elegant. 20 units. 3 stories (no elevator), interior corridors. **Terms:** check-in 4 pm, cancellation fee imposed. **Dining:** restaurant, see separate listing. **Guest Services:** valet laundry.

SAVE 🍴 🛄 Y BIZ 📶 ✕ / SOME UNITS 🛆

(See map & index p. 152.)

WHERE TO EAT

THE BERNARDS INN
908/766-0002 (117)

American
Fine Dining
$14-$48

AAA Inspector Notes: *Historic.* A fine meal awaits in this elegant dining room, intimately lit by brass chandeliers and furnished with stately oil paintings hanging above a stone fireplace. The progressive menu includes items like dry-aged beef, lamb loin, locally farmed chicken, local seafood and produce from area farms. **Features:** full bar. **Reservations:** suggested. **Address:** 27 Mine Brook Rd 07924 **Location:** Jct US 202 and CR 525 (Mt Airy Rd), just s; downtown. *Menu on AAA.com* [B] [L] [D]

OSTERIA MORINI
908/221-0040 (115)

Regional Italian. Casual Dining. $15-$32 **AAA Inspector Notes:** Renowned chef Michael White brings this casual Italian restaurant from Manhattan to a cozy and inviting spot tucked away next to shops and car dealerships. The menu focuses on the Emilia Romagna region and offers items like garganelli pasta with truffle butter, prosciutto and roasted mushrooms, margherita pizza and oven roasted Branzino with arugula and salsa verde. **Features:** full bar, Sunday brunch. **Reservations:** suggested. **Address:** 107 Morristown Rd (US 202) 07924 **Location:** 0.5 mi e of jct US 202 and CR 525 (Mt Airy Rd). [L] [D] CALL [&M]

SETTE CUCINA ITALIANA
908/502-5054 (116)

Italian. Fine Dining. $12-$30 **AAA Inspector Notes:** You may feel like you have found a hidden gem at this tiny but very charming dining room right on the main street. The chef-owner prepares excellent dishes including a welcoming bruschetta, fresh antipasto and mozzarella and pastas like the fettuccine with shrimp, petit peas and truffle cream or the pillowy ricotta gnocchi with speck. Other entrées may include pork scaloppine with pancetta, sage and marsala jus or grey snapper with tomato ratatouille. A tasting menu is also available. **Reservations:** suggested. **Address:** 7 Mine Brook Rd 07924 **Location:** Jct US 202 and CR 525 (Mt Airy Rd), just s; downtown. **Parking:** street only. [L] [D] CALL [&M]

BLACKWOOD pop. 4,545

HAMPTON INN-TURNERSVILLE
(856)228-4200

Hotel $109-$182 **Address:** 5800 Black Horse Pike 08012 **Location:** Just w of SR 42. **Facility:** 76 units. 5 stories, interior corridors. **Terms:** 1-7 night minimum stay, cancellation fee imposed.

AAA Benefit:
Members save 5% or more!

Pool(s): heated indoor. **Activities:** exercise room. **Guest Services:** valet and coin laundry.
[T+] CALL [&M] [≥] [BIZ] [HS] [🛜] [✕] [🖥] [🖥] [🖥]

BLOOMFIELD pop. 47,315
• Hotels & Restaurants map & index p. 162

THE ORANGE SQUIRREL
973/337-6421 (98)

New American. Casual Dining. $19-$46 **AAA Inspector Notes:** This is a popular little chef-owned place with a casual, relaxed atmosphere and great food that ranges from delicate salmon tartare to rustic bone in rib-eye with chipotle butter and garlic confit served in a cast iron dish. A well-chosen wine list, engaged servers and creative cocktails add to an air of metropolitan sophistication. **Features:** full bar. **Address:** 412 Bloomfield Ave 07003 **Location:** Garden State Parkway exit 148, just s. **Parking:** street only.
[L] [D] CALL [&M]

BOONTON (G-5) pop. 8,347, elev. 407'

NEW JERSEY FIREMEN'S HOME MUSEUM is n. on Washington St., then .7 mi. e. to 565 Lathrop Ave. The two-story museum, housed in a brick building dating from 1878, stands on an 88-acre site. It features artifacts and memorabilia from fire companies throughout the state, including antique fire trucks, hose carts, tools and uniforms as well as awards and medals.

The Firemen's Home was established in the early 1900s and serves as a residence for the state's aged and disabled firefighters. **Time:** Allow 1 hour minimum. **Hours:** Daily 8-4. Closed major holidays. **Cost:** Donations. **Phone:** (973) 334-0024.

BORDENTOWN pop. 3,924
• Restaurants p. 92

BEST WESTERN BORDENTOWN INN
(609)298-8000

Motel
$80-$120

Best Western

AAA Benefit:
Members save up to 20%!

Address: 1068 US Hwy 206 S 08505 **Location:** New Jersey Tpke exit 7, 0.8 mi n. Next to a park. **Facility:** 100 units. 2 stories (no elevator), exterior corridors. **Pool(s):** heated indoor. **Activities:** sauna, hot tub, exercise room. **Guest Services:** valet and coin laundry.

DAYS INN-BORDENTOWN
(609)298-6100

Motel
$70-$99

Address: 1073 US Hwy 206 N 08505 **Location:** New Jersey Tpke exit 7, 0.8 mi n. **Facility:** 129 units. 2 stories (no elevator), exterior corridors. **Amenities:** safes. **Pool(s):** outdoor. **Activities:** exercise room. **Guest Services:** coin laundry.

HAMPTON INN BORDENTOWN
(609)298-4000

Hotel $99-$199 **Address:** 2004 US Hwy 206 S 08505 **Location:** New Jersey Tpke exit 7, just s. **Facility:** 72 units. 4 stories, interior corridors. **Terms:** 1-7 night minimum stay, cancellation fee imposed. **Pool(s):** heated indoor. **Activities:** exercise room. **Guest Services:** valet and coin laundry.

AAA Benefit:
Members save 5% or more!

[T+] CALL [&M] [≥] [BIZ] [HS] [🛜] [🖥] [🖥] [🖥]

WHERE TO EAT

THE FARNSWORTH HOUSE RESTAURANT 609/291-9232

▼▼ ▼▼ Italian. Casual Dining. $11-$43 **AAA Inspector Notes:** Outside, a large likeness of an Early American fellow in a powdered wig—presumably Thomas Farnsworth, who settled the area in 1682—welcomes diners. However, the menu is all Italian. Try the chicken prepared several different ways, including chicken Francaise and chicken Marsala. The tortellini and linguine are a hit, as well as various versions of seafood, veal and steak. **Features:** full bar. **Reservations:** suggested. **Address:** 135 Farnsworth Ave 08505 **Location:** Center. ⓛ ⓓ CALL ⓔM

MASTORIS DINER RESTAURANT 609/298-4650

▼▼ ▼▼ American. Casual Dining. $6-$49 **AAA Inspector Notes:** This casual family eatery with faux windows draped with curtains offers a simple dining room featuring meals with exceptional value. In addition to Italian and Greek fare, the menu includes heaping servings of wholesome food such as burgers, wraps, seafood, steak and sandwiches. The on-site bakery displays attractive desserts and breads. The servers are fast and efficient. **Features:** full bar. **Address:** 144 Rt 130 08505 **Location:** N of jct US 206 and 130; I-295 exit 56 (US 130); New Jersey Tpke exit 7, 3 mi n.

ⓑ ⓛ ⓓ LATE CALL ⓔM

BRANCHBURG

HOLIDAY INN EXPRESS HOTEL & SUITES BRANCHBURG 908/252-1000

▼▼ ▼▼
Hotel
Rates not provided

Address: 947 US 202 N 08876 **Location:** Just s of jct Milltown Rd. **Facility:** 79 units. 4 stories, interior corridors. **Activities:** exercise room. **Guest Services:** valet laundry, area transportation. **Featured Amenity:** continental breakfast.

SAVE CALL ⓔM BIZ HS 📶 ✕
🖨 📠 💻

HYATT HOUSE BRANCHBURG (908)704-2191

▼▼ ▼▼
Hotel
$89-$329

  H HYATT house™

AAA Benefit: Members save 10%!

Address: 3141 Rt 22 E 08876 **Location:** I-287 exit 14B northbound, 6.7 mi w; exit 17 southbound, 3.7 mi w. **Facility:** 139 efficiencies. 3 stories, interior corridors. **Terms:** check-in 4 pm, cancellation fee imposed. **Pool(s):** heated outdoor. **Activities:** hot tub, exercise room. **Guest Services:** valet and coin laundry, area transportation. **Featured Amenity:** breakfast buffet. *(See ad this page.)*

SAVE ➥ BIZ HS 📶 ✕ 🖨 📠 💻
/ SOME UNITS S⃠ 🐾

▼ See AAA listing this page ▼

BRANT BEACH

DADDY O BOUTIQUE HOTEL, BAR & RESTAURANT
(609)494-1300

 Boutique Contemporary Hotel $152-$467 **Address:** 4401 Long Beach Blvd 08008 **Location:** Garden State Pkwy exit 63 to SR 72, e to causeway, then 4 mi s. **Facility:** More swanky than the seashore, this stylish hotel is the traveler's alternative to the roadside motel or beach bungalow. Rooms include all-white bedding, flat-screen TVs and glass-enclosed rainfall showers. 22 units. 3 stories, interior corridors. **Bath:** shower only. **Terms:** closed 11/15-4/17, age restrictions may apply, 30 day cancellation notice-fee imposed. **Amenities:** safes. **Dining:** restaurant, see separate listing, entertainment. ⎕ ⎕ CALL ⎕ ⎕ ⎕ ⎕

WHERE TO EAT

DADDY O BOUTIQUE HOTEL, BAR & RESTAURANT
609/494-1300

American Casual Dining $12-$37

AAA Inspector Notes: A more sophisticated and trendy version of the beach restaurant, this place has modern decor with red accent walls and stylish seating. The menu offers a good mix of seafood, sandwiches and salads with a few creative twists. There is also a large and lively bar area. **Features:** full bar, patio dining, happy hour. **Reservations:** suggested. **Address:** 4401 Long Beach Blvd 08008 **Location:** Garden State Pkwy exit 63 to SR 72, e to causeway, then 4 mi s. ⎕ L ⎕ D ⎕

BRICK

WINDMILL RESTAURANTS
732/458-7774

⎕ Hot Dogs Burgers. Quick Serve. $3-$8 **AAA Inspector Notes:** This is a local favorite haunt for their top hot dogs, charbroiled burgers, and gooey but oh so good cheese fries. There is a fixin's bar to dress that dog up however you desire such as a little relish and onion. Seating is limited and sometimes cramped, but the service is fast and should have you in and out in no time. **Address:** 856 Rt 70 08724 **Location:** Garden State Pkwy exit 90, 1.3 mi s on Chambers Bridge Rd, 0.7 mi e, then just w. ⎕ L ⎕ D ⎕ CALL ⎕

BRIDGEPORT

HAMPTON INN-BRIDGEPORT
(856)467-6200

⎕ **Hotel** $139-$159 **Address:** 2 Pureland Dr 08085 **Location:** I-295 exit 10, just se. **Facility:** 95 units. 4 stories, interior corridors. **Terms:** 1-7 night minimum stay, cancellation fee imposed.

AAA Benefit:
Members save 5% or more!

Pool(s): heated outdoor. **Activities:** exercise room. **Guest Services:** coin laundry.

⎕ CALL ⎕ ⎕ ⎕ ⎕ ⎕ ⎕ ⎕ ⎕ ⎕ / SOME UNITS ⎕

BRIDGETON (G-2) pop. 25,349, elev. 40'

Quakers settled the area around present-day Bridgeton in the late 1600s, and within 50 years constructed the bridge across Cohansey Creek that would give the town its name. By the 19th century Bridgeton was the seat of Cumberland County and boasted a woolen mill, a nail factory and an ironworks. Prosperous residents constructed still-standing Colonial, Federal and Victorian edifices; today more than 2,200 period houses and commercial buildings crowd the town's historic district.

Bridgeton Area Chamber of Commerce: 76 Magnolia Ave., P.O. Box 1063, Bridgeton, NJ 08302. **Phone:** (856) 455-1312.

Self-guiding tours: Brochures outlining self-guiding tours past period houses on Bridgeton's historic east and west sides are available at the chamber of commerce.

Shopping areas: On W. Commerce Street, a row of restored Victorian buildings contains a variety of shops.

BRIDGETON CITY PARK is at jct. W. Commerce St. and Mayor Aitken Dr. The 1,100-acre park offers summer recreational facilities. Also on the grounds is Nail Mill Museum, which houses a diverse collection of memorabilia and items related to local history. **Note:** The museum is currently closed for renovations; phone ahead for information. **Hours:** Park open daily dawn-dusk. **Cost:** Free. **Phone:** (856) 455-3230, ext. 280.

Cohanzick Zoo is in Bridgeton City Park on Mayor Aitken Dr. The zoo focuses on wildlife native to New Jersey but also exhibits primates and felines, including a white-headed gibbon, a white Siberian tiger and Asiatic bears. Large special events take place in May, October and December. **Hours:** Daily 9-5, during daylight savings time; 8-4, rest of year. Closed Thanksgiving and Christmas. **Cost:** Donations. **Phone:** (856) 453-1658.

WOODRUFF MUSEUM OF INDIAN ARTIFACTS is in the Bridgeton Public Library at 150 E. Commerce St. Some 20,000 Native American artifacts, all collected within a 30-mile radius of Bridgeton, comprise the museum's collection. Although found locally, many of the implements were transported to the region during tribal meetings, migrations and conflicts.

Some Folsom Point arrowheads date back 10,000 years; more recent artifacts include Lenni Lenape Indian ceramic pipes, cooking utensils, fishing bobs, axes and gorgets, the latter a collar worn to protect the throat during warfare. Guides are on hand to explain the exhibits on Wednesdays. **Hours:** Mon.-Fri. 1-4, Sat. 11-2. Closed major holidays. Phone ahead to confirm schedule. **Cost:** Donations. **Phone:** (856) 451-2620.

BRIDGEWATER
- **Restaurants p. 94**
- **Hotels & Restaurants map & index p. 152**

BRIDGEWATER MARRIOTT
(908)927-9300

Hotel $119-$401

AAA Benefit: Members save 5% or more!

Address: 700 Commons Way 08807 **Location:** I-287 exit 17 to US 202/206 S, 0.5 mi to Commons Way, then 0.4 mi e. **Facility:** 347 units. 8 stories, interior corridors. **Pool(s):** heated indoor. **Activities:** exercise room. **Guest Services:** valet and coin laundry, boarding pass kiosk, area transportation.

⎕ ⎕ ⎕ ⎕ ⎕ CALL ⎕

/ SOME UNITS ⎕ ⎕

(See map & index p. 152.)

DAYS INN CONFERENCE CENTER

(908)526-9500

Hotel
S66-S73

Address: 1260 US 22 E 08807 **Location:** I-287 exit 17 to US 202/206 S, just s, exit US 22, then 2 mi e; exit 14B northbound, 1 mi w on US 22, U-turn at Adamsville Rd, then 1 mi e. **Facility:** 164 units. 2-3 stories, interior corridors. **Terms:** cancellation fee imposed. **Pool(s):** heated outdoor. **Activities:** exercise room. **Guest Services:** valet and coin laundry. **Featured Amenity:** continental breakfast.

HILTON GARDEN INN-BRIDGEWATER

(732)271-9030

 Hotel $99-$279 **Address:** 500 Promenade Blvd 08807 **Location:** I-287 exit 13B northbound, just w; exit 13 southbound. **Facility:** 129 units. 4 stories, interior corridors. **Terms:** 1-7 night minimum stay, cancellation fee imposed. **Pool(s):** heated indoor. **Activities:** hot tub, exercise room. **Guest Services:** valet and coin laundry.

AAA Benefit: Members save 5% or more!

HYATT HOUSE BRIDGEWATER

(908)725-0800

Extended Stay Hotel
S89-$299

H HYATT house

AAA Benefit: Members save 10%!

Address: 530 US 22 E 08807 **Location:** I-287 exit 14B northbound, 4.7 mi w; exit 17 southbound, 1.8 mi w. **Facility:** 128 kitchen units, some two bedrooms. 3 stories (no elevator), exterior corridors. **Terms:** cancellation fee imposed. **Pool(s):** heated outdoor. **Activities:** hot tub, exercise room. **Guest Services:** valet and coin laundry, area transportation. **Featured Amenity:** breakfast buffet.

    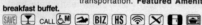

WHERE TO EAT

MCCORMICK & SCHMICK'S

908/707-9996 (160)

Seafood. Fine Dining. $11-$46 **AAA Inspector Notes:** This place is all about seafood, which is imported from all over the world. Among good choices are Washington state oysters, Maine clams, delicate Hawaiian escolar and tuna from Ecuador. The clublike decor is cozy and the staff are attentive. **Features:** full bar, happy hour. **Address:** 400 Commons Way 08807 **Location:** In Bridgewater Commons Mall. (L) (D) CALL

BRIGANTINE (G-4) pop. 9,450, elev. 6'
• Part of Atlantic City area — see map p. 73

"It is a very good land to fall in with, and a pleasant land to see," first mate Robert Juet penned in his journal aboard English explorer Henry Hudson's *Half Moon* in 1608. The excerpt is thought to be a very early appreciation of Brigantine, a scenic rendezvous on Brigantine Beach Island, about 6 miles north of Atlantic City.

The town is a hot spot for water sports, biking, hiking and just plain relaxing. (Little did the Lenape Indians of the 1500s know that their so-called *Watamoonica*, or "summer playground," would fulfill the same purpose 5 centuries later.) To get a real feel for the area's natural beauty, grab a camera and head to the sea wall at the north end of Brigantine Avenue, where you can behold rollicking dolphins and sensational sunrises. Situated 3 miles northwest, the 20,000-acre Brigantine Unit of the Edwin B. Forsythe National Wildlife Refuge *(see attraction listing p. 175)* also boasts some outstanding views.

The three-story concrete-and-stucco lighthouse at the center of a downtown traffic circle was built not to warn ships away but to attract customers; a real estate company erected it as a sales office in 1926. It served as Brigantine Police Department headquarters during the Great Depression and a museum and gift shop in the 1940s. Although closed to the public since its increasingly busy location became a safety issue, the historic landmark is still illuminated nightly.

The Marine Mammal Stranding Center, just south of the lighthouse at 3625 Brigantine Blvd., is devoted to the rescue and rehabilitation of stranded or distressed marine mammals such as whales, dolphins, seals and sea turtles that come ashore along the New Jersey coast; phone (609) 266-0538.

Catch another glimpse of local history at Brigantine Beach Historical Museum, 3607 Brigantine Blvd.; phone (609) 266-9339. Among the collection of artifacts and photos is an exhibit about Brigantine Castle, a beachside bar turned haunted mansion that spooked millions of visitors in the 1970s and '80s. The attraction, at 14th Street N. and Brigantine Avenue, burned down in 1987, 3 years after shutting its doors.

Along with ghouls and goblins, ferocious storms and seafaring scoundrels are woven into Brigantine's story. The town was named after a type of 1600s ship—quite possibly one of the first of hundreds of vessels destroyed along the shoreline's treacherous shallows. A particularly interesting wreck was the *Florida*, which had been toting 15 hefty bundles of ostrich feathers when it was victimized by an 1847 tempest. Practical islanders retrieved the dispersed plumes and used them as wall insulation.

The Brigantine area was once a hangout of Edward Teach, alias Blackbeard; the notorious pirate evaded British capturers by submerging himself in nearby meadow waters, relying solely on a hollow reed for oxygen. In 1698 Scottish buccaneer Captain Kidd and his crew allegedly hid a massive treasure chest under some dunes near Brigantine Inlet; shortly thereafter Kidd and his first mate, Timothy Jones, secretly reburied the loot elsewhere. Legend holds that Kidd killed Jones during a subsequent altercation and interred him next to the trunk. Both booty and body have yet to be found.

BUDD LAKE pop. 8,968

DAYS INN BUDD LAKE   (973)426-0800
▼▼ **Hotel** $80-$130 **Address:** 138 US 46 W 07828 **Location:** I-80 exit 26 (Budd Lake/US 46 W) westbound, 1 mi w; exit 27 eastbound, U-turn to I-80 westbound exit 26. **Facility:** 44 units. 3 stories, interior corridors. **Amenities:** safes. **Activities:** exercise room.

⊞ 🛜 🖥 🖳 🖵 / SOME UNITS HS

WHERE TO EAT

BUDD LAKE DINER-RESTAURANT   973/691-9100
▼▼ Comfort Food. Family Dining. $7-$27 **AAA Inspector Notes:** Drive past the usual fast food places and check out this friendly little town diner that is just a short way from I-80. The large menu offers an array of fresh salads, any kind of sandwich imaginable and many home-style entrées all served in ample portions. The enticing dessert case alone is reason for a pit stop. **Address:** 120 US 46 W 07828 **Location:** I-80 exit 26 westbound (Budd Lake/US 46 W), 0.5 mi w; exit 27 eastbound, U-turn, then just w.

B   L   D   24 CALL ▧M

BURLINGTON (E-3) pop. 9,920, elev. 13'

One of the first permanent settlements in the western part of the colony, Burlington was established by members of the Society of Friends in 1677. It became the capital of West Jersey and shared that status with Perth Amboy after East and West Jersey united. A strategic location on the Delaware River between Trenton and Camden made the flourishing port so prosperous that its citizens—primarily Quaker settlers and pacifists—were relatively uninvolved in the Revolution.

Venerable buildings that are open to the public by appointment include the 1703 Old St. Mary's Church, at Broad and Wood streets; the 1685 Revell House, in the 200 block of Wood Street; the 1785 Friends Meeting House, on High Street near Broad Street; the John Hoskins House, 202 High St.; the 1792 Friend's School, at York and Penn streets; and the restored carriage house on Smith's Alley between High and Wood streets.

Burlington County Chamber of Commerce: 100 Technology Way, Suite 110, Mount Laurel, NJ 08054. **Phone:** (856) 439-2520.

BURLINGTON COUNTY HISTORICAL SOCIETY COMPLEX is 2 blks. n. of US 130 at 451-459 High St. The Corson Poley Center contains a library, museum, Children's History Center and three historic houses: the Bard-How House, the Capt. James Lawrence House and the James Fenimore Cooper House. The museum displays a locally made jinrikisha—an Asian hand-pulled carriage—as well as a collection of tall case clocks and quilts. Another exhibit, The American Revolution: A Global Conflict, explores early American history. The Children's History Center offers interactive experiences for children ages 2 and up.

The library's genealogical records are available for research. **Hours:** Guided museum and 40-minute house tours are offered Tues.-Sat. 10-5. Children's History Center open Tues.-Sat. 10-5. Library open Wed.-Thurs. 1-5. Closed major holidays. **Cost:** Fee for house tour, Children's History Center

or library and gallery $5. House tour, library and gallery $5. **Phone:** (609) 386-4773.

Bard-How House, 453 High St. in the Burlington County Historical Society Complex, was built around 1743 for merchant Bennett Bard and his wife, Sarah Pattison Bard. It was purchased in 1756 by butcher and tavern owner Samuel How. Period furnishings and other accessories decorate the restored house, including a tall case clock that dates from 1740.

Hours: Guided house tours are offered Tues.-Sat. 10-5. Closed major holidays. **Cost:** (includes Capt. James Lawrence House, James Fenimore Cooper House, and Burlington County Historical Society Complex library and gallery) $5. Tour only (includes Capt. James Lawrence House and James Fenimore Cooper House) $5. **Phone:** (609) 386-4773.

Capt. James Lawrence House, 459 High St. in the Burlington County Historical Society Complex, is the birthplace of the American naval hero of the War of 1812. The commander of the USS *Chesapeake* engaged in battle against the HMS *Shannon,* and the mortally wounded Lawrence issued his famous last command, remembered as "Don't give up the ship." The house is furnished in period and also contains a toy collection.

Hours: Guided house tours are offered Tues.-Sat. 10-5. Closed major holidays. **Cost:** (includes Bard-How House, James Fenimore Cooper House, and Burlington County Historical Society Complex library and gallery) $5. Tour only (includes Bard-How House and James Fenimore Cooper House) $5. **Phone:** (609) 386-4773.

James Fenimore Cooper House, 457 High St. in the Burlington County Historical Society Complex, is the birthplace of the author of the "Leatherstocking Tales," novels depicting the era of American frontiersmen and Native Americans. "The Last of the Mohicans" and "The Deerslayer" are among the best known titles in the series, written 1826-41. The 1780 Cooper House has five museum rooms.

Hours: Guided house tours are offered Tues.-Sat. 10-5. Closed major holidays. **Cost:** (includes Bard-How House, Capt. James Lawrence House, and Burlington County Historical Society Complex library and gallery) $5. Tour only (includes Bard-How House and Capt. James Lawrence House) $5. **Phone:** (609) 386-4773.

CALDWELL (G-5) pop. 7,822, elev. 411'
• Restaurants p. 96
• Hotels & Restaurants map & index p. 152

GROVER CLEVELAND BIRTHPLACE STATE HISTORIC SITE is at 207 Bloomfield Ave. The 22nd and 24th president of the United States was born here in 1837 and lived in the house until 1841. The restored house contains many of his possessions. **Time:** Allow 45 minutes minimum. **Hours:** Wed.-Sat. 10-noon and 1-4, Sun. 1-4. Closed state holidays and

(See map & index p. 152.)

also periodically without advance notice; phone ahead to confirm schedule. **Cost:** Donations. Reservations are recommended. **Phone:** (973) 226-0001. GT

LUCÉ ECLECTIC-ITALIAN   973/403-8500 6
▼▼▼ Italian. Casual Dining. $7-$29 **AAA Inspector Notes:** Chic decor accentuates the upscale dining room, which has an open kitchen as its centerpiece. The menu centers on contemporary Italian preparations of fish, veal, pork and pasta. Chicken Mezzanotte is the signature dish. In-house desserts are divine. **Reservations:** suggested. **Address:** 115 Bloomfield Ave 07006 **Location:** I-280 exit 7, 1.5 mi n to Bloomfield Ave, then 1.5 mi w. **Parking:** valet only.

L   D   CALL ⚑M

CAMDEN (E-2) pop. 77,344, elev. 25'

The site of William Cooper's ferryboat operation on the Delaware River in the 1680s grew into a city well-established in industry and transportation, especially after becoming the terminus for the Camden & Amboy Railroad in 1834. Yet echoes of the city's shipbuilding past remain ever-present.

The arrival of the **Tall Ships Philadelphia Camden 2015** offers those in the Delaware River region a glimpse into history—12 massive vessels, to be exact—at Penn's Landing and the Camden Waterfront from June 24-28.

Port facilities along the deep, broad Delaware River led to a boom in shipbuilding during World Wars I and II. The first nuclear-powered merchant ship, the *Savannah,* was built in Camden. On the cultural side, poet Walt Whitman—whose unfettered, subjective style revolutionized poetic expression in the mid-19th century—lived his last years in Camden. The tomb of the good gray poet is in Harleigh Cemetery on Haddon Avenue.

The Camden Riversharks play minor league baseball at Campbell's Field, 401 N. Delaware Ave., from late April through late September; for ticket and schedule information phone the box office at (866) 742-7579.

ADVENTURE AQUARIUM is on the banks of the Delaware River at 1 Riverside Dr. Sea life and wildlife can be seen and touched in a variety of exhibits, including the new KidZone, an interactive exhibit designed specifically for kids. Shark Realm, a 40-foot walk-through tunnel, houses more than 20 sharks and 850 other marine animals. The West African River Experience houses hippopotamuses and porcupines as well as a variety of African birds in an aviary. Films shown in a 4-D theater depict the wonders of underwater life. A Swim with the Sharks snorkeling program and special behind-the-scenes animal adventures also are offered.

Ferry/trolley service to the museum is available to and from the riverfront in Philadelphia May through September. **Time:** Allow 2 hours minimum. **Hours:** Daily 10-5. **Cost:** $25.95; $18.95 (ages 2-12). Adventure Combo with 4-D theater ticket $28.95; $21.95 (ages 2-12). **Parking:** $10. **Phone:** (856) 365-3300 or (800) 616-5297. ⬜ ⬜ City Hall, 144

SAVE **BATTLESHIP *NEW JERSEY*** is berthed at 62 Battleship Pl. on the Camden waterfront. This Iowa Class vessel, launched from the Philadelphia Navy Yard in 1942, is celebrated as the U.S. Navy's most decorated battleship. After serving in World War II, Korea, Vietnam and the Persian Gulf, the ship was decommissioned in 1990. Gun turrets, bridge communications, captain's and admiral's cabins, and enlisted men's bunks and mess area can be seen.

The 2-hour Fire Power Tour offers an in-depth look at the ship's weapons systems and the combat engagement center. The 90-minute Turret II Experience explores the battleship's legendary 16-inch gun turret.

Note: Video cameras, bags, backpacks and baby strollers are not permitted. Comfortable dress and shoes are recommended. A video version is available for those physically unable to take the tour. **Time:** Allow 2 hours minimum. **Hours:** Tours are offered every 15 minutes daily 9:30-5, May 1-Labor Day; daily 9:30-3, in Apr., day after Labor Day-Oct. 31 and Dec. 26-Dec. 31; Sat.-Sun. 9:30-3, Nov. 1-Dec. 31 and early Feb.-Mar. 31. Turret II Experience tours are offered Sat.-Sun. at 11 and 1. Closed Jan. 1, Thanksgiving and Christmas. **Cost:** Fire Power Tour $21.95; $17 (ages 6-11, 65+ and retired military with ID); free (ages 0-5 and active military with ID). Turret II Experience $29.95; $25.95 (ages 6-11, 65+ and retired military with ID); free (ages 0-5 and active military with ID). **Parking:** Fees vary by garage. **Phone:** (856) 966-1652 or (866) 877-6262. ⬜ City Hall, 144

CAMDEN CHILDREN'S GARDEN is on the riverfront at 3 Riverside Dr., adjacent to Adventure Aquarium. It features a variety of themed gardens designed for children ages 12 and under, including a dinosaur garden, a fitness garden and a picnic garden. Storybook Gardens features the Giant's Garden, Three Little Pigs Garden and an English-style garden like the one depicted in the different versions of the movie "The Secret Garden." There also is a butterfly garden, a maze and a tree house. Indoor exhibits include the Philadelphia Eagles Butterfly House, Benjamin Franklin's Secret Workshop and the tropically landscaped Plaza de Aibonito.

Visitors also can ride the Garden Carousel, the Arrow River Train and the Spring Butterfly Ride, which raises riders 30 feet in the air to provide a butterfly's-eye view of the gardens. **Time:** Allow 2 hours minimum. **Hours:** Wed.-Sun. 10-4, July-Aug.; Thurs.-Sun. 10-4, Sept.-Dec.; phone for schedule, late Mar.-June 30. Closed Thanksgiving and Christmas. **Cost:** $6; $4 (visitors with a paid admission to Adventure Aquarium arriving through the Garden Gate); free (ages 0-2). **Phone:** (856) 365-8733. ⬜ ⬜ City Hall, 144

CAMDEN COUNTY HISTORICAL SOCIETY is .5 mi. n.w. on Haddon Ave. off US 130, .2 mi. n.e. on Vesper Blvd., then .2 mi. n.w. to 1900 Park Blvd.

The society's museum contains fire-fighting equipment, Civil War artifacts, working Victrolas and a large collection of other vintage RCA items.

The brick, Georgian-style Pomona Hall, a Quaker mansion built in 1726 and extensively enlarged in 1788, is authentically restored and furnished in period. The society's library has maps, 18th- and 19th-century newspapers and an extensive collection of genealogical data. **Note:** The museum is currently closed and house tours have been temporarily suspended due to weather-related damage; phone for updates. **Hours:** House tours are given Thurs. and Sun. 12:30-3:30. Library open Wed. and Fri. 10-3, Thurs. 10-noon, Sun. noon-5. Closed major holidays. Phone ahead to confirm schedule. **Cost:** Museum or library $5; $4 (ages 65+ and students with ID). Pomona Hall tour $5. Museum and Pomona Hall $8; $6 (students with ID). **Phone:** (856) 964-3333. ⏷ Ferry Ave, 146

CAPE MAY (H-2) pop. 3,607, elev. 10'
• Hotels p. 98 • Restaurants p. 100

Have you ever wondered how Cape May got its name? Explorer Cornelius Jacobsen May, sent by the Dutch East India Co. to explore the then-mysterious East Coast, found the climate "charming" and lent his moniker to the shore area.

Victorian gingerbread is a recurrent architectural theme; the prevalence of well-preserved late 19th-century structures led to Cape May being designated a national historic landmark in 1976. Representative of this florid style is the Emlen Physick Estate (see attraction listing). The Pink House on Perry Street exemplifies the ornate "wedding cake" architectural style.

At New Jersey's southernmost tip, Cape May is one of the oldest seashore resorts on the Atlantic Coast. During the first half of the 19th century it rivaled Newport, R.I., as a favored summer retreat for Philadelphia and New York socialites. Presidents Buchanan, Grant, Harrison and Pierce were among the notables who vacationed here. Another, more infamous visitor was pirate Captain Kidd, who filled his water casks near Lily Pond.

In addition to the pleasures of the beach and the amusements of the promenade, Cape May offers good boating and fishing. Various craft can be rented for fishing in the ocean or in Delaware Bay. Rockhounds pursue their interest also; the tide-worn quartz pebbles known as "Cape May Diamonds" can be found on the beach at nearby Cape May Point and along lower Delaware Bay.

Those who prefer entertainment rather than sand with their food should try Elaine's Famous Dinner Theater at Elaine's Victorian Inn, 513 Lafayette St.; phone (609) 884-4358. Visitors also can enjoy a number of special events throughout the year. Three major celebrations are the ⏷ Cape May Food and Wine Celebration in September; ⏷ Victorian Weekend, a 4-day festival held in October; and

⏷ Christmas Candlelight House Tours in December, a self-guiding tour of fancifully decorated Victorian inns, hotels, guesthouses and churches.

At Cape May Point State Park (see Recreation Areas Chart), 1.2 miles west via Sunset Boulevard (CR 606), is the historic Cape May Lighthouse, erected in 1859 (see attraction listing). The state park is one of three prime bird-watching areas adjacent to Cape May Bird Observatory in nearby Cape May Point. Higbee's Beach Wildlife Management Area and Cape May Migratory Bird Refuge are other observation points.

The World War II Lookout Tower (see attraction listing), formerly Fire Control Tower No. 23, off Sunset Boulevard on the state park grounds, is one of two artillery lookout towers remaining in the area and the only one accessible to the public. Interpretive signs at each level along the ascent to the top (via a spiral staircase) provide background about the tower's history and purpose; phone (609) 884-5404 or (800) 275-4278.

Explore this charming community with guided tours conducted by the Mid-Atlantic Center for the Arts & Humanities. The organization's Cape May Trolley Tours (see attraction listing) features the historic district as well as carriage tours, historic house tours and guided walking tours that depart from the Washington Street Mall information booth.

Of special interest in nearby Cold Spring is The Cemetery at Cold Spring Presbyterian Church, where the oldest grave dates to 1742 and the present church building to 1823; phone (609) 884-5130 or (609) 884-4065. Also nearby, north of Cape May near Rio Grande, is the Naval Air Station Wildwood Aviation Museum. This former training facility for dive-bomber squadrons during World War II remembers the Navy airmen who died during training (see attraction listing p. 188).

The Cape May-Lewes Ferry runs daily between Cape May and Lewes, Del. The New Jersey terminal is at the junction of Lincoln Boulevard and US 9, about 2.5 miles west of the southern end of the Garden State Parkway. The 17-mile trip takes 85 minutes. Reservations are recommended and should be made at least 1 day in advance; phone (800) 643-3779.

Cape May Welcome Center: 609 Lafayette St., Cape May, NJ 08204. **Phone:** (609) 884-9562.

Self-guiding tours: Brochures outlining a walking tour of Cape May's historic sites are available at the welcome center.

CAPE MAY LIGHTHOUSE is at jct. Lighthouse Ave. and Sunset Blvd. in Cape May Point State Park. The lighthouse was built in 1859 and has been fully restored. Visitors who choose to climb the 199 steps to the top will be rewarded with a view of the Jersey Cape, where the Delaware Bay and Atlantic Ocean meet. Information about the lighthouse's structure and history is posted along the ascent. A visitor orientation center also is on site.

Time: Allow 1 hour minimum. **Hours:** Open daily with varying hours, Apr.-Nov.; Sat.-Sun. with varying hours, rest of year (weather permitting). Closed Thanksgiving and Christmas. **Cost:** $8; $3 (ages 3-12). Combination ticket with Hereford Inlet Lighthouse in North Wildwood $10; $3 (ages 0-11). **Phone:** (609) 884-5404, (800) 275-4278 or TTY (805) 882-7899.

CAPE MAY TROLLEY TOURS depart from the Washington Street Mall information booth at Ocean St. The Mid-Atlantic Center for the Arts provides scenic tours around the Cape May area ranging from 45 minutes to 2 hours in length. Offerings include historic districts, children's attractions and even supernatural hot spots. The popular 90-minute War at the Shore Trolley Tour displays a 1941 fire control tower, a bunker, the Cape May Canal, the U.S. Coast Guard base and the Naval Air Station Wildwood Aviation Museum. Seasonal and holiday tours also are available.

Inquire about wheelchair-accessible trolley tours; offerings may vary. **Time:** Allow 1 hour minimum. **Hours:** Tours depart in spring, summer and fall; phone ahead for specific schedule. **Cost:** Fares vary depending on the tour chosen. The 1.5-hour War at the Shore Trolley Tour (includes admission to Naval Air Station Wildwood Aviation Museum in Rio Grande) $20; $15 (ages 3-12). Reservations are recommended. **Phone:** (609) 884-5404 or (800) 275-4278. GT

EMLEN PHYSICK ESTATE is at 1048 Washington St. at Lafayette St. This 18-room, 1879 Victorian house was designed by notable Philadelphia architect Frank Furness. Emlen Physick Jr., a gentleman farmer, was the grandson of Dr. Philip Syng Physick, a surgeon who invented procedures and instruments that are still used. Tours through restored rooms provide insight into the lifestyles of two distinct Victorian classes: the wealthy and the servants. The Victorian Luxuries tour explores the differences between this house and a middle-class home. A combination ticket with the Cape May Trolley also is available.

Time: Allow 1 hour minimum. **Hours:** Guided tours Mon.-Fri. (hours vary), Sat.-Sun. at 11:45, 1, 2:15 and 3:30, Mar.-Dec.; Sat.-Sun. (hours vary), rest of year. Closed Thanksgiving and Christmas. Phone ahead to confirm schedule. **Cost:** $12; $7 (ages 3-12). Combination ticket with the Cape May Trolley $20; $12 (ages 3-12). **Phone:** (609) 884-5404 or (800) 275-4278.

SAVE **HISTORIC COLD SPRING VILLAGE** is at 720 US 9S. This open-air, living-history museum portrays 19th-century lifestyles, trades, crafts and architecture in a South Jersey rural community. The 22-acre wooded village consists of 25 restored buildings. Interpreters demonstrate such trades and crafts as pottery making, blacksmithing, yarn spinning, woodworking, broom making, basket weaving,

printing and book binding. A welcome center features exhibits, a 7-minute video and interactive stations highlighting the village's history.

Time: Allow 3 hours minimum. **Hours:** Tues.-Sun. 10-4:30, late June-Labor Day; phone for schedule in spring in fall. Hours may vary during special events; phone ahead to verify schedule. **Cost:** $10; $8 (ages 3-12). Combination tickets are available with Cape May Lighthouse, Naval Air Station Wildwood Aviation Museum, Hereford Lighthouse, WWII Lookout Tower and the Emlem Physick Estate; phone ahead for prices. **Phone:** (609) 898-2300. ⊞

WORLD WAR II LOOKOUT TOWER is 1 mi. w. on CR 606 (Sunset Blvd.) at Sunset Beach. Providing sweeping views, this tall, slender concrete tower was constructed in 1942 as part of Fort Miles. Known as Fire Control Tower No. 23, it took aim for large shore guns by using triangulation. This is the only surviving public example of the 15 towers constructed along the coast from Cape May to Bethany Beach, Del.

Displays show regional and military history along the wooden walkway and throughout the six levels of the tower. The adjacent All Veteran's Memorial, featuring a copper cauldron and eternal brass flames by craftsman Stephen D. Bradway, is a contemplative sculpture dedicated to all veterans. **Note:** Full mobility is required to climb the narrow staircase in the tower. **Time:** Allow 30 minutes minimum. **Hours:** All Veteran's Memorial is open 24 hours daily. Tower open daily 9-8, in summer; otherwise varies. **Cost:** $6; free (one child ages 3-12); $3 (each additional child ages 3-12); $2 (active and retired military with ID). **Phone:** (609) 884-5404 or (800) 275-4278.

CARROLL VILLA HOTEL   609/884-9619
▼▼ **Historic Country Inn.** Rates not provided. **Address:** 19 Jackson St 08204 **Location:** Just w of Beach Ave. **Facility:** A bustling restaurant dominates the front of this 1882 Victorian country inn. 21 units. 3 stories (no elevator), interior corridors. **Dining:** The Mad Batter Restaurant, see separate listing.
🍽 📶 ✕ / SOME UNITS 🛗

CONGRESS HALL   609/884-8421
▼▼▼ **Historic Hotel.** Rates not provided. **Address:** 251 Beach Ave 08204 **Location:** Between Congress and Perry sts; entrance at Congress Pl. Across from ocean. **Facility:** You'll enjoy both elegant and grand touches at this lovingly restored 1879 property with tastefully decorated guest rooms. 108 units. 4 stories, interior corridors. **Parking:** on-site and valet. **Amenities:** safes. **Dining:** The Blue Pig Tavern, see separate listing. **Pool(s):** heated outdoor. **Activities:** beach access, recreation programs in summer, bicycles, exercise room, spa. **Guest Services:** valet laundry.
🍽 🛒 📞 CALL ☾M 🏊 📶 ✕ 🎥 / SOME UNITS 🛗 🖼

GINGERBREAD HOUSE   609/884-0211
▼▼▼ **Historic Bed & Breakfast.** Rates not provided. **Address:** 28 Gurney St 08204 **Location:** Just w of Beach Ave; center. **Facility:** This Carpenter Gothic-style home, dating from 1869, is furnished with many antiques. The owner's fine woodworking is displayed throughout the house. Beach chairs and towels are provided for an extra charge. 6 units. 3 stories (no elevator), interior corridors. *Bath:* some shared. **Parking:** street only. **Terms:** age restrictions may apply. 🍽 📶 ✕ 🅿

THE HUMPHREY HUGHES HOUSE
609/884-4428

▼▼▼ **Historic Bed & Breakfast.** Rates not provided. **Address:** 29 Ocean St 08204 **Location:** Jct Columbia Ave and Ocean St. **Facility:** Occupied by the Hughes family until 1980, this large late-Victorian home features expansive guest rooms and parlors, wrap-around verandas and elegant antiques. 10 units. 3 stories (no elevator), interior/exterior corridors. **Parking:** street only. **Terms:** age restrictions may apply.

LA MER BEACHFRONT INN
609/884-9000

Hotel
Rates not provided

Address: 1317 Beach Ave 08204 **Location:** Jct Pittsburgh and Beach aves. Across from ocean. **Facility:** 141 efficiencies. 4 stories, interior corridors. **Amenities:** safes. **Pool(s):** heated outdoor. **Activities:** beach access, exercise room, spa. **Guest Services:** coin laundry.

MADISON AVENUE BEACH CLUB MOTEL
609/884-8266

▼▼ **Motel.** Rates not provided. **Address:** 605 Madison Ave 08204 **Location:** Jct Columbia Ave. **Facility:** 42 units, some efficiencies and kitchens. 2 stories (no elevator), exterior corridors. *Bath:* shower only. **Pool(s):** heated outdoor. **Activities:** hot tub. **Guest Services:** coin laundry.

THE MAINSTAY INN
609/884-8690

▼▼▼ **Historic Bed & Breakfast.** Rates not provided. **Address:** 635 Columbia Ave 08204 **Location:** Jct Stockton Pl and Columbia Ave. **Facility:** Operating as one of the first B&Bs in Cape May since the last 1970s, this property's upscale common areas and beautiful wrap-around porch make for great spots to relax and socialize with others. 13 units. 3 stories (no elevator), interior corridors. **Terms:** age restrictions may apply.

MARQUIS DE LAFAYETTE HOTEL
609/884-3500

▼▼▼
Hotel
Rates not provided

Address: 501 Beach Ave 08204 **Location:** Between Decatur and Ocean sts. Across from ocean. **Facility:** 84 units, some efficiencies and kitchens. 3-6 stories, interior/exterior corridors. **Terms:** check-in 4 pm. **Pool(s):** heated outdoor. **Activities:** beach access, exercise room. **Guest Services:** coin laundry. **Featured Amenity:** breakfast buffet.

MONTREAL BEACH RESORT
609/884-7011

▼▼▼
Hotel
Rates not provided

Address: 1025 Beach Ave 08204 **Location:** Between Madison Ave and Queen St. Across from ocean. **Facility:** 69 units, some efficiencies. 4 stories, exterior corridors. **Amenities:** safes. **Pool(s):** heated outdoor. **Activities:** sauna, hot tub, beach access, exercise room. **Guest Services:** coin laundry. **Featured Amenity:** continental breakfast.

PALACE HOTEL OF CAPE MAY
(609)898-8100

▼▼▼
Hotel
$89-$339

Address: 1101 Beach Ave 08204 **Location:** Jct Beach and Philadelphia aves. Across from ocean. **Facility:** 56 units, some efficiencies. 4 stories, interior corridors. **Terms:** closed 11/1-3/31, 2 night minimum stay - seasonal and/or weekends, 7 day cancellation notice-fee imposed. **Activities:** beach access. **Featured Amenity:** continental breakfast.

PERIWINKLE INN
609/884-9200

▼▼ **Motel.** Rates not provided. **Address:** 1039 Beach Ave 08204 **Location:** Between Madison and Philadelphia aves. Across from ocean. **Facility:** 50 units, some efficiencies. 3 stories, exterior corridors. **Pool(s):** outdoor. **Activities:** beach access.

THE QUEEN VICTORIA
609/884-8702

▼▼▼ **Historic Bed & Breakfast.** Rates not provided. **Address:** 102 Ocean St 08204 **Location:** Jct Columbia Ave and Ocean St. **Facility:** The rooms here are spread among five 1880s Victorian homes filled with antique furnishings. Guests are treated to evening turn-down service and afternoon tea. 35 units. 3 stories (no elevator), interior/exterior corridors. **Parking:** street only. **Terms:** age restrictions may apply. **Amenities:** safes. **Activities:** bicycles.

SEA CREST INN
609/884-4561

▼▼ **Motel.** Rates not provided. **Address:** 101 Beach Ave 08204 **Location:** Between Patterson Ave and Broadway. Across from ocean. **Facility:** 56 units, some two bedrooms and efficiencies. 4 stories, exterior corridors. **Pool(s):** heated outdoor. **Activities:** hot tub, beach access. **Guest Services:** coin laundry.

THE SOUTHERN MANSION
(609)884-7171

▼▼▼ ▼▼▼
Historic Bed & Breakfast
$145-$415

Address: 720 Washington St 08204 **Location:** Jct Jefferson and Washington sts. **Facility:** A grand mansion on picturesque grounds, this renovated property features polished wood floors, high ceilings, elaborate moldings and several verandas. 24 units. 4 stories (no elevator), interior/exterior corridors. **Terms:** closed 1/3-2/14, 2-3 night minimum stay - weekends, age restrictions may apply, 21 day cancellation notice-fee imposed.

THE STAR INN
609/884-8421

▼▼▼ **Motel.** Rates not provided. **Address:** 29 Perry St 08204 **Location:** Between Congress Pl and Beach Ave. **Facility:** 21 units, some efficiencies and cottages. 2-3 stories (no elevator), interior/exterior corridors.

VICTORIAN LACE INN
609/884-1772

▼▼▼ **Historic Bed & Breakfast** $135-$395 **Address:** 901 Stockton Ave 08204 **Location:** At Jefferson St; just w of Beach Ave. **Facility:** This cozy family home dating from 1869 has a wood-burning fireplace in the parlor and offers carriage house apartments and suites with gas fireplaces. 7 units, some two bedrooms, kitchens and cottages. 2-3 stories (no elevator), interior/exterior corridors. **Parking:** street only. **Terms:** closed 1/1-3/15, 2-3 night minimum stay - seasonal and/or weekends, 14 day cancellation notice-fee imposed.

THE VIRGINIA HOTEL   609/884-5700

▼▼▼ **Historic Country Inn.** Rates not provided. **Address:** 25 Jackson St 08204 **Location:** Between Washington Square Mall and Beach Ave; center. **Facility:** Verandas span the front of this restored inn dating from 1879. The guest rooms are elegantly furnished. A beautifully appointed dining area just off the lobby provides a complimentary breakfast each morning. 24 units. 3 stories (no elevator), interior corridors. **Parking:** street only. **Amenities:** safes. **Dining:** The Ebbitt Room at the Virginia Hotel, see separate listing.

⊞ ⊉ 📶 ⊠ ⋣

WHERE TO EAT

410 BANK STREET   609/884-2127

▼▼▼ Creole. Fine Dining. $27-$40 **AAA Inspector Notes:** *Historic.* In a charming, restored 1840 carriage house, just a block from a pedestrian shopping mall, this restaurant offers intimate dining rooms, including an enclosed porch and patio. Innovative cuisine blends the flavors of France, the Caribbean and New Orleans. The friendly, knowledgeable waitstaff aims to please. **Features:** wine only, patio dining. **Reservations:** suggested. **Address:** 410 Bank St 08204 **Location:** Between Broad and Lafayette sts; just w of Pedestrian Mall. D

ALEATHEA'S   609/884-5555

▼▼ American. Casual Dining. $7-$39 **AAA Inspector Notes:** Directly across from the beach, this pretty eatery is destined to become a Cape May favorite. Its location makes it a worthy destination for anyone with a preference for a water view, while its Victorian décor appeals to those with refined sensibilities. The bill of fare lists something for everyone, including sandwiches, soups and salads for lunch and varied entrées for dinner. **Features:** full bar, patio dining, early bird specials. **Reservations:** suggested. **Address:** 7 Ocean St 08204 **Location:** At Beach Dr. B L D

AXELSSONS'S BLUE CLAW RESTAURANT   609/884-5878

▼▼▼ Seafood. Fine Dining. $25-$35 **AAA Inspector Notes:** Preparations of seafood, chicken, veal, pasta and hand-selected beef, as well as occasional game specialties, line this restaurant's varied menu. From the modestly sophisticated dining room, guests can watch the working fishing fleet. **Features:** full bar, happy hour. **Reservations:** suggested. **Address:** 991 Ocean Dr 08204 **Location:** From southern terminus of Garden State Pkwy, 1.3 mi e on CR 621 (Ocean Dr). D

THE BLUE PIG TAVERN   609/884-8422

▼▼▼
American
Casual Dining
$16-$36

AAA Inspector Notes: Generous portions of hearty American cuisine are served in this cozy dining room, originally a tavern for whalers in the 1700s. From crab cakes and macaroni and cheese to lobster and burgers, diners surely can find something from the extensive menu or from the list of blue plate specials. **Features:** full bar, patio dining. **Reservations:** suggested, for dinner. **Address:** 251 Beach Ave 08204 **Location:** Between Congress and Perry sts; entrance at Congress Pl; in Congress Hall.

B L D CALL ⓎM

CAPE MAY FISH MARKET   609/770-3790

▼▼ Seafood. Casual Dining. $10-$38 **AAA Inspector Notes:** This is a good stop for simple and casual fresh seafood meals, or to pick up some fresh fish to cook at home. The crab cakes are popular, and there are other treasures from local waters including flounder and scallops. **Address:** 408 Washington St 08204 **Location:** On Washington St Mall; between Decatur and Jackson sts. **Parking:** street only. L D

THE EBBITT ROOM AT THE VIRGINIA HOTEL   609/884-5700

▼▼▼▼ American. Fine Dining. $28-$33 **AAA Inspector Notes:** Creatively presented dishes here reflect influences from Asia to the American Southwest. Professional servers and a softly-lit dining room enhance the relaxed experience. The restaurant's name honors the inn's founder. Home-baked desserts are wonderful. **Features:** full bar, patio dining, happy hour. **Reservations:** suggested. **Address:** 25 Jackson St 08204 **Location:** Between Washington Square Mall and Beach Ave; center; in The Virginia Hotel. **Parking:** on-site (fee) and valet. D

FRESCOS SEAFOOD TRATTORIA   609/884-0366

▼▼▼ Seafood. Fine Dining. $18-$40 **AAA Inspector Notes:** *Historic.* Patrons can unwind in this restored 1880 Victorian cottage, which is bustling on the inside and quiet on the broad veranda. Excellent Northern and regional Italian cuisine, such as osso buco, is at the heart of the menu along with fresh local seafood. **Features:** wine only. **Reservations:** suggested. **Address:** 412 Bank St 08204 **Location:** Between Broad and Lafayette sts; just w of Pedestrian Mall. D

GODMOTHERS RESTAURANT   609/884-4543

▼▼ Italian. Casual Dining. $15-$26 **AAA Inspector Notes:** This spot, one of Cape May's original Italian restaurants opening in 1983, is located in a residential neighborhood. Come in as soon as they open at 5 pm and enjoy a three-course early bird special menu until 5:30. The restaurant features a selection of dry white and dry red wine from the local Cape May Winery, sold only by the bottle not by the glass. The restaurant is closed on certain weekdays during the off season. **Features:** full bar, early bird specials. **Reservations:** suggested. **Address:** 413 S Broadway 08204 **Location:** Corner of W Perry St. **Parking:** street only. D

LOBSTER HOUSE   609/884-8296

▼▼ Seafood. Casual Dining. $10-$40 **AAA Inspector Notes:** Overlooking the harbor, the restaurant is a local favorite for fresh seafood, particularly lobster. Nautical appointments decorate the informal dining room, while the outside patio is even more relaxed. A fresh fish market is on the grounds. **Features:** full bar, patio dining. **Address:** 906 Schellenger Landing 08204 **Location:** At wharf; east of south end of Cold Spring Bridge. L D CALL ⓎM

THE MAD BATTER RESTAURANT   609/884-5970

▼▼ American. Casual Dining. $13-$33 **AAA Inspector Notes:** *Historic.* Request a seat on the charming front porch in nice weather to savor Jackson Street crab cakes, a house specialty at this casually upscale restaurant. The kitchen is known for its eclectic, flavorful preparations and friendly servers. **Features:** full bar, early bird specials, happy hour. **Reservations:** suggested, for dinner. **Address:** 19 Jackson St 08204 **Location:** Just w of Beach Ave; in Carroll Villa Hotel. **Parking:** street only. B L D

MERION INN   609/884-8363

▼▼ American. Casual Dining. $17-$50 **AAA Inspector Notes:** *Historic.* Located in the heart of Cape May's Victorian historic district, the restaurant, constructed in 1885, features charming restored dining rooms and a beautiful turn-of-the-20th-century bar, where guests may enjoy cocktails and live music. **Features:** full bar, patio dining. **Reservations:** suggested. **Address:** 106 Decatur St 08204 **Location:** Jct Decatur St and Columbia Ave; center. **Parking:** valet only. D

OYSTER BAY STEAK & SEAFOOD RESTAURANT   609/884-2111

▼▼ American. Casual Dining. $21-$39 **AAA Inspector Notes:** On the road into town, the casual spot offers a pleasant evening out. Some of the dishes--which include steak, seafood and a few pasta preparations--show refinement. Specials round out the offerings. **Features:** full bar, happy hour. **Reservations:** suggested. **Address:** 615 Lafayette St 08204 **Location:** Just e of Elmira St. D

PILOT HOUSE   609/884-3449

▼▼ American. Casual Dining. $9-$27 **AAA Inspector Notes:** Located in the heart of the Victorian historic district, this restaurant is aptly decorated with brass lanterns, lace curtains and floral wallpaper. Guests can request seating on the enclosed patio or next to the dining room's wood-burning fireplace. Menu offerings include well-prepared veal, steaks and burgers. **Features:** full bar, early bird specials, happy hour. **Reservations:** suggested. **Address:** 142 Decatur St 08204 **Location:** Jct Carpenters Ln and Decatur St; at Washington Street Mall. **Parking:** street only. L D

UNION PARK DINING ROOM   609/884-8811

▼▼▼ American. Fine Dining. $19-$39 **AAA Inspector Notes:** Located in the lobby of an historic hotel, this restaurant offers seating on the veranda during the summer months so be sure to reserve it. The menu highlights lamb, veal tenderloin, short ribs, filet mignon, scallops and lobster. Desserts all are made in-house. **Features:** full bar, patio dining, early bird specials. **Reservations:** suggested. **Address:** 727 Beach Ave 08204 **Location:** Between Howard St and Stockton Pl; in Hotel Macomber. **Parking:** street only. D

THE WASHINGTON INN   609/884-5697

▼▼▼▼ American. Fine Dining. $24-$40 **AAA Inspector Notes:** *Historic.* Flowers, classical music and candlelight add to the romance in this 1848 Colonial plantation home. Selections from the well-stocked wine cellar complement such dishes as cocoa chile-rubbed New York steak and herb-crusted New Zealand rack of lamb. The waitstaff specializes in gracious, knowledgeable service. Cape May's famed historic district offers a nice after-dinner stroll. **Features:** full bar. **Reservations:** suggested. **Address:** 801 Washington St 08204 **Location:** Jct Jefferson St; center. **Parking:** valet and street only.

D

CAPE MAY COURT HOUSE (H-3)
pop. 5,338, elev. 19'

The county seat, Cape May Court House is a good place to begin a tour of the Victorian and historic houses throughout Cape May County.

Cape May County Chamber of Commerce and Visitor Information Center: 13 Crest Haven Rd., P.O. Box 74, Cape May Court House, NJ 08210. **Phone:** (609) 465-7181.

CAPE MAY COUNTY HISTORICAL MUSEUM is .7 mi. n. at 504 US 9N. The Cresse-Holmes House, built about 1704, contains furnishings, costumes, tools and other artifacts that provide a survey of life in early Cape May County. An 1800s barn houses a collection of local Native American artifacts, whaling implements, maritime exhibits and carriages. The Alexander Memorial Library contains documents and photographs pertaining to Cape May County families and local history.

Time: Allow 1 hour minimum. **Hours:** Museum Tues.-Sat. 10-3 (tours at 11 and 2), early Apr. to mid-Oct.; tours by appointment, rest of year. Library Wed.-Fri. 10:30-3:30. Closed major holidays. Phone ahead to confirm schedule. **Cost:** Free. **Phone:** (609) 465-3535.

CAPE MAY COUNTY PARK AND ZOO is off Garden State Pkwy. exit 11 at 707 US 9N. This 200-acre park contains a zoo that is home to some 250 species of animals including bison, camels, deer, exotic birds, foxes, giraffes, lemurs, leopards, lions, monkeys, mountain bongos, oryxes, reptiles, tigers and zebras. Many of the animals are rare or endangered species. An 800-foot boardwalk leads to an African savanna habitat. *See Recreation Areas Chart.*

Hours: Park open daily 9-dusk. Zoo open daily 10-4:45, mid-Mar. to early Nov.; 10-3:45, rest of year. Closed Christmas. **Cost:** Donations. **Phone:** (609) 465-5271. ⬚⬚

ECOGARDENS AT LEAMING'S RUN is off Garden State Pkwy. exit 13, then 1 mi. n. to 1845 US 9N. A winding path leads visitors through themed gardens surrounded by 30 acres of preserved native woodlands and wild plants. Educational demonstration gardens cover a variety of eco-friendly, sustainable gardening techniques. Ruby-throated hummingbirds visit the flowers in late summer.

At Thimblefull Discovery Farm, farming techniques from the 17th century are depicted and farm animals, cotton and tobacco can be seen. Interactive displays include re-created Colonial log buildings, an herb garden and educational exhibits of modern-day organic farming practices. **Time:** Allow 2 hours minimum. **Hours:** Daily 10-4, mid-May to late Sept. (weather permitting). **Cost:** Ecogardens admission $8; $5 (ages 5-14). Thimblefull Discovery Farm admission $5; free (ages 0-4). Combination ticket for both attractions $10; free (ages 0-5) . Cash only. **Phone:** (609) 465-5871.

THE DOCTORS INN   (609)463-9330

▼▼▼ **Historic Bed & Breakfast** $99-$250 **Address:** 2 N Main St 08210 **Location:** At Main (US 9) and Mechanic sts; just s of Garden State Pkwy. **Facility:** Built in 1854, the home's huge basement was used as part of the Underground Railroad. The owners are happy to discuss the fascinating history of this home. Guest rooms are very spacious for a B&B. 8 units, some three bedrooms. 3 stories (no elevator), interior corridors. **Terms:** 2 night minimum stay - seasonal and/or weekends, 14 day cancellation notice-fee imposed.

CARLSTADT   pop. 6,127
• **Hotels & Restaurants map & index p. 162**

HAMPTON INN-MEADOWLANDS   (201)935-9000   [61]

▼▼▼ Hotel $129-$179 **Address:** 304 Paterson Plank Rd 07072 **Location:** New Jersey Tpke exit 16W to SR 3 W, then 2 mi n on SR 120 (Paterson Plank Rd). **Facility:** 122 units. 5 stories, interior corridors. **Terms:** 1-7 night minimum stay, cancellation fee imposed. **Amenities:** safes. **Activities:** exercise room. **Guest Services:** valet and coin laundry, area transportation.

AAA Benefit: Members save 5% or more!

CALL ⬚ ⬚ ⬚ ⬚ ⬚ ⬚ ⬚ ⬚

HOLIDAY INN EXPRESS HOTEL & SUITES   201/460-9292   [60]

▼▼▼ Hotel. Rates not provided. **Address:** 100 Paterson Plank Rd 07072 **Location:** New Jersey Tpke exit 16W to SR 3 W to SR 17 N, 1.3 mi n to SR 120 (Paterson Plank Rd), then just e. **Facility:** 99 units. 5 stories, interior corridors. **Pool(s):** heated indoor. **Activities:** exercise room. **Guest Services:** valet and coin laundry.

CARNEYS POINT   pop. 7,382

COMFORT INN & SUITES   (856)299-8282

▼▼▼ Hotel $99-$150 **Address:** 634 Sodders Rd 08069 **Location:** I-295 exit 2B, just e on Pennsville-Auburn Rd, then 0.3 mi s. **Facility:** 63 units, some efficiencies. 3 stories, interior corridors. **Activities:** exercise room. **Guest Services:** coin laundry.

⬚ CALL ⬚ ⬚ ⬚ ⬚ ⬚ ⬚ ⬚ / SOME UNITS ⬚

HOLIDAY INN EXPRESS HOTEL & SUITES   (856)351-9222

▼▼▼
Hotel
$110-$140

Address: 506 S Pennsville-Auburn Rd 08069 **Location:** I-295 exit 2B, just e. **Facility:** 78 units. 3 stories, interior corridors. **Guest Services:** valet and coin laundry. **Featured Amenity:** breakfast buffet.

CARTERET pop. 22,844
• Hotels & Restaurants map & index p. 152

HOLIDAY INN OF CARTERET-RAHWAY   732/541-9500   **102**
▼▼▼ **Hotel.** Rates not provided. **Address:** 1000 Roosevelt Ave 07008 **Location:** I-95 (New Jersey Tpke) exit 12, just s of toll booths. **Facility:** 118 units. 2 stories (no elevator), interior corridors. **Pool(s):** outdoor. **Activities:** exercise room. **Guest Services:** valet and coin laundry, boarding pass kiosk, area transportation.

HOTEL EXECUTIVE SUITES   (732)541-2005   **103**
▼▼▼ **Hotel** $99-$299 **Address:** 30 Minue St 07008 **Location:** I-95 (New Jersey Tpke) exit 12, 0.3 mi e on Roosevelt Ave, just s. **Facility:** 117 units. 6 stories, interior corridors. **Terms:** cancellation fee imposed. **Activities:** exercise room. **Guest Services:** valet laundry, area transportation.

CEDAR GROVE pop. 12,411
• Hotels & Restaurants map & index p. 152

LU NELLO   973/837-1660   **22**
▼▼▼ Northern Italian. Casual Dining. $16-$34 **AAA Inspector Notes:** Servers, dressed in formal attire, amaze with their ability to recite the specials, which on most nights, is somewhere around twenty. The largely traditional menu of Northern Italian specialties includes linguine with littleneck clams, tripe with polenta and a delicate veal dish with shiitake mushrooms and Fontina. **Features:** full bar. **Reservations:** suggested. **Address:** 182 Stevens Ave 07009 **Location:** Jct SR 23, 0.5 mi e at Lindsley Rd. **Parking:** valet only.

CHATHAM pop. 8,962
• Hotels & Restaurants map & index p. 152

A TASTE OF ASIA   973/701-8821   **87**
▼▼ Asian. Casual Dining. $8-$20 **AAA Inspector Notes:** Malaysian food is pungent, fragrant and spicy, and those in-the-know line up for the traditional dishes served in this charming storefront. Flavors are vibrant in dishes seasoned with chili, lemongrass, kaffir lime leaves and galangal. Noodles, curries and soups are top rate, as are satays and stir-fries. **Reservations:** suggested. **Address:** 245 Main St 07928 **Location:** At N Passaic Ave. **Parking:** street only.

BEAN CURD   973/635-5333   **86**
▼▼ Chinese. Casual Dining. $7-$20 **AAA Inspector Notes:** This restaurant is a casual place to bring the kids for a well-prepared Chinese meal. Choices on the large menu suit varying preferences. **Address:** 275 Main St 07928 **Location:** Center, at Fairmount Ave. **Parking:** street only.

CHARLIE BROWN'S STEAKHOUSE   973/822-1800
▼▼ Steak. Casual Dining. $9-$30 **AAA Inspector Notes:** This budget-friendly steakhouse, famous for its prime rib, offers top quality fare without hurting your pocketbook. The young ones will not be disappointed with the kids' menu, and just might even try something green from the salad bar. Adults will love the quality steaks, chicken and rib dishes. The express lunches are great for those saddled with time constraints. **Features:** full bar, happy hour. **Address:** 522 Southern Blvd 07928 **Location:** Just s on Fairmount Ave, 2.5 mi ne on Shunpike Rd, then just s.

RESTAURANT SERENADE   973/701-0303   **85**

▼▼▼▼ New American Fine Dining $18-$38   **AAA Inspector Notes:** Although it can be a bit loud on busy nights, the subdued upscale décor with modern art create warm, modern dining rooms in which to enjoy creative and inspired contemporary cuisine. Try one of the tasting menus for the best experience. Themes may include seasonal market items or an all-seafood menu. Expert wine pairings also are offered for each course. **Features:** full bar. **Reservations:** suggested. **Address:** 6 Roosevelt Ave 07928 **Location:** Just n off SR 124 (Main St). **Parking:** valet and street only.

SCALINI FEDELI   973/701-9200   **88**
▼▼▼ Northern Italian. Fine Dining. $14-$54 **AAA Inspector Notes:** *Historic.* The restaurant name, which translates from Italian to little steps of faith, is a destination spot for intimate, candle-lit dinners. Located in a 260-year-old farmhouse that evokes a distinctly Tuscan feel, the menu offers a three course, prix fixe dinner of Italian-inspired fare with American and French influences. Menu highlights include delicious giant ravioli filled with ricotta, truffles and a lightly cooked egg, topped with Parmesan and brown butter. **Features:** full bar. **Reservations:** required, weekends. **Address:** 63 Main St 07928 **Location:** At Parrot Mill Rd. **Parking:** valet only.

CHERRY HILL (E-2) elev. 56'

GARDEN STATE DISCOVERY MUSEUM is at 2040 Springdale Rd., Suite 100. More than 20 interactive exhibit areas provide an entertaining and educational experience for children, especially for ages 1-10. The exhibits include re-creations of a diner, farmers market, newsroom, veterinary hospital, restaurant construction site, newspaper office and a miniature Philadelphia Flyers hockey rink. Other features include a rock wall, puppet shows, face painting and a variety of hands-on activities. There also is a collection of reptiles, insects and fish. The Little Discoveries area, which has a farmhouse and a barn, is suitable for toddlers under age 4.

Time: Allow 2 hours minimum. **Hours:** Mon.-Thurs. 9:30-8:30, Fri.-Sun. 9:30-5:30, July-Aug.; daily 9:30-5:30 (also Sat. 5:30-8:30, Oct.-Apr.), rest of year. Closed Thanksgiving and Christmas. **Cost:** $12.95; $11.95 (ages 55+ and grandparents); $5 (Mon.-Thurs. 5-8:30, July-Aug.); free (ages 0-1). Buy-one-get-one-free admission, active and retired military and their spouses and dependents with ID. **Phone:** (856) 424-1233.

CROWNE PLAZA PHILADELPHIA/CHERRY HILL   856/665-6666
▼▼▼ **Hotel.** Rates not provided. **Address:** 2349 W Marlton Pike (SR 70) 08002 **Location:** SR 70 at Cuthbert Blvd (SR 38 E); I-295 exit 34B southbound, 4 mi w. **Facility:** 408 units. 14 stories, interior corridors. **Terms:** check-in 4 pm. **Pool(s):** outdoor. **Activities:** exercise room. **Guest Services:** valet and coin laundry, boarding pass kiosk.

DAYS INN & SUITES (856)663-0100

Motel
$80-$155

Address: 525 SR 38 E 08002 **Location:** I-295 exit 34B, 4 mi w on SR 70 to Cuthbert Blvd (SR 38 E), then just ne. **Facility:** 86 units. 2 stories (no elevator), exterior corridors. **Terms:** cancellation fee imposed. **Pool(s):** outdoor. **Activities:** exercise room. **Guest Services:** coin laundry. **Featured Amenity:** continental breakfast.

SAVE [YI+] [🏊] [BIZ] [HS] [🛜] [✕] [🔒] [🖨] [🖵]

EXTENDED STAY AMERICA-PHILADELPHIA/CHERRY HILL
856/616-1200

◆◆ **Extended Stay Hotel.** Rates not provided. **Address:** 1653 E SR 70 (Marlton Pike) 08034 **Location:** I-295 exit 34A, just e. **Facility:** 77 efficiencies. 3 stories, interior corridors. **Guest Services:** coin laundry. [🛜] [🔒] [🖨] / SOME UNITS [S] [🖵]

HOLIDAY INN PHILADELPHIA-CHERRY HILL
856/663-5300

Hotel
Rates not provided

Address: 2175 W Marlton Pike 08002 **Location:** I-295 exit 34B, 2.5 mi w. **Facility:** 186 units. 6 stories, interior corridors. **Amenities:** safes. **Pool(s):** outdoor, heated indoor. **Activities:** exercise room. **Guest Services:** valet and coin laundry, rental car service.

SAVE [YI] [👥] [工] CALL [&M] [🏊]
[BIZ] [🛜] [✕] [🔒] [🖵]
/ SOME UNITS [🐾] [🖨]

WHERE TO EAT

BRIO TUSCAN GRILLE 856/910-8166 [134]

◆◆◆ Italian. Fine Dining. $10-$29 **AAA Inspector Notes:** While the atmosphere is casual, upscale Tuscan villa-style décor lends a sophisticated touch to the dining experience. Both lunch and dinner offer all the attentiveness a diner expects. From the garlic, spinach and artichoke dip starter to beef, chicken, veal, seafood and homemade pasta entrées, there is a selection to satisfy all tastes. Among specialties are homemade mozzarella, crisp flatbreads and wood-fired oven-baked pizza, in addition to a selection of steak. **Features:** full bar, patio dining, Sunday brunch, happy hour. **Reservations:** suggested. **Address:** 901 Haddonfield Rd 08002 **Location:** I-295 exit 34B, 2.5 mi w. [L] [D]

CAFFE' ALDO LAMBERTI 856/663-1747 [136]

◆◆◆ Italian. Fine Dining. $10-$38 **AAA Inspector Notes:** Contemporary describes both the décor and special dishes served at this café. The menu lists such traditional options as scampi, fra diavolo and many veal and pasta choices. Try the wild sea bass caramelized in a butter-lemon-wine sauce. Competent, crisply-dressed servers navigate the comfortable, modern dining room. **Features:** full bar, happy hour. **Reservations:** suggested. **Address:** 2011 Rt 70 W 08002 **Location:** I-295 exit 34B, 2.5 mi w; across from Garden State Park. **Parking:** valet and street only. [L] [D] CALL [&M]

IL VILLAGGIO 856/795-1778 [139]

◆◆◆ Italian. Fine Dining. $9-$32 **AAA Inspector Notes:** This bring-your-own-bottle establishment offers a warm, fine dining ambience with coordinating Italian artwork and an attractive brick fireplace. The menu does not disappoint with imported Italian meats and cheeses to provide all of the traditional favorites. Banquet facilities are available for any special occasion. **Features:** patio dining. **Reservations:** suggested, weekends. **Address:** 211 Haddonfield-Berlin Rd 08034 **Location:** I-295 exit 28, 1 mi n. [🚇] Haddonfield, 149. [L] [D] CALL [&M] [🚇]

NORMA'S 856/795-1373 [137]

◆◆◆ Eastern Mediterranean. Casual Dining. $6-$27 **AAA Inspector Notes:** This spot is two restaurants in one. Lunch offers a casual taste of Lebanon, with familiar salads and starters, shawarma, chicken kebabs, lamb shish and kafta kebabs, gyros and falafel. Dinner is Moroccan, with couscous specialties, kebabs, tagine and other favorites served in a bejeweled tented room of low tables with cushioned seating, traditional music and customs. Dinner could be an event. **Address:** 145 Barclay Farms Shopping Center (SR 70) 08002 **Location:** 0.4 mi w of jct SR 70 and I-295; 3.2 mi w of jct SR 70 and 73. [L] [D]

OH YOKO! SUSHI 856/857-9050 [138]

◆◆◆ Japanese. Casual Dining. $9-$20 **AAA Inspector Notes:** Beatles music and posters, friendly staff and a large but pricey special maki menu can all be found here in this warm, cozy environment. Dressings, green tea ice cream and soy sauce are made in house. Very fresh fish and ingredients are utilized in the dishes offered. **Address:** 1428 Marlton Pike E 08034 **Location:** I-295 exit 34B, just w on SR 70; in Pine Tree Shopping Center. [L] [D]

SEASONS 52 FRESH GRILL 856/665-1052 [133]

◆◆◆◆ New American. Fine Dining. $10-$30 **AAA Inspector Notes:** Embracing a distinctive concept, this restaurant focuses entirely on calorie-conscious dishes that reflect the current season. The menu changes 52 times a year. Modern and tasty dishes include several types of flatbreads, salmon, chicken and an unusual offering of novelty dessert shots. Many by-the-glass options are among selections on the wine list. **Features:** full bar, patio dining, happy hour. **Address:** 2000 Rt 38, Suite 1145 08002 **Location:** I-295 exit 34B, 4 mi w on SR 70 to Cuthbert Blvd to SR 38 E, then 1.2 mi ne; in Cherry Hill Mall. **Parking:** on-site and valet. [L] [D] CALL [&M]

SILVER DINER 856/910-1240

◆◆ American. Family Dining. $7-$17 **AAA Inspector Notes:** The eatery with its chrome and glass plate exterior and the glow of neon, provides the traditional diner setting. Booths with juke boxes, counter service and friendly waitstaff add to the diner experience. The menu is extensive with salads, sandwiches and full meals. The desserts are made fresh and the fountain treats, shakes, floats and malts make for a great ending. Breakfast is available all day. **Address:** 2131 SR 38 E 08002 **Location:** I-295 exit 34B, 4 mi w on SR 70 to Cuthbert Blvd to SR 38 E, then 1.2 mi ne. [B] [L] [D] [LATE] CALL [&M]

SIRI'S THAI FRENCH CUISINE 856/663-6781 [135]

◆◆ Thai. Casual Dining. $9-$29 **AAA Inspector Notes:** Through the storefront window, passersby cannot help but notice the elegant dining room filled with patrons enjoying sophisticated Thai and French cuisine. Asian seasonings are evident in the seafood bouillabaisse spiked with lemongrass, as well as chicken with green curry. French influences can be found in the rack of lamb with Madeira rosemary au jus and the roast duck with berry glaze. Desserts are lovely and typically French. The restaurant implements a bring your own alcohol policy. **Reservations:** suggested. **Address:** 2117 Rt 70 W 08002 **Location:** I-295 exit 34B, 2.8 mi w on SR 70; at Track Town Shopping Center; opposite Garden State Park. [L] [D]

CHESTER (C-3) pop. 1,649, elev. 846'

BAMBOO BROOK OUTDOOR EDUCATION CENTER is 3 mi. s. on US 206, .4 mi. w. on Spring Lake Dr., .1 mi. s. on Bamboo Ln., then .2 mi. e. to 170 Longview Rd. Gardeners, landscape architects and nature lovers will all find something to enjoy on this 100-acre site that was once known as Merchiston Farm. Nature trails meander by the brook and through meadows, where birds, butterflies and other creatures can be discovered. Along with formal gardens and native plants, there are mature trees, including the Japanese Scholar Tree (Sophora japonica) and American hophornbean (Ostrya virginiana).

The delightful water features and white cedar allée, or walkway, add to the experience. **Note:** Pets are not permitted. **Time:** Allow 2 hours minimum. **Hours:** Daily 9 a.m.-dusk. **Cost:** Free. **Phone:** (973) 326-7600. 🏧

Willowwood Arboretum is 3 mi. s. on US 206, .4 mi. w. on Spring Lake Dr., .3 mi. s. on Bamboo Ln., then .2 mi. e. to 300 Longview Rd. The 130-acre of rolling farmland, designed in 1908 by brothers Henry and Robert Tubbs, contains 3,500 native and exotic plants. In addition to virgin forest, one can find oak, maple, willow, magnolia, lilac, cherry, fir, pine and a dawn redwood (Metasequoia) now more than 98 feet tall. Other sights include ferns as well as wildflowers.

Both wild and cultivated plantings can be seen on self-guiding tours; pick up a map with a list of identified trees at the parking lot. **Note:** Dogs and horses are not permitted. **Time:** Allow 2 hours minimum. **Hours:** Daily 8 a.m.-dusk. **Cost:** Free. **Phone:** (908) 234-1815. 🏧

COOPER GRISTMILL is 1 mi. w. of jct. US 206 at 66 Washington Tpke., in Black River Park. The site's original mill was used for grinding flour in the late 1700s; the present structure was built in 1826 by Nathan Cooper. Interpreters in period attire explain the mill's history and the working mill stones that once produced 1,600 pounds of wheat flour and corn meal an hour.

Hours: Guided 30- to 45-minute tours are offered Wed.-Sat. 10-5, Sun. noon-5, July-Aug.; Sat. 10-5, Sun. noon-5, Sept.-Oct.; Sat. 10-5, Apr.-June. Last tour begins 1 hour, 30 minutes before closing. **Cost:** $3; $2 (ages 65+); $1 (ages 4-16). **Phone:** (908) 879-5463.

CINNAMINSON

SLEEP INN   (856)829-0717
🔻🔻🔻
Hotel
$80-$150
Address: 208 Rt 130 N 08077 **Location:** 0.9 mi n of jct SR 73. **Facility:** 52 units. 2 stories, interior corridors. *Bath:* shower only. **Activities:** limited exercise equipment. **Featured Amenity:** full hot breakfast.

WHERE TO EAT

THE JUG HANDLE INN   856/665-9464   (105)
🔻🔻 American. Casual Dining. $7-$20 **AAA Inspector Notes:** Fill up on hearty portions of tasty food, such as fried Buffalo-style wings, at this sports pub—a great place to catch a game with friends over a few brews. **Features:** full bar, happy hour. **Address:** 10118 S Fork Landing Rd 08077 **Location:** 0.9 mi s of jct US 130.
L D LATE

Choose real ratings you can trust from

professional inspectors who've been there

CLARK pop. 14,756
• **Hotels & Restaurants map & index p. 152**

HOLIDAY INN CLARK-NEWARK   (732)574-0100 (96)
🔻🔻🔻🔻 Hotel $109-$209 **Address:** 36 Valley Rd 07066 **Location:** Garden State Pkwy exit 135, just e. **Facility:** 192 units. 6 stories, interior corridors. **Terms:** cancellation fee imposed. **Pool(s):** heated outdoor. **Activities:** exercise room. **Guest Services:** valet and coin laundry, area transportation.

WHERE TO EAT

THAILAND RESTAURANT   732/388-4441 (141)
🔻🔻 Thai. Casual Dining. $9-$20 **AAA Inspector Notes:** The '50s-style chrome streamline resembles a diner more than a popular Thai joint. The interior is equally unexpected, but folks get down to business with the menu, which lists fragrant and well-prepared classics, as well as creative chef's specials that offer additional promise. Children with adventurous palates are welcome. **Address:** 291 Central Ave 07066 **Location:** Garden State Pkwy exit 135, 0.5 mi w.
L D

CLEMENTON (F-2) pop. 5,000, elev. 96'

CLEMENTON PARK & SPLASH WORLD, .7 mi. w. of US 30 on White Horse Ave., is set on the shore of a small lake. The amusement park has rides, carnival games and a children's section; the water park has a variety of waterslides and a wave pool.

Note: Bathing suits are required at the water park; lockers and changing facilities are available. **Hours:** Amusement park Mon.-Thurs. 11-8, Fri.-Sun. 11-9, July-Aug. Water park Mon.-Thurs. 11-8, Fri.-Sun. 11-7, July-Aug. Hours vary May-June and in Sept.; phone ahead. **Cost:** (includes both parks) $39.99; $29.99 (under 48 inches tall, ages 65+ and physically impaired individuals); free (under 36 inches tall). Phone ahead to verify rates. **Parking:** $10. **Phone:** (856) 783-0263.

CLIFTON pop. 84,136
• **Hotels & Restaurants map & index p. 162**

CHENGDU 46   973/777-8855 (46)
🔻🔻🔻 Chinese. Casual Dining. $12-$42 **AAA Inspector Notes:** Diners may be familiar with most of the dishes here, but the quality of the food is uncommon. The menu centers on classic Szechuan food such as orange beef or kung pao chicken. The excellent Peking duck is expertly prepared and elaborately presented tableside by the formal service staff who also do showy flambé desserts. **Features:** full bar. **Reservations:** suggested. **Address:** 1105 US Hwy 46 07013 **Location:** Garden State Pkwy exit 154 southbound, 1 mi e; exit 153B northbound to first U-turn, then e.
L D CALL ⛽M

TICK TOCK DINER   973/777-0511 (47)
🔻🔻 American. Casual Dining. $9-$20 **AAA Inspector Notes:** *Classic.* Long considered the king of New Jersey diners—no small status in this diner-rich state—this 1949 eatery was a pioneer in diner design. Although fully renovated with a modern chrome facade, the original rooftop clock, with the words "eat heavy" aglow in neon, remains unchanged. It still holds sway over patrons who stop in at all hours for their fix of classic diner grub, including hefty sandwiches, great burgers, lumberjack breakfasts and sinfully rich desserts. **Features:** full bar. **Address:** 281 Allwood Rd 07012 **Location:** Garden State Pkwy exit 153A northbound; exit 153 southbound, 1.7 mi e on SR 3 W, then just w of Passaic Ave.
B L D (24) CALL ⛽M

CLINTON (C-2) pop. 2,719, elev. 160'

Clinton was a prominent mill town and stage-coach stop in the mid-19th century. The historic Red Mill and Stone Mill, which stand on opposite banks of the Raritan River, are picturesque reminders of its past. Nearby Spruce Run and Round Valley recreation areas *(see Recreation Areas Chart)* offer a variety of recreational opportunities.

HUNTERDON ART MUSEUM is at 7 Lower Center St. Housed in the restored 1836 Stone Mill, the museum exhibits works by established and emerging contemporary artists, with a strong focus on works on paper. Educational programs and guided tours also are offered. **Time:** Allow 1 hour, 30 minutes minimum. **Hours:** Tues.-Sun. 11-5. Closed major holidays. **Cost:** $5. **Phone:** (908) 735-8415.

RED MILL MUSEUM VILLAGE is at 56 Main St. Built around 1810, the mill was used for grist milling, plaster and talc grinding and graphite processing. Displays from a 40,000-item collection depict early 19th-century life, methods of agriculture and local industries. Other buildings on the 10-acre site include a working blacksmith shop, a quarry office, a general store, a log cabin and a one-room schoolhouse.

Time: Allow 1 hour minimum. **Hours:** Tues.-Sat. 10-4, Sun. noon-5, Apr.-Sept.; Tues.-Sat. noon-4, Sun. noon-4, Nov.-Dec.; Sat.-Sun. noon-4, Jan.-Mar. Phone ahead for Haunted Mill hours in Oct. Closed major holidays. **Cost:** Admission Apr.-Sept. $8; $6 (ages 65+); $5 (ages 6-12); $5 rest of year. Admission varies during special events. **Phone:** (908) 735-4101.

HOLIDAY INN-CLINTON   (908)735-5111

WWW **Hotel** $99-$199 **Address:** 111 Rt 173 08809 **Location:** I-78 exit 15, just nw. **Facility:** 142 units. 5 stories, interior corridors. **Terms:** cancellation fee imposed. **Dining:** nightclub. **Pool(s):** heated indoor. **Activities:** exercise room. **Guest Services:** valet laundry.

[icons]

WHERE TO EAT

THE CLINTON HOUSE   908/730-9300

WWW W Traditional American. Casual Dining. $11-$45 **AAA Inspector Notes:** *Historic.* This historic restaurant offers the cozy ambience of a classic Colonial tavern and has pleasant, warm service to match. The menu here features many traditional dishes such as beef Wellington, crab cakes, broiled flounder and a selection of steaks and prime rib. **Features:** full bar. **Address:** 2 W Main St 08809 **Location:** I-78 exit 15, 0.3 mi on SR 173 E. [L] [D] CALL [&M]

COUNTRY GRIDDLE RESTAURANT & LOUNGE   908/713-1200

WWW American. Family Dining. $8-$17 **AAA Inspector Notes:** Locals flock here for fresh, oversized traditional favorites (chicken and dumplings, meatloaf and mashed potatoes and apple pie) at more than fair prices, but breakfast may be the best choice. The attached cocktail lounge hosts weekly quiz nights and karaoke. **Features:** full bar. **Address:** 190 Center St 08809 **Location:** I-78 E exit 16, just ne; I-78 W exit 17, just w. [B] [L] [D]

COLLINGSWOOD pop. 13,926

THE POP SHOP   856/869-0111 [130]

WWW WW Comfort Food. Casual Dining. $5-$11 **AAA Inspector Notes:** Sample creative takes on classic grilled cheese at this retro-style neighborhood soda shop which stakes a claim to fame in that celebrity chef Bobby Flay once challenged the owners on his show. Locals and tourists frequent this place for its warm service, upbeat candy-colored dining area and family-friendly environment. Check the website for fun weekly events such as team trivia. **Address:** 729 Haddon Ave 08108 **Location:** 1.2 mi e of jct US 30; on the main street. [R] Collingswood, 147. **Parking:** street only.

[B] [L] [D] [icon]

COOKSTOWN

QUALITY INN MCGUIRE AFB   (609)723-6500

WWW WW **Hotel** $80-$159 **Address:** 21 Wrightstown/Cookstown Rd 08511 **Location:** 0.3 mi n of main entrance to McGuire Air Force Base. **Facility:** 102 units. 2 stories, interior corridors. **Amenities:** safes. **Pool(s):** outdoor. **Activities:** exercise room. **Guest Services:** coin laundry.

[icons] / SOME UNITS [icon]

WHERE TO EAT

LOCAL SMOKE BBQ   609/286-2298

WW Barbecue. Quick Serve. $7-$22 **AAA Inspector Notes:** The menu here features all the great 'cue you would find at a BBQ competition because that's where the owners started out and honed their craft. There is great variety including St. Louis-style ribs, pulled pork, smoked chicken and the truly outstanding Texas slow-smoked beef brisket that is as tender as a love song. Sample a few items and then give out your own awards. **Address:** 19 Wrightstown Cookstown Rd 08511 **Location:** 0.3 mi n of main entrance to McGuire Air Force Base. [L] [D] CALL [&M]

CRANBURY (D-3) pop. 2,181, elev. 103'
• Restaurants p. 106

THE PLAINSBORO PRESERVE is 3 mi. w. on Dey Rd., then .8 mi. n. to 80 Scotts Corner Rd. Visitors can view various plants, some of which are rare or endangered, and more than 150 species of birds. More than 5 miles of trails traverse beech woods, wet meadows and the McCormack Lake shoreline. The Education Center has interactive displays, an observation deck and a resource library.

Time: Allow 2 hours minimum. **Hours:** Trails daily 7-7. Education Center Tues.-Sat. 9-5, Sun. noon-5, mid-Mar. to mid-Nov.; Tues.-Sat. 9-4, Sun. noon-4, rest of year. Closed major holidays. Phone ahead to confirm schedule. **Cost:** Donations. **Phone:** (609) 897-9400.

COURTYARD BY MARRIOTT CRANBURY/SOUTH BRUNSWICK   (609)655-9950

WWW
Hotel
$125-$206

COURTYARD Marriott

AAA Benefit: Members save 5% or more!

Address: 420 Forsgate Dr 08512 **Location:** New Jersey Tpke exit 8A to SR 32 W toward town, just s. **Facility:** 144 units. 4 stories, interior corridors. **Pool(s):** heated indoor. **Activities:** hot tub, exercise room. **Guest Services:** valet and coin laundry, boarding pass kiosk.

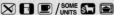

RESIDENCE INN BY MARRIOTT/CRANBURY-SOUTH BRUNSWICK
(609)395-9447

Extended Stay Hotel
$111-$229

AAA Benefit:
Members save 5% or more!

Address: 2662 US 130 08512 **Location:** New Jersey Tpke exit 8A to SR 32 W toward town, 2 mi s on River Rd. **Facility:** 108 units, some two bedrooms, efficiencies and kitchens. 3 stories, interior corridors. **Terms:** check-in 4 pm. **Pool(s):** heated indoor. **Activities:** hot tub, exercise room. **Guest Services:** valet and coin laundry. **Featured Amenity:** breakfast buffet.

STAYBRIDGE SUITES/CRANBURY (609)409-7181

Extended Stay Hotel $130-$150 **Address:** 1272 S River Rd 08512 **Location:** New Jersey Tpke exit 8A to SR 32 W toward town, 2 mi s. **Facility:** 87 efficiencies, some two bedrooms. 3 stories, interior corridors. **Pool(s):** outdoor. **Activities:** exercise room. **Guest Services:** valet and coin laundry.

WHERE TO EAT

ZINNA'S BISTRO 609/860-9600

Italian. Casual Dining. $8-$30 **AAA Inspector Notes:** This casual eatery others a wide-ranging menu with something for everyone. The setting is friendly and comfortable, with a nice patio for outdoor dining and the location is very close to local hotels. **Features:** patio dining. **Address:** 1275 S River Rd 08512 **Location:** New Jersey Tpke exit 8A to SR 32 W, 2 mi w.

DENVILLE
• Hotels & Restaurants map & index p. 152

HAMPTON INN DENVILLE (PARSIPPANY AREA) (973)664-1050

Hotel $109-$149 **Address:** 350 Morris Ave 07834 **Location:** I-80 exit 37 westbound, just s on Green Pond Rd, then just e; exit eastbound, just n on Hibernia Ave, then just e. **Facility:** 119 units. 5 stories, interior corridors. **Terms:** 1-7 night minimum stay, cancellation fee imposed. **Pool(s):** heated indoor. **Activities:** hot tub, exercise room. **Guest Services:** valet laundry.

AAA Benefit:
Members save 5% or more!

WHERE TO EAT

CHARLIE BROWN'S STEAKHOUSE 973/586-3095

Steak. Casual Dining. $9-$30 **AAA Inspector Notes:** This budget-friendly steakhouse, famous for its prime rib, offers top quality fare without hurting your pocketbook. The young ones will not be disappointed with the kids' menu, and just might even try something green from the salad bar. Adults will love the quality steaks, chicken and rib dishes. The express lunches are great for those saddled with time constraints. **Features:** full bar, happy hour. **Address:** 167 W Main St 07834 **Location:** Corner of Franklin Rd and US 46.

THAI CHEF RESTAURANT 973/983-0800 ⑲

Thai. Casual Dining. $10-$23 **AAA Inspector Notes:** Lazy bamboo ceiling fans set the tone for an unhurried and delightful dining experience. In addition to the usual Thai favorites, the kitchen is adept at preparing inventive dishes with a Thai flair, including tamarind duck, spicy calamari and snapper with chili, basil and lime. **Address:** 28A Diamond Spring Rd 07834 **Location:** Just w of jct Broadway; center. **Parking:** street only.

DEPTFORD

FAIRFIELD INN BY MARRIOTT PHILADELPHIA/DEPTFORD (856)686-9050

Hotel $97-$160 **Address:** 1160 Hurffville Rd 08096 **Location:** SR 42 exit Deptford, Runnemede, Woodbury to CR 544, just e to SR 41 S. **Facility:** 102 units. 4 stories, interior corridors. **Amenities:** safes. **Pool(s):** heated indoor. **Activities:** exercise room. **Guest Services:** valet laundry.

AAA Benefit:
Members save 5% or more!

RESIDENCE INN BY MARRIOTT DEPTFORD (856)686-9188

Extended Stay Hotel $125-$229 **Address:** 1154 Hurffville Rd 08096 **Location:** SR 42 exit Deptford, Runnemede, Woodbury to CR 544, just e to SR 41 S. **Facility:** 102 efficiencies, some two bedrooms. 3 stories, interior corridors. **Pool(s):** heated indoor. **Activities:** exercise room. **Guest Services:** valet and coin laundry.

AAA Benefit:
Members save 5% or more!

DOVER pop. 18,157
• Hotels & Restaurants map & index p. 152

HOMEWOOD SUITES BY HILTON DOVER-ROCKAWAY (973)989-8899 ㊳

Extended Stay Hotel $135-$175 **Address:** 2 Commerce Center Dr 07801 **Location:** 1.2 mi n on Mt Hope Ave, just w on Mt Pleasant Ave. Across from Rockaway Townsquare Mall. **Facility:** 108 efficiencies, some two bedrooms. 4 stories, interior corridors. **Terms:** 1-7 night minimum stay, cancellation fee imposed. **Pool(s):** heated indoor. **Activities:** exercise room. **Guest Services:** valet and coin laundry.

AAA Benefit:
Members save 5% or more!

EASTAMPTON

CHARLEY'S OTHER BROTHER 609/261-1555

American. Casual Dining. $9-$38 **AAA Inspector Notes:** Families often drop in to this casual spot where there is something for everyone. Nosh on such daily specials as stuffed flounder Oscar, fried oysters, buffalo shrimp and stuffed or Milanese pork chops—pork chop preparation and homemade soup choice changes every day. Youngsters can order from the array of kid food on the children's menu while adults narrow down their selection of steak, prime rib, crab cakes or seafood of all kinds. **Features:** full bar, happy hour. **Address:** 1383 Monmouth Rd 08060 **Location:** Jct CR 537 and Jacksonville Rd.

AAA Vacations® packages ...
unforgettable experiences and unrivaled value

EAST BRUNSWICK pop. 47,512

BEST WESTERN EAST BRUNSWICK INN   (732)238-4900

Hotel
$90-$300

 AAA Benefit: Members save up to 20%!

Address: 764 SR 18 N 08816 **Location:** Between Rue Ln and Racetrack Rd; New Jersey Tpke exit 9 (SR 18 N), 4 mi s. Across from a shopping mall. **Facility:** 105 units. 2 stories (no elevator), interior/exterior corridors. **Activities:** exercise room.

[SAVE] [↑↓] CALL [&M] [📶] [🖥] [🖨] [📺] [🖥] / SOME UNITS [🐕]

COMFORT SUITES EAST BRUNSWICK   (732)967-1505

Hotel
$90-$189

Address: 555 Old Bridge Tpke 08816 **Location:** New Jersey Tpke exit 9 (SR 18), 1 mi s to Edgeboro Rd exit, then just s. **Facility:** 66 units, some efficiencies. 3 stories, interior corridors. **Activities:** exercise room. **Guest Services:** coin laundry. **Featured Amenity:** breakfast buffet.

[SAVE] CALL [&M] [BIZ] [HS] [📶] [✕] [🖨] [🖥] [🖨]

HILTON EAST BRUNSWICK HOTEL & EXECUTIVE MEETING CENTER   (732)828-2000

Hotel $99-$249 **Address:** 3 Tower Center Blvd 08816 **Location:** New Jersey Tpke exit 9 (SR 18 N), first right on service road. **Facility:** 405 units. 15 stories, interior corridors. **Parking:** on-site (fee). **Terms:** check-in 4 pm, 1-7 night minimum stay, cancellation fee imposed. **Amenities:** Some: safes. **Dining:** 2 restaurants. **Pool(s):** heated indoor. **Activities:** sauna, hot tub, exercise room. **Guest Services:** valet laundry, area transportation.

AAA Benefit: Members save 5% or more!

[↑↓] [🛎] [Y] CALL [&M] [🏊] [BIZ] [📶] [✕] [🖥] / SOME UNITS [🖨]

MOTEL 6 EAST BRUNSWICK #1083   732/390-4545

Motel. Rates not provided. **Address:** 244 SR 18 N 08816 **Location:** New Jersey Tpke exit 9 (SR 18), 1 mi s, U-turn at Edgeboro Rd, then just e. **Facility:** 111 units. 2 stories (no elevator), interior/exterior corridors. **Guest Services:** coin laundry.

CALL [&M] [🐕] / SOME UNITS [🐕] [🖨] [🖥]

STUDIO 6 EAST BRUNSWICK #6020   732/238-3330

Extended Stay Hotel. Rates not provided. **Address:** 246 Rt 18 at Edgeboro Rd 08816 **Location:** New Jersey Tpke exit 9 (SR 18), 1 mi s, U-turn at Edgeboro Rd, then just e. **Facility:** 124 efficiencies. 2 stories, interior corridors. **Guest Services:** coin laundry.

CALL [&M] [🐕] [🖨] [🖥] [🖥] / SOME UNITS [🐕]

EAST HANOVER
• Hotels & Restaurants map & index p. 152

THE GODFATHER SEAFOOD BAR & GRILL   973/887-4830

Seafood. Casual Dining. $8-$24 **AAA Inspector Notes:** This long time local favorite is a great casual spot for all manner of fresh seafood from live lobster to crab cakes and oysters baked in the brick oven. The menu also features some Italian specialties, small pizzas and at lunch a good selection of panini. The atmosphere is relaxed and friendly with a popular bar and lots of TVs. Right next door they also operate a classic brick-oven pizzeria that serves pizza you cannot refuse. **Features:** full bar, happy hour. **Address:** 200 Rt 10 W 07936 **Location:** 2.1 mi w of jct CR 609 (Eisenhower Pkwy).

[L] [D] CALL [&M]

MR. CHU   973/887-7555

Chinese. Casual Dining. $6-$19 **AAA Inspector Notes:** Light green walls, flowing floor-to-ceiling curtains and a distinctive Asian serenity transport diners from the busy highway just outside the doors to a relaxed and civilized setting, where tea service and attentive staff take care of harried souls. Scallion pancakes offer nothing but unabashed comfort, and the wonton soup warms to the core. A fine moo shu will not disappoint, nor will the orange-flavored beef or any of the noodle dishes. **Address:** 44 SR 10 W 07936 **Location:** I-287 exit 39, 2.5 mi e. [L] [D]

EAST RUTHERFORD (G-6) pop. 8,913, elev. 60'
• Restaurants p. 108
• Hotels & Restaurants map & index p. 162

The Meadowlands Sports Complex, at the intersection of New Jersey Turnpike exit 16W and SR 3, includes MetLife Stadium, home of both the New York Giants and the New York Jets of the National Football League. Meadowlands Racetrack offers both thoroughbred and harness racing.

Guided tours of MetLife Stadium are offered by appointment; phone (201) 559-1500 for tour information, (201) 559-1515 for general information, (201) 559-1300 for the arena/stadium box office or (201) 843-2446 for the racetrack.

Note: Policies concerning admittance of children to pari-mutuel betting facilities vary. Phone for information.

Meadowlands Regional Chamber of Commerce: 201 SR 17N, 2nd Floor, Rutherford, NJ 07070. **Phone:** (201) 939-0707 or (877) 652-8287.

FAIRFIELD INN BY MARRIOTT MEADOWLANDS   (201)507-5222 [64]

Hotel $132-$217 **Address:** 850 Paterson Plank Rd 07073 **Location:** New Jersey Tpke E exit 16W (from western spur) to SR 3 W to SR 17 N, 1.5 mi n to Paterson Plank Rd (SR 120), then just e; I-80 exit 64B, 3 mi s on SR 17 to Paterson Plank Rd, then just e. **Facility:** 141 units. 5 stories, interior corridors. **Activities:** exercise room. **Guest Services:** valet and coin laundry, boarding pass kiosk.

AAA Benefit: Members save 5% or more!

CALL [&M] [HS] [📶] [✕] [Y] [🖨] [🖥] [🖥]

HOMEWOOD SUITES BY HILTON-EAST RUTHERFORD/ MEADOWLANDS   (201)460-9030 [66]

Extended Stay Hotel $189-$269 **Address:** 125 Rt 17 S 07073 **Location:** 1 mi n of Meadowlands Sport Complex. **Facility:** 126 efficiencies, some two bedrooms. 7 stories, interior corridors. **Terms:** 1-7 night minimum stay, cancellation fee imposed. **Pool(s):** heated indoor. **Activities:** sauna, exercise room. **Guest Services:** valet and coin laundry, area transportation.

AAA Benefit: Members save 5% or more!

[↑↓] CALL [&M] [🏊] [BIZ] [HS] [📶] [Y] [🖨] [🖥] [🖥]

(See map & index p. 162.)

RESIDENCE INN BY MARRIOTT EAST RUTHERFORD MEADOWLANDS
(201)939-0020 **65**

Extended Stay Hotel $195-$321 **Address:** 10 Murray Hill Pkwy 07073 **Location:** New Jersey Tpke exit 16W (from western spur) to SR 3 W to SR 17 N, 1.5 mi n to Paterson Plank Rd (SR 120), then just e. **Facility:** 133 units, some two bedrooms, efficiencies and kitchens. 6 stories, interior corridors. **Pool(s):** heated indoor. **Activities:** hot tub, exercise room. **Guest Services:** valet and coin laundry.

AAA Benefit: Members save 5% or more!

WHERE TO EAT

PARK & ORCHARD
201/939-9292 **56**

American. Casual Dining. $9-$36 **AAA Inspector Notes:** You do not have to go to an upscale restaurant to find farm fresh food prepared in a health conscious manner. This popular spot serves food with no bleached flour, no refined sugar and no preservatives, and the menu is filled with fresh produce and organic items. Dishes include such items as grilled or blackened fish, pirogies, chile noncarne, chicken Parmesan and crayfish pasta. Vegetarians will find several good options. The food, like the dining room, is very straightforward in presentation. **Features:** full bar. **Reservations:** suggested. **Address:** 240 Hackensack St 07073 **Location:** SR 3 W exit 16W (Park Ave and Orchard St). L D

VESTA WOOD FIRED PIZZA & BAR
201/939-6012 **55**

Italian. Casual Dining. $12-$23 **AAA Inspector Notes:** Of course the pizza here is good—crisp from the wood-fired oven and topped with fresh premium fresh ingredients like the excellent prosciutto and arugula pie with cherry tomatoes and fresh homemade mozzarella. Entrées include classics like veal saltimbocca, flounder oreganata or hearty homemade lasagna. The stylish restaurant is definitely a few steps up from the typical Jersey pizza place, and the warm friendly service makes this place a great pick. **Features:** full bar. **Address:** 64 Hoboken Rd 07073 **Location:** Just w of jct SR 17 and 120 (Paterson Plank Rd); at Enoch St. L D CALL

EAST WINDSOR

DAYS INN EAST WINDSOR
(609)448-3200

Hotel $69-$149 **Address:** 460 Rt 33 E 08520 **Location:** New Jersey Tpke exit 8, just e. **Facility:** 100 units. 3 stories, interior corridors. **Amenities:** video games. **Pool(s):** outdoor. **Guest Services:** valet and coin laundry.

HAMPTON INN EAST WINDSOR
(609)426-1600

Hotel $129-$259 **Address:** 384 Monmouth St 08520 **Location:** New Jersey Tpke exit 8, just e, just n via Woodside Ave, then just w. **Facility:** 80 units. 3 stories, interior corridors. **Terms:** 1-7 night minimum stay, cancellation fee imposed. **Pool(s):** heated indoor. **Activities:** exercise room. **Guest Services:** valet and coin laundry.

AAA Benefit: Members save 5% or more!

HOLIDAY INN OF EAST WINDSOR
(609)448-7000

Hotel $99-$174

Address: 399 Monmouth St 08520 **Location:** New Jersey Tpke exit 8, just e, then just n via Woodside Ave. **Facility:** 201 units. 4 stories, interior corridors. **Terms:** cancellation fee imposed. **Amenities:** video games, safes. **Pool(s):** outdoor. **Activities:** sauna, game room, exercise room. **Guest Services:** valet and coin laundry.

QUALITY INN EAST WINDSOR
(609)448-7399

Hotel $70-$199

Address: 351 Franklin St 08520 **Location:** New Jersey Tpke exit 8, just w. **Facility:** 54 units. 2 stories (no elevator), interior/exterior corridors. **Amenities:** safes. **Activities:** limited exercise equipment. **Guest Services:** valet and coin laundry.

EATONTOWN pop. 12,709

SHERATON EATONTOWN HOTEL
(732)542-6500

Hotel $99-$199

Sheraton HOTELS & RESORTS

AAA Benefit: Members save up to 15%, plus Starwood Preferred Guest® benefits!

Address: 6 Industrial Way E 07724 **Location:** Garden State Pkwy exit 105, 0.7 mi e on SR 36, then 1 mi s on SR 35. **Facility:** 208 units, interior corridors. **Terms:** check-in 4 pm. **Pool(s):** outdoor, heated indoor. **Activities:** hot tub, exercise room. **Guest Services:** valet and coin laundry, area transportation.

STAYBRIDGE SUITES HOTEL EATONTOWN-TINTON FALLS
(732)380-9300

Extended Stay Hotel $89-$259

Address: 4 Industrial Way E 07724 **Location:** Garden State Pkwy exit 105, 0.7 mi e on SR 36, then 1 mi s on SR 35. **Facility:** 131 efficiencies, some two bedrooms. 5 stories, interior corridors. **Terms:** cancellation fee imposed. **Pool(s):** heated outdoor. **Activities:** exercise room. **Guest Services:** valet and coin laundry. **Featured Amenity:** breakfast buffet.

WHERE TO EAT

BOBBY'S BURGER PALACE   732/544-0200

Burgers. Quick Serve. $6-$9 **AAA Inspector Notes:** In an effort to top his already skyrocketing culinary career, Bobby Flay naturally turned to burgers. True to form, Flay does not cook up the run-of-the-mill patty melt; these burgers are positively top shelf. The L.A. burger makes a name for itself with avocado relish and watercress. Of course, fancy and creamy milk shakes and a side of fries pair nicely with the whole bunch. **Address:** 180 SR 35 S 07724 **Location:** Just s of jct SR 36; at Monmouth Mall. L D CALL M

EDGEWATER pop. 11,513
• Hotels & Restaurants map & index p. 162

HOMEWOOD SUITES BY HILTON/EDGEWATER
(201)941-4700 57

Extended Stay Hotel
$214-$264 **Address:** 10 The Promenade 07020 **Location:** Jct Gorge and River rds. **Facility:** 122 efficiencies. 8 stories, interior corridors. **Terms:** 1-7 night minimum stay, cancellation fee imposed. **Activities:** sauna, exercise room. **Guest Services:** valet and coin laundry, area transportation.

AAA Benefit:
Members save 5% or more!

M CALL M BIZ HS

WHERE TO EAT

THE CRAB HOUSE   201/840-9311 51

Seafood. Casual Dining. $10-$41 **AAA Inspector Notes:** Seafood lovers can get crabby in a good way at this great spot that offers lively yet laid-back dining. The savory crustaceans are prepared in nearly every way imaginable, including the trademark South Florida-style blue crabs with garlic and butter. Daily fresh catches also are well-prepared hits. **Features:** full bar, happy hour. **Reservations:** suggested, weekends. **Address:** 541 River Rd 07020 **Location:** I-95 exit 73 (Lemoine Ave), service ramp to end, s on Hudson Terr to Main St (which becomes River Rd), then 3 mi s; behind Edgewater Commons Shopping Center. SAVE L D CALL M

FLEMING'S PRIME STEAKHOUSE & WINE BAR
201/313-9463 52

Steak. Fine Dining. $32-$50 **AAA Inspector Notes:** The warm, clubby atmosphere is the ideal setting for perfectly grilled steaks and seafood. Side dishes come in hearty portions, and salads are fresh and crisp. More than 100 wine selections are available. **Features:** full bar. **Reservations:** suggested. **Address:** 90 The Promenade 07020 **Location:** Jct Gorge and River rds; in The Promenade Shopping Center. D CALL M

THE RIVER PALM TERRACE   201/224-2013 50

Steak. Fine Dining. $10-$47 **AAA Inspector Notes:** This outpost of the popular chain has a noticeably different feel from all the others—Porsches and Jaguars line the parking lot. Inside, well-dressed suit-types are making deals, trades and cell phone calls. All bets are off when the steaks arrive: fine, dry-aged, rib-eyes, porterhouses and New York strips. Nothing can interfere with the pure enjoyment that comes from perfectly marbled meats, unless it's the hearty home-fried potatoes or the sumptuous creamed spinach. **Features:** full bar. **Reservations:** suggested. **Address:** 1416 River Rd 07020 **Location:** I-95 exit 73 (Lemoine Ave), 1 mi s of George Washington Bridge, service ramp to end, s on Hudson Terr to Main St (which becomes River Rd). **Parking:** valet only.

L D CALL M

Get AAA/CAA travel

information in the digital and

printed formats you prefer

EDISON pop. 99,967
• Restaurants p. 110
• Hotels & Restaurants map & index p. 152

COMFORT INN EDISON   (732)287-0171 143

Hotel
$69-$115

Address: 831 US 1 S 08817 **Location:** 1.3 mi s of I-287. **Facility:** 99 units. 3 stories, interior corridors. **Activities:** limited exercise equipment. **Featured Amenity: full hot breakfast.**

SOME UNITS

COURTYARD BY MARRIOTT EDISON/WOODBRIDGE
(732)738-1991 138

Hotel $132-$217 **Address:** 3105 Woodbridge Ave 08837 **Location:** New Jersey Tpke exit 10, 0.5 mi se on CR 514, then just e. **Facility:** 146 units. 4 stories, interior corridors. **Pool(s):** heated indoor. **Activities:** hot tub, exercise room. **Guest Services:** valet and coin laundry.

AAA Benefit:
Members save 5% or more!

CALL M BIZ / SOME UNITS

CROWNE PLAZA EDISON   732/287-3500 142

Hotel. Rates not provided. **Address:** 2055 Lincoln Hwy (SR 27) 08817 **Location:** I-287 exit 2B (SR 27 S) northbound, 1 mi s; exit 3 southbound, 0.5 mi w, then 1 mi s on Talmadge Rd. **Facility:** 169 units. 5 stories, interior corridors. **Amenities:** safes. **Activities:** exercise room. **Guest Services:** valet laundry, area transportation.

CALL M BIZ / SOME UNITS

FAIRFIELD INN & SUITES BY MARRIOTT EDISON SOUTH PLAINFIELD   (732)650-0011 137

Hotel
$104-$171

FAIRFIELD INN & SUITES Marriott

AAA Benefit:
Members save 5% or more!

Address: 875 New Durham Rd 08817 **Location:** I-287 exit 2A northbound, 0.3 mi w via Bridge St, then left; exit 3 southbound, just w. **Facility:** 105 units. 3 stories, interior corridors. **Pool(s):** heated indoor. **Activities:** hot tub, exercise room. **Guest Services:** valet and coin laundry. **Featured Amenity: full hot breakfast.**

SAVE CALL M BIZ HS

HILTON GARDEN INN EDISON/RARITAN CENTER
(732)225-0900 140

Hotel
$89-$199

Hilton Garden Inn

AAA Benefit:
Members save 5% or more!

Address: 50 Raritan Center Pkwy 08837 **Location:** I-287 exit CR 514 to King Georges Post Rd. **Facility:** 132 units. 5 stories, interior corridors. **Terms:** 1-7 night minimum stay, cancellation fee imposed. **Pool(s):** heated indoor. **Activities:** hot tub, exercise room. **Guest Services:** valet and coin laundry, area transportation.

SAVE CALL M BIZ

HS

(See map & index p. 152.)

QUALITY INN EDISON   (732)548-7000 **139**

▼▼ **Hotel** $80-$95 **Address:** 21 Cortlandt St 08837 **Location:** I-287 exit 1B, just s to Prince St. **Facility:** 108 units. 2 stories, interior corridors. **Activities:** limited exercise equipment. **Guest Services:** valet and coin laundry.

RED ROOF INN EDISON   732/248-9300 **136**

▼ **Motel.** Rates not provided. **Address:** 860 New Durham Rd 08817 **Location:** I-287 exit 2A northbound, 0.3 mi w via Bridge St, then left; exit 3 southbound, just w. **Facility:** 132 units. 2 stories (no elevator), exterior corridors. **Amenities:** safes.

SHERATON EDISON HOTEL RARITAN CENTER
                                      (732)225-8300 **141**

▼▼▼
Hotel
$149-$299

(Ⓢ) **Sheraton** HOTELS & RESORTS

AAA Benefit: Members save up to 15%, plus Starwood Preferred Guest® benefits!

Address: 125 Raritan Center Pkwy 08837 **Location:** New Jersey Tpke exit 10, 0.5 mi se on CR 514, keep right after tolls. **Facility:** 276 units. 12 stories, interior corridors. **Terms:** cancellation fee imposed. **Pool(s):** heated indoor. **Activities:** sauna, hot tub, exercise room. **Guest Services:** valet laundry, boarding pass kiosk, rental car service, area transportation.

WHERE TO EAT

AKBAR   732/632-8822 **166**

▼▼ Indian. Fine Dining. $8-$20 **AAA Inspector Notes:** This restaurant borrows its name from the greatest of the grand Moghul emperors who ruled India in the sixteenth century. He was famous for the splendor of his table, and here those splendors are of the Northern Indian variety where tandoori (clay oven cooking) reigns supreme. The pleasant and attractive dining room, with illuminated stained glass, a trickling fountain and fresh flowers, together with polished service, make for a royal dining experience. **Features:** full bar. **Address:** 21 Cortlandt St 08837 **Location:** I-287 exit 1B, just s to Prince St; next to Quality Inn Edison. L D

CHARLIE BROWN'S STEAKHOUSE   732/494-6135

▼▼ Steak. Casual Dining. $9-$30 **AAA Inspector Notes:** This budget-friendly steakhouse, famous for its prime rib, offers top quality fare without hurting your pocketbook. The young ones will not be disappointed with the kids' menu, and just might even try something green from the salad bar. Adults will love the quality steaks, chicken and rib dishes. The express lunches are great for those saddled with time constraints. **Features:** full bar, happy hour. **Address:** 222 Plainfield Rd 08820 **Location:** Jct Park Ave. L D

EDISON DINER   732/985-3335

▼▼ American. Casual Dining. $6-$25 **AAA Inspector Notes:** After choosing a meal from the large and varied menu that has just about anything diners can think of, take a look at the enormous case of desserts made in house. The menu offers breakfast all day, sandwiches, pastas, familiar blue plate dinners, Greek items and even some Mexican-style dishes. **Address:** 101 US 1 S 08817 **Location:** Jct I-287, 3.3 mi s; jct SR 18, 1 mi n. B L D 24

MING PAN ASIAN CUISINE   732/549-5051 **164**

▼▼ Asian. Casual Dining. $15-$24 **AAA Inspector Notes:** The restaurant offers patrons a unique blend of Thai, Chinese and Indian dishes with entrées of lamb, chicken and seafood. Vegetarians will especially appreciate the creative menu offerings. **Reservations:** suggested. **Address:** 1655-195 Oak Tree Rd 08820 **Location:** Garden State Pkwy exit 151B, 1.2 mi n. L D

MOGHUL FINE INDIAN CUISINE   732/549-5050 **163**

▼▼▼ Indian. Casual Dining. $10-$25 **AAA Inspector Notes:** Though it seems out of the way, people wait outside before the doors open for this lunch buffet and crowds steadily arrive, many drawn from the local Indian community for fragrant and authentic flavors which are cooked into varied dishes, many of which are new to lovers of Indian cuisine. Beautifully garnished dishes of brightly colored fresh food exude tantalizing aromas. Copper lanterns dress up the very presentable, yet casual, dining room. **Reservations:** suggested. **Address:** 1655-195 Oak Tree Rd 08820 **Location:** Garden State Pkwy exit 131B, 1.2 mi n. L D

PENANG   732/287-3038 **167**

▼▼ Asian. Casual Dining. $9-$23 **AAA Inspector Notes:** This attractive modern dining room fills up quickly at lunchtime with guests ordering from the large menu of Thai, Malaysian and Chinese dishes. Service is quick and efficient. Try starting with one of the excellent noodle soups or roti canai and then move on to the Rendang curry or the Chiang Mai jumbo shrimp. **Address:** 505 Old Post Rd 08817 **Location:** Garden State Pkwy exit 130, 3.9 mi s on SR 1, then just w; 1.1 mi s of jct SR 1 and US 287. L D

SHEZAN RESTAURANT   732/548-6111 **165**

▼▼ Indian. Casual Dining. $9-$16 **AAA Inspector Notes:** Tandoor dishes prepared in the clay oven and fresh ground spices flavor the menu at this colorful restaurant. The weekend brunch buffet is a great way to sample many of the exotic dishes. **Features:** Sunday brunch. **Address:** 1673 Oak Tree Rd 08820 **Location:** Garden State Pkwy exit 131, 0.4 mi w to Wood Ave, 0.5 mi n to Oak Tree Rd, then just w. L D

SKYLARK FINE DINER & LOUNGE   732/777-7878 **168**

▼▼ American. Casual Dining. $8-$27 **AAA Inspector Notes:** As the name implies, this is not your typical roadside greasy spoon. The menu is not huge but shows some sophistication without straying too far from familiar diner favorites. The breakfast is extensive with a focus on sandwiches and entrées at lunch and dinner. There are also desserts, pastries and good, fresh-baked bread. The retro-cool 1960s architecture and decor really adds to the experience and has made this a local landmark. **Features:** full bar. **Address:** 17 Wooding Ave 08817 **Location:** At US 1 N. B L D LATE CALL

EGG HARBOR CITY (F-3) pop. 4,243, elev. 58'
• Part of Atlantic City area — see map p. 73

Egg Harbor City's hallmark is neither eggs nor a harbor but acres of vineyards. The 1858 discovery that soil in the vicinity was conducive to growing wine grapes attracted German and Italian vintners to the area, and the town prospered. Some of the vineyards are still operated by the original founding families.

WINERIES

• **Historic Renault Winery** is just n. of US 30 at 72 N. Bremen Ave. **Hours:** Tours with tasting offered on the hour Sun.-Thurs. 11-4, Fri. 11-5, Sat. 11-7, early July to mid-Oct.; Mon.-Thurs. at noon, 2 and 4; Fri. on the hour 11-5; Sat. on the hour 11-7; Sun. on the hour 11-4, rest of year. Closed Jan. 1 and Christmas. Phone ahead to confirm schedule. **Phone:** (609) 965-2111. GT

EGG HARBOR TOWNSHIP (G-3)
• Part of Atlantic City area — see map p. 73

STORYBOOK LAND is 2 mi. w. of the Garden State Pkwy. at 6415 Black Horse Pike (US 40/322). This 20-acre park offers rides as well as more than 50 buildings and displays depicting scenes from children's literature. Rides include Bubbles the Coaster, Turtle Twirl, The Rockin' Tug and Whirly-Bug. Operating seasonally is Storybook Seaport, a water play area with water sprayers and misters.

Hours: Mon.-Sat. 10-5:30, Sun. 11-5:30, July 1-Labor Day; Mon.-Fri. 10-5, Sat.-Sun. 11 to 5, mid-June through June 30; Mon.-Fri. 10-3, Sat.-Sun. 11-5, May 1 through mid-June; Thurs.-Fri. 10-3, Sat.-Sun. 11-5, day after Labor Day-Oct. 31; Sat.-Sun. 11-5, Nov. 1 through mid-Nov. and in Apr.; Sat.-Sun. 2-9, mid-Nov. through day before Thanksgiving; Mon.-Fri. 4:30-9, Sat.-Sun. 2-9, day after Thanksgiving through Dec. 23; daily 4:30-9, Dec. 26-30. Closed Thanksgiving, Christmas Eve and Christmas. Phone ahead to confirm schedule. **Cost:** $24.50; $21.50 (ages 65+ and active and retired military and their family members); free (ages 0-1). **Phone:** (609) 641-7847.

DAYS HOTEL ATLANTIC CITY-EGG HARBOR TOWNSHIP
(609)641-4500
▼▼ ▼▼ **Hotel** $70-$300 **Address:** 6708 Tilton Rd 08234 **Location:** Garden State Pkwy exit 36, at Tilton Rd on CR 563; just s of US 40. **Facility:** 115 units, some kitchens. 5 stories, interior corridors. **Amenities:** safes. **Pool(s):** outdoor. **Activities:** playground, exercise room. **Guest Services:** coin laundry.

HOLIDAY INN EXPRESS ATLANTIC CITY WEST   609/484-1500
▼▼▼▼ **Hotel.** Rates not provided. **Address:** 6811 Black Horse Pike (US 40/322) 08234 **Location:** Garden State Pkwy exit 36 northbound, 0.3 mi e; exit 37 southbound, 1 mi w of US 9. **Facility:** 197 units. 4 stories, interior corridors. **Terms:** check-in 4 pm. **Amenities:** safes. **Pool(s):** heated outdoor. **Activities:** exercise room. **Guest Services:** valet and coin laundry.

WHERE TO EAT

A TOUCH OF ITALY RESTAURANT & LOUNGE   609/646-1855
▼▼ Italian. Casual Dining. $14-$36 **AAA Inspector Notes:** For some 25 years, this eatery has provided a taste of Italy to its clientèle. This family-owned establishment offers an extensive selection of traditional Italian fare along with nightly specials. An impressive wine list complements the diverse menu. **Features:** full bar, happy hour. **Address:** 6629 Black Horse Pike 08234 **Location:** Garden State Pkwy exit 36 northbound, 0.6 mi ne on Fire Rd, then 1.8 mi w on US 40/322; exit 37 southbound, 2 mi w. (D)

THE BERKSHIRE GRILL   609/272-8808
▼▼ American. Casual Dining. $9-$33 **AAA Inspector Notes:** Since 2000, this grill has provided a casual and relaxed atmosphere in which to enjoy a wide range of mouth-watering steaks, seafood entrées and hearty pasta dishes. The nightly specials and seasonally changing menu keeps customers returning time and time again. **Features:** full bar. **Address:** 6105 Black Horse Pike 08234 **Location:** Jct US 40/322 and CR 575, just e. (D)

EAST BAY CRAB & GRILLE   609/272-7721
▼▼ Seafood. Casual Dining. $9-$50 **AAA Inspector Notes:** It is hard to miss the bright pink crab on the roof of this inviting spot, where plates overflow with fresh seafood offerings, including the namesake crab dishes. Guests can choose just claws, whole Maryland crabs, Alaskan king crab legs by the pound or all-you-can-eat on special nights. Welcoming staff members serve the many hungry diners who frequent this spot. **Features:** full bar, early bird specials, happy hour. **Reservations:** suggested. **Address:** 6701 Black Horse Pike 08234 **Location:** Black Horse Pike (US 40/322) at Cardiff Cir; in Fashion Shopping Plaza. (L) (D) CALL ⓛM

ELIZABETH (H-5) pop. 124,969, elev. 38'
• Hotels & Restaurants map & index p. 162

Elizabeth is part of metropolitan New York City's extensive, densely populated urban conurbation. The city's marine terminal is one of the largest container ports in the world; it was here that John Philip Holland assembled the first successful submarine, later purchased by the U.S. Navy. The College of New Jersey, the school that would eventually become Princeton University, was founded in Elizabeth by Jonathan Dickinson in 1746.

Notable early residents include Alexander Hamilton and Aaron Burr, both of whom attended the old academy on the site now occupied by the First Presbyterian Church parish house; James Caldwell, the fiery "Fighting Parson" of the Revolution; and Gen. Winfield Scott, the 1852 Whig party presidential candidate.

Nearly two dozen pre-Revolutionary War structures remain standing in a city that suffered many attacks and skirmishes. Several of them, identified by plaques, are located in the 1000 and 1100 blocks of E. Jersey Street. The Bonnell House, 1045 E. Jersey St., dates from about 1682 and is one of the city's oldest buildings. Boxwood Hall, 1073 E. Jersey St., was built around 1750 and is the former home of Elias Boudinot, president of the Continental Congress 1782-83. In 1789 George Washington visited the Boudinot home en route to New York for his presidential inauguration. Hamilton also was a frequent visitor, having lived for a time with the Boudinot family while attending school.

Enjoy the floriferous beauty at Henry S. Chatfield Memorial Garden; the spring display of tulips in late April and early May is particularly noteworthy. The garden is in Warinanco Park, designed by noted landscape architect Frederick Law Olmsted. The city's largest park is an oasis of huge old trees, winding paths and recreational facilities that include tennis courts, an ice-skating rink and football, baseball and soccer fields. The park is off Garden State Parkway exit 137 at the intersection of Rahway and Park avenues; for directions and other information phone (908) 527-4900.

Greater Elizabeth Chamber of Commerce: 456 N. Broad St., Elizabeth, NJ 07208. **Phone:** (908) 355-7600.

COUNTRY INN & SUITES BY CARLSON
(908)282-0020 104
▼▼ ▼▼ ▼▼
Hotel
$109-$169
Address: 100 Glimcher Realty Way 07201 **Location:** New Jersey Tpke exit 13A, 1 mi se on Jersey Garden Blvd, just n on Kapkowski Rd, then just w. **Facility:** 210 units. 7 stories, interior corridors. **Amenities:** safes. **Pool(s):** heated indoor. **Activities:** hot tub, exercise room. **Guest Services:** valet and coin laundry, area transportation. **Featured Amenity:** breakfast buffet.

(See map & index p. 162.)

COURTYARD BY MARRIOTT NEWARK ELIZABETH
(908)436-9800 **105**

Hotel
$174-$286

AAA Benefit: Members save 5% or more!

Address: 87 Glimcher Realty Way 07201 **Location:** New Jersey Tpke exit 13A, 1 mi se on Jersey Garden Blvd, just n on Kapkowski Rd, then just w. **Facility:** 203 units. 6 stories, interior corridors. **Parking:** on-site (fee). **Pool(s):** heated indoor. **Activities:** exercise room. **Guest Services:** valet and coin laundry, boarding pass kiosk, area transportation.

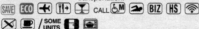

CROWNE PLAZA NEWARK AIRPORT   (908)527-1600 **102**
Hotel $110-$249 **Address:** 901 Spring St 07201 **Location:** New Jersey Tpke exit 13A to US 1 and 9 S; exit North Ave W, right at 2nd light, then 0.3 mi n. **Facility:** 260 units. 11 stories, interior corridors. **Parking:** on-site (fee). **Terms:** 2 night minimum stay - weekends, 4 day cancellation notice, resort fee. **Pool(s):** heated indoor. **Activities:** exercise room. **Guest Services:** valet and coin laundry, area transportation.

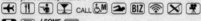

EMBASSY SUITES NEWARK AIRPORT   (908)558-0752 **106**
Extended Stay Contemporary Hotel $159-$259 **Address:** 95 Glimcher Realty Way 07201 **Location:** New Jersey Tpke exit 13A, 1 mi se on Jersey Garden Blvd, just n on Kapkowski Rd, then just w. **Facility:** 189 units. 8 stories, interior corridors. **Parking:** on-site (fee). **Terms:** 1-7 night minimum stay, cancellation fee imposed. **Pool(s):** heated indoor. **Activities:** hot tub, exercise room. **Guest Services:** valet and coin laundry, boarding pass kiosk, area transportation.

AAA Benefit: Members save 5% or more!

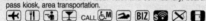

HAMPTON INN-NEWARK AIRPORT   (908)355-0500 **100**
Hotel $119-$259 **Address:** 1128-38 Spring St 07207 **Location:** New Jersey Tpke exit 14, 2.5 mi s on US 1 and 9, on service/local lane. **Facility:** 151 units. 5 stories, interior corridors. **Terms:** 1-7 night minimum stay, cancellation fee imposed. **Activities:** exercise room. **Guest Services:** valet laundry.

AAA Benefit: Members save 5% or more!

HILTON NEWARK AIRPORT   (908)351-3900 **99**

Hotel
$119-$229

AAA Benefit: Members save 5% or more!

Address: 1170 Spring St 07201 **Location:** exit 14 New Jersey Tpke exit 14, 2.3 mi s on US 1 and 9. **Facility:** 378 units. 12 stories, interior corridors. **Parking:** on-site (fee). **Terms:** 1-7 night minimum stay, cancellation fee imposed. **Amenities:** video games, safes. **Pool(s):** heated indoor. **Activities:** exercise room. **Guest Services:** valet and coin laundry, boarding pass kiosk.

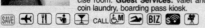

RENAISSANCE NEWARK AIRPORT HOTEL
(908)436-4600 **101**

Contemporary Hotel
$202-$332

R
RENAISSANCE*
HOTELS

AAA Benefit: Members save 5% or more!

Address: 1000 Spring St 07201 **Location:** New Jersey Tpke exit 14, 2.5 mi s on US 1 and 9, on service/local lane. **Facility:** 396 units. 10 stories, interior corridors. **Terms:** check-in 4 pm. **Amenities:** safes. **Pool(s):** heated indoor. **Activities:** exercise room. **Guest Services:** valet and coin laundry.

RESIDENCE INN BY MARRIOTT NEWARK ELIZABETH/ LIBERTY INTERNATIONAL AIRPORT
(908)352-4300 **103**

Extended Stay Hotel
$174-$286

Residence
Inn
Marriott

AAA Benefit: Members save 5% or more!

Address: 83 Glimcher Realty Way 07201 **Location:** New Jersey Tpke exit 13A, 1 mi se on Jersey Garden Blvd, just n on Kapkowski Rd, then just w. **Facility:** 198 units, some two bedrooms, efficiencies and kitchens. 6 stories, interior corridors. **Parking:** on-site (fee). **Pool(s):** heated indoor. **Activities:** exercise room. **Guest Services:** valet and coin laundry, area transportation. **Featured Amenity:** breakfast buffet.

ENGLEWOOD pop. 27,147
• Hotels & Restaurants map & index p. 162

CROWNE PLAZA ENGLEWOOD   (201)871-2020 **35**

Hotel
$129-$209

Address: 401 S Van Brunt St 07631 **Location:** SR 4 exit Van Brunt St westbound, just n; exit Grand Ave/Englewood eastbound, just n to U-turn. **Facility:** 194 units. 9 stories, interior corridors. **Pool(s):** heated indoor. **Activities:** exercise room. **Guest Services:** valet and coin laundry, area transportation.

EWING pop. 35,790

COURTYARD BY MARRIOTT EWING/PRINCETON
(609)771-8100

Hotel
$169-$277

AAA Benefit: Members save 5% or more!

Address: 360 Scotch Rd 08628 **Location:** I-95 exit 3A, just e. **Facility:** 130 units. 5 stories, interior corridors. **Pool(s):** heated indoor. **Activities:** hot tub, exercise room. **Guest Services:** valet and coin laundry, boarding pass kiosk, area transportation.

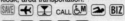

ELEMENT BY WESTIN EWING PRINCETON
(609)671-0050

Extended Stay Contemporary Hotel
$109-$199

AAA Benefit: Members save up to 15%, plus Starwood Preferred Guest® benefits!

Address: 1000 Sam Weinroth Rd E 08628 **Location:** I-95 exit 3A, just e. **Facility:** 127 units, some efficiencies. 4 stories, interior corridors. *Bath:* shower only. **Terms:** cancellation fee imposed, resort fee. **Amenities:** safes. **Pool(s):** heated indoor. **Activities:** hot tub, bicycles, exercise room. **Guest Services:** valet and coin laundry, boarding pass kiosk, area transportation.

SPRINGHILL SUITES BY MARRIOTT EWING/PRINCETON SOUTH
(609)530-0900

Hotel $132-$217 **Address:** 1000 Charles Ewing Blvd 08628 **Location:** I-95 exit 4 (SR 31 S), just s. **Facility:** 134 units. 4 stories, interior corridors. **Pool(s):** heated indoor. **Activities:** exercise room. **Guest Services:** valet laundry, area transportation.

AAA Benefit: Members save 5% or more!

WHERE TO EAT

METRO GRILL   609/882-2800

Italian. Casual Dining. $9-$29 **AAA Inspector Notes:** This casual restaurant has a comfortable menu with many familiar favorites including steaks, veal Marsala or Parmesan, burgers and salads. The easy feeling extends to the friendly service and the laid-back but updated décor of the dining room and bar. **Features:** full bar. **Address:** 172 Scotch Rd 08628 **Location:** Jct Upper Ferry Rd.

FAIRFIELD pop. 7,466
• Hotels & Restaurants map & index p. 152

BEST WESTERN PLUS FAIRFIELD EXECUTIVE INN
973/575-7700 **14**

Hotel
Rates not provided

AAA Benefit: Members save up to 20%!

Address: 216-234 Rt 46 E 07004 **Location:** I-80 exit 52 westbound, 1.5 mi w; exit 47B (Caldwells) eastbound, 5.5 mi e. **Facility:** 170 units. 4 stories, interior corridors. **Amenities:** safes. **Dining:** entertainment. **Pool(s):** heated indoor. **Activities:** hot tub, exercise room. **Guest Services:** valet and coin laundry, area transportation.

COMFORT INN FAIRFIELD
(973)227-4333 **13**

Hotel
$85-$149

Address: 286 US Hwy 46 07004 **Location:** I-80 exit 52 westbound, 1 mi w on US 46 E; exit 47B (Caldwells) eastbound, 6 mi e. **Facility:** 70 units. 3 stories, interior corridors. **Amenities:** safes. **Activities:** exercise room. **Guest Services:** coin laundry. **Featured Amenity: full hot breakfast.**

CROWNE PLAZA FAIRFIELD
973/227-9200 **12**

Hotel. Rates not provided. **Address:** 690 US 46 E 07004 **Location:** I-80 exit 52 westbound; exit 47B (Caldwells) eastbound, 5.6 mi e. **Facility:** 204 units. 5 stories, interior corridors. **Activities:** exercise room. **Guest Services:** valet and coin laundry, area transportation.

HAMPTON INN & SUITES
(973)575-5777 **15**

Hotel $149-$299 **Address:** 118-124 Rt 46 E 07004 **Location:** I-80 exit 52 westbound to US 46 W, U-turn at Clinton Rd; exit 47 eastbound, U-turn to US 46 E, then 4.3 mi e. **Facility:** 154 units, some efficiencies. 3 stories, interior corridors. **Terms:** 1-7 night minimum stay, cancellation fee imposed. **Amenities:** video games. **Pool(s):** heated indoor. **Activities:** hot tub, exercise room. **Guest Services:** valet and coin laundry, area transportation.

AAA Benefit: Members save 5% or more!

LA QUINTA INN & SUITES FAIRFIELD
(973)575-1742 **11**

Hotel $85-$225 **Address:** 38 Two Bridges Rd 07004 **Location:** I-80 exit 52 westbound; exit 47B (Caldwells) eastbound, 7 mi e on US 46 exit Passaic Ave. **Facility:** 176 units. 2 stories, interior corridors. **Pool(s):** heated indoor. **Activities:** hot tub, limited exercise equipment. **Guest Services:** valet and coin laundry, area transportation.

Enjoy great member rates and benefits

at AAA/CAA Preferred Hotels

FAIR LAWN pop. 32,457
• Hotels & Restaurants map & index p. 162

HYATT PLACE FAIR LAWN/PARAMUS
(201)475-3888 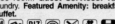 32

Hotel
$74-$209

H HYATT PLACE°
AAA Benefit: Members save 10%!

Address: 41-01 Broadway (Rt 4 W) 07410 **Location:** Garden State Pkwy exit 161 northbound, 0.7 mi w. exit 163 southbound; entrance from SR 4 W. **Facility:** 143 units. 4 stories, interior corridors. **Terms:** cancellation fee imposed. **Pool(s):** heated indoor. **Activities:** exercise room. **Guest Services:** valet laundry. **Featured Amenity:** breakfast buffet.

WHERE TO EAT

MEI SUSHI   201/398-9882 24
▼▼ Sushi. Casual Dining. $9-$22 **AAA Inspector Notes:** Great sushi and sashimi can be had at the simple storefront eatery on a busy downtown street just steps from the train station. Service is personable and efficient, and the sushi chefs' artistry entices commuters, locals and sushi lovers of every stripe. **Address:** 14-20 Plaza Rd 07410 **Location:** Jct SR 4 and 208, 1.3 mi n on SR 208 exit Plaza Rd/Fair Lawn, 0.4 mi n. L   D

THE RIVER PALM TERRACE   201/703-3500 25
▼▼▼ Steak. Casual Dining. $17-$47 **AAA Inspector Notes:** Well-prepared porterhouse steak for two is the specialty at this moderately upscale restaurant, known locally for succulent, aged steaks. Also on the menu are such dishes as Chilean sea bass, Maine lobster and Dover sole. **Features:** full bar. **Reservations:** suggested. **Address:** 41-11 Rt 4 W 07410 **Location:** Jct Paramus Rd, just w. **Parking:** valet only. L   D

FAR HILLS (C-3) pop. 919, elev. 140'

On the western edge of the northeastern New Jersey metropolitan urban area, Far Hills is in an area of rolling hills and grand estates where wealthy residents originally engaged in farming and fox hunting. In more recent years many of the estate homes have been converted into corporate headquarters offices.

LEONARD J. BUCK GARDEN is 1 mi. s.e. of US 202 via Liberty Corner Rd. to 11 Layton Rd. Wooded trails connect gardens that have been incorporated into natural rock outcroppings. Themed areas are landscaped with alpine and woodland plants. Highlights include extensive collections of ferns and wildflowers; peak wildflower blooming season is mid-April to mid-June.

Pets are not permitted. **Time:** Allow 1 hour minimum. **Hours:** Mon.-Fri. 10-4, Sat. 10-5, Sun. noon-5, Apr.-Nov.; Mon.-Fri. 10-4, rest of year. Closed holidays Dec.-Mar. **Cost:** Donations. **Phone:** (908) 234-2677.

USGA MUSEUM is at 77 Liberty Corner Rd. The 1919 John Russell Pope residence, now home to the Arnold Palmer Center for Golf History, features rooms dedicated to such legendary golfers as Arnold Palmer, Robert Tyre "Bobby" Jones Jr. and Ben Hogan and a room dedicated to female golfer Mickey Wright.

The Pynes Putting Course is open early spring to late fall. **Time:** Allow 2 hours minimum. **Hours:** Tues.-Sun. 10-5. Closed major holidays. **Cost:** $7; $5 (USGA members); $3.50 (ages 13-17). **Phone:** (908) 234-2300, ext. 1057.

FARMINGDALE (D-4) pop. 1,329, elev. 79'

ALLAIRE STATE PARK is off CR 547, 1.5 mi. w. of Garden State Pkwy. exit 98 or 1 mi. n. of I-195 exit 31B. The park is the site of the historic Howell Works, a bog ore furnace and iron forge operated by industrialist James P. Allaire in the early 19th century.

Allaire Village, built 1822-37, includes a carpenter shop, a smithy, a general store, an enameling furnace, a carriage house, a bakery, a church and a mansion. Pine Creek Railroad displays antique trains, two of which offer 20-minute rides. Also on site are a nature center, a visitor center housing historical exhibits and 23 miles of trails. *See Recreation Areas Chart.*

Allow a full day. **Hours:** Park open daily 8-6, during daylight saving time; 8-4:30, rest of year. Allaire Village open Wed.-Sun. noon-4, Memorial Day-Labor Day; Sat.-Sun. noon-4, May 1-day before Memorial day and day after Labor Day through mid-Dec. Nature center open daily 10-4, Memorial Day weekend-Labor Day. Train rides are offered Mon.-Fri. noon-4, Sat.-Sun. noon-4:30, July-Aug.; Sat.-Sun. noon-4:30, early Apr.-June 30 and Sept. 1-early Nov.; Sat.-Sun. noon-4, early-late Nov.

Cost: Village buildings $3; $2 (ages 6-12). Train ride $4; free (ages 0-2). **Parking:** $7 (New Jersey residents $5), Sat.-Sun. and holidays, Memorial Day weekend-Labor Day. **Phone:** (732) 938-2371 for the park, (732) 938-5524 for Pine Creek Railroad, or (732) 919-3500 for Allaire Village.

FLEMINGTON (C-3) pop. 4,581, elev. 179'

Flemington became widely known in the early 20th century for the manufacture of pottery and cut glass, but notoriety of a different sort came to town in 1935 when the much-publicized Lindbergh kidnapping trial was held in the county courthouse.

Steam and vintage diesel locomotives provide the power for 11-mile round trips aboard the Black River & Western Railroad. Summer weekend and holiday trips depart from Flemington Station, 12 Stangl Rd. off SR 12W, and travel to the Ringoes Station on CR 579. Seasonal themed excursions also are available. For information and reservations phone (908) 782-6622.

Shopping areas: Liberty Village, at 1 Church St., features specialty shops and outlet stores housed in

Colonial-style buildings on the site of an old railroad turntable.

NORTHLANDZ is at 495 US 202. This 16-acre complex features one of the world's most extensive model railroads. The Great American Railway is a miniature world of cities and towns, landscapes that include 35-foot-tall mountains, more than 100 trains comprising some 10,000 freight cars, and 8 miles of track. Also on the premises is a 94-room dollhouse, a doll museum, a music hall and an art gallery. Outdoor train rides are offered as well.

Time: Allow 1 hour, 30 minutes minimum. **Hours:** Mon. and Wed.-Fri. 10:30-4 (also Tues. 10:30-4 during Christmas week), Sat.-Sun. and holidays 10:30-5:30. Closed Easter, Thanksgiving and Christmas. **Cost:** $13.75; $12.50 (ages 62+); $9.75 (ages 2-12). Train ride $2.75. **Phone:** (908) 782-4022.

HAMPTON INN   (908)284-9427

Hotel $140-$160 **Address:** 14B Royal Rd 08822 **Location:** US 202 to Church St; 0.5 mi n of jct SR 31 and US 202. **Facility:** 83 units. 3 stories, interior corridors. **Terms:** 1-7 night minimum stay, cancellation fee imposed. **Pool(s):** heated indoor. **Activities:** hot tub, exercise room. **Guest Services:** valet and coin laundry.

> **AAA Benefit:**
> Members save 5%
> or more!

MAIN STREET MANOR BED & BREAKFAST   908/782-4928

Historic Bed & Breakfast. Rates not provided. **Address:** 194 Main St 08822 **Location:** Downtown. **Facility:** Within walking distance of outlets and town shops, this restored Queen Anne Victorian, built in 1901, is furnished with period antiques. 5 units. 3 stories (no elevator), interior corridors. **Activities:** massage.

WHERE TO EAT

ANGELO'S CUCINA ITALIANA   908/788-6833

Italian. Family Dining. $5-$18 **AAA Inspector Notes:** This casual pizza place also prepares a variety of pasta, chicken, seafood and veal dishes. While only counter service is offered at lunch, there is seated service at dinner. The no-nonsense décor and family-friendly menu make this a nice place to bring kids. **Address:** 164 Rt 31 08817 **Location:** 1.6 mi n of jct SR 31 and US 202.

COUNTRY GRIDDLE RESTAURANT & BAKERY   908/788-8779

American. Family Dining. $8-$17 **AAA Inspector Notes:** Locals flock here for breakfast and fresh, oversized traditional favorites (think chicken and dumplings, meatloaf and mashed potatoes and apple pie) at more than fair prices. Try one of the Greek specialties for a tasty change of pace. **Address:** 289 Rt 202/31 08822 **Location:** Jct SR 31 and 12; just s of traffic circle.

ORVIETO   908/788-0119

Italian. Casual Dining. $7-$30 **AAA Inspector Notes:** Dishes, such as orecchiette with fresh broccoli, olive oil and garlic, show influences from all regions of Italy. Live jazz music filters through the relaxed dining room Thursdays and Saturdays. The homemade chocolate cake is decadent. **Features:** wine only. **Reservations:** suggested. **Address:** 148 Main St 08822 **Location:** Downtown.

FLORHAM PARK (G-5) pop. 11,696, elev. 240'
• Hotels & Restaurants map & index p. 152

The name Florham Park was derived from the first names of millionaire Hamilton Twombly and his wife, Florence; "Park" was added in honor of Dr. Leslie D. Ward's estate, Brooklake Park.

The College of St. Elizabeth, a Catholic liberal arts college founded in Morris County in 1899, is said to be the oldest women's college in the state. The 200-acre campus is partially in the town of Convent Station; phone (973) 290-4000.

Shared by the town of Madison, the Florham-Madison campus of Fairleigh Dickinson University occupies 187 acres on the site of the former Twombly estate. The 100-room Twombly Mansion, begun in 1893 and completed in 1896, is a replica of one wing of Hampton Court in England. The manor house serves as a campus administration building. Tours of the campus are available by appointment; phone (973) 443-8500.

The Little Red Schoolhouse, Ridgedale Avenue and Columbia Turnpike, was built in 1866 and used as a school until 1914. The schoolhouse is now a museum operated by the Florham Park Historical Society; phone (973) 377-3713.

IMAGINE THAT!!! DISCOVERY MUSEUM FOR CHILDREN is 1.7 mi. e. on Columbia Tpke. (CR 510), then .5 mi. n. to 4 Vreeland Rd. Hands-on activities encourage youngsters to learn about computers and science and express their creative side via art, drama and music. Children can imagine themselves being a doctor, dentist, nurse or veterinarian, and "fly" a real plane and "drive" a real firetruck in the transportation area. Other exhibits include a post office, T.V. news room, three-level train exhibit and a multicultural area with items from around the world. A Medieval castle includes a dress-up area. **Time:** Allow 2 hours minimum. **Hours:** Daily 10-5:30. Phone ahead for holiday schedule. **Cost:** $10.95 (ages 1-12); $9.95 (ages 13+). **Phone:** (973) 966-8000.

WYNDHAM HAMILTON PARK HOTEL & CONFERENCE CENTER   (973)377-2424 68

Hotel
$135-$289

Address: 175 Park Ave 07932 **Location:** SR 24 exit 2A, 0.4 mi w on CR 510, then 1 mi s on CR 623. **Facility:** 219 units. 5 stories, interior corridors. **Terms:** check-in 4 pm. **Amenities:** safes. **Dining:** 2 restaurants. **Pool(s):** heated outdoor, heated indoor. **Activities:** sauna, hot tub, massage. **Guest Services:** valet laundry, area transportation.

Visit the AAA and CAA senior driving websites for valuable resources

FORKED RIVER (E-4) pop. 5,244, elev. 13'

 POPCORN PARK ZOO is off Garden State Pkwy. exit 74, then 7 mi. w. on Lacey Rd. to 1 Humane Way. The zoo provides a refuge for more than 200 wild and domestic animals, including exotic pets unable to return to their natural habitats. Many animals roam freely; Chinese geese greet visitors and "escort" them around the grounds. Among the animals living in comfortable compounds are Bengal tigers, pythons, monkeys, wallabies and a Bactrian camel. **Time:** Allow 1 hour, 30 minutes minimum. **Hours:** Daily 11-5 (holidays 11-2). **Cost:** $5; $4 (ages 3-11 and 62+). **Phone:** (609) 693-1900.

FORT LEE (G-6) pop. 35,345, elev. 313'
• Hotels & Restaurants map & index p. 162

Situated on the Hudson River palisades, Fort Lee was a critical point in Gen. George Washington's unsuccessful attempts to stem the tide of British forces in 1776. The convenient and dramatic location also made Fort Lee the motion picture capital of America from 1910 until the mid-1920s. The borough's striking scenery and a ready labor force made it a lucrative filming site; talent scouts often waited outside local schools to ask children to appear in movies under production. At the peak of activity before World War I, seven studios and 21 companies produced the silent films that revolutionized entertainment around the world.

Realizing that New Jersey winters were not conducive to movie production, the studios eventually relocated to Hollywood. Fire destroyed many of the buildings in the Coytesville area, where companies such as Universal Studios got their start, and the remaining structures were converted to other uses. Fort Lee, however, earned its place in pop culture when Gilda Radner, as recurring character Roseanne Roseannadanna on the Weekend Update segment of "Saturday Night Live," would begin one of her monologues by reading a letter from "a Mr. Richard Fader of Fort Lee, New Jersey."

This residential suburb of New York City is connected to the metropolis by the George Washington Bridge. The bridge serves as the southern terminus of Palisades Interstate Parkway, a scenic section of highway that skirts the Hudson River and continues north into New York.

Greater Fort Lee Chamber of Commerce: 210 Whiteman St., Fort Lee, NJ 07024. **Phone:** (201) 944-7575.

FORT LEE HISTORIC PARK is off Hudson Terr. in Palisades Interstate Park. The 33-acre site atop the Palisades was chosen by Gen. George Washington in 1776 to defend New York and the Hudson River against British warships. Washington's army was forced into retreat by the British army under Gen. Charles Cornwallis.

The visitor center chronicles Fort Lee's role in the Revolutionary War. Trails lead to two points overlooking the New York skyline. Gun batteries, a rifle parapet and a soldier's hut have been restored. **Time:** Allow 30 minutes minimum. **Hours:** Grounds daily 8 a.m.-dusk (weather permitting). Visitor center Sun. 10-4:45. **Cost:** Free. **Parking:** $5 Sat.-Sun., May-Nov., and during special events. **Phone:** (201) 461-1776.

BEST WESTERN FORT LEE   (201)461-7000   **45**

Motel
$100-$250

AAA Benefit:
Members save up to 20%!

Address: 2300 Rt 4 W 07024 **Location:** 0.5 mi w of George Washington Bridge (SR 4 W). **Facility:** 63 units. 2 stories (no elevator), interior corridors. **Terms:** 3 day cancellation notice. **Activities:** exercise room. **Guest Services:** valet laundry.

DOUBLETREE BY HILTON FORT LEE-GEORGE
WASHINGTON BRIDGE   (201)461-9000   **46**

Hotel $139-$269 **Address:** 2117 Rt 4 E 07024 **Location:** 1 mi w of George Washington Bridge (SR 4 W), U-turn on Jones Rd; I-95 and 80 eastbound, local lanes exit 71 (Broad Ave-Leonia) to Broad Ave, 0.5 mi e. **Facility:** 242 units. 15 stories, interior corridors. **Terms:** 1-7 night minimum stay, cancellation fee imposed. **Amenities:** safes. **Dining:** 2 restaurants. **Pool(s):** heated indoor. **Activities:** hot tub, exercise room. **Guest Services:** valet laundry, area transportation.

AAA Benefit:
Members save 5% or more!

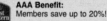

HOLIDAY INN FORT LEE   201/944-5000   **44**

Hotel. Rates not provided. **Address:** 2339 Rt 4 E 07024 **Location:** 1.2 mi s of George Washington Bridge (SR 4 W), U-turn on Jones Rd; I-95 and 80 eastbound local lanes exit 71 (Broad Ave-Leonia) to Broad Ave, 0.3 mi e. **Facility:** 185 units. 6 stories, interior corridors. **Pool(s):** outdoor. **Activities:** exercise room. **Guest Services:** valet and coin laundry, area transportation.

FRANKLIN (B-3) pop. 5,045, elev. 621'

Rockhounds exploring old mine dumps in the vicinity of Franklin are often rewarded; nearly 300 different minerals can be found. Zinc contributed to the city's initial development; for nearly a century, until the body of ore was depleted in the 1950s, New Jersey Zinc Co. mined 500,000 tons of zinc ore annually.

FRANKLIN MINERAL MUSEUM is .5 mi. n.w. of jct. SR 23 and Franklin Ave. at 32 Evans St. Samples of minerals mined from the area are displayed at the museum, which features the Fluorescent Room, where ores and minerals produce brilliant colors under ultraviolet light. An adjacent mine replica demonstrates zinc mining. Artifacts, dinosaur footprints and fossils from around the world also are displayed. Visitors can prospect on site during museum hours.

Time: Allow 1 hour minimum. **Hours:** Mon.-Fri. 10-4, Sat. 10-5, Sun. 11-5, Apr.-Nov.; Sat. 10-5, Sun. 11-5, in Mar. Rock collecting ends 30 minutes before closing. Closed Easter and Thanksgiving. **Cost:** Museum $7; $6 (ages 65+); $5 (ages 3-12). Rock collecting $8; $7 (ages 65+); $6 (ages 3-12). Additional collected rock charge of $1.50 per pound. Museum and rock collecting (up to 2 pounds) combination ticket $12; $10 (ages 65+); $8 (ages 3-12). Additional fee for fossil dig and gem panning. **Phone:** (973) 827-3481. ⟨GT⟩ ⟨⟩

FRANKLINVILLE

FRANKLINVILLE INN RESTAURANT   856/694-1577
▼▼▼▼ Steak Seafood. Fine Dining. $25-$46 **AAA Inspector Notes:** This traditional American restaurant has kept the locals coming back with its warm, inviting atmosphere and outstanding selection of food. All the steaks are aged and cut in-house to provide the highest degree of flavor. The New York strip steak is highly recommended. Seafood selections include flounder stuffed with lump crab and twin Brazilian lobster tails. Knowledgeable and friendly staff members assist your every need. **Features:** full bar. **Reservations:** suggested. **Address:** 2526 Delsea Dr 08322 **Location:** Jct SR 47 and Swedesboro Rd. ⟨D⟩ CALL ⟨&M⟩

FREEHOLD (D-4) pop. 12,052, elev. 178'

The Battle of Monmouth occurred in Freehold on June 28, 1778, when Gen. George Washington's army overtook Sir Henry Clinton's army as it retreated from Philadelphia. During this battle Molly Pitcher—so called because she brought water to the battlefield for the soldiers—helped to keep her husband's cannon in action when he was overcome by the 100-degree heat.

Just before the battle, Clinton used the house of a local farmer as his headquarters. Covenhoven House, 150 W. Main St., dates from the early 1750s and contains period furnishings. The house is open May through September; phone (732) 462-1466.

Outdoor recreation is available at nearby Turkey Swamp Park (see Recreation Areas Chart). Camping is available early Apr. to mid-November, while boat rentals are offered daily in the summer and on fall weekends; phone (732) 462-7286.

Harness racing takes place at Freehold Raceway, US 9 and SR 33, during most of the year; phone (732) 462-3800.

Note: Policies concerning admittance of children to pari-mutuel betting facilities vary. Phone for information.

Greater Monmouth Chamber of Commerce: Pinho Professional Center, 57 Schanck Rd., Suite C-3, Freehold, NJ 07728. **Phone:** (732) 462-3030.

MONMOUTH BATTLEFIELD STATE PARK is 3 mi. w. on SR 33 Bus. Rte. One of the longest Revolutionary War battles was fought here on June 28, 1778, when British troops on their way to New York were met by Gen. George Washington's troops from Valley Forge. The Americans matched British regulars in pitched battles for the first time. Exhibits at the visitor center relate the conflict. Guided tours of the Craig House, a 1746 farmhouse, are available.

The privately owned Battleview Orchards, which have been farmed by the same local family since 1908, also are on the grounds. Visitors may pick their own strawberries in late May, cherries in late June, nectarines and peaches from mid- to late July, apples in early September and pumpkins in early October.

Hours: Park open daily 8-8, Memorial Day weekend-Labor Day; 8-6, day after Labor Day through mid-Oct. and early Apr.-day before Memorial Day weekend; 8-4:30, rest of year. Visitor center open daily 9-4. Phone ahead to confirm schedule. **Cost:** Free. **Phone:** (732) 462-9616 for the park, or (732) 462-0970 for the orchards' fruit-picking schedule. ⟨⟩

MONMOUTH COUNTY HISTORICAL ASSOCIATION MUSEUM AND LIBRARY is at 70 Court St. Founded in 1898, the museum exhibits collections of furniture, paintings and decorative arts, most of which were owned or made in Monmouth County. Highlights include artifacts from the American Revolution, Chinese export porcelain and folk art. A research library houses historical documents, photographs, manuscripts and genealogical materials. **Hours:** Museum Tues.-Sat. 10-4. Library Wed.-Sat. 10-4. **Cost:** $5; $2.50 (ages 62+ and students with ID); free (ages 0-5). **Phone:** (732) 462-1466.

RADISSON HOTEL FREEHOLD   732/780-3400
▼▼▼ Hotel. Rates not provided. **Address:** 50 Gibson Pl 07728 **Location:** Jct US 9 and CR 537 (W Main St), 0.7 mi w. **Facility:** 121 units. 5 stories, interior corridors. **Amenities:** safes. **Pool(s):** outdoor. **Activities:** exercise room. **Guest Services:** valet and coin laundry.
⟨⟩ ⟨⟩ ⟨⟩ CALL ⟨&M⟩ ⟨⟩ ⟨BIZ⟩ ⟨HS⟩ ⟨⟩ ⟨⟩ ⟨⟩ ⟨⟩ ⟨⟩/SOME UNITS ⟨⟩

⟨WHERE TO EAT⟩

EL MESON CAFE   732/308-9494
▼▼ Mexican. Casual Dining. $8-$18 **AAA Inspector Notes:** Choices on both the lunch and dinner menus are plentiful. Offerings include varied tacos, enchiladas, quesadillas and burritos. The lively music and bright, festive decor are suited to a relaxed meal. **Features:** patio dining. **Address:** 40 W Main St 07728 **Location:** Jct CR 522 (Throckmorton St) and 537 (W Main St); center. **Parking:** street only. ⟨L⟩ ⟨D⟩

FRENCHTOWN pop. 1,373

THE FRENCHTOWN INN   908/996-3300
▼▼▼ French. Fine Dining. $14-$39 **AAA Inspector Notes:** Historic. A country simplicity prevails in this charming, upscale dining room, a nice riverside retreat in a quiet, small town. Hints of creativity mark dishes on the limited menu. The wine list represents a good selection of countries. **Features:** full bar, patio dining. **Reservations:** suggested. **Address:** 7 Bridge St 08825 **Location:** Just w of jct SR 12; center. ⟨L⟩ ⟨D⟩

GALLOWAY
• Part of Atlantic City area — see map p. 73

COUNTRY INN & SUITES BY CARLSON, ABSECON
(609)652-4050

▼▼▼ Hotel $59-$499 Address: 100 White Horse Pike 08205 Location: Atlantic City Expwy exit 12, just n; Garden State Pkwy exit 40, just e. Facility: 68 units, some efficiencies. 3 stories, interior corridors. Terms: cancellation fee imposed. Pool(s): heated indoor. Activities: hot tub, exercise room. Guest Services: coin laundry.

CALL 🄼 ➋ BIZ 🛜 ✕ 🛋 🖼 🖵

STOCKTON SEAVIEW HOTEL & GOLF CLUB-A DOLCE
RESORT   (609)652-1800

▼▼▼ Historic Resort Hotel $99-$379 Address: 401 S New York Rd 08205 Location: US 9, 2.5 mi ne of White Horse Pike (US 30). Facility: A historic property in operation since 1914, the resort offers a traditional atmosphere and two beautiful golf courses of championship caliber. 297 units. 3-4 stories, interior corridors. Parking: on-site and valet. Terms: check-in 4 pm, cancellation fee imposed. Dining: 2 restaurants. Pool(s): heated outdoor, heated indoor. Activities: sauna, hot tub, regulation golf, tennis, game room, exercise room, spa. Guest Services: valet and coin laundry.

🍴 🏋 ⅄ ➋ BIZ 🛜 ✕ 🎥 🖵
/SOME UNITS 🆒 🛋 🖼

WHERE TO EAT

RAM'S HEAD INN RESTAURANT   609/652-1700

▼▼▼ American. Fine Dining. $12-$39 AAA Inspector Notes: Set amid lush, landscaped grounds, this elegant restaurant is a favorite for special occasions. The spacious dining room is lovely and bright with a hint of Colonial spirit in the spindle-back chairs and stone fireplace. There is a garden room, nice for a cheerful lunch. The seasonally changing menu lists such well-prepared dishes as rack of lamb, beef Wellington, Chateaubriand and chicken pot pie served in a copper kettle. Features: full bar, happy hour. Reservations: suggested. Semiformal attire. Address: 9 W White Horse Pike (US 30) 08205 Location: Garden State Pkwy exit 40 southbound, 2.8 mi w of US 9. Parking: on-site and valet. [L] [D]

W. L. GOODFELLOWS AND CO.   609/652-1942

▼▼ American. Casual Dining. $8-$36 AAA Inspector Notes: Since 1984 and following a five-generation family tradition, this establishment has become one of the Atlantic City areas most popular restaurants. Its menu shows an Italian influence, and its widely diverse offerings ensure there will be something to please everyone. Features: full bar. Address: 310 E White Horse Pike 08205 Location: Garden State Pkwy exit 40, 0.8 mi e. [L] [D] CALL 🄼

GARFIELD pop. 30,487
• Hotels & Restaurants map & index p. 162

GOODFELLAS RISTORANTE   973/478-4000 �37

▼▼ Italian. Casual Dining. $11-$37 AAA Inspector Notes: This comfortable neighborhood restaurant offers tried-and-true Italian favorites including zuppa de pesce, linguine with clams and Bolognese. The owner appeared in the film "Goodfellas" hence the name of the restaurant. Features: full bar. Reservations: suggested. Address: 661 Midland Ave 07026 Location: US 46, 1 mi sw via Outwater Ln to Midland Ave, then just n. Parking: valet only.
[L] [D]

GATEWAY NATIONAL RECREATION AREA (I-6)

Comprising the Breezy Point, Jamaica Bay and Staten Island units in New York City and Sandy Hook Unit in New Jersey, Gateway National Recreation Area offers urban residents and visitors a chance to enjoy nature and the sea.

So named because it is at the entrance to the great New York-New Jersey estuary, the recreation area was created by Congress in 1972 to reclaim the parkland's ocean beaches, dunes, wooded uplands and bays from the effects of urbanization, which had decimated the region's bird, fish and animal populations.

Among the numbers of replenished wildlife are more than 300 species of birds that frequent the Jamaica Bay Wildlife Refuge and Sandy Hook Unit along the Atlantic flyway.

The Breezy Point Unit, on Rockaway Peninsula, includes Jacob Riis Beach, historic Fort Tilden and the westernmost point of the peninsula. The Jamaica Bay Unit includes Jamaica Bay Wildlife Refuge in Queens, Canarsie Pier, Plumb Beach and Floyd Bennett Field in Brooklyn. The Staten Island Unit consists of Fort Wadsworth, Great Kills Park and Miller Field. The Sandy Hook Unit in Highlands, N.J., includes a beach, a lighthouse and Fort Hancock.

Historical, educational, cultural and recreational events are presented throughout the year. The beaches are open daily and lifeguards are on duty Memorial Day weekend-Labor Day. For further information contact the Public Affairs Office, Gateway National Recreation Area, 210 New York Ave., Staten Island, NY 10305. Phone (718) 354-4606 . See Recreation Areas Chart.

SANDY HOOK UNIT is entered by bridge from SR 36 at Highlands, N.J. The barrier beach peninsula extends into the entrance of Lower New York Harbor. Recreational activities include bird-watching (approximately 340 bird species migrate through Sandy Hook during spring and fall), hiking, kiteboarding, swimming and windsurfing. Bicyclists, in-line skaters and pedestrians are afforded a 5-mile multipurpose trail.

The 1764 Sandy Hook Lighthouse is reputedly the oldest working light tower in the nation. During the American Revolution the site was occupied by British Loyalists. Today the keeper's quarters houses exhibits about New Jersey's lighthouses and maritime, military, and natural history. The History House, an 1898 former lieutenant's home, is furnished with period pieces.

A visitor center is housed in a former U.S. Life-Saving Service station at Spermaceti Cove which offers exhibits, programs and park information. Also housing displays is Fort Hancock, established in 1895. It is still largely intact, as are gun emplacements that defended the harbor during the Spanish-American War and World Wars I and II. See Recreation Areas Chart.

Hours: Sandy Hook Unit daily 5 a.m.-10 p.m., Apr.-Oct.; 5 a.m.-8 p.m., rest of year. Visitor Center at Spermaceti Cove daily 9-5, Apr.-Sept. Visitor Center at Lighthouse Keepers Quarters daily 9-5, Oct.-Mar. Guided lighthouse tours are given daily 1-4:30. History House Sat.-Sun. 1-5. Rangers are available daily 24 hours. Closed Jan. 1, Thanksgiving and Christmas.

Cost: Free. Under 48 inches tall are not permitted to climb the lighthouse tower. **Parking:** Beach Center parking $15 daily, Memorial Day weekend-Labor Day. **Phone:** (732) 872-5970. 🍽 🏕

GIBBSBORO pop. 2,274

THE CHOPHOUSE   856/566-7300   (157)
▼▼▼ Steak. Fine Dining. $13-$50 **AAA Inspector Notes:** As you might expect, steaks rise to the top of the menu at this spot, which has come to be known for its food, classic martinis and outstanding service. Splurge on the delicious sides and sinful desserts. Floor-to-ceiling windows add to the bright, airy feel of the dining area, which is enhanced with wood accents and an inviting hearth. **Features:** full bar, patio dining, happy hour. **Reservations:** suggested. **Address:** 4 S Lakeview Dr 08026 **Location:** I-295 exit 32, 4 mi e on Haddonfield-Berlin Rd (CR 561). **Parking:** valet and street only.
Ⓛ Ⓓ

GLASSBORO pop. 18,579

COURTYARD BY MARRIOTT GLASSBORO ROWAN UNIVERSITY   (856)881-0048
▼▼▼ Hotel $90-$183

AAA Benefit: COURTYARD Marriott Members save 5% or more!

Address: 325 Rowan Blvd 08028 **Location:** 2.6 mi e of jct SR 55 and US 322. **Facility:** 129 units. 4 stories, interior corridors. **Pool(s):** heated indoor. **Activities:** hot tub, exercise room. **Guest Services:** valet and coin laundry, boarding pass kiosk.

SAVE 🍽 CALL 📞 🚐 (BIZ) (HS) 📶 ✕ 🎒 🍽 🖨 / SOME UNITS

GLOUCESTER CITY pop. 11,456

QUALITY INN   (856)456-7400
▼▼ Hotel $75-$126 **Address:** 1200 Crescent Blvd 08030 **Location:** I-295 exit 23, 3 mi n on US 130. **Facility:** 63 units. 2 stories (no elevator), interior/exterior corridors. **Activities:** exercise room. **Guest Services:** valet and coin laundry.
(BIZ) 📶 🎒 🍽 🖨

GREENWICH (G-1) elev. 14'

American colonists burned a cargo of East India tea in the Greenwich town square on Dec. 22, 1774. It was one of six "tea parties"—Boston's being the most famous—held to protest British taxation that led up to the Revolutionary War. The Tea Burners Monument, erected in 1908 at the corner of Ye Greate Street and Market Lane, commemorates the historic event. The Cumberland County Prehistoric Museum, 1461 Bridgeton Rd., offers a one-room display of stone and bone artifacts, pottery and marine fossils; phone (856) 455-8141.

GIBBON HOUSE is at 960 Ye Greate St. Built in 1730 by wealthy merchant Nicholas Gibbon and patterned after a London townhouse, the house is furnished with 18th- and 19th-century items, including locally made rush-seated "Ware" chairs. The 1740 kitchen and its 10-foot working fireplace is still used to prepare special meals. **Hours:** Guided tours are given Tues.-Sat. 1-4 and by appointment, Apr.-Dec. Closed major holidays. **Cost:** Donations. **Phone:** (856) 455-4055.

HACKENSACK (G-6) pop. 43,010, elev. 22'
• Restaurants p. 120
• Hotels & Restaurants map & index p. 162

Remembering where their journeys had begun, the Manhattan Dutchmen who crossed the Hudson to establish a trading post on a lesser river about 4 miles west called their site New Barbados. For 274 years the name as well as the architecture of some buildings and institutions retained the Dutch stamp. Not until 1921, in an act that traded euphony for a city charter, did New Barbados become Hackensack, a Native American term meaning "place of sharp ground."

Due to its location on the road that linked Manhattan and its bastion at Fort Lee *(see place listing p. 116)* with the Passaic River, the village was a strategic point during the Revolution. Gen. George Washington and his troops stopped there after evacuating Fort Lee. Intrigue and skirmishes were common throughout the war; in 1780 a plundering party of Hessians and Britons burned the New Barbados courthouse.

The Green at the south end of Main Street was the core of New Barbados. It contained in one small area a courthouse for government and justice, pillories for punishment and the Church on the Green for absolution. Built at the Green's northeast corner in 1696 and reconstructed several times since, the church is one of the oldest in the state. Its Dutch Colonial architecture served as a prototype for several churches in the area.

The New Jersey Naval Museum, home of the USS *Ling*, is a memorial to those who served aboard U.S. submarines during World War II. The museum at 78 River St. offers guided tours year-round and conducts Memorial Day and Pearl Harbor Day services; phone (201) 342-3268.

On the east side of the Hackensack River in nearby Teaneck, the Hackensack Riverwalk is a 3.5-mile pedestrian walkway and nature trail connecting Terhune Memorial Park in nearby Wayne to Andreas and Brett parks in Teaneck (not all segments of the trail are complete). The trail offers views of the Hudson River, the New York City skyline and nearby mountains. Guided walking tours are available; for more information write Friends of the Greenway, P.O. Box 3028, Teaneck, NJ 07666.

Hackensack Regional Chamber of Commerce: 5 University Plaza Dr., Hackensack, NJ 07601. **Phone:** (201) 489-3700.

(See map & index p. 162.)

THE CHEESECAKE FACTORY   201/488-0330 32

▼▼▼▼ International. Casual Dining. $9-$30 **AAA Inspector Notes:** What started as a small bakery in Los Angeles in the 1970s has since blossomed into one of the most recognizable restaurant chains today. Known for their large portion sizes and seemingly never-ending menu, this restaurant features over 200 selections to choose from! The "SkinnyLicious" menu options may appeal to those counting calories. **Features:** full bar, patio dining, Sunday brunch. **Address:** 197 Riverside Square 07601 **Location:** In Riverside Square Mall. L D LATE

MORTON'S THE STEAKHOUSE   201/487-1303 33

▼▼▼▼ Steak. Fine Dining. $26-$56 **AAA Inspector Notes:** Patrons should make sure to reserve ahead for the popular, well-known steakhouse. Large portions, including huge cuts of fine beef and plentiful seafood, are the norm. Even the vegetables are oversized, with baked potatoes big enough for sharing. **Features:** full bar. **Reservations:** suggested. **Address:** One Riverside Square 07601 **Location:** In Riverside Square Mall. D CALL 🔊M

P.F. CHANG'S CHINA BISTRO   201/646-1565 31

▼▼▼ Chinese. Fine Dining. $9-$26 **AAA Inspector Notes:** Trendy, upscale decor provides a pleasant backdrop for New Age Chinese dining. Appetizers, soups and salads are a meal by themselves. Vegetarian plates and sides, noodles, chow meins, chicken and meat dishes are created from exotic, fresh ingredients. **Features:** full bar, happy hour. **Reservations:** suggested. **Address:** 390 Hackensack Ave, Suite 50 07601 **Location:** In Riverside Square Mall. L D CALL 🔊M

STONY HILL INN   201/342-4085 34

▼▼▼ Continental. Fine Dining. $14-$40 **AAA Inspector Notes:** *Historic.* Listed on the National Register of Historic Places, the circa 1818 white clapboard Dutch Colonial farmhouse with shuttered arched windows--which has lush plantings, a velvety lawn and a garden gazebo within the stone walls--sits on a hill and looks charming. A stately center hallway leads to elegant and handsomely appointed dining rooms. The menu lists a large selection of sophisticated Italian cuisine, with specialty dishes such as Chateaubriand for two and charcoal-grilled double veal chop. **Features:** full bar, Sunday brunch. **Reservations:** suggested. **Address:** 231 Polifly Rd 07601 **Location:** I-80 local lanes from George Washington Bridge exit 64B westbound, then right; exit 64 (SR 17 S) eastbound exit Terrace Ave, 0.3 mi n. **Parking:** valet only. L D

HADDONFIELD (E-2) pop. 11,593, elev. 74'

In 1701, Elizabeth Haddon was sent from England by her father—who had no sons—to develop 550 acres southeast of Camden. In less than a year the industrious Quaker lass had built a house, begun the colony and proposed marriage to Quaker missionary John Estaugh (he accepted). Their romance is at the center of "The Theologian's Tale" in Henry Wadsworth Longfellow's "Tales of a Wayside Inn."

INDIAN KING TAVERN HOUSE MUSEUM, 1.5 blks. n. of Haddon Ave. at 233 Kings Hwy. E., was built in 1750 and was for many years an important social, political and military gathering place along the historic Kings Highway. The three-and-a-half-story structure is furnished in period and contains historical displays. **Time:** Allow 30 minutes minimum. **Hours:** Thurs.-Sat. 10-noon and 1-4, Apr.-Sept. Hours vary rest of year. Closed Jan. 1, Thanksgiving and Christmas. Phone ahead to confirm schedule. **Cost:** Free. **Phone:** (856) 429-6792.
🏛 Haddonfield, 149

HADDONFIELD INN   856/428-2195

▼▼▼▼ Bed & Breakfast. Rates not provided. **Address:** 44 W End Ave 08033 **Location:** I-295 exit 28, 0.7 mi n on SR 168, 2.6 mi e on Kings Hwy, then just n. 🏛 Haddonfield, 149. **Facility:** You can walk around the shops of the historic district before retiring to your room, which features a fireplace and themed décor ranging from Tokyo to Cape Cod. 9 units. 3 stories, interior corridors. **Guest Services:** valet laundry.
📶 CALL 🔊M 📶 ✕ /SOME UNITS 🔊 🅿 🛗

HALEDON (G-6) pop. 8,318, elev. 300'

During the 1913 Paterson Silk strike, Haledon received national attention when the town's socialist mayor invited strikers to meet at co-worker Pietro Botto's home. Thousands gathered, unmolested by Paterson authorities, to hear labor organizer William "Big Bill" Haywood and writers John Reed and Upton Sinclair. Although the workers' petitions were not immediately met, the Paterson Silk strike was a major turning point in the history of unionized labor.

[SAVE] **AMERICAN LABOR MUSEUM/BOTTO HOUSE NATIONAL LANDMARK** is at 83 Norwood St. The museum occupies the 1908 Botto House, the former home of an Italian immigrant silk mill worker. Period rooms and changing exhibits illustrate the history of the world labor movement and the lifestyle of immigrant workers and their families in early 20th-century America.

An 18-minute video precedes a guided tour. An exhibit about the 1913 Paterson Silk strike is in the building's library. **Time:** Allow 1 hour, 30 minutes minimum. **Hours:** Wed.-Sat. 1-4 and by appointment. Closed holidays except Labor Day. **Cost:** $5. **Phone:** (973) 595-7953.

HAMBURG pop. 3,277

GRAND CASCADES LODGE   973/823-6500

▼▼▼ ▼▼▼ Resort Hotel. Rates not provided. **Address:** 3 Wild Turkey Way 07419 **Location:** Jct SR 23, 0.7 mi n; entrance off SR 94. Located in Crystal Springs Resort. **Facility:** Prepare to be impressed as you drive up to this striking mountain resort. A full array of first-class recreational facilities, upscale dining and sweeping views of lush green hills and valleys await. 285 units, some two bedrooms, efficiencies and kitchens. 5 stories, interior corridors. **Parking:** on-site and valet. **Terms:** check-in 4 pm. **Amenities:** safes. **Dining:** 3 restaurants. **Pool(s):** outdoor, heated indoor. **Activities:** sauna, hot tub, steamroom, cabanas, regulation golf, miniature golf, lawn sports, trails, exercise room, spa. **Guest Services:** complimentary laundry, area transportation.
🛏 📶 🍸 🛥 BIZ HS 🔊 📹 💻
/SOME UNITS 🅿 📷

HAMILTON (MERCER COUNTY) (D-3) elev. 80'

Hamilton, in the southern part of Mercer County, is adjacent to the Trenton metropolitan area.

Kuser Farm Mansion and Park has entrances at 390 Newkirk Ave. and on Kuser Road. The Fred Kuser family, which manufactured the Mercer Motor Car in Hamilton, helped finance the movie company that would become 20th Century Fox. A private projection room in the 1892 mansion is among rooms open to visitors on weekends. The 22-acre estate eatures a formal garden, tennis house, laundry ouse, coach house, barn, corn crib, shower house, indmill and gazebo; phone (609) 890-3630.

GROUNDS FOR SCULPTURE is off I-295 exit 65B, .2 mi. w. on Sloan Ave. to Klockner d., s. to E. State St., .8 mi. e. to Sculptor's Way, en .2 mi. s. to 18 Fairgrounds Rd. The 42-acre culpture park, built on the site of the former New ersey State Fairgrounds, features three buildings, ach of which houses museum galleries whose ex-ibitions rotate seasonally with contemporary art culptures. The Domestic Arts Building offers two xhibit spaces; the steel-framed Museum Building ffers the largest gallery; a third structure, the eward Johnson Center for the Arts, contains a isitor center and educational areas at which work-hops are offered, as well as the 7,500 square foot ast Gallery. More than 270 large-scale contempo-ary sculptures by American and international artists n such media as bronze, wood, stone and steel are lisplayed outdoors in both formal and naturalistic andscape settings.

The park contains lotus ponds, waterfalls, misting eatures, a water garden, bridges, a courtyard of lapanese maples, winding pathways and two allées. Peacocks roam the grounds. An arboretum features nany unusual conifers, bamboos and ornamental grasses. A Tree Tour brochure of 78 interesting pecimens is available. Touch tours for the visually mpaired and cart rides for the mobility impaired are available with advance notice.

Note: Comfortable shoes are recommended. Time: Allow 1 hour minimum. **Hours:** Thurs.-Sat. 10-9, Tues., Wed. and Sun. 10-6, early May-day be-ore Labor Day; Tues.-Sun. (also Memorial Day and Labor Day) 10-6, rest of year. Guided 1-hour tours are dependent on docent availability and depart from the visitor center Tues.-Sun. at 1 and 3 (also Sat. at 11), Apr.,-Oct. Phone ahead to confirm tour schedule. Closed Jan. 1, Thanksgiving and Christmas. **Cost:** $15; $12 (ages 65+); $10 (ages 6-17). **Phone:** (609) 586-0616. 🍴

HILTON GARDEN INN HAMILTON   (609)585-6789

▼▼▼ **Hotel** $139-$209 **Address:** 800 US 130 08690 **Location:** I-195 exit 5A or 5B onto US 130, 0.8 mi s. **Facility:** 105 units. 4 stories, interior corridors. **Terms:** 1-7 night minimum stay, cancellation fee imposed. **Pool(s):** heated indoor. **Activities:** hot tub, exercise room. **Guest Services:** complimentary and valet laundry.

AAA Benefit: Members save 5% or more!

🍴 CALL 📶 �. BIZ HS 📶 ✕ 🎁 📷 🖥

WHERE TO EAT

BROTHER'S PIZZA ON RT. 33   609/586-2707

◈ Pizza Sandwiches. Quick Serve. $8-$18 **AAA Inspector Notes:** Bring the family to this casual hometown pizzeria for a quick dinner out. Counter or sit-down service is available. Although the local newspaper deemed the pizza here—particularly the popular thin-crust creations—the best in town, the menu offers plenty more variety with sandwiches, calzones, pasta dishes and baked dinners. **Address:** 871 SR 33 08619 **Location:** I-295 exit 63 (southbound); 63A (northbound), 1.5 mi e. L D LATE

RAT'S RESTAURANT   609/584-7800

▼▼▼ ▼▼▼ French. Fine Dining. $13-$38 **AAA Inspector Notes:** In one word—unforgettable. Set amid a 22-acre sculpture and water garden, this whimsical dining room is reminiscent of the 19th-century French village of Giverny, made famous by Claude Monet, and the not-so-humble home of dapper Mr. Rat of 'Wind in the Willows' fame. Locally grown organic produce is used in seasonally changing, creative dishes to great acclaim. Al fresco dining in warmer months is serene and lovely. **Features:** full bar, patio dining, Sunday brunch. **Reservations:** suggested. **Address:** 16 Fairgrounds Rd 08619 **Location:** I-295 exit 63, 1 mi w on SR 33 (Nottingham Way) to Sculptors Way; in Grounds for Sculpture park. L D CALL 📶

HAMPTON (C-2) pop. 1,401, elev. 500'

TOWNSHIP OF LEBANON MUSEUM is 7 mi. n. of I-78 off SR 31 at 57 Musconetcong River Rd. This Greek Revival structure was built in 1825 as a one-room schoolhouse; a second story was added in the 1870s. The first floor is a re-created schoolroom with period furnishings, and the second floor displays changing exhibits. **Hours:** Tues. and Thurs. 9:30-5, Sat. 1-5. Closed major holidays. **Cost:** Free. **Phone:** (908) 537-6464.

HARRISON pop. 13,620
• Hotels & Restaurants map & index p. 162

ELEMENT HARRISON-NEWARK   (973)484-1500   **90**

Contemporary Hotel
$139-$299

AAA Benefit: Members save up to 15%, plus Starwood Preferred Guest® benefits!

Address: 399 Somerset St 07029 **Location:** I-95 exit 15W; I-280 exit 16 (Essex St), just s on Frank E Rodgers Blvd S. **Facility:** 138 units, some two bedrooms and efficiencies. 7 stories, interior corridors. **Bath:** shower only. **Parking:** on-site (fee). **Terms:** cancellation fee imposed. **Amenities:** safes. **Pool(s):** heated indoor. **Activities:** bicycles, exercise room. **Guest Services:** valet and coin laundry, boarding pass kiosk. **Featured Amenity:** full hot breakfast. *(See ad this page.)*

SAVE CALL ⎗M ⤻ BIZ HS 🛜 ✕ 🛏 ▭ ▯ / SOME UNITS 🐾

NEWARK/HARRISON RIVERWALK HAMPTON INN & SUITES
(973)483-1900   **89**

Hotel $149-$239 **Address:** 100 Passaic Ave 07029 **Location:** Jct SR 21 and Bridge St, just w, then just n. **Facility:** 165 units. 6 stories, interior corridors. **Terms:** 1-7 night minimum stay, cancellation fee imposed. **Pool(s):** heated indoor. **Activities:** exercise room. **Guest Services:** valet and coin laundry, area transportation.

AAA Benefit: Members save 5% or more!

✈ 🍽 CALL ⎗M ⤻ BIZ HS 🛜 ✕ 🛏 ▭ ▯

WHERE TO EAT

SPANISH PAVILLION   973/485-7750   **89**

Spanish. Casual Dining. $8-$36 **AAA Inspector Notes:** Paella aficionados will not be disappointed with one of the several preparations offered at this restaurant, where the service is warm and attentive and the portions robust. The kitchen puts out a top-notch mariscada, a garlicky and oh-so-good green sauce, and killer clams casino. **Features:** full bar, patio dining. **Address:** 31 Harrison Ave 07029 **Location:** Jct SR 21 and Bridge St, 0.4 mi w.

L D

HARVEY CEDARS pop. 337

PLANTATION RESTAURANT & BAR   609/494-8191

New American. Fine Dining. $11-$38 **AAA Inspector Notes:** The palm fronds, slowly revolving ceiling fans, rattan and shuttered windows might make guests think they are in a Tommy Bahama store. Seafood, of course, is a mainstay of the menu which also features a few Caribbean-influenced items. The bar is a lively spot for happy hour and there is live music on some nights. **Features:** full bar, happy hour. **Reservations:** suggested. **Address:** 7908 Long Beach Blvd 08008 **Location:** SR 72 Cswy, 4 mi n. L D

▼ *See AAA listing this page* ▼

Ask about on-the-go vehicle battery testing and replacement

HASBROUCK HEIGHTS pop. 11,842

• Hotels & Restaurants map & index p. 162

HILTON HASBROUCK HEIGHTS/ MEADOWLANDS
(201)288-6100 **53**

 **Hotel** $114-$199 **Address:** 650 Terrace Ave 07604 **Location:** I-80 exit 64B westbound; exit 64 eastbound, just s on SR 17 S. **Facility:** 355 units. 14 stories, interior corridors. **Terms:** check-in 4 pm, 1-7 night minimum stay, cancellation fee imposed. **Amenities:** safes. **Pool(s):** heated outdoor. **Activities:** exercise room. **Guest Services:** valet laundry, area transportation.

AAA Benefit: Members save 5% or more!

HOLIDAY INN MEADOWLANDS AREA
(201)288-9600 **54**

Hotel $129-$199

Address: 283 Rt 17 S 07604 **Location:** I-80 exit 64B westbound; exit 64 eastbound, 1 mi s. **Facility:** 244 units. 2-5 stories, interior corridors. **Terms:** 3 day cancellation notice-fee imposed. **Amenities:** safes. **Dining:** entertainment. **Pool(s):** outdoor. **Activities:** exercise room. **Guest Services:** valet and coin laundry, area transportation. **Featured Amenity:** breakfast buffet.

Just minutes from MetLife Stadium and Izod Center. NYC sightseeing tours leave hotel daily.

 WHERE TO EAT

BENSI RISTORANTE ITALIANO
201/727-9525

Italian. Family Dining. $8-$20 **AAA Inspector Notes:** A quick and tasty meal can be had at the casual Italian restaurant, which satisfies hankerings for crusty pizza, hearty bowls of pasta and more substantial entrees, including veal piccata, shrimp scampi and grilled rib-eye steak. Plentiful portions result in many doggie bags heading back out the door. **Features:** full bar. **Address:** 459 SR 17 S 07604 **Location:** I-80 exit 64B westbound; exit 64A eastbound, 1 mi s.

IVY INN
201/393-7699 **43**

Continental. Fine Dining. $11-$36 **AAA Inspector Notes:** *Historic.* This former stagecoach stop now offers a rustic and cozy dining experience, great for romantic dinners or lunch with friends. The dinner menu features familiar and well-prepared steaks, pastas and seafood done with just enough creative twists to keep it interesting. The prix fixe lunch menu may be the best deal in all of New Jersey, with two delicious courses for one price. **Features:** full bar, patio dining, early bird specials, Sunday brunch, happy hour. **Reservations:** suggested. **Address:** 268 Terrace Ave 07604 **Location:** Between Kipp Ave and Washington Pl; just nw of Teterboro Airport.

HAZLET

BEST WESTERN HAZLET INN
(732)888-2800

Hotel $89-$149

AAA Benefit: Members save up to 20%!

Address: 3215 SR 35 N 07730 **Location:** Garden State Pkwy exit 117, 1.5 mi s. **Facility:** 85 units. 3 stories, interior corridors. **Terms:** 3 day cancellation notice-fee imposed. **Activities:** limited exercise equipment. **Featured Amenity:** continental breakfast.

Conveniently located within minutes from GS Parkway. Complimentary breakfast & free wifi access.

HOLIDAY INN/HAZLET
732/888-2000

Hotel. Rates not provided. **Address:** 2870 SR 35 07730 **Location:** Garden State Pkwy exit 117 to SR 35 S, 2.5 mi s. **Facility:** 121 units. 2 stories, interior corridors. **Pool(s):** heated outdoor. **Activities:** exercise room. **Guest Services:** valet and coin laundry.

HIGHLANDS (D-5) pop. 5,005, elev. 10'

Summer vacationers and anglers flock to Highlands, connected by bridge to the Sandy Hook Unit of Gateway National Recreation Area *(see place listing p. 118).* Like neighboring Highlands Beach and Atlantic Highlands, the town's name refers to hills that rise abruptly from the shore.

Nearby 266-foot Mount Mitchill is one of the first points of land sighted by ships bound for New York Harbor. Ocean Boulevard, a scenic drive off SR 36, connects Highlands to Atlantic Highlands. The Highlands hills provided the setting for James Fenimore Cooper's 1831 novel "The Water Witch"; the title refers to the hero's vessel, which hid among the coves of Sandy Hook.

TWIN LIGHTS STATE HISTORIC SITE is on Lighthouse Rd. off Highland Ave. The twin-towered 1862 lighthouse replaced a structure built in 1828. An important site in terms of lighthouse technology, the tower once was the primary light source for New York harbor. A museum contains historical exhibits. Visitors can climb the north tower.

Time: Allow 1 hour minimum. **Hours:** North tower and museum daily 10-4:30, Memorial Day-Labor Day; Wed.-Sun. 10-4:30, rest of year. Closed major holidays. **Cost:** Donations. **Phone:** (732) 872-1814.

HILLSBOROUGH (C-3)

DUKE FARMS is at 1112 Dukes Pkwy. W. First developed by tobacco and hydropower magnate James Buchanan Duke in 1893 and later enhanced by his daughter, Doris, this 2,700-acre estate features wetlands, buildings, fountains and stone walls. Open to the public, it allows recreational opportunities such as geocaching and biking, as well as environmental programs.

Many buildings have been repurposed with eco-friendly power and water systems. The Orientation Center, which is on the first floor of the Farm Barn, presents interactive exhibits on land stewardship and sustainability. Orchids and exotic flowers from around the world can be seen in Doris Duke's greenhouses.

Note: Trails and paths may require full mobility as they are undeveloped, with loose gravel or wood chips. Motor vehicle traffic is limited, but a tram makes regular stops, including at the conservatory/greenhouse. **Time:** Allow 2 hours minimum. **Hours:** Thurs.-Tues. 8:30-6, Apr.-Oct.; 8:30-4:30, rest of year. Tram operates 8:30-4:30, Apr. 1-Oct. 31 (weather permitting). Closed Thanksgiving and Christmas. Phone ahead to confirm schedule. **Cost:** Free. **Phone:** (908) 722-3700.

HOBOKEN (H-6) pop. 50,005, elev. 5'
• Hotels & Restaurants map & index p. 162

Squeezed into little more than a square mile of land between the Hudson River and North Bergen, Hoboken is nevertheless a major railroad terminal and seaport across the river from New York City. West of the Hudson River is Stevens Institute of Technology, founded in 1870 as an engineering academy. The college has expanded from its original location at Castle Point to include centers for science, research, management and engineering.

While beer gardens and fireworks attracted revelers to Hoboken's River Walkway, the scenic countryside called out to such literary, artistic and society figures as John Jacob Astor, Washington Irving and William Cullen Bryant. John Stevens, a prominent Hoboken native, built the country's first steam locomotive in 1824.

Hoboken Historical Museum, 1301 Hudson St., offers changing exhibits, activities and events and a self-guiding walking tour of historic buildings and homes; phone (201) 656-2240.

Hoboken Chamber of Commerce: 50 Harrison St., Suite 212 D, P.O. Box 349, Hoboken, NJ 07030. **Phone:** (201) 222-1100.

Keep a current AAA/CAA

Road Atlas in every vehicle

W HOBOKEN   (201)253-2400 [86]

Boutique
Contemporary
Hotel
S209-S619

AAA Benefit: Members save up to 15%, plus Starwood Preferred Guest® benefits!

Address: 225 River St 07030 **Location** Waterfront. Between 1st and 2nd sts. **Facility:** The hip upscale lobby here gives way to equally stylish modern rooms, many with spectacular views of Manhattan across the Hudson River. 225 units, some two bedrooms. 17-26 stories, interior corridors. **Parking:** valet only. **Amenities:** safes. **Dining:** Zylo, Hoboken, see separate listing. **Activities:** exercise room, spa. **Guest Services:** valet laundry, boarding pass kiosk.

WHERE TO EAT

AMANDA'S   201/798-0101 [81]

American. Fine Dining. $18-$32 **AAA Inspector Notes:** The enchanting and romantic brownstone setting invites a meal of fine contemporary American cuisine. Savvy, well-heeled crowds appreciate the tempting and versatile menu, with dishes such as seared diver scallops and braised short ribs with roasted vegetables and celery root puree. Service is poised and professional. **Features:** full bar, Sunday brunch. **Reservations:** suggested. **Address:** 908 Washington St 07030 **Location:** At 9th St. **Parking:** street only.

THE BRASS RAIL RESTAURANT & BAR   201/659-7074 [85]

Continental. Fine Dining. $10-$32 **AAA Inspector Notes:** In an early 1900s landmark building, this restaurant has a comfortable neighborhood feel with lots of polished wood and large windows looking out on the bustling downtown street. The seasonal and slightly eclectic menu offers familiar items but with some creative twists and flavors to make it fun and interesting. Fresh ingredients, including market fresh shellfish and local produce, might be paired with Thai or Moroccan flavors, or try a hearty pasta or roasted duck. **Features:** full bar, patio dining, Sunday brunch. **Reservations:** suggested, weekends. **Address:** 135 Washington St 07030 **Location:** Corner of Washington and 2nd sts; downtown. **Parking:** street only.

ELYSIAN CAFE   201/798-5898 [80]

American. Casual Dining. $8-$26 **AAA Inspector Notes:** This former dive bar epitomized Hoboken's seedier days when it appeared in the classic Kazan film "On the Waterfront." After a lengthy restoration, the café now radiates beauty. The bistro-style menu lists such classics as steak frites, slow-roasted duck confit with Roquefort risotto and roasted salmon with wild mushroom vinaigrette. Lobster bisque, oysters on the half-shell, croque monsieur and burgers can be ordered from the bar menu until closing. **Features:** full bar, patio dining, Sunday brunch. **Address:** 1001 Washington St 07030 **Location:** At 10th St. **Parking:** street only.

GRIMALDI'S COAL BRICK OVEN PIZZERIA   201/792-0010 [82]

Pizza. Casual Dining. $12-$21 **AAA Inspector Notes:** The old-style coal-fired brick oven here makes for light and crisp pizzas that are best enjoyed with a minimum of toppings. The simple menu here offers whole pies, calzones and salads in a comfortable setting with red-and-white tablecloths and cozy booths. The naming and lineage of famous pizza places in New York City is vague and confusing at best, but it's safe to say that this place has at least some distant connection to the original owner of the famous Grimaldi's in Brooklyn. **Features:** full bar. **Address:** 411 Washington St 07030 **Location:** Between 4th and 5th sts. **Parking:** street only.

(See map & index p. 162.)

IT'S GREEK TO ME   201/216-1888

♥♥ Greek. Casual Dining. $10-$35 **AAA Inspector Notes:** This restaurant is a veritable find for those in search of authentic Greek cuisine. Start with the creamy, garlicky and oh-so-good gigantes, giant white beans cooked with tomato and sage. Gyros are, as they should be, good and messy. Servers are happy to bring over extra napkins, or anything else you may need. The dining room is reminiscent of a sunny Greek Island and is bedecked with the country's official blue and white colors. **Features:** patio dining. **Address:** 538 Washington St 07030 **Location:** At 6th St. **Parking:** street only.

L D

NAPOLI'S BRICK OVEN PIZZA & RESTAURANT
                                        201/216-0900   79

♥♥ Italian Pizza. Casual Dining. $6-$17 **AAA Inspector Notes:** In the tradition of great New York pizza, this clean and friendly place turns out beautiful, crisp, brick-oven-baked pies topped with the best ingredients. Keep it traditional and have a margherita pizza with San Marzano tomato, fresh mozzarella and basil. The menu also includes a good selection of panini, hoagies and traditional Italian entrées. **Address:** 1118 Washington St 07030 **Location:** Between 11th and 12th sts. **Parking:** street only.   L D

THE TACO TRUCK   201/850-1400   86

♥ Mexican. Quick Serve. $5-$8 **AAA Inspector Notes:** The popular mobile food trucks came first, but now there is also a small permanent restaurant in which to enjoy this great Mexican street food. Besides the mainstay—authentic-style tacos—there is a selection of salads and tortas such as the Barbacoa de Costilla with pasilla chile-braised shredded beef and chipotle salsa. The restaurant has a strong commitment to sustainability, including using hormone- and antibiotic-free meats, biodegradable packaging and a LEED-certified restaurant space. **Address:** 62 Newark St 07030 **Location:** Between Washington and Hudson sts; 1 blk n of Hoboken train station. **Parking:** street only.   L D LATE CALL ♿M

ZAFRA   201/610-9801   83

♥♥ Cuban. Casual Dining. $9-$23 **AAA Inspector Notes:** Patrons who know this small, cheerful bring-your-own-bottle Cuban charmer sing its praises, though quietly because it is crowded enough. A large hot and cold starter menu could make a meal, but then guests would miss the excellent skirt steak and other well-prepared entrées. Some prefer to just pop in for the tasty Cuban sandwich or a Latin coffee. **Address:** 301 Willow St 07030 **Location:** Corner of 3rd St. **Parking:** street only.   B L D

ZYLO HOBOKEN   201/253-2500   84

♥♥♥ Mediterranean. Casual Dining. $11-$48 **AAA Inspector Notes:** You will probably spend most of your time gawking at the striking view of the Manhattan skyline from this dining room, which is right on the Hudson river, but the food also makes Zylo worth the visit. Mediterranean flavors color the creative menu. Located right on the waterfront promenade, this is a good place to stop for a drink and a stroll afterward even if you don't plan to have a whole meal. **Features:** full bar, patio dining, Sunday brunch, happy hour. **Address:** 225 River St 07030 **Location:** Between 1st and 2nd sts; in W Hoboken. **Parking:** valet and street only.

B L D CALL ♿M

HO-HO-KUS (B-4) pop. 4,078, elev. 113'

SAVE **THE HERMITAGE** is at 335 N. Franklin Tpke. Originally an 18th-century stone house, The Hermitage was remodeled 1847-48 in the romantic Gothic Revival style. George Washington, the Marquis de Lafayette, Alexander Hamilton and James Monroe were among the notables who paid a visit during the Revolutionary War.

The Rosencrantz family owned the house for 163 years. The family's upper-middle-class lifestyle during the late Victorian era is portrayed through an extensive collection of furnishings, personal items and papers.

Time: Allow 1 hour minimum. **Hours:** Wed.-Sun. 1-4. Closed Jan. 1, July 4, Thanksgiving, day after Thanksgiving, Christmas Eve and Christmas. Guided tours are given at 1:15, 2:15 and 3:15. Phone ahead to confirm schedule. **Cost:** $7; $5 (ages 55+); $4 (ages 6-12). **Phone:** (201) 445-8311.

HOLMDEL (D-4) elev. 100'

The tree-shaded village of Holmdel is one of the oldest communities in Monmouth County, originally settled by the Holmes family in the mid-1600s. The Holmes-Hendrickson House, built by William Holmes about 1754, still stands at 62 Longstreet Rd. and is a fine example of local Dutch building traditions. Visitors can tour the house from May through September; phone (732) 462-1466.

VIETNAM ERA MUSEUM & EDUCATIONAL CENTER is off Garden State Pkwy. exit 116 on the grounds of the PNC Bank Arts Center, following signs to 1 Memorial Ln. The museum's exhibits offer a comprehensive overview of the Vietnam era and its cultural complexities and lasting impact on American culture. A display of personal letters and photos of New Jersey residents underscores the larger issues of the era.

Time: Allow 1 hour, 30 minutes minimum. **Hours:** Tues.-Sat. 10-4 and by appointment. Closed Jan. 1, July 4, Thanksgiving, day after Thanksgiving and Christmas. **Cost:** $7; $5 (senior citizens and students with ID); free (ages 0-10, veterans and military with ID). **Phone:** (732) 335-0033.

SAVE **New Jersey Vietnam Veterans' Memorial** is off Garden State Pkwy. exit 116 on the grounds of the PNC Bank Arts Center, following signs. The memorial features an emotionally moving bronze statue that depicts a nurse tending to a wounded soldier. Also on view are 366 black granite panels inscribed with the names of 1,562 New Jerseyans who were either killed or listed as missing. **Time:** Allow 30 minutes minimum. **Hours:** Daily 24 hours. Guided tours offered first Sat. of the month at 11 and 1. **Cost:** Free. **Phone:** (732) 335-0033.

HOPE (B-2) elev. 433'

"Jenny, jump!" Apparently the young girl did, foiling the Native Americans her father had spotted sneaking up on her. The true story remains unknown, but the warning cry is commemorated in the name of the mountain that rises above Hope. The village was settled in 1769 by Moravians from Bethlehem, Pa. They built a sturdy, self-sustaining community with mills, a church, a public inn, a brewery and a distillery.

Several old structures remain, their stone walls contrasting with more recent buildings. The Moravians' position as conscientious objectors during the Revolution did not endear them to Patriot forces, but they won respect by caring for sick and wounded soldiers. The colony—diminished by a smallpox epidemic—returned to Pennsylvania in 1808.

Self-guiding tours: Brochures outlining a walking tour past Hope's Moravian architecture can be obtained at stores and banks throughout town and at the Municipal Building Clerk's Office at 407 Great Meadows Rd. (CR 611); phone (908) 459-5011.

LAND OF MAKE BELIEVE is at 354 Great Meadows Rd. This 30-acre family amusement and water park offers rides, shows, attractions and play areas geared to children under 13 and their parents. Highlights include Middle Earth Theater, a talking scarecrow, a Ferris wheel, a roller coaster, the Grand Carousel, an enchanted Christmas Village, an 1862 train, hayrides and Old McDonald's Farm, as well as water slides, river tubing and a life-size pirate ship in a wading pool.

Time: Allow 3 hours minimum. **Hours:** Daily 10-6, third weekend in June-Labor Day; Sat.-Sun. 10-6, Memorial Day weekend-second weekend in June and the weekend after Labor Day. **Cost:** $28 (ages 2-18); $26 (ages 19-61); $24 (ages 62+). **Phone:** (908) 459-9000. *(See ad this page.)* 🍴 🎡

ISELIN   pop. 18,695

• Hotels & Restaurants map & index p. 152

RENAISSANCE WOODBRIDGE HOTEL
(732)634-3600 **111**

Hotel
$160-$263

R
RENAISSANCE®
HOTELS

AAA Benefit:
Members save 5%
or more!

Address: 515 US 1 S 08830 **Location:** Garden State Pkwy exit 131A northbound; exit 130 southbound, 0.7 mi n. Located diagonal to Woodbridge Center. **Facility:** 311 units. 7 stories, interior corridors. **Terms:** check-in 4 pm. **Pool(s):** heated outdoor, heated indoor. **Activities:** exercise room. **Guest Services:** valet laundry, area transportation.

[SAVE] [🍴] [🛗] [Y] [🏊] [BIZ] [📶]
[✕] [🎦] [▣] / SOME UNITS [♿]

JACKSON   (E-4) elev. 120'

A township at the northern fringes of the Pine Barrens, Jackson has several campgrounds and parks. The New Jersey Forest Nursery is off CR 527-528. Prospertown Lake, a wildlife management area west on CR 537, offers fishing and hunting. Canoeing is available on the Upper Toms River.

In nearby Lakewood, the Sister Mary Grace Burns Arboretum of Georgian Court University, 900 Lakewood Ave., features formal gardens, impressive sculptures and fountains; phone (732) 364-2200. A 50-room Georgian-style mansion that was once the winter home of George Jay Gould, the son of a 19th-century railroad tycoon, also is on the premises but is not open to the public.

Jackson Chamber of Commerce: 1021 W. Commodore Blvd., Jackson, NJ 08527. **Phone:** (732) 833-0005.

[GEM] [SAVE] **SIX FLAGS GREAT ADVENTURE & SAFARI**, 1 Six Flags Blvd., has more than 100 rides, shows and attractions in the themed areas. Highlights encompass roller coasters, including the wooden coaster El Toro and the mega coaster Nitro; children's areas that offer various rides and activities; and shows featuring sea lions and sea otters.

The park also offers Safari Off Road Adventure, a guided off-road tour through a 350-acre wildlife preserve. From safari-style vehicles, visitors can view 1,200 species of animals from around the world, including lions, elephants, rhinoceroses, bears and giraffes.

Allow a full day. **Hours:** Opens daily at 10:30, late May-Labor Day; Sat.-Sun. at 10:30, early Apr.-late May; otherwise varies. Closing times vary between 6 and 11 p.m. **Cost:** (Includes Safari Off Road Adventure) $67.99; $42.99 (under 54 inches tall); free (ages 0-2). Prices and schedule may vary; phone ahead. **Parking:** $25. **Phone:** (732) 928-1821. [🍴]

[SAVE] **Six Flags Hurricane Harbor**, 1 Six Flags Blvd., is a 45-acre water park featuring thrill rides, slides, a million-gallon wave pool and a half-mile lazy river. The Tornado launches riders on a four-person raft into a 60-foot-tall, 132-foot-long funnel filled with gushing water. On Big Wave Racer, guests climb 4 stories and then race to the end in water toboggans. For little ones there's Discovery Bay, an activity lagoon with kiddie slides and water gadgets.

Time: Allow 3 hours minimum. **Hours:** Opens daily at 10:30, Memorial Day weekend-Labor Day; otherwise varies. Closing times vary between 5 and 7 p.m. **Cost:** $42.99; $32.99 (under 48 inches tall); free (ages 0-2). Prices and schedule may vary; phone ahead. **Parking:** $25. **Phone:** (732) 928-1821. [🍴]

JAMESBURG   pop. 5,915

CROWNE PLAZA MONROE
(609)655-4775

▼▼▼▼ Hotel $109-$189 **Address:** 390 Forsgate Dr 08831 **Location:** New Jersey Tpke exit 8A (SR 32 E), follow signs. **Facility:** 150 units. 6 stories, interior corridors. **Terms:** cancellation fee imposed. **Pool(s):** heated indoor. **Activities:** exercise room. **Guest Services:** valet and coin laundry.

[🍴] [🛗] [Y] [CALL] [✱M] [🏊] [📶] [✕] [▣]
/ SOME UNITS [♿] [🖨]

WHERE TO EAT

FIDDLEHEADS RESTAURANT
732/521-0878

▼▼▼ New American. Casual Dining. $8-$34 **AAA Inspector Notes:** This small, quaint local restaurant offers a menu that is familiar, yet just creative enough to keep it interesting. Dinner includes such dishes as orange brandied salmon, jambalaya or rack of lamb basted with honey mustard and nuts. Lunch brings a nice selection of sandwiches and salads as well as a few entrées. Service is attentive and friendly in the cozy dining room. **Features:** Sunday brunch. **Reservations:** suggested. **Address:** 27 E Railroad Ave (CR 522) 08831 **Location:** New Jersey Tpke exit 8A (SR 32 E), 3 mi e to Railroad Ave, then just n. **Parking:** street only. [L] [D]

JERSEY CITY   (H-6) pop. 247,597, elev. 83'

• Hotels p. 129 • Restaurants p. 130
• Hotels & Restaurants map & index p. 162

Jersey City, a major manufacturing and transportation center, occupies a peninsula in the Hudson River west of Manhattan Island. More than $1.3 billion annually in steel, chemicals, soaps, perfumes, elevators and myriad other products pour from the city's approximately 600 industrial plants. Completion of the Hudson River railroad tunnels in 1910 cemented Jersey City's position as the transportation and distribution heart of the New York-New Jersey megalopolis.

The Paulus Hook peninsula first was settled by the Dutch about 1630, but less-than-friendly relations with American Indians delayed the establishment of the first permanent settlement at Bergen until 1660. The hook became a strategic link between New York and cities to the west and south, and therefore played an important role in the American Revolution; it was the 1779 site of the Battle of Paulus Hook.

(See map & index p. 162.)

Urban revitalization rescued such architectural treasures as the brownstone houses that were home to the city's elite during the late 19th and early 20th centuries. A number of these restored houses are in the Hamilton Park neighborhood.

The octagonal Colgate Clock, at the foot of Essex Street on the Hudson River, was first set in motion in December 1924. It stands at the former site of Colgate-Palmolive & Company, a symbol of an era when factories dominated the Jersey City waterfront. The clock faces Manhattan and is best viewed from the water. Its dial is 50 feet in diameter; the minute hand is 25 feet, 10 inches long, weighs 2,200 pounds and moves 23 inches every minute.

Hudson County Chamber of Commerce: 857 Bergen Ave., Third Floor, Jersey City, NJ 07306. **Phone:** (201) 386-0699.

LIBERTY STATE PARK is off New Jersey Tpke. exit 14B at Audrey Zapp Dr. and Phillip St. This urban park faces Liberty Island, site of the Statue of Liberty and Ellis Island, and offers a view of the New York City skyline. Facilities include a bicycle trail; an interpretive center; a playground; and Liberty Walk, a 1.3-mile promenade lining the harbor. The pathway leads to the historic Central Railroad of New Jersey Terminal, from which early settlers departed. *See Recreation Areas Chart.*

Statue Cruises makes daily trips to the Statue of Liberty and Ellis Island. **Note:** At press time The Central Railroad of New Jersey Terminal and the interpretive center were closed due to damage from Hurricane Sandy; phone for updates. **Hours:** Park open daily 6 a.m.-10 p.m. Closed holidays. Ferry operates daily 8:30-3:30, Memorial Day-Labor Day; 9:30-3:30, rest of year (weather permitting). No ferry service Christmas Day. Ferry schedule may vary; phone ahead. **Cost:** Park free. Ferry $18; $14 (ages 62+); $9 (ages 4-12). **Parking:** $7. **Phone:** (201) 915-3402, ext. 109 for the interpretive center, or (877) 523-9849 for ferry information. 🏕

Liberty Science Center is off New Jersey Tpke. exit 14C at 222 Jersey City Blvd., in Liberty State Park. With hundreds of interactive exhibits—and at 88 feet tall, the nation's largest IMAX dome screen—the center allows visitors to explore nature, science and technology. Four floors feature 12 museum exhibition halls with permanent and changing displays. Exhibits cover the importance of health, inventions, the conservation of natural resources and eco-friendly lifestyles.

At the Skyscraper! exhibit, courageous visitors can walk an I-beam 18 feet above the floor, learn about how enormous buildings are built, and brave simulated hurricane-force winds and rain. The Eat and Be Eaten exhibit showcases creatures from around the globe, including poison dart frogs and ultra-toxic puffer fish, and illustrates how animals evolve to eat prey while avoiding becoming hunted themselves.

Changing live science demonstrations are presented throughout the day. A ride simulator and 3-D films also are available for an additional fee.

Time: Allow 3 hours minimum. **Hours:** Daily 9-5:30, Apr.-Aug.; Tues.-Fri. 9-4, Sat.-Sun. 9-5:30, rest of year. Schedules for IMAX and 3-D shows vary; phone ahead. Closed Thanksgiving and Christmas. **Cost:** Exhibits $19.75; $16.75 (ages 62+); $14.75 (ages 2-12); $9.75 (educators with ID). IMAX or 3-D show $10; $9 (educators with ID); $8 (ages 2-12 and 62+). Combination ticket (exhibits and one IMAX show) $25.75; $22.75 (ages 62+); $19.75 (ages 2-12); $15.75 (educators with ID). Other combination tickets are available. Science demonstrations free with paid admission. Prices may vary. Under 18 must be with an adult. Under 2 are not permitted in the IMAX theater. **Parking:** $7. **Phone:** (201) 200-1000. 🍴

STATUE OF LIBERTY NATIONAL MONUMENT is in Upper New York Bay on Liberty Island. The Statue of Liberty is accessible only by ferry service from Battery Park; take the subway to the South Ferry stop to reach the departure point. The statue was presented to the United States by France and dedicated in 1886 in commemoration of the two countries' alliance during the American Revolution. Measuring 151 feet high on a 154-foot-high pedestal, it is the tallest statue of modern times. Ellis Island *(see attraction listing p. 129)* is nearby.

Visitors can take ranger-led or self-guiding tours of Liberty Island. Audio tours that can be used on both Liberty and Ellis islands are available as part of the ferry ticket. Free timed passes for entrance inside the pedestal are available but must be reserved at time of ferry ticket purchase; a limited quantity is available. A Flex ticket permits the user to visit the park once within 3 consecutive days.

Only 10 people at a time are permitted to ascend the 377 steps from the main lobby to the crown platform. The walk is strenuous and is not recommended for the physically impaired. The crown's stairwell is a tightly enclosed area and is not air-conditioned.

Note: Visitors to the Statue of Liberty and Ellis Island must pass through primary security screening (similar to airport security procedures) before boarding the ferry. As part of security procedures, it is recommended that you allow ample time and maintain a flexible schedule to include security screening and boarding the ferry. Tickets can be purchased in advance as wait times can be several hours, particularly during peak seasons. Liberty Island is accessible only by ferry service, available daily from Battery Park in Lower Manhattan and from Liberty State Park in Jersey City. A round-trip ticket includes stops at both Liberty and Ellis islands.

Time: Allow 3 hours minimum. **Hours:** Boats depart from Battery Park and Liberty State Park daily

(See map & index p. 162.)

8:30-3:30, Memorial Day-Columbus Day; daily 9:30-3:30, rest of year (weather permitting). Closed Christmas. Phone ahead to confirm schedule.

Cost: Ferry $18; $14 (ages 62+); $9 (ages 4-12). Crown access $3; ages 0-3 are not permitted and reservations are required. **Phone:** (212) 363-3200 for the National Park Service's information line, or (877) 523-9849 for ferry departures from N.J. and N.Y. and for crown reservations.

ELLIS ISLAND is in New York Harbor north of the Statue of Liberty. Ellis Island is accessible only by ferry service from Battery Park and Liberty State Park; take the subway to the South Ferry stop to reach the ferry departure point. This was the nation's main point of entry for millions of immigrants 1892-1954. Some 30 galleries and exhibits in the museum chronicle the history of immigration into the United States.

Highlights include the baggage, registry and hearing rooms; the American Family Immigration History Center, a computerized genealogy center with the names of immigrants processed during the peak years, 1892-1924; and the American Immigrant Wall of Honor, containing the names of more than 700,000 individuals. The Peopling of America Center features exhibits dedicated to those who arrived before the immigration station opened in 1892, including early Native Americans, colonists and Europeans. Ranger-led and audio tours are available.

The 28-minute film, "Island of Hope, Island of Tears," tells the story of immigrants traveling via steerage to the United States.

Note: Due to the effects of Hurricane Sandy in late October 2012, some exhibits will not be available. Ferry service is available daily from Battery Park in Lower Manhattan and from Liberty State Park in Jersey City, N.J. A round-trip ticket includes stops at both Liberty and Ellis islands. **Time:** Allow 3 hours minimum. **Hours:** Boats depart from Battery Park and Liberty State Park daily (weather permitting) 8:30-3:30, Memorial Day-Columbus Day; 9:30-3:30, rest of year. Museum open daily 9:30-5. Film runs continuously throughout the day. All schedules may vary; phone ahead to confirm. Closed Christmas.

Cost: Ferry $18; $14 (ages 62+); $9 (ages 4-12). Museum, film and audio tour are free. **Phone:** (212) 363-3200 for the National Park Service's information line, or (877) 523-9849 for N.J. and N.Y. ferry departures. GT

COURTYARD BY MARRIOTT JERSEY CITY NEWPORT
(201)626-6600   94

▼▼▼ Hotel $209-$459

COURTYARD Marriott

AAA Benefit: Members save 5% or more!

Address: 540 Washington Blvd 07310 **Location:** From end of US 1 and 9 at Holland Tunnel, s on Jersey Ave, e to Washington Blvd, then 0.3 mi e. **Facility:** 187 units. 10 stories, interior corridors. **Parking:** valet only. **Pool(s):** heated indoor. **Activities:** hot tub, exercise room. **Guest Services:** valet and coin laundry, boarding pass kiosk.

DOUBLETREE BY HILTON HOTEL & SUITES JERSEY CITY
(201)499-2400   95

▼▼▼ Hotel $137-$389 **Address:** 455 Washington Blvd 07310 **Location:** Between 4th and 6th sts; at The Waterfront. **Facility:** 198 units. 14 stories, interior corridors. **Parking:** on-site (fee) and valet. **Terms:** 1-7 night minimum stay, cancellation fee imposed. **Amenities:** safes. **Activities:** exercise room. **Guest Services:** valet laundry, rental car service, area transportation.

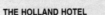

AAA Benefit: Members save 5% or more!

THE HOLLAND HOTEL
(201)963-6200   93

▼▼ Motel $105-$155

Address: 175 12th St 07310 **Location:** New Jersey Tpke exit 14C, 3 mi e, follow signs to Holland Tunnel; in toll plaza. **Facility:** 71 units. 3 stories (no elevator), interior corridors. **Terms:** cancellation fee imposed. **Amenities:** safes.

THE WESTIN JERSEY CITY NEWPORT
(201)626-2900   96

▼▼▼ ▼▼▼ Contemporary Hotel $199-$569

WESTIN HOTELS & RESORTS

AAA Benefit: Members save up to 15%, plus Starwood Preferred Guest® benefits!

Address: 479 Washington Blvd 07310 **Location:** At The Waterfront, just n of 6th St. **Facility:** Close to the PATH train, shops and the riverfront, this Westin is the "in" place to stay on the Jersey City harbor. From its dramatic center staircase to its zen-like guest rooms, this place has it all. 429 units. 23 stories, interior corridors. **Parking:** on-site (fee) and valet. **Amenities:** safes. **Dining:** Fire & Oak, see separate listing. **Pool(s):** heated indoor. **Activities:** hot tub, exercise room, massage. **Guest Services:** valet laundry.

(See map & index p. 162.)

WHERE TO EAT

CASA DANTE 201/795-2750 (92)
▼▼▼▼ Italian. Fine Dining. $15-$31 **AAA Inspector Notes:** Tucked away in a busy commercial downtown neighborhood packed with ethnic shops and take-out restaurants, this long-established restaurant serves classic Italian dishes that are well-prepared and presented in savory sauces. A European décor punctuates the dining room, which has a casually upscale feel. Service is prompt and attentive. **Features:** full bar, happy hour. **Reservations:** suggested. **Address:** 737 Newark Ave 07306 **Location:** Just e of jct Kennedy Blvd; downtown. **Parking:** valet only. (L) (D)

FIRE & OAK 201/610-9610 (93)
▼▼ ▼▼ American. Casual Dining. $13-$44 **AAA Inspector Notes:** There just might be something for everyone at this popular, casual restaurant. The décor is modern yet relaxed and comfortable, while the menu offers a little bit of everything including burgers, sushi, large salads, flatbread pizza, pastas and even a little barbecue. **Features:** full bar, Sunday brunch, happy hour. **Address:** 485 Washington Blvd 07310 **Location:** At 6th St; in The Westin Jersey City Newport. **Parking:** on-site (fee) and valet. (L) (D) CALL (C,M)

JOHN'S PIZZERIA 201/433-4411 (94)
▼▼ Pizza. Casual Dining. $6-$14 **AAA Inspector Notes:** This is an outpost of the popular NYC pizzeria. The table service here ranges from basic to nonexistent, but the excellent thin crust pizza makes up for it and then some. There are no slices served here but you can get a smaller, personal-sized pie. Your best bet is to keep it simple and get the margherita with fresh mozzarella and basil. They also have a menu of sandwiches and pastas. **Features:** full bar, patio dining. **Address:** 87 Sussex St 07302 **Location:** Between Greene and Washington sts; in Paulus Hook. **Parking:** street only. (L) (D)

LIGHT HORSE TAVERN 201/946-2028 (95)
▼▼▼▼ American. Casual Dining. $11-$29 **AAA Inspector Notes:** This tavern takes its name from Henry Lee, a soldier who attracted the admiration of Gen. George Washington through his adroit horsemanship that earned him the nickname "Light Horse Harry." Some 200 years later, diners beat a path to the beautiful, lovingly restored dining room for sublime food, from a terrific saffron-infused fisherman's stew to a fine-aged New York sirloin. **Features:** full bar, patio dining, Sunday brunch. **Reservations:** suggested. **Address:** 199 Washington St 07302 **Location:** Between Sussex and Morris sts. **Parking:** street only. (L) (D)

KEANSBURG (I-6) pop. 10,105, elev. 13'

[SAVE] **RUNAWAY RAPIDS WATERPARK** is at 275 Beachway Ave. The water park features high-speed waterslides, a lazy river and a play space designed for toddlers. Volcanic Revenge is a waterslide that runs uphill. Pairs can ride together in a double tube on the double-wide Mountain Blast.

Time: Allow 2 hours minimum. **Hours:** Opens daily at 10, mid-June through Labor Day; Sat.-Sun. (also Memorial Day) at 10, Memorial Day weekend to mid-June and day after Labor Day-Sept. 30. Closing time varies (generally closes Mon.-Fri. at 11 p.m., Sat.-Sun. at midnight). Phone ahead to confirm schedule. **Cost:** $26.95 (for 3 hours); $24.95 (for 2 hours); $11.95 (under 42 inches tall). After 4 p.m. $11.95. Locker rental $5. **Parking:** $5. **Phone:** (732) 495-1400. (TI)

Pick up vibrant, top-quality travel guides

and atlases at AAA/CAA offices

[SAVE] **Keansburg Amusement Park** is adjacent to Runaway Rapids Waterpark at 275 Beachway Ave. Operating more than 100 years, the park offers a variety of rides for children and adults, several thrill rides and roller coasters and classic Jersey boardwalk food. Boardwalk-style games of chance, arcades, go-carts and a haunted house also are available.

Time: Allow 2 hours minimum. **Hours:** Opens daily at 10, mid-June through Labor Day; Sat.-Sun. (also Memorial Day) at 10, Memorial Day weekend to mid-June and day after Labor Day-Sept. 30. Closing time varies; the park generally closes Mon.-Fri. at 11 p.m. and Sat.-Sun. at midnight. Phone ahead to confirm schedule. **Cost:** Free, but fare for ride tickets may vary by day of week and time of year. Book of 200 tickets $94.95; 100 tickets $54.95; 50 tickets $29.95; single ticket 75c. Locker rental $5. **Parking:** $5. **Phone:** (732) 495-1400. (TI)

KENILWORTH pop. 7,914
• **Hotels & Restaurants map & index p. 152**

LE RENDEZ VOUS 908/931-0888 (108)
▼▼▼▼ French. Fine Dining. $28-$32 **AAA Inspector Notes:** The seasonal menu represents an exciting interpretation of modern French cuisine. Food is lovingly prepared and served by an attentive staff. The room is tiny but distinctly Provençal in charm. **Reservations:** suggested. **Address:** 520 Boulevard 07033 **Location:** Jct 21st St; downtown. (D)

STAR OF INDIA RESTAURANT 908/272-6633 (109)
▼▼ ▼▼ Indian. Casual Dining. $7-$15 **AAA Inspector Notes:** The dining room is dark, lit only by votives and jewel-tone lanterns that illuminate the colorful painted wall murals. Locals keep the kitchen busy preparing the creamy chicken tikka masala, shrimp in sweet and spicy honey sauce, lamb in fragrant spinach, and many other aromatic dishes. **Address:** 496 Boulevard 07033 **Location:** Garden State Pkwy exit 138, w on Kenilworth Blvd, then 0.7 mi e. (D)

KINGSTON (D-3) pop. 1,493, elev. 110'

Gen. George Washington and his officers met at the Kingston Presbyterian church cemetery in January 1777, where they decided to break winter camp at Morristown instead of engaging British forces in New Brunswick. Washington made at least two other trips to Kingston: one on his way to the Battle of Monmouth in 1778 and an extended stay during the Continental Congress convention in Princeton in the summer of 1783.

ROCKINGHAM STATE HISTORIC SITE is on Laurel Ave./Kingston-Rocky Hill Rd. (CR 603) between CR 518 and SR 27. Washington wrote his "Farewell Orders to the Armies of the United States" at this site. He lived in the 18th-century house between late August and early November 1783 while Congress was in session in Princeton. While here, Washington received word that the final version of the Treaty of Paris had been signed, making this his final wartime headquarters.

The restored house contains a collection of period furnishings and reproductions of Washington's military equipment. Also at the site is a kitchen garden typical of the late 18th century, filled with vegetables, herbs and flowers.

Hours: Guided tours are given Wed.-Sat. on the hour 10-11 and 1-3, Sun. 1-3. Closed state and federal holidays and Wed. after Mon. or Tues. holidays. Phone ahead to confirm schedule. **Cost:** Free. **Phone:** (609) 683-7132.

ENO TERRA RESTAURANT & ENOTECA   609/497-1777

 New Italian. Fine Dining. $15-$36 **AAA Inspector Notes:** The cuisine here is vaguely Italian, yet clearly fresh and sophisticated. The menu is made up of excellent farm fresh and organic produce, grass-fed meats and market fresh seafood—the restaurant has its own two-acre farm just down the road. The wine list continues the theme of eat local, drink global with some well selected and comfortably priced fine wines. The restaurant itself is a beautiful blend of Old World exterior and contemporary interiors. **Features:** full bar. **Reservations:** suggested. **Address:** 4484 Rt 27 08528 **Location:** 2 mi n of Princeton on Old Lincoln Hwy (SR 27).

LAKEHURST (E-4) pop. 2,654, elev. 72'

Surrounded by fish and wildlife management areas, Lakehurst is best known for its role in aviation history. The community was the American terminal for huge, transatlantic lighter-than-air craft during the 1920s and 1930s. The Naval Air Engineering Station at Lakehurst was a landing site for the German airship *Hindenburg*, which caught fire and crashed to the field in 1937, resulting in the loss of 36 lives. The event is commemorated by a small monument on the grounds.

Self-guiding tours: The Lakehurst Historical Society offers information about a walking tour of the downtown area's historic sites; phone (732) 657-8864.

LAKEWOOD pop. 53,805

BEST WESTERN LEISURE INN   (732)367-0900

Hotel
$80-$179

AAA Benefit: Members save up to 20%!

Address: 1600 Rt 70 E 08701 **Location:** Garden State Pkwy exit 88 southbound, just w; 2.5 mi e of US 9. **Facility:** 104 units. 2 stories (no elevator), interior/exterior corridors. **Pool(s):** outdoor. **Guest Services:** coin laundry. **Featured Amenity:** continental breakfast.

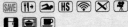

HILTON GARDEN INN OF LAKEWOOD   (732)262-5232

 Hotel $129-$309 **Address:** 1885 SR 70 W 08701 **Location:** 3.5 mi e of jct US 9. **Facility:** 110 units. 4 stories, interior corridors. **Terms:** 1-7 night minimum stay, cancellation fee imposed. **Amenities:** safes. **Pool(s):** heated indoor. **Activities:** hot tub, exercise room. **Guest Services:** valet and coin laundry.

AAA Benefit: Members save 5% or more!

WHERE TO EAT

CHARLIE BROWN'S STEAKHOUSE   732/367-4818

 Steak. Casual Dining. $9-$30 **AAA Inspector Notes:** This budget-friendly steakhouse, famous for its prime rib, offers top quality fare without hurting your pocketbook. The young ones will not be disappointed with the kids' menu, and just might even try something green from the salad bar. Adults will love the quality steaks, chicken and rib dishes. The express lunches are great for those saddled with time constraints. **Features:** full bar, happy hour. **Address:** 400 Rt 70 08701 **Location:** Garden State Pkwy exit 88, 3 mi w.

LAMBERTVILLE (D-2) pop. 3,906, elev. 71'
• Restaurants p. 132

Collectors from the mid-Atlantic come for antiques, crafts and art galleries that fill Bridge, Union and Coryell sts. The tree-lined neighborhood looks like a movie set from a New England town, and if you arrive from Pennsylvania over the Delaware River, the Lambertville Station should remind guests about the borough's railroad history. It has now turned into a popular hotel and restaurant to go along with all of the shops, coffee bars and other bistros.

Lambertville Area Chamber of Commerce: 59 N. Union St., Lambertville, NJ 08530. **Phone:** (609) 397-0055.

Self-guiding tours: A guide outlining the various shops and things to do in the area is available at the convention and visitors bureau.

Shopping areas: The Antique Center at The People's Store at the corner of Church and Union features three floors that's seen selling action since 1839. If you arrive from the Washington Crossing Park side of town, you'll pass right by the Golden Nugget Antique Flea Market, a much higher end "flea" than you're used to, with 60 shops.

HOWELL LIVING HISTORY FARM, A FACILITY OF THE MERCER COUNTY PARK COMMISSION is 2 mi. s. via SR 29, 1.5 mi. e. on Valley Rd., then just n. to 70 Wooden's Ln. With farmhands tilling the fields and tending livestock just as their ancestors did, this 130-acre homestead replicates a rural lifestyle practiced during the late 19th and early 20th centuries. A self-guiding tour brochure is available at the visitor center. **Hours:** Tues.-Sat. 10-4, Sun. noon-4, Apr.-Nov.; Tues.-Sat. 10-4, Feb.-Mar. Time may be reduced in summer; phone to confirm schedule. Closed major holidays. **Cost:** Free. **Phone:** (609) 737-3299.

CHIMNEY HILL ESTATE INN   609/397-1516

 Historic Bed & Breakfast. Rates not provided. **Address:** 207 Goat Hill Rd 08530 **Location:** Jct SR 29 and Swan St, just n to Studdiford St to Goat Hill Rd, then 0.4 mi e. **Facility:** This fieldstone house sits on a hill high above Lambertville. The dining room features a large fireplace, beamed ceilings and elegant table settings. 13 units. 2-3 stories (no elevator), interior/exterior corridors. **Terms:** age restrictions may apply.

LAMBERTVILLE HOUSE-A NATIONAL HISTORIC INN
(609)397-0200

▼▼▼ ▼▼▼
Historic Hotel
$185-$360

Address: 32 Bridge St 08530 **Location:** Downtown. **Facility:** Historic is an understatement as this lodging has been in operation for more than 200 years. Built in 1812 as a stagecoach stop near the Delaware River, this charming inn features original fieldstone walls. 26 units. 4 stories, interior/exterior corridors. **Terms:** 5 day cancellation notice-fee imposed. **Guest Services:** valet laundry. **Featured Amenity:** continental breakfast.

[SAVE] [YI] [Y] [HS] [📶] [X]
/ SOME UNITS [🖥]

LAMBERTVILLE STATION INN
609/397-4400

▼▼▼
Hotel
$150-$350

Address: 11 Bridge St 08530 **Location:** South of Free Bridge; center. **Facility:** 46 units. 3 stories, interior corridors. **Terms:** cancellation fee imposed. **Amenities:** safes. **Dining:** Lambertville Station Restaurant, see separate listing. **Guest Services:** valet laundry.

[SAVE] [YI] [Y] [BIZ] [📶] [X]
/ SOME UNITS [🖥] [💻]

WHERE TO EAT

HAMILTON'S GRILL ROOM
609/397-4343

▼▼▼ American. Casual Dining. $13-$42 **AAA Inspector Notes:** Sophisticated food is served in a charming location beside a pedestrian path along the Delaware River Canal. The seasonal patio is enchanting. Grilled seafood is the specialty on a menu that also includes satisfying grilled meats and nightly specials. **Features:** Sunday brunch. **Reservations:** suggested. **Address:** 8 Coryell St 08530 **Location:** Downtown. **Parking:** street only. [L] [D]

INN OF THE HAWKE
609/397-9555

▼▼▼ American. Casual Dining. $11-$25 **AAA Inspector Notes:** Classic American fare, including steaks, burgers, hearty sandwiches and chili, make up the bill of fare at this downtown eatery set in a historic house with a garden patio for al fresco dining in fair weather. A simple décor and straightforward preparations make this spot a local favorite. **Features:** full bar, patio dining. **Address:** 74 S Union St 08530 **Location:** At Mt Hope St. [L] [D]

LAMBERTVILLE STATION RESTAURANT
609/397-8300

▼▼ ▼▼
American
Family Dining
$7-$25

AAA Inspector Notes: Historic. Along the scenic Delaware River, this restaurant occupies a restored train station sitting next to infrequently used tracks. Tourists flock here for wild game dishes, especially during the winter months. There also are hearty standbys such as meatloaf, burgers, chicken salad and French dip sandwiches. Brunch is served on Sunday. Friendly staffers carry out casual service. **Features:** full bar, patio dining, Sunday brunch, happy hour. **Address:** 11 Bridge St 08530 **Location:** South of Free Bridge; center; in The Inn at Lambertville Station.
[L] [D]

OTA-YA
609/397-9228

▼▼ ▼▼ Sushi. Casual Dining. $4-$27 **AAA Inspector Notes:** This casual eatery is a favorite among locals, who are greeted by name by the proficient sushi chefs working behind the bar. The sizable sushi boat appears to be the town favorite. The staff makes newcomers feel welcome. Diners who are interested in a drink may bring along some sake. **Address:** 21 Ferry St 08530 **Location:** Jct S Union St. **Parking:** no self-parking. [L] [D]

SIAM
609/397-8128

▼▼ ▼▼ Thai. Casual Dining. $10-$16 **AAA Inspector Notes:** What this spot may lack in ambience more than makes up for by serving some of the best food in town. The small, rather plain storefront packs a one-two chili-garlic punch. Dishes such as garlic and pepper shrimp or sautéed bean sprouts with tofu have folks lining up at the door. Guests may bring their own alcohol, but credit cards are not accepted. The restaurant also is open for lunch Thursday through Sunday. **Reservations:** suggested. **Address:** 61 N Main St 08530 **Location:** At Church St. **Parking:** no self-parking. [D] CALL [📱M]

LAWRENCEVILLE pop. 3,887

RED ROOF INN PRINCETON
609/896-3388

▼▼
Motel
Rates not provided

Address: 3203 Brunswick Pike (US 1) 08648 **Location:** I-295 exit 67A, just n. **Facility:** 144 units. 2 stories (no elevator), exterior corridors.

[SAVE] [YI+] [📶] [X] [📷]
/ SOME UNITS [🐾] [🖥] [🖥] [💻]

WHERE TO EAT

ACACIA
609/895-9885

▼▼▼ New American. Casual Dining. $12-$34 **AAA Inspector Notes:** The dining room décor is plush and the progressive American menu mouthwatering at this charming little bistro. Lunch offers a few entrées, sandwiches and such fresh salads as poached apple and arugula salad with orange yogurt dressing. The dinner menu expands with creative entrées including Colorado lamb rack, herb-roasted salmon and walnut-crusted Chilean sea bass with seared shrimp, roasted zucchini and black couscous. Bring your own bottle service is available. **Features:** patio dining. **Reservations:** suggested. **Address:** 2637 Main St 08648 **Location:** I-95 exit 7B, 0.7 mi n on US 206. [L] [D]

KC PRIME STEAKHOUSE
609/275-5418

▼▼▼ Steak. Casual Dining. $9-$42 **AAA Inspector Notes:** This restaurant has a contemporary décor and casual atmosphere. The menu offers all the usual suspects for a steakhouse, but also has some other options like sandwiches and the popular baby back ribs. **Features:** full bar, Sunday brunch, happy hour. **Address:** 4160 Quakerbridge Rd 08648 **Location:** 5 mi e of US 1 N; behind Quaker Bridge Mall. [L] [D] CALL [📱M]

LEBANON pop. 1,358

COURTYARD BY MARRIOTT LEBANON
(908)236-8500

▼▼▼
Hotel
$181-$298

COURTYARD®
Marriott

AAA Benefit: Members save 5% or more!

Address: 300 Corporate Dr 08833 **Location:** I-78 exit 20A (Cokesbury Rd) westbound; exit 18 eastbound, 2 mi e on US 22, U-turn to Cokesbury Rd, then just n. **Facility:** 125 units. 4 stories, interior corridors. **Pool(s):** heated indoor. **Activities:** exercise room. **Guest Services:** valet and coin laundry, boarding pass kiosk.

[SAVE] [ECO] [Y] CALL [📱M] [🐾] [BIZ]
[HS] [📶] [X] [🖥] [💻] / SOME UNITS [🍽]

LINDEN pop. 40,499
• Hotels & Restaurants map & index p. 152

HAMPTON INN LINDEN   (908)862-3222 [87]

WWW **Hotel** $109-$189 **Address:**
501 W Edgar Rd 07036 **Location:** US 1
N and Stiles St. Located in a shopping
plaza. **Facility:** 149 units. 4 stories, interior corridors. **Terms:** check-in 4 pm, 1-7
night minimum stay, cancellation fee imposed. **Pool(s):** heated outdoor. **Activities:** exercise room. **Guest Services:** valet and coin
laundry, area transportation.

| **AAA Benefit:** |
| Members save 5% |
| or more! |

LITTLE FALLS (G-5) pop. 14,432, elev. 360'

YOGI BERRA MUSEUM & LEARNING CENTER is
.3 mi. s. of jct. SRs 3 and 46 via Valley Rd. to 8 Yogi
Berra Dr., at the entrance to Montclair State University. Overlooking the baseball stadium of the minor-
league New Jersey Jackals, this museum traces the
history of baseball and commemorates Berra's legendary career. Highlight films are shown daily.

Guided tours are available by appointment. **Time:**
Allow 30 minutes minimum. **Hours:** Wed.-Sun.
noon-5. Closed major holidays. **Cost:** $6; $5 (ages
65+); $4 (ages 5-17). **Phone:** (973) 655-2378.

LIVINGSTON pop. 29,366
• Hotels & Restaurants map & index p. 152

WESTMINSTER HOTEL   (973)533-0600 [58]

WWWWW
Boutique
Contemporary
Hotel
$139-$459

Address: 550 W Mount Pleasant Ave
07039 **Location:** Between Daven Ave
and Microlab Rd; just w of jct CR 508.
Facility: Original art and contemporary
design combined with richly appointed
rooms contribute to the boutique style of
this suburban hotel. Baths offer limited
space, but the fixtures are ultra modern.
183 units. 4 stories, interior corridors.
Parking: on-site and valet. **Terms:** cancellation fee imposed. **Amenities:** safes.
Dining: Strip House, see separate
listing. **Pool(s):** heated indoor. **Activities:** hot tub, exercise room, spa. **Guest
Services:** valet laundry, boarding pass
kiosk, area transportation. **Featured
Amenity: continental breakfast.**

WHERE TO EAT

PANEVINO RISTORANTE   973/535-6160 [51]
WW Italian. Casual Dining. $14-$29 **AAA Inspector Notes:**
Relaxed and family-friendly, this Italian eatery offers a menu with familiar pastas, salads, seafood and pizza cooked in a wood oven. The
rustic dining room is comfortable but the outdoor patio is a real draw
in warmer months. They even have an outdoor bocce ball court. **Features:** full bar, patio dining, happy hour. **Address:** 637 W Mount
Pleasant Ave 07039 **Location:** On SR 10; 0.8 mi w of Eisenhower
Pkwy. [L] [D] CALL 🖥M

STRIP HOUSE   973/548-0050 [52]
WWW Steak. Fine Dining. $13-$49 **AAA Inspector Notes:** The
double entendre of the Strip House name is not lost on the owners,
who play up both angles. Patterned red wallpaper shows silhouettes
of lithe figures in a 1940s Hollywood setting, while the menu centers
on such dishes as well-seasoned filet mignon and indulgent New
York strip. **Features:** full bar. **Reservations:** suggested. **Address:**
550 W Mount Pleasant Ave 07039 **Location:** Between Daven Ave
and Microlab Rd; just w of jct CR 508; in Westminster Hotel. **Parking:**
on-site and valet. [B] [L] [D]

THAVMA MEDITERRANEAN GRILL   973/992-8999 [50]
WW Mediterranean. Casual Dining. $8-$26 **AAA Inspector
Notes:** The menu here covers more than just Greek cuisine and has
a good selection of seafood entrées, steaks, sandwiches and salads.
There is a nice terrace for outdoor dining when the weather permits.
Address: 6230 Town Center Way 07039 **Location:** Jct SR 10 and N
Livingston Ave (CR 527); in Livingston Town Center.
[L] [D] CALL 🖥M

LONG BRANCH (D-5) pop. 30,719, elev. 19'
• Hotels p. 134 • Restaurants p. 134

One of America's earliest seashore resorts, Long
Branch rivaled Saratoga, N.Y., in popularity during
its heyday. The stiff Philadelphia moral codes of the
late 18th century required that a female beachgoer
be escorted to the water by a male companion.
Wealthy socialites preferring to choose their own
partners created a lucrative business for available
young men, a custom that lasted until the Gay '90s.

Once mores relaxed Long Branch boomed with
coed beaches, gambling and other adult amuse-
ments. Such colorful personalities as Diamond Jim
Brady and Lily Langtry frequented the resort. Long
Branch also was the preferred summer home of
Presidents Ulysses S. Grant, Rutherford B. Hayes,
James A. Garfield, Chester A. Arthur, Benjamin Har-
rison, William McKinley and Woodrow Wilson.

Attractions here include a 2-mile boardwalk and 5
miles of oceanfront good for swimming, sunbathing
and surf fishing. Seven Presidents Oceanfront Park
embraces 38 acres along the coast; phone (732)
229-0924 Memorial Day-Labor Day.

Greater Long Branch Chamber of Commerce:
228 Broadway, P.O. Box 628, Long Branch, NJ
07740. **Phone:** (732) 222-0400.

OCEAN PLACE RESORT & SPA 732/571-4000

Resort Hotel
Rates not provided

Address: 1 Ocean Blvd 07740 **Location:** Oceanfront. Jct SR 71, 3 mi e on SR 36, then 0.5 mi s. **Facility:** Rooms with ocean views coupled with expansive conference facilities, a sunny pool deck and a laid-back tiki bar make this a great option for fun or business. 255 units. 12 stories, interior corridors. **Terms:** check-in 4 pm. **Amenities:** safes. **Dining:** 3 restaurants, entertainment. **Pool(s):** heated outdoor, heated indoor. **Activities:** sauna, hot tub, steamroom, tennis, exercise room, spa. **Guest Services:** valet laundry, area transportation.

WHERE TO EAT

MCLOONE'S PIER HOUSE 732/923-1006

▼▼ American. Casual Dining. $11-$34 **AAA Inspector Notes:** You can't get a table any closer to the water without getting wet. Located at a bustling oceanfront shopping/dining complex, this casual and welcoming place offers a menu with everything you might be looking for at the beach—a raw bar, a good selection of sandwiches and salads and some creative dinner entrées. **Features:** full bar, patio dining, Sunday brunch. **Reservations:** suggested. **Address:** 1 Ocean Ave 07740 **Location:** At Laird St; in Pier Village. **Parking:** street only. L D CALL M

ROONEY'S 732/870-1200

▼▼ Seafood. Casual Dining. $13-$45 **AAA Inspector Notes:** Looking for casual oceanfront dining? Here it is with a large menu of fresh seafood that is sure to cover any craving. A full raw bar with oyster selections, clams and crab, live lobsters and a full array of fresh and seasonal fish are offered in a friendly and relaxed atmosphere. Grab a seat at the bar or a table in the enclosed glass patio for great views of the beach and the rolling waves. Convenient free parking only adds to the appeal. **Features:** full bar, patio dining. **Reservations:** suggested. **Address:** 100 Ocean Ave N 07740 **Location:** At Cooper Ave. L D CALL M

SURF TACO 732/229-7873

▼ Southwestern. Casual Dining. $3-$11 **AAA Inspector Notes:** This laid-back taco shop serves up tasty West Coast, Baja-style burritos, tacos, enchiladas, salads and wraps filled with everything you might expect and a few items you may not. The blackened mahi or the chicken teriyaki tacos are a great choice, or if you're up for an eating challenge, try to finish the monster "tsunami" burrito in 15 minutes and get your picture on the wall of fame. **Features:** patio dining. **Address:** 94 Brighton Ave 07740 **Location:** Between Ocean and 2nd aves. **Parking:** street only. L D CALL M

WINDMILL RESTAURANTS 732/229-9863

▼ Hot Dogs Burgers. Quick Serve. $3-$8 **AAA Inspector Notes:** This is a local favorite haunt for the area's top hot dogs, charbroiled burgers, and gooey but oh so good cheese fries. There is a fixin's bar to dress that dog however you desire such as a little relish and onion. Seating is limited and sometimes cramped, but the service is fast and should have you in and out in no time. **Address:** 586 Ocean Blvd 07740 **Location:** Jct SR 71, 3 mi e on SR 36, then 2 mi s. L

WINDMILL RESTAURANTS 732/870-6098

▼ Hot Dogs Burgers. Quick Serve. $3-$8 **AAA Inspector Notes:** This is a local favorite haunt for the area's top hot dogs, charbroiled burgers, and gooey but oh so good cheese fries. There is a fixin's bar to dress that dog however you desire such as a little relish and onion. Seating is limited and sometimes cramped, but the service is fast and should have you in and out in no time. **Features:** beer only. **Address:** 200 Ocean Ave N 07740 **Location:** Jct SR 71, 3 mi on SR 36, then just s; in Krauser's Shopping Center. L CALL M

LONG VALLEY pop. 1,879

THE NEIGHBOUR HOUSE B&B 908/876-3519

▼▼ Historic Bed & Breakfast. Rates not provided. **Address:** 143 W Mill Rd (CR 513) 07853 **Location:** Just s of jct CR 513 and 517. **Facility:** This rural 1830 Greek Revival high-style farmhouse with a large front porch sits adjacent to 800 acres of corn fields and exudes a lovely simple country charm. 4 units. 2 stories (no elevator), interior corridors. **Bath:** some shared.

WHERE TO EAT

LONG VALLEY PUB & BREWERY 908/876-1122

▼▼ American. Casual Dining. $10-$30 **AAA Inspector Notes:** Some of the fine handcrafted ales served in this cozy converted 1771 stone barn have won awards. In addition to the requisite burgers, the menu lists pulled pork barbecue, entrée salads, grilled steaks, duck and cedar plank salmon. There is a nice outdoor patio open in warmer months. **Features:** full bar, patio dining, happy hour. **Address:** 1 Fairmount Rd (CR 513) 07853 **Location:** Corner of CR 513 and 517. L D

LUMBERTON (E-3) elev. 20'

AIR VICTORY MUSEUM is 2 mi. s. on Main St., .3 mi. n.w. on Fostertown Rd. (CR 612), then .7 mi. w. to 68 Stacy Haines Rd. at South Jersey Regional Airport. This hands-on museum features restored aircraft, flight simulators, a wind tunnel and aviation artifacts. A collection of more than 1,000 plastic, balsa and fabric flying models includes the Wright *Flyer*, the *Spirit of St. Louis*, the X-15 and the Delta-Thor rocket. Among the restored aircraft displayed are an F-14 Tomcat and an F-86 Sabre.

Time: Allow 1 hour minimum. **Hours:** Wed.-Sat. 10-4, Sun. 11-4, mid-Apr. through Oct. 31; Wed.-Sat. 10-4, Nov.-Dec. Closed Easter, Thanksgiving and Christmas. **Cost:** $4; $3 (ages 62+); $2 (ages 4-13). **Phone:** (609) 267-4488.

LYNDHURST (G-6) pop. 20,554, elev. 101'
• Hotels & Restaurants map & index p. 162

Nearby Kingsland was the site of the Canadian Car and Foundry Plant, a munitions factory set ablaze by German saboteurs in 1917, 4 months before America's entry into World War I. Despite the explosion of a half-million artillery shells, no one was killed. Exhibits about the terrorist attack are displayed at the 1893 Little Red Schoolhouse on Riverside Avenue; phone (201) 804-2513.

MEDIEVAL TIMES DINNER & TOURNAMENT is off New Jersey Tpke. exit 16W, w. on SR 3, then s. on SR 17 to 149 Polito Ave. In a building resembling an 11th-century European castle, visitors consume a four-course dinner sans silverware and then watch an arena performance of live jousting, swordplay, horsemanship and falconry. Guests are encouraged to cheer for one of six "Knights of the Realm," named after historic regions of medieval Spain.

Time: Allow 3 hours minimum. **Hours:** Seatings Wed.-Fri. (times vary), Sat. at 5 and 8, Sun. at 4:30;

(See map & index p. 162.)

additional show times are offered on some weekends. **Cost:** $61.95; $36.95 (ages 3-12). Reservations are required. **Phone:** (201) 933-2220 or (888) 935-6878.

COURTYARD BY MARRIOTT LYNDHURST MEADOWLANDS
(201)896-6666 **20**

▼▼▼▼ **Hotel** $146-$240 **Address:** 1 Polito Ave 07071 **Location:** New Jersey Tpke exit 16W (SR 3 W), stay left exit SR 17 S. **Facility:** 227 units. 6 stories, interior corridors. **Pool(s):** heated indoor. **Activities:** exercise room. **Guest Services:** valet and coin laundry, area transportation.

AAA Benefit: Members save 5% or more!

MADISON (H-4) pop. 15,845, elev. 261'
• Hotels & Restaurants map & index p. 152

Madison, settled about 1685, was first known as Bottle Hill after a local tavern that existed in Colonial days. It was renamed for President James Madison in 1834. Tours of the Drew University and Fairleigh Dickinson University campuses can be arranged; phone (973) 408-3739 for Drew University or (973) 443-8500 for Fairleigh Dickinson University.

The Shakespeare Theatre of New Jersey, in residence at Drew University, presents Shakespeare's works as well as classical and modern plays from late May through December; phone (973) 408-5600.

MUSEUM OF EARLY TRADES & CRAFTS is on SR 124 (Main St.) at Green Village Rd. The museum preserves the tools and techniques used by ordinary people before the rise of industrialization in the 19th century. Housed in the historic James Library Building, this 1899 Richardsonian Romanesqe Revival building is listed on the New Jersey and National Registers and is one of the finest secular examples of this style in the state. Displays include implements used by farm families as well as tools and products found in trades such as cabinetmaking, coopering, distilling, shoemaking and other crafts that have either died out or become mechanized. Changing exhibitions exploring the shifting cultural and technological fabric of American life tying the past to the modern era are presented twice a year.

Hours: Tues.-Sat. 10-4, Sun. noon-5, Sept.-June; Tues.-Sat. 10-4, rest of year. Closed major holidays. **Cost:** $5; $3 (ages 6-17, ages 62+ and students with ID); $13 (family). **Phone:** (973) 377-2982.

54 MAIN BAR & GRILLE   973/966-0252 **74**

▼▼ American. Casual Dining. $11-$28 **AAA Inspector Notes:** Friendly and picturesque Main Street now has a casual spot for the collegiate sort (Drew and Fairleigh are a stone's throw). Here guests can catch a game on one of the many TVs, grab a drink or linger over dinner in the pub-style dining room. Live music is offered in the bar on most nights. The large menu has hefty burgers, salads and such entrées as steak frites or broiled mahi mahi with an asparagus, potato, leek salad and mustard tarragon vinaigrette. **Features:** full bar, Sunday brunch, happy hour. **Address:** 54 Main St 07940 **Location:** Center.

BEGUM PALACE   973/660-9100 **78**

▼▼ Indian. Casual Dining. $13-$26 **AAA Inspector Notes:** The large menu holds some surprises, such as an unusual number of dosa and uthpam-filled crepes, which are not so common in the area. Among other choices are tandoori, kormas, masalas and murg with prawns, lamb and chicken. Sauces are rich with flavor and texture. **Address:** 300 Main St 07940 **Location:** In Madison Plaza at Staples Shopping Center.

BLUE WAZABI   973/845-2086 **76**

▼▼ Sushi. Casual Dining. $11-$24 **AAA Inspector Notes:** A full selection of fresh sushi bar items are offered here, along with various Asian dishes from the kitchen. The Black Ninja roll is a good choice with shrimp tempura, avocado, spicy kani and black tobiko on top. Space is a little tight in the dining room, but the charming downtown area is great for strolling, and there are a few wine shops nearby where you can pick up a bottle to have with dinner. **Address:** 20 Waverly Pl 07940 **Location:** Just w of SR 124 (Main St); downtown. **Parking:** street only.

IL MONDO VECCHIO RISTORANTE ITALIANO
973/301-0024 **75**

▼▼▼ Italian. Casual Dining. $16-$36 **AAA Inspector Notes:** Although the atmosphere is somewhat relaxed at this long-time local favorite, guests also find smooth refined service and simply excellent upscale Italian cuisine. The chef-owner and his wife have gone on to open some other successful restaurants such as Scalini Fedeli (in Chatham, New Jersey and Manhattan), but they still maintain a close presence here. This is a bring-your-own-bottle restaurant with several good wine shops in the immediate vicinity. **Reservations:** suggested. **Address:** 72 Main St 07940 **Location:** Just e of Waverly Pl; downtown. **Parking:** street only.

L' ALLEGRIA   973/377-4692 **77**

▼▼▼ Italian. Fine Dining. $13-$36 **AAA Inspector Notes:** This is classic Italian dining in a traditional atmosphere. The staff is very professional and attentive and the menu features all the usual suspects. The veal is excellent and there also is a good selection of daily seafood specials. **Features:** full bar. **Reservations:** suggested. **Address:** 11 Prospect St 07940 **Location:** Just w of SR 124; center. **Parking:** street only. CALL

SHANGHAI JAZZ RESTAURANT & BAR   973/822-2899 **73**

▼▼▼ Chinese. Casual Dining. $16-$35 **AAA Inspector Notes:** Locals in this small charming, upscale town flock to this gem to hear live jazz while tasting colorful and flavorful dishes from a menu offering dim sum, seafood, meat and vegetarian entrées. The atmosphere is fun and relaxed, with a very welcoming staff. The performances are top-notch with many well-known jazz players on the schedule. **Features:** full bar. **Reservations:** suggested, Fri & Sat. **Address:** 24 Main St 07940 **Location:** Center.

MAHWAH

COURTYARD BY MARRIOTT MAHWAH   (201)529-5200

Hotel
$139-$229

COURTYARD
Marriott

AAA Benefit: Members save 5% or more!

Address: 140 SR 17 S 07430 **Location:** I-287 exit 66, just s. **Facility:** 146 units. 3 stories, interior corridors. **Pool(s):** heated indoor. **Activities:** exercise room. **Guest Services:** valet and coin laundry, boarding pass kiosk.

DOUBLETREE BY HILTON HOTEL MAHWAH   (201)529-5880

Hotel $129-$179 **Address:** 180 Rt 17 S 07430 **Location:** I-287 exit 66, 0.8 mi s. **Facility:** 139 units. 4 stories, interior corridors. **Terms:** 1-7 night minimum stay, cancellation fee imposed.

AAA Benefit: Members save 5% or more!

Pool(s): heated indoor. **Activities:** exercise room. **Guest Services:** valet and coin laundry, rental car service, area transportation.

HAMPTON INN & SUITES MAHWAH   201/828 2031

Hotel. Rates not provided. **Address:** 290 SR 17 S 07430 **Location:** I-287 exit 66, 1 mi s. **Facility:** 111 units. 3 stories, interior corridors. **Pool(s):** heated indoor. **Activities:** exercise room.

AAA Benefit: Members save 5% or more!

Guest Services: valet and coin laundry, area transportation.

HOMEWOOD SUITES BY HILTON   (201)760-9994

Extended Stay Hotel $113-$179 **Address:** 375 Corporate Dr 07430 **Location:** I-287 exit 66, 1.7 mi on SR 17 S to MacArthur Blvd, then 0.4 mi w. **Facility:** 110 efficiencies, some two bedrooms. 3 stories, interior corridors. **Terms:** 1-7 night minimum stay, cancellation fee imposed. **Pool(s):** heated outdoor. **Activities:** exercise room. **Guest Services:** valet and coin laundry, area transportation.

AAA Benefit: Members save 5% or more!

SHERATON MAHWAH HOTEL   (201)529-1660

Hotel
$129-$309

Sheraton
HOTELS & RESORTS

AAA Benefit: Members save up to 15%, plus Starwood Preferred Guest® benefits!

Address: 1 International Blvd (Rt 17) 07495 **Location:** I-287 exit 66, at SR 17 N. **Facility:** 225 units. 22 stories, interior corridors. **Terms:** cancellation fee imposed. **Pool(s):** heated indoor. **Activities:** hot tub, tennis, exercise room. **Guest Services:** valet and coin laundry, boarding pass kiosk, rental car service.

SUPER 8 MAHWAH   (201)512-0800

Hotel $80-$120 **Address:** 160 Rt 17 S 07430 **Location:** I-287 exit 66, 0.7 mi s. **Facility:** 78 units. 3 stories, interior corridors. **Amenities:** safes. **Guest Services:** coin laundry.

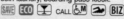
THE RIVER PALM TERRACE   201/529-1111

Steak. Casual Dining. $13-$52 **AAA Inspector Notes:** The Mahwah outpost of the popular Jersey steakhouse serves top-quality steaks and fresh seafood in casual surroundings. Meat lovers will encounter too many options, including a marvelous prime rib, a tantalizing T-bone and a perfect porterhouse. Roasted salmon, steamed lobster and other seafood dishes vie for competition, as do the lamb, veal and chicken selections. Service is casual and efficient, and the wine list is substantial. **Features:** full bar, patio dining. **Reservations:** suggested. **Address:** 209 Ramapo Valley Rd 07430 **Location:** Jct SR 17 S and US 202 (Ramapo Valley Rd), just w. **Parking:** valet only.

MANAHAWKIN pop. 2,303

HOLIDAY INN   609/481-6100

Hotel. Rates not provided. **Address:** 151 SR 72 W 08050 **Location:** Garden State Pkwy exit 63, 2 mi e. **Facility:** 116 units. 5 stories, interior corridors. **Pool(s):** heated indoor. **Activities:** hot tub, exercise room. **Guest Services:** valet and coin laundry.

MAKOTO JAPANESE STEAK HOUSE   609/978-9986

Japanese. Casual Dining. $8-$32 **AAA Inspector Notes:** While the exterior may suggest otherwise to fans of the White Castle chain, inside guests can find Japanese dishes rather than bite-size burgers. Diners watch in delight as talented hibachi chefs chop, toss, stir-fry and ham it up while preparing food. Fine sushi offerings are included. **Address:** 297 SR 72 E 08050 **Location:** Garden State Pkwy exit 63, 1 mi e.

MANCHESTER

COMFORT INN TOMS RIVER / MANCHESTER   (732)657-7100

Hotel $75-$999 **Address:** 2016 Rt 37 W 08759 **Location:** Garden State Pkwy exit 82A, 5 mi w. **Facility:** 44 units. 2 stories (no elevator), interior corridors. **Activities:** limited exercise equipment. **Guest Services:** coin laundry.

MAPLE SHADE

CHARLIE BROWN'S STEAKHOUSE   856/779-8003

Steak. Casual Dining. $9-$30 **AAA Inspector Notes:** This budget-friendly steakhouse, famous for its prime rib, offers top quality fare without hurting your pocketbook. The young ones will not be disappointed with the kids' menu, and just might even try something green from the salad bar. Adults will love the quality steaks, chicken and rib dishes. The express lunches are great for those saddled with time constraints. **Features:** full bar, happy hour. **Address:** 114-116 E Main St 08052 **Location:** Corner of Main and Spruce (CR 537) sts.

P.J. WHELIHAN'S PUB & RESTAURANT   856/234-2345 [124]

American. Casual Dining. $6-$19 **AAA Inspector Notes:** Sports lovers will rejoice at the sight of the island bar surrounded with flat-screen TVs. Hefty plates of wings, nachos, burgers and gooey desserts round out the menu. Food and drink specials are offered daily. **Features:** full bar. **Address:** 396 S Lenola Rd 08052 **Location:** I-295 exit 40, 3.4 mi w on SR 38.

Use travel time to share driving tips and rules of the road with your teens

MARGATE CITY (G-3) pop. 6,354, elev. 8'
• Part of Atlantic City area — see map p. 73

LUCY THE ELEPHANT is at 9200 Atlantic Ave. Built in the shape of an elephant, this six-story wooden structure is complete with a canopied seat called a howdah. The 90-ton historic landmark was constructed in 1881 by real estate developer James V. Lafferty to draw prospective buyers to his holdings. It has served as a real estate office, a residence and a tavern. A climb up to the howdah is rewarded by scenic views.

Hours: Twenty-minute guided tours are offered Mon.-Sat. every 30 minutes 10-8, Sun. and Labor Day 10-5, mid-June through Labor Day; Mon.-Fri. 11-4, Sat.-Sun. 10-5, May 1 to mid-June and day after Labor Day-Oct. 31; Wed.-Fri. 11-4, Sat.-Sun. 10-5, in Apr. and Nov.-Dec.; Sat.-Sun. 10-5, rest of year (weather permitting). Last tour begins 30 minutes before closing. Closed Thanksgiving and Christmas. Phone ahead to confirm schedule. **Cost:** $8; $4 (ages 3-12); free (ages 0-3 and military with ID). **Phone:** (609) 823-6473.

MARLTON pop. 10,133

JOE'S PEKING DUCK HOUSE   856/985-1551   (143)
♦♦ Chinese. Casual Dining. $8-$29 **AAA Inspector Notes:** Guests probably would not come to this small storefront restaurant for its looks, nor its service. However, the tasty noodle platters, soups and create-your-own entrées draw crowds. And we did not even mention the Peking duck—the memorable, standout signature dish. **Address:** 145 Rt 73 S 08053 **Location:** Jct SR 70, just s; in Marlton Crossing Shopping Center. [L] [D]

MEXICAN FOOD FACTORY   856/983-9222   (142)
♦♦ Mexican. Casual Dining. $6-$17 **AAA Inspector Notes:** This restaurant is a great place to enjoy varied and creative dishes, many featuring fish as well as traditional favorites. Guacamole is homemade and good. Choices include grilled orange roughy with garlic and capers, grilled salmon or tuna with red onion and cilantro marmalade and jumbo shrimp over black pepper fettuccine with sweet chipotle cream sauce. Interesting art and great music give this place character. **Features:** full bar. **Address:** 601 W SR 70 08053 **Location:** Jct SR 73, 0.3 mi sw. [L] [D]

MATAWAN pop. 8,810

BART'S RESTAURANT   732/566-0267
♦♦ Italian. Casual Dining. $7-$27 **AAA Inspector Notes:** This place is notable mainly for being in a small, old restored church. The bar is dotted with regulars, as this place is popular with locals. The menu offers familiar items with sandwiches and some Italian entrées including the signature specialty ravioli. **Features:** full bar. **Reservations:** suggested, weekends. **Address:** 74 Main St (CR 516) 07747 **Location:** 0.8 mi n of jct SR 34 and Main St (CR 516).

[L] [D]

MENDHAM pop. 4,981
• Hotels & Restaurants map & index p. 152

THE BLACK HORSE TAVERN   973/543-7300   (94)
♦♦♦ American. Fine Dining. $17-$44 **AAA Inspector Notes:** Historic. Dating to 1740, this former stagecoach stop retains much of its original English country and early American ambience. An eclectic menu is served in the cozy dining rooms with fireplaces and exposed beamed ceilings. Entrées include caramelized rack of venison, pan-seared Barnegat Bay scallops and USDA Prime steaks. The adjacent pub is a more casual and family friendly option with a lively scene and a menu that includes lots of fresh seafood and an oyster bar. **Features:** full bar. **Reservations:** suggested. **Address:** 1 W Main St 07945 **Location:** On SR 24; center. **Parking:** valet only. [D]

MENLO PARK (I-5) elev. 140'

A suburb at the fringe of the northeastern New Jersey industrial metropolis, Menlo Park was markedly less congested when Thomas Alva Edison set up shop in 1876. For the next decade the "Wizard of Menlo Park" astonished his neighbors by conducting field experiments on an electric railway and by creating the first Christmas holiday light display in the area; he amazed the world with such innovations as the dynamo, the phonograph, the automatic telegraph and the incandescent light bulb (see Thomas Edison National Historical Park in West Orange p. 209).

THOMAS ALVA EDISON MENLO PARK MUSEUM AND TOWER is .6 mi. w. of Garden State Pkwy. exit 131 to 37 Christie St. On the site of Edison's laboratory is Edison Memorial Tower, designed to incorporate the devices pioneered by the inventor. The museum, known as the birthplace of recorded sound, exhibits some of Edison's early inventions and memorabilia.

Time: Allow 1 hour minimum. **Hours:** Thurs.-Sat. 10-4. **Cost:** Donations. **Phone:** (732) 549-3299.

MIDDLETOWN (D-4) elev. 100'
• Hotels p. 138

On Raritan Bay, Middletown is the largest township in the Northern Monmouth area. A semblance of Colonial-era atmosphere manages to prevail along some residential streets, where ancient shade trees tower over large old houses. A few 17th-century structures still stand, including Marlpit Hall, a 1756 Dutch Colonial house at 137 Kings Hwy., that contains furnishings from the mid-18th century. The house is open to the public Thursday through Saturday from May through September; phone (732) 462-1466.

PORICY PARK CONSERVANCY nature center and farmhouse are w. of SR 35S on Oak Hill Rd., following signs; the fossil beds are on Middletown-Lincroft Rd., between Dwight Rd./Nutswamp Rd. and Oak Hill Rd. The conservancy's 250 acres preserve wildlife, native habitats, prehistoric fossil beds and a historic farmhouse.

Fossils approximately 72 million years old from the Cretaceous period of the Mesozoic era, mainly of shellfish, can be found in Poricy Brook; the best time to find fossils is in early spring. The nature center has displays of the different types of fossils found in the brook as well as live turtles and fish. Open during scheduled programs, the 1770 Murray farmhouse is typical of a middle-class lifestyle during the Colonial period.

Note: Only basic hand tools are permitted. Restrictions apply to the number of fossils that can be removed from the site; phone ahead for specific details. **Time:** Allow 30 minutes minimum. **Hours:** Park trails daily dawn-10 p.m. Nature center Mon.-Fri. 9-4. Fossil beds daily dawn-dusk, Apr.-Oct. Phone for information about farmhouse tours and other programs. Closed Jan. 1, Memorial Day, July 4, Labor Day weekend, Thanksgiving, day after Thanksgiving, Christmas Eve and Christmas. Phone ahead to confirm schedule. **Cost:** Donations. **Phone:** (732) 842-5966. GT ⊠ ☂

COMFORT INN MIDDLETOWN-RED BANK
(732)671-3400

Hotel
S89-S250

Address: 750 State Rt 35 S 07748 **Location:** Garden State Pkwy exit 114, 2 mi e on Red Hill Rd, 1 mi s on Kings Hwy to SR 35, then 0.3 mi s. **Facility:** 81 units. 2 stories, interior corridors. **Amenities:** safes. **Pool(s):** heated outdoor. **Activities:** game room, exercise room. **Guest Services:** valet and coin laundry. **Featured Amenity: full hot breakfast.**

Great location to Red Bank and Jersey Shore Beaches. Free hot breakfast daily. Pet friendly hotel.

MILFORD pop. 1,233

THE SHIP INN RESTAURANT & BREWERY
908/995-0188

English
Casual Dining
S8-$25

AAA Inspector Notes: An old-time feel prevails in this English-style pub, which harks back to fishing days of old in a seaside town. The menu lists a variety of pasties, beer-battered fish and chips and shepherd's pie, which pair with many types of beer from across the channel, in addition to non-filtered ales and hard ciders on draft. **Features:** full bar, happy hour. **Address:** 61 Bridge St 08848 **Location:** Downtown. **Parking:** street only. L D

MILLBURN (H-5) pop. 20,149, elev. 140'
• Hotels & Restaurants map & index p. 152

Millburn came into existence via a 1664 land grant by Charles II and was settled in the 1720s. Stewart Hartshorn, inventor of the window shade, acquired more than 1,500 acres in town in 1877 and designed a village called Short Hills. Although it likely cut into sales of his invention, Hartshorn's meandering street plan called for the preservation of as many trees as possible. The Cora Hartshorn Arboretum, 324 Forest Dr. S. in Short Hills, was founded in 1923 by Hartshorn's daughter. The 16.5-acre site offers good bird-watching and has a natural amphitheater; phone (973) 376-3587.

The success of many lumber, paper, cloth and hat mills was assured with the arrival of the Morris and Essex Railroad, later called the Erie-Lackawanna Railroad. The tracks linked Millburn with Newark, New York City and the coal industry to the northwest.

A former mill on Brookside Drive is now the home of the Paper Mill Playhouse, New Jersey's designated state theater. The season runs from October through June. Phone (973) 376-4343.

Millburn-Short Hills Chamber of Commerce: 343 Millburn Ave., Suite 303, P.O. Box 651, Millburn, NJ 07041. **Phone:** (973) 379-1198.

BASILICO
973/379-7020 82

Italian. Casual Dining. $10-$35 **AAA Inspector Notes:** A touch of class punctuates this friendly, comfortable restaurant which serves contemporary Italian dishes. Cream of wild mushroom soup and delicate fried calamari and vegetables are popular staples on the menu. The great pasta selection includes such dishes as spaghettini Arrabbiata, bucatini Amatriciana and gnocchi Sorrentina. Entrées include veal chops, whole grilled branzino and braised short ribs. A limited wine list is offered by the bottle only; guests also can bring their own. **Features:** wine only. **Reservations:** suggested. **Address:** 324 Millburn Ave 07041 **Location:** Just e of jct Main St and Millburn Ave. **Parking:** street only. L D

CHARLIE BROWN'S STEAKHOUSE
973/376-1724

Steak. Casual Dining. $9-$30 **AAA Inspector Notes:** This budget-friendly steakhouse, famous for its prime rib, offers top quality fare without hurting your pocketbook. The young ones will not be disappointed with the kids' menu, and just might even try something green from the salad bar. Adults will love the quality steaks, chicken and rib dishes. The express lunches are great for those saddled with time constraints. **Features:** full bar, happy hour. **Address:** 35 Main St 07041 **Location:** Corner of Essex and Main sts. L D

TINGA TAQUERIA
973/218-9500 81

Mexican. Casual Dining. $7-$19 **AAA Inspector Notes:** The simple family-friendly Mexican restaurant offers a good menu of tacos, salads, burritos and some daily specials. **Address:** 321 Millburn Ave 07041 **Location:** Just n of Main St. **Parking:** no self-parking. L D

MILLVILLE (G-2) pop. 28,400, elev. 37'

At the head of the tidewater on the Maurice (MOR-ris) River, Millville was initially a river port. The discovery of silica sand fostered the growth of glassmaking; by the end of the 19th century the only American city to produce more glassware was Pittsburgh. Glass remains among Millville's diversified industries. The designation "The Holly City" rests on a holly farm in neighboring East Millville that once produced 14 varieties of the ornamental shrub for shipment around the world.

The region also is noted for having been the home of hunter and woodsman "Stretch" Garrison, whose alleged feats included riding sharks and porpoises up the Maurice River and raising a rooster so tall that it ate from the porch roof. Although his nickname resulted from what was done to the truth, "Stretch" remains a local folk hero.

Greater Millville Chamber of Commerce: 321 N. High St., P.O. Box 831, Millville, NJ 08332. **Phone:** (856) 825-2600.

MILLVILLE ARMY AIR FIELD MUSEUM is at 1 Leddon St. at the Millville Airport. Dedicated by the U.S. War Department in 1941, the Millville Army Air Field was known as "America's First Defense Airport." Some 10,000 men and women served in Millville during World War II, including 1,500 fighter pilots. Exhibits include aviation artifacts and displays dedicated to the Tuskegee airmen, USO women and veterans of World Wars I and II, Korea and Vietnam. **Hours:** Tues.-Sun. 10-4, Mon. by appointment. Closed Jan. 1, Thanksgiving and Christmas. **Cost:** Free. **Phone:** (856) 327-2347.

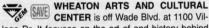 **WHEATON ARTS AND CULTURAL CENTER** is off Wade Blvd. at 1100 Village Dr. It focuses on the art of and history behind American glass and glassmaking and traditional southern New Jersey crafts. Artist demonstrations take place throughout the day.

The complex includes the Museum of American Glass; glass, ceramics and woodcarving studios; and a picnic and playground area.

Time: Allow 3 hours minimum. **Hours:** Tues.-Sun. 10-5, Apr.-Dec.; Fri.-Sun. 10-5, rest of year. Glassmaking demonstrations are offered at 11, 1:30 and 3:30. Closed Jan. 1, Easter, Thanksgiving and Christmas. Phone ahead to confirm schedule.

Cost: Shopping and strolling free except during outdoor special events. Admission to village facilities and artist studios $10; $9 (ages 62+); $7 (students with ID); free (ages 0-5 and to all Jan.-Mar.). **Phone:** (856) 825-6800 or (800) 998-4552.

Museum of American Glass is at 1100 Village Dr., in the Wheaton Arts and Cultural Center. More than 7,000 objects span the history of American glass from the early 1700s to the present. Exhibits include pieces by the New England, Tiffany, Boston & Sandwich and Steuben glass companies, and by contemporary artists Dale Chihuly and Paul Stankard.

Hours: Tues.-Sun. 10-5, Apr.-Dec.; Fri.-Sun. 10-5, rest of year. Guided 45-minute tours depart at 2:30. Closed Jan. 1, Easter, Thanksgiving and Christmas. **Cost:** Included with Wheaton Arts and Cultural Center. **Phone:** (856) 825-6800 or (800) 998-4552.

COUNTRY INN & SUITES BY CARLSON   856/825-3100
 Hotel. Rates not provided. **Address:** 1125 Village Dr 08332 **Location:** SR 55 exit 26, just w to Wade Blvd, then 0.7 mi s. Located in a quiet area. **Facility:** 100 units. 2 stories (no elevator), interior corridors. **Pool(s):** outdoor. **Guest Services:** valet and coin laundry.

QUALITY INN & SUITES   (856)327-3300
 **Motel** $70-$200 **Address:** 1701 N 2nd St 08332 **Location:** SR 55 exit 27, 0.7 mi s. **Facility:** 102 units, some two bedrooms and efficiencies. 2 stories (no elevator), exterior corridors. **Pool(s):** outdoor. **Activities:** exercise room. **Guest Services:** coin laundry.

MONMOUTH JUNCTION pop. 2,887

BEST WESTERN PRINCETON MANOR INN & SUITES
(732)329-4555

Motel
$72-$161

AAA Benefit: Members save up to 20%!

Address: 4191 US 1 S 08852 **Location:** 0.5 mi n of Raymond Rd. **Facility:** 63 units. 2 stories (no elevator), exterior corridors. **Terms:** check-in 4 pm. **Activities:** exercise room.

RESIDENCE INN BY MARRIOTT PRINCETON-SOUTH BRUNSWICK   (732)329-9600
 **Extended Stay Hotel** $104-$207 **Address:** 4225 US 1 S 08543 **Location:** 0.5 mi s of Raymond Rd. **Facility:** 208 kitchen units, some two bedrooms. 2 stories (no elevator), interior corridors. **Terms:** check-in 4 pm. **Pool(s):** outdoor. **Activities:** exercise room. **Guest Services:** valet and coin laundry, area transportation.

AAA Benefit: Members save 5% or more!

MONTCLAIR (G-5) pop. 37,669, elev. 300'

• Restaurants p. 140
• Hotels & Restaurants map & index p. 152, 162

Because the town of West Bloomfield wanted a rail link to New York City and the town of Bloomfield did not, the former separated from the latter in 1868, renamed itself Montclair and built the railroad. The result is a prosperous suburban business center, of which little could be purchased with the original price paid the Native Americans for the region—"two guns, three coats and 13 cans of rum."

For a backdrop Montclair has First Mountain, from which the British were denied entry to the upper Passaic River Valley during the Revolution.

In nearby Upper Montclair a normal school was established in 1908; today Montclair State University

(See maps & indexes p. 152, 162.)

is New Jersey's second-largest college. Mountainside Park on Upper Mountain Avenue includes the Presby Memorial Iris Gardens, which usually bloom in May.

MONTCLAIR ART MUSEUM is off I-280 exit 8B, 2.5 mi. n.e. on Prospect Ave., then s.e. on Bloomfield Ave. to 3 S. Mountain Ave. The museum's collection includes American paintings and Native American art and artifacts. Works by the Hudson River School, Adolph Gottlieb, Georgia O'Keeffe, Andy Warhol and Montclair native George Inness are augmented by examples from the Hudson River School, Realism and Abstract Expressionism. The museum also presents a series of solo exhibitions of contemporary art.

Time: Allow 1 hour minimum. **Hours:** Wed.-Sun. noon-5 (also first Thurs. of the month 5-9, Oct.-June). Closed major holidays. **Cost:** $12; $10 (ages 65+ and students with ID); free (ages 0-11 and to all first Fri. of the month, year-round, and first Thurs. of the month 5-9, Oct.-June). **Phone:** (973) 746-5555.

AOZORA   973/233-9400 [68]

▼▼▼ Japanese. Fine Dining. $10-$35 **AAA Inspector Notes:** With its stark white walls, high-back booths and bonsai plants tucked into tiny alcoves throughout the dining room, this restaurant offers a cool, hip place to sample some of Montclair's best sushi and most innovative Asian-inspired dishes. Do not pass up the beautiful ruby red tuna carpaccio, sprinkled with black pearls of caviar; or the shumai, bursting with shrimp and pork. The seared scallops with wild mushrooms, Japanese risotto and tomato coulis is a must. **Reservations:** required, weekends. **Address:** 407 Bloomfield Ave 07042 **Location:** Between Glen Ridge Ave and Willow St. **Parking:** street only.
[L] [D]

DAI-KICHI JAPANESE RESTAURANT   973/744-2954 [62]

▼▼ Japanese. Casual Dining. $16-$24 **AAA Inspector Notes:** This simple storefront has been a local favorite for years, not only because of its central location, but also because of the top-notch sushi prepared by the skilled chefs behind the counter. You will find all your favorites here, including spicy tuna and dragon rolls, as well as tempura and teriyaki dishes. Minimalist décor and casual, efficient service make this a great spot for a quick business lunch, or a relaxed evening out with friends. **Features:** beer & wine. **Address:** 608 Valley Rd 07043 **Location:** Just s of jct Bellevue Ave; center. **Parking:** street only. [L] [D]

FASCINO   973/233-0350 [70]

▼▼▼▼ Italian. Fine Dining. $40-$45 **AAA Inspector Notes:** The storefront restaurant borrows its name from the Italian, and it lives up to its definition on a nightly basis. There is a certain charm, glamour and fascination, with its saffron-colored walls, minimalist decor and cosmopolitan menu. Pastas are made in-house, and the pappardelle with braised beef, caramelized onions and shredded Gorgonzola just about nears perfection. A chef's tasting menu allows patrons to sample the chef's handiwork, which is positively fascino. **Reservations:** suggested. **Address:** 331 Bloomfield Ave 07042 **Location:** Just w of jct Grove St; center. **Parking:** street only. [D]

MESOB   973/655-9000 [66]

▼▼ Ethiopian. Casual Dining. $10-$26 **AAA Inspector Notes:** In Ethiopia, friends and family gather at small, woven tables, called mesob, to share communal meals. Diners here sample Ethiopian fare, including hearty stews and fragrant vegetable dishes, in an attractive dining room furnished with Africa-inspired art and a few mesob for those who dare to dine in the traditional manner. The silverware is not missing—everything is eaten with injera, a spongy-textured Ethiopian flatbread used to scoop up the exotic foods. **Reservations:** suggested, weekends. **Address:** 515 Bloomfield Ave 07042 **Location:** Jct Park St; center. **Parking:** street only.
[L] [D]

THE OFFICE BEER BAR & GRILL   973/783-2929

▼▼▼ American. Casual Dining. $10-$18 **AAA Inspector Notes:** The extensive beer list makes this office different from the one most folks visit from 9 to 5. Vintage typewriters, shelves of books and other office bric-a-brac contribute to the workaday theme, while the friendly staff and menu of favorites, including quesadillas, ribs and burgers, prompt patrons to put in a little overtime. **Features:** full bar, Sunday brunch, happy hour. **Address:** 619 Bloomfield Ave 07042 **Location:** Just s of jct Valley Rd; center. **Parking:** street only.
[L] [D] [LATE]

PIG & PRINCE   973/233-1006 [69]

▼▼▼ New American. Gastropub. $18-$36 **AAA Inspector Notes:** Chef Michael Carrino shows a good mix of creative compositions done with well-prepared ingredients.. The menu ranges from house-cured meats, appetizers like braised pork cheeks with heirloom carrots, mascarpone and chervil to entrées like a wild boar chop or Norwegian salmon with carrot, pumpkin and sweet potato hash. The setting in an old train station provides lots of character and the lively bar offers a great selection of craft beers, wines and creative cocktails. **Features:** full bar, patio dining, Sunday brunch. **Address:** 1 Lackawanna Plaza St 07042 **Location:** Just e of Bloomfield Ave; center. **Parking:** street only.
[D] CALL [&M]

RAYMOND'S   973/744-9263 [67]

▼▼ American. Casual Dining. $8-$23 **AAA Inspector Notes:** This casual spot reflects an old soda fountain in the décor, although it is most popular for its outdoor sidewalk tables set on a charming downtown side street. The menu offers updated comfort foods done with fresh ingredients. Popular dinner items include grits with wild mushrooms and truffle oil, macaroni and cheese with Vermont cheddar, fish tacos and meatloaf. Some good vegetarian options also are offered. Breakfast offers many of the usual suspects done with upgraded ingredients. **Features:** patio dining, Sunday brunch. **Address:** 28 Church St 07042 **Location:** Just sw of Bloomfield Ave; center. **Parking:** street only.
[B] [L] [D] CALL [&M]

THAI CHEF RESTAURANT   973/783-4994 [64]

▼▼▼ Thai. Casual Dining. $13-$28 **AAA Inspector Notes:** As welcoming to families as it is to couples in search of a quiet spot, the sophisticated Thai restaurant, recently expanded to include a separate, classic French menu, delivers quality food. Fragrant and colorful dishes are delivered steaming to tables, and empty dishes return to the kitchen. The outdoor patio is lovely during nice weather. A "bring your own" alcohol policy is in place. **Reservations:** suggested, weekends. **Address:** 664 Bloomfield Ave 07042 **Location:** Jct CR 506 and SR 23, just se. **Parking:** street only. [L] [D]

TINGA TAQUERIA   973/509-8226 [63]

▼▼ Tex-Mex. Casual Dining. $7-$15 **AAA Inspector Notes:** This taqueria's rendition of Tex-Mex fare is downright terrific. The super-casual eatery is a great spot for a quick meal that is anything but fast food. The guacamole is homemade and the tacos, burritos and enchiladas are all made to order using only fresh ingredients. Ribs also are on the menu, as is a pulled pork taco that is positively sublime. No trouble finding something for the bambinos, either—the kids' menu makes it easy on everyone. **Features:** Sunday brunch. **Address:** 215 Bellevue Ave 07043 **Location:** Jct Valley Rd and Bellevue Ave; center. **Parking:** street only. [L] [D]

TUPTIM THAI CUISINE   973/783-3800 [65]

▼▼ Thai. Casual Dining. $10-$19 **AAA Inspector Notes:** This casual spot is a local favorite for satisfying dishes fragrant with herbs and spices. Curry puffs and spring rolls are great starters. Tempting dinner choices include daily specials as well as chicken with ginger and scallion, green curry beef with coconut milk and basil, and shrimp with noodles, bean sprouts and peanuts. A large vegetarian menu offers healthy alternatives. Thai artwork and ornaments lend an air of authenticity to the dining room. Diners may bring their own wine. **Reservations:** suggested. **Address:** 600 Bloomfield Ave 07042 **Location:** Garden State Pkwy exit 148, 2.3 mi w. **Parking:** street only.
[L] [D]

MONTVALE pop. 7,844

COURTYARD BY MARRIOTT MONTVALE   (201)391-7700

▼▼▼ Hotel $174-$286 **Address:** 100 Chestnut Ridge Rd 07645 **Location:** Garden State Pkwy exit 172 northbound, just w on Grande Ave, then just s. **Facility:** 184 units. 3 stories, interior corridors. **Dining:** Fire & Oak, see separate listing. **Pool(s):** heated outdoor. **Activities:** exercise room. **Guest Services:** valet and coin laundry, area transportation.

AAA Benefit: Members save 5% or more!

[icons]

WHERE TO EAT

FIRE & OAK   201/307-1100

▼▼▼ American. Casual Dining. $11-$32 **AAA Inspector Notes:** This relaxed restaurant brings American grill fare to new heights. The menu offers a good range of comfortable items including fresh burgers, simply grilled fresh fish, steaks and large entrée salads like the sesame-seared tuna with soba noodles, mango, avocado, citrus vinaigrette and peanut sauce. Sushi also is offered at dinner. The casual dining room, with reclaimed barn wood paneling, candle light and spacious lounge suggests that guests have settled on the right spot. **Features:** full bar. **Reservations:** suggested. **Address:** 100 Chestnut Ridge Rd 07645 **Location:** Garden State Pkwy exit 172 northbound, just w on Grande Ave, then just s; in Courtyard by Marriott Montvale. [L] [D] CALL [GM]

MORRIS PLAINS (G-4) pop. 5,532, elev. 390'
• Hotels & Restaurants map & index p. 152

THE STICKLEY MUSEUM AT CRAFTSMAN FARMS is off I-287 exit 39, then 3 mi. w. to 2352 SR 10 at Manor Ln. Gustav Stickley, a key proponent of the American Arts and Crafts movement, built this log house on his 650-acre farm in 1911. Best known for his elegantly simple Craftsman, or Mission, furniture, Stickley was a major influence in home design and helped popularize the Bungalow movement in the United States. His house, situated on 35 acres, has been preserved, and many original furnishings have been reacquired.

Time: Allow 1 hour minimum. **Hours:** Museum open Thurs.-Sun. noon-4. Guided tours are offered Thurs.-Sun. on the hour 12:15-3:15. Other tours are offered; phone for details. Grounds open daily dawn-dusk. Phone ahead to confirm schedule. **Cost:** $10; $5 (ages 62+ and students with ID); $4 (ages 3-12). **Phone:** (973) 540-1165.

CANDLEWOOD SUITES PARSIPPANY-MORRIS PLAINS   973/984-9960   41

▼▼ Extended Stay Hotel. Rates not provided. **Address:** 100 Candlewood Dr 07950 **Location:** I-287 exit 39 northbound; exit 39B southbound, 2 mi w on SR 10. **Facility:** 122 efficiencies. 3 stories, interior corridors. **Terms:** check-in 4 pm. **Activities:** exercise room. **Guest Services:** valet and coin laundry, area transportation.

[icons]

WHERE TO EAT

ARTHUR'S TAVERN   973/455-9705   34

▼▼ American. Casual Dining. $7-$24 **AAA Inspector Notes:** This popular and crowded local tavern is known for its thick rib-eye steak, but also has great burgers, deli sandwiches and daily specials. The atmosphere is relaxed and very casual. **Features:** full bar. **Address:** 700 Speedwell Ave 07950 **Location:** Across from train station; center. **Parking:** on-site and street. [L] [D]

GRATO   973/267-4006   33

▼▼▼ Italian. Fine Dining. $10-$25 **AAA Inspector Notes:** There is a warm ambience at this comfortable restaurant with an inviting fireplace in the middle of the dining room and lots of rustic wood and stone accents. There are some hearty pastas on the menu such as bucatini with veal and ricotta meatballs as well as such other entrées as steamy cioppino or grilled pork chop with Swiss chard, ceci beans, soffrito and fig marmalade. Service here is skilled and attentive. **Features:** full bar. **Reservations:** suggested. **Address:** 2230 Rt 10 W 07950 **Location:** At Tabor Rd (SR 53). **Parking:** on-site and valet. [L] [D] CALL [GM]

MINADO   973/734-4900   31

▼▼ Japanese. Cafeteria. $18-$32 **AAA Inspector Notes:** This place calls itself the ultimate sushi buffet and it is hard to argue that claim. There is a huge selection of high-quality sushi and rolls, as well as a full buffet of Japanese salads and hot entrées. Items can be grilled to order on a hibachi and there also are made-to-order crepes for dessert. The restaurant itself is large and clean. The dinner buffet offers a bit more selection than lunch, and is priced accordingly. Children are priced by height. **Features:** beer & wine. **Address:** 2888 Rt 10 W 07950 **Location:** 1.2 mi w of SR 53. [L] [D] CALL [GM]

TABOR ROAD TAVERN   973/267-7004   32

▼▼▼ American. Casual Dining. $11-$39 **AAA Inspector Notes:** This beautiful restaurant has a warm and inviting feel with lots of woodwork, stone fireplaces and high ceilings reminiscent of a luxury mountain lodge. The menu offers familiar dishes with some creative tweaks such as halibut with grits, roasted yellow corn, pesto and bacon vinaigrette, or the roasted duck breast with pumpkin risotto and an orange-cranberry relish. **Features:** full bar, patio dining. **Address:** 510 Tabor Rd 07950 **Location:** 1.5 mi n on SR 53 (Tabor Rd), just n of jct SR 10. **Parking:** on-site and valet. [L] [D] CALL [GM]

MORRISTOWN (G-4) pop. 18,411, elev. 327'
• Hotels p. 142 • Restaurants p. 144
• Hotels & Restaurants map & index p. 152

The Revolutionary War demanded iron, and a lot of it was processed at the furnaces and forges in Morristown. Much of the powder used by the Continental Army was made at Jacob Ford's powder mill. These operations were attractive targets for the British, who made several attempts to take the town. This led Gen. George Washington to select Morristown for his army's winter quarters in 1777 and again 2 years later (see Morristown National Historical Park p. 145). Elaborate Victorian houses still stand in some of the oldest neighborhoods.

(See map & index p. 152.)

Morris County Visitors Center: 6 Court St., Morristown, NJ 07960. **Phone:** (973) 631-5151.

ACORN HALL is at jct. Morris Ave. and Whippany Rd. at 68 Morris Ave. The 1853 Victorian Italianate mansion is decorated and furnished in period and features a research library with information about the Victorian era, a Victorian-style garden and changing exhibits focusing on local history.

Pieces from the Crane-Hone and Schermerhorn families—both of whom lived in the mansion—constitute the majority of the furnishings, which also include contributions from other notable Morris County families. Special events and workshops hosted by the Morris County Historical Society also are offered.

Time: Allow 1 hour minimum. **Hours:** Guided tours are offered Wed.-Thurs. 11-4, Sun. 1-4. Last tour begins 30 minutes before closing. **Cost:** $6; $5 (ages 65+); $3 (students with ID); free (ages 0-11). **Phone:** (973) 267-3465.

FOSTERFIELDS LIVING HISTORICAL FARM is off I-287 exit 35, w. on SR 124 (Madison Ave.), then 1.1 mi. w. of the Morristown Green on CR 510 to 73 Kahdena Rd. The farm was purchased in 1852 by the grandson of Paul Revere. Joseph Warren Revere built The Willows, a 19th-century Gothic Revival house.

Visitors can watch an introductory film; view exhibits; explore the farm on a self-guiding tour; see draft horses, Jersey cows, sheep, pigs, chickens and a 1920s farmhouse; and observe demonstrations of late 19th- and early 20th-century farming practices.

Time: Allow 1 hour, 30 minutes minimum. **Hours:** Grounds Tues.-Sat. 10-5, Apr.-June; Wed.-Sat. 10-5, Sun. noon-5, July-Oct. Guided afternoon tours of The Willows are by reservation only. Closed July 4. Phone ahead to confirm schedule. **Cost:** $6; $5 (ages 65+); $4 (ages 4-16); $2 (ages 2-3). **Phone:** (973) 326-7645.

FRELINGHUYSEN ARBORETUM is 3 mi. e. on Morris Ave., then n. on Ridgedale Ave. and e. to 353 E. Hanover Ave., opposite the Morris County Library. Contrasts between field and woodland, naturalized plantings and formal gardens characterize the 127-acre preserve, which surrounds a historic Colonial Revival mansion. Trees and shrubs are labeled. Demonstration gardens include a Blue Garden, an Alpine Garden and a French Intensive Vegetable Garden. An education center displays exhibits and a carriage house.

Pets are not permitted. **Time:** Allow 1 hour, 30 minutes minimum. **Hours:** Grounds daily 8-dusk. Education center daily 9-4:30. Closed major holidays. **Cost:** Donations. **Phone:** (973) 326-7601.

HISTORIC SPEEDWELL, 333 Speedwell Ave., preserves the homestead estate of Stephen Vail, including the factory building where his son, Alfred, assisted Samuel Morse with perfecting the telegraph and Morse code. The complex includes an exhibit about the Speedwell Iron Works, built in the early 1800s, three farm buildings and three historic houses. A timeline of modern communication and an exhibit about the telegraph also are on view.

Time: Allow 1 hour minimum. **Hours:** Wed.-Sat. 10-5 and select Sun., Apr.-Oct. Guided tours of the Vail house are available. Last tour begins 1 hour, 30 minutes before closing. **Cost:** $5; $4 (ages 65+); $3 (ages 4-16). **Phone:** (973) 285-6550.

 MORRIS MUSEUM is 2.5 mi. e. on CR 510 at 6 Normandy Heights Rd. Housed in the Frelinghuysen mansion at Twin Oaks, the collection includes some 48,000 items representing the decorative and fine arts, costumes and textiles, natural science, anthropology, mineralogy and paleontology. A highlight is the Murtogh D. Guinness Collection: Musical Machines & Living Dolls, a permanent exhibit that displays more than 150 mechanical musical instruments and automata, most dating to the 19th century; a viewable storage area houses another 550 pieces.

Other permanent exhibitions are Dinosaur Den, an exploration of dinosaurs that lived 65 million years ago, the American Indian Gallery and galleries devoted to rocks, minerals and mammals. The museum also has a significant costume collection, which is drawn on for annual costume exhibitions. Changing exhibits are featured as well.

Time: Allow 2 hours minimum. **Hours:** Tues.-Sat. 11-5 (also second and third Thurs. of the month 5-8), Sun. noon-5. Musical Machines & Living Dolls demonstrations are offered Tues.-Sun. at 2. Closed Jan. 1, Easter, Memorial Day, July 4, Labor Day, Thanksgiving, Christmas Eve and Christmas. **Cost:** $10; $7 (ages 3-12 and 65+); free (ages 0-2 and military and up to five family members with ID); by donation (second and third Thurs. of the month 5-8 p.m.). **Phone:** (973) 971-3700.

▼ See AAA listing this page ▼

(See map & index p. 152.)

HYATT HOUSE MORRISTOWN   (973)971-0008   62

Extended Stay Hotel
$99-$359

H HYATT house™

AAA Benefit: Members save 10%!

Address: 194 Park Ave 07960 **Location:** SR 24 exit 2A (Morristown), just w. **Facility:** 132 units, some two bedrooms, efficiencies and kitchens. 3 stories, interior corridors. **Terms:** cancellation fee imposed. **Amenities:** *Some:* safes. **Pool(s):** outdoor. **Activities:** hot tub, exercise room. **Guest Services:** valet and coin laundry, area transportation. **Featured Amenity:** breakfast buffet. *(See ad this page.)*

SAVE CALL 🅜 🚐 BIZ 🛜 ✕ 🛏 📠 💻 / SOME UNITS 🐾

HYATT MORRISTOWN   (973)647-1234   63

Hotel
$89-$429

HYATT®

AAA Benefit: Members save 10%!

Address: 3 Speedwell Ave (US 202 N) 07960 **Location:** Just n of Morristown Green. **Facility:** 256 units. 16 stories, interior corridors. **Parking:** on-site and valet. **Terms:** cancellation fee imposed. **Amenities:** safes. **Pool(s):** heated indoor. **Activities:** sauna, massage. **Guest Services:** valet and coin laundry, rental car service, area transportation. **Featured Amenity:** full hot breakfast.

SAVE 🍴 👤 🍸 CALL 🅜 🚐 👥 BIZ 🛜 ✕ 🎬 🛏 💻 / SOME UNITS 📠

THE MADISON HOTEL   (973)285-1800   65

Hotel
$135-$399

Address: 1 Convent Rd 07960 **Location:** I-287 exit 35 northbound, 1.5 mi e on SR 124 (Madison Ave). **Facility:** 186 units. 4 stories, interior corridors. **Terms:** check-in 4 pm, cancellation fee imposed. **Dining:** Rod's Steak & Seafood Grille, see separate listing. **Pool(s):** heated indoor. **Activities:** hot tub, exercise room. **Guest Services:** valet laundry, area transportation. **Featured Amenity:** continental breakfast.

SAVE 🍴 👤 🍸 🚐 BIZ HS 🛜 ✕ 💻 / SOME UNITS 🛏 📠

THE WESTIN GOVERNOR MORRIS   (973)539-7300   61

Hotel
$139-$499

WESTIN® HOTELS & RESORTS   **AAA Benefit:** Members save up to 15%, plus Starwood Preferred Guest® benefits!

Address: 2 Whippany Rd 07960 **Location:** I-287 exit 36 southbound, left lane to light, left to stop sign, then 1 mi e; exit 36A northbound to Morris Ave, 0.8 mi e, follow signs. **Facility:** 224 units. 6 stories, interior corridors. **Terms:** cancellation fee imposed. **Amenities:** safes. **Dining:** Blue Morel Restaurant and Wine Bar, see separate listing. **Pool(s):** heated outdoor. **Activities:** exercise room. **Guest Services:** valet laundry, boarding pass kiosk, area transportation.

SAVE 🍴 👤 🍸 CALL 🅜 🚐 BIZ 🛜 ✕ 🛏 💻 / SOME UNITS 🐾

morristown.house.hyatt.com

Located in the beautiful rolling hills and broad valley of northern New Jersey, yet within walking distance of the Morristown Municipal Airport and easy access to popular local attractions.

- Complimentary Full Hot Breakfast
- Free Parking
- Free high-speed wireless Internet Access
- 24-hour Guest Market
- Outdoor pool and 24-hour Fitness Center

H HYATT house™
Morristown

HYATT house Morristown
194 Park Avenue
Morristown, NJ 07960
973-971-0008

(See map & index p. 152.)

WHERE TO EAT

BLUE MOREL RESTAURANT AND WINE BAR
973/451-2619 (55)

New American. Casual Dining. $11-$44 **AAA Inspector Notes:** The menu theme at this upscale hotel restaurant is farm-to-table foods, although they also have a large seafood selection with raw bar and sushi items. The attractive wine bar has a wide range of fine selections from all over the world and all are available in smaller portions for those who just want to sample. The setting is modern and a little bit cosmopolitan, while the service is relaxed and casual. **Features:** full bar, Sunday brunch. **Reservations:** suggested. **Address:** 2 Whippany Rd 07960 **Location:** I-287 exit 36 southbound, left lane to light, left to stop sign, then 1 mi e; exit 36A northbound to Morris Ave, 0.8 mi e, follow signs; in The Westin Governor Morris. [B] [L] [D] CALL &M

DAVID TODD'S CITY TAVERN
973/993-8066 (69)

New American. Casual Dining. $10-$37 **AAA Inspector Notes:** A great combination of upscale, stylish and yes, comfortable. The progressive American menu has interesting preparations with such highlights as braised short ribs, seared ahi tuna and an excellent duck entrée. The restaurant has two sections, a comfortable loungy tavern room and a slightly more chic dining room. Both have a modern, cosmopolitan décor with subdued lighting and artistic accents. The beverage list is another highlight with well-chosen wines and high-end beer selections. **Features:** full bar, patio dining, happy hour. **Address:** 150 South St 07960 **Location:** 0.3 mi s of Morristown Green on SR 124 (South St). **Parking:** street only. [L] [D] CALL &M

END OF ELM
973/998-4534 (58)

Small Plates. Gastropub. $11-$18 **AAA Inspector Notes:** This comfortable little place next to the train station offers a nice selection of craft beers, wines and cocktails to go with a creative menu of small plates. Dishes range from sashimi tuna "pizza" on crisp sticky rice or chicken and waffles with maple hollandaise to slightly simpler items like roasted vegetable Caesar salad or truffled Parmesan cheese fries. **Features:** full bar, Sunday brunch, happy hour. **Address:** 140 Morris St 07960 **Location:** Just e of Morristown train station; center. **Parking:** street only. [L] [D] [LATE] CALL &M

MILLIE'S OLD WORLD MEATBALLS & PIZZA
973/267-9616 (67)

Pizza. Casual Dining. $12-$22 **AAA Inspector Notes:** This pizza and meatball palace boasts not one but two specialty pizza ovens—one coal-fired and one wood-fired—to create different styles of crusts. A range of fresh, creative toppings is offered, and the meatballs are also worth a try, accompanied by your choice of sauces and cheeses. **Features:** patio dining. **Address:** 60 South St 07960 **Location:** Center; just s of Morristown Green. **Parking:** street only. [L] [D] CALL &M

THE OFFICE TAVERN GRILL
973/285-0220 (65)

American. Casual Dining. $9-$34 **AAA Inspector Notes:** The extensive beer list makes this office different from the one most folks visit from 9 to 5. The menu of fresh salads, stone oven pizzas, creative burgers and a raw bar prompt patrons to put in a little overtime. **Features:** full bar, Sunday brunch, happy hour. **Address:** 3 South St 07960 **Location:** At South Park Pl; east of Morristown Green. **Parking:** street only. [L] [D] [LATE]

ORIGIN
973/971-9933 (64)

Thai. Casual Dining. $10-$30 **AAA Inspector Notes:** A longtime city favorite for Thai food with a French flair, the busy storefront packs in patrons at lunch and dinner. Papaya salad is all it should be--sweet, salty, spicy and sour--and is a perfect start to a meal that bursts with flavor from start to finish. **Reservations:** suggested, weekends. **Address:** 10 South St 07960 **Location:** Just e of Morristown Green; center. [L] [D]

PAMIR
973/605-1095 (66)

Afghan. Casual Dining. $8-$27 **AAA Inspector Notes:** This simple, family-run restaurant, draped in colorful rugs, offers authentic dishes from Afghanistan. Though mildly spiced, the food is fragrant and rich in flavors of coriander, cardamom, cilantro, onion and garlic. In addition to the regular menu, a buffet is offered at lunch which is a good way to sample several different dishes. **Features:** patio dining. **Address:** 11 South St 07960 **Location:** At South Park Pl; east of Morristown Green. **Parking:** street only. [L] [D]

ROD'S STEAK & SEAFOOD GRILLE
973/539-6666 (70)

American. Casual Dining. $11-$42 **AAA Inspector Notes:** It may prove difficult to focus on Rod's menu with the ornate Victorian dining room and its stunning woodwork providing a distraction. Highlights on a menu of steak and seafood include a prime porterhouse, herb-crusted diver scallops and roast chicken with olives and lemon. Side orders, whether they be roasted wild mushrooms, rosti potatoes or grilled asparagus brushed with garlic butter, dress up each dish nicely. **Features:** full bar, Sunday brunch. **Reservations:** suggested. **Address:** 1 Convent Rd 07960 **Location:** I-287 exit 35 northbound, 1.5 mi e on SR 124 (Madison Ave); in The Madison Hotel. [B] [L] [D]

ROOTS STEAKHOUSE
973/326-1800 (62)

Steak. Fine Dining. $12-$80 **AAA Inspector Notes:** The dark and clubby dining room and lively bar fill up with a sophisticated crowd of city diners. Naturally the steaks are the main attraction here—first rate, aged USDA Prime beef with a good variety of cuts offered. There also is a good selection of chilled shellfish, including a great crab cocktail and live Maine lobsters. **Features:** full bar. **Reservations:** suggested. **Address:** 40 Park Pl W 07960 **Location:** Across from Morristown Green; center. **Parking:** street only. [L] [D] CALL &M

SEBASTIAN'S THE STEAKHOUSE
973/539-8545 (59)

Steak. Fine Dining. $11-$37 **AAA Inspector Notes:** This is the classic city steakhouse experience with seared USDA Prime steaks and all the accompaniments, as well as such items as organic chicken, tuna and swordfish. The atmosphere is sophisticated, yet comfortable with exposed brick and lots of wood in the multi-level dining room and clubby bar. **Features:** full bar, patio dining. **Reservations:** suggested. **Address:** 80 Elm St 07960 **Location:** At Morris St; across from Morristown train station. **Parking:** street only. [L] [D]

SIRIN
973/993-9122 (68)

Thai. Casual Dining. $10-$26 **AAA Inspector Notes:** The three cozy dining rooms that make up this lovely restaurant located in a stately brownstone are warm, colorful and inviting. The same can be said for the soul-satisfying Thai fare prepared by the kitchen. Dishes are prepared with care, and attention is given to the balance of spices so that they don't overwhelm the main ingredients or the palate. The food, casual atmosphere and friendly service all add up to an enjoyable, relaxing dining experience. **Address:** 3 Pine St 07960 **Location:** I-287 exit 35, 0.4 mi w on SR 124 (Madison Ave), then just n. **Parking:** street only. [L] [D]

SUSHI LOUNGE
973/539-1135 (61)

Sushi. Casual Dining. $15-$37 **AAA Inspector Notes:** They have a good selection of ultra fresh fish here as well as a nice menu of creative Japanese dishes from the kitchen. The sushi is taken seriously here with selections covering all the usual items and may include sea urchin, bluefin toro, striped bass or ivory salmon. The best way to dine here is to match your sushi selections with one of the great hot dishes from the kitchen like the steamed Chilean sea bass with black bean-fig-vodka sauce or some of the silky udon noodle dishes. **Features:** full bar. **Address:** 12 Schuyler Pl 07960 **Location:** 1 blk w of Morristown Green, just s of Washington St. **Parking:** street only. [L] [D]

THE TACO TRUCK
862/260-9300 (57)

Mexican. Quick Serve. $5-$8 **AAA Inspector Notes:** This a larger permanent outlet for the popular roaming food trucks. Besides the mainstay authentic-style tacos there is a selection of salads and tortas such as the barbacoa de costilla with pasilla chile-braised shredded beef and chipotle salsa. The restaurant has a strong commitment to sustainability including using hormone and antibiotic-free meats, biodegradable packaging and restaurant space that makes use of recycled materials and eco friendly systems. **Address:** 50 Morris St 07960 **Location:** Just w of train station; in Midtown Shopping Center. [L] [D] [LATE] CALL &M

(See map & index p. 152.)

TIM SCHAFER'S CUISINE   973/538-3330 **56**

▼▼▼▼ American. Casual Dining. $14-$38 **AAA Inspector Notes:** Bring your own wine to this quaint, little restaurant which offers intriguing dishes with some unusual combinations that work well together. Hearty flavors and attractive presentations characterize dishes, particularly the beer-enhanced choices and the game meats. Delicious desserts are homemade. **Reservations:** suggested. **Address:** 82 Speedwell Ave (US 202) 07960 **Location:** Between Spring St and Cattano Ave; just n of circle at SR 124 (Madison Ave) and US 202. **Parking:** street only. Ⓛ Ⓓ

TITO'S BURRITOS   973/267-8486 **60**

▼ Mexican. Casual Dining. $4-$10 **AAA Inspector Notes:** This small shop serves up tasty West Coast-style burritos and tacos as well as a few salads and some great chicken wings. Seating is limited, but take-out is offered. **Address:** 26 Washington St 07960 **Location:** Center; just w of Morristown Green. **Parking:** street only.

Ⓛ Ⓓ

URBAN TABLE   973/326-9200 **63**

▼▼ Comfort Food. Casual Dining. $9-$23 **AAA Inspector Notes:** This casual eatery has a fun urban theme and an interesting menu that includes great burgers, large entrée salads, a little sushi and also some healthy entrées like pan-roasted mahi mahi with toasted farro, kale and Mediterranean salsa verde. **Features:** full bar, patio dining, Sunday brunch. **Reservations:** suggested. **Address:** 40 West Park Pl 07960 **Location:** Center; across from Morristown Green. **Parking:** street only. Ⓛ Ⓓ CALL Ⓜ

♦ MORRISTOWN NATIONAL HISTORICAL PARK (B-3)

Consisting of four units, two in Morristown and two 6 miles southwest, Morristown National Historical Park includes the Ford Mansion (Washington's Headquarters), the site of Fort Nonsense, Jockey Hollow and the New Jersey Brigade Area. Gen. George Washington selected this easily defensible site for his military headquarters and the main encampment of the Continental Army of the Middle Colonies in the "Hard Winter" of 1779-80.

Despite starvation, disease and mutiny, he reorganized his weary and depleted forces almost within sight of strong British lines in New York. For a time this village was the U.S. military capital. Most park buildings are open daily 9-5. Closed Jan. 1, Thanksgiving and Christmas. A combination ticket offering a guided tour of Ford Mansion and admittance to the museum and library is $4; under 16 free with adult. Phone (973) 539-2016, ext. 210.

FORD MANSION (WASHINGTON'S HEADQUARTERS) is at 30 Washington Pl. Built 1772-74 for Col. Jacob Ford Jr., the Colonial house is furnished in period and has a few original 18th-century pieces. During the winter of 1779-80 it was the home of Gen. and Mrs. George Washington. Entrance to the mansion is by guided tour only.

Hours: Tours depart from the headquarters museum daily on the hour 10-11 and 1-4, when staff is available. Phone ahead to confirm tour times. Closed Jan. 1, Thanksgiving and Christmas. **Cost:** $4 (includes Washington's Headquarters Museum and Library); free (ages 0-15 with adult). **Phone:** (973) 539-2016, ext. 210.

Washington's Headquarters Museum and Library is at 30 Washington Pl. The museum's three exhibit galleries display material relating to the 1779-80 encampment. The library, open to the public only by appointment, houses some 40,000 manuscripts and more than 20,000 printed works dealing with both the Colonial and Revolutionary eras. Park headquarters is on the premises.

Time: Allow 2 hours minimum. **Hours:** Museum open daily 9-5. Library open by appointment. Closed Jan. 1, Thanksgiving and Christmas. Phone ahead to confirm schedule. **Cost:** $4 (includes tour fee for Ford Mansion); free (ages 0-15 with adult). **Phone:** (973) 539-2016, ext. 210.

FORT NONSENSE, off Ann St. near Western Ave., was built on a hill overlooking Morristown at Washington's order in 1777 as a defense for supplies stored in the village. The fort had cannons to protect the town below and the main roads leading north and south. Legend has it that the fort's name derived from Washington's intent to keep his troops busy, thus preventing idleness and desertion. Visitors will see a cannon, waysides describing historical events and an outline of the fort. **Hours:** Daily 8-dusk. Closed Jan. 1, Thanksgiving and Christmas. **Cost:** Free.

JOCKEY HOLLOW is 5 mi. s.w. of Morristown at jct. Jockey Hollow and Tempe Wick rds. The hollow contains most of the sites occupied by the Continental Army 1779-80. That "Hard Winter" proved to be one of the harshest of the 18th century. The army stripped the surrounding woods to build more than 1,000 huts, each housing 12 men. Five of these soldier huts have been re-created. The 1,200-acre area is also a wildlife sanctuary with several hiking trails. A visitor center offers displays and DVD presentations.

Time: Allow 1 hour minimum. **Hours:** Park grounds open daily 8-8, early May-Labor Day; 8-7, day after Labor Day-early Oct. and late Mar.-early May; 8-6, early Oct.-early Nov. and late Feb.-late Mar.; 8-5, rest of year. Tour road closes 30 minutes before park closing. Visitor center open daily 9-5. Closed Jan. 1, Thanksgiving and Christmas. **Cost:** Free. **Phone:** (973) 543-4030.

Wick House and Garden is in Jockey Hollow, 5 mi. s.w. of Morristown at jct. Jockey Hollow and Tempe Wick rds., off Jockey Hollow Rd. The 1750 farmhouse was occupied by Maj. Gen. Arthur St. Clair 1779-80. Henry Wick's 1,400-acre farm of timberland and open fields was central to the army occupation. The restored six-room house and adjacent herb garden reflect the life of a relatively prosperous farmer during the Revolutionary period. **Hours:** Open daily 9:30-noon and 1-4:30, May-Oct.; Tues.-Sun. 9:30-noon and 1-4:30, rest of year, when staff is available; phone ahead to confirm schedule. Closed Jan. 1, Thanksgiving and Christmas. **Cost:** Free. **Phone:** (973) 543-4030.

NEW JERSEY BRIGADE AREA is 1.5 mi. s. on Leddell Rd. to Old Jockey Hollow Rd. in Bernardsville. Some 900 men belonging to the New Jersey Brigade camped here during the winter of 1779-80. The four regiments of the "Jersey Blues," the last brigade to arrive, spent Christmas building log huts. Hiking trails and the Cross Estate Gardens are on the grounds. **Hours:** Daily 8 a.m.-30 minutes before dusk. **Cost:** Free.

MOUNTAINSIDE (H-5) pop. 6,685, elev. 142'
• Hotels & Restaurants map & index p. 152

TRAILSIDE NATURE AND SCIENCE CENTER is off the US 22 New Providence Rd. exit n. to Ackerman Ave., then n. on Coles Ave. to 452 New Providence Rd. Within the Watchung Reservation, the 2,065-acre preserve has a visitor center with changing exhibits about human and natural history as well as a collection of live reptiles and fish. A museum contains taxidermy displays, fossils and a hands-on discovery room for preschoolers. Miles of trails surround the facility.

Hours: Grounds daily dawn-dusk. Visitor center daily noon-5. Closed Jan. 1, Easter, July 4, Thanksgiving, day after Thanksgiving and Christmas. Holiday hours may vary; phone ahead. **Cost:** Donations. **Phone:** (908) 789-3670.

ARIRANG HIBACHI STEAKHOUSE   908/518-9733 (112)
 Japanese. Casual Dining. $16-$39 AAA Inspector **Notes:** Lush greenery, a tropical waterfall and tranquil pools greet patrons at the entry of this steakhouse. The sushi dining room, just beyond, is quiet and serene, with bamboo reeds scattered about for privacy. The lively, almost raucous hibachi room features the flamboyant antics of skilled chefs, showing off their prowess at the grill. The menu offers lots of dishes to choose from, including various teriyaki, hibachi dinners and sushi rolls. **Features:** full bar. **Address:** 1230 SR 22 W 07092 **Location:** Garden State Pkwy exit 140 northbound, 5 mi w; exit 140A southbound. [D]

MOUNT ARLINGTON pop. 5,050
• Hotels & Restaurants map & index p. 152

COURTYARD BY MARRIOTT ROCKAWAY/MT. ARLINGTON
(973)770-2000 (35)

 Hotel $132-$217 **Address:** 15 Howard Blvd 07856 **Location:** I-80 exit 30, just n. Located in a business park. **Facility:** 125 units. 5 stories, interior corridors. **Pool(s):** heated indoor. **Activities:** hot tub, exercise room. **Guest Services:** valet and coin laundry.

AAA Benefit: Members save 5% or more!

HOLIDAY INN EXPRESS & SUITES   973/770-7880 (34)

Hotel
Rates not provided

Address: 176 Howard Blvd 07856 **Location:** I-80 exit 30, 0.3 mi n. **Facility:** 76 units. 3 stories, interior corridors. **Activities:** sauna, hot tub, exercise room. **Guest Services:** valet and coin laundry.

MOUNT HOLLY (E-3) elev. 45'

Sharing the name of a nearby hill, Mount Holly was first settled by Quakers in 1676 and served as the capital of the state for 2 months in 1779. John Woolman, a Quaker abolitionist known for his 1774 journal, taught at the Old School House at 35 Brainerd St. Other historic buildings include the 18th- and 19th-century county buildings on High Street between Garden and Union streets.

Smithville Mansion, 2 miles east at 803 Smithville Rd. in nearby Eastampton, was the Victorian home of Hezekiah B. Smith, former owner of a local foundry and operator of the factory that produced the first "American Star" bicycles. Guided tours of the restored mansion are available May through October; phone (609) 265-5858. Also on the estate grounds is a building devoted to Smith's bicycles and an art gallery. Christmas and candlelight tours are offered in December.

HISTORIC BURLINGTON COUNTY PRISON MUSEUM is at 128 High St. The museum's interior still looks much the same as it did during its years as a prison. Exhibits includes a re-created warden's office and adjacent home, a maximum-security cell and a kitchen. One display details changes to American prison cells throughout history. Architect Robert Mills also designed several Washington, D.C.-area buildings as well as the Washington Monument.

Time: Allow 45 minutes minimum. **Hours:** Thurs.-Sat. 10-4, Sun. noon-4. Closed major holidays. **Cost:** $4; $2 (ages 55+ and students with ID); free (ages 0-4). **Phone:** (609) 265-5476 or (609) 518-7667.

CHARLIE BROWN'S STEAKHOUSE   609/265-1100
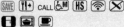 Steak. Casual Dining. $9-$30 AAA Inspector **Notes:** This budget-friendly steakhouse, famous for its prime rib, offers top quality fare without hurting your pocketbook. The young ones will not be disappointed with the kids' menu, and just might even try something green from the salad bar. Adults will love the quality steaks, chicken and rib dishes. The express lunches are great for those saddled with time constraints. **Features:** full bar, happy hour. **Address:** 949 Rt 541 08060 **Location:** To Burrs Rd jughandle and crossover. [L] [D]

ROBIN'S NEST   609/261-6149 (88)
 American. Casual Dining. $9-$29 AAA Inspector Notes: Eclectic Victorian furnishings and prints of Mount Holly from the first half of the 20th century decorate the quaint dining rooms. In addition to fantastic homemade desserts (seriously, take some home for later), the menu offers quiche, sandwiches, salads and soups. Sunday brunch is popular. **Features:** full bar, patio dining, Sunday brunch, happy hour. **Reservations:** suggested. **Address:** 2 Washington St 08060 **Location:** Downtown. [L] [D]

MOUNT LAUREL

• Restaurants p. 148

ALOFT MOUNT LAUREL   856/234-1880

Hotel
Rates not provided

AAA Benefit: Members save up to 15%, plus Starwood Preferred Guest® benefits!

Address: 558 Fellowship Rd 08054 **Location:** I-295 exit 36A, just se on SR 73 to Fellowship Rd, then just n. **Facility:** 154 units. 6 stories, interior corridors. *Bath:* shower only. **Amenities:** safes. **Pool(s):** heated indoor. **Activities:** exercise room. **Guest Services:** valet and coin laundry, area transportation.

CANDLEWOOD SUITES MT. LAUREL   856/642-7567

Extended Stay Hotel. Rates not provided. **Address:** 4000 Crawford Pl 08054 **Location:** New Jersey Tpke exit 4, 1 mi s on SR 73 S. **Facility:** 123 efficiencies. 3 stories, interior corridors. **Activities:** exercise room. **Guest Services:** valet and coin laundry.

COMFORT INN & SUITES   (856)727-0010

Hotel $89-$129 **Address:** 6000 Crawford Pl 08054 **Location:** New Jersey Tpke exit 4, 1 mi on SR 73 S. **Facility:** 90 units, some efficiencies. 3 stories, interior corridors. **Activities:** exercise room. **Guest Services:** valet and coin laundry.

COURTYARD BY MARRIOTT MT. LAUREL

(856)273-4400

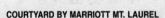
Hotel
$132-$252

AAA Benefit: Members save 5% or more!

Address: 1000 Century Pkwy 08054 **Location:** New Jersey Tpke exit 4, just nw on SR 73 to Fellowship Rd, then just s; I-295 exit 36A, just se on SR 73 to Fellowship Rd, then just s. **Facility:** 151 units. 4 stories, interior corridors. **Pool(s):** heated indoor. **Activities:** hot tub, exercise room. **Guest Services:** valet and coin laundry, boarding pass kiosk.

DOUBLETREE SUITES BY HILTON HOTEL MT. LAUREL

(856)778-8999

Hotel
$109-$309

AAA Benefit: Members save 5% or more!

Address: 515 Fellowship Rd N 08054 **Location:** I-295 exit 36A, just se on SR 73 to Fellowship Rd, then just n. **Facility:** 204 units. 3 stories, interior corridors. **Terms:** 1-7 night minimum stay, cancellation fee imposed. **Amenities:** safes. **Pool(s):** heated indoor. **Activities:** hot tub, exercise room. **Guest Services:** valet and coin laundry.

EXTENDED STAY AMERICA PACILLI PLACE PHILADELPHIA/MT. LAUREL

856/608-9820

Extended Stay Hotel. Rates not provided. **Address:** 500 Diemer Dr 08054 **Location:** New Jersey Tpke exit 4, 1 mi se on SR 73, just n on Crawford Pl, then just e. Located in a corporate office park. **Facility:** 85 kitchen units. 3 stories, interior corridors. **Activities:** exercise room. **Guest Services:** coin laundry.

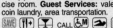

FAIRFIELD INN & SUITES BY MARRIOTT MT. LAUREL

(856)642-0600

Hotel $132-$217 **Address:** 350 Century Pkwy 08054 **Location:** New Jersey Tpke exit 4 to SR 73 N, just s. **Facility:** 118 units. 4 stories, interior corridors. **Pool(s):** heated indoor. **Activities:** hot tub, exercise room. **Guest Services:** valet and coin laundry.

AAA Benefit: Members save 5% or more!

HAMPTON INN PHILADELPHIA/MT. LAUREL   (856)778-5535

Hotel $89-$149 **Address:** 5000 Crawford Pl 08054 **Location:** New Jersey Tpke exit 4, 1 mi se on SR 73; I-295 exit 36A, 1.7 mi se on SR 73. Located behind Chili's. **Facility:** 125 units.

AAA Benefit: Members save 5% or more!

4 stories, interior corridors. **Terms:** 1-7 night minimum stay, cancellation fee imposed. **Pool(s):** outdoor. **Activities:** exercise room. **Guest Services:** valet and coin laundry.

HILTON GARDEN INN-MT. LAUREL   (856)234-4788

Hotel $109-$179 **Address:** 4000 Atrium Way 08054 **Location:** New Jersey Tpke exit 4, 1 mi se on SR 73, then just w. **Facility:** 140 units. 5 stories, interior corridors. **Terms:** 1-7 night minimum stay, cancellation fee imposed. **Pool(s):** heated indoor. **Activities:** hot tub, exercise room. **Guest Services:** valet and coin laundry, boarding pass kiosk.

AAA Benefit: Members save 5% or more!

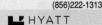

HOTEL ML   (856)234-7300

Hotel
$99-$299

Address: 915 SR 73 N 08054 **Location:** New Jersey Tpke exit 4, northeast corner; I-295 exit 36A, just se. **Facility:** 280 units. 10 stories, interior corridors. **Terms:** check-in 4 pm. **Pool(s):** heated outdoor, heated indoor. **Activities:** hot tub, exercise room. **Guest Services:** valet and coin laundry, area transportation.

HYATT HOUSE MT. LAUREL   (856)222-1313

Extended Stay Hotel
$99-$189

AAA Benefit: Members save 10%!

Address: 3000 Crawford Pl 08054 **Location:** I-295 exit 36A, 1.5 mi s on SR 73. **Facility:** 116 kitchen units, some two bedrooms. 3 stories (no elevator), exterior corridors. **Terms:** cancellation fee imposed. **Pool(s):** outdoor. **Activities:** exercise room. **Guest Services:** valet and coin laundry. **Featured Amenity:** breakfast buffet.

HYATT PLACE MT. LAUREL (856)840-0770

Hotel
$99-$199

HYATT PLACE
AAA Benefit: Members save 10%!

Address: 8000 Crawford Pl 08054 **Location:** New Jersey Tpke exit 4, 1 mi se on SR 73; I-295 exit 36A, 1.7 mi se on SR 73. **Facility:** 124 units. 6 stories, interior corridors. **Pool(s):** outdoor. **Activities:** exercise room. **Guest Services:** valet laundry. **Featured Amenity:** breakfast buffet.

LA QUINTA MT. LAUREL-PHILADELPHIA (856)235-7500

Hotel
$79-$249

Address: 5000 Clover Rd 08054 **Location:** New Jersey Tpke exit 4, just se; I-295 exit 36A, 0.8 mi se. **Facility:** 63 units. 3 stories, interior corridors. **Amenities:** video games, safes. **Activities:** exercise room. **Guest Services:** valet and coin laundry. **Featured Amenity:** full hot breakfast.

PHILADELPHIA/MOUNT LAUREL HOMEWOOD SUITES BY HILTON (856)222-9001

Extended Stay Hotel $109-$199 **Address:** 1422 Nixon Dr 08054 **Location:** I-295 exit 36B, follow ramp to end, then just n. **Facility:** 118 efficiencies, some two bedrooms. 3 stories, interior corridors. **Terms:** 1-7 night minimum stay, cancellation fee imposed. **Pool(s):** heated indoor. **Activities:** hot tub, exercise room. **Guest Services:** valet and coin laundry.

AAA Benefit: Members save 5% or more!

RED ROOF INN #7066 856/234-5589

Motel
Rates not provided

Address: 603 Fellowship Rd 08054 **Location:** I-295 exit 36A, just se on SR 73 to Fellowship Rd, then just s. **Facility:** 108 units. 2 stories (no elevator), exterior corridors. **Amenities:** video games, safes.

RESIDENCE INN BY MARRIOTT MOUNT LAUREL AT BISHOP'S GATE (856)234-1025

Extended Stay Hotel $118-$194 **Address:** 1000 Bishops Gate Blvd 08054 **Location:** I-295 exit 40A, just e. **Facility:** 144 units, some two bedrooms, efficiencies and kitchens. 3 stories, interior corridors. **Pool(s):** heated indoor. **Activities:** hot tub, exercise room. **Guest Services:** valet and coin laundry, boarding pass kiosk.

AAA Benefit: Members save 5% or more!

STAYBRIDGE SUITES (856)722-1900

Extended Stay Hotel
$149-$359

Address: 4115 Church Rd 08054 **Location:** New Jersey Tpke exit 4, 0.5 mi s on SR 73, then 0.5 mi w. **Facility:** 99 efficiencies, some two bedrooms. 3 stories, interior corridors. **Terms:** check-in 4 pm. **Pool(s):** heated indoor. **Guest Services:** valet and coin laundry. **Featured Amenity:** full hot breakfast.

SUPER 8 (856)802-2800

Hotel $69-$109 **Address:** 560 Fellowship Rd 08054 **Location:** New Jersey Tpke exit 4, just s to Fellowship Rd. **Facility:** 80 units. 2 stories, interior corridors. *Bath:* shower only. **Guest Services:** coin laundry.

THE WESTIN MOUNT LAUREL (856)778-7300

Hotel
$99-$399

WESTIN HOTELS & RESORTS
AAA Benefit: Members save up to 15%, plus Starwood Preferred Guest® benefits!

Address: 555 Fellowship Rd 08054 **Location:** I-295 exit 36A, just se on SR 73 to Fellowship Rd, then just n. **Facility:** 173 units. 7 stories, interior corridors. **Parking:** on-site and valet. **Amenities:** safes. **Pool(s):** heated indoor. **Activities:** hot tub. **Guest Services:** valet laundry.

WYNDHAM PHILADELPHIA-MOUNT LAUREL (856)234-7000

Hotel
$109-$189

Address: 1111 SR 73 08054 **Location:** New Jersey Tpke exit 4; I-295 exit 36A, 0.5 mi se. **Facility:** 243 units. 9 stories, interior corridors. **Amenities:** video games, safes. **Pool(s):** heated indoor. **Activities:** exercise room. **Guest Services:** valet laundry, rental car service, area transportation.

WHERE TO EAT

CHULICIOUS 856/780-5240 [120]

Chinese. Casual Dining. $8-$20 **AAA Inspector Notes:** Painted a bright red color, this casual spot is popular for their authentic spices and flavors. The crystal wonton in chili oil is the signature appetizer and is highly recommended. An $8 lunch special is available Monday through Friday and includes a variety of poultry, tofu and seafood options. **Address:** 1200 S Church St 08054 **Location:** New Jersey Tpke exit 4, 2.1 mi e, then just n; in Village II.

L D

AAA Vacations® packages ...
unforgettable experiences
and unrivaled value

MILLER'S NJ ALE HOUSE
856/722-5690 (117)

▼▼ ▼▼ American. Casual Dining. $8-$20 **AAA Inspector Notes:** This casual pub and restaurant provides an almost lodge-like feel with their wood paneling and large wraparound bar at the center of the restaurant. Flat-panel televisions flood the ceiling to provide guests with ample viewing angles from any table. The large menu touches on a bit of everything and includes pastas, burgers, steaks, fajitas, and fresh seafood. **Features:** full bar, happy hour. **Address:** 554 Fellowship Rd 08054 **Location:** I-295 exit 36A, just se on SR 73 to Fellowship Rd, then just n. [L] [D] CALL [⅃M]

SAGE DINER
856/727-0770 (119)

▼▼ ▼▼ American. Casual Dining. $5-$27 **AAA Inspector Notes:** A favorite with the local crowd, this casual, unassuming diner serves corned beef and cabbage, split pea soup, meatloaf, lasagna, chicken cutlets, pasta and other home-style comfort foods. The menu features a page of breakfast choices and numerous sandwiches and salads. Fluffy meringue towers above the lemon pie. Art Deco touches decorate the dining room. **Address:** 1170 Rt 73 & Church Rd 08054 **Location:** New Jersey Tpke exit 4, just se; I-295 exit 36A, 1 mi se. [B] [L] [D] [LATE]

SINGAPORE RESTAURANT AND SUSHI BAR
856/802-2888 (121)

▼▼ ▼▼ Japanese. Casual Dining. $5-$20 **AAA Inspector Notes:** If you're looking to get away from the local chain restaurants, you will find this small, cozy Japanese restaurant a great value. The menu is filled with an array of sushi rolls, bento boxes and traditional favorites. Great for a quick bite and convenient to many nearby hotels. **Address:** 1215 SR 73 08054 **Location:** I-295 exit 36A, 2 mi se, off SR 73. [L] [D]

STEFANO'S RISTORANTE
856/778-3663 (118)

▼▼ ▼▼ Italian. Casual Dining. $12-$27 **AAA Inspector Notes:** A small, cozy Italian restaurant with friendly service and a warm atmosphere. You will often find the owner and chef, Paolo, cooking up homemade favorites for her patrons. On the menu you will find Sicilian style pizza, an array of pasta dishes, homemade soups and much more. Remember to bring your own wine and beer at this BYOB establishment. **Reservations:** suggested, for dinner. **Address:** 3815 Church Rd 08054 **Location:** I-295 exit 36A, 0.4 mi s on Beaver Ave, then just w. [L] [D]

MOUNT OLIVE

RESIDENCE INN BY MARRIOTT MT. OLIVE AT THE INTERNATIONAL TRADE CENTER
(973)691-1720

▼▼ ▼▼ ▼▼ Extended Stay Hotel $140-$230 **Address:** 271 Continental Dr 07828 **Location:** I-80 exit 25, just n, follow signs for International Trade Center. Located in a business park. **Facility:** 123 units, some two bedrooms, efficiencies and kitchens. 4 stories, interior corridors. **Pool(s):** heated indoor. **Activities:** hot tub, exercise room. **Guest Services:** valet and coin laundry.

AAA Benefit: Members save 5% or more!

CALL [⅃M] [➔] [HS] [🛰] [✕] [🔌] [▣] [▯] / SOME UNITS [🔧]

NATIONAL PARK (E-2) pop. 3,036, elev. 16'

RED BANK BATTLEFIELD PARK (FORT MERCER)
is 2 mi. w. of I-295 at 100 Hessian Ave., on the riverfront. During the Revolutionary War Fort Mercer was hastily built at this site to protect the Delaware River and the port of Philadelphia from British forces. In October 1777, 400 Patriots under Gen. Christopher Greene vanquished 1,200 Britons and Hessians led by Count Van Donop. Also at the site is the restored dwelling of Ann Whitall, who allegedly spun wool while the battle raged around her home. **Hours:** Park open daily dawn-dusk. House Thurs.-Sun. 1-4, Apr. 1 to mid-Oct. Phone ahead to confirm schedule. **Cost:** Free. **Phone:** (856) 853-5120.

NEPTUNE

HAMPTON INN NEPTUNE/WALL
732/643-0500

▼▼ ▼▼ ▼▼ Hotel. Rates not provided. **Address:** 4 McNamara Way 07753 **Location:** Garden State Pkwy exit 100B southbound; exit 100A northbound, just e. **Facility:** 109 units. 5 stories, interior corridors. **Pool(s):** heated indoor. **Activities:** exercise room. **Guest Services:** valet and coin laundry.

AAA Benefit: Members save 5% or more!

CALL [⅃M] [➔] [BIZ] [🛰] [✕] [🔌] [▣] [▯]

HOLIDAY INN EXPRESS NEPTUNE
732/922-9600

▼▼ ▼▼ ▼▼ Hotel. Rates not provided. **Address:** 3510 Route 66 07753 **Location:** Garden State Pkwy exit 100A northbound; exit 100B southbound, 0.5 mi e. **Facility:** 95 units. 4 stories, interior corridors. **Amenities:** safes. **Pool(s):** heated indoor. **Activities:** game room, exercise room. **Guest Services:** coin laundry.

CALL [⅃M] [➔] [BIZ] [🛰] [✕] [🔌] [▯] / SOME UNITS [▣]

RESIDENCE INN BY MARRIOTT NEPTUNE AT GATEWAY CENTRE
(732)643-9350

▼▼ ▼▼ ▼▼ Extended Stay Hotel $118-$206 **Address:** 230 Jumping Brook Rd 07753 **Location:** Garden State Pkwy exit 100B, 0.5 mi e on SR 33, then 0.5 mi n. **Facility:** 105 units, some two bedrooms, efficiencies and kitchens. 4 stories, interior corridors. **Pool(s):** heated indoor. **Activities:** hot tub, exercise room. **Guest Services:** valet and coin laundry, rental car service.

AAA Benefit: Members save 5% or more!

CALL [⅃M] [➔] [BIZ] [HS] [🛰] [✕] [🎥] [🔌] [▣] [▯] / SOME UNITS [🔧]

NEWARK (H-6) pop. 277,140, elev. 95'
• Hotels p. 168 • Restaurants p. 169
• Hotels & Restaurants map & index p. 162

New Jersey's largest city had a humble start: two streets laid out by Puritans from Connecticut in 1666. A major land, sea and air transportation center, Newark is a headquarters for leading insurance companies, banks and retail operations, as well as many federal and state agencies.

The city's midtown college complex is the home of four institutions of higher learning: Rutgers University at Newark, which includes the University of Medicine and Dentistry of New Jersey; Seton Hall University School of Law; the New Jersey Institute of Technology; and Essex County College. The Rutgers Institute of Jazz Studies maintains an extensive collection of jazz recordings, while a gallery in Rutgers' Paul Robeson Cultural Center, 600 Bartholomew Rd. (adjacent to the Busch Campus Center), displays changing art exhibits. Phone (973) 353-5595 and (848) 445-3545, respectively.

Inspiring statues in wedged-shaped Military Park, downtown between Broad Street, Center Street and Park Place, includes the monumental "Wars of America" by Mount Rushmore sculptor Gutzon Borglum and a bust of President John F. Kennedy by Jacques Lipchitz. Parking is available at the Military Park Garage, 4250 Park Pl.; phone (973) 643-4700.

Conceived by renowned landscape architect Frederick Law Olmstead in 1867, 360-acre Branch Brook Park is known for its necklace of waterways— streams, ponds and open lakes—that are traversed

(See map & index p. 162.)

by 19 bridges. Branch Brook Park Lake is stocked with trout, and the park has miles of winding pathways and more than 4,000 Japanese cherry trees that put on an extravagant floral display in the spring. There are multiple entrances for cars along the park's 2-mile length; parking is available off Bloomfield Avenue. For park information phone (973) 268-2300.

City Hall, 920 Broad St., is a fine example of Beaux Arts architecture. Dedicated in 1906, the building features a grand central staircase and a skylight. James Street Commons, next to Washington Park, is a 20-block area that contains a number of well-preserved Victorian row houses.

Newark was the birthplace of Whitney Houston, who became one of the world's best-selling recording artists in the 1980s. She also starred in "The Bodyguard"; the 1992 movie's theme song, the Dolly Parton-penned "I Will Always Love You," became Houston's signature hit. The six-time Grammy winner died Feb. 11, 2012, on the eve of the 54th annual awards ceremony.

The New Jersey State Opera performs at venues around the state. The New Jersey Symphony Orchestra gives concerts at the New Jersey Performing Arts Center, 1 Center St.; for more information about the symphony phone (973) 624-3713 or (800) 255-3476 for the box office.

The Prudential Center, 25 Lafayette St., is home to the National Hockey League's New Jersey Devils, who hit the ice from mid-October to mid-April, and the Seton Hall University Pirates men's basketball team. The arena seats more than 18,500 for concerts, family shows and sporting events; phone (973) 757-6000 for general information, (973) 757-6600 for the Prudential Center box office or (973) 275-4255 for the Seton Hall ticket office.

Greater Newark Convention & Visitors Bureau: 60 Park Pl., Suite 104, Newark, NJ 07012. **Phone:** (973) 735-2135.

CATHEDRAL BASILICA OF THE SACRED HEART, 89 Ridge St., is a French Gothic-style cathedral comparable in size to London's Westminster Abbey and resembling the basilica at Rheims, France. Dedicated by the Roman Catholic Archdiocese of Newark in 1953, more than 50 years after construction started, the cathedral features hand-carved *reredos* (altar screens), more than 200 stained-glass windows, bronze doors and 14 bells cast in Italy. The towers are 232 feet high. **Hours:** Mon.-Sat. 9-7, Sun. 1-5. **Cost:** Donations. **Phone:** (973) 484-4600.

THE NEWARK MUSEUM is at 49 Washington St. (at Central Ave.). The museum's 80 galleries exhibit collections of art representing ancient Egypt, Greece and Rome as well as Africa, Asia, the Pacific and the Americas.

The Asian wing features an extensive collection of Tibetan art, including a Buddhist altar that the 14th Dalai Lama consecrated in 1990. American art includes Colonial-era pieces as well as contemporary works, including paintings by Mary Cassatt, Thomas Cole, Edward Hopper, Georgia O'Keeffe, Joseph Stella and Henry Ossawa Tanner. Rocks, minerals, fossils, insects and shells are among the extensive collections in the museum's Natural Science Collection. The complex also includes the Alice and Leonard Dreyfuss Planetarium and a memorial garden.

Time: Allow 3 hours minimum. **Hours:** Wed.-Sun. noon-5. Closed Jan. 1, July 4, Thanksgiving and Christmas. **Cost:** $12 (includes Ballantine House); $7 (ages 62+, children, college students with ID and veterans and their families); free (Newark residents). Planetarium additional $5; $3 (ages 62+, children under 12 and college students with ID). **Phone:** (973) 596-6550. [T]

Ballantine House is at 49 Washington St., adjacent to The Newark Museum. This restored 1885 Victorian mansion, which belonged to brewer John H. Ballantine, contains eight rooms furnished as they would have been in 1891. Six galleries and two hallways display a collection of decorative arts.

Hours: Wed.-Sun. noon-5. Closed Jan. 1, July 4, Thanksgiving and Christmas. **Cost:** $12 (includes The Newark Museum); $7 (ages 62+, children, college students with ID and veterans and their families); free (Newark residents). **Phone:** (973) 596-6550.

NEWARK PUBLIC LIBRARY is at 5 Washington St. opposite Washington Park. One of the largest public libraries in the state and a major resource center, it has large collections of material about the history of the city and state. Also housed in the 1901 building are more than 1 million books, pictures and periodicals. Changing exhibits are presented regularly.

Time: Allow 1 hour minimum. **Hours:** Mon.-Sat. 9-5:30 (also Tues.-Thurs. 5:30-8:30). Closed major holidays. Phone ahead to confirm schedule. **Cost:** Free. **Phone:** (973) 733-7784.

NEW JERSEY HISTORICAL SOCIETY is at 52 Park Pl. in Military Park. The Georgian-style building houses the society's historical collections, which were established in 1845. Among the displays are original land grants, prints and decorative arts, and furniture. Among the 32,000-plus items are a turn-of-the-20th-century woman's bathing suit, a teapot from the mid-1700s and a vintage baseball glove. Visitors also can browse the historic publications in the society's reference and research library. **Time:** Allow 1 hour minimum. **Hours:** Museum open Tues.-Sat. 10-5. Library open Tues.-Sat. noon-5. Reservations are required for the library. **Cost:** Museum $3. Library $5. **Phone:** (973) 596-8500.

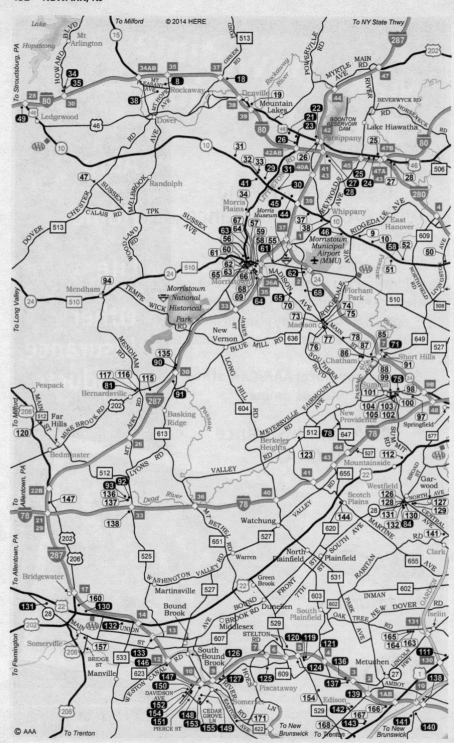

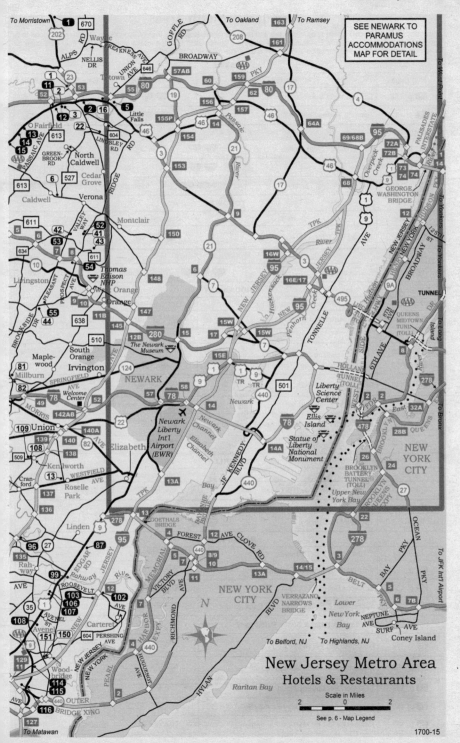

New Jersey Metro Area
Hotels & Restaurants

Scale in Miles

See p. 6 - Map Legend

1700-15

New Jersey Metro Area

This index helps you to "spot" where approved hotels and restaurants are located on the corresponding detailed maps. Hotel daily rate range is for comparison only. Restaurant price range is a combination of lunch and/or dinner. Turn to the listing page for more detailed rate and price information and consult display ads for special promotions.

WAYNE

Map Page	Hotels	Diamond Rated	Rate Range	Page
1 p. 152	La Quinta Inn & Suites	◈◈	$72-$185	206
2 p. 152	Ramada Wayne Fairfield Area	◈◈	$90-$150	206

Map Page	Restaurants	Diamond Rated	Cuisine	Price Range	Page
① p. 152	Izumi Hibachi Steak House	◈◈	Japanese	$9-$37	207
② p. 152	Jyoti	◈◈	Indian	$12-$17	207
③ p. 152	The Cheesecake Factory	◈◈◈	International	$9-$30	207

TOTOWA

Map Page	Hotel	Diamond Rated	Rate Range	Page
5 p. 152	Holiday Inn-Totowa	◈◈◈	Rates not provided	201

Map Page	Restaurant	Diamond Rated	Cuisine	Price Range	Page
⑯ p. 152	Sushi Lounge	◈◈◈	Sushi	$11-$37	201

ROCKAWAY

Map Page	Hotel	Diamond Rated	Rate Range	Page
8 p. 152	Hilton Garden Inn Rockaway	◈◈◈	$109-$194 SAVE	189

FAIRFIELD

Map Page	Hotels	Diamond Rated	Rate Range	Page
11 p. 152	La Quinta Inn & Suites Fairfield	◈◈	$85-$225	113
12 p. 152	Crowne Plaza Fairfield	◈◈◈	Rates not provided	113
13 p. 152	Comfort Inn Fairfield	◈◈	$85-$149 SAVE	113
14 p. 152	BEST WESTERN PLUS Fairfield Executive Inn	◈◈◈	Rates not provided SAVE	113
15 p. 152	Hampton Inn & Suites	◈◈◈	$149-$299	113

DENVILLE

Map Page	Hotel	Diamond Rated	Rate Range	Page
18 p. 152	Hampton Inn Denville (Parsippany Area)	◈◈◈	$109-$149	106

Map Page	Restaurant	Diamond Rated	Cuisine	Price Range	Page
⑲ p. 152	Thai Chef Restaurant	◈◈	Thai	$10-$23	106

PARSIPPANY

Map Page	Hotels	Diamond Rated	Rate Range	Page
21 p. 152	Courtyard by Marriott Parsippany	◈◈◈	$181-$298 SAVE	177
22 p. 152	Embassy Suites Parsippany	◈◈◈	$101-$256	177
23 p. 152	Fairfield Inn & Suites by Marriott Parsippany	◈◈◈	$146-$240	177
24 p. 152	Holiday Inn Hotel & Suites Parsippany	◈◈◈	$99-$149 SAVE	177
25 p. 152	Red Roof Inn Parsippany	◈◈	Rates not provided SAVE	178
26 p. 152	Sonesta ES Suites Parsippany	◈◈◈	Rates not provided SAVE	179
27 p. 152	Sheraton Parsippany Hotel	◈◈◈	$75-$369 SAVE	178
28 p. 152	HYATT house Parsippany-East *(See ad p. 178.)*	◈◈◈	$109-$299 SAVE	178
29 p. 152	Residence Inn by Marriott Parsippany	◈◈◈	$188-$309 SAVE	178

PARSIPPANY (cont'd)

Map Page	Hotels (cont'd)	Diamond Rated	Rate Range	Page
30 p. 152	**Hilton Parsippany**	◇◇◇	$139-$299 [SAVE]	177
31 p. 152	Hampton Inn Parsippany	◇◇◇	$139-$299	177

Map Page	Restaurants	Diamond Rated	Cuisine	Price Range	Page
25 p. 152	Eccola Italian Bistro	◇◇◇	Northern Italian	$15-$25	179
26 p. 152	Baadshah	◇◇	Indian	$8-$19	179
27 p. 152	Marakesh	◇◇	Moroccan	$9-$23	179
28 p. 152	Keo Ku Korean Restaurant	◇◇	Korean	$9-$30	179

MOUNT ARLINGTON

Map Page	Hotels	Diamond Rated	Rate Range	Page
34 p. 152	**Holiday Inn Express & Suites**	◇◇◇	Rates not provided [SAVE]	146
35 p. 152	Courtyard by Marriott Rockaway/Mt. Arlington	◇◇◇	$132-$217	146

DOVER

Map Page	Hotel	Diamond Rated	Rate Range	Page
38 p. 152	Homewood Suites by Hilton Dover-Rockaway	◇◇◇	$135-$175	106

MORRIS PLAINS

Map Page	Hotel	Diamond Rated	Rate Range	Page
41 p. 152	Candlewood Suites Parsippany-Morris Plains	◇◇	Rates not provided	141

Map Page	Restaurants	Diamond Rated	Cuisine	Price Range	Page
31 p. 152	Minado	◇◇	Japanese	$18-$32	141
32 p. 152	Tabor Road Tavern	◇◇◇	American	$11-$39	141
33 p. 152	Grato	◇◇◇	Italian	$10-$25	141
34 p. 152	Arthur's Tavern	◇◇	American	$7-$24	141

WHIPPANY

Map Page	Hotels	Diamond Rated	Rate Range	Page
44 p. 152	**HYATT house Parsippany/Whippany** *(See ad p. 211.)*	◇◇◇	$99-$299 [SAVE]	211
45 p. 152	Hanover Marriott	◇◇◇	$209-$344	211
46 p. 152	**Courtyard by Marriott Hanover Whippany**	◇◇◇	$202-$332 [SAVE]	211

Map Page	Restaurants	Diamond Rated	Cuisine	Price Range	Page
37 p. 152	Nikko	◇◇◇	Japanese	$8-$26	212
38 p. 152	Il Capriccio	◇◇◇◇	Italian	$16-$32	212

WEST ORANGE

Map Page	Hotels	Diamond Rated	Rate Range	Page
52 p. 152	Residence Inn by Marriott-West Orange	◇◇◇	$139-$286	210
53 p. 152	**The Wilshire Grand Hotel**	◇◇◇	$199-$449 [SAVE]	210
54 p. 152	Courtyard by Marriott West Orange	◇◇◇	$139-$252	210
55 p. 152	**BEST WESTERN Turtle Brook Inn**	◇◇	$130-$160 [SAVE]	210

Map Page	Restaurants	Diamond Rated	Cuisine	Price Range	Page
41 p. 152	**The Manor**	◇◇◇◇	Continental	$11-$53	210
42 p. 152	Primavera Ristorante	◇◇◇	Italian	$11-$28	210

Map Page	Restaurants (cont'd)	Diamond Rated	Cuisine	Price Range	Page
43 p. 152	Highlawn Pavilion	♦♦♦	American	$13-$45	210
44 p. 152	McLoone's Boathouse	♦♦	American	$10-$35	210

LIVINGSTON

Map Page	Hotel	Diamond Rated	Rate Range	Page
58 p. 152	**Westminster Hotel**	♦♦♦♦	$139-$459 [SAVE]	133

Map Page	Restaurants	Diamond Rated	Cuisine	Price Range	Page
50 p. 152	Thavma Mediterranean Grill	♦♦	Mediterranean	$8-$26	133
51 p. 152	Panevino Ristorante	♦♦	Italian	$14-$29	133
52 p. 152	Strip House	♦♦♦	Steak	$13-$49	133

MORRISTOWN

Map Page	Hotels	Diamond Rated	Rate Range	Page
61 p. 152	**The Westin Governor Morris**	♦♦♦	$139-$499 [SAVE]	143
62 p. 152	**HYATT house Morristown** *(See ad p. 143.)*	♦♦♦	$99-$359 [SAVE]	143
63 p. 152	**Hyatt Morristown**	♦♦♦	$89-$429 [SAVE]	143
64 p. 152	**BEST WESTERN PLUS Morristown Inn**	♦♦♦	$99-$189 [SAVE]	142
65 p. 152	**The Madison Hotel**	♦♦♦	$135-$399 [SAVE]	143

Map Page	Restaurants	Diamond Rated	Cuisine	Price Range	Page
55 p. 152	Blue Morel Restaurant and Wine Bar	♦♦♦	New American	$11-$44	144
56 p. 152	Tim Schafer's Cuisine	♦♦♦	American	$14-$38	145
57 p. 152	The Taco Truck	♦	Mexican	$5-$8	144
58 p. 152	End of Elm	♦♦	Small Plates	$11-$18	144
59 p. 152	Sebastian's The Steakhouse	♦♦♦	Steak	$11-$37	144
60 p. 152	Tito's Burritos	♦	Mexican	$4-$10	145
61 p. 152	Sushi Lounge	♦♦♦	Sushi	$15-$37	144
62 p. 152	Roots Steakhouse	♦♦♦	Steak	$12-$80	144
63 p. 152	Urban Table	♦♦	Comfort Food	$9-$23	145
64 p. 152	Origin	♦♦	Thai	$10-$30	144
65 p. 152	The OFFICE Tavern Grill	♦♦	American	$9-$34	144
66 p. 152	Pamir	♦♦	Afghan	$8-$27	144
67 p. 152	Millie's Old World Meatballs & Pizza	♦♦	Pizza	$12-$22	144
68 p. 152	Sirin	♦♦	Thai	$10-$26	144
69 p. 152	David Todd's City Tavern	♦♦♦	New American	$10-$37	144
70 p. 152	Rod's Steak & Seafood Grille	♦♦♦	American	$11-$42	144

FLORHAM PARK

Map Page	Hotel	Diamond Rated	Rate Range	Page
68 p. 152	**Wyndham Hamilton Park Hotel & Conference Center**	♦♦♦	$135-$289 [SAVE]	115

SHORT HILLS

Map Page	Hotel	Diamond Rated	Rate Range	Page
71 p. 152	**Hilton Short Hills**	♦♦♦♦	$170-$341 [SAVE]	193

Map Page	Restaurant	Diamond Rated	Cuisine	Price Range	Page
91 p. 152	Legal Sea Foods	♦♦♦	Seafood	$12-$45	193

SUMMIT

Map Page	Hotel	Diamond Rated	Rate Range	Page
75 p. 152	The DeBary Inn	◈◈◈	Rates not provided	198

Map Page	Restaurants	Diamond Rated	Cuisine	Price Range	Page
97 p. 152	Huntley Taverne	◈◈◈	American	$11-$34	198
98 p. 152	Tito's Burritos	◈	Mexican	$4-$10	198
99 p. 152	Roots Steakhouse	◈◈◈	Steak	$11-$43	198
100 p. 152	Taka Sushi	◈◈	Sushi	$11-$24	198
101 p. 152	Monster Sushi	◈◈	Japanese	$9-$31	198
102 p. 152	Pizza Vita	◈◈	Pizza	$8-$16	198
103 p. 152	Anna's Ristorante	◈◈	Italian	$9-$32	198
104 p. 152	Fiorino Ristorante	◈◈◈	Italian	$14-$36	198
105 p. 152	FIN Rawbar & Kitchen	◈◈◈	Seafood	$22-$32	198

NEW PROVIDENCE

Map Page	Hotel	Diamond Rated	Rate Range	Page
78 p. 152	**BEST WESTERN PLUS Murray Hill Inn & Suites**	◈◈◈	$129-$189 SAVE	171

BERNARDSVILLE

Map Page	Hotel	Diamond Rated	Rate Range	Page
81 p. 152	**The Bernards Inn**	◈◈◈◈	$167-$356 SAVE	90

Map Page	Restaurants	Diamond Rated	Cuisine	Price Range	Page
115 p. 152	Osteria Morini	◈◈◈	Regional Italian	$15-$32	91
116 p. 152	Sette Cucina Italiana	◈◈◈	Italian	$12-$30	91
117 p. 152	**The Bernards Inn**	◈◈◈◈	American	$14-$48	91

WESTFIELD

Map Page	Hotel	Diamond Rated	Rate Range	Page
84 p. 152	**BEST WESTERN Westfield Inn**	◈◈	$129-$179 SAVE	208

Map Page	Restaurants	Diamond Rated	Cuisine	Price Range	Page
126 p. 152	Tinga Taqueria	◈◈	Tex-Mex	$9-$15	209
127 p. 152	Fujiyama Mama	◈◈◈	Japanese	$8-$34	208
128 p. 152	Theresa's	◈◈◈	Northern Italian	$10-$28	209
129 p. 152	Cod Almighty Chippery	◈	Seafood	$7-$17	208
130 p. 152	Mojave Grille	◈◈◈	Southwestern	$8-$26	209
131 p. 152	Ferraro's	◈◈◈	Italian	$9-$30	208
132 p. 152	Chez Catherine	◈◈◈	Traditional French	$33-$68	208

LINDEN

Map Page	Hotel	Diamond Rated	Rate Range	Page
87 p. 152	Hampton Inn Linden	◈◈◈	$109-$189	133

BASKING RIDGE

Map Page	Hotels	Diamond Rated	Rate Range	Page
90 p. 152	The Olde Mill Inn	◈◈◈	Rates not provided	87
91 p. 152	Dolce Basking Ridge	◈◈◈◈	Rates not provided	87
92 p. 152	**Courtyard by Marriott Basking Ridge**	◈◈◈	$207-$339 SAVE	87
93 p. 152	Hotel Indigo Basking Ridge	◈◈◈	Rates not provided	87

Map Page	Restaurants	Diamond Rated	Cuisine	Price Range	Page
(135) p. 152	The Grain House at The Olde Mill Inn	◆◆◆	American	$7-$29	87
(136) p. 152	Urban Table	◆◆	American	$11-$23	88
(137) p. 152	3 West	◆◆◆	American	$10-$30	87
(138) p. 152	Trattoria Bolu	◆◆	Italian	$9-$25	88

CLARK

Map Page	Hotel	Diamond Rated	Rate Range	Page
(96) p. 152	Holiday Inn Clark-Newark	◆◆◆	$109-$209	104

Map Page	Restaurant	Diamond Rated	Cuisine	Price Range	Page
(141) p. 152	Thailand Restaurant	◆◆	Thai	$9-$20	104

RAHWAY

Map Page	Hotel	Diamond Rated	Rate Range	Page
(99) p. 152	**BEST WESTERN Riverview Inn & Suites**	◆◆◆	$120-$160 [SAVE]	186

CARTERET

Map Page	Hotels	Diamond Rated	Rate Range	Page
(102) p. 152	Holiday Inn of Carteret-Rahway	◆◆◆	Rates not provided	102
(103) p. 152	Hotel Executive Suites	◆◆◆	$99-$299	102

AVENEL

Map Page	Hotels	Diamond Rated	Rate Range	Page
(106) p. 152	Fairfield Inn & Suites by Marriott Woodbridge	◆◆◆	$111-$183	86
(107) p. 152	**Comfort Suites at Woodbridge**	◆◆◆	$99-$159 [SAVE]	86
(108) p. 152	Holiday Inn Express-Woodbridge	◆◆◆	Rates not provided	86

ISELIN

Map Page	Hotel	Diamond Rated	Rate Range	Page
(111) p. 152	**Renaissance Woodbridge Hotel**	◆◆◆	$160-$263 [SAVE]	127

WOODBRIDGE

Map Page	Hotels	Diamond Rated	Rate Range	Page
(114) p. 152	Residence Inn by Marriott-Woodbridge Edison/Raritan Center	◆◆◆	$160-$263	222
(115) p. 152	Hampton Inn	◆◆◆	$119-$149	222
(116) p. 152	Extended Stay America Woodbridge-Newark	◆◆	Rates not provided	222

Map Page	Restaurants	Diamond Rated	Cuisine	Price Range	Page
(150) p. 152	Mie Thai	◆◆	Thai	$12-$21	222
(151) p. 152	Ristorante Venezia	◆◆◆	Italian	$16-$36	222

SOUTH PLAINFIELD

Map Page	Hotels	Diamond Rated	Rate Range	Page
(119) p. 152	Hampton Inn South Plainfield/Piscataway	◆◆◆	$144-$169	196
(120) p. 152	**BEST WESTERN The Garden Executive Hotel**	◆◆	$94-$124 [SAVE]	196
(121) p. 152	Holiday Inn South Plainfield/Piscataway	◆◆◆	Rates not provided	196

PISCATAWAY

Map Page	Hotels	Diamond Rated	Rate Range	Page
(124) p. 152	Motel 6 Piscataway #1084	◆	Rates not provided	180
(125) p. 152	Extended Stay America Piscataway-Rutgers University	◆◆	Rates not provided	180

PISCATAWAY (cont'd)

Map Page	Hotels (cont'd)	Diamond Rated	Rate Range	Page
126 p. 152	Radisson Hotel Piscataway Somerset	◆◆◆	$110-$199	180
127 p. 152	Embassy Suites Hotel Piscataway-Somerset	◆◆◆	$119-$209	180

Map Page	Restaurant	Diamond Rated	Cuisine	Price Range	Page
154 p. 152	Al Dente	◆◆◆	Italian	$16-$30	181

BRIDGEWATER

Map Page	Hotels	Diamond Rated	Rate Range	Page
130 p. 152	**Bridgewater Marriott**	◆◆◆	$119-$401 SAVE	93
131 p. 152	**HYATT house Bridgewater**	◆◆◆	$89-$299 SAVE	94
132 p. 152	**Days Inn Conference Center**	◆	$66-$73 SAVE	94
133 p. 152	Hilton Garden Inn-Bridgewater	◆◆◆	$99-$279	94

Map Page	Restaurant	Diamond Rated	Cuisine	Price Range	Page
160 p. 152	McCormick & Schmick's	◆◆◆	Seafood	$11-$46	94

EDISON

Map Page	Hotels	Diamond Rated	Rate Range	Page
136 p. 152	Red Roof Inn Edison	◆	Rates not provided	110
137 p. 152	**Fairfield Inn & Suites by Marriott Edison South Plainfield**	◆◆◆	$104-$171 SAVE	109
138 p. 152	Courtyard by Marriott Edison/Woodbridge	◆◆◆	$132-$217	109
139 p. 152	Quality Inn Edison	◆◆	$80-$95	110
140 p. 152	**Hilton Garden Inn Edison/Raritan Center**	◆◆◆	$89-$199 SAVE	109
141 p. 152	**Sheraton Edison Hotel Raritan Center**	◆◆◆	$149-$299 SAVE	110
142 p. 152	Crowne Plaza Edison	◆◆◆	Rates not provided	109
143 p. 152	**Comfort Inn Edison**	◆◆	$69-$115 SAVE	109

Map Page	Restaurants	Diamond Rated	Cuisine	Price Range	Page
163 p. 152	Moghul Fine Indian Cuisine	◆◆◆	Indian	$10-$25	110
164 p. 152	Ming Pan Asian Cuisine	◆◆	Asian	$15-$24	110
165 p. 152	Shezan Restaurant	◆◆	Indian	$9-$16	110
166 p. 152	Akbar	◆◆	Indian	$8-$20	110
167 p. 152	Penang	◆◆	Asian	$9-$23	110
168 p. 152	Skylark Fine Diner & Lounge	◆◆	American	$8-$27	110

SOMERSET

Map Page	Hotels	Diamond Rated	Rate Range	Page
146 p. 152	La Quinta Inn & Suites Somerset	◆◆◆	$74-$224	194
147 p. 152	**Holiday Inn-Somerset**	◆◆◆	Rates not provided SAVE	194
148 p. 152	**DoubleTree by Hilton Hotel & Executive Meeting Center Somerset**	◆◆◆	$99-$209 SAVE	194
149 p. 152	Candlewood Suites	◆◆	Rates not provided	194
150 p. 152	**Sonesta ES Suites Somerset**	◆◆	$125-$225 SAVE	195
151 p. 152	Courtyard by Marriott Somerset	◆◆◆	$230-$378	194
152 p. 152	Comfort Inn & Suites Somerset	◆◆◆	$79-$139	194

SOMERSET (cont'd)

Map Page	Hotels (cont'd)	Diamond Rated	Rate Range	Page
153 p. 152	**Residence Inn by Marriott-Somerset**	◈◈◈	$167-$275 SAVE	194
154 p. 152	Fairfield Inn & Suites by Marriott Somerset	◈◈◈	$146-$240	194
155 p. 152	Homewood Suites by Hilton-Somerset	◈◈◈	$109-$179	194

Map Page	Restaurant	Diamond Rated	Cuisine	Price Range	Page
171 p. 152	Pooja	◈◈	Indian	$12-$18	195

CALDWELL

Map Page	Restaurant	Diamond Rated	Cuisine	Price Range	Page
6 p. 152	Lucé eclectic-italian	◈◈◈	Italian	$7-$29	96

EAST HANOVER

Map Page	Restaurants	Diamond Rated	Cuisine	Price Range	Page
9 p. 152	Mr. Chu	◈◈	Chinese	$6-$19	107
10 p. 152	The Godfather Seafood Bar & Grill	◈◈	Seafood	$8-$24	107

ROSELLE PARK

Map Page	Restaurant	Diamond Rated	Cuisine	Price Range	Page
13 p. 152	Costas Restaurant & Pizzeria	◈◈	Italian	$11-$25	189

CEDAR GROVE

Map Page	Restaurant	Diamond Rated	Cuisine	Price Range	Page
22 p. 152	Lu Nello	◈◈◈◈	Northern Italian	$16-$34	102

RANDOLPH

Map Page	Restaurant	Diamond Rated	Cuisine	Price Range	Page
47 p. 152	Casa de Pasta	◈◈	Italian	$11-$20	186

MADISON

Map Page	Restaurants	Diamond Rated	Cuisine	Price Range	Page
73 p. 152	Shanghai Jazz Restaurant & Bar	◈◈◈	Chinese	$16-$35	135
74 p. 152	54 Main Bar & Grille	◈◈	American	$11-$28	135
75 p. 152	Il Mondo Vecchio Ristorante Italiano	◈◈◈	Italian	$16-$36	135
76 p. 152	Blue Wazabi	◈◈	Sushi	$11-$24	135
77 p. 152	L' Allegria	◈◈◈	Italian	$13-$36	135
78 p. 152	Begum Palace	◈◈	Indian	$13-$26	135

MILLBURN

Map Page	Restaurants	Diamond Rated	Cuisine	Price Range	Page
81 p. 152	Tinga Taqueria	◈◈	Mexican	$7-$19	138
82 p. 152	Basilico	◈◈	Italian	$10-$35	138

CHATHAM

Map Page	Restaurants	Diamond Rated	Cuisine	Price Range	Page
85 p. 152	**Restaurant Serenade**	◈◈◈◈	New American	$18-$38	102
86 p. 152	Bean Curd	◈◈	Chinese	$7-$20	102
87 p. 152	A Taste of Asia	◈◈	Asian	$8-$20	102
88 p. 152	Scalini Fedeli	◈◈◈	Northern Italian	$14-$54	102

MENDHAM

Map Page	Restaurant	Diamond Rated	Cuisine	Price Range	Page
94 p. 152	The Black Horse Tavern	◈◈◈	American	$17-$44	137

KENILWORTH

Map Page	Restaurants	Diamond Rated	Cuisine	Price Range	Page
(108) p. 152	Le Rendez Vous	▽▽▽	French	$28-$32	130
(109) p. 152	Star of India Restaurant	▽▽	Indian	$7-$15	130

MOUNTAINSIDE

Map Page	Restaurant	Diamond Rated	Cuisine	Price Range	Page
(112) p. 152	Arirang Hibachi Steakhouse	▽▽▽	Japanese	$16-$39	146

PEAPACK

Map Page	Restaurant	Diamond Rated	Cuisine	Price Range	Page
(120) p. 152	Ninety Acres	▽▽▽▽	Regional American	$19-$39	180

BERKELEY HEIGHTS

Map Page	Restaurant	Diamond Rated	Cuisine	Price Range	Page
(123) p. 152	Trap Rock Restaurant & Brewery	▽▽▽	American	$12-$34	90

SCOTCH PLAINS

Map Page	Restaurant	Diamond Rated	Cuisine	Price Range	Page
(144) p. 152	Stage House Restaurant & Tavern	▽▽	American	$11-$30	191

BEDMINSTER

Map Page	Restaurant	Diamond Rated	Cuisine	Price Range	Page
(147) p. 152	**Pluckemin Inn**	▽▽▽▽	New American	$14-$38	90

SOMERVILLE

Map Page	Restaurant	Diamond Rated	Cuisine	Price Range	Page
(157) p. 152	Origin	▽▽▽	Thai	$10-$31	196

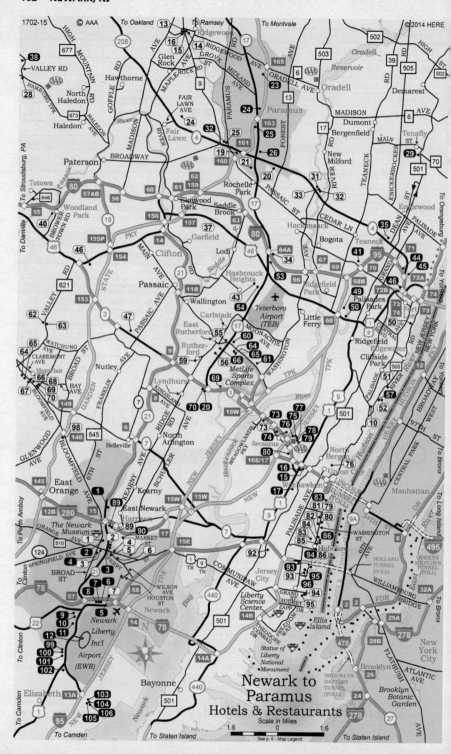

Newark to Paramus
Hotels & Restaurants
Scale in Miles
1.6   0   1.6
See p. 6 - Map Legend

✈ Airport Hotels

Map Page	NEWARK LIBERTY INTERNATIONAL AIRPORT (Maximum driving distance from airport: 4.7 mi)	Diamond Rated	Rate Range	Page
104 p. 162	Country Inn & Suites By Carlson, 3.6 mi	▽▽▽	$109-$169 SAVE	111
105 p. 162	Courtyard by Marriott Newark Elizabeth, 3.6 mi	▽▽▽	$174-$286 SAVE	112
102 p. 162	Crowne Plaza Newark Airport, 3.2 mi	▽▽▽	$110-$249	112
106 p. 162	Embassy Suites Newark Airport, 3.6 mi	▽▽▽	$159-$259	112
100 p. 162	Hampton Inn-Newark Airport, 2.8 mi	▽▽▽	$119-$259	112
99 p. 162	Hilton Newark Airport, 2.7 mi	▽▽▽	$119-$229 SAVE	112
101 p. 162	Renaissance Newark Airport Hotel, 2.9 mi	▽▽▽	$202-$332 SAVE	112
103 p. 162	Residence Inn by Marriott Newark Elizabeth/ Liberty International Airport, 3.6 mi	▽▽▽	$174-$286 SAVE	112
9 p. 162	BEST WESTERN PLUS Newark Airport West, 3.5 mi	▽▽▽	$120-$199 SAVE	168
2 p. 162	BEST WESTERN PLUS Robert Treat Hotel, 4.4 mi	▽▽▽	$99-$249 SAVE	168
4 p. 162	Courtyard by Marriott Newark Downtown, 3.9 mi	▽▽▽	$164-$269 SAVE	168
8 p. 162	Courtyard by Marriott Newark Liberty International Airport, 4.6 mi	▽▽▽	$169-$278 SAVE	168
5 p. 162	DoubleTree by Hilton Newark Airport, 3.9 mi	▽▽▽	$129-$299 SAVE	169
7 p. 162	Fairfield Inn & Suites by Marriott Newark Liberty International Airport, 4.6 mi	▽▽▽	$108-$177	169
3 p. 162	Hilton Newark Penn Station, 4.3 mi	▽▽▽	$169-$399	169
11 p. 162	Holiday Inn Newark Airport, 1.8 mi	▽▽▽	Rates not provided	169
12 p. 162	Marriott Newark Airport, 1.4 mi	▽▽▽	$230-$378	169
6 p. 162	SpringHill Suites by Marriott Newark Liberty International Airport, 4.7 mi	▽▽▽	$125-$229	169
10 p. 162	Wyndham Garden Hotel Newark Airport, 3.4 mi	▽▽▽	$149-$369	169

Newark To Paramus

This index helps you "spot" where approved hotels and restaurants are located on the corresponding detailed maps. Hotel daily rate range is for comparison only. Restaurant price range is a combination of lunch and/or dinner. Turn to the listing page for more detailed rate and price information and consult display ads for special promotions.

NEWARK

Map Page	Hotels	Diamond Rated	Rate Range	Page
1 p. 162	Comfort Suites Newark	▽▽	$120-$190 SAVE	168
2 p. 162	BEST WESTERN PLUS Robert Treat Hotel	▽▽▽	$99-$249 SAVE	168
3 p. 162	Hilton Newark Penn Station	▽▽▽	$169-$399	169
4 p. 162	Courtyard by Marriott Newark Downtown	▽▽▽	$164-$269 SAVE	168
5 p. 162	DoubleTree by Hilton Newark Airport	▽▽▽	$129-$299 SAVE	169
6 p. 162	SpringHill Suites by Marriott Newark Liberty International Airport	▽▽▽	$125-$229	169
7 p. 162	Fairfield Inn & Suites by Marriott Newark Liberty International Airport	▽▽▽	$108-$177	169
8 p. 162	Courtyard by Marriott Newark Liberty International Airport	▽▽▽	$169-$278 SAVE	168
9 p. 162	BEST WESTERN PLUS Newark Airport West	▽▽▽	$120-$199 SAVE	168
10 p. 162	Wyndham Garden Hotel Newark Airport	▽▽▽	$149-$369	169

NEWARK (cont'd)

Map Page	Hotels (cont'd)	Diamond Rated	Rate Range	Page
⓫ p. 162	Holiday Inn Newark Airport	▽▽▽	Rates not provided	169
⓬ p. 162	Marriott Newark Airport	▽▽▽	$230-$378	169

Map Page	Restaurants	Diamond Rated	Cuisine	Price Range	Page
① p. 162	Maize	▽▽▽	Portuguese	$15-$30	170
② p. 162	Don Pepe Restaurant	▽▽	Spanish	$10-$35	169
③ p. 162	Dinosaur Bar-B-Que	▽▽	Barbecue	$8-$28	169
④ p. 162	Spain Restaurant	▽▽	Spanish	$10-$25	170
⑤ p. 162	Fornos of Spain Restaurant	▽▽	Spanish	$13-$36	169
⑥ p. 162	Adega Grill	▽▽	Portuguese	$16-$35	169
⑦ p. 162	Tony da Caneca	▽▽	Portuguese	$9-$29	170

NORTH BERGEN

Map Page	Hotels	Diamond Rated	Rate Range	Page
⓯ p. 162	Super 8	▽▽	$72-$220 [SAVE]	172
⓰ p. 162	Meadowlands View Hotel	▽▽	$99-$152	172
⓱ p. 162	Comfort Suites	▽▽▽	$119-$329 [SAVE]	172

Map Page	Restaurant	Diamond Rated	Cuisine	Price Range	Page
⑩ p. 162	Sabor Latin Bistro	▽▽▽	Latin American	$10-$36	172

LYNDHURST

Map Page	Hotel	Diamond Rated	Rate Range	Page
⑳ p. 162	Courtyard by Marriott Lyndhurst Meadowlands	▽▽▽	$146-$240	135

PARAMUS

Map Page	Hotels	Diamond Rated	Rate Range	Page
㉓ p. 162	Crowne Plaza Paramus	▽▽▽	$99-$199 [SAVE]	176
㉔ p. 162	Courtyard by Marriott Paramus	▽▽▽	$139-$229 [SAVE]	176
㉕ p. 162	Comfort Inn & Suites of Paramus	▽▽▽	$100-$180 [SAVE]	176
㉖ p. 162	Holiday Inn Express	▽▽▽	$130-$159 [SAVE]	176

Map Page	Restaurants	Diamond Rated	Cuisine	Price Range	Page
⑲ p. 162	Chakra Restaurant	▽▽▽	American	$16-$42	176
⑳ p. 162	Bobby's Burger Palace	▽	Burgers	$6-$9	176
㉑ p. 162	Legal Sea Foods	▽▽▽	Seafood	$12-$45	177

TENAFLY

Map Page	Hotel	Diamond Rated	Rate Range	Page
㉙ p. 162	Clinton Inn Hotel & Event Center	▽▽▽	Rates not provided	199

FAIR LAWN

Map Page	Hotel	Diamond Rated	Rate Range	Page
㉜ p. 162	Hyatt Place Fair Lawn/Paramus	▽▽▽	$74-$209 [SAVE]	114

Map Page	Restaurants	Diamond Rated	Cuisine	Price Range	Page
㉔ p. 162	Mei Sushi	▽▽	Sushi	$9-$22	114
㉕ p. 162	The River Palm Terrace	▽▽▽	Steak	$17-$47	114

ENGLEWOOD

Map Page	Hotel	Diamond Rated	Rate Range	Page
㉟ p. 162	Crowne Plaza Englewood	▽▽▽	$129-$209 [SAVE]	112

WAYNE

Map Page	Hotel	Diamond Rated	Rate Range	Page
38 p. 162	Residence Inn by Marriott Wayne	◈◈◈	$146-$240	206

Map Page	Restaurant	Diamond Rated	Cuisine	Price Range	Page
28 p. 162	Aldo's Cucina Ristorante Italiano	◈◈	Italian	$9-$29	206

TEANECK

Map Page	Hotel	Diamond Rated	Rate Range	Page
41 p. 162	Teaneck Marriott at Glenpointe	◈◈◈	$167-$275	199

FORT LEE

Map Page	Hotels	Diamond Rated	Rate Range	Page
44 p. 162	Holiday Inn Fort Lee	◈◈◈	Rates not provided	116
45 p. 162	**BEST WESTERN Fort Lee**	◈◈	$100-$250 SAVE	116
46 p. 162	DoubleTree by Hilton Fort Lee-George Washington Bridge	◈◈◈	$139-$269	116

RIDGEFIELD PARK

Map Page	Hotels	Diamond Rated	Rate Range	Page
49 p. 162	Hilton Garden Inn Ridgefield Park	◈◈◈	$169-$239	187
50 p. 162	Hampton Inn at Ridgefield Park	◈◈◈	$124-$189	187

HASBROUCK HEIGHTS

Map Page	Hotels	Diamond Rated	Rate Range	Page
53 p. 162	Hilton Hasbrouck Heights/ Meadowlands	◈◈◈	$114-$199	123
54 p. 162	**Holiday Inn Meadowlands Area**	◈◈◈	$129-$199 SAVE	123

Map Page	Restaurant	Diamond Rated	Cuisine	Price Range	Page
43 p. 162	Ivy Inn	◈◈	Continental	$11-$36	123

EDGEWATER

Map Page	Hotel	Diamond Rated	Rate Range	Page
57 p. 162	Homewood Suites by Hilton/Edgewater	◈◈◈	$214-$264	109

Map Page	Restaurants	Diamond Rated	Cuisine	Price Range	Page
50 p. 162	The River Palm Terrace	◈◈◈	Steak	$10-$47	109
51 p. 162	The Crab House	◈◈	Seafood	$10-$41 SAVE	109
52 p. 162	Fleming's Prime Steakhouse & Wine Bar	◈◈◈	Steak	$32-$50	109

CARLSTADT

Map Page	Hotels	Diamond Rated	Rate Range	Page
60 p. 162	Holiday Inn Express Hotel & Suites	◈◈◈	Rates not provided	101
61 p. 162	Hampton Inn-Meadowlands	◈◈◈	$129-$179	101

EAST RUTHERFORD

Map Page	Hotels	Diamond Rated	Rate Range	Page
64 p. 162	Fairfield Inn by Marriott Meadowlands	◈◈◈	$132-$217	107
65 p. 162	Residence Inn by Marriott East Rutherford Meadowlands	◈◈◈	$195-$321	108
66 p. 162	Homewood Suites by Hilton-East Rutherford/ Meadowlands	◈◈◈	$189-$269	107

Map Page	Restaurants	Diamond Rated	Cuisine	Price Range	Page
55 p. 162	Vesta Wood Fired Pizza & Bar	◈◈◈	Italian	$12-$23	108
56 p. 162	Park & Orchard	◈◈	American	$9-$36	108

RUTHERFORD

Map Page	Hotels	Diamond Rated	Rate Range	Page
69 p. 162	Extended Stay America-Meadowlands-Rutherford	◆◆	Rates not provided	190
70 p. 162	Renaissance Meadowlands Hotel	◆◆◆	$202-$332	190

Map Page	Restaurant	Diamond Rated	Cuisine	Price Range	Page
59 p. 162	Cafe Matisse	◆◆◆	New Small Plates	$60-$95	190

SECAUCUS

Map Page	Hotels	Diamond Rated	Rate Range	Page
73 p. 162	**Meadowlands Plaza Hotel**	◆◆	$114-$169 SAVE	192
74 p. 162	La Quinta Inn & Suites Secaucus Meadowlands	◆◆	$125-$434	192
75 p. 162	**Courtyard by Marriott Secaucus Meadowlands**	◆◆◆	$186-$305 SAVE	191
76 p. 162	Meadowlands River Inn	◆◆	$109-$359	193
77 p. 162	Embassy Suites-Secaucus-Meadowlands	◆◆◆	$169-$269	191
78 p. 162	**Holiday Inn Secaucus Meadowlands**	◆◆◆	Rates not provided SAVE	192
79 p. 162	**Hyatt Place Secaucus/Meadowlands** (See ad p. 192.)	◆◆◆	$109-$349 SAVE	192
80 p. 162	Hilton Garden Inn Secaucus/Meadowlands	◆◆◆	Rates not provided	192

Map Page	Restaurant	Diamond Rated	Cuisine	Price Range	Page
73 p. 162	Bareli's	◆◆◆	Italian	$17-$50	193

WEEHAWKEN

Map Page	Hotel	Diamond Rated	Rate Range	Page
83 p. 162	**Sheraton Lincoln Harbor Hotel**	◆◆◆	$189-$449 SAVE	207

HOBOKEN

Map Page	Hotel	Diamond Rated	Rate Range	Page
86 p. 162	**W Hoboken**	◆◆◆◆	$209-$619 SAVE	124

Map Page	Restaurants	Diamond Rated	Cuisine	Price Range	Page
79 p. 162	Napoli's Brick Oven Pizza & Restaurant	◆◆	Italian Pizza	$6-$17	125
80 p. 162	Elysian Cafe	◆◆	American	$8-$26	124
81 p. 162	Amanda's	◆◆◆	American	$18-$32	124
82 p. 162	Grimaldi's Coal Brick Oven Pizzeria	◆◆	Pizza	$12-$21	124
83 p. 162	Zafra	◆◆	Cuban	$9-$23	125
84 p. 162	Zylo Hoboken	◆◆◆	Mediterranean	$11-$48	125
85 p. 162	The Brass Rail Restaurant & Bar	◆◆◆	Continental	$10-$32	124
86 p. 162	The Taco Truck	◆	Mexican	$5-$8	125

HARRISON

Map Page	Hotels	Diamond Rated	Rate Range	Page
89 p. 162	Newark/Harrison Riverwalk Hampton Inn & Suites	◆◆◆	$149-$239	122
90 p. 162	**Element Harrison-Newark** (See ad p. 122.)	◆◆◆	$139-$299 SAVE	122

Map Page	Restaurant	Diamond Rated	Cuisine	Price Range	Page
89 p. 162	Spanish Pavillion	◆◆◆	Spanish	$8-$36	122

JERSEY CITY

Map Page	Hotels	Diamond Rated	Rate Range	Page
93 p. 162	**The Holland Hotel**	◆◆	$105-$155 SAVE	129
94 p. 162	**Courtyard by Marriott Jersey City Newport**	◆◆◆	$209-$459 SAVE	129

JERSEY CITY (cont'd)

Map Page	Hotels (cont'd)	Diamond Rated	Rate Range	Page
95 p. 162	DoubleTree by Hilton Hotel & Suites Jersey City	▼▼▼	$137-$389	129
96 p. 162	**The Westin Jersey City Newport**	▼▼▼▼	$199-$569 SAVE	129

Map Page	Restaurants	Diamond Rated	Cuisine	Price Range	Page
92 p. 162	Casa Dante	▼▼▼	Italian	$15-$31	130
93 p. 162	Fire & Oak	▼▼	American	$13-$44	130
94 p. 162	John's Pizzeria	▼	Pizza	$6-$14	130
95 p. 162	Light Horse Tavern	▼▼▼	American	$11-$29	130

ELIZABETH

Map Page	Hotels	Diamond Rated	Rate Range	Page
99 p. 162	**Hilton Newark Airport**	▼▼▼	$119-$229 SAVE	112
100 p. 162	Hampton Inn-Newark Airport	▼▼▼	$119-$259	112
101 p. 162	**Renaissance Newark Airport Hotel**	▼▼▼	$202-$332 SAVE	112
102 p. 162	Crowne Plaza Newark Airport	▼▼▼	$110-$249	112
103 p. 162	**Residence Inn by Marriott Newark Elizabeth/ Liberty International Airport**	▼▼▼	$174-$286 SAVE	112
104 p. 162	**Country Inn & Suites By Carlson**	▼▼▼	$109-$169 SAVE	111
105 p. 162	**Courtyard by Marriott Newark Elizabeth**	▼▼▼	$174-$286 SAVE	112
106 p. 162	Embassy Suites Newark Airport	▼▼▼	$159-$259	112

RIDGEWOOD

Map Page	Restaurants	Diamond Rated	Cuisine	Price Range	Page
13 p. 162	Kailash	▼▼	Indian	$8-$20	187
14 p. 162	Raymond's	▼▼	Comfort Food	$8-$16	187
15 p. 162	Latour	▼▼▼	Traditional French	$12-$36	187
16 p. 162	MaLee Fine Thai Cuisine	▼▼	Thai	$12-$25	187

HACKENSACK

Map Page	Restaurants	Diamond Rated	Cuisine	Price Range	Page
31 p. 162	P.F. Chang's China Bistro	▼▼▼	Chinese	$9-$26	120
32 p. 162	The Cheesecake Factory	▼▼▼	International	$9-$30	120
33 p. 162	Morton's The Steakhouse	▼▼▼	Steak	$26-$56	120
34 p. 162	Stony Hill Inn	▼▼▼	Continental	$14-$40	120

GARFIELD

Map Page	Restaurant	Diamond Rated	Cuisine	Price Range	Page
37 p. 162	Goodfellas Ristorante	▼▼	Italian	$11-$37	118

WOODLAND PARK

Map Page	Restaurant	Diamond Rated	Cuisine	Price Range	Page
40 p. 162	Castalia 997 Restaurant & Lounge	▼▼▼	Italian	$9-$23	223

CLIFTON

Map Page	Restaurants	Diamond Rated	Cuisine	Price Range	Page
46 p. 162	Chengdu 46	▼▼▼	Chinese	$12-$42	104
47 p. 162	Tick Tock Diner	▼▼	American	$9-$20	104

MONTCLAIR

Map Page	Restaurants	Diamond Rated	Cuisine	Price Range	Page
62 p. 162	Dai-Kichi Japanese Restaurant	▼▼	Japanese	$16-$24	140

MONTCLAIR (cont'd)

Map Page	Restaurant	Diamond Rated	Cuisine	Price Range	Page
⑥③ p. 162	Tinga Taqueria	▼▼	Tex-Mex	$7-$15	140
⑥④ p. 162	Thai Chef Restaurant	▼▼	Thai	$13-$28	140
⑥⑤ p. 162	Tuptim Thai Cuisine	▼▼	Thai	$10-$19	140
⑥⑥ p. 162	Mesob	▼▼	Ethiopian	$10-$26	140
⑥⑦ p. 162	Raymond's	▼▼	American	$8-$23	140
⑥⑧ p. 162	Aozora	▼▼	Japanese	$10-$35	140
⑥⑨ p. 162	Pig & Prince	▼▼▼	New American	$18-$36	140
⑦⓪ p. 162	Fascino	▼▼▼	Italian	$40-$45	140

UNION CITY

Map Page	Restaurant	Diamond Rated	Cuisine	Price Range	Page
⑦⑥ p. 162	Beyti Kebab Restaurant	▼▼	Turkish	$14-$26	203

BLOOMFIELD

Map Page	Restaurant	Diamond Rated	Cuisine	Price Range	Page
⑨⑧ p. 162	The Orange Squirrel	▼▼▼	New American	$19-$46	91

BEST WESTERN PLUS NEWARK AIRPORT WEST
(973)621-6200 **9**

▼▼▼
Hotel
$120-$199

AAA Benefit: Members save up to 20%!

Address: 101 International Way 07114 **Location:** I-95 (New Jersey Tpke) exit 14 to US 1 and 9 S, then 1 mi s. Located in an industrial area set back from the highway. **Facility:** 83 units. 6 stories, interior corridors. **Amenities:** safes. **Activities:** exercise room. **Guest Services:** valet and coin laundry, area transportation.

BEST WESTERN PLUS ROBERT TREAT HOTEL
(973)622-1000 **2**

▼▼▼
Hotel
$99-$249

AAA Benefit: Members save up to 20%!

Address: 50 Park Pl 07102 **Location:** At Center St. Across from Arts Center. **Facility:** 169 units. 15 stories, interior corridors. **Amenities:** safes. **Dining:** Maize, see separate listing. **Activities:** exercise room. **Guest Services:** valet and coin laundry, area transportation.

COMFORT SUITES NEWARK
(973)481-5200 **1**

▼▼
Hotel
$120-$190

Address: 1348 McCarter Hwy (Rt 21) 07104 **Location:** 3.6 mi n of jct US 1, 9 and SR 21. **Facility:** 86 units. 4 stories, interior corridors. **Activities:** exercise room. **Guest Services:** valet and coin laundry. **Featured Amenity:** full hot breakfast.

COURTYARD BY MARRIOTT NEWARK DOWNTOWN
(973)848-0070 **4**

▼▼▼
Hotel
$164-$269

AAA Benefit: Members save 5% or more!

Address: 858 Broad St 07102 **Location:** Between Branford Pl and William St; downtown. **Facility:** 150 units. 7 stories, interior corridors. **Parking:** on-site (fee). **Activities:** exercise room. **Guest Services:** valet and coin laundry, boarding pass kiosk, area transportation.

COURTYARD BY MARRIOTT NEWARK LIBERTY INTERNATIONAL AIRPORT
(973)643-8500 **8**

▼▼▼
Hotel
$169-$278

AAA Benefit: Members save 5% or more!

Address: 600 Rt 1 & 9 S 07114 **Location:** I-95 (New Jersey Tpke) exit 14, 1 mi sw via US 1 and 9 S. **Facility:** 146 units. 3 stories, interior corridors. **Parking:** on-site (fee). **Pool(s):** heated indoor. **Activities:** hot tub, exercise room. **Guest Services:** valet and coin laundry, boarding pass kiosk.

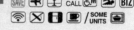

(See map & index p. 162.)

DOUBLETREE BY HILTON NEWARK AIRPORT
(973)690-5500 **5**

Hotel
$129-$299

DOUBLETREE BY HILTON

AAA Benefit: Members save 5% or more!

Address: 128 Frontage Rd 07114 **Location:** I-95 (New Jersey Tpke) exit 14, 2nd right after toll booth, then just w. **Facility:** 502 units. 12 stories, interior corridors. **Parking:** on-site (fee). **Terms:** 1-7 night minimum stay, cancellation fee imposed. **Pool(s):** heated indoor. **Activities:** exercise room. **Guest Services:** valet laundry, rental car service.

FAIRFIELD INN & SUITES BY MARRIOTT NEWARK LIBERTY INTERNATIONAL AIRPORT
(973)242-2600 **7**

Hotel $108-$177 **Address:** 618-50 Rt 1 & 9 S 07114 **Location:** I-95 (New Jersey Tpke) exit 14, 1 mi sw via US 1 and 9 S. **Facility:** 162 units. 6 stories, interior corridors. **Pool(s):** heated indoor. **Activities:** hot tub, exercise room.

AAA Benefit: Members save 5% or more!

Guest Services: valet and coin laundry, boarding pass kiosk.

HILTON NEWARK PENN STATION
(973)622-5000 **3**

Contemporary Hotel $169-$399 **Address:** Gateway Center - 1048 Raymond Blvd 07102 **Location:** I-95 (New Jersey Tpke) exit 15E, 3 mi w via Raymond Blvd. Connects to Penn Station. **Facility:** 253 units. 10 stories, interior corridors. **Parking:** on-site (fee). **Terms:** 1-7 night minimum stay, cancellation fee imposed. **Amenities:** safes. **Guest Services:** valet laundry, rental car service.

AAA Benefit: Members save 5% or more!

HOLIDAY INN NEWARK AIRPORT
973/242-0900 **11**

Hotel. Rates not provided. **Address:** 450 US 1 & 9 S 07114 **Location:** I-95 (New Jersey Tpke) exit 14 to US 1 and 9 S, then 1.6 mi s. **Facility:** 191 units. 8 stories, interior corridors. **Amenities:** safes. **Activities:** exercise room. **Guest Services:** valet and coin laundry, boarding pass kiosk.

MARRIOTT NEWARK AIRPORT
(973)623-0006 **12**

Hotel $230-$378 **Address:** Newark Liberty Int'l Airport, 1 Hotel Rd 07114 **Location:** I-95 (New Jersey Tpke) exit 13A northbound; exit 14 southbound to airport. **Facility:** 591 units. 10 stories, interior corridors. **Parking:** on-site (fee) and valet. **Terms:** check-in 4 pm. **Amenities:** Some: safes. **Pool(s):** outdoor, heated indoor. **Activities:** exercise room. **Guest Services:** valet and coin laundry, boarding pass kiosk.

AAA Benefit: Members save 5% or more!

SPRINGHILL SUITES BY MARRIOTT NEWARK LIBERTY INTERNATIONAL AIRPORT
(973)624-5300 **6**

Hotel $125-$229 **Address:** 652 Rt 1 & 9 S 07114 **Location:** I-95 (New Jersey Tpke) exit 14, 1 mi sw via US 1 and 9 S. **Facility:** 200 units. 6 stories, interior corridors. **Pool(s):** heated indoor. **Activities:** hot tub, exercise room. **Guest Services:** valet and coin laundry.

AAA Benefit: Members save 5% or more!

WYNDHAM GARDEN HOTEL NEWARK AIRPORT
(973)824-4000 **10**

Hotel $149-$369 **Address:** 550 US 1 & 9 S 07114 **Location:** I-95 (New Jersey Tpke) exit 14 to US 1 and 9 S, then 1.4 mi s. **Facility:** 349 units. 5 stories, interior corridors. **Amenities:** safes. **Pool(s):** outdoor. **Activities:** exercise room. **Guest Services:** valet and coin laundry, boarding pass kiosk, rental car service.

WHERE TO EAT

ADEGA GRILL
973/589-8830 **6**

Portuguese. Casual Dining. $16-$35 **AAA Inspector Notes:** A world away from the city streets just outside its door, the pretty dining room is wonderfully romantic, and its vineyard-cum-wine-cellar theme is warm, rustic and utterly cozy. The food, much like the neighborhood, is Portuguese and wonderfully satisfying. Among good choices are bacalao, roasted chicken or chorizo flambé, which is grilled tableside. **Features:** full bar. **Reservations:** suggested, weekends. **Address:** 130 Ferry St 07105 **Location:** Between Madison and Monroe sts; in Ironbound section. **Parking:** street only. L D

DINOSAUR BAR-B-QUE
862/214-6100 **3**

Barbecue. Casual Dining. $8-$28 **AAA Inspector Notes:** This outpost of the legendary Syracuse, New York barbecue joint brings all of the flavor and atmosphere to a location right next to the Prudential Center. Excellent pit-smoked brisket, chicken, fall-off-the-bone ribs and juicy pulled pork are served up and accompanied by great sides and sauces. **Features:** full bar. **Address:** 224 Market St 07102 **Location:** At Mulberry St; downtown; next to Prudential Center. **Parking:** street only. L D CALL

DON PEPE RESTAURANT
973/623-4662 **2**

Spanish. Family Dining. $10-$35 **AAA Inspector Notes:** Warm wall murals lend a feeling of the Spanish countryside. Fresh seafood specialties and lobster specials are local favorites. Portions are large and easily shared. The garlic shrimp starter is a solid choice, while garlic chicken, shellfish casserole and seafood paella are popular entrees. **Features:** full bar. **Address:** 844 McCarter Hwy (SR 21) 07102 **Location:** Just n of Raymond Blvd. L D

FORNOS OF SPAIN RESTAURANT
973/589-4767 **5**

Spanish. Casual Dining. $13-$36 **AAA Inspector Notes:** This impressively-sized restaurant, which practically takes up an entire city block, has been a long-time favorite in the Ironbound. Diners can sample what all the locals have come to love, including the Spanish tortilla, one of the paellas and the seafood mariscada (a tomato-based brew bolstered with calamari, clams, shrimp and lobster). Carnivores will not be shut out—steaks, chops, pork and game are carefully prepared and artfully presented, too. **Features:** full bar, patio dining. **Reservations:** suggested. **Address:** 47 Ferry St 07105 **Location:** Between Union and McWhorter sts; in Ironbound section. L D

(See map & index p. 162.)

MAIZE 973/733-2202
▼▼▼ Portuguese. Casual Dining. $15-$30 **AAA Inspector Notes:** The location is unexpected, but this place is suave and so-phisticated with a contemporary décor with tones of black and tan. Flavorful dishes mingle Portuguese and American influences. The menu presents many options but is heavy on fresh seafood. Across from the performing arts center, the restaurant is a popular pre-show choice. **Features:** full bar. **Reservations:** suggested. **Address:** 50 Park Pl 07102 **Location:** At Center St; in BEST WESTERN PLUS Robert Treat Hotel. **Parking:** no self-parking.

L D CALL ⓖM

SPAIN RESTAURANT 973/344-0994 ④
▼▼ ▼ Spanish. Casual Dining. $10-$25 **AAA Inspector Notes:** This is a casual place to have sangria and a hearty meal of shellfish drizzled in various Spanish sauces and served with thinly sliced fried potatoes, vegetables and yellow rice. If seafood is not your thing, try a dish of meat flavored with traditional, rich, garlic-scented sauces. The clams in green sauce are a great way to start off. Portions seem designed for sharing. **Features:** full bar. **Address:** 419 Market St 07105 **Location:** At Raymond Blvd. **Parking:** on-site and street.

L D

TONY DA CANECA 973/589-6882 ⑦
▼▼ ▼ Portuguese. Casual. Dining. $9-$29 **AAA Inspector Notes:** *Classic.* This nearly 50-year-old restaurant continues the long traditions of Portuguese immigrants in the Ironbound district. The comfortable dining room offers up a large menu with a good selection of shellfish appetizers ranging from clams in green sauce to king crab legs with garlic sauce. Entrées include broiled squid with clams and cilantro sauce, roast suckling pig, broiled rack of lamb and rabbit stew. **Features:** full bar. **Reservations:** suggested. **Address:** 72 Elm Rd 07105 **Location:** Corner of Elm Rd and Houston St; in Ironbound section. **Parking:** on-site and street. L D

NEW BRUNSWICK (I-4) pop. 55,181, elev. 80'

New Brunswick originated in 1686 as a ferry crossing in an area known as Prigmore's Swamp. A port and water power afforded by the Raritan River made the settlement a major shipping and milling depot by the 1750s.

Queen's College opened in 1771 in a tavern. After years of monetary struggles and shifting locations and monetary struggles, it was renamed Rutgers in 1825. The State University of New Jersey now occupies several campuses in the city.

Buccleuch Park, at the north end of College Avenue, overlooks the Raritan River. On the grounds is a house built in 1729 by a British officer. The birthplace of Alfred Joyce Kilmer, best known for his poem "Trees," is at 17 Joyce Kilmer Ave.

Middlesex County Regional Chamber of Commerce: 109 Church St., New Brunswick, NJ 08901. **Phone:** (732) 745-8090.

RUTGERS UNIVERSITY comprises five campuses: the Busch and Livingston campuses, n. off SR 18; the College Avenue Campus downtown; and the Cook and Douglass campuses, s. off SR 18 and n.w. of US 1. Chartered as a Colonial college in 1766, the state university at New Brunswick has an enrollment of approximately 35,000 students. The first formal collegiate football game in the country was held here in 1869; Rutgers beat Princeton six goals to four. Old Queens, a three-story brownstone building that once housed all of the college's facilities, now serves as the president's office. **Hours:** A variety of campus tours are available; phone ahead for details. **Cost:** Tours free; reservations are required. **Phone:** (732) 445-1000.

Zimmerli Art Museum at Rutgers is at 71 Hamilton St. on the College Avenue Campus of Rutgers, the State University of New Jersey. The museum houses more than 60,000 works of art, ranging from ancient to contemporary art. The permanent collection features particularly rich holdings in 19th-century French art; Russian art from icons to the avant-garde; Soviet nonconformist art from the Dodge Collection; and American art with notable holdings of prints. In addition, small groups of antiquities, old master paintings and art inspired by Japan and original illustrations for children's books provide representative examples of the museum's research and teaching message at Rutgers.

Hours: Tues.-Fri. 10-4:30, Sat.-Sun. noon-5 (also first Tues. of the month 4:30-9), Sept.-July. Closed Jan. 1, July 4, Thanksgiving, day after Thanksgiving, Christmas Eve and Christmas. **Cost:** Free. **Phone:** (848) 932-7237. 🏛

Rutgers Gardens is s. on US 1 from SR 18, then e. to 112 Ryders Ln. Dating to 1927, the 50-acre gardens feature a diverse series of botanical collections, including flowers and vegetables, rhododendrons and azaleas, American hollies, evergreens, ornamental and shade trees, a terrace garden and a bamboo forest. The Frank G. Helyar Woods is a 41-acre old-growth forest with a marked trail.

Hours: Gardens daily dawn-dusk. Guided 1-hour tours are offered Mon.-Fri. mornings and afternoons and Sat. mornings. **Cost:** Gardens free. Guided tours Mon.-Fri. $10; $8 (ages 65+); $5 (children). Guided tours Sat. $12; $10 (ages 65+); $5 (children). Reservations are required for guided tours. **Phone:** (732) 932-8451.

Rutgers Geology Museum is at 85 Somerset St. on the College Avenue Campus of Rutgers University. Exhibits pertain to geology, natural history and anthropology. **Hours:** Tues.-Thurs. 10-5, Fri. 10-4, Sat. 10-2, Sept.-July. Closed major holidays and the weeks of Thanksgiving, Christmas and Jan. 1. Phone for schedule during school breaks. **Cost:** Free. **Phone:** (848) 932-7243.

HYATT REGENCY NEW BRUNSWICK (732)873-1234

▼▼▼ Contemporary Hotel $79-$339

 HYATT REGENCY®
AAA Benefit: Members save 10%!

Address: Two Albany St 08901 **Location:** Between Neilson and Burnet sts. **Facility:** 288 units. 6 stories, interior corridors. **Parking:** on-site (fee) and valet. **Terms:** cancellation fee imposed. **Pool(s):** heated indoor. **Activities:** hot tub, exercise room. **Guest Services:** complimentary laundry, boarding pass kiosk, area transportation.

 SAVE ECO ⌴ ⌴ ⌴ CALL ⓖM
 ⌴ BIZ ⌴ ⌴ ⌴ ⌴ / SOME UNITS ⌴ ⌴

CATHERINE LOMBARDI
732/296-9463

▽▽▽ ▽▽▽

Italian
Casual Dining
$20-$40

AAA Inspector Notes: The successful restaurateurs who brought us Stage Left are behind this restaurant which sits just upstairs. The warm, rich dining room, enhanced by fireplaces, ruby red walls, soft lighting and stacked stone accents makes for a lovely setting. The menu features a large selection of salumi and entrées like pork osso buco or wood-grilled swordfish with creamy farro and puttanesca sauce. **Features:** full bar. **Reservations:** suggested. **Address:** 3 Livingston Ave 08901 **Location:** Between George and New sts. **Parking:** street only. [D] [LATE]

DELTA'S
732/249-1551

▽▽▽▽ Soul Food. Casual Dining. $18-$27 **AAA Inspector Notes:** Before sneaking a peak at the menu, take in this beautiful space—a soaring ceiling, exposed brick and a sleek bar and lounge sets the stage for a cool, hip menu that takes its cues from Southern fare with a soul food nouveau twist. Case in point—try the Asian-style steamed dumplings, stuffed with crayfish, collard greens, fennel and sweet potato. The Carolina barbecue platter is big enough for the next day's lunch. **Features:** full bar. **Reservations:** suggested. **Address:** 19 Dennis St 08901 **Location:** Just w of jct SR 27 and 18 via Albany St to Neilson St, then just e. [D] [LATE]

DESTINATION DOGS
732/993-1016

▽▽ ▽▽ Hot Dogs. Casual Dining. $5-$11 **AAA Inspector Notes:** This fun, casual place takes diners on a journey around the world with more than 25 theme hot dogs and sausages on a creative menu. Try a Newark-style beef hot dog topped with fried potatoes, onions, peppers and yellow mustard, or a Vietnamese creation with pork sausage, shaved foie gras, pickled vegetables, jalapeños and sriracha mayo. There are also some interesting daily special sausages, which could be anything from antelope to python. You can build your own or just have it plain. **Address:** 101 Paterson St 08901 **Location:** At Joyce Kilmer Ave N. **Parking:** street only. [L] [D]

DUE MARI
732/296-1600

▽▽▽▽ Italian. Fine Dining. $18-$34 **AAA Inspector Notes:** This upscale outpost of the restaurant group led by chef Michael White offers a menu studded with ultra fresh seafood and refined pasta. Daily selections of east and west coast oysters are offered and dinner entrées might include such items as grilled Mediterranean branzino with escarole, roasted tomatoes, Caribbean white shrimp and black olive vinaigrette. There also are meat dishes with duck and dry-aged steaks. The dining room has a cosmopolitan flair and a lively bar scene. **Features:** full bar. **Reservations:** suggested. **Address:** 78 Albany St 08901 **Location:** 1 blk w of Memorial Pkwy (SR 18); downtown. **Parking:** street only. [L] [D] CALL [&][M]

THE FROG AND THE PEACH
732/846-3216

▽▽▽ ▽▽▽ New American. Fine Dining. $10-$35 **AAA Inspector Notes:** *Historic.* Named for a Dudley Moore and Peter Cook comedy routine about a restaurant that serves only frogs and peaches, this fine dining experience will entertain taste buds. The romantic setting includes lush plants, votive lights and finely-set tables. During the summer, the covered patio is a nice seating alternative. Servers are knowledgeable and polite. **Features:** full bar, patio dining. **Reservations:** suggested. **Address:** 29 Dennis St 08901 **Location:** Just w of jct SR 27 and 18 via Albany St to Neilson St, just e. **Parking:** valet and street only. [L] [D]

MAKEDA ETHIOPIAN RESTAURANT
732/545-5115

▽▽ ▽▽ Ethiopian. Casual Dining. $9-$37 **AAA Inspector Notes:** Woven baskets and African masks decorate the large, airy restaurant, located on a busy commercial street in this college town. Live music draws a crowd around the bar, as does the exotic fare. Low tables and chairs offer the traditional way to share an Ethiopian meal, but diners can opt for contemporary seating. Meals are served with injera, an Ethiopian sourdough flatbread with a soft and spongy texture that's used to scoop up the spicy, fragrant meat and vegetable stews. **Features:** full bar. **Reservations:** suggested, weekends. **Address:** 338 George St 08901 **Location:** Between Bayard St and Livingston Ave. **Parking:** street only. [L] [D]

OLD BAY RESTAURANT
732/246-3111

▽▽ ▽▽ Creole. Casual Dining. $14-$28 **AAA Inspector Notes:** For a taste of New Orleans and an atmosphere that is all about laissez les bons temps rouler (let the good times roll), this restaurant will more than fit the bill. The Cajun/Creole menu offers all dishes that has made New Orleans the dining destination it always will be. This is a great spot to unwind and sample some brews from the extensive beer list. **Features:** full bar. **Reservations:** suggested. **Address:** 61-63 Church St 08901 **Location:** At Albany St. **Parking:** street only. [D]

PANICO'S
732/545-6100

▽▽▽▽ Italian. Fine Dining. $10-$39 **AAA Inspector Notes:** An award-winning wine list complements this kitchen's lusty Italian cuisine. The softly-lit dining room, attended by a polished and professional staff, exudes an air of elegant simplicity; warm and mellow with shades of mauve and rose-colored mirrors scattered about the room. Soft tones and votive candles create a soothing and somewhat sophisticated dining room. Banquette seating is comfortable. Service is polite, professional and eager to please. **Features:** full bar, early bird specials, happy hour. **Reservations:** suggested. **Address:** 103 Church St 08901 **Location:** SR 18 exit New St to Neilson St; downtown. **Parking:** street only. [L] [D]

STAGE LEFT
732/828-4444

▽▽▽ ▽▽▽

American
Fine Dining
$24-$42

AAA Inspector Notes: The restaurant, which sits to the left of the city's professional theaters, is a theater of sorts in its own right, with show-stopping innovative cuisine taking center stage. Plump diver scallops drizzled in blood orange reduction are exquisite, as is a juicy filet mignon served with wilted spinach and chanterelle mushrooms. There is an extensive, award-winning wine list and a dessert menu to die for. First-rate service and a well-appointed dining room contribute to a stellar dining experience. **Features:** full bar, patio dining. **Reservations:** suggested. **Address:** 5 Livingston Ave 08901 **Location:** Between George and New sts. **Parking:** valet only. [D]

NEW EGYPT pop. 2,512

INN AT LAURITA WINERY
609/752-0303

▽▽ ▽▽ Bed & Breakfast $190-$310 **Address:** 19 Archertown Rd 08533 **Location:** I-195 exit 16, 4 mi w on CR 537, 2 mi s on CR 539, 2 mi w on CR 528, just s on Applegate Ln, then just s. **Facility:** Surrounded by 250 acres of farmland, this beautiful B&B exudes country charm and also delivers on comfort with a gourmet breakfast and spacious rooms, many with balconies, fireplaces and jetted tubs. 10 units. 2 stories (no elevator), interior corridors. **Terms:** age restrictions may apply, 15 day cancellation notice-fee imposed. **Activities:** massage. [📶] [✕] / SOME UNITS [🛗]

NEW PROVIDENCE pop. 12,171
• Hotels & Restaurants map & index p. 152

BEST WESTERN PLUS MURRAY HILL INN & SUITES
(908)665-9200 [78]

▽▽▽ ▽▽▽

Hotel
$129-$189

AAA Benefit: Members save up to 20%!

Address: 535 Central Ave 07974 **Location:** I-78 exit 43 westbound to Diamond Hill Rd, 0.6 mi e on Mountain Ave, 0.8 mi to South Ave, then 0.8 mi n. **Facility:** 76 units, some efficiencies and kitchens. 2 stories, interior corridors. **Amenities:** *Some:* safes. **Activities:** sauna, exercise room. **Guest Services:** valet and coin laundry, area transportation.

[SAVE] [🍴] [🛎️] CALL [&][M] [BIZ] [📶]
[✕] [🖥️] / SOME UNITS [🛗] [📠]

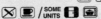

NEWTON pop. 7,997

HOLIDAY INN EXPRESS HOTEL & SUITES   973/940-8888
🎗🎗🎗 **Hotel. Rates not provided. Address:** 8 N Park Dr 07860 **Location:** 0.5 mi n of jct US 206 and SR 94, then just w. **Facility:** 79 units. 3 stories, interior corridors. **Activities:** exercise room.

THE WOODEN DUCK BED & BREAKFAST   973/300-0395
🎗🎗🎗 **Bed & Breakfast. Rates not provided. Address:** 140 Goodale Rd 07860 **Location:** I-80 exit 25, 8.2 mi n on US 206 to Goodale Rd, then 1.5 mi e. **Facility:** Set on 17 acres of woodsy tranquility surrounded by a state park, this B&B has handsomely appointed guest rooms with ample seating areas; several rooms include a fireplace and soaking tub. 10 units. 2 stories (no elevator), interior/exterior corridors. **Terms:** age restrictions may apply. **Pool(s):** outdoor. **Activities:** trails.

NEWTONVILLE (F-2) elev. 102'

AFRICAN AMERICAN HERITAGE MUSEUM OF SOUTHERN NEW JERSEY is at 661 Jackson Rd. The museum's collection includes more than 3,000 regional and national African-American cultural artifacts, including manuscripts, photographs, art and documents. Changing exhibits display artwork created by local artists and students. Guided tours offer an enlightening perspective on African-American history. **Time:** Allow 1 hour minimum. **Hours:** Tues.-Fri. 10-4, Sat. by appointment. Closed major holidays. Phone ahead to confirm schedule. **Cost:** Donations. **Phone:** (609) 704-5495.

NORTH BERGEN
• **Hotels & Restaurants map & index p. 162**

COMFORT SUITES   (201)392-0008
🎗🎗🎗 Hotel $119-$329 **Address:** 1200 Tonnelle Ave 07047 **Location:** I-495 exit US 1 and 9, 1 mi s, U-turn, then 0.4 mi n. **Facility:** 67 units, some efficiencies. 5 stories, interior corridors. **Amenities:** safes. **Activities:** exercise room. **Guest Services:** valet and coin laundry.

MEADOWLANDS VIEW HOTEL   (201)348-3600
🎗🎗 Hotel $99-$152 **Address:** 2750 Tonnelle Ave 07047 **Location:** Jct SR 3, 0.4 mi s. **Facility:** 250 units. 12 stories, interior corridors. **Amenities:** Some: safes. **Dining:** 2 restaurants. **Guest Services:** valet and coin laundry, boarding pass kiosk.

Visit AAA.com/searchfordiscounts

to save on dining, attractions,

hotels and more

SUPER 8   (201)864-4500
🎗🎗🎗 **Address:** 2800 Columbia Ave 07047 **Location:** New Jersey Tpke exit 16E (Lincoln Tunnel) northbound to JFK Blvd exit; exit 17 (Lincoln Tunnel) southbound to JFK Blvd exit. **Facility:** 89 units. 2 stories (no elevator), interior/exterior corridors. **Amenities:** safes. **Featured Amenity: continental breakfast.**

Motel
$72-$220

WHERE TO EAT

SABOR LATIN BISTRO   201/943-6366
🎗🎗🎗 Latin American. Casual Dining. $10-$36 **AAA Inspector Notes:** Bright red walls and trendy decor set the stage for refined dining with flair. Top sellers include grilled Mojito pork tenderloin, skirt steak with chimichurri sauce and roasted duck breast with fig and pineapple wild rice pilaf. Thursdays offer Latin music and dancing; al fresco dining is an option in warmer months. **Features:** full bar, patio dining, early bird specials, Sunday brunch, happy hour. **Address:** 8809 River Rd 07047 **Location:** I-95 exit 16E (Lincoln Tunnel) to SR 495, 1.2 mi e to Weehawken/Hoboken exit, 1.5 mi n on JFK Blvd, just e on Hillside Rd (CR 505), then 1.6 mi n. **Parking:** valet only.

NORTH BRUNSWICK

COMFORT SUITES   (732)297-7400
🎗🎗 Hotel $89-$149 **Address:** 2880 US 1 N 08902 **Location:** Between Finnegan and Black Horse Ins. **Facility:** 71 units. 3 stories, interior corridors. **Activities:** limited exercise equipment. **Guest Services:** valet and coin laundry.

HAMPTON INN NORTH BRUNSWICK   (732)246-3555
🎗🎗🎗 Hotel $109-$149 **Address:** 841 Georges Rd 08902 **Location:** I-95 (New Jersey Tpke) exit 9, SR 18 N, 2 mi s on US 1 to SR 130, then just n. **Facility:** 83 units. 3 stories, interior corridors. **Terms:** 1-7 night minimum stay, cancellation fee imposed. **Pool(s):** heated indoor. **Activities:** exercise room. **Guest Services:** valet and coin laundry.

AAA Benefit: Members save 5% or more!

WHERE TO EAT

ARTHUR'S STEAKHOUSE & PUB   732/828-1117
🎗🎗 Steak. Casual Dining. $8-$27 **AAA Inspector Notes:** A tin ceiling and lots of wood accents decorate this bustling tavern, which draws a diverse crowd. The dining rooms include brick fireplaces. Familiar steakhouse fare, such as steak, sandwiches and burgers, mingles with such seafood choices as lobster and scrod. Service is casual and friendly. **Features:** full bar. **Address:** 644 Georges Rd 08902 **Location:** 0.3 mi n of jct US 1.

NORTHVALE pop. 4,640

MADELEINE'S PETIT PARIS   201/767-0063
🎗🎗🎗 French. Casual Dining. $16-$37 **AAA Inspector Notes:** The bright and cheerful room offers a traditional French menu reminiscent of grandma's home cooking—that is, if your grandma is French. Mussels with garlic wine sauce, seared foie gras with sherry vinegar, coquilles St. Jacques, escargot and onion soup start the meal. Then opportunity presents itself by way of rack of lamb with herbs, Dijon and garlic, steak au poivre, sautéed calf liver with apples, shallots and Calvados or Dover sole meunière. **Features:** full bar, Sunday brunch. **Reservations:** suggested. **Address:** 416 Tappan Rd 07647 **Location:** Just n of jct Tappan Rd and Paris Ave. **Parking:** valet and street only.

NORTH WILDWOOD (H-3) pop. 4,041
• Hotels & Restaurants map & index p. 215

At the northern end of the Wildwoods' "Five Mile Island" is North Wildwood, founded in the 1890s as the tiny fishing village of Anglesea. Along with its sister boroughs, Wildwood Crest *(see place listing p. 218)* and Wildwood *(see place listing p. 212),* the town boasts a packed strip of 1950s and '60s-era Doo Wop architecture—neon Sputnik signs, pastel facades, tiki roofs and angled glass buildings abound.

More residential than adjacent Wildwood, North Wildwood nevertheless offers many recreational activities, from hiking to beachcombing to just ambling along the fun-filled boardwalk. Guided saltwater fishing trips are popular; boat rentals are easily arranged. Local outfitters include Dad's Place Marina, 501 Ocean Dr., phone (609) 729-5438; Jersey Bait & Tackle, 124 W. Chestnut Ave., phone (609) 522-7060; and Tuna Teaser Charters Inc., 217 Hoffman Ave., phone (609) 522-5140.

The New Jersey Coastal Heritage Trail Route stretches nearly 300 miles south, as far as Cape May, then continues west along the shore of Delaware Bay. The Hereford Inlet Lighthouse is a stop on the scenic drive as it passes through the Wildwoods resort area.

HEREFORD INLET LIGHTHOUSE is at 111 N. Central Ave. The lighthouse began operation in 1874 when this area was known as the fishing village of Anglesea. The restored Victorian lighthouse is notable for its five fireplaces. On the lighthouse grounds are cottage-style flower and herb gardens and a gazebo; paths lead to the nearby shore.

Time: Allow 30 minutes minimum. **Hours:** Daily 9-5, mid-May to mid-Oct.; Wed.-Sun. 10-2 (weather permitting), rest of year. Last admission is 1 hour before closing. Phone ahead to confirm schedule. **Cost:** $5; $2 (ages 0-11); free (U.S. Coast Guard personnel with ID). Combination ticket with Cape May Lighthouse $10; $3 (ages 0-11). **Phone:** (609) 522-4520. GT

CANDLELIGHT INN   609/522-6200 12
Historic Bed & Breakfast. Rates not provided. Address: 2310 Central Ave 08260 Location: At 24th Ave. Facility: a turn-of-the-20th-century Queen Anne Victorian, this inn features a wrap-around veranda and some antique furnishings. Pets are accepted upon request during the off-season. 10 units. 4 stories (no elevator), interior/exterior corridors. Terms: age restrictions may apply. Activities: hot tub.

SUMMER NITES   609/846-1955 11
Historic Bed & Breakfast. Rates not provided. Address: 2110 Atlantic Ave 08260 Location: Rio Grand Ave/SR 47, 1.3 mi n on Atlantic Ave; corner of 22nd and Atlantic aves. Facility: Guests will marvel as they step back to the 1950s at this modern yet uniquely-themed property located in a quiet residential area. 8 units. 3 stories (no elevator), interior corridors. Terms: age restrictions may apply. Activities: hot tub, bicycles, game room.

PIRO'S VILLAGE RESTAURANT   609/729-0401 8
Italian. Casual Dining. $15-$40 AAA Inspector Notes: Stained mahogany accents and art pieces showing turn-of-the-20th-century European cathedrals decorate this intimate dining room. An extensive selection of wines complements preparations of seafood, steak, veal and pasta. The restaurant is renowned for its excellent crab spinach chowder. Features: full bar. Reservations: suggested. Address: 1901 New York Ave 08260 Location: Garden State Pkwy exit 6, 3 mi se on SR 147 (which becomes New Jersey Ave) to 19th Ave, then just w.

OCEAN CITY (G-3) pop. 11,701, elev. 6'
• Hotels p. 174 • Restaurants p. 174

When the Lake brothers—ministers all—established Ocean City as a proper Christian summer resort in 1879, they decreed that no liquor would be sold. The injunction, which is still in effect, might account in part for the town's long-standing popularity with families. Other reasons the area is a favorite vacation spot are obvious: the 8-mile-long beach, an equable climate, excellent sport fishing and all the standard amenities of a summer seashore vacation community.

At the north end of an island between the Atlantic and Great Egg Harbor, Ocean City offers easy access to both the ocean and to inland waterways, making it a favored summer port for yacht owners. Chief among the many recreational facilities is the town boardwalk, lined with shops and amusements. Marinas accommodate visiting craft as well as charter boats for sightseeing and fishing, and the downtown area has numerous boutiques and restaurants to browse.

The Music Pier is Ocean City's primary entertainment center; band concerts take place regularly in summer. Gillian's Wonderland Pier and Playland's Castaway Cove have family-oriented amusement parks that operate from early April to mid-October. The Ocean City Arts Center, 1735 Simpson Ave., presents monthly art exhibits; phone (609) 399-7628.

Ocean City Regional Chamber of Commerce: P.O. Box 1706, Ocean City, NJ 08226. The Roy Gillian Welcome Center is on the route 52 Causeway. **Phone:** (609) 399-1412.

OCEAN CITY HISTORICAL MUSEUM, 1735 Simpson Ave. in the Ocean City Community Center, features an extensive collection of memorabilia. There are exhibits about Grace Kelly (Princess Grace of Monaco), whose family had a home in Ocean City; a shipwreck filled with Far East treasures; and Ocean City's beaches, founding, community and boardwalk. A cellphone audio tour is offered. A research library also is available. **Hours:** Tues.-Sat. 10-4 (also Thurs. 4-7). Closed major holidays. Phone ahead to confirm schedule. **Cost:** Donations. **Phone:** (609) 399-1801.

ATLANTIS INN LUXURY B&B (609)399-9871

▼▼▼ **Bed & Breakfast.** Rates not provided. **Address:** 601 Atlantic Ave 08226 **Location:** Jct 6th St and Atlantic Ave. **Facility:** This beautiful Victorian with a wraparound covered porch exudes luxury and sophistication with chic décor, cherry hardwood floors, decorative crown molding and wainscoting. 13 units, some two bedrooms and kitchens. 3 stories (no elevator), interior corridors. **Activities:** massage.

BISCAYNE SUITES (609)391-8800

▼▼▼
Hotel
$99-$619

Address: 820 Ocean Ave 08226 **Location:** Between 8th and 9th sts. **Facility:** 64 units, some two bedrooms, efficiencies and kitchens. 4 stories, interior corridors. **Terms:** 7 day cancellation notice-fee imposed. **Pool(s):** heated outdoor. **Guest Services:** coin laundry.

THE FLANDERS HOTEL (609)399-1000

▼▼▼▼
Historic Hotel
$149-$349

Address: 719 E 11th St 08226 **Location:** Waterfront. Garden State Pkwy exit 30, 3 mi e to Ocean Ave, then 0.3 mi s. **Facility:** This historic property has spacious suites that have an appealing beach-theme décor. Families will love the location, which is near multiple attractions. 117 units, some two bedrooms, three bedrooms, efficiencies and kitchens. 9 stories, interior corridors. **Terms:** 2 night minimum stay - seasonal and/or weekends, cancellation fee imposed. **Amenities:** safes. **Pool(s):** heated outdoor. **Activities:** beach access, exercise room, spa. **Guest Services:** coin laundry.

NORTHWOOD INN (609)399-6071

▼▼▼ **Historic Bed & Breakfast.** Rates not provided. **Address:** 401 Wesley Ave 08226 **Location:** Garden State Pkwy exit 30, e on 9th St to Wesley Ave, then 0.5 mi n at 4th St. **Facility:** This property is a charming Queen Anne-style Victorian offering wicker filled rooms and modern amenities such as a rooftop hot tub and a guest pantry. 7 units. 3 stories (no elevator), interior corridors. **Terms:** age restrictions may apply. **Activities:** bicycles.

SCARBOROUGH INN (609)399-1558

▼▼▼ **Historic Bed & Breakfast.** Rates not provided. **Address:** 720 Ocean Ave 08226 **Location:** Garden State Pkwy exit 30, e on SR 52 to Ocean Ave, then just n of 7th St. Located in a historic district. **Facility:** This Victorian-style inn dating from 1895 is a short walk from the beach and has high-back wooden rockers lining the cozy porch. Inside there is an inviting common room and a library. 24 units, some efficiencies. 4 stories (no elevator), interior corridors. **Guest Services:** coin laundry.

SERENDIPITY BED & BREAKFAST 609/399-1554

▼▼ **Historic Bed & Breakfast.** Rates not provided. **Address:** 712 9th St 08226 **Location:** Garden State Pkwy exit 30, 3 mi e, then just e of Ocean Ave. **Facility:** Thoughtful extras lend charm to this 1912 inn not far from the beach; some rooms feature large baths. 5 units. 3 stories (no elevator), interior corridors.

Enjoy great member rates and benefits
at AAA/CAA Preferred Hotels

WATSON'S REGENCY SUITES (609)398-4300

▼▼▼ **Condominium** $99-$309 **Address:** 901 Ocean Ave 08226 **Location:** Garden State Pkwy exit 30, e to Ocean Ave; at 9th St. **Facility:** All rooms at this beach-area property have sleeper sofas and private balconies. 80 condominiums. 5 stories, interior corridors. **Terms:** 2 night minimum stay - seasonal and/or weekends, 7 day cancellation notice-fee imposed. **Amenities:** safes. **Pool(s):** heated indoor. **Activities:** hot tub. **Guest Services:** coin laundry.

CAFE BEACH CLUB 609/398-7700

▼▼ American. Casual Dining. $8-$23 **AAA** You will not find a fluffier omelet or a better bowl of crab chowder anywhere else on the Ocean City boardwalk. Burgers, sandwiches, pastas and a variety of chicken and veal dishes are deftly prepared and served by a courteous and pleasant staff who cannot do enough to please their customers. And it goes without saying that the ocean view is second to none, especially from the outside tables right next to the boardwalk. **Features:** patio dining, early bird specials. **Address:** 1282 Boardwalk 08226 **Location:** At 13th St; on the Boardwalk. **Parking:** street only. B L D

COUSIN'S RESTAURANT & CATERING 609/399-9462

▼▼ Continental. Casual Dining. $14-$28 **AAA Inspector Notes:** Popular with locals, this restaurant delivers an extensive offering of homemade favorites, including lasagna and pasta Alfredo as well as chicken, seafood and steak. Tasty braided bread is crusty outside and chewy inside. Homemade desserts are yummy. **Features:** patio dining. **Reservations:** suggested. **Address:** 104 Asbury Ave 08226 **Location:** Just s of 1st St. **Parking:** street only. D

THE HULA RESTAURANT & SAUCE CO. 609/399-2400

▼ Hawaiian. Casual Dining. $6-$17 **AAA Inspector Notes:** This simple and casual place is a nice departure from the usual pizza and sandwich joints on the boardwalk. The menu offers salads and sandwiches made with the signature Hula sauces as well as such entrées as salmon teriyaki, Hawaiian chicken, pulled pork and grilled ahi tuna. **Address:** 940 Boardwalk 08226 **Location:** Between 9th and 10th sts. **Parking:** street only. L D

KATINA'S RESTAURANT 609/399-5525

▼▼ Greek. Casual Dining. $7-$17 **AAA Inspector Notes:** Locals visit this place for something a little different and tasty. Hummus and taramasalata are served with a warm, soft pita. Kebabs, moussaka, falafel and an assortment of sandwiches and salads are popular entrees. **Address:** 9th St & Central Ave 08226 **Location:** Corner of 9th St and Central Ave. **Parking:** street only. L D

SZECHWAN GARDEN CHINESE RESTAURANT 609/398-5456

▼▼ Chinese. Casual Dining. $6-$29 **AAA Inspector Notes:** Casual and equipped for children, this mom-and-pop storefront restaurant is a short walk from the beach. Although it offers no surprises, the food is savory and is served with a smile. **Address:** 503 E 9th St 08226 **Location:** At Central Ave. **Parking:** street only. L D

OCEAN GROVE (D-5) pop. 3,342, elev. 20'

Ocean Grove, a family-oriented seaside resort, has been under the leadership of the Camp Meeting Association of the United Methodist Church since 1869. Pop music and symphony concerts, cultural events, and religious services and programs take place throughout the summer at the 6,500-seat Great Auditorium, 21 Pilgrim Pathway. Organ concerts are given Wednesday nights and Saturday afternoons on a 1908 Hope-Jones pipe organ. For Great Auditorium schedule and ticket information phone the box office at (800) 590-4064.

Many of the community's houses exhibit a Victorian architectural style. Centennial Cottage, a restored 1879 vacation home at Central Avenue and McClintock Street, is maintained by the local historical society and is open to visitors in the summer. The Museum of the Historical Society of Ocean Grove, 50 Pitman Ave., has a collection of about 15,000 items, including photographs, postcards, glass negatives, maps, artwork and furniture; phone (732) 774-1869.

Also of interest is the tent colony that surrounds the Great Auditorium; both are part of the historical society's guided 90-minute Ocean Grove walking tour. A tabernacle, a chapel, pavilions, parks, the boardwalk and the beach make up Ocean Grove's chautauqua-like setting. The walking tour is available mid-June to mid-September; for information phone (732) 774-1869.

Ocean Grove Chamber of Commerce: 45 Pilgrim Pathway, Ocean Grove, NJ 07756. **Phone:** (732) 774-1391 or (800) 388-4768.

OCEANVILLE (G-4) elev. 41'
• Part of Atlantic City area — see map p. 73

EDWIN B. FORSYTHE NATIONAL WILDLIFE REFUGE is 1 mi. e. of US 9 on Great Creek Rd. More than 320 species of waterfowl and other birds have been identified within this refuge's 47,000 acres of tidal marshes and forests. Two observation towers can be climbed; the best seasons for wildlife observation are spring and fall.

Visitors can view wetland and upland areas on an 8-mile drive. There also are four trail loops ranging from a quarter-mile to 5 miles in length. **Hours:** Grounds open daily dawn-dusk. Visitor Information Center open Mon.-Fri. 10-3, Sat.-Sun. 9-4. **Cost:** $4 (per private vehicle); $2 (per visitor arriving by bicycle or on foot). **Phone:** (609) 652-1665.

SAVE **THE NOYES MUSEUM OF ART,** off US 9 to 733 Lily Lake Rd., displays American fine and folk art as well as a collection of vintage bird decoys. The museum also features rotating exhibits of fine arts and crafts by leading regional and national artists. **Time:** Allow 30 minutes minimum. **Hours:** Mon.-Sat. 10-4:30 (also Thurs. 4:30-8), Sun. noon-5. Closed major holidays. **Cost:** $5; $4 (ages 60+ and students with ID); free (ages 0-6). **Phone:** (609) 652-8848.

OGDENSBURG (B-3) pop. 2,410, elev. 693'

SAVE **STERLING HILL MINE TOUR & MUSEUM** is .6 mi. w. on Passaic Ave. from jct. CR 517, then .1 mi. past Plant St. The entrance is on Passaic Ave., just under the railroad bridge. Visitors can learn about the mining process during a guided 2-hour walking tour through the last underground mine to operate in New Jersey. Stops include the mine, including "Rainbow Tunnel"; a 5,000-square-foot mining history exhibit hall; and the museum of fluorescence. Also available are the Rock, Fossil and Gem Discovery Centers as well as opportunities for mineral collecting.

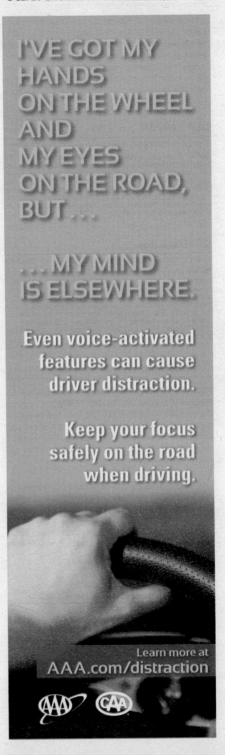

Time: Allow 2 hours, 30 minutes minimum. **Hours:** Daily 10-3, Apr.-Nov.; Sat.-Sun. 10-3, rest of year (weather permitting). Two-hour guided tours depart at 1 (also at 10 a.m., July-Aug.). Closed Jan. 1, Easter, Thanksgiving and Christmas. Phone ahead to confirm schedule. **Cost:** $11 (includes tour fee); $10 (ages 65+ and military with ID); $8 (ages 4-12). **Phone:** (973) 209-7212.

OLD TAPPAN pop. 5,750

CHARLIE BROWN'S STEAKHOUSE   201/767-6106

▼▼ Steak. Casual Dining. $9-$30 **AAA Inspector Notes:** This budget-friendly steakhouse, famous for its prime rib, offers top quality fare without hurting your pocketbook. The young ones will not be disappointed with the kids' menu, and just might even try something green from the salad bar. Adults will love the quality steaks, chicken and rib dishes. The express lunches are great for those saddled with time constraints. **Features:** full bar. **Address:** 203 Old Tappan Rd 07675 **Location:** Just e of center. [L] [D]

ORADELL pop. 7,978

CHARLIE BROWN'S STEAKHOUSE   201/265-0403

▼▼ Steak. Casual Dining. $9-$30 **AAA Inspector Notes:** This budget-friendly steakhouse, famous for its prime rib, offers top quality fare without hurting your pocketbook. The young ones will not be disappointed with the kids' menu, and just might even try something green from the salad bar. Adults will love the quality steaks, chicken and rib dishes. The express lunches are great for those saddled with time constraints. **Features:** full bar. **Address:** 2 Kinderkamack Rd 07649 **Location:** SR 17 exit Midland Ave, follow signs to River Edge, 3 mi e on Midland Ave, then just n. [L] [D] CALL [&M]

OXFORD (B-2) pop. 1,090, elev. 554'

PEQUEST TROUT HATCHERY AND NATURAL RESOURCE EDUCATION CENTER is 3 mi. n.e. on Pequest Rd. More than 600,000 trout are raised for release into state waters. Visitors learn about egg collection, fertilization and hatching. "Raceways," large concrete tanks, hold smaller fish until they are ready for release.

A brochure detailing a short, self-guiding tour of the grounds is available. River fishing and hiking also can be enjoyed. **Time:** Allow 30 minutes minimum. **Hours:** Daily 10-4, May-Oct.; Mon.-Fri. 9-4, rest of year. Closed state holidays. Phone ahead to confirm schedule. **Cost:** Free. **Phone:** (908) 637-4125. [⛽]

PARAMUS pop. 26,342, elev. 56'
• Hotels & Restaurants map & index p. 162

COMFORT INN & SUITES OF PARAMUS
   (201)261-8686   **25**

▼▼▼ Hotel $100-$180

Address: 211 Rt 17 S 07652 **Location:** 1 mi n of jct SR 4. **Facility:** 76 units. 2 stories (no elevator), interior corridors. **Activities:** exercise room. **Guest Services:** valet laundry. **Featured Amenity:** breakfast buffet.

SAVE ⑪ ⏲ HS 🛜 📞 📷
💻

COURTYARD BY MARRIOTT PARAMUS
   (201)599-1414   **24**

▼▼▼ Hotel $139-$229

AAA Benefit: Members save 5% or more!

Address: 320 SR 17 N 07652 **Location:** 1.5 mi n of jct SR 4. **Facility:** 154 units. 4 stories, interior corridors. **Pool(s):** heated indoor. **Activities:** exercise room. **Guest Services:** valet and coin laundry.

SAVE ⏲ CALL [&M] 〰 BIZ HS
🛜 ⊠ 🎿 📷 💻

CROWNE PLAZA PARAMUS   (201)262-6900   **23**

▼▼▼ Hotel $99-$199

Address: 601 From Rd 07652 **Location:** Garden State Pkwy exit 165, on service road toward Garden State Pkwy S; exit Ridgewood (shopping center) northbound; exit Oradell (shopping center) southbound. Next to Paramus Mall. **Facility:** 120 units. 2 stories (no elevator), interior corridors. **Activities:** exercise room. **Guest Services:** valet laundry, area transportation.

SAVE ⑪ ⏲ CALL [&M] BIZ
HS 🛜 ⊠ 💻 / SOME UNITS 📷

Prime location next to Paramus Park Mall, free Wi-Fi, Fitness Center, Bonefish Grill on-site.

HOLIDAY INN EXPRESS   (201)843-5400   **26**

▼▼▼ Hotel $130-$159

Address: 50 Rt 17 N 07652 **Location:** Garden State Pkwy exit 161 northbound; exit 163 northbound, 0.4 mi e on SR 4, then just n. **Facility:** 89 units. 2 stories, interior corridors. **Activities:** limited exercise equipment. **Guest Services:** valet laundry. **Featured Amenity:** continental breakfast.

SAVE CALL [&M] BIZ HS 🛜 ⊠
🎿 📷 💻 / SOME UNITS 📷

WHERE TO EAT

BOBBY'S BURGER PALACE   201/368-7001   **20**

▼ Burgers. Quick Serve. $6-$9 **AAA Inspector Notes:** First came the restaurants, fame, books and TV spots followed by his Iron Chef win. In an effort to top his skyrocketing culinary career, Bobby Flay turned to burgers! True to form, Flay does not cook up run-of-the-mill patty melts—these burgers are positively top shelf. Yes, there is kitsch, exemplified in the homage to childhood's crunchburger (topped with American cheese and potato chips), but there also is the very grown up Bobby burger with blue cheese and bacon. **Address:** 610 Bergen Town Center 07652 **Location:** Garden State Pkwy exit 161 northbound; exit 163 southbound, 1 mi e on SR 4. [L] [D] CALL [&M]

CHAKRA RESTAURANT   201/556-1530   **19**

▼▼▼ American. Fine Dining. $16-$42 **AAA Inspector Notes:** There is a sultry, somewhat romantic vibe at this popular restaurant. The dimly-lit dining room is lined with cabana-style booths and decorated with an eclectic mix of art and fabrics. The interesting menu covers a lot of ground with varied culinary influences from around the globe including sushi, Italian, Asian and Latin. Service is knowledgeable, but relaxed and slow paced. **Features:** full bar. **Reservations:** suggested. **Address:** W 144 Rt 4 E 07652 **Location:** 0.2 mi w of Garden State Pkwy. **Parking:** valet only. [D] [LATE] CALL [&M]

(See map & index p. 162.)

JOE'S AMERICAN BAR & GRILL
201/843-8858

American. Casual Dining. $9-$36 **AAA Inspector Notes:** If it's Americana you want, you'll get all that and more at Joe's, where the bill of fare includes all-American favorites like hearty burgers, fresh-from-the-oven chicken pot pies, Maryland lump crab cakes, and Joe's classic meatloaf. Pizzas, pastas, steaks and salads round out the extensive menu, giving diners the freedom to choose from a vast selection of offerings. There's nothing more American than that, except, of course, for apple pie, so save some room. **Features:** full bar, patio dining, Sunday brunch. **Address:** 298 Garden State Plaza 07652 **Location:** In Garden State Plaza Mall.

LEGAL SEA FOODS
201/843-8483 **21**

Seafood. Casual Dining. $12-$45 **AAA Inspector Notes:** Legal prides itself on a reputation for freshness and consistency. More than 40 varieties of seafood can be grilled, broiled, fried or prepared Cajun style. Try the clam chowder that has been served at every presidential inauguration since 1981. The nautically inspired dining room is upscale and attractive with its rich cherry wood paneling and intricately detailed model ships. **Features:** full bar. **Address:** 1 Garden State Plaza 07653 **Location:** In Garden State Plaza Mall.

PAPA RAZZI
201/843-0990

Italian. Casual Dining. $11-$33 **AAA Inspector Notes:** Italy has changed and so has authentic Italian food. It's lighter, fresher, more exciting Italian, and it's just what you'll find amid the elegant yet comfortable atmosphere that is Papa Razzi. If the steamy bowls of pasta don't tempt you, one of the aromatic pizzas or a warm panini sandwich definitely will. In addition there is a fine wine list, an array of salads, chicken, and fish options to choose from. **Features:** full bar, patio dining, Sunday brunch, happy hour. **Address:** 298 Garden State Plaza 07652 **Location:** Jct SR 4 and 17; in Garden State Plaza Mall.

PARK RIDGE pop. 8,645

PARK RIDGE MARRIOTT HOTEL
(201)307-0800

Hotel $188-$309 **Address:** 300 Brae Blvd 07656 **Location:** Garden State Pkwy southbound U-turn through Food Fuel Service Plaza; exit 172 northbound, 0.5 mi e on Grand Ave, then 0.8 mi s on Phillips Pkwy. **Facility:** 289 units. 4 stories, interior corridors. **Terms:** check-in 4 pm. **Dining:** 2 restaurants. **Pool(s):** heated outdoor, heated indoor. **Activities:** sauna, hot tub, exercise room. **Guest Services:** valet and coin laundry, area transportation.

AAA Benefit: Members save 5% or more!

PARSIPPANY
• Restaurants p. 179
• Hotels & Restaurants map & index p. 152

COURTYARD BY MARRIOTT PARSIPPANY
(973)394-0303 **21**

Hotel $181-$298

AAA Benefit: Members save 5% or more!

Address: 3769 Rt 46 E 07054 **Location:** I-80 exit 42B, 0.5 mi n to US 46, then 0.3 mi w. **Facility:** 151 stories, interior corridors. **Pool(s):** heated indoor. **Activities:** hot tub, exercise room. **Guest Services:** valet and coin laundry, area transportation.

EMBASSY SUITES PARSIPPANY
(973)334-1440 **22**

Hotel $101-$256 **Address:** 909 Parsippany Blvd 07054 **Location:** I-80 exit 42 to US 202 N; just ne of jct US 202 and 46 W. **Facility:** 274 units, some two bedrooms. 5 stories, interior corridors. **Terms:** 1-7 night minimum stay, cancellation fee imposed. **Pool(s):** heated indoor. **Activities:** hot tub, exercise room. **Guest Services:** valet and coin laundry, area transportation.

AAA Benefit: Members save 5% or more!

FAIRFIELD INN & SUITES BY MARRIOTT PARSIPPANY
(973)263-0095 **23**

Hotel $146-$240 **Address:** 3535 Rt 46 E 07054 **Location:** I-80 exit 42, 0.5 mi e to jct US 46 and Cherry Hill Rd; southwest corner. **Facility:** 108 units. 4 stories, interior corridors. **Activities:** exercise room. **Guest Services:** valet and coin laundry, area transportation.

AAA Benefit: Members save 5% or more!

HAMPTON INN PARSIPPANY
(973)290-9058 **31**

Hotel $139-$299 **Address:** 1 Hilton Ct 07054 **Location:** I-287 exit 39 northbound; exit 39B southbound, 1.3 mi w on SR 10 to Dryden Way; behind Hilton Parsippany. Located in an office park. **Facility:** 152 units. 6 stories, interior corridors. **Terms:** 1-7 night minimum stay, cancellation fee imposed. **Dining:** 2 restaurants. **Pool(s):** outdoor, heated indoor. **Activities:** hot tub, exercise room, spa. **Guest Services:** valet and coin laundry, area transportation.

AAA Benefit: Members save 5% or more!

HILTON PARSIPPANY
(973)267-7373 **30**

Hotel $139-$299

AAA Benefit: Members save 5% or more!

Hilton
HOTELS & RESORTS

Address: 1 Hilton Ct 07054 **Location:** I-287 exit 39 northbound; exit 39B southbound, 1.3 mi w on SR 10 to Dryden Way. Located in an office park. **Facility:** 353 units. 6 stories, interior corridors. **Terms:** 1-7 night minimum stay, cancellation fee imposed. **Amenities:** safes. **Dining:** 2 restaurants. **Pool(s):** outdoor, heated indoor. **Activities:** hot tub, exercise room, spa. **Guest Services:** valet and coin laundry, area transportation.

HOLIDAY INN HOTEL & SUITES PARSIPPANY
(973)263-2000 **24**

Hotel $99-$149

Address: 707 US Hwy 46 E 07054 **Location:** I-80 exit 47 westbound, just w; exit 45 eastbound, 0.8 mi e. **Facility:** 184 units. 4 stories, interior corridors. **Terms:** cancellation fee imposed. **Amenities:** safes. **Pool(s):** outdoor. **Activities:** exercise room. **Guest Services:** valet and coin laundry, area transportation.

Use travel time to share driving tips and rules of the road with your teens

(See map & index p. 152.)

HYATT HOUSE PARSIPPANY-EAST

(973)428-8875 **28**

Extended Stay Hotel
$109-$299

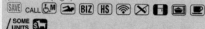

AAA Benefit: Members save 10%!

Address: 299 Smith Rd 07054 **Location:** I-287 exit 41A northbound; exit 42 southbound to US 46 E, 0.5 mi s. **Facility:** 140 efficiencies. 3 stories, interior corridors. **Terms:** cancellation fee imposed. **Pool(s):** heated outdoor. **Activities:** hot tub, exercise room. **Guest Services:** valet and coin laundry, area transportation. **Featured Amenity:** breakfast buffet.

(See ad this page.)

RED ROOF INN PARSIPPANY

973/334-3737 **25**

Motel
Rates not provided

Address: 855 US Hwy 46 E 07054 **Location:** I-80 exit 47 westbound; exit 45 eastbound, 0.5 mi e. **Facility:** 108 units. 2 stories (no elevator), exterior corridors. **Amenities:** safes.

RESIDENCE INN BY MARRIOTT PARSIPPANY

(973)984-3313 **29**

Extended Stay Hotel
$188-$309

Residence Inn Marriott

AAA Benefit: Members save 5% or more!

Address: 3 Gatehall Dr 07054 **Location:** I-287 exit 39 northbound; exit 39B southbound, 2 mi w on SR 10. Located in an office park. **Facility:** 156 units, some two bedrooms, efficiencies and kitchens. 3 stories, interior/exterior corridors. **Terms:** check-in 4 pm. **Pool(s):** heated indoor. **Activities:** hot tub, playground, game room, exercise room. **Guest Services:** valet and coin laundry, area transportation. **Featured Amenity:** breakfast buffet.

SHERATON PARSIPPANY HOTEL

(973)515-2000 **27**

Hotel
$75-$369

Sheraton STARWOOD HOTELS RESORTS

AAA Benefit: Members save up to 15%, plus Starwood Preferred Guest® benefits!

Address: 199 Smith Rd 07054 **Location:** I-287 exit 41A northbound; exit 42 to US 46 E, 0.4 mi s. **Facility:** 370 units. 6 stories, interior corridors. **Terms:** 2-3 night minimum stay - seasonal, cancellation fee imposed. **Pool(s):** outdoor, heated indoor. **Activities:** sauna, hot tub, steamroom, massage. **Guest Services:** valet laundry, boarding pass kiosk, area transportation.

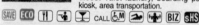

Ask about on-the-go vehicle battery testing and replacement

(See map & index p. 152.)

SONESTA ES SUITES PARSIPPANY 973/334-2907 (26)

▼▼▼▼
Extended Stay
Hotel
Rates not provided

Address: 61 Interpace Pkwy 07054 **Location:** I-80 exit 42, 0.3 mi s on Cherry Hill Rd, then just w. **Facility:** 150 efficiencies, some two bedrooms. 5 stories, interior corridors. **Pool(s):** heated indoor. **Activities:** exercise room. **Guest Services:** valet and coin laundry, area transportation.

[SAVE] CALL [&M] [🛒] [BIZ] [HS] [📶]
[✕] [🔔] [📷] [💻] / SOME UNITS [🍽]

WHERE TO EAT

BAADSHAH 973/331-1616 (26)

▼▼ Indian. Casual Dining. $8-$19 **AAA Inspector Notes:** Weekday lunch and weekend brunch buffets attract crowds eager for the cardamom, cumin, curry and mustard seeds that flavor the food and perfume the air at this restaurant. Typical tandoori, korma, vindaloo, panir and makhani dishes are here, and guests should feel comfortable with the casual, clean décor, which hints of a former life as another type of restaurant. **Reservations:** suggested. **Address:** 3079 Rt 46 E 07054 **Location:** I-80 exit 42, 0.5 mi n on Cherry Hill Rd, then 0.6 mi e; 0.5 mi e of jct US 202 and 46; in Morris Hills Shopping Center. [L] [D]

ECCOLA ITALIAN BISTRO 973/334-8211 (25)

▼▼▼ Northern Italian. Casual Dining. $15-$25 **AAA Inspector Notes:** This popular, bustling bistro serves home-style Italian standards like hearty lasagna and a rich and lusty osso buco. The long list of daily specials may include items like grilled calamari or seasonal preparations of gnocchi and seafood dishes. The dining room can be a bit loud and crowded but service is professional and attentive. **Features:** full bar. **Address:** 1082 Rt 46 W 07054 **Location:** I-80 exit 47 westbound, just w; exit 45 eastbound, 0.3 mi e. [L] [D]

KEO KU KOREAN RESTAURANT 973/244-0032 (28)

▼▼ Korean. Casual Dining. $9-$30 **AAA Inspector Notes:** This spot is known for its barbecue—Korean barbecue, that is—where patrons take part in the cooking at their table top grill. Also offered are traditional Korean fare, including jap chae, bibimbap and dok boki, as well as a full sushi bar with all the usual suspects. **Features:** full bar. **Address:** 245 Rt 46 E 07054 **Location:** I-80 exit 47 westbound; exit 45 eastbound, 1.5 mi e. [L] [D] CALL [&M]

MARAKESH 973/808-0062 (27)

▼▼ Moroccan. Casual Dining. $9-$23 **AAA Inspector Notes:** Settle in to a plush, communal banquette draped in vibrantly colored fabrics, or opt for a stool or pillow adorned in the same bright fashion. Either way, guests have a comfy spot from which to enjoy varied tagines and grilled meats. Continuing the upbeat, colorful theme, decorative bowls, baskets, instruments and tapestries hang from the walls, and live music entertains on Friday and Saturday nights. **Reservations:** required, weekends. **Address:** 321 Rt 46 E 07054 **Location:** I-80 exit 47 westbound; exit 45 eastbound, 1.4 mi e. [L] [D]

PATERSON (G-6) pop. 146,199, elev. 70'

Harnessing the potential water power of the Great Falls of the Passaic River, which can be viewed at McBride Avenue and Spruce Street, inspired statesman and economist Alexander Hamilton to organize the Society for Establishing Useful Manufactures (S.U.M.) and to plan Paterson as the new nation's first industrial city.

Pierre L'Enfant, planner of Washington, D.C., submitted the original design for a raceway to harness the falls and supply water power to the city's mills. Deemed too expensive and time consuming by investors who wanted a quicker return on their investment, L'Enfant's design was shelved in favor of a more workable recovery system designed by Peter Colt.

A section of the restored upper raceway parallels a section of Spruce Street. In the Old Gun Mill, at Van Houten and Mill streets, Samuel Colt created the first successful repeating revolver, and John Ryle launched the silk industry for which the city became well-known. Parts of this old industrial area are being preserved as part of Paterson Great Falls National Historical Park, where restorations on Mill and Van Houten streets are forerunners of an ongoing effort to encourage adaptive re-use of the old mills.

Greater Paterson Chamber of Commerce: 100 Hamilton Plaza, Suite 1201, Paterson, NJ 07505. **Phone:** (973) 881-7300.

Self-guiding tours: A brochure outlining a walking and/or driving tour as well as information and appointments for guided walking tours can be obtained at Great Falls Historic District Cultural Center, 65 McBride Ave., Paterson, NJ 07501; phone (973) 279-9587.

[SAVE] **LAMBERT CASTLE MUSEUM** is off I-80 exit 57, then s. on SR 19 to 3 Valley Rd. Built in 1892 by Catholina Lambert, a silk mill owner, the 24-room stone mansion houses the Passaic County Historical Society Museum. Furnishings, textiles, costumes and works of art include original family pieces. Period rooms are adorned with ornate plaster moldings, carved fireplace mantels and stained glass.

Permanent and changing exhibits about the county's history also are featured. **Time:** Allow 1 hour minimum. **Hours:** Wed.-Sun. noon-4, July 5-day before Labor Day; Wed.-Sun 1-4, Jan. 2-July 3, day after Labor Day to mid-Oct. and mid-Dec. through Dec. 31. Phone for schedule rest of year. Closed major holidays. **Cost:** $5; $4 (ages 65+); $3 (ages 5-17). **Phone:** (973) 247-0085.

PATERSON MUSEUM is at 2 Market St. Housed in the 1873 Thomas Rogers Locomotive Erecting Shop, the museum features exhibits about local history, archeology and mineralogy. Exhibits highlighting Paterson's silk industry, locomotive manufacturing, Colt firearms and the Holland submarine reflect the city's role as a machinery and textile center. An art gallery displays photographs and paintings inspired by the Great Falls. **Hours:** Tues.-Fri. 10-4, Sat.-Sun. 12:30-4:30. Closed major holidays. **Cost:** $2; free (ages 0-17). **Phone:** (973) 321-1260.

Add AAA or CAA Associate Members

to bring home the benefits of membership

PEAPACK pop. 2,582
• Hotels & Restaurants map & index p. 152

NINETY ACRES   908/901-9500 (120)
♦♦♦ ♦♦♦ Regional American. Fine Dining. $19-$39 AAA Inspector Notes: This standout restaurant is in the restored carriage house of the sprawling Natirar estate once owned by the king of Morocco and now backed in part by Sir Richard Branson. The dinner here is all about sustainable organic and local foods, many of which are sourced from the estate's own farms and greenhouses; in fact, they like to describe it as 'a table at the farm.' The beautiful dining room and outdoor patio have a relaxed sophistication, and the refined service is detailed but never stuffy. Reservations: suggested. Address: 2 Main St 07977 Location: I-287 exit 22 southbound; 22B northbound, 1.5 mi n on US 206, 0.8 mi ne on Hillside Ave/Old Dutch Rd, then 0.5 mi n on Peapack Rd (CR 512). Parking: valet only. (D)

PENNINGTON pop. 2,585

PICCOLO TRATTORIA   609/737-9050
♦♦♦ Italian. Casual Dining. $7-$22 AAA Inspector Notes: This casual spot has a huge menu with all manner of salads, pastas, entrées and, of course, pizza. Address: 800 R Denow Rd 08534 Location: I-95 exit 4, 0.6 mi n; in Hopewell Crossing Shopping Center.
(L) (D) CALL ⌖M

PENNSVILLE (F-1) pop. 11,888, elev. 19'

FORT MOTT STATE PARK, 454 Fort Mott Rd., encompasses 104 acres on the Delaware River. Next to the park is Finns Point National Cemetery, burial ground for some 3,000 Confederate and Union soldiers. Visitors can walk along ramparts of the 1896 fort, which was built as a river defense during the Spanish American War.

Seasonal ferry service connects Fort Mott and Fort Delaware State Park on Pea Patch Island; phone ahead for schedule. Hours: Daily 8-7:30, Memorial Day-Labor Day; 8-4, rest of year. Cost: Free. Phone: (856) 935-3218.

HAMPTON INN   (856)351-1700
♦♦♦ ♦♦♦ Hotel $109-$209 Address:
429 N Broadway 08070 Location: I-295   **AAA Benefit:**
exit 1, just se. Facility: 103 units. 4 sto-   Members save 5%
ries, interior corridors. Terms: 1-7 night   or more!
minimum stay, cancellation fee imposed.
Pool(s): outdoor. Activities: exercise room. Guest Services: valet and coin laundry.
(🍴) (Y) CALL ⌖M (➔) (BIZ) (📶) (🔒) (📷) (📺)

SUPER 8 PENNSVILLE/WILMINGTON   (856)299-2992
♦♦♦ ♦♦♦ Hotel $79-$124 Address: 413 N Broadway 08070 Location: I-295 exit 1, just se. Facility: 100 units. 4 stories, interior corridors. Guest Services: coin laundry.
(🍴) (📶) (🔒) (📺)

PEQUANNOCK

TIFF'S CASUAL GRILL & BAR   973/686-6040
♦♦♦ ♦♦♦ American. Casual Dining. $7-$23 AAA Inspector Notes: This casual and relaxed sports-themed restaurant offers a menu with all the usual suspects: wings, burgers, salads, sandwiches, ribs and a few pastas. This is a great place to catch a game or meet up with friends for drinks and a bite to eat. Features: full bar, happy hour. Address: 23 SR 23 07440 Location: 6 mi n of US 46, SR 23 and I-80; 3 mi s of jct I-287 and SR 23. (L) (D) CALL ⌖M

PHILLIPSBURG pop. 14,950

FRANK'S TRATTORIA   908/454-8790
♦♦♦ Italian. Quick Serve. $5-$20 AAA Inspector Notes: This casual, counter-service pizzeria offers the requisite pizza as well as such familiar dishes as eggplant parmigiana, scampi, Marsala and fra diavolos. Grilled sandwiches also are tasty. Address: 1250 Rt 22 (E Laneco) 08865 Location: I-78 exit 3, 0.7 mi to St. James Ave, left U-turn to US 22 E, then just e; in strip mall. (L) (D)

PISCATAWAY (I-4) elev. 98'
• Hotels & Restaurants map & index p. 152

CORNELIUS LOW HOUSE/MIDDLESEX COUNTY MUSEUM is on the Rutgers University New Brunswick/Piscataway campus at 1225 River Rd. This two-story stone building was constructed in 1741 for Cornelius Low, a prosperous Dutch merchant and prominent Raritan Landing citizen; the Low family owned the home until 1793. The museum presents changing exhibits pertaining to local and state history.

Time: Allow 1 hour minimum. Hours: Tues.-Fri. and Sun. 1-4. Closed state holidays. Cost: Donations. Phone: (732) 745-4177 or TTY (732) 745-3888.

EMBASSY SUITES HOTEL PISCATAWAY-SOMERSET
                                  (732)980-0500 (127)
♦♦♦ ♦♦♦ Hotel $119-$209 Address:
121 Centennial Ave 08854 Location: **AAA Benefit:**
I-287 exit 9 (Highland Park), just s to   Members save 5%
Centennial Ave. Located in a business   or more!
park. Facility: 221 units, some two bed-
rooms. 5 stories, interior corridors. Terms: check-in 4 pm, 1-7 night minimum stay, cancellation fee imposed. Pool(s): heated indoor. Activities: hot tub, exercise room. Guest Services: valet and coin laundry, area transportation.
(🍴) (🔥) (Y) (➔) (BIZ) (📶) (📷) (🔒) (📺) (💻) / SOME UNITS (🐾)

EXTENDED STAY AMERICA PISCATAWAY-RUTGERS
UNIVERSITY   732/235-1000 (125)
♦♦♦ ♦♦♦ Extended Stay Hotel. Rates not provided. Address: 410 S Randolphville Rd 08854 Location: I-287 exit 7, 0.4 mi s. Facility: 112 efficiencies. 3 stories, interior corridors. Pool(s): heated outdoor. Activities: exercise room. Guest Services: coin laundry, area transportation.
(➔) (📶) (🔒) (📺) (💻) / SOME UNITS (🐾)

MOTEL 6 PISCATAWAY #1084   732/981-9200 (124)
♦♦♦ Hotel. Rates not provided. Address: 1012 Stelton Rd 08854 Location: I-287 exit 5, just e. Facility: 137 units. 2 stories (no elevator), interior/exterior corridors. Guest Services: coin laundry.
(🍴) (📶) / SOME UNITS (🐾) (🔒) (📺)

RADISSON HOTEL PISCATAWAY SOMERSET
                                  (732)980-0400 (126)
♦♦♦ ♦♦♦ Hotel $110-$199 Address: 21 Kingsbridge Rd 08854 Location: I-287 exit 9 (Highland Park), just s to Centennial Ave. Facility: 206 units. 5 stories, interior corridors. Terms: cancellation fee imposed. Amenities: Some: safes. Pool(s): heated indoor. Activities: hot tub, exercise room. Guest Services: valet and coin laundry, area transportation.
(🍴) (🔥) (Y) (➔) (BIZ) (📶) (✕) (🔒) (📺) (💻)

Keep a current AAA/CAA
Road Atlas in every vehicle

(See map & index p. 152.)

WHERE TO EAT

AL DENTE 732/985-8220 154
▼▼▼ Italian. Casual Dining. $16-$30 **AAA Inspector Notes:** The casually elegant restaurant gives a nod to the Old World with grapevines, grappa bottles and statuary. Locals frequent the place for stylish preparations of traditional Italian cuisine, including items like linguine pescatore and tender veal saltimbocca. There is usually a long list of specials with daily preparations of risotto, gnocchi and fresh fish. Several vegetarian entrées also are offered. Many by-the-glass selections and grappas are on the impressive wine list. **Features:** full bar, patio dining. **Reservations:** suggested. **Address:** 1665 Stelton Rd 08854 **Location:** I-287 exit 5, 1.7 mi s; jct US 1 and Plainfield Ave, 3 mi nw. L D 🐾

PLAINFIELD (H-4) pop. 49,808, elev. 110'

A few reminders of the Revolutionary War period remain in this Elizabeth/Newark metropolitan area suburb. While planning the Battle for the Watchungs, Gen. George Washington often stayed at the Plainfield home of a friend, the Rev. Nathaniel Drake; today the 1746 house, at 602 W. Front St., is the headquarters of the local historical society. Another 18th-century building still in use is the 1788 Friends Meeting House on Dover-Chester Road; phone (973) 361-9427.

PLAINSBORO (D-3) elev. 80'

In the early 20th century, visitors from around the world flocked to the Walker-Gordon Dairy Farm, where a rotary machine milked 50 cows in 12 minutes. Borden Milk's original mascot Elsie, a Jersey cow intriguingly named "You'll Do Lobelia," is buried at the farm on Plainsboro Road.

The 17-room Wicoff House, built in the 1880s by one of the town's founding fathers, now houses the museum of the Plainsboro Historical Society; phone (609) 799-0909.

In 1982, road construction unearthed an archeological site at Plainsboro estimated to be up to 3,700 years old. Some 25,000 artifacts have been excavated, including the remains of structures indicating a permanent settlement.

PLEASANTVILLE pop. 20,249
• Part of Atlantic City area — see map p. 73

BEST WESTERN PLUS ATLANTIC CITY WEST EXTENDED STAY & SUITES 609/646-5515

Extended Stay Hotel
Rates not provided

AAA Benefit: Members save up to 20%!

Address: 701 Black Horse Pike (US 40/322) 08232 **Location:** 1 mi w of US 9. **Facility:** 68 kitchen units. 3 stories, interior/exterior corridors. **Amenities:** safes. **Pool(s):** heated indoor. **Activities:** steamroom, exercise room. **Guest Services:** coin laundry.
SAVE ❗️ CALL 💪M 🍽 BIZ 🛜
📱 📷 🖨

WHERE TO EAT

SHORE DINER 609/641-3669
▼▼ American. Casual Dining. $7-$21 **AAA Inspector Notes:** In a setting of shiny chrome and marble, sit back in soft booths and peruse the lengthy menu that makes choices difficult. Great entrée selections and super sandwiches are impossible to resist. Sample some of the in-house baked goods, mile-high cakes and other rich desserts displayed in glass cases. **Features:** full bar, Sunday brunch. **Address:** 6710 Tilton Rd 08234 **Location:** Garden State Pkwy exit 36. B L D

POINT PLEASANT (E-5) pop. 18,392, elev. 16'

NEW JERSEY MUSEUM OF BOATING is at the Johnson Brothers Boat Works at 1800 Bay Ave., Bldgs. #12 and #13. Dedicated to New Jersey's boating industry and its role in the nation's maritime history, the museum features an array of nautical artifacts. Included in the collection are boats, motors, rudders, equipment, models and miniature replicas, photos and documents.

Life preservers and an oar from one of the lifeboats of the *Morro Castle* also are displayed. The cruise ship caught fire off the Jersey coast in 1934; 134 people lost their lives. **Time:** Allow 1 hour minimum. **Hours:** Wed. and Fri.-Sun. noon-4, mid-Apr. through Nov. 30; Wed. and Sat.-Sun. noon-4, rest of year. Closed major holidays. **Cost:** Free. **Phone:** (732) 606-7605.

CAPT'N ED'S PLACE 732/892-4121
▼▼ Seafood. Casual Dining. $17-$30 **AAA Inspector Notes:** Steamers or mussels in sherry and garlic, crab and spinach dip and crayfish in spicy cream sauce are a few starters. The main draw is the mix-and-match surf and turf, snow and king crab legs, fish prepared to the diner's liking and steak and seafood that the diner prepares on a hot stone. Reservations are accepted every day except Saturday. **Address:** 1001 Arnold Ave 08742 **Location:** 1.2 mi w of jct SR 35 and Arnold Ave; corner of Pine Bluff Ave. D

WOODCHUCKS BBQ 732/714-1400
▼▼ Barbecue. Casual Dining. $7-$21 **AAA Inspector Notes:** The ribs here are well smoked and come out tasty and tender. The rest of the menu rounds out nicely with familiar barbecue items like pulled pork, brisket and chicken. To top it off, there is a popular Italian ice stand right next door for a cool summer treat. **Address:** 3009 SR 88 08742 **Location:** 0.3 mi e of Bridge Ave. L D

POINT PLEASANT BEACH (E-5)
pop. 4,665, elev. 10'
• Hotels p. 182 • Restaurants p. 182

The Unami Indians spent spring and summer fishing and collecting shells along the coast of what is now Point Pleasant Beach, a livelihood that was disrupted in the 18th century with the arrival of the first European settlers. This area began to take on the air of a seaside resort by the mid-19th century. The completion of the Garden State Parkway turned Point Pleasant Beach into one of New Jersey's leading summer vacation destinations.

Family-oriented amusements prevail along mile-long Jenkinson's Boardwalk. Neighboring Manasquan Inlet provides ocean access and boating opportunities.

Everyone looks forward to the ▼ Festival of the Sea, a street fair complete with goodies like funnel cakes and fried Oreos, not to mention clam chowder, shrimp skewers and other seafood favorites. The event, which takes place in mid-September along Arnold and Bay avenues downtown, also offers pony rides, hundreds of craft booths and live entertainment courtesy of local musicians.

Point Pleasant Beach Chamber of Commerce: 517A Arnold Ave., Point Pleasant Beach, NJ 08742. **Phone:** (732) 899-2424 or (888) 772-3862.

JENKINSON'S AQUARIUM is at 300 Ocean Ave. The aquarium features a touch tank, a live coral reef and exhibits featuring Atlantic and Pacific shark species, penguins, seals and American alligators. Animal feedings take place throughout the day.

Time: Allow 1 hour minimum. **Hours:** Daily 10-10, late June-Labor Day; Mon.-Fri. 9:30-5, Sat.-Sun. 10-5, rest of year. Closed Jan. 1, Thanksgiving and Christmas. Phone ahead to confirm schedule. **Cost:** $11; $6.50 (ages 3-12 and 62+). **Parking:** $5-$15, Memorial Day to mid-Sept. **Phone:** (732) 899-1212 or (732) 892-0600.

RIVER BELLE CRUISES is 1.7 mi. s. on SR 35, then .5 mi. e. to 47 Broadway. The *River Belle*, a replica of a Mississippi riverboat, departs on sightseeing cruises along the Manasquan River, Point Pleasant Canal and Barnegat Bay. Bridges, native wildlife and distinctive land formations are among the sights. Brunch, lunch, dinner, and pizza and fireworks cruises also are offered. **Time:** Allow 1 hour, 30 minutes minimum. **Hours:** Sightseeing cruises depart Tues. and Thurs.-Fri. at 2, Wed. and Sat.-Sun. at 3:30, July 1-Labor Day. **Cost:** Sightseeing fare $24; $22 (ages 65+); $12 (ages 4-11). Phone for other departure times and fares. **Phone:** (732) 892-3377.

SURFSIDE MOTEL   732/899-1109

Motel
$69-$299

Address: 101 Broadway 08742 **Location:** 0.5 mi e of jct SR 35, follow signs to beach area; just w of ocean. **Facility:** 31 units, some two bedrooms. 2 stories (no elevator), exterior corridors. **Terms:** 2 night minimum stay - seasonal and/or weekends, 7 day cancellation notice-fee imposed. **Pool(s):** heated outdoor. **Activities:** beach access.

WHITE SANDS OCEANFRONT RESORT & SPA 732/899-3370

▼▼ ▼▼ **Resort Hotel.** Rates not provided. **Address:** 1205 Ocean Ave 08742 **Location:** Oceanfront. SR 35 N, 1 mi e. **Facility:** Both hotel- and motel-style rooms in different buildings provide comfortable accommodations, some with a balcony and some with oceanfront views. The two oceanfront pools provide swimming options. 126 units, some two bedrooms, efficiencies and kitchens. 2-3 stories, interior/exterior corridors. **Amenities:** safes. **Dining:** 2 restaurants. **Pool(s):** heated outdoor, heated indoor. **Activities:** sauna, hot tub, steamroom, beach access, exercise room, spa.

WHERE TO EAT

THE ARK PUB & EATERY   732/295-1122

▼▼ ▼▼ Seafood. Casual Dining. $9-$22 **AAA Inspector Notes:** The rustic, old-shore standby is one of the most popular joints around. High wooden booths, low ceilings, wood plank floors and a fireplace in winter make for cozy casual appeal. Despite the lively bar scene, this is a good place for families at lunch and dinner. The menu focuses heavily on steak and seafood, sandwiches and burgers. The daily specials feature fresh, catch-of-the-day fish. **Features:** full bar. **Address:** 401 Sea Ave (SR 35) 08742 **Location:** 0.4 mi s of center on SR 35. [L] [D] [LATE]

JACK BAKER'S LOBSTER SHANTY & WHARFSIDE
732/892-9100

▼▼ ▼▼ Seafood. Family Dining. $14-$45 **AAA Inspector Notes:** This family-oriented restaurant, with an unbeatable view of the Manasquan Inlet, is prone to long waits in season. A wide variety of seafood dishes are served such as stuffed salmon, flounder and shrimp, shrimp scampi, crab cakes, baked and broiled fish, steamers and a few dishes for landlubbers. Cobbler, pie and crisps are available for dessert. **Features:** full bar, patio dining. **Address:** 101 Channel Dr 08742 **Location:** 0.5 mi e of SR 35, follow signs to beach area, left on Boston Ave. [L] [D] CALL [&M]

THE SHRIMP BOX   732/899-1637

▼▼ ▼▼ Seafood. Family Dining. $9-$45 **AAA Inspector Notes:** This is a family restaurant located on the Manasquan Inlet with nautical theme decor and large picture windows with views of docked fishing boats. The menu is mainly fish and shellfish, baked, broiled, fried, and scampied with other meat options available. **Features:** full bar, patio dining. **Reservations:** suggested. **Address:** 75 Inlet Dr 08742 **Location:** 0.5 mi e of SR 35 via Broadway, just n. [L] [D] CALL [&M]

SPIKES FISH MARKET & RESTAURANT   732/295-9400

▼▼ ▼▼ Seafood. Casual Dining. $8-$24 **AAA Inspector Notes:** Known for fresh seafood, this casual shore spot is part retail, part restaurant sporting large benches and tables. The menu eschews deep-fried dishes in favor of broiled, blackened, stuffed, seared and served scampi-style with tasty sauces. Creative specials typically are served with outstanding slaw, potato salad, rice or roasted potatoes. Lobster bisque makes an excellent starter. **Address:** 415 Broadway Dr 08742 **Location:** Just e of jct SR 35 and Manasquan River Bridge. **Parking:** on-site and street. [L] [D]

POMPTON PLAINS

BEST WESTERN PLUS REGENCY HOUSE HOTEL
(973)696-0900

Hotel
$90-$119

AAA Benefit: Members save up to 20%!

Address: 140 SR 23 N 07444 **Location:** 6 mi n of jct I-80, US 46 and SR 23. **Facility:** 104 units, some efficiencies. 2 stories (no elevator), interior corridors. **Pool(s):** outdoor. **Activities:** exercise room. **Guest Services:** valet and coin laundry.

PRINCETON (D-3) pop. 12,307, elev. 215'
• Hotels p. 184 • Restaurants p. 185

The key to Princeton's future was turned in 1756 when the College of New Jersey, founded in Elizabeth by royal charter in 1746, was moved to the town; it was not officially renamed Princeton University until 1896. The school's Nassau Hall was the site of another pivotal event: the 1776 meeting of the first New Jersey state legislature at which William Livingston was inaugurated as governor.

A short time afterward Gen. Charles Cornwallis' troops occupied Nassau Hall as they pushed Gen. George Washington's army westward. Early the next year Washington followed up his victory at Trenton by surprising and defeating the British in the Battle of Princeton. A monument at Mercer, Nassau and Stockton streets commemorates the battle.

In 1783 the Continental Congress met in Nassau Hall when mutinous American soldiers drove its members from Philadelphia. It was during this time that members received news of the treaty of peace with Great Britain.

Community life has long melded with that of the university and other institutions of higher education. Albert Einstein spent his last years at the Institute for Advanced Study.

The Historical Society of Princeton offers a 2-hour guided walking tour of historic Princeton every Sunday at 2; phone (609) 921-6748. The Princeton Tour Company *(see attraction listing)* offers self-guiding audio and guided bus, bicycle and walking tours of Princeton University and the city's historic areas.

Princeton Regional Chamber of Commerce: 182 Nassau St., Suite 301, Princeton, NJ 08542. **Phone:** (609) 924-1776.

Self-guiding tours: The Historical Society of Princeton has brochures outlining walking tours around such topics as 18th-century houses and architecture. These brochures can be obtained at the society's museum shop in the Bainbridge House, 158 Nassau St.

BAINBRIDGE HOUSE is at 158 Nassau St. The birthplace of William Bainbridge, commander of the USS *Constitution* during the War of 1812, serves as a museum with changing exhibitions, a library and photographic archives. The restored 1766 house is the headquarters of the Historical Society of Princeton. **Hours:** Wed.-Sun. noon-4. **Cost:** $4. **Phone:** (609) 921-6748.

PRINCETON TOUR COMPANY is at 116 Nassau St.; walking tours depart from inside Princeton University U-Store. This indie tour company offers 1.5- to 2-hour walking tours and biking tours as well as bus tours, air tours, holiday trolley tours and pre-recorded versions. Ghost tours also are offered. All tours view—but not enter—the buildings that make up historic Princeton.

Depending on the tour, stops may include Princeton University, the main business district and Revolutionary War sites. Famous residents, students and alumni also are covered; presidents Woodrow Wilson, James Madison and Grover Cleveland found their way here as have numerous Pulitzer and Nobel Prize winners.

Note: One walking tour may cover about 3 miles over 2 hours with only brief informational stops; phone ahead about accessibility. **Time:** Allow 2 hours, 30 minutes minimum. **Hours:** Public tours are offered daily Apr.-Dec.; by appointment, rest of year. Phone ahead for information regarding specific tours and their availability. Participants should arrive 15 minutes prior to their scheduled tour's departure. **Cost:** $25; $20 (ages 0-12). Rates may vary depending on tour type; phone ahead to confirm prices. A free self-guiding cellphone tour is available online. **Parking:** $1-$2 per hour. Limited free parking is available on the Princeton campus. **Phone:** (855) 743-1415. GT

PRINCETON UNIVERSITY is off US 1 at jct. Washington Rd. and Nassau St. The university enrolls some 7,900 students on its 500-acre campus. The original 1756 building, Nassau Hall, served as a barracks and hospital during the Revolutionary War. Sculptures from the John B. Putnam Jr. Memorial Collection, including works by Alexander Calder, Henry Moore, Louise Nevelson and Pablo Picasso, are displayed on campus.

Visitor information is available at the Frist Campus Center. Points of interest on guided 1-hour campus tours include Nassau Hall and Princeton University Chapel. **Hours:** Campus tours given daily. Closed holidays, Jan. 1-early Jan. and mid-Dec. through Dec. 31. Phone ahead to confirm schedule. **Cost:** Free. **Phone:** (609) 258-1766 for tour information.

Princeton University Art Museum is in McCormick Hall near jct. Nassau and Witherspoon sts., at the center of the Princeton University campus. The outstanding collection of 80,000 works spans the globe from ancient to modern times. Especially noteworthy are Chinese paintings and bronzes, Pre-Columbian art, Impressionist paintings and photography. Guided tours are available by appointment. **Hours:** Tues.-Sat. 10-5 (also Thurs. 5-10), Sun. 1-5. Closed Jan. 1, July 4, Thanksgiving and Christmas. **Cost:** Free. **Phone:** (609) 258-3788.

Princeton University Chapel is at jct. Washington Rd. and William St., near Firestone Library. One of the world's largest university chapels, the Gothic building was completed in 1928. The pulpit, which dates from the mid-16th century, was brought from France. Also of interest are the chapel's pews and stained-glass windows.

Hours: Daily 7 a.m.-11 p.m., during the academic year; 7-4, rest of the year and during school breaks. Phone ahead to confirm schedule. **Cost:** Free. **Phone:** (609) 258-3047.

THE THOMAS CLARKE HOUSE is at 500 Mercer Rd. in Princeton Battlefield State Park, where Gen. George Washington led his forces to victory in 1777. Gen. Hugh Mercer died in the house from wounds suffered in the battle. Built by a Quaker farmer in

1772, the Georgian-style dwelling contains period furniture and Revolutionary War exhibits. **Hours:** Guided house tours Wed.-Sat. 10-noon and 1-4, Sun. 1-4. Park open daily dawn-dusk. Closed Jan. 1, Thanksgiving and Christmas. **Cost:** Free. **Phone:** (609) 921-0074.

CHAUNCEY HOTEL AND CONFERENCE CENTER
609/921-3600

Hotel
Rates not provided

Address: 660 Rosedale Rd 08541 **Location:** 0.5 mi w on Stockton Rd, 0.5 mi n on Elm Rd, 1.8 mi w. Located in Educational Testing Service campus. **Facility:** 100 units. 2 stories, interior corridors. **Terms:** check-in 4 pm. **Amenities:** safes. **Activities:** bicycles, exercise room. **Guest Services:** valet and coin laundry, area transportation. **Featured Amenity: full hot breakfast.**

CLARION HOTEL PALMER INN
(609)452-2500

Hotel
$80-$263

Address: 3499 US 1 S 08540 **Location:** 2 mi s of jct CR 526 and 571. **Facility:** 105 units, some efficiencies. 2 stories, interior/exterior corridors. **Amenities:** safes. **Pool(s):** outdoor. **Activities:** exercise room. **Guest Services:** valet and coin laundry, area transportation. **Featured Amenity: full hot breakfast.**

COURTYARD BY MARRIOTT PRINCETON
(609)716-9100

Hotel $167-$275 **Address:** 3815 US 1 S 08540 **Location:** 0.4 mi s of Scudders Mill Rd at Mapleton Rd. **Facility:** 154 units. 3 stories, interior corridors. **Pool(s):** heated indoor. **Activities:** hot tub, exercise room. **Guest Services:** valet and coin laundry, boarding pass kiosk.

| AAA Benefit: |
| Members save 5% |
| or more! |

DOUBLETREE BY HILTON HOTEL PRINCETON
(609)452-2400

Hotel
$89-$349

AAA Benefit: Members save 5% or more!

Address: 4355 US 1 Rd 08540 **Location:** On US 1 southbound at Ridge Rd, 3 mi n of CR 571. **Facility:** 238 units. 6 stories, interior corridors. **Terms:** 1-7 night minimum stay, cancellation fee imposed. **Pool(s):** heated indoor. **Activities:** exercise room. **Guest Services:** valet and coin laundry, area transportation.

HAMPTON INN PRINCETON
(609)951-0066

Hotel $99-$179 **Address:** 4385 US 1 S 08540 **Location:** Just past Ridge Rd. **Facility:** 110 units. 3 stories, interior corridors. **Terms:** 1-7 night minimum stay, cancellation fee imposed. **Pool(s):** heated outdoor. **Activities:** exercise room. **Guest Services:** valet and coin laundry.

| AAA Benefit: |
| Members save 5% |
| or more! |

HOLIDAY INN PRINCETON
609/520-1200

Hotel. Rates not provided. **Address:** 100 Independence Way 08540 **Location:** I-295 exit 67A (SR 1) northbound; exit 67 (SR 1) southbound, 7 mi n. Located in Princeton Corporate Center. **Facility:** 182 units. 4 stories, interior corridors. **Amenities:** video games. **Pool(s):** outdoor. **Activities:** exercise room. **Guest Services:** valet and coin laundry, area transportation.

HOMEWOOD SUITES PRINCETON
(609)720-0550

Extended Stay Hotel $119-$409 **Address:** 3819 US 1 S 08540 **Location:** 0.4 mi s of Scudders Mill Rd at Mapleton Rd. **Facility:** 142 efficiencies, some two bedrooms. 4 stories, interior corridors. **Terms:** 1-7 night minimum stay, cancellation fee imposed. **Pool(s):** heated indoor. **Activities:** hot tub, exercise room. **Guest Services:** valet and coin laundry, area transportation.

| AAA Benefit: |
| Members save 5% |
| or more! |

HYATT PLACE PRINCETON
(609)720-0200

Hotel
$89-$379

HYATT PLACE
AAA Benefit: Members save 10%!

Address: 3565 US 1 S 08540 **Location:** 1.5 mi s of jct CR 526 and 571. **Facility:** 122 units. 5 stories, interior corridors. **Terms:** cancellation fee imposed. **Amenities:** safes. **Pool(s):** heated indoor. **Activities:** exercise room. **Guest Services:** valet laundry, area transportation. **Featured Amenity: breakfast buffet.**

HYATT REGENCY PRINCETON
(609)987-1234

Contemporary Hotel
$79-$369

HYATT REGENCY
AAA Benefit: Members save 10%!

Address: 102 Carnegie Center 08540 **Location:** US 1 N, 0.5 mi s of CR 571. Located in Carnegie Office Complex. **Facility:** 330 units, some two bedrooms. 4 stories, interior corridors. **Parking:** on-site and valet. **Terms:** cancellation fee imposed. **Dining:** entertainment. **Pool(s):** heated indoor. **Activities:** tennis, exercise room. **Guest Services:** valet laundry, rental car service, area transportation.

NASSAU INN
(609)921-7500

Historic Hotel
$199-$305

Address: 10 Palmer Square E 08542 **Location:** Center. **Facility:** This charming 1756 hotel features restored Colonial-style lobby areas. The rustic tavern features an authentic Norman Rockwell mural and photographs of famed Princeton grads. 188 units. 5 stories, interior corridors. **Parking:** on-site (fee). **Terms:** cancellation fee imposed. **Amenities:** video games, safes. **Dining:** Yankee Doodle Tap Room, see separate listing, entertainment. **Activities:** exercise room. **Guest Services:** valet laundry.

PRINCETON MARRIOTT AT FORRESTAL
(609)452-7800

Hotel
$167-$275

MARRIOTT

AAA Benefit: Members save 5% or more!

Address: 100 College Rd E 08540 **Location:** US 1 N, 2.5 mi n of CR 571. Located in Princeton Forrestal Center. **Facility:** 302 units, some two bedrooms. 3 stories, interior corridors. **Parking:** on-site and valet. **Amenities:** video games. **Dining:** 2 restaurants. **Pool(s):** heated indoor. **Activities:** sauna, hot tub, steamroom, tennis, exercise room, spa. **Guest Services:** valet and coin laundry.

RESIDENCE INN BY MARRIOTT-PRINCETON AT CARNEGIE CENTER
(609)799-0550

Extended Stay Hotel
$174-$286 **Address:** 3563 US 1 S 08540 **Location:** 1.5 mi s of jct CR 527 and 571. **Facility:** 120 units, some two bedrooms, efficiencies and kitchens. 4 stories, interior corridors. **Pool(s):** heated indoor. **Activities:** hot tub, exercise room. **Guest Services:** valet and coin laundry, area transportation.

AAA Benefit: Members save 5% or more!

SONESTA ES SUITES PRINCETON
609/951-0009

Extended Stay Hotel
Rates not provided

Address: 4375 US 1 S 08543 **Location:** Just past Ridge Rd. **Facility:** 124 kitchen units, some two bedrooms. 2-3 stories (no elevator), exterior corridors. **Terms:** check-in 4 pm. **Amenities:** safes. **Pool(s):** outdoor. **Activities:** exercise room. **Guest Services:** valet and coin laundry, area transportation.

Find thousands of pet-friendly places to stay, play and dine with *The AAA PetBook*

WESTIN PRINCETON AT FORRESTAL VILLAGE
(609)452-7900

Hotel
$139-$299

WESTIN
HOTELS & RESORTS

AAA Benefit: Members save up to 15%, plus Starwood Preferred Guest® benefits!

Address: 201 Village Blvd 08540 **Location:** On US 1 southbound, 1.5 mi n of CR 571. Located in a shopping village. **Facility:** 296 units. 6 stories, interior corridors. **Amenities:** safes. **Pool(s):** outdoor, heated indoor. **Activities:** tennis, exercise room. **Guest Services:** valet laundry, area transportation.

WHERE TO EAT

THE ALCHEMIST & BARRISTER
609/924-5555

American. Casual Dining. $9-$34 **AAA Inspector Notes:** This lovely, intimate dining room lets guests sample simple, yet well-prepared dishes. The atmosphere shows a hint of refinement, but there also is a casual pub room serving relaxed fare. **Features:** full bar, patio dining, Sunday brunch. **Address:** 28 Witherspoon St 08542 **Location:** Center. **Parking:** street only. L D

BIG FISH SEAFOOD BISTRO
609/919-1179

Seafood. Casual Dining. $10-$36 **AAA Inspector Notes:** Popular with local corporate types, the eclectic restaurant is dotted with stylized fish and nautical memorabilia. Specializing in fresh seafood, the daily catch menu changes constantly, but the varied steak, chicken and pasta dishes are reliable choices. Hot and cold soups, varied appetizers and creative desserts complement such innovatively prepared seafood entrees as whitefish Oscar. **Features:** full bar, patio dining, Sunday brunch, happy hour. **Address:** 3535 US Route One, Suite 370 08540 **Location:** 1.5 mi s of jct CR 526 and 571; in Market Fair Mall. L D CALL

CONTE'S PIZZA
609/921-8041

Pizza. Casual Dining. $7-$13 **AAA Inspector Notes:** *Classic.* It's not fancy at this local pizza joint and bar that has been in business since the 1950s. There are no fancy toppings, exotic crusts or cheeses—just tasty traditional pies with familiar toppings and a few simple red-sauce pasta dishes. The décor here is simple and slightly retro with a large bar on one side of the room serving cold beers or soft drinks to wash down your pizza. **Features:** full bar. **Address:** 339 Witherspoon St 08540 **Location:** 0.7 mi n of Nassau St; at Guyot Ave. L D

MEDITERRA RESTAURANT AND TAVERNA
609/252-9680

Mediterranean. Casual Dining. $14-$35 **AAA Inspector Notes:** Scenes of the Mediterranean decorate the chic, upscale bistro, a warm spot for families and couples alike. Italian, Greek and Spanish flavors blend on the varied menu. In addition to an extensive wine list, the restaurant has several draft beers. **Features:** full bar. **Reservations:** suggested. **Address:** 29 Hulfish St 08540 **Location:** Jct Nassau and Witherspoon sts, just w; downtown. **Parking:** on-site (fee). L D

TERESA CAFFE
609/921-1974

Italian. Casual Dining. $11-$23 **AAA Inspector Notes:** After dining here you will wonder why there are not more places like this. This bright and bustling café serves simple, rustic Italian cuisine made from fresh, local and organic ingredients, some of which are sourced from their own nearby farm. Individual pizza is the specialty such as the perfecta with Fontina, prosciutto, arugula, grana padano, lemon zest and organic olive oil. Fresh salads and pastas such as cavatelli salsa and lasagna Bolognese round out the menu. **Features:** full bar. **Address:** 23 Palmer Square E 08542 **Location:** Just w of jct Nassau St on Palmer Square; downtown; opposite entrance to Nassau Inn. **Parking:** street only. L D

TORTUGA'S MEXICAN VILLAGE   609/924-5143

▼▼ ▼▼ Mexican. Casual Dining. $9-$20 **AAA Inspector Notes:** Authentic Mexican favorites have made up the menu here since the mid-1980s. Chiles rellenos, chimichangas and a variety of grilled entrées, including chipotle carne asada, attract a crowd at lunch even though the restaurant is slightly off the beaten path in a simple neighborhood. The casual spot lures people with its food. Guests can bring their own bottle, but also need to bring cash because credit cards are not accepted. **Address:** 44 Leigh Ave 08540 **Location:** 0.5 mi e, just s of jct Witherspoon St. **Parking:** street only. L | D

TRIUMPH BREWING COMPANY   609/924-7855

▼▼ ▼▼ American. Gastropub. $10-$16 **AAA Inspector Notes:** This is the place to sample excellent craft beers that are brewed right on premises. The multi-level dining and bar space affords views of the sparkling, stainless steel brewing kettles. The menu offers familiar tavern-style items, but they are enhanced by some creative twists and use of locally grown ingredients. **Features:** full bar. **Address:** 138 Nassau St 08542 **Location:** Between Vendeventer Ave and Tulane St; across from main campus. **Parking:** street only.
L | D | CALL &M

WITHERSPOON GRILL   609/924-6011

▼▼ ▼▼ ▼▼ Steak Seafood. Casual Dining. $14-$42 **AAA Inspector Notes:** This casual but sophisticated steak and seafood grill makes use of many local products from the area in serving up familiar dishes like braised short ribs, crab cakes, sesame tuna and a full range of USDA Prime steaks. The relaxed bar is a great spot for drinks and appetizers. **Features:** full bar, patio dining, Sunday brunch. **Reservations:** suggested. **Address:** 57 Witherspoon St 08542 **Location:** Center; next to public library. **Parking:** street only.
L | D | CALL &M

YANKEE DOODLE TAP ROOM   609/921-7500

▼▼ ▼▼ Comfort Food. Casual Dining. $12-$28 **AAA Inspector Notes:** The atmosphere at this old tavern takes diners back to Colonial times with lots of wood and a rustic brick fireplace. The most notable feature is the original Norman Rockwell "Yankee Doodle" mural behind the bar. The menu offers the usual pub fare with sandwiches, burgers, salads and a few entrées. They also have a great outdoor patio that opens to the charming Palmer Square shopping district. **Features:** full bar, patio dining, happy hour. **Address:** 10 Palmer Square E 08542 **Location:** Center; in Nassau Inn. **Parking:** street only. B | L | D | CALL &M

RAHWAY pop. 27,346
• Hotels & Restaurants map & index p. 152

BEST WESTERN RIVERVIEW INN & SUITES
(732)381-7650 **99**

▼▼ ▼▼ ▼▼
Hotel
$120-$160

AAA Benefit:
Members save up to 20%!

Address: 1747 Paterson St 07065 **Location:** Jct Paterson St and US 1/9. **Facility:** 74 units. 5 stories, interior corridors. **Terms:** 3 day cancellation notice-fee imposed. **Pool(s):** heated indoor. **Activities:** exercise room. **Guest Services:** valet laundry. **Featured Amenity:** continental breakfast.

SAVE CALL &M ⊷ BIZ HS 📶
✕ 🔌 📷 📺

RAMSEY pop. 14,473

BEST WESTERN THE INN AT RAMSEY   (201)327-6700

▼▼ ▼▼
Hotel
$89-$129

AAA Benefit:
Members save up to 20%!

Address: 1315 Rt 17 S 07446 **Location:** Jct I-287 and SR 17 S, 3 mi s. **Facility:** 81 units. 2 stories (no elevator), interior corridors. **Parking:** winter plug-ins. **Terms:** check-in 4 pm. **Guest Services:** valet laundry. **Featured Amenity:** full hot breakfast.

SAVE 🍴 🍽 ⊻ CALL &M 📶
🔌 📷 📺 / SOME UNITS 🛏 HS

HOLIDAY INN EXPRESS RAMSEY/MAHWAH   (201)934-9250

▼▼ ▼▼ ▼▼ $129-$599 **Address:** 946 Rt 17 07446 **Location:** At Airmont Rd. **Facility:** 79 units. 3 stories, interior corridors. **Guest Services:** valet laundry.

🍴 CALL &M HS 📶 ✕ 🔌 📷 📺

WHERE TO EAT

CAFE PANACHE   201/934-0030

▼▼ ▼▼ ▼▼ New American. Casual Dining. $12-$38 **AAA Inspector Notes:** The attractive and comfortable dining room is the setting for upscale cuisine at this bring-your-own-bottle restaurant. The ever-changing menu includes signature items such as pecan chicken with Dijon mustard sauce, crispy wasabi halibut or braised short ribs with dark beer and molasses. At lunch there are some creative entrée salads as well as fish and pasta dishes. **Reservations:** suggested. **Address:** 130 E Main St 07446 **Location:** Downtown.
L | D

KINCHLEY'S TAVERN   201/934-7777

▼▼ ▼▼ Pizza. Casual Dining. $6-$13 **AAA Inspector Notes:** It's cash only at this long-time local favorite, but the pizza here is on the money. The menu has some other well-known sandwiches and entrées, most with red sauce, but you would really be missing out here if you did not have the pizza. The thin, crispy crust is best topped with just one or two items, so keep it simple and order multiple pies. Try the fra diavolo sauce for a little more kick. Service is quick but friendly, even when it gets very busy in the evenings. **Features:** full bar. **Address:** 586 N Franklin Tpke 07446 **Location:** 0.5 mi n of SR 17.
L | D

RANDOLPH
• Hotels & Restaurants map & index p. 152

CASA DE PASTA   973/584-3700 **47**

▼▼ ▼▼ Italian. Casual Dining. $11-$20 **AAA Inspector Notes:** Red brick, roadside tavern with rough-hewn beams and varnished wood tabletops, flickering wall lanterns and a popular bar with locals serves traditional dishes including homemade specialties of manicotti, cheese and meat ravioli, stuffed shells and lasagna. **Features:** full bar. **Address:** 1438 Sussex Tpke 07869 **Location:** Just n of jct Dover-Chester Rd and Sussex Tpke. D

RED BANK pop. 12,206

COURTYARD BY MARRIOTT LINCROFT/RED BANK
(732)530-5552

Hotel
$125-$206

COURTYARD Marriott

AAA Benefit: Members save 5% or more!

Address: 245 Half Mile Rd 07701 **Location:** Garden State Pkwy exit 109, just ne. **Facility:** 146 units. 3 stories, interior corridors. **Pool(s):** heated indoor. **Activities:** exercise room. **Guest Services:** valet and coin laundry.

MOLLY PITCHER INN
732/747-2500

Historic Hotel. Rates not provided. **Address:** 88 Riverside Ave 07701 **Location:** Waterfront. 0.3 mi s of Navesink River Bridge on SR 35. **Facility:** Built in 1928, this landmark riverfront inn offers traditional décor and great views that make it a popular site for weddings. 106 units. 4 stories, interior corridors. **Parking:** on-site and valet. **Amenities:** safes. **Pool(s):** outdoor. **Activities:** boat dock, exercise room. **Guest Services:** valet laundry.

THE OYSTER POINT HOTEL
732/530-8200

Hotel. Rates not provided. **Address:** 146 Bodman Pl 07701 **Location:** Waterfront. 0.3 mi s of Navesink River Bridge on SR 35, just e. **Facility:** 56 units. 5 stories, interior corridors. **Amenities:** safes. **Activities:** boat dock, fishing, exercise room. **Guest Services:** valet laundry.

WHERE TO EAT

BASIL T'S BREWERY & ITALIAN GRILL
732/842-5990

Traditional Italian. Casual Dining. $13-$40 **AAA Inspector Notes:** This family-owned Italian cucina has been a local favorite for more than 25 years. The menu is like an old friend with familiar pastas, pizzas, great chicken Parmesan, steak and fish. The relaxed dining room and bar have a warm welcoming ambience. There is an impressive wine list, and they even brew their own beer on site. **Features:** full bar. **Reservations:** suggested. **Address:** 183 Riverside Ave 07701 **Location:** 0.3 mi s of Navesink River Bridge on SR 35.

RESTAURANT NICHOLAS
732/345-9977

New American. Fine Dining. $65-$85 **AAA Inspector Notes:** The husband and wife team of Melissa and Nicholas Harary ensure an exquisite dining experience from start to finish. Melissa and the dining room staff see that patrons want for nothing, offering seamless service. Guests are welcomed to the table by Chef Nicholas's amuse-bouche, followed by his two- or three-course menus, as well as the chef's degustation. Dishes, such as the fabulous big eye tuna with tabbouleh and caramelized lemon, are beautifully presented and expertly prepared. **Features:** full bar. **Reservations:** suggested. **Address:** 160 SR 35 07701 **Location:** 0.7 mi n of Navesink River Bridge. **Parking:** valet only.

RIDGEFIELD PARK pop. 12,729
• Hotels & Restaurants map & index p. 162

HAMPTON INN AT RIDGEFIELD PARK
(201)641-2900 **50**

Hotel $124-$189 **Address:** 100 Rt 46 E 07660 **Location:** New Jersey Tpke exit 18W to US 46 E (Ridgefield/Palisades Park), just e. **Facility:** 83 units. 4 stories, interior corridors. **Terms:** 1-7 night minimum stay, cancellation fee imposed. **Pool(s):** heated indoor. **Activities:** exercise room. **Guest Services:** valet laundry.

AAA Benefit: Members save 5% or more!

HILTON GARDEN INN RIDGEFIELD PARK
(201)641-2024 **49**

Hotel $169-$239 **Address:** 70 Challenger Rd 07660 **Location:** I-95 exit 68, follow signs. **Facility:** 140 units. 5 stories, interior corridors. **Terms:** 1-7 night minimum stay, cancellation fee imposed. **Pool(s):** heated indoor. **Activities:** hot tub, exercise room. **Guest Services:** valet and coin laundry, area transportation.

AAA Benefit: Members save 5% or more!

RIDGEWOOD pop. 24,958
• Hotels & Restaurants map & index p. 162

IT'S GREEK TO ME
201/612-2600

Greek. Casual Dining. $10-$35 **AAA Inspector Notes:** This restaurant is a veritable find for those in search of authentic Greek cuisine. Start with the creamy, garlicky and oh-so-good gigantes, giant white beans cooked with tomato and sage. Gyros are, as they should be, good and messy. Servers are happy to bring over extra napkins, or anything else you may need. The dining room is reminiscent of a sunny Greek Island and is bedecked with the country's official blue and white colors. **Features:** patio dining. **Address:** 21 E Ridgewood Ave 07450 **Location:** Between Chestnut and Broad sts; center. **Parking:** street only.

KAILASH
201/251-9693 **13**

Indian. Casual Dining. $8-$20 **AAA Inspector Notes:** The city's first Indian restaurant is still second to none. Hindus and Buddhists consider the legendary Mount Kailash in the Himalayan range to be the center of the universe, and devotees of classic Indian fare are apt to think the same of this delightful restaurant, where soothing Indian music and aromatic curries and biryanis are transporting experiences in their own right. **Address:** 22 Oak St 07450 **Location:** Between E Ridgewood and Franklin aves; center. **Parking:** street only.

LATOUR
201/445-5056 **15**

Traditional French. Fine Dining. $12-$36 **AAA Inspector Notes:** An intimate and formal atmosphere is the setting for upscale cuisine prepared by the chef-owner. Think escargots a la Bourguignonne, sautéed Atlantic salmon, Grand Marnier duck and beef Wellington interspersed with a few lighter and more modern dishes. The food is excellent, service refined and location in the quaint downtown makes for a nice after-dinner stroll. **Reservations:** suggested. **Address:** 6 E Ridgewood Ave 07450 **Location:** Adjacent to train station; center. **Parking:** on-site (fee).

MALEE FINE THAI CUISINE
201/612-7797 **16**

Thai. Casual Dining. $12-$25 **AAA Inspector Notes:** Set along the tracks of the Ridgewood Train Station, this eatery brings a taste of exotic Bangkok to those who crave the flavors of Thai cuisine. The aroma of cilantro, curry and jasmine rice greets diners as they enter the storefront dining room furnished with colorful Thai tapestries and bric-a-brac. **Features:** patio dining. **Address:** 2 E Ridgewood Ave 07450 **Location:** Center. **Parking:** street only.

THE OFFICE BEER BAR & GRILL
201/652-1070

American. Casual Dining. $9-$18 **AAA Inspector Notes:** The extensive beer list makes this office different from the one most folks visit from 9 to 5. Vintage typewriters, shelves of books and other office bric-a-brac contribute to the workaday theme, while the friendly staff and menu of favorites, including quesadillas, ribs and burgers, prompt patrons to put in a little overtime. **Features:** full bar, happy hour. **Address:** 32-34 Chestnut St 07450 **Location:** Between E Ridgewood and Franklin aves; center. **Parking:** street only.

RAYMOND'S
201/445-5125 **14**

Comfort Food. Casual Dining. $8-$16 **AAA Inspector Notes:** Comfortable, familiar foods are on the menu at this popular and attractive downtown eatery, which has a retro, soda-fountain-style decor. Items like chicken dumpling soup, meatloaf, patty melts and mac & cheese are all done with quality, fresh ingredients. The popular breakfast items, including French toast and omelets, are available until 4 pm. **Features:** patio dining, Sunday brunch. **Address:** 101 E Ridgewood Ave 07450 **Location:** At Oak St; center. **Parking:** street only.

RINGOES

HARVEST MOON INN   908/806-6020
▼▼▼ Continental. Fine Dining. $10-$37 **AAA Inspector Notes:** This restaurant retains much of the Colonial-era appeal of the Federal-style stone building which dates to 1811. The modern menu offers such entrées as sautéed pork tenderloin with maple-glazed celery root and squash with a crisp potato fritter, in an apple cider and walnut vinaigrette. Or try the seared tuna with cracked black pepper, Napa cabbage, broccoli, sliced red onions and shiitake mushrooms with spicy red pepper miso vinaigrette. A casual tavern menu also is offered. **Features:** full bar. **Reservations:** suggested. **Address:** 1039 Old York Rd 08551 **Location:** 1 mi e of jct US 202.

L D

RINGWOOD (A-4) pop. 12,228, elev. 470'

Claiming a colorful past as an iron-mining and forging center, Ringwood has been described as "more a company than a town, and more a tradition than a company." The iron-rich Ramapo Mountains were responsible for Ringwood's early importance as a mining and forging center. The first forge was built in 1739; by 1771 it had become the lucrative, London-based American Iron Co. Wealthy mine and forge owners built homes on vast tracts of land.

When the Revolutionary War erupted, ironmaster Robert Erskine sided with the Colonies and became the surveyor general for the Continental Armies. Meanwhile his forges worked overtime turning out munitions, cannons and most of the huge chain that was stretched across the Hudson to prevent British ships from reaching West Point. The Ringwood iron mine continued to produce until 1931.

Ringwood Chamber of Commerce: P.O. Box 62, Ringwood, NJ 07456.

RINGWOOD STATE PARK is 2.5 mi. n. via Skyline Dr. and CR 511 at 1304 Sloatsburg Rd. The park's three units total 6,199 acres. The Shepherd Lake unit, 14 miles north of Pompton Lakes, offers water recreation. *See Recreation Areas Chart.* **Hours:** Park open daily 8 a.m.-dusk. Shepherd Lake unit open daily 10-6. **Cost:** Park free. **Parking:** Shepherd Lake unit $10 (New Jersey residents $5) Mon.-Fri., $20 (New Jersey residents $10) Sat.-Sun., Memorial Day weekend-Labor Day. **Phone:** (973) 962-7031.

New Jersey State Botanical Garden is off Sloatsburg Rd. at jct. Sloatsburg and Morris rds. in Ringwood State Park. The 44-room Skylands Manor is surrounded by 96 acres of formal and informal gardens and more than 1,000 acres of native woodlands. Clarence McKenzie Lewis built the Tudor-style mansion in the 1920s and collected flowering trees and plants from around the world to beautify

the grounds. Marked trails wind through the gardens; annuals and perennials bloom from spring through the first frost.

Hours: Gardens daily 8-8. Guided garden tours are offered Sun. at 2, May-Oct. Woodland walks are offered on the third Sun. of the month at 1. Forty-five minute guided tours of the manor's first floor are offered one Sun. per month 11-3, Mar.-Nov.; phone for schedule. **Cost:** Garden and garden tours free. Guided manor tour $7; $5 (ages 13-18 and 62+); $3 (ages 6-12). **Parking:** Sat.-Sun. and holidays, Memorial Day weekend-Labor Day $7 (out-of-state residents); $5 (N.J. residents); free, all other times. **Phone:** (973) 962-9534.

Ringwood Manor is at 1304 Sloatsburg Rd. in Ringwood State Park. Martin J. Ryerson began construction of the manor house in 1807 on the estate once owned by Robert Erskine, George Washington's mapmaker. Later owners included industrialist Peter Cooper and ironmaster Abram S. Hewitt. Additions to the 51-room mansion exhibit a variety of architectural styles. Some 8,000 objects can be found in the home, ranging from the 1490s to 1920s. The grounds include formal gardens, as well as woodlands traversed by hiking and mountain biking trails.

Hours: Grounds open daily dawn-dusk. Guided manor tours are given Wed.-Sun. on the hour 10-11 and 1-3. Manor closed major holidays except Memorial Day, July 4 and Labor Day. Because there are few staff members, phone ahead to verify holiday hours and guided tour schedule. **Cost:** Guided manor tour $3; $1 (ages 6-12). **Parking:** Sat.-Sun. $7 (New Jersey residents $5), Memorial Day weekend-Labor Day. **Phone:** (973) 962-7031.

GT 🎁

RIO GRANDE (H-2) pop. 2,670, elev. 22'

SAVE **NAVAL AIR STATION WILDWOOD AVIATION MUSEUM** is located at the Cape May County Airport at 500 Forrestal Rd. Throughout World War II Naval Air Station Wildwood was used as a training facility for dive-bomber squadrons. The museum honors the 42 airmen who lost their lives here. The museum, housed in an all-wood hangar, displays aircraft and aircraft engines as well as aviation artifacts and military memorabilia.

Time: Allow 30 minutes minimum. **Hours:** Daily 9-5, Apr. 1-Columbus Day; daily 9-4, day after Columbus Day-Nov. 30; Mon.-Fri. 9-4, rest of year. Closed Jan. 1, Thanksgiving, Christmas Eve, Christmas and Dec. 31. Phone ahead to confirm schedule. **Cost:** $10; $8 (ages 3-12); free (military with ID). **Phone:** (609) 886-8787.

ROBBINSVILLE

HAMPTON INN & SUITES   (609)259-0300

▼▼▼▼ **Hotel** $119-$159 **Address:** 153 W Manor Way 08691 **Location:** I-195 exit 7, just n. **Facility:** 104 units. 4 stories, interior corridors. **Terms:** 1-7 night minimum stay, cancellation fee imposed. **Amenities:** *Some:* safes. **Pool(s):** heated indoor. **Activities:** exercise room. **Guest Services:** complimentary and valet laundry.

AAA Benefit: Members save 5% or more!

CALL 🔍M 🛪 BIZ 📶 ✖ 🖵
/ SOME UNITS 🍴 HS 🖪 🖨

ROCKAWAY pop. 6,438
• Hotels & Restaurants map & index p. 152

HILTON GARDEN INN ROCKAWAY   (973)328-0600   8

Hilton Garden Inn

Hotel
$109-$194

AAA Benefit: Members save 5% or more!

Address: 375 Mount Hope Ave 07866 **Location:** I-80 exit 35 eastbound; exit 35A westbound, 0.6 mi s. Located in Rockaway Townsquare Mall. **Facility:** 162 units. 5 stories, interior corridors. **Terms:** 1-7 night minimum stay, cancellation fee imposed. **Pool(s):** heated indoor. **Activities:** hot tub, exercise room. **Guest Services:** valet and coin laundry. **Featured Amenity:** breakfast buffet.

SAVE 🍴 ▼ CALL 🔍M 🛪 BIZ HS 📶 ✖ 🎣
🖪 🖨 🖵

ROSELLE PARK pop. 13,297
• Hotels & Restaurants map & index p. 152

COSTAS RESTAURANT & PIZZERIA   908/241-1131   13

▼▼▼ Italian. Casual Dining. $11-$25 **AAA Inspector Notes:** The established neighborhood landmark is a local favorite for traditional Italian cuisine--plenty of pasta dishes with tasty sauces and huge portions. Pretty china and nice table settings enhance the appearance of the relaxed dining room. Servers are clean and prompt. **Features:** full bar. **Reservations:** suggested, weekends. **Address:** 120 Chestnut St 07204 **Location:** Garden State Pkwy exit 137, 1 mi e on SR 28, then just n. **Parking:** street only.   L   D

RUMSON pop. 7,122

DAVID BURKE FROMAGERIE   732/842-8088

▼▼▼▼ New American. Fine Dining. $25-$39 **AAA Inspector Notes:** A creative and seasonally changing menu focuses on herbs, reductions and infusions which enhance and highlight the flavors of the fish, poultry and game being offered. The comfy dining room invites guests to linger over a cheese course or some of the excellent desserts. **Features:** full bar, Sunday brunch, happy hour. **Reservations:** suggested. Semiformal attire. **Address:** 26 Ridge Rd 07760 **Location:** Garden State Pkwy exit 109, 7.5 mi e on CR 520 to Two Rivers Ave, then 0.3 mi n; jct SR 34 (Ridge Rd) and Two Rivers Ave. **Parking:** valet only.   L   D

SALT CREEK GRILLE   732/933-9272

▼▼▼ American. Casual Dining. $15-$39 **AAA Inspector Notes:** An enchanting outdoor fireplace and comfortable bench seating make any table wait easy to bear at this popular, contemporary grill specializing in mesquite-grilled steak and seafood. Gazing out the dining room's big picture windows, guests take in a wonderful view of the Navesink River. **Features:** full bar, Sunday brunch. **Address:** 4 Bingham Ave 07760 **Location:** Garden State Pkwy exit 109, 5.2 mi e on River Rd, W Front St to Bingham Ave, then just n to Oceanic Bridge.   D   CALL 🔍M

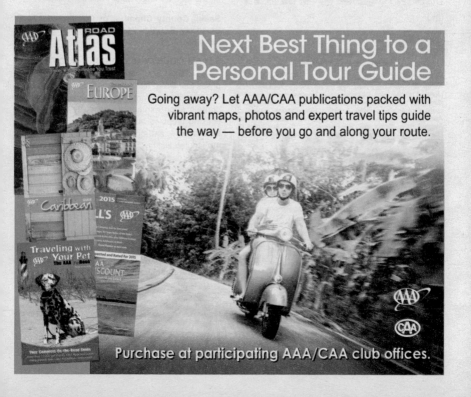

Next Best Thing to a Personal Tour Guide

Going away? Let AAA/CAA publications packed with vibrant maps, photos and expert travel tips guide the way — before you go and along your route.

Purchase at participating AAA/CAA club offices.

RUNNEMEDE pop. 8,468

LA QUINTA INN & SUITES RUNNEMEDE (856)312-8521

Hotel
$89-$239

Address: 109 E 9th Ave 08078 **Location:** New Jersey Tpke exit 3, 0.3 mi se, then just e; I-295 exit 28, 1.2 mi se. **Facility:** 146 units. 7 stories, interior corridors. **Pool(s):** outdoor. **Activities:** game room, exercise room. **Guest Services:** coin laundry. **Featured Amenity:** breakfast buffet.

RUTHERFORD pop. 18,061
• Hotels & Restaurants map & index p. 162

EXTENDED STAY AMERICA-MEADOWLANDS-RUTHERFORD
201/635-0266 69

Extended Stay Hotel. Rates not provided. **Address:** 750 Edwin L Ward Sr Memorial Hwy 07070 **Location:** I-95 exit 16W, 1.5 mi w on SR 3 to SR 17 N service road exit, then 0.5 mi e. **Facility:** 127 efficiencies. 5 stories, interior corridors. **Guest Services:** coin laundry.

RENAISSANCE MEADOWLANDS HOTEL (201)231-3100 70

Hotel $202-$332 **Address:** 801 Rutherford Ave 07070 **Location:** New Jersey Tpke exit 16W, SR 3 W to SR 5. **Facility:** 167 units. 9 stories, interior corridors. **Amenities:** safes. **Pool(s):** heated indoor. **Activities:** hot tub, exercise room. **Guest Services:** valet and coin laundry, area transportation.

AAA Benefit:
Members save 5% or more!

WHERE TO EAT

CAFE MATISSE 201/935-2995 59

New Small Plates. Fine Dining. $60-$95 **AAA Inspector Notes:** A prix fixe menu features creative American cuisine, served in a renovated brick firehouse. An interesting menu of multiple grazing courses, or smaller portions, is offered. **Reservations:** suggested. **Address:** 167 Park Ave 07070 **Location:** SR 3 W exit Ridge Rd/Park Ave, 0.8 mi n; eastbound to exit Riverside Ave/Park Ave, just e on Riverside Ave to Park Ave, then 0.8 mi n. **Parking:** street only.

D

SADDLE RIVER pop. 3,152

SADDLE RIVER INN 201/825-4016

New American. Fine Dining. $34-$48 **AAA Inspector Notes:** Set well off the road down a small embankment, this converted old barn is a long-lived local favorite with plenty of charm. The sophisticated menu incorporates many seasonal items, local seafood and meats done in a modern style with some French accents. The intimate dining room with subdued lighting sets an upscale yet relaxed tone. It is bring-your-own-bottle here so do not forget to pick up that special bottle of wine. **Reservations:** required. **Address:** 2 Barnstable Ct 07458 **Location:** SR 17 exit Saddle River/Woodcliff Lake, just w. D CALL

SALEM (F-1) pop. 5,146, elev. 14'

Settled in 1675 by Quakers, Salem is one of the oldest English settlements on the Delaware River. Its early importance as a port made it a prize during the Revolutionary War, when the city was occupied by the British. After the war Camden surpassed

Salem as a shipping center, and attention turned to agriculture.

The restored 1721 Alexander Grant House, 4 miles south of town at 79-83 Market St., displays objects from the Colonial and Federal periods. Hancock House State Historic Site was the scene of a British-led massacre during the Revolutionary War. In retaliation against the Quaker community for supplying cattle to Gen. George Washington's starving troops at Valley Forge, 300 men under Maj. John Simcoe surprised and killed some 30 local militiamen asleep in the house; among the dead was homeowner Judge William Hancock.

Built in 1734, the Hancock House is an excellent example of the English Quaker style of dwelling once prominent in the Lower Delaware Valley, which incorporated a distinctive feature of zigzagging lines of bricks at each end. The house is located at 3 Front St. in the nearby town of Hancocks Bridge, south of Salem via SR 49 to CR 658. It is open Wed.-Sat. 10-noon and 1-4, Sun. 1-4; phone (856) 935-4373.

One survivor of this bygone era is an oak tree estimated to be more than 5 centuries old. It stands at the entrance to the Friends Burial Ground, 112 W. Broadway. Beneath its branches early settler John Fenwick bargained with the Lenni Lenape Indians for the land on which Salem was established.

Salem County Chamber of Commerce 174 E. Broadway, P.O. Box 71, Salem, NJ 08079. **Phone:** (856) 351-2245.

SALEM COUNTY HISTORICAL SOCIETY is at 79-83 Market St. Founded in 1884, the site comprises four linked historic homes, one of which is the 1721 Alexander Grant Mansion House. Three rooms contain such exhibits as an early 18th-century cooking fireplace and kitchen utensils as well as local artwork and pottery. Other highlights include the reputed first law office in the U.S., a log cabin, a stone barn, and a genealogical and local history library. Changing exhibits also are presented.

Time: Allow 30 minutes minimum. **Hours:** Tues.-Sat. noon-4. Closed major holidays. **Cost:** Museum $5. Library research fee $5. **Phone:** (856) 935-5004. GT

SCOTCH PLAINS pop. 23,510
• Hotels & Restaurants map & index p. 152

CHARLIE BROWN'S STEAKHOUSE 908/232-3443

Steak. Casual Dining. $9-$30 **AAA Inspector Notes:** This budget-friendly steakhouse, famous for its prime rib, offers top quality fare without hurting your pocketbook. The young ones will not be disappointed with the kids' menu, and just might even try something green from the salad bar. Adults will love the quality steaks, chicken and rib dishes. The express lunches are great for those saddled with time constraints. **Features:** full bar, happy hour. **Address:** 2376 North Ave 07076 **Location:** Garden State Pkwy exit 137, 5 mi w on SR 28. L D

(See map & index p. 152.)

STAGE HOUSE RESTAURANT & TAVERN
908/322-4224 (144)

♥♥ ♥♥ American. Casual Dining. $11-$30 **AAA Inspector Notes:** *Historic.* In a small antique village, the quaint 1746 stagecoach stop features white clapboard walls, a brick garden courtyard, wide plank floors, Hitchcock chairs and early American tavern-style décor. The familiar fare is eminently satisfying, from the grilled striped bass to the steamed clams and a knockout burger. **Features:** full bar. **Reservations:** suggested. **Address:** 366 Park Ave 07076 **Location:** Corner of Park Ave and Front St, 0.3 mi e of jct US 22.

L   D   LATE   CALL ⊑ M

SEABROOK (G-2) elev. 100'

After the attack on Pearl Harbor in 1941, more than 100,000 Japanese Americans were sent to internment camps. At the same time, farms such as the one owned by Charles Franklin Seabrook were in need of help, and an arrangement allowed them to leave the camps and work as seasonal farm employees. After the internment camps were shut down many workers chose to stay on at Seabrook Farms, where prefabricated homes and a Buddhist temple were built.

Migrant workers from the South, Estonian immigrants and German prisoners of war also were employed by Seabrook Farms Co., which went on to become one of the world's largest producers of packaged frozen fruits and vegetables.

SEABROOK EDUCATIONAL & CULTURAL CENTER is at 1325 SR 77 in the Upper Deerfield Township Municipal Building. This museum chronicles the settlement of Upper Deerfield and Charles Seabrook's role in the growth of the multicultural community. Exhibits include scale models of Seabrook Village in the 1950s, cultural artifacts, photographs and oral histories. **Time:** Allow 30 minutes minimum. **Hours:** Mon.-Thurs. 9-noon. Closed major holidays. Phone ahead to confirm schedule. **Cost:** Donations. **Phone:** (856) 451-8393.

SEASIDE HEIGHTS (E-5) pop. 2,887, elev. 7'

Established in 1913, Seaside Heights lies between the Atlantic Ocean and Barnegat Bay. Most businesses are open daily Memorial Day weekend through Labor Day. Activities such as fishing and Wednesday night fireworks during the summer occur at the boardwalk; portions of the structure have been rebuilt after 2012's Hurricane Sandy and a September 2013 fire. Phone ahead (800) 365-6933.

CASINO PIER AND JENKINSON'S BREAK-WATER BEACH is at 800 Ocean Terr. The amusement park and water park offer more than 30 rides, including the Super Storm, which spins around and upside down. The Surf Shack is a multilevel walkthrough fun house geared toward families. The Wave Swinger offers views of the Atlantic Ocean from swings suspended from a carousel. Other attractions include the Sky Ride, a chairlift that takes you high above the beach and boardwalk; and the

Skyscraper for adventure seekers. Water park slides include The Nor'Easter, a speed slide with a big drop; Minuteman Express, a two-person tube slide; and Patriot's Plunge, a six-lane racing slide.

Hours: Breakwater Beach open daily 9-7, late June-Labor Day. Casino Pier open daily at noon, June 1-Labor Day; Sat.-Sun, Apr.-May (closing times vary and opening hours may be expanded). Phone ahead to confirm schedule.

Cost: All-day water park admission $31.95; $25.95 (under 48 inches tall); $15.95 (ages 65+). Twilight admission after 3 p.m. $23.95; $19.95 (under 48 inches tall); $15.95 (ages 65+). Amusement park rides are priced individually and require three to eight tickets per ride; ticket books can be purchased. Combination ticket for all water park and amusement rides $49.95; $44.95 (under 48 inches tall); $31.95 (ages 65+). Prices may vary; phone ahead to confirm. **Phone:** (732) 793-6488.

SEASIDE PARK (E-5) pop. 1,579, elev. 6'

Seaside Park is a shore community of beaches on the Barnegat Peninsula. South of town on SR 35 is Island Beach State Park, which protects 10 miles of pristine coastal dunes and is a great place for hiking, swimming, bicycling and fishing. Home to the state's largest osprey colony, the park offers glimpses of peregrine falcons, wading birds, waterfowl and migrating songbirds *(see Recreation Areas Chart).*

SECAUCUS pop. 16,264
• Restaurants p. 193
• Hotels & Restaurants map & index p. 162

COURTYARD BY MARRIOTT SECAUCUS MEADOWLANDS
(201)617-8888 (75)

♥♥ ♥♥ Hotel $186-$305

COURTYARD Marriott

AAA Benefit: Members save 5% or more!

Address: 455 Harmon Meadow Blvd 07094 **Location:** New Jersey Tpke eastern spur exit 16E northbound; exit 17 southbound, just e on SR 3. **Facility:** 168 units. 7 stories, interior corridors. **Activities:** exercise room. **Guest Services:** valet and coin laundry, area transportation.

SAVE 🍴 CALL ⊑ M 📶 ✕ 🛗
🖥 / SOME UNITS 🖨

EMBASSY SUITES-SECAUCUS-MEADOWLANDS
(201)864-7300 (77)

♥♥ ♥♥ Hotel $169-$269 **Address:** 455 Plaza Dr 07094 **Location:** New Jersey Tpke eastern spur exit 16E northbound; exit 17 southbound, just e on SR 3 to Harmon Meadow Blvd. **Facility:** 261 units. 9 stories, interior corridors. **Terms:** 1-7 night minimum stay, cancellation fee imposed. **Amenities:** video games, safes. **Pool(s):** heated indoor. **Activities:** hot tub, exercise room. **Guest Services:** valet and coin laundry, area transportation.

AAA Benefit: Members save 5% or more!

🍴 🧖 🍸 🏊 BIZ 📞 🛗 🖨 🖥

▼ See AAA listing this page ▼

HYATT PLACE Secaucus/Meadowlands

Located just 3 miles outside New York City, the HYATT PLACE Secaucus/Meadowlands hotel is centrally located near top attractions and public transportation.

- Complimentary hotel-wide Wi-Fi Internet access
- Gallery Menu, Fresh 24/7
- Complimentary a.m. Kitchen Skillet™ served daily, with hot breakfast items, fresh fruit, oatmeal and plenty more to choose from.

HYATT PLACE®
secaucus meadowlands

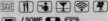

HILTON GARDEN INN SECAUCUS/MEADOWLANDS
201/864-1400 **80**

Hotel. Rates not provided.
Address: 875 Rt 3 E Service Rd 07094
Location: New Jersey Tpke exit 16E northbound; exit 17 southbound, follow signs to SR 3/Secaucus, then just e at light. **Facility:** 124 units. 5 stories, interior corridors. **Pool(s):** heated indoor. **Activities:** hot tub, exercise room. **Guest Services:** valet and coin laundry.

AAA Benefit:
Members save 5% or more!

HOLIDAY INN SECAUCUS MEADOWLANDS
201/348-2000 **78**

Hotel
Rates not provided

Address: 300 Plaza Dr 07094 **Location:** New Jersey Tpke exits 16E, 17 or 16W via SR 3 to Harmon Meadow Blvd. **Facility:** 161 units. 8 stories, interior corridors. **Parking:** on-site and valet. **Activities:** exercise room. **Guest Services:** valet and coin laundry, area transportation.

HYATT PLACE SECAUCUS/MEADOWLANDS
(201)422-9480 **79**

Hotel
$109-$349

HYATT PLACE®
AAA Benefit: Members save 10%!

Address: 575 Park Plaza Dr 07094 **Location:** New Jersey Tpke exits 16E, 17 or 16W via SR 3 to Harmon Meadow Blvd, then just w. **Facility:** 159 units. 9 stories, interior corridors. **Terms:** cancellation fee imposed. **Amenities:** safes. **Activities:** exercise room. **Guest Services:** valet laundry, area transportation. **Featured Amenity:** breakfast buffet.

(See ad this page.)

LA QUINTA INN & SUITES SECAUCUS MEADOWLANDS
(201)863-8700 **74**

Hotel $125-$434 **Address:** 350 Lighting Way 07094 **Location:** Between eastern and western spurs of New Jersey Tpke exits 16E, 17 or 16W via SR 3 W and Harmon Meadow Blvd; in Mill Creek Mall. **Facility:** 151 units. 9 stories, interior corridors. **Pool(s):** heated indoor. **Activities:** exercise room. **Guest Services:** valet and coin laundry, area transportation.

MEADOWLANDS PLAZA HOTEL　(201)272-1000 **73**

Hotel
$114-$169

Address: 40 Wood Ave 07094 **Location:** New Jersey Tpke exit 16W to SR 3 E exit Meadowlands Pkwy. **Facility:** 176 units. 9 stories, interior corridors. **Terms:** cancellation fee imposed. **Activities:** game room, exercise room. **Guest Services:** valet laundry, area transportation. **Featured Amenity:** breakfast buffet.

(See map & index p. 162.)

MEADOWLANDS RIVER INN   (201)867-4400 **76**

▼▼ **Hotel** $109-$359 **Address:** 250 Harmon Meadow Blvd 07094 **Location:** New Jersey Tpke eastern spur exit 16E northbound; exit 17 southbound, just e on SR 3. Located in a light-commercial area. **Facility:** 149 units. 7 stories, interior corridors. **Terms:** cancellation fee imposed. **Amenities:** *Some:* safes. **Activities:** exercise room. **Guest Services:** valet and coin laundry.

[icons]

WHERE TO EAT

BARELI'S   201/865-0473 **73**

▼▼▼ Italian. Casual Dining. $17-$50 **AAA Inspector Notes:** The fleet of high-end cars parked out front hints to the clientele within: movers, shakers and power brokers, all hungry for a taste of classic Italian fare. The restaurant exudes a confidence that appeals to the glitterati, from the warm greeting of the hosts to the unobtrusive yet attentive service of the staff. The kitchen deftly prepares delectable pasta, wonderful fish dishes and succulent veal preparations, ensuring a full parking lot, no matter the time of day. **Features:** full bar, Sunday brunch. **Reservations:** suggested. **Address:** 219 Rt 3 E 07094 **Location:** New Jersey Tpke exits 16E, 17 or 16W to SR 3 E, on service road. **Parking:** valet only. [L] [D] CALL [M]

SHORT HILLS pop. 13,165
• Hotels & Restaurants map & index p. 152

HILTON SHORT HILLS   (973)379-0100 **71**

▼▼▼▼ ▼▼▼▼
Hotel
$170-$341

(H) Hilton **HOTELS & RESORTS**

AAA Benefit: Members save 5% or more!

Address: 41 John F Kennedy Pkwy 07078 **Location:** I-78 exit 48 (SR 24), 2.5 mi nw. **Facility:** There are many elegant and luxurious enhancements to this hotel, especially in the public areas where you will find lots of marble, rich woods and extra amenities. 304 units. 10 stories, interior corridors. **Parking:** on-site and valet. **Terms:** 1-7 night minimum stay, cancellation fee imposed. **Amenities:** safes. **Dining:** 2 restaurants. **Pool(s):** heated outdoor, heated indoor. **Activities:** sauna, hot tub, tennis, exercise room, spa. **Guest Services:** valet laundry, rental car service, area transportation.

[icons]

WHERE TO EAT

JOE'S AMERICAN BAR & GRILL   973/379-4444

▼▼ American. Casual Dining. $9-$36 **AAA Inspector Notes:** If it's Americana you want, you'll get all that and more at Joe's, where the bill of fare includes all-American favorites like hearty burgers, fresh-from-the-oven chicken pot pies, Maryland lump crab cakes, and Joe's classic meatloaf. Pizzas, pastas, steaks and salads round out the extensive menu, giving diners the freedom to choose from a vast selection of offerings. There's nothing more American than that, except, of course, for apple pie, so save some room. **Features:** full bar, Sunday brunch. **Address:** 1200 Morris Tpke 07078 **Location:** Jct SR 24 and Morris Tpke; in Mall at Short Hills. [L] [D] CALL [M]

LEGAL SEA FOODS   973/467-0089 **91**

▼▼▼ Seafood. Casual Dining. $12-$45 **AAA Inspector Notes:** Legal prides itself on a reputation for freshness and consistency. More than 40 varieties of seafood can be grilled, broiled, fried or prepared Cajun style. Try the clam chowder that has been served at every presidential inauguration since 1981. The nautically inspired dining room is upscale and attractive with its rich cherry wood paneling and intricately detailed model ships. **Features:** full bar. **Reservations:** suggested. **Address:** 1200 Morris Tpke 07078 **Location:** Jct SR 24 and Morris Tpke; in Mall at Short Hills.

[L] [D] CALL [M]

PAPA RAZZI   973/467-5544

▼▼ ▼▼ Italian. Casual Dining. $11-$33 **AAA Inspector Notes:** Italy has changed and so has authentic Italian food. It's lighter, fresher, more exciting Italian, and it's just what you'll find amid the elegant yet comfortable atmosphere that is Papa Razzi. If the steamy bowls of pasta don't tempt you, one of the aromatic pizzas or a warm panini sandwich definitely will. In addition there is a fine wine list, an array of salads, chicken, and fish to choose from. **Features:** full bar, Sunday brunch. **Address:** 1200 Morris Tpke 07078 **Location:** Jct SR 24 and Morris Tpke; in Mall at Short Hills.

[L] [D] CALL [M]

SHREWSBURY pop. 3,809

AMERICANA DINER   732/542-1658

▼▼ ▼▼ American. Casual Dining. $5-$34 **AAA Inspector Notes:** Glitzy neon and shiny metal are the hallmarks of this classic Jersey diner. Split pea soup and spinach mushroom cheddar quiche are good choices on a large menu of tried-and-true comfort food classics. Reasonable prices and big portions make this place popular with families. **Address:** 1160 Rt 35 S 07702 **Location:** Just n of CR 537. [B] [L] [D] [LATE] CALL [M]

SILVERTON

CHARLIE BROWN'S STEAKHOUSE   732/279-0216

▼▼ ▼▼ Steak. Casual Dining. $9-$30 **AAA Inspector Notes:** This budget-friendly steakhouse, famous for its prime rib, offers top quality fare without hurting your pocketbook. The young ones will not be disappointed with the kids' menu, and just might even try something green from the salad bar. Adults will love the quality steaks, chicken and rib dishes. The express lunches are great for those saddled with time constraints. **Features:** full bar. **Address:** 11 Kettle Creek Rd 08753 **Location:** Off CR 549 (Hooper Ave). [L] [D] [icon]

SMITHVILLE pop. 7,242
• Part of Atlantic City area — see map p. 73

COLONIAL INN AT HISTORIC SMITHVILLE   609/748-8999

▼▼▼ ▼▼▼ Bed & Breakfast. Rates not provided. **Address:** 615 E Moss Mill Rd 08205 **Location:** Garden State Pkwy exit 48, 4 mi s on US 9, then just w. **Facility:** Set amid the quaint shops of historic Smithville, this charming Colonial inn offers modern and comfortable lodgings decorated with a Colonial/Americana flourish. 27 units. 2 stories (no elevator); interior/exterior corridors. **Terms:** age restrictions may apply.

[icons] / SOME UNITS [icons]

WHERE TO EAT

THE HISTORIC SMITHVILLE INN   609/652-7777

▼▼▼▼ ▼▼▼▼
Regional American Casual Dining
$10-$38

AAA Inspector Notes: *Historic.* This Colonial inn dates to 1787 when it was constructed on a popular carriage route where it operated until being abandoned in 1864. In 1952, it was reborn and has been thriving ever since. Expect a hearty early American inspired bill of fare such as prime rib, stuffed pork chops and chicken pot pie all served with the inn's glazed raisin bread. **Features:** full bar, Sunday brunch, happy hour. **Reservations:** suggested. **Address:** 1 N New York Rd 08205 **Location:** Jct US 9 and Moss Mill Rd. **Parking:** street only. [L] [D]

SOMERSET (C-3) pop. 22,083, elev. 92'
• Hotels p. 194 • Restaurants p. 195
• Hotels & Restaurants map & index p. 152

COLONIAL PARK is 2.7 mi. w. on Amwell Rd. (CR 514), then .5 mi. n. to 150 Mettlers Rd. This 685-acre facility features an arboretum displaying ornamental trees and shrubs from around the world; a

(See map & index p. 152.)

rose garden decorated with arches, gazebos and trellises; a perennial garden; and a fragrance and sensory garden.

Paddleboats can be rented for use on one of the park's three ponds; fishing is permitted on all three. There are tennis courts, bocce courts, a softball field, grills and picnic tables, a leash-free dog park, a 1.4-mile fitness track, an ADA-accessible playground, and 18-hole and miniature golf courses. A nature trail can be hiked in summer and is used for cross-country skiing and ice skating in winter.

Hours: Arboretum and perennial garden daily dawn-dusk. Fragrance, rose garden and sensory garden daily 8 a.m.-dusk. Maintenance may delay rose garden opening on Wed. **Cost:** Arboretum and perennial garden free. Rose garden and fragrance and sensory garden by donation. **Phone:** (732) 873-2459 or (732) 873-2695.

CANDLEWOOD SUITES   732/748-1400 **149**

▼▼ **Extended Stay Hotel.** Rates not provided. **Address:** 41 Worlds Fair Dr 08873 **Location:** I-287 exit 10 (CR 527), left on ramp (CR 527 S/Easton Ave), 0.3 mi, then 0.5 mi w. **Facility:** 110 efficiencies. 3 stories, interior corridors. **Activities:** exercise room. **Guest Services:** complimentary and valet laundry.

COMFORT INN & SUITES SOMERSET   (732)563-1600 **152**

▼▼▼ Hotel $79-$139 **Address:** 255 Davidson Ave 08873 **Location:** I-287 exit 10 (CR 527), just n toward Bound Brook, then 0.7 mi sw. **Facility:** 109 units. 5 stories, interior corridors. **Pool(s):** heated outdoor. **Activities:** hot tub, exercise room. **Guest Services:** valet laundry, area transportation.

COURTYARD BY MARRIOTT SOMERSET
                                  (732)271-4555 **151**

▼▼▼ Hotel $230-$378 **Address:** 250 Davidson Ave 08873 **Location:** I-287 exit 10 (CR 527), just n toward Bound Brook to Davidson Ave, then 0.6 mi sw. **Facility:** 162 units. 5 stories, interior corridors. **Pool(s):** heated indoor. **Activities:** exercise room. **Guest Services:** valet and coin laundry, boarding pass kiosk, area transportation.

AAA Benefit: Members save 5% or more!

DOUBLETREE BY HILTON HOTEL & EXECUTIVE MEETING CENTER SOMERSET   (732)469-2600 **148**

Hotel $99-$209

AAA Benefit: Members save 5% or more!

Address: 200 Atrium Dr 08873 **Location:** I-287 exit 10 (CR 527), just n toward Bound Brook to Davidson Ave, then 0.5 mi sw; in Atrium Corp Park. **Facility:** 364 units. 6 stories, interior corridors. **Terms:** 1-7 night minimum stay, cancellation fee imposed. **Dining:** 2 restaurants. **Pool(s):** heated outdoor, heated indoor. **Activities:** hot tub, tennis, exercise room. **Guest Services:** valet and coin laundry, rental car service, area transportation.

FAIRFIELD INN & SUITES BY MARRIOTT SOMERSET
                                  (732)627-8483 **154**

▼▼▼ Hotel $146-$240 **Address:** 315 Davidson Ave 08873 **Location:** I-287 exit 10 (CR 527), just n toward Bound Brook to Davidson Ave, then 1 mi sw. **Facility:** 100 units. 4 stories, interior corridors. **Amenities:** safes. **Activities:** exercise room. **Guest Services:** valet and coin laundry, area transportation.

AAA Benefit: Members save 5% or more!

HOLIDAY INN-SOMERSET   732/356-1700 **147**

▼▼▼ Hotel Rates not provided

Address: 195 Davidson Ave 08873 **Location:** I-287 exit 10 (CR 527), just n toward Bound Brook, then 0.5 mi sw. **Facility:** 284 units. 6 stories, interior corridors. **Pool(s):** outdoor. **Activities:** exercise room. **Guest Services:** valet and coin laundry, rental car service, area transportation.

HOMEWOOD SUITES BY HILTON-SOMERSET
                                  (732)868-9155 **155**

▼▼▼ **Extended Stay Hotel** $109-$179 **Address:** 101 Pierce St 08873 **Location:** I-287 exit 10 (CR 527), left on ramp (CR 527 S/Easton Ave), 0.3 mi, 0.7 mi w on Worlds Fair Dr, then just s. **Facility:** 123 efficiencies, some two bedrooms. 4 stories, interior corridors. **Terms:** 1-7 night minimum stay, cancellation fee imposed. **Pool(s):** heated indoor. **Activities:** hot tub, exercise room. **Guest Services:** valet and coin laundry.

AAA Benefit: Members save 5% or more!

LA QUINTA INN & SUITES SOMERSET   (732)560-9880 **146**

▼▼▼ Hotel $74-$224 **Address:** 60 Cottontail Ln 08873 **Location:** I-287 exit 12, just sw via Weston Canal Rd. **Facility:** 126 units. 5 stories, interior corridors. **Pool(s):** heated indoor. **Activities:** sauna, exercise room. **Guest Services:** valet and coin laundry.

RESIDENCE INN BY MARRIOTT-SOMERSET
                                  (732)627-0881 **153**

▼▼▼ Extended Stay Hotel $167-$275

Residence Inn Marriott

AAA Benefit: Members save 5% or more!

Address: 37 Worlds Fair Dr 08873 **Location:** I-287 exit 10 (CR 527), 0.3 mi left on ramp (CR 527 S/Easton Ave), then 0.5 mi w. **Facility:** 108 units, some two bedrooms, efficiencies and kitchens. 4 stories, interior corridors. **Pool(s):** heated indoor. **Activities:** hot tub, exercise room. **Guest Services:** valet and coin laundry. **Featured Amenity:** breakfast buffet.

Gear up with head-to-toe savings

at AAA.com/searchfordiscounts

(See map & index p. 152.)

SONESTA ES SUITES SOMERSET (732)356-8000

WWW WWW
Extended Stay Hotel
$125-$225

Address: 260 Davidson Ave 08873 **Location:** I-287 exit 10 (CR 527), just n toward Bound Brook to Davidson Ave, then 0.8 mi sw. **Facility:** 140 kitchen units, some two bedrooms. 2 stories (no elevator), exterior corridors. **Terms:** 3 day cancellation notice. **Amenities:** Some: safes. **Pool(s):** heated outdoor. **Activities:** hot tub, exercise room. **Guest Services:** valet and coin laundry.

SAVE ⋔ 🚣 BIZ HS 🛜 📶
🖨 💻 / SOME UNITS 🅂

WHERE TO EAT

POOJA 732/220-0051 (171)
WWW WWW Indian. Casual Dining. $12-$18 **AAA Inspector Notes:** At the casual mom-and-pop restaurant, the menu lists curries, kormas, tandoori, dhosa and biryanis. There's nothing to surprise the palate, but familiar tastes are complemented by enjoyable ethnic music. **Features:** Sunday brunch. **Address:** 1075 Easton Ave 08873 **Location:** I-287 exit 10 (CR 527), 1.8 mi se. L D

STAGE HOUSE TAVERN 732/873-3990
WWW WWW American. Casual Dining. $10-$30 **AAA Inspector Notes:** This is an easy combination of casual setting and tasty food. The menu covers a lot of ground with a raw bar, salads, hearty sandwiches, pastas and entrées including some wood-fired grilled steaks. There is a large patio for outdoor dining in season. **Features:** full bar, early bird specials, Sunday brunch, happy hour. **Address:** 1719 Amwell Rd 08873 **Location:** 8 mi e of Cedar Grove Ln.
L D CALL 🅼

SOMERS POINT (G-3) pop. 10,795, elev. 27'
• Part of Atlantic City area — see map p. 73

ATLANTIC COUNTY HISTORICAL SOCIETY is at 907 Shore Rd. (CR 585). A 20,000-item collection includes Native American stone implements, weapons, furniture and turn-of-the-20th-century clothing. Shipbuilding, one of Atlantic County's major 19th-century industries, is represented by boat models, paintings and tools. The historical society's library is open to the public for genealogical research and local history.

Time: Allow 30 minutes minimum. **Hours:** Guided 30-minute museum tours are offered Wed.-Sat. 10-3:30. Last tour begins 30 minutes before closing. Closed major holidays. **Cost:** Free. Fee for library research $5. **Phone:** (609) 927-5218.

SOMERS MANSION is at 1000 Shore Rd. (CR 585). Built around 1725 by Richard Somers, son of an early area settler, the three-story brick dwelling is reputed to be the oldest house in Atlantic County and was continuously inhabited by the Somers family until 1937. Displays include 18th-century furnishings. An interesting architectural detail is the interior woodwork decorated with heart-shaped perforations.

Time: Allow 30 minutes minimum. **Hours:** Sat.-Sun. 9-3:30. Operating schedule may be extended; phone to confirm opening days. Closed major holidays. **Cost:** Free. **Phone:** (609) 927-2212.

PIER 4 HOTEL ON THE BAY 609/927-9141
WWW WWW Hotel $65-$299 **Address:** 6 Broadway & The Bay 08244 **Location:** Waterfront. Garden State Pkwy exit 30 southbound; exit 29 northbound, 1.5 mi e; jct SR 52 and CR 559, at circle. **Facility:** 69 units. 4 stories, interior corridors. **Terms:** check-in 4 pm, 2 night minimum stay - seasonal and/or weekends. **Dining:** Crab Trap Restaurant, see separate listing. **Pool(s):** heated outdoor. **Guest Services:** coin laundry.

⋔ 🍴 🚣 🛜 ✕ 📶 🖨 🛒 💻

RESIDENCE INN BY MARRIOTT ATLANTIC CITY SOMERS POINT (609)927-6400

WWW WWW Extended Stay Hotel $139-$344 **Address:** 900 Mays Landing Rd 08244 **Location:** Garden State Pkwy exit 30 southbound; exit 29 northbound, 1 mi e. **Facility:** 120 kitchen units, some

AAA Benefit: Members save 5% or more!

two bedrooms. 2 stories (no elevator), exterior corridors. **Terms:** check-in 4 pm. **Pool(s):** heated outdoor. **Activities:** limited exercise equipment. **Guest Services:** valet and coin laundry.
⋔ 🚣 🛜 ✕ 📶 🖨 💻 / SOME UNITS 🅂

WHERE TO EAT

CRAB TRAP RESTAURANT 609/927-7377
WWW WWW Seafood. Casual Dining. $7-$37 **AAA Inspector Notes:** Crab is a favorite at this nautically-themed restaurant, which overlooks Great Egg Harbor Bay. In addition to such dishes as crab imperial and deviled crab, the menu offers other seafood, live Maine lobsters and some steaks. The friendly and efficient staff are used to the crowds and still offer a smile and a smooth meal. **Features:** full bar, early bird specials, happy hour. **Address:** 2 Broadway 08244 **Location:** Garden State Pkwy exit 30 southbound; exit 29 northbound, 1.5 mi e; jct SR 52 and CR 559, at circle; in Pier 4 Hotel On the Bay. L D CALL 🅼

SOMERVILLE (C-3) pop. 12,098, elev. 54'
• Restaurants p. 196
• Hotels & Restaurants map & index p. 152

The Somerville area was first settled by Native Americans who eventually negotiated with European settlers for a peaceful withdrawal. Soldiers in the Continental Army were frequent visitors to the region then known as Raritan while Gen. George Washington was a guest at the Wallace House. Somerville began to take shape with the construction of a courthouse in 1787.

A great way to learn about local history is to participate in 🐾 Somerset County's Weekend Journey Through the Past, held the second weekend in October. More than 20 historic sites, many with significant Revolutionary War histories, feature special exhibits, programs and tours.

Somerset County Business Partnership: 360 Grove St., Bridgewater, NJ 08807. **Phone:** (908) 218-4300.

OLD DUTCH PARSONAGE STATE HISTORIC SITE is at 71 Somerset St. Built in 1751, the parsonage was the 1756-81 home of the Rev. Mr. Jacob Hardenbergh, founder of Queens College in New Brunswick. The college later became Rutgers University. The site is furnished as it might have appeared in 1780. **Hours:** Wed.-Sat. 10-noon and 1-4, Sun. 1-4. Closed major holidays and Wed. after Mon. or Tues. holidays. Phone ahead to confirm schedule. **Cost:** Donations. **Phone:** (908) 725-1015.

(See map & index p. 152.)

WALLACE HOUSE STATE HISTORIC SITE is at 71 Somerset St. The building, furnished in period, was used as a headquarters by Gen. George Washington during the winter of 1778-79 while his Continental Army stayed at the Middlebrook encampment. **Hours:** Wed.-Sat. 10-noon and 1-4, Sun. 1-4. Closed major holidays and Wed. after Mon. or Tues. holidays. Phone ahead to confirm schedule. **Cost:** Donations. **Phone:** (908) 725-1015.

ORIGIN   908/685-1344 (157)

▼▼▼ Thai. Casual Dining. $10-$31 **AAA Inspector Notes:** Diners hungry for flavor-filled dishes—be they French or Thai—might start with French onion or tom kha kai soup, escargot or satay, then move on to such savory entrées as tamarind duck, wild boar with Thai basil, steak au poivre, duck a l'orange and lamb. Efficient service, pretty presentations of tasty food and casual décor, which shows a hint of sophistication and energy, add up to full tables. **Features:** patio dining. **Reservations:** suggested. **Address:** 25 Division St 08876 **Location:** Just s of W Main St. **Parking:** street only.

L   D

SOUTH PLAINFIELD pop. 23,385
• Hotels & Restaurants map & index p. 152

BEST WESTERN THE GARDEN EXECUTIVE HOTEL
(908)561-4488 (120)

Hotel
$94-$124

AAA Benefit:
Members save up to 20%!

Address: 101 New World Way 07080 **Location:** I-287 exit 5, just s. **Facility:** 100 units. 2 stories (no elevator), interior corridors. **Activities:** exercise room. **Guest Services:** valet and coin laundry.

SAVE ⏹ ⓨ CALL ♿M 📶 🖨
🍽 / SOME UNITS 🖥

HAMPTON INN SOUTH PLAINFIELD/PISCATAWAY
(908)561-2600 (119)

▼▼▼ Hotel $144-$169 **Address:** 205 New World Way 07080 **Location:** I-287 exit 5, just s. **Facility:** 107 units. 5 stories, interior corridors. **Terms:** 1-7 night minimum stay, cancellation fee imposed. **Pool(s):** heated indoor. **Activities:** hot tub, exercise room. **Guest Services:** valet and coin laundry.

AAA Benefit:
Members save 5% or more!

⏹➕ CALL ♿M ⚓ BIZ HS 📶 🖥 / SOME UNITS 🖨

HOLIDAY INN SOUTH PLAINFIELD/PISCATAWAY
908/753-5500 (121)

▼▼▼ Hotel. Rates not provided. **Address:** 4701 Stelton Rd 07080 **Location:** I-287 exit 5, just s. Adjacent to Middlesex Mall. **Facility:** 181 units. 4 stories, interior corridors. **Pool(s):** heated indoor. **Activities:** sauna, exercise room. **Guest Services:** valet and coin laundry.

⏹ 🐕 ⓨ CALL ♿M ⚓ BIZ 📶 📹 🖨 🖥
🖥

Remember, car seats,
booster seats and seat
belts save lives

SPARTA

KROGH'S RESTAURANT & BREW PUB   973/729-8428

▼▼ American. Casual Dining. $7-$25 **AAA Inspector Notes:** Historic. Along the boardwalk across from Lake Mohawk, this charming place brings friends together for casual interaction and a glass of local brew. The food is uncomplicated but good, with offerings such as pizza and grilled chicken sandwiches. **Features:** full bar, patio dining, happy hour. **Reservations:** suggested. **Address:** 23 White Deer Plaza 07871 **Location:** Jct Winona Pkwy; center.

L   D

SPRING LAKE pop. 2,993

BREAKERS HOTEL ON THE OCEAN   732/449-7700

▼▼▼ Hotel $100-$435 **Address:** 1507 Ocean Ave 07762 **Location:** Across from beach. **Facility:** 75 units. 4 stories, interior corridors. **Parking:** street only. **Terms:** 2-3 night minimum stay - seasonal and/or weekends, 14 day cancellation notice-fee imposed. **Amenities:** safes. **Dining:** entertainment. **Pool(s):** heated outdoor. **Activities:** beach access, bicycles.

⏹ 🐕 ⓨ ⚓ BIZ HS 📶 ✕ 🖨

THE CHATEAU INN & SUITES   732/974-2000

▼▼▼ Historic Bed & Breakfast $99-$279 **Address:** 500 Warren Ave 07762 **Location:** Jct SR 71 and Warren Ave, 0.5 mi e, just w of Lake Divine Park. **Facility:** This lovely inn, shaded by majestic pines and 100-year-old sycamore trees, exudes both Old World charm and modern sophistication. 36 units, some kitchens. 3 stories (no elevator), interior/exterior corridors. **Terms:** 2-3 night minimum stay - seasonal and/or weekends, 10 day cancellation notice-fee imposed. **Amenities:** safes. **Activities:** bicycles.

HS 📶 ✕ 🖨 / SOME UNITS 🖥 🖥

NORMANDY INN   732/449-7172

▼▼ Classic Historic Bed & Breakfast. Rates not provided. **Address:** 21 Tuttle Ave 07762 **Location:** Between Ocean and 1st aves. **Facility:** A local treasure listed on the National Register of Historic Places, this gorgeous 1888 Victorian with a large wraparound porch is filled with antiques, including some rooms with huge canopy beds. 18 units. 3 stories (no elevator), interior corridors. **Parking:** on-site and street. 📶 ✕ 🅿 / SOME UNITS 🖨

SPRING LAKE INN   732/449-2010

▼▼ Classic Historic Bed & Breakfast. Rates not provided. **Address:** 104 Salem Ave 07762 **Location:** Just w of Ocean Ave. **Facility:** A charming, classic inn at the beach. Individual tables in the dining area allow for privacy at breakfast but a comfortable living room and front porch invites mingling, as well. 16 units. 3 stories (no elevator), interior corridors. **Activities:** beach access.

HS 📶 ✕ 🅿 🖨

SPRING LAKE HEIGHTS pop. 4,713

THE MILL AT SPRING LAKE HEIGHTS   732/449-1800

▼▼▼ American. Casual Dining. $10-$38 **AAA Inspector Notes:** Both dining rooms—one casual, one slightly upscale—overlook Old Mill Pond, a scenic lake spot. The menu delivers a large selection of steaks and seafood, particularly fresh fish. The wine selection is excellent. Enjoy live entertainment on weekends during summer. **Features:** full bar, Sunday brunch. **Reservations:** suggested. **Address:** 101 Old Mill Rd 07762 **Location:** Between SR 35 and 71; at Ocean Ave. L   D

ST. STEPHEN'S GREEN PUBLICK HOUSE   732/449-2626

▼▼ Irish. Casual Dining. $10-$29 **AAA Inspector Notes:** This very popular pub charms with warm décor including lots of wood and a stone fireplace. The menu has all of the traditional dishes you would expect as well as fresh shellfish and a good selection of sandwiches and salads. There is live entertainment on most nights, often Irish music. **Features:** full bar, happy hour. **Address:** 2031 SR 71 07762 **Location:** Between Allaire and Wall rds. L   D   CALL ♿M

STANHOPE (B-3) pop. 3,610, elev. 882'

Stanhope dates from Revolutionary War times, when the Sussex Iron Works was a major industry. The nation's first anthracite furnace was built in town around 1821. Hopatcong State Park *(see Recreation Areas Chart)* is on the shore of nearby Lake Hopatcong. Stanhope is at the eastern end of a scenic stretch of I-80 that runs 28 miles to the Delaware Water Gap and continues into Pennsylvania.

WILD WEST CITY is .5 mi. e. of jct. US 206 and CR 607 (Lackawanna Dr.). Visitors to this re-creation of the Old West can board a stagecoach, see Pony Express riders race into town, witness gunslingers in action and view a re-enactment of the gunfight at the O.K. Corral. Other activities include train and pony rides, a petting zoo and gold panning. Live entertainment is presented, and costumed interpreters also give living-history demonstrations.

Time: Allow 3 hours minimum. **Hours:** Daily 10:30-6, mid-June through Labor Day; Sat.-Sun. and holidays 10:30-6, May 1 through mid-June and day after Labor Day-Columbus Day. **Cost:** $16; $14 (ages 2-11); $11 (ages 62+). Miniature golf, stagecoach, pony ride and train ride $3.50 each. Prices may vary; phone ahead. **Phone:** (973) 347-8900. 🍴 🎡

THE WHISTLING SWAN INN   973/347-6369

💎💎💎 **Historic Bed & Breakfast. Rates not provided. Address:** 110 Main St 07874 **Location:** I-80 exit 27B westbound, 1 mi on SR 183 N; exit 25 eastbound, 1.5 mi on SR 183 S. Located in a residential area. **Facility:** A wraparound porch and beautiful guest rooms with Art Deco or Oriental antiques are featured at this 1900s Queen Anne-style home located in a quiet residential area. Many rooms have a fireplace. 9 units. 3 stories (no elevator), interior corridors. **Activities:** bicycles.
🍴 📶 ✕ / SOME UNITS 🐾 ⊟

WHERE TO EAT

BLACK FOREST INN   973/347-3344

💎💎💎 German. Casual Dining. $15-$37 **AAA Inspector Notes:** A delightful Old World charm permeates the cozy, relaxed dining room, which is appointed with Bavarian décor. The menu centers on finely prepared European and German cuisines, including the specialty sauerbraten. Freshly made desserts test the willpower of those watching their weight. **Features:** full bar. **Reservations:** suggested. **Address:** 249 US Rt 206 N 07874 **Location:** I-80 exit 25 to US 206 N, 0.7 mi n. D CALL 📶M

STOCKTON pop. 538

WOOLVERTON INN   609/397-0802

💎💎💎 **Historic Bed & Breakfast** $150-$435 **Address:** 6 Woolverton Rd 08559 **Location:** Jct CR 523 N and SR 29 N, just n to Woolverton Rd, then just w. **Facility:** Attention to detail is evident in the renovation and décor of this 18th-century inn featuring feather beds, large porches, fireplaces, charming nooks and gardens. 13 units, some cottages. 3 stories (no elevator), interior corridors. **Terms:** 2 night minimum stay - weekends, 10 day cancellation notice-fee imposed.
📶 ✕ 🅆 / SOME UNITS 🐾 🐾 ⊟ 🖵

STONE HARBOR (H-3) pop. 866, elev. 10'
• Restaurants p. 198

THE WETLANDS INSTITUTE is 3 mi. e. of Garden State Pkwy. exit 10B on CR 657 to 1075 Stone Harbor Blvd. Dedicated to promoting appreciation, understanding and stewardship of wetlands and coastal ecosystems through programs in research, education and conservation, this facility features aquariums, a live turtle observation station and a horseshoe crab aquaculture display. Visitors can walk along a salt marsh trail and view the marsh from an elevated walkway.

Time: Allow 1 hour minimum. **Hours:** Daily 9:30-4:30 (also Tues.-Thurs. 4:30-8, mid-June through Labor Day), early May to mid-Oct.; Fri.-Sun. 9:30-4:30, rest of year. Closed Dec. 23–Jan 2.; phone for holiday closures rest of year. **Cost:** $8; $6 (ages 2-11). **Phone:** (609) 368-1211.

COLONIAL LODGE   609/368-2202

Motel
Rates not provided

Address: 181 93rd St 08247 **Location:** Garden State Pkwy exit 10B, 3.5 mi e on CR 657, then just n. **Facility:** 17 units, some efficiencies. 2 stories (no elevator), interior corridors.

SAVE 📶 ✕ 🍴 🖵 🖵

DUNES MOTEL   609/368-4121

Motel
Rates not provided

Address: 9801 Second Ave 08247 **Location:** Garden State Pkwy exit 10B, 3.5 mi e on CR 657, then just s. **Facility:** 14 units, some efficiencies. 2 stories (no elevator), exterior corridors.

SAVE CALL 📶M 📶 ✕ ⊟ 🍴
🖵

SEAWARD MOTEL   609/368-5900

Motel
Rates not provided

Address: 9720 Second Ave 08247 **Location:** Garden State Pkwy exit 10B, 3.5 mi e on CR 657, then just s. **Facility:** 20 units, some efficiencies. 3 stories (no elevator), exterior corridors. **Pool(s):** heated outdoor. **Guest Services:** coin laundry.
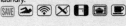
SAVE 🏊 📶 ✕ ⊟ 🍴 🖵

WHERE TO EAT

STONE HARBOR BAR & GRILL   609/368-8800
▼▼ American. Casual Dining. $9-$34 **AAA Inspector Notes:** This casual sports pub offers a familiar menu of finger foods, sandwiches and pizza along with a few entrées. Located right in the center of the charming shopping district. **Features:** full bar, happy hour. **Address:** 261 96th St 08247 **Location:** Between 2nd and 3rd aves. **Parking:** street only. L D

STRATHMERE pop. 158

LA FONTANA DEL MARE   609/263-7700
fyi Not evaluated. The dining room has scenes of Italian villas hanging on the walls. Limited parking is available. **Address:** 1 Commonwealth 08248

SUMMIT pop. 21,457
• Hotels & Restaurants map & index p. 152

THE DEBARY INN   908/277-0005   75
▼▼▼ **Historic Country Inn.** Rates not provided. **Address:** 265 Springfield Ave 07901 **Location:** Just e of downtown. **Facility:** The owners refer to this as an "executive boutique inn." Offering high-quality lodgings in an intimate and relaxed setting, this is a great alternative for both business travelers and tourists alike. 16 units. 3 stories (no elevator), interior corridors. **Activities:** bicycles.

🍴 BIZ 🛜 ✕ 🕿

WHERE TO EAT

ANNA'S RISTORANTE   908/273-4448   103
▼▼ Italian. Casual Dining. $9-$32 **AAA Inspector Notes:** The menu at this restaurant covers many of the familiar Italian dishes and offers something for everyone all served in a casual atmosphere. Here diners can find crisp pizza as well as such entrées as fettuccine primavera and veal saltimbocca. **Address:** 67 Union Pl 07901 **Location:** Center; across from train station. **Parking:** street only.

L D CALL 🖐M

FIN RAWBAR & KITCHEN   908/277-1414   105
▼▼▼ Seafood. Casual Dining. $22-$32 **AAA Inspector Notes:** This place is cozy and somewhat trendy with a great menu of market-fresh seafood that includes a selection of fresh oysters, lobster, crab and such fish as bigeye tuna, Norwegian salmon and Pacific cod. The menu includes options for simple, wood-grilled fish as well as entrées complete with creative sauces and accompaniments, some of which have an Asian flavor. **Reservations:** suggested. **Address:** 37 Maple St 07901 **Location:** Just s of Springfield Ave; center. **Parking:** street only. D

FIORINO RISTORANTE   908/277-1900   104
▼▼▼ Italian. Casual Dining. $14-$36 **AAA Inspector Notes:** This upscale restaurant, in the middle of the charming downtown shopping/dining district, retains a comfortable neighborhood feel. The menu is loaded with options for many Tuscan-inspired dishes and some fresh seasonal items. The lively bar is great for cocktails or for a single diner. The somewhat clubby atmosphere is echoed in the polished wood walls with Italian-themed murals and in the well-seasoned waitstaff who dote on some of the regular customers. **Features:** full bar. **Address:** 38 Maple St 07901 **Location:** Just s of Springfield Ave; center. **Parking:** street only. L D

HUNTLEY TAVERNE   908/273-3166   97
▼▼▼ American. Casual Dining. $11-$34 **AAA Inspector Notes:** The interior here is visually striking with Craftsman-style décor, large wood-burning fireplaces and an inviting bar area. Tables on the porch are especially popular. Dishes are prepared with a strong focus on using locally sourced ingredients whenever possible, so menus vary with the season. Expect to see such items as corn chowder, ahi tuna tartare, hanger steak, seared duck breast and wood-fired pizza. **Features:** full bar, patio dining. **Reservations:** suggested. **Address:** 3 Morris Ave 07901 **Location:** 0.9 mi e on Broad St; center. L D

MONSTER SUSHI   908/598-1100   101
▼▼ Japanese. Casual Dining. $9-$31 **AAA Inspector Notes:** Like the name says, this restaurant serves monster sushi, oversized slices of fish on large pods of rice and a large variety of generously-sized special rolls. In addition there are many choices of teriyaki, tempura, sukiyaki hot pots and other chef specials such as black cod with miso paste, broiled sea bass with soy and marinated and grilled steaks. The bright and friendly atmosphere enhanced by fun monster memorabilia make it a good place for well-behaved children. **Address:** 395 Springfield Ave 07901 **Location:** Corner of Maple St. **Parking:** street only. L D CALL 🖐M

PIZZA VITA   908/277-1400   102
▼▼ Pizza. Casual Dining. $8-$16 **AAA Inspector Notes:** This lively and family-friendly place serves up authentic and tasty Napoletana-style pizza along with fresh salads, panini, pastas and gelato. The wood-burning oven cooks the pies in 90 seconds delivering a softer, lighter crust that is topped with premium imported ingredients. The dining room can get busy but the table service is warm and friendly. **Features:** patio dining. **Address:** 7 Union Place 07901 **Location:** Just w of Summit Ave; across from train station. **Parking:** street only. L D

ROOTS STEAKHOUSE   908/273-0027   99
▼▼ Steak. Fine Dining. $11-$43 **AAA Inspector Notes:** This dark and clubby dining room and lively bar fills up with a sophisticated crowd of city diners. Naturally the steaks are the main attraction here—first rate, aged USDA Prime beef with a good variety of cuts offered. There also is a good selection of chilled shellfish, including a great crab cocktail and live Maine lobster. **Features:** full bar. **Reservations:** suggested. **Address:** 401 Springfield Ave 07901 **Location:** At Maple St; center. **Parking:** street only. L D

TAKA SUSHI   908/277-0886   100
▼▼ Sushi. Casual Dining. $11-$24 **AAA Inspector Notes:** The simple, reserved decor and polite service at this restaurant set the tone for a comfortable meal. There is nothing really groundbreaking, and the fish selections don't stray too far from the familiar species. The quality is excellent, though, and you'll find creativity in the long list of specialty sushi rolls. **Address:** 95 Summit Ave 07901 **Location:** Between Springfield Ave and Franklin Pl; downtown. **Parking:** street only. L D CALL 🖐M

TITO'S BURRITOS   908/277-3710   98
▼ Mexican. Quick Serve. $4-$10 **AAA Inspector Notes:** This small shop in the middle of the downtown shopping district serves up tasty West Coast-style burritos and tacos, as well as a few salads and some great chicken wings. **Address:** 356 Springfield Ave 07901 **Location:** Between Beechwood Rd and Summit Ave; downtown. **Parking:** street only. L D CALL 🖐M

WINBERIE RESTAURANT & BAR   908/277-4224
▼▼ American. Casual Dining. $9-$29 **AAA Inspector Notes:** The restaurant's varied menu echoes French and Italian favorites. The black Angus beef burger with brie and peppered bacon on a brioche bun is popular, as are such decadent desserts as gingered crème brûlée, chocolate fondue and sinful Toll House pie. **Features:** full bar, patio dining, Sunday brunch, happy hour. **Address:** 2 Kent Place Blvd 07901 **Location:** At Springfield Ave. **Parking:** street only. L D CALL 🖐M

SURF CITY pop. 1,205

YELLOW FIN   609/494-7001
▼▼▼ Seafood. Fine Dining. $25-$38 **AAA Inspector Notes:** This restaurant's creative menu showcases the talents of its skilled chef, Greg Mann, and his winning way with seafood. Succulent roasted cod with escarole and white bean stew is top-notch, as are coriander-dusted day boat scallops with sweet corn succotash. The seared tuna has become legendary, and a fried green tomato appetizer, topped with poached lobster, is destined for similar greatness. **Reservations:** required, weekends. **Address:** 104 24th St 08008 **Location:** SR 72 Cswy, 1.7 mi n. D CALL 🖐M

SUSSEX (A-3) pop. 2,130, elev. 449'

SPACE FARMS ZOO & MUSEUM is .4 mi. w. on Loomis Ave., 1.1 mi. s.w. on CR 639, 2.8 mi. n.w. on CR 628, then 1.5 mi. s.w. to 218 CR 519 in Beemerville. The 100-acre preserve is home to more than 500 animals and 100 species of North American wildlife, including bears, bobcats and otters; exotic animals, birds and reptiles also can be seen. The museum displays such Americana as antique automobiles, motorcycles and horse-drawn vehicles.

Hours: Daily 9-5, early Apr.-Oct. 31. Last admission 1 hour before closing. **Cost:** $15.50; $14.50 (ages 65+); $11 (ages 3-12). **Phone:** (973) 875-5800. 🍴 🏕

SWEDESBORO pop. 2,584

HOLIDAY INN   856/467-3322
▼▼▼ **Hotel.** Rates not provided. **Address:** 1 Pureland Dr 08085 **Location:** I-295 exit 10, 0.4 mi e. **Facility:** 161 units. 4 stories, interior corridors. **Dining:** entertainment. **Pool(s):** outdoor. **Activities:** exercise room. **Guest Services:** coin laundry.

🍴 🍷 🏊 BIZ 🛜 ✖ 🐾 💻
/SOME UNITS 🐄 🛆 📺

TEANECK pop. 39,776
• Hotels & Restaurants map & index p. 162

TEANECK MARRIOTT AT GLENPOINTE   (201)836-0600   **41**
▼▼▼ **Hotel** $167-$275 **Address:** 100 Frank W Burr Blvd 07666 **Location:** New Jersey Tpke northbound, just after toll, follow signs to George Washington Bridge in local lane exit 70 to 70B; I-95 southbound local lanes exit 70 (Teaneck). **Facility:** 345 units. 15 stories, interior corridors. **Terms:** check-in 4 pm. **Pool(s):** heated indoor. **Activities:** sauna, hot tub, massage. **Guest Services:** valet laundry, boarding pass kiosk.

AAA Benefit: Members save 5% or more!

🍴 🛆 CALL 🅼 🏊 👪 BIZ 🆂HS 📶 ✖
🐾 💻 /SOME UNITS 🛆

TENAFLY (G-6) pop. 14,488
• Hotels & Restaurants map & index p. 162

The area now occupied by present-day Tenafly was discovered in 1609 by Henry Hudson, but it wasn't until 1894 that the town was incorporated. Many Victorian and Gothic homes dating back to the mid-19th century still stand in this primarily residential community. The notable Gothic-style home of New York architect Daniel Topping Atwood is located in the Highwood Park Historic District. The 1874 Tenafly Railroad Station, another example of Atwood's Gothic design, was restored in the early 1990s; made of sandstone, it has a cupola with intricate woodwork.

Past residents include women's suffrage pioneer Elizabeth Cady Stanton and big band leader Glenn Miller, who vanished in 1944 when his plane disappeared while flying over the English Channel.

AFRICAN ART MUSEUM OF THE SOCIETY OF AFRICAN MISSIONS, 23 Bliss Ave., was founded by the Society of African Missions, an international Roman Catholic missionary organization that serves the people of Africa. The collections explore sub-Saharan costumes, decorative arts, folklore, painting, religion, sculpture and textiles. Pieces on display include carved masks, fabrics, jewelry and sculptures. **Time:** Allow 1 hour minimum. **Hours:** Daily 10-5. Closed major holidays. Phone ahead to confirm schedule. **Cost:** Free. **Phone:** (201) 894-8611.

CLINTON INN HOTEL & EVENT CENTER   201/871-3200   **29**
▼▼▼ Hotel. Rates not provided. **Address:** 145 Dean Dr 07670 **Location:** Just s of Clinton Ave; center. **Facility:** 119 units. 3 stories, interior corridors. **Terms:** check-in 4 pm. **Activities:** exercise room. **Guest Services:** valet and coin laundry, area transportation.

🍴 🛆 🍷 🛜 ✖ 🛆 💻

TETERBORO (G-6) pop. 67, elev. 5'

AVIATION HALL OF FAME & MUSEUM OF NEW JERSEY is e. off SR 46 following signs at Teterboro Airport to 400 Fred Wehran Dr. The museum contains aviation memorabilia and historic aircraft equipment and depicts the roles played in aviation history by New Jerseyans. Seven historic aircraft are on display, as is an airport fire truck. A short film is shown, and visitors can listen to radio transmissions between air-traffic controllers and pilots.

Hours: Tues.-Sun. 10-4. Closed Jan. 1, Easter, July 4, Thanksgiving, Christmas Eve, Christmas and Dec. 31. **Cost:** $8; $6 (ages 3-12 and 62+). **Phone:** (201) 288-6344.

THOROFARE

BEST WESTERN WEST DEPTFORD INN   (856)848-4111
▼▼▼
Hotel
$110

AAA Benefit: Members save up to 20%!

Address: 98 Friars Blvd 08086 **Location:** I-295 exit 20, just e on Mid Atlantic Pkwy, then 0.4 mi n. **Facility:** 100 units. 2 stories, interior corridors. **Pool(s):** outdoor. **Activities:** limited exercise equipment. **Guest Services:** valet and coin laundry.

SAVE 🏊 BIZ HS 🛜 💻
/SOME UNITS 🆂 🛆 📺

TINTON FALLS pop. 17,892

COURTYARD BY MARRIOTT TINTON FALLS-EATONTOWN
(732)389-2100

Hotel
$118-$194

COURTYARD
Marriott

AAA Benefit:
Members save 5% or more!

Address: 600 Hope Rd 07724 **Location:** Garden State Pkwy exit 105, 1st jughandle after toll, then just n. **Facility:** 121 units. 3 stories, interior corridors. **Pool(s):** heated outdoor. **Activities:** exercise room. **Guest Services:** valet and coin laundry, boarding pass kiosk.

[SAVE] [ECO] [🛗] [📺] CALL [♿M] [♒]
[BIZ] [📶] [✕] [🍴] [🖨] [🖥]

DOUBLETREE BY HILTON HOTEL TINTON FALLS-EATONTOWN
(732)544-9300

[🏨🏨🏨] Hotel $89-$189 **Address:** 700 Hope Rd 07724 **Location:** Garden State Pkwy exit 105, just s. **Facility:** 179 units. 5 stories, interior corridors. **Terms:** 1-7 night minimum stay, cancellation fee imposed. **Amenities:** safes. **Pool(s):** outdoor. **Activities:** exercise room. **Guest Services:** valet and coin laundry.

AAA Benefit:
Members save 5% or more!

[🍴] [🛗] [📺] CALL [♿M] [♒] [BIZ] [📶] [✕] [🎬] [🖨]
[🖥] /SOME UNITS [🖥]

RED ROOF INN TINTON FALLS JERSEY SHORE
732/389-4646

[🏨] Motel. Rates not provided. **Address:** 11 Centre Plaza 07724 **Location:** Garden State Pkwy exit 105, just right at 1st light after toll. **Facility:** 119 units. 3 stories, exterior corridors. **Amenities:** safes.

[🛗] CALL [♿M] [📶] [✕] /SOME UNITS [🐾] [🖨] [🖥] [🖥]

RESIDENCE INN BY MARRIOTT TINTON FALLS
(732)389-8100

[🏨🏨🏨] Extended Stay Hotel $111-$206 **Address:** 90 Park Rd 07724 **Location:** Garden State Pkwy exit 105, 1st jughandle after toll, then just n. **Facility:** 96 kitchen units. 2 stories (no elevator), exterior corridors. **Pool(s):** outdoor. **Activities:** exercise room. **Guest Services:** valet and coin laundry.

AAA Benefit:
Members save 5% or more!

[♒] [📶] [✕] [🖨] [🖥] [🖥] /SOME UNITS [💵]

TITUSVILLE (D-2)

WASHINGTON CROSSING STATE PARK is 1.1 mi. s.e. on River Rd. (SR 29), then 1.5 mi. n.e. to 355 Washington Crossing-Pennington Rd. The park marks the site of the historic Delaware River crossing by Gen. George Washington and the Continental Army prior to the Battle of Trenton. The Visitor Center Museum houses an extensive collection of Revolutionary War artifacts.

Exhibits also are displayed at the Nelson House and the Johnson Ferry House (see sub-attraction listing). A nature center offers guided nature walks by appointment. Additional park features include the George Washington Memorial Arboretum, the John W.H. Simpson Observatory and the Open Air Theatre, where summer performances take place.

Check DrivingLaws.AAA.com for local motor vehicle laws when traveling

Hours: Park open daily 8-8, in summer; 8-6, in fall and spring; 8-4:30, in winter. Visitor center open daily 9-4. Nature center open Wed.-Sat. 9-4, Sun. noon-4. Nelson House open Sat.-Sun. 11-6, in summer; otherwise varies. Observatory open during special programs. **Cost:** Free. **Parking:** $7 Sat.-Sun. and holidays, Memorial Day-Labor Day; $5 (New Jersey residents). **Phone:** (609) 737-0623 for the park, (609) 737-9303 for the visitor center, or (609) 737-0609 for the nature center. [GT]

Johnson Ferry House is at the s. end of Continental Ln. in Washington Crossing State Park. Restored to resemble a Dutch farmhouse, the building contains a winter kitchen, a pantry, a parlor and three bed chambers with period furnishings. Also on site is a kitchen garden. Guided tours are available by appointment. **Time:** Allow 30 minutes minimum. **Hours:** Wed.-Sat. 10-noon and 1-4, Sun. 1-4. **Cost:** Free. **Parking:** $7 (New Jersey residents $5), Sat.-Sun. and holidays, Memorial Day-Labor Day. **Phone:** (609) 737-2515.

TOMS RIVER (E-4) pop. 88,791, elev. 40'

Founded in the early 18th century, the village of Toms River was a haven from which privateers wreaked havoc on British shipping early in the Revolutionary War. It rose to brief post-Revolutionary prominence in 1782 when Tories tried to seize the highly prized local saltworks and warehouses by burning the blockhouse, killing its defenders and hanging its commander, Capt. Joshua Huddy. Huddy Park and a replica of the original blockhouse, both near the waterfront in downtown Toms River, commemorate this event.

Whaling and shipping were major local industries. The first tourists, adventurous harbingers of today's thriving industry, reputedly arrived aboard empty seafood carts following the morning's deliveries to Philadelphia. Today locals and visitors alike enjoy the shops, coffee houses and waterfront restaurants that line Main and Water streets downtown.

Winding River Park, north on Main Street to SR 37 then 1 mile west to Hospital Road, straddles the Toms River. Within the park are two picnic areas, a small fishing pond, hiking and biking trails, a skating rink, playgrounds and a lighted softball field.

Ocean County Department of Tourism: 101 Hooper Ave., P.O. Box 2191, Toms River, NJ 08754-2191. **Phone:** (732) 929-2000 or (800) 722-0291.

CATTUS ISLAND COUNTY PARK is at 1170 Cattus Island Blvd. The island is actually a peninsula jutting into Barnegat Bay. The habitat in the 500-acre park is a quintessential transition zone between land and sea, with salt marsh blending into pine-oak uplands. The Cooper Environmental Center presents exhibits that relate to the area. Six miles of marked trails wind through the preserve, which also features a butterfly garden. Boat tours are offered in July and August. **Note:** The Cooper Environmental Center was closed at press time due to damage sustained during Hurricane Sandy. It is expected to reopen in fall 2015; phone for updates. **Hours:** Park open daily dawn-dusk. **Cost:** Free. **Phone:** (732) 270-6960 or TTY (732) 270-5573.

INSECTROPOLIS is at 1761 Lakewood Rd. Filled with bugs—both live creepy crawlers and preserved specimens from around the globe—the museum focuses on the impact insects have had on the human world. Home to ants, beetles, butterflies, moths, spiders and termites, the learning center also features hands-on displays in several themed exhibit areas, including Bug University, Caterpillar Café and the Rubber Tree Power Plant.

Time: Allow 1 hour minimum. **Hours:** Tues.-Sat. 10-3. Closed major holidays and Dec. 24-31. **Cost:** $8; free (ages 0-2). **Phone:** (732) 349-7090.

RIVER LADY **CRUISE AND DINNER BOAT** is .5 mi. e. of Garden State Pkwy. exit 81, just e. of SR 166 (Main St.) at 1 Robbins Pkwy., overlooking the Toms River. Historical sightseeing, dinner, dance and lunch cruises are offered along Barnegat Bay and the Toms River aboard a reproduction of a paddle-wheel riverboat. The historical sightseeing cruise provides narration about area history. Cruises vary in length from 90 minutes to 3 hours.

Hours: Historical sightseeing cruises depart Tues. and Thurs.-Fri. at 11, early May to mid-Oct. Lunch cruises depart Tues.-Fri. at 11, Sat. at 12:30, early May to mid-Oct. Dinner cruises depart Tues. and Thurs. at 6, Wed. and Fri.-Sat. at 7, early May to mid-Oct. Phone ahead to confirm schedule.

Cost: Historical sightseeing cruise $18; $15 (ages 65+); $12 (ages 0-11). Lunch cruise $40; $34-$40 (ages 65+); $25 (ages 0-11). Dinner cruise $40-$60; $34-$55 (ages 65+); $25-$40 (ages 0-11). Inquire about special reduced fares. Tickets must be purchased at least 1 day in advance. Passengers should arrive 30 minutes before departure. **Phone:** (732) 349-8664.

ROBERT J. NOVINS PLANETARIUM is on the campus of Ocean County College on College Dr. at SR 549 (Hooper Ave.). Changing 3-D video shows emphasize the night sky, the solar system, the human body and aquatic life. **Hours:** One-hour shows are presented on a varying schedule; phone ahead for dates and show times. **Cost:** $10; $8 (ages 60+); $7 (ages 0-12); $35 (family, two adults and three children). **Phone:** (732) 255-0342.

CLARION HOTEL AND CONFERENCE CENTER
(732)341-2400

▼▼▼▼ **Hotel** $115-$289 **Address:** 815 SR 37 W 08755 **Location:** Garden State Pkwy exit 82A, 1.5 mi w. **Facility:** 100 units. 2 stories, interior corridors. **Terms:** check-in 4 pm. **Amenities:** safes. **Pool(s):** outdoor. **Activities:** exercise room. **Guest Services:** valet and coin laundry.

HOWARD JOHNSON HOTEL-TOMS RIVER
(732)244-1000

Hotel
$99-$399

Address: 955 Hooper Ave 08753 **Location:** Garden State Pkwy exit 82, 1 mi e on SR 37. **Facility:** 96 units. 2 stories, interior corridors. **Terms:** cancellation fee imposed. **Amenities:** safes. **Dining:** 2 restaurants. **Pool(s):** heated indoor. **Guest Services:** valet laundry. **Featured Amenity: continental breakfast.**

RAMADA TOMS RIVER
(732)905-2626

▼▼▼ **Hotel** $84-$199 **Address:** 2373 Rt 9 N 08755 **Location:** Jct US 9 and SR 70 exit 88 (Garden State Pkwy) southbound, 2.5 mi w; exit 83 northbound, 4.4 mi n. **Facility:** 153 units, some efficiencies. 3 stories, interior corridors. **Amenities:** *Some:* safes. **Dining:** Angles Cafe Grille, see separate listing. **Pool(s):** outdoor. **Activities:** hot tub, tennis, game room, exercise room. **Guest Services:** valet and coin laundry.

TR HOTEL
732-244-4000

▼▼▼▼ **Hotel.** Rates not provided. **Address:** 290 Rt 37 E 08753 **Location:** Garden State Pkwy exit 82, 1.5 mi e. **Facility:** 173 units. 4 stories, interior corridors. **Pool(s):** heated indoor. **Activities:** sauna, game room, exercise room. **Guest Services:** valet and coin laundry.

WHERE TO EAT

ANGLES CAFE GRILLE
732/367-6400

▼▼ American. Casual Dining. $8-$20 **AAA Inspector Notes:** This café offers a familiar menu which ranges from full-course hot meals to quick sandwiches. **Features:** full bar. **Address:** 2373 Rt 9 08755 **Location:** Jct US 9 and SR 70 exit 88 (Garden State Pkwy) southbound, 2.5 mi w; exit 83 northbound, 4.4 mi n; in Ramada Toms River.

TOTOWA pop. 10,804
• Hotels & Restaurants map & index p. 152, 162

HOLIDAY INN-TOTOWA
973/785-9000 **5**

▼▼▼ **Hotel.** Rates not provided. **Address:** 1 Rt 46 W 07512 **Location:** 2.5 mi w of jct SR 3; I-80 exit 55A westbound, 1st left; exit eastbound to US 46 E to Totowa Union Blvd exit, then 1st right. **Facility:** 155 units. 5 stories, interior corridors. **Amenities:** video games. **Pool(s):** outdoor. **Activities:** exercise room. **Guest Services:** valet and coin laundry, area transportation.

WHERE TO EAT

SUSHI LOUNGE
973/890-0007 **16**

▼▼▼ Sushi. Casual Dining. $11-$37 **AAA Inspector Notes:** Located on busy strip along the highway, this former diner now is home to a sleek and sophisticated restaurant that is worlds away from eggs-over-easy. The stone and metal accents contribute to the minimalist décor and serve as an apt backdrop to the sushi and Japanese preparations on the menu. Diners can choose between raw and cooked, the latter of which goes far beyond the traditional teriyaki dishes typically found on sushi menus. **Features:** full bar, happy hour. **Address:** 235 US 46 W 07511 **Location:** I-80 exit 55A westbound, 0.5 mi s on Union Blvd to US 46 W, then just w; exit 54 eastbound, just s on Minnisink Rd, then just e on Furler St.

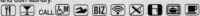

TRENTON (D-3) pop. 84,913, elev. 54'

The New Jersey state capital's location was selected in 1679 because it was the highest navigable point on the Delaware River. The site's potential for industry, trade and shipping was recognized by Philadelphia merchant William Trent, who in 1714 purchased 1,600 acres and a mill built by the original settlers. The village came to be known as Trent's Town, later modified to Trenton.

In 1776 Hessian troops occupied the city for the British as Gen. George Washington and his army crossed New Jersey into Pennsylvania. On Dec. 26, 1776, after crossing the Delaware 8 miles upstream, Washington surprised the Hessian garrison, taking about 1,000 prisoners. The victory at the Battle of Trenton was his first in the Revolutionary War.

The city was designated the state capital in 1790; the State House was constructed in 1792. The 1883 opening of the Brooklyn Bridge brought fame to Trenton-based John A. Roebling's Sons Co., also designers of the George Washington and Golden Gate bridges. Trenton was the center of the American pottery industry for 60 years after the Civil War, and porcelain from Boehm and Cybis ranks among the city's major manufacturing products.

Seven historic districts preserve many key sites. The Mill Hill Historic District, between Mercer and Jackson streets, has brick sidewalks, gaslights and restored Victorian houses. The State House Historic District, W. State Street between Willow and Calhoun streets, is an architecturally rich area where 19th-century Trenton's prominent families have been supplanted by 21st-century Trenton's prominent lobbyists.

Veterans' Park, 2206 Kuser Rd., is dedicated to area residents who served in the U.S. Armed Forces. The 320-acre park contains the Camp Olden Civil War and Native American Museum, which features Civil War and Delaware Indian exhibits, and the John Abbott II House, a two-story home built in 1730 that served as a repository for funds as the British advanced on Trenton in 1776. For museum schedule information phone (609) 585-8900.

Destination: Trenton Visitor Center: 102 Barracks St., Trenton, NJ 08608. **Phone:** (609) 292-2261.

THE 1719 WILLIAM TRENT HOUSE is at the intersection of Market St. and William Trent Pl. Said to be city's oldest still-standing house, the residence was built in 1719 by William Trent. It was subsequently the home of a number of prominent individuals, including the first Colonial governor of New Jersey, Lewis Morris. **Time:** Allow 1 hour minimum. **Hours:** Wed.-Sun. 12:30-4. Closed municipal holidays. **Cost:** $5; $4 (ages 5-11 and 65+). **Phone:** (609) 989-3027. 🏛 Trenton, 259

CADWALADER PARK is at Parkside and Stuyvesant aves. The park honors Dr. Thomas Cadwalader, a pioneer in the development of preventive inoculation; he vaccinated citizens against smallpox in the late 1740s. Laid out in 1891 by landscape designer Frederick Law Olmsted, the park features a deer paddock, a stream, a small lake and an arm of the historic Delaware-Raritan Canal. **Hours:** Daily dawn-dusk. **Cost:** Free.

The Trenton City Museum at Ellarslie Mansion is in Cadwalader Park, near the Parkside Ave. entrance. The Italianate villa contains galleries with changing art and history displays as well as a permanent Trenton ceramics exhibit and a period Victorian room. **Time:** Allow 30 minutes minimum. **Hours:** Tues.-Sat. 11-3, Sun. 1-4. Closed city holidays. Phone ahead to confirm schedule. **Cost:** Donations. **Phone:** (609) 989-3632 or (609) 989-1191.

NEW JERSEY STATE HOUSE is at 125 W. State St. A gold dome crowns the 1792 building, which has undergone many changes since its construction. Visitors can view the rotunda, legislative chambers, caucus rooms and the governor's reception room, all of which have noteworthy decorative treatments. Collections of art and period rooms also can be seen.

Note: Visitors must show a photo ID and undergo a security screening. **Time:** Allow 1 hour minimum. **Hours:** One-hour guided tours are given Mon.-Fri. on the hour 10-3, first and third Sat. of the month noon-3. Closed state holidays. Phone ahead to confirm schedule. **Cost:** Free. **Phone:** (609) 847-3150. 🏛 Trenton, 259

NEW JERSEY STATE MUSEUM is at 205 W. State St., in the State House Historic District. Three floors of exhibits focus on archeology, fine arts, cultural history and natural science. Highlights include Native American artifacts, mastodon skeletons, a full-size model of a dinosaur and a mine replica with fluorescent minerals. Changing art exhibits as well as films, concerts and lectures are presented. The museum's planetarium offers changing programs emphasizing the solar system and the night sky.

Time: Allow 1 hour minimum. **Hours:** Main museum building and auditorium galleries Tues.-Sun. 9-4:45. Planetarium shows are presented Sat.-Sun. on the hour noon-3. Closed state holidays. **Cost:** Donations. Main museum building free. Fees are charged for special exhibits and programs. Planetarium show $7; $5 (ages 0-12). **Phone:** (609) 292-6464.

OLD BARRACKS MUSEUM is at 101 Barrack St. near the New Jersey State Capitol Complex. The army barracks, constructed in 1758, served as winter quarters for British "regulars" returning from fighting in the frontier regions of the French and Indian War. The structure also was occupied at various times by Hessian and Continental troops during the Revolutionary War. Following the Battles of Trenton, the barracks served as a military hospital for smallpox inoculations.

The museum offers 18th-century furnishings in restored officers' quarters, soldiers' barracks rooms and a hospital room. Rotating special exhibitions also are presented. Historical interpreters portray Trentonians circa 1777—including nurses, doctors and Continental Army soldiers—who describe the Battles of Trenton and medical techniques of the day.

Hours: Mon.-Sat. 10-5. Closed Jan. 1, Easter, Thanksgiving, Christmas Eve and Christmas. **Cost:** $8; $6 (ages 62+ and students with ID); free (ages 0-5). **Phone:** (609) 396-1776 Mon.-Fri., or (609) 777-3599 on Sat. Trenton, 259

WYNDHAM GARDEN TRENTON   (609)421-4000
Hotel $89-$140 **Address:** 1 W Lafayette St 08608 **Location:** At Warren St. Trenton, 259. **Facility:** 164 units. 7 stories, interior corridors. **Parking:** on-site (fee). **Activities:** exercise room. **Guest Services:** valet and coin laundry.

WHERE TO EAT

SETTIMO CIELO   609/656-8877
Traditional Italian. Fine Dining. $13-$27 **AAA Inspector Notes:** The setting is traditional and formal at this downtown restaurant. A menu of familiar, classic dishes is very well prepared by the chef-owner and includes veal, chicken, pastas and steak. **Features:** full bar. **Reservations:** suggested. **Address:** 17 E Front St 08608 **Location:** Between S Broad and S Warren sts. Trenton, 259. **Parking:** street only.

TUCKERTON (F-4) pop. 3,347, elev. 23'

Settled by Quakers in the late 1600s, the town of Tuckerton has gone by many names, including Clamtown, Fishtown, Quakertown, Andrew's Mill and Middle-of-the-Shore. In 1791 the busy Colonial seaport was designated by George Washington as America's third port of entry. Although constantly shifting tides and ferocious storms have taken their toll—the Tucker's Island Lighthouse collapsed into the ocean in 1927—the town perseveres as a historic seaport village with a distinctively maritime air.

TUCKERTON SEAPORT is s. of jct. CR 539 and SR 9 at 120 W. Main St. This 40-acre site brings to life the history and heritage of the Jersey shore. Restored and re-created structures include a clamming shack, a hunting shanty, decoy-carving shops and boat works.

A replica of Tucker's Island Lighthouse displays permanent and temporary exhibits. The Tuckerton Yacht Club also houses interpretive exhibits. Two other buildings—one featuring the history of South Jersey Shore hotels and resorts and the other showcasing an extensive decoy collection—are on site. Boat tours are offered May through August. **Time:** Allow 1 hour minimum. **Hours:** Daily 10-5. Closed Thanksgiving and Christmas. **Cost:** $8; $6 (ages 62+); $5 (ages 5-12). **Phone:** (609) 296-8868.

THE GRAPEVINE   609/296-7799
American. Casual Dining. $13-$30 **AAA Inspector Notes:** A popular place with locals, especially for the early-bird specials, this comfortable family restaurant is warm and inviting with a simple décor. Preparations are straightforward and portions are plentiful. Baked stuffed flounder, cheesy crab casserole, seafood étouffee, chicken Marsala or parmigiana, pork ribs, steaks and pasta are just a sample of the large menu. Servers are casual, yet attentive. **Features:** full bar, early bird specials. **Reservations:** suggested. **Address:** 364 E Main St 08087 **Location:** US 9, 1 mi n.

UNION (H-5) pop. 56,642, elev. 93'

LIBERTY HALL MUSEUM AT KEAN UNIVERSITY is at 1003 Morris Ave. Built in 1772 by New Jersey's first elected governor (1776-90), William Livingston, Liberty Hall was home to seven generations of the Livingston/Kean family. The 14-room Georgian manor, expanded in the 1800s to a Victorian Italianate-style 50-room mansion, contains furnishings from the pre-Revolutionary era to the turn of the 20th century. The 12-acre grounds include a carriage house, the Liberty Hall Museum Firehouse and gardens.

Time: Allow 1 hour, 30 minutes minimum. **Hours:** Mon.-Sat. 10-4. Last tour departs 1 hour, 30 minutes before closing. Closed Jan. 1, July 4, Thanksgiving, day after Thanksgiving and Christmas. **Cost:** $10; $6 (ages 3-17 and 65+ and college students with ID); free (ages 0-2). **Phone:** (908) 527-0400.

UNION CITY pop. 66,455
• Hotels & Restaurants map & index p. 162

BEYTI KEBAB RESTAURANT   201/865-6281 (76)
Turkish. Casual Dining. $14-$26 **AAA Inspector Notes:** This ethnic eatery, with piquant aromas of mingled spices hanging in the air, offers a large selection of assorted salads that include baba ghanoush, hummus, tarama, stuffed eggplant and yogurt sauces. Numerous appetizers are served with soft strips of chewy bread and can easily make a meal in themselves. Fresh, vibrant shepherd salad is a treat, as are the ground meat and lamb kebabs. **Reservations:** required, Sat only. **Address:** 4105 Park Ave 07087 **Location:** I-495 viaduct toward Lincoln Tunnel exit John F Kennedy Blvd, 0.4 mi n to 42nd St, 0.4 mi e to Park Ave, then just right. **Parking:** street only.

VERNON (A-3) elev. 564'
• Hotels p. 204

MOUNTAIN CREEK WATERPARK is at 200 SR 94. This recreational theme park features more than 20 major attractions. Several slides, including Cannonball Falls and Vortex, will get thrill-seekers' adrenaline pumping, while water play areas and miniature slides keep younger visitors occupied. Also within the park are rope swings, cliffs from which adventurous guests can plunge into a mountain spring, and a wave pool.

Hours: Water park opens daily, late June-Labor Day; Sat.-Sun., early-late June. Opening and closing times vary; phone ahead for specific schedule information. **Cost:** $39.99; $27.99 (ages 65+ and under 48 inches tall); free (ages 0-2). Twilight rate (3 hours before the park closes) $19.99.

Admission rates may vary; phone ahead to confirm. **Phone:** (973) 827-2000. [🍴]

RECREATIONAL ACTIVITIES
Skiing and Snowboarding

- **Mountain Creek** is at 200 SR 94 (McAfee Vernon Rd.). Other activities are offered. **Hours:** Ski resort Sun.-Thurs. 9-9, Fri.-Sat. 9 a.m.-10 p.m., mid-Dec. to late Mar. Hours may be extended during holiday periods. Phone ahead to confirm schedule. **Phone:** (973) 827-2000.

APPALACHIAN MOTEL   (973)764-6070

Motel
$55-$125

Address: 367 Rt 94 N 07462 **Location:** 1 mi n. **Facility:** 10 units. 1 story, exterior corridors. *Bath:* shower only. **Terms:** 2-3 night minimum stay - seasonal and/or weekends, 3 day cancellation notice-fee imposed.

[SAVE] [📶] [🔌] [🖨] [💻] / SOME UNITS [🐘]

MINERALS RESORT & SPA AT CRYSTAL SPRINGS
                                        (973)827-5996

▼▼▼▼ **Resort Hotel** $179-$269 **Address:** 2 Chamonix Dr 07462 **Location:** Jct SR 23, 4.5 mi n on SR 94. **Facility:** A plethora of swimming pools, great golfing, lots of skiing and a state-of-the-art health club keeps active guests on the go. 178 units. 3-4 stories, interior corridors. **Terms:** check-in 4 pm, 2 night minimum stay - seasonal and/or weekends, 3 day cancellation notice-fee imposed. **Amenities:** safes. **Pool(s):** outdoor, heated indoor. **Activities:** sauna, hot tub, steamroom, regulation golf, tennis, downhill skiing, snowboarding, sledding, recreation programs, playground, game room, trails, spa. **Guest Services:** area transportation.

[🍴] [💻] [🛗] CALL [&M] [�] [🛕] [HS] [📶] [✕]
[🎥] [💻] / SOME UNITS [🔌] [🖨]

VINELAND (G-2) pop. 60,724, elev. 106'

Vineland has plenty of room to grow: At 69 square miles, geographically it's the largest city in the state. And as the name implies, this busy manufacturing center was originally intended to be the focus of a wine-producing region. In 1861, promoter Charles K. Landis attracted farmers from other mid-Atlantic states as well as Italian immigrants familiar with grape production to the area.

After a quarter-century of growth, disease struck the vines, and the wine-grape industry was all but abandoned. But an enterprising dentist named Thomas Welch developed a non-fermentative method of preserving grape juice, one that became permanently associated with his name.

In 1868 female citizens staged one of the earliest women's suffrage demonstrations in the country. Unwilling to have their opinions go unheard during that year's presidential election, 172 women defiantly cast their token votes, a number of them supporting suffrage pioneer Elizabeth Cady Stanton for president.

Landis, Howard Pagliughi, Gittone and Giampietro city parks all have recreational facilities. Six

miles west of town via CR 540 is Parvin State Park *(see Recreation Areas Chart).*

Greater Vineland Chamber of Commerce: 2115 S. Delsea Dr., Vineland, NJ 08360-0489. **Phone:** (856) 691-7400.

VINELAND HISTORICAL AND ANTIQUARIAN SOCIETY is at 108 S. 7th St. Exhibits relate to Vineland and its surroundings, including items belonging to town founder Charles K. Landis and his family, locally crafted glassware, military memorabilia, a music room, old firefighting equipment, Native American relics, and period furniture and clothing. Archives are available for genealogical research.

Hours: Museum open Sat. 1-4. Archives open Tues.-Fri. 1-4 by appointment. Closed major holidays. **Cost:** Museum free. Archives fee $5. **Phone:** (856) 691-1111. [GT]

COMFORT INN   (856)692-8070

▼▼▼ **Hotel** $68-$170 **Address:** 29 W Landis Ave 08360 **Location:** SR 55 exit 32A, 2 mi e. **Facility:** 40 units. 3 stories, interior corridors. **Amenities:** safes. **Activities:** exercise room. **Guest Services:** valet laundry.

[📶+] [BIZ] [📶] [🔌] [🖨] [💻] / SOME UNITS [🐘]

HAMPTON INN & SUITES VINELAND   (856)405-0600

▼▼▼ **Hotel** $119-$229 **Address:** 2134 W Landis Ave 08360 **Location:** 0.5 mi w of SR 55. **Facility:** 130 units. 5 stories, interior corridors. **Terms:** 1-7 night minimum stay, cancellation fee imposed.

AAA Benefit: Members save 5% or more!

Amenities: safes. **Pool(s):** heated indoor. **Activities:** hot tub, miniature golf, exercise room. **Guest Services:** valet and coin laundry.

[📶+] [🛗] CALL [&M] [�
] [BIZ] [HS] [📶] [✕] [🎥] [🔌]
[🖨] [💻]

HOLIDAY INN EXPRESS & SUITES   856/293-8888

▼▼▼ **Hotel.** Rates not provided. **Address:** 398 Smith St 08360 **Location:** SR 55 exit 27, just e on SR 47. Adjacent to Cumberland Mall. **Facility:** 100 units. 3 stories, interior corridors. **Pool(s):** heated indoor. **Activities:** hot tub, exercise room. **Guest Services:** valet and coin laundry.

[📶+] [�
] [BIZ] [📶] [✕] [🎥] [🔌] [🖨] [💻]

RAMADA VINELAND   (856)696-3800

Hotel
$69-$160

Address: 2216 W Landis Ave 08360 **Location:** SR 55 exit 32A, just e. **Facility:** 102 units. 2 stories (no elevator), interior corridors. **Dining:** 2 restaurants. **Pool(s):** outdoor. **Activities:** exercise room. **Guest Services:** valet laundry. **Featured Amenity:** full hot breakfast.

[SAVE] [🍴] [🛗] [🍽] CALL [&M] [�
]
[BIZ] [📶] [💻] / SOME UNITS [🔌] [🖨]

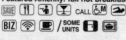

WINGATE BY WYNDHAM

(856)690-9900

Hotel
$79-$159

Address: 2196 W Landis Ave 08360 **Location:** SR 55 exit 32A, just e. **Facility:** 116 units. 4 stories, interior corridors. **Amenities:** video games, safes. **Pool(s):** outdoor. **Activities:** exercise room. **Guest Services:** valet and coin laundry. **Featured Amenity: breakfast buffet.**

[SAVE] [↑↓] CALL [&M] [🔌] [BIZ] [HS]
[📶] [✕] [🛏] [🖨] [▣]
/ SOME UNITS [🐘]

WHERE TO EAT

MAPLEWOOD III

856/692-2011

Italian. Casual Dining. $14-$31 **AAA Inspector Notes:** This casual Italian spot offers traditional dishes and a variety of seafood options including sea scallops and Maryland crab scampi, crab imperial-stuffed flounder and an 8.5-ounce Brazilian lobster tail. Courteous staff attend to every request and can assist with recommendations. Be sure to check the new specials daily. **Features:** full bar. **Address:** 200 N Delsea Dr 08360 **Location:** SR 55 exit 32A, 1.7 mi e. [D]

OLYMPIA RESTAURANT

856/691-6095

Greek. Casual Dining. $10-$22 **AAA Inspector Notes:** Bright blue colors provide a Mediterranean feel at this casual restaurant. The engaging staff are happy to assist with menu recommendations and ensure the meal is satisfactory. The menu is filled with all traditional Greek favorites including gyros, souvlaki, calamari and spanakopita. **Address:** 739 S Delsea Expwy 08360 **Location:** SR 55 exit 32A, 1.6 mi e, then 0.7 mi s. [L] [D]

VOORHEES

HAMPTON INN-CHERRY HILL/VOORHEES

(856)346-4500

Hotel $89-$189 **Address:** 121 Laurel Oak Rd 08043 **Location:** I-295 exit 32, 2.3 mi e on Haddonfield-Berlin Rd, then s on White Horse Rd. Located in Voorhees Corporate Center. **Facility:** 120 units. 4 stories, interior corridors. **Terms:** 1-7 night minimum stay, cancellation fee imposed. **Amenities:** video games. **Pool(s):** outdoor. **Activities:** exercise room. **Guest Services:** valet and coin laundry, area transportation.

AAA Benefit: Members save 5% or more!

[↑↓] CALL [&M] [🔌] [BIZ] [📶] [✕] [✦] [🛏] [🖨] [▣]
/ SOME UNITS [HS]

HAMPTON INN PHILADELPHIA/VOORHEES

(856)751-1212

Hotel $109-$149 **Address:** 320 Rt 73 S 08043 **Location:** I-295 exit 32, 1.7 mi e on Haddonfield-Berlin Rd, 2.5 mi n on E Evesham Rd, 1.5 mi e on Kresson Rd, then just s. **Facility:** 118 units. 4 stories, interior corridors. **Terms:** 1-7 night minimum stay, cancellation fee imposed. **Pool(s):** heated indoor. **Activities:** exercise room. **Guest Services:** valet and coin laundry.

AAA Benefit: Members save 5% or more!

[↑↓] CALL [&M] [🔌] [BIZ] [📶] [✕] [▣] / SOME UNITS [HS]

WHERE TO EAT

A LITTLE CAFE

856/784-3344 (151)

American. Casual Dining. $22-$32 **AAA Inspector Notes:** Bring your favorite wine from home and enjoy sophisticated Asian-influenced American dishes at this small, quaint spot, which rises above its humble location in a strip mall. The cozy dining room lacks size, but provides a warm, inviting atmosphere. **Reservations:** suggested. **Address:** 118 White Horse Rd E 08043 **Location:** I-295 exit 32, 3.8 mi e on CR 561 to White Horse Rd, then 1.1 mi s; in Plaza Shoppes. [🅿] Lindenwold, 152. [D] [🚆]

PASSARIELLO'S PIZZERIA & ITALIAN EATERY

856/784-7272 (150)

Italian. Cafeteria. $7-$16 **AAA Inspector Notes:** Pick up a passport card upon entry, then prepare to enjoy a delicious meal of homemade Italian or American favorites. From baked gnocchi and calamari marinara to Buffalo wings and hoagies, this restaurant has a wide variety of affordable and satisfying dishes for the whole family. **Address:** 111 Laurel Oak Rd 08043 **Location:** I-295 exit 32, 2.3 mi e on Haddonfield-Berlin Rd, then just s on White Horse Rd. [L] [D] CALL [&M]

RITZ SEAFOOD

856/566-6650 (149)

Seafood. Casual Dining. $9-$25 **AAA Inspector Notes:** Step inside this charming little storefront restaurant to find a casual, Asian-influenced dining room. Grab a seat to sample mainly seafood dishes with a similar Asian flair. Garlic and ginger-crusted salmon with Indonesian black beans, flash-fried devil fish with sweet chile scallion sauce and seafood stew with Asian noodles in Korean-style broth are a few such choices. However, there also are seafood shepherd's pie with lobster sauce and a few meat, rice and noodle dishes. **Reservations:** suggested, weekends. **Address:** 910 Rt 561 08043 **Location:** I-295 exit 32, 2.2 mi e; in Ritz Center. [L] [D]

WALL

COURTYARD BY MARRIOTT WALL AT MONMOUTH SHORES

(732)919-2780

Hotel $111-$194 **Address:** 1302 Campus Pkwy 07753 **Location:** Garden State Pkwy exit 100B southbound; exit 100A northbound, 0.4 mi w on SR 66 (which becomes SR 33), then 1 mi w. **Facility:** 113 units. 3 stories, interior corridors. **Pool(s):** heated indoor. **Activities:** hot tub, exercise room. **Guest Services:** valet and coin laundry.

AAA Benefit: Members save 5% or more!

[🍽] CALL [&M] [🔌] [BIZ] [HS] [📶] [✕] [🛏] [▣]
/ SOME UNITS [🐘]

WANTAGE

HIGH POINT COUNTRY INN

973/702-1860

Motel. Rates not provided. **Address:** 1328 SR 23 N 07461 **Location:** 1 mi n of Colesville Village Center. **Facility:** 14 units. 1 story, exterior corridors. **Activities:** picnic facilities.

[📶] [✕] [🈂] [🛏] [🖨] / SOME UNITS [🐘] [▣]

WARETOWN (F-4) pop. 1,569, elev. 13'

Every Saturday night a whole lot of pickin' and grinnin' takes place at Albert Music Hall, 131 Wells Mills Rd., courtesy of live acoustic country and bluegrass music served up by the Pinelands Cultural Society. Shows feature seven sets, each lasting about 30 minutes. Before the 7:30 p.m. show begins music lovers stage their own impromptu jam sessions on the grounds. For more information contact the Pinelands Cultural Society, P.O. Box 657, Waretown, NJ 08758; phone (609) 971-1593.

WELLS MILLS COUNTY PARK is 5 mi. w. on CR 532 to 905 Wells Mills Rd. Situated in the southern New Jersey Pine Barrens, this 910-acre park contains pine and oak forests, swamps and freshwater bogs that are ideal for activities like hiking, bird-watching, bicycling, canoeing and fishing. In winter the trails are used for cross-country skiing. A nature center offers environmental exhibits and an observation deck. *See Recreation Areas Chart.*

Hours: Grounds open daily 7 a.m.-dusk. Nature center open daily 8-4; phone to confirm schedule. Closed Jan. 1, Easter, Thanksgiving and Christmas. **Cost:** Free. **Phone:** (609) 971-3085. 🏚

WASHINGTON (C-2) pop. 6,461, elev. 463'

THE BLUE ARMY SHRINE OF THE IMMACULATE HEART OF MARY is off SR 31, 1 mi. w. on CR 632, 1 mi. n. on Cemetery Hill Rd., then .2 mi. w. on Mountain View Rd., following signs. Featured are the shrine, Blessed Sacrament Chapel, Rosary Garden, Outdoor Way of the Cross and Angel Pond. The Holy House Chapel is a replica of the Holy House of Loreto, Italy; the Capelinha is a replica of the chapel at Fatima, Portugal.

Hours: Grounds daily 9-7, June-Aug.; 9-3, rest of year. Shrine open daily 9-5, May-Oct.; 10-4, rest of year. Rosary mass is held daily at noon. Phone ahead to confirm schedule. **Cost:** Free. **Phone:** (908) 689-1700.

MERRILL CREEK RESERVOIR VISITORS CENTER is at 34 Merrill Creek Rd. In addition to wildlife exhibits and dioramas, the center features environmental education programs. A large dam, 650-acre reservoir, 290-acre environmental preserve and 200 acres of woodland surround the center. Recreational options include boating, fishing and hiking. **Time:** Allow 30 minutes minimum. **Hours:** Visitor center Mon.-Fri. 8:30-4:30, Sat.-Sun. 10-4. Outdoor areas daily dawn-dusk. Closed Jan. 1, Easter, Thanksgiving, day after Thanksgiving, Christmas Eve and Christmas. **Cost:** Free. **Phone:** (908) 454-1213. 🍽 🏚

WASHINGTON TOWNSHIP

CHARLIE BROWN'S STEAKHOUSE   201/666-3080
▼▼ Steak. Casual Dining. $9-$30 **AAA Inspector Notes:** This budget-friendly steakhouse, famous for its prime rib, offers top quality fare without hurting your pocketbook. The young ones will not be disappointed with the kids' menu, and just might even try something green from the salad bar. Adults will love the quality steaks, chicken and rib dishes. The express lunches are great for those saddled with time constraints. **Features:** full bar, happy hour. **Address:** 95 Linwood Ave 07676 **Location:** Garden State Pkwy exit 166.
Ⓛ Ⓓ

WAYNE (G-5) pop. 54,717, elev. 180'
• Hotels & Restaurants map & index p. 152, 162

The Wayne area is the setting for Albert Payson Terhune's "Lad: A Dog" and other books about the collies he raised until his death in 1942. Sunnybank, Terhune's estate, is 4 miles north of Wayne on US 202; it is now part of Terhune Memorial Park, featuring gardens and a picnic ground.

Shopping areas: Willowbrook, at 1400 Willowbrook Mall, offers Bloomingdale's, Lord & Taylor, Macy's and Sears among its stores.

DEY MANSION is at 199 Totowa Rd. in Preakness Valley Park. The Georgian manor was built by Dirck Dey, a Dutch-born planter, in the 1740s. His son

Theunis, commander of the Bergen County militia, invited Gen. George Washington to use the mansion as his headquarters in 1780. The stately house is furnished in period. On the 2-acre site are a blacksmith shop, a plantation house, a formal garden and a family cemetery.

Note: The museum was closed for restoration at press time. Phone for updates. **Hours:** Guided 30-minute tours are offered Wed.-Fri. 1-4, Sat.-Sun. 10-noon and 1-4. Last tour begins 30 minutes before closing. Closed Jan. 1, Easter, Thanksgiving and Christmas. **Cost:** $1; free (ages 0-9). **Phone:** (973) 696-1776. 🏚

LA QUINTA INN & SUITES   (973)696-8050 ❶
▼▼▼ Hotel $72-$185 **Address:** 1850 SR 23 07470 **Location:** I-80 exit 53 (Butler-Verona) westbound to SR 23 N, 3 mi to Ratzer Rd (service road), then just n; exit 54 eastbound to Minnisink Rd, U-turn for US 80 W exit 53. **Facility:** 146 units. 2 stories, interior corridors. **Pool(s):** outdoor. **Activities:** exercise room. **Guest Services:** coin laundry.
CALL 🛄 🚭 🛜 ▦ ▦ / SOME UNITS 🐾 🚪 🖨

RAMADA WAYNE FAIRFIELD AREA   (973)256-7000 ❷
▼▼▼ Hotel $90-$150 **Address:** 334 Rt 46 E/Service Rd 07470 **Location:** I-80 exit 53 (Butler-Verona) westbound to SR 23 S, service road off US 46 eastbound Caldwells; exit 47B eastbound, 7 mi e on US 46 to service road. **Facility:** 136 units. 2 stories (no elevator), exterior corridors. **Amenities:** Some: safes. **Pool(s):** outdoor. **Guest Services:** valet and coin laundry, area transportation.
🚭 BIZ 🛜 ▦ / SOME UNITS 🅂🄻 🚪 🖨

RESIDENCE INN BY MARRIOTT WAYNE (973)872-7100 ❸❽
▼▼▼▼ Extended Stay Hotel $146-$240 **Address:** 30 Nevins Rd 07470 **Location:** Jct CR 640 (Riverview Dr) and 681 (Valley Rd), 3.5 mi n, just w on Barbour Pond Dr, then just n. **Facility:** 119 units, some two bedrooms, efficiencies and kitchens. 4 stories, interior corridors. **Pool(s):** heated indoor. **Activities:** hot tub, exercise room. **Guest Services:** valet and coin laundry, area transportation.

> **AAA Benefit:**
> Members save 5% or more!

CALL 🛄 🚭 HS 🛜 ✕ 🍴 🚪 🖨 ▦
/ SOME UNITS 🅂🄻

WHERE TO EAT

ALDO'S CUCINA RISTORANTE ITALIANO 973/872-1842 ㉘
▼▼ Italian. Casual Dining. $9-$29 **AAA Inspector Notes:** This casual storefront may not look impressive from the outside, but the neighborhood favorite has garnered a legion of local devotees who have come to love the hearty pasta, delicate veal dishes and a host of daily specials. Bring your own bottle and settle in for a night of Italian cooking, served by an attentive and courteous staff. **Reservations:** suggested. **Address:** 777 Hamburg Tpke 07470 **Location:** Jct Valley Rd and Hamburg Tpke (CR 504); in Ramapo Plaza Shopping Center. Ⓛ Ⓓ CALL 🛄

BENSI RISTORANTE ITALIANO   973/904-3004
▼▼ Italian. Fine Dining. $8-$20 **AAA Inspector Notes:** Home-cooked Italian fare served in casual storefront digs make this place a must for anyone looking for a quick meal but not fast food. Wholesome pasta, veal, seafood and steaks are freshly prepared and served by a staff eager to please. Diners are encouraged to bring their own bottle of wine and linger over cannoli or an espresso. **Features:** full bar. **Address:** 669 Hamburg Tpke 07470 **Location:** US 46 exit Riverview Dr, 2.1 mi n on Riverview Dr (CR 640), 3.2 mi w on Valley Rd (CR 681), then 0.3 mi s on Hamburg Tpke (CR 504); in Shop Rite Plaza. Ⓛ Ⓓ CALL 🛄

(See maps & indexes p. 152, 162.)

CHARLIE BROWN'S STEAKHOUSE　973/686-1901

▼▼ ▼▼ Steak. Casual Dining. $9-$30 **AAA Inspector Notes:** This budget-friendly steakhouse, famous for its prime rib, offers top quality fare without hurting your pocketbook. The young ones will not be disappointed with the kids' menu, and just might even try something green from the salad bar. Adults who love the quality steaks, chicken and rib dishes. The express lunches are great for those saddled with time constraints. **Features:** full bar, happy hour. **Address:** 1207 Hamburg Tpke 07470 **Location:** SR 23 exit Alps Rd, 3.7 mi e on CR 670 (Alps Rd), then just s on Hamburg Tpke (CR 504).

L　D　CALL 🅼

THE CHEESECAKE FACTORY　973/890-1400　③

▼▼▼▼ International. Casual Dining. $9-$30 **AAA Inspector Notes:** What started as a small bakery in Los Angeles in the 1970s has since blossomed into one of the most recognizable restaurant chains today. Known for their large portion sizes and seemingly never-ending menu, this restaurant features over 200 selections to choose from! The "SkinnyLicious" menu options may appeal to those counting calories. **Features:** full bar, Sunday brunch. **Address:** 1700 Willowbrook Blvd 07470 **Location:** Just w of I-80, US 46 and SR 23 interchange; in Willowbrook Mall.　L　D　CALL 🅼 \

IZUMI HIBACHI STEAK HOUSE　973/628-1888　①

▼▼ ▼▼ Japanese. Casual Dining. $9-$37 **AAA Inspector Notes:** Both sushi lovers and fans of hibachi-style cooking will find their bliss at the Japanese steakhouse. A kimono-clad hostess acknowledges diners' arrivals by banging a gong before directing them to the serene sushi room or the main dining area, where hibachi chefs entertain patrons with their wild antics at the grill. Service is gracious and accommodating. **Features:** full bar. **Address:** 517 SR 23 S 07470 **Location:** 0.5 mi n of jct I-80, US 46 and SR 23; on service road.

L　D

JYOTI　973/890-2224　②

▼▼ ▼▼ Indian. Casual Dining. $12-$17 **AAA Inspector Notes:** The intoxicating aroma of Indian curries permeates the gilded dining room, where friendly waiters hustle to and fro, delivering freshly baked breads, including a heavenly onion kulcha, delicious soups and fabulous tandoori dishes. Thick and frothy mango lassi is a great partner to fiery lamb masala or chicken vindaloo. Fear not, the kitchen is happy to adjust seasonings to accommodate diners' preferences. **Address:** 24 Rt 46 E 07470 **Location:** I-80 exit 52 westbound; exit 47B eastbound, 5.8 mi e.　L　D

WAYNE HILLS DINER AND RESTAURANT　973/628-1824

▼▼ ▼▼ Continental. Casual Dining. $5-$21 **AAA Inspector Notes:** The diner truly has something for everyone: great salads, interesting pasta, triple-decker sandwiches, a bit of Italian, and maybe even moussaka. This place may just have an answer to that age-old question, "What's for dinner?"—with treasures from both land and sea, breakfast served all day and enough pastries and cakes to make a grown man cry. **Features:** full bar. **Address:** 1465 Hamburg Tpke 07470 **Location:** 0.4 mi w of Alps Rd.　B　L　D　24

WEEHAWKEN (H-6) elev. 189'

• Hotels & Restaurants map & index p. 162

Alexander Hamilton and Aaron Burr met on a dueling ground in Weehawken on July 11, 1804, the result of a minor insult exacerbated by a long-standing enmity. Hamilton was mortally wounded; Burr's political career suffered a fatal blow. In a tragic twist of fate, Hamilton's 19-year-old son had been killed on the same field 3 years earlier, and Hamilton chose his son's dueling pistol as a weapon.

Weehawken is the home of the Lincoln Tunnel, which links central New Jersey and midtown Manhattan beneath the Hudson River. Each year some 22 million commuters travel through Weehawken via the world's only three-portal underwater vehicular tunnel.

SPIRIT OF NEW JERSEY departs from Lincoln Harbor Marina at 1500 Harbor Blvd. Sightseeing cruises tour the New York City harbor. The Statue of Liberty, Empire State Building, Ellis Island and the Brooklyn Bridge are among landmarks seen on 2-hour narrated lunch and 3-hour dinner cruises. DJ music and live performances are provided.

Hours: Lunch cruises depart daily at noon. Dinner cruise departure times vary with the season. Boarding is a half-hour prior to departure. Phone ahead to confirm schedule. **Cost:** Lunch cruise $49.90. Dinner cruise $89.90, Sun.-Thurs.; $94.90, Fri.; $99.90, Sat. Rates may vary; phone ahead to confirm. Reservations are required. **Phone:** (866) 483-3866.

SHERATON LINCOLN HARBOR HOTEL

(201)617-5600　83

 Hotel $189-$449

 Sheraton

AAA Benefit: Members save up to 15%, plus Starwood Preferred Guest® benefits!

Address: 500 Harbor Blvd 07086 **Location:** Waterfront. Just se of Lincoln Tunnel entrance, at 19th St. **Facility:** 343 units. 10 stories, interior corridors. **Parking:** on-site (fee). **Amenities:** safes. **Pool(s):** heated indoor. **Activities:** exercise room. **Guest Services:** valet laundry.

 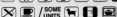

WESTAMPTON

BEST WESTERN BURLINGTON INN

(609)261-3800

 Hotel $99-$139

AAA Benefit: Members save up to 20%!

Address: 2020 Burlington Mt Holly Rd 08060 **Location:** New Jersey Tpke exit 5, just n. **Facility:** 88 units. 2 stories, interior corridors. **Pool(s):** heated indoor. **Activities:** exercise room. **Guest Services:** valet laundry.

COURTYARD BY MARRIOTT BURLINGTON MT. HOLLY/ WESTAMPTON
(609)261-6161

▼▼▼▼ **Hotel** $130-$213 **Address:** 30 Western Dr 08060 **Location:** New Jersey Tpke exit 5, 0.3 mi n. **Facility:** 119 units. 4 stories, interior corridors. **Pool(s):** heated indoor. **Activities:** exercise room. **Guest Services:** valet and coin laundry, area transportation.

AAA Benefit: Members save 5% or more!

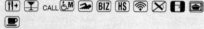
/ SOME UNITS

HILTON GARDEN INN MT. HOLLY/WESTAMPTON
609/702-1600

▼▼▼▼ **Hotel.** Rates not provided. **Address:** 111 Hancock Ln 08060 **Location:** New Jersey Tpke exit 5. **Facility:** 113 units. 3 stories, interior corridors. **Terms:** check-in 4 pm. **Pool(s):** heated indoor. **Activities:** exercise room. **Guest Services:** valet and coin laundry.

AAA Benefit: Members save 5% or more!

HOLIDAY INN EXPRESS HOTEL & SUITES
(609)702-5800

▼▼▼ **Hotel** $99-$149 **Address:** 18 Western Dr 08060 **Location:** New Jersey Tpke exit 5, 0.3 mi n. **Facility:** 76 units. 3 stories, interior corridors. **Amenities:** safes. **Pool(s):** heated indoor. **Activities:** exercise room. **Guest Services:** valet and coin laundry.

QUALITY INN & SUITES
(609)845-9400

▼▼ **Hotel** $85-$150 **Address:** 2015 Burlington Mt Holly Rd 08060 **Location:** New Jersey Tpke exit 5, just n. **Facility:** 78 units. 2 stories (no elevator), interior corridors. **Activities:** exercise room. **Guest Services:** valet and coin laundry.

WEST ATLANTIC CITY
• Part of Atlantic City area — see map p. 73

COMFORT INN & SUITES ATLANTIC CITY WEST
(609)484-1900

Hotel
$60-$300

Address: 7079 Black Horse Pike 08232 **Location:** Garden State Pkwy exit 38 (Atlantic City Expwy), 2 mi e to exit 5, 0.5 mi s on US 9 to US 40/322, then 1.5 mi e. **Facility:** 124 units. 6 stories, interior corridors. **Amenities:** safes. **Activities:** exercise room. **Guest Services:** coin laundry. **Featured Amenity:** continental breakfast.

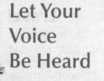

AAA.com/ TourBook Comments

Let Your Voice Be Heard

If your visit to a TourBook-listed property doesn't meet your expectations, tell us about it.

AAA.com/TourBookComments

WEST CAPE MAY pop. 1,024

THE BLACK DUCK ON SUNSET
609/898-0100

▼▼▼ American. Casual Dining. $28-$34 **AAA Inspector Notes:** Nestled in a residential neighborhood is this quaint, casually-upscale restaurant set in a Victorian home. Inside, guests will find a cozy, white-theme décor with contemporary touches. The menu focuses on fresh, local seafood and offers outstanding dishes such as dry-rubbed black pearl salmon and seared yellow fin tuna. Guests are able to bring their favorite wine from home and those looking for the best deal should try to come during their early-bird special. **Features:** early bird specials. **Reservations:** suggested. **Address:** 1 Sunset Blvd 08204 **Location:** Between Broadway and Pacific aves.
D

WESTFIELD pop. 30,316
• Hotels & Restaurants map & index p. 152

BEST WESTERN WESTFIELD INN
(908)654-5600 84

Hotel
$129-$179

AAA Benefit: Members save up to 20%!

Address: 435 North Ave W 07090 **Location:** Garden State Pkwy exit 137, 4 mi w on SR 28. **Facility:** 40 units, some efficiencies. 3 stories, interior corridors. **Amenities:** Some: safes. **Guest Services:** valet and coin laundry.

WHERE TO EAT

CHEZ CATHERINE
908/654-4011 132

▼▼▼▼ Traditional French. Fine Dining. $33-$68 **AAA Inspector Notes:** This small, cozy, slightly formal and very traditional French dining room serves up all the classics in expert fashion. Think escargot, seafood crepes, braised beef short rib and sautéed Dover sole prepared at your table by the well-seasoned French staff. Although the recipes are more Old World, the chef retains a modern sensibility for balance. A prix fixe menu is offered for lunch and dinner, and there also is an optional seven-course chef's tasting menu available at dinner. **Features:** full bar. **Reservations:** suggested. **Address:** 431 North Ave W 07090 **Location:** Garden State Pkwy exit 137, 4 mi w on SR 28. L D

COD ALMIGHTY CHIPPERY
908/233-5533 129

▼ Seafood. Quick Serve. $7-$17 **AAA Inspector Notes:** You can get your fish grilled or choose from a few nice salads on the menu, but the reason to come here is the battered, fried seafood. Some of the standouts on the menu include the simple fried cod and chips, the fat fish sandwich and the fried clam po' boy. The setting is modest with limited seating, but service is quick and friendly. **Features:** patio dining. **Address:** 231 South Ave E 07090 **Location:** Just e of Central Ave. L D

FERRARO'S
908/232-1105 131

▼▼▼ Italian. Casual Dining. $9-$30 **AAA Inspector Notes:** Grab a sidewalk table and enjoy this location in the center of the shopping district or sit in the attractive dining room lined with warm brick and woods. The menu offers something for everyone—veal scaloppine Francese, chicken rollatini, shrimp oreganato, eggplant parmigiana, pasta of all sorts, fresh oysters and crowd-pleasing pizzas. **Features:** full bar. **Address:** 14 Elm St 07090 **Location:** Center. **Parking:** valet and street only. L D CALL

FUJIYAMA MAMA
908/232-6598 127

▼▼▼ Japanese. Casual Dining. $8-$34 **AAA Inspector Notes:** Purists of Japanese cuisine may find this large restaurant a bit too Americanized, but the place is popular for good reason. The sushi selections are excellent and include some very creative rolls made by the staff at the bar. Families and groups will enjoy the hibachi-style tableside cooking in the dining room. **Features:** full bar. **Address:** 341 South Ave E 07090 **Location:** Just e of Central Ave. L D CALL

(See map & index p. 152.)

MOJAVE GRILLE   908/233-7772 (130)
▼▼▼▼ Southwestern. Casual Dining. $8-$26 **AAA Inspector Notes:** Take in the Southwest setting at this storefront spot, where clay-textured walls, original art and mod tables and chairs give the room a decidedly retro look. The menu is comprised of nouveau takes on Southwestern standards, including charred tomato soup, chipotle-lime Caesar salad, spiced tuna ceviche and wild mushroom tacos. **Features:** patio dining, Sunday brunch. **Address:** 35 Elm St 07090 **Location:** Center. **Parking:** street only. [L] [D]

THERESA'S   908/233-9133 (128)
▼▼▼▼ Northern Italian. Casual Dining. $10-$28 **AAA Inspector Notes:** This longstanding restaurant in the Westfield shopping area offers a solid menu of mostly Northern Italian dishes and is known for its great salads and fresh made pasta. The décor in the cozy dining room is simple but comfortable. **Features:** patio dining. **Address:** 47 Elm St 07090 **Location:** At Quimby St. **Parking:** street only.
[L] [D] CALL [&M]

TINGA TAQUERIA   908/301-0100 (126)
▼▼ Tex-Mex. Casual Dining. $9-$15 **AAA Inspector Notes:** This spot's rendition of Tex-Mex fare is downright terrific. The super casual eatery is a great spot for a quick meal that is anything but fast food. The guacamole is homemade, and the tacos, burritos and enchiladas are all made to order, using only fresh ingredients. Ribs also are on the menu, as is a pulled pork taco that is positively sublime. No trouble finding something for the bambinos—the kids' menu will make it easy on everyone. **Features:** Sunday brunch. **Address:** 110 Central Ave 07090 **Location:** Just s of Broad St; center. **Parking:** street only. [L] [D]

WEST LONG BRANCH pop. 8,097

HOLIDAY INN EXPRESS HOTEL & SUITES   732/542-1234
▼▼▼▼ Hotel. Rates not provided. **Address:** 294 SR 36 E 07764 **Location:** Garden State Pkwy exit 105, 2.5 mi e. **Facility:** 128 units. 4 stories, interior corridors. **Amenities:** safes. **Pool(s):** heated indoor. **Activities:** exercise room. **Guest Services:** valet and coin laundry.
CALL [&M] [🖨] [BIZ] [HS] [🛜] [✕] [🛏] [📶] [📠] / SOME UNITS [🐾]

LA QUINTA INN   (732)403-8700
▼▼▼ Hotel $85-$294 **Address:** 109 Rt 36 07764 **Location:** 1.9 mi w of jct SR 35. **Facility:** 98 units. 2 stories, interior corridors. **Pool(s):** heated indoor. **Activities:** hot tub, exercise room. **Guest Services:** coin laundry.
[🖨] [BIZ] [HS] [🛜] [✕] [🛏] [📶] [📠] / SOME UNITS [🐾]

WEST ORANGE (G-5) pop. 46,207, elev. 500'
• Hotels p. 210 • Restaurants p. 210
• Hotels & Restaurants map & index p. 152

Along with its sibling municipalities—Orange, South Orange, East Orange and Maplewood—the city of West Orange is a primarily residential Newark suburb. Eagle Rock Reservation, at Prospect and Eagle Rock Avenues, is a tract of wooded land on the crest of First Mountain—part of the Watchung Mountains, a series of long, low hills in northeastern New Jersey. Lookout Point provides a grand view of the New York City skyline from the George Washington Bridge to the Verrazano Bridge. Also within the park is a memorial to 9/11; the sculpture and plaza commemorate the site where hundreds of people watched the horrific events of Sept. 11, 2001, unfold. The wooded areas are crisscrossed with bridle paths and hiking trails. For park information phone (973) 268-3500.

▼GEM ▼ **THOMAS EDISON NATIONAL HISTORICAL PARK** is at Main St. and Lakeside Ave. The Laboratory Complex includes 14 structures, many of which contain their original furnishings. The collection of 400,000-plus artifacts includes Edison's prototype and commercial inventions. The archives house millions of documents, sound recordings, rare books and photographs.

Most notable inside Glenmont, where Edison and wife Mina Miller Edison lived, is the second-floor living room. Here Edison often conceived inventions at his "thought bench." A greenhouse, barn, stables and garage stand on the landscaped grounds as well as the couple's graves.

Video cameras and strollers are not allowed on tours. **Time:** Allow 2 hours, 30 minutes minimum. **Hours:** Park open Wed.-Sun. 9:30-5, July 4-Aug. 31; 10-4, rest of year. Glenmont open Fri.-Sun. 11-5, July 4-Aug. 31; 11:30-4, rest of year. Guided mansion tour tickets are distributed on a first-come first-served basis from the visitor center. Closed Jan. 1, Thanksgiving and Christmas. **Cost:** $7 (valid for 7 days and includes Edison Laboratory Complex); free (ages 0-15). Audio tour $5. Cash only. **Phone:** (973) 736-0550.

Edison Laboratory Complex is at Main St. and Lakeside Ave. in Thomas Edison National Historical Park. Built in 1887, the complex includes chemical, physics and metallurgical laboratories, a machine shop, a stockroom and even the inventor's library/office. His personal desk is preserved in the exact condition it was in at the time of his death. Many original inventions—phonographs as well as a full-size reproduction of the Black Maria, the world's first motion picture studio—are on display.

Hours: Wed.-Sun. 9:30-5, July 4-Aug. 31; Wed.-Sun. 10-4, rest of year. Closed Jan. 1, Thanksgiving and Christmas. Phone ahead to confirm schedule. **Cost:** $7 (valid for 7 days and includes Thomas Edison National Historical Park and Glenmont); free (ages 0-15). Audio tour $5. Cash only. **Phone:** (973) 736-0550.

Glenmont is at 15 Honeysuckle in Llewellyn Park. Grounds include the greenhouse, garage, barn, stables and Edison's home from 1886 until his death in 1931. The 29-room Queen Anne-style mansion is on the 15-acre estate and contains its original furnishings. The graves of Edison and his wife Mina are behind the house.

Note: Full mobility is required. **Hours:** Grounds Fri.-Sun. 11:30-4. Guided mansion tour tickets are distributed on a first-come first-served basis from the visitor center. Closed Jan. 1, Thanksgiving and Christmas. **Cost:** (Includes Edison Laboratory Complex and Edison National Historic Site visitor center) $7; free (ages 0-15). Gate pass must be obtained at the visitors center. Cash only. Reservations are required. **Phone:** (973) 324-9973 or (973) 736-0550.

(See map & index p. 152.)

TURTLE BACK ZOO is on South Mountain Reservation at 560 Northfield Ave. (CR 508) between Cherry Ln. and Prospect Ave. The zoo contains a variety of animals in outdoor paddock enclosures as well as an animal nursery. From April through November a miniature train offers a scenic 1-mile ride around the grounds.

Time: Allow 2 hours minimum. **Hours:** Mon.-Sat. 10-5, Sun. 11-6 (weather permitting). Last admission 30 minutes before closing. Closed Jan. 1, Thanksgiving and Christmas. **Cost:** Admission Apr.-Nov. $11; $8 (ages 2-12 and 62+). Admission rest of year $9; $7 (ages 2-12 and 62+). Carousel $2. Pony ride $2. **Phone:** (973) 731-5800 to verify schedule.

BEST WESTERN TURTLE BROOK INN
(973)731-5300   **55**

Hotel
$130-$160

AAA Benefit: Members save up to 20%!

Address: 555 Northfield Ave 07052 **Location:** 2 mi s on CR 577 (Prospect Ave), 0.7 mi w. **Facility:** 56 units. 2 stories (no elevator), interior corridors. **Activities:** exercise room. **Guest Services:** valet and coin laundry.

COURTYARD BY MARRIOTT WEST ORANGE
(973)669-4725   **54**

Hotel $139-$252 **Address:** 8 Rooney Cir 07052 **Location:** I-280 exit 8A, 0.5 mi s on CR 577 (Prospect Ave); in Essex Green Shopping Center. **Facility:** 131 units. 3 stories, interior corridors. **Pool(s):** heated indoor. **Activities:** hot tub, exercise room. **Guest Services:** valet and coin laundry, boarding pass kiosk.

AAA Benefit: Members save 5% or more!

RESIDENCE INN BY MARRIOTT-WEST ORANGE
(973)669-4700   **52**

Extended Stay Hotel $139-$286 **Address:** 107 Prospect Ave 07052 **Location:** I-280 exit 8B, 1 mi n on CR 577 (Prospect Ave). **Facility:** 128 units, some two bedrooms, efficiencies and kitchens. 3 stories, interior corridors. **Terms:** check-in 4 pm. **Pool(s):** heated indoor. **Activities:** hot tub, exercise room. **Guest Services:** valet and coin laundry.

AAA Benefit: Members save 5% or more!

THE WILSHIRE GRAND HOTEL
(973)731-7007   **53**

Hotel
$199-$449

Address: 350 Pleasant Valley Way 07052 **Location:** I-280 exit 8B, just n to Eagle Rock Ave, 0.9 mi w, then just n. **Facility:** 89 units. 3 stories, interior corridors. **Terms:** 3 day cancellation notice. **Amenities:** safes. **Dining:** Primavera Ristorante, see separate listing. **Activities:** bicycles, exercise room. **Guest Services:** valet laundry, area transportation. **Featured Amenity:** breakfast buffet.

WHERE TO EAT

HIGHLAWN PAVILION
973/731-3463   **43**

American. Fine Dining. $13-$45 **AAA Inspector Notes:** *Historic.* Vast picture windows throughout the Mediterranean-style dining room afford views of the wooded hillside and the spectacular New York City skyline. Upon entry, guests are treated to a view of the open kitchen and a cadre of chefs hard at work behind large stoves, brick ovens and roasting spits. The eclectic menu is thoughtful and intriguing, and includes slow-roasted duck with lavender glaze, sea bass with chamomile flower sauce and linguine with cockle clams in a verbena tomato sauce. **Features:** full bar. **Reservations:** suggested. **Address:** 381 Eagle Rock Ave 07052 **Location:** I-280 exit 8B, 0.3 mi n, then 0.3 mi e. **Parking:** valet only.

THE MANOR
973/731-2360   **41**

Continental
Fine Dining
$11-$53

AAA Inspector Notes: Lush grounds, formal gardens and romantic gazebos surround elegant buildings which comprise this luxury retreat. Seasonal menus feature classic dishes of fish and game. Service is formal and sophisticated. Guests have options of the a la carte dining room or the buffet-only room which features a nightly lobster buffet and a Sunday family dinner buffet. **Features:** full bar, Sunday brunch. **Reservations:** required. Semiformal attire. **Address:** 111 Prospect Ave 07052 **Location:** I-280 exit 8B, 1 mi n on CR 577 (Prospect Ave). **Parking:** on-site and valet. *Menu on AAA.com*

MCLOONE'S BOATHOUSE
862/252-7108   **44**

American. Casual Dining. $10-$35 **AAA Inspector Notes:** The menu offers familiar items with some fresh seafood, burgers and entrées, but the beautiful restaurant and relaxed lakefront setting are reason enough to stop here. Soaring ceilings and picture windows look out on the Orange Reservoir and make you feel like you are miles away at a mountain camp. McLoone's is a great stop after exploring the adjacent, family-friendly Turtle Back Zoo. **Features:** full bar, patio dining, Sunday brunch. **Reservations:** suggested. **Address:** 9 Cherry Ln 07052 **Location:** I-280 exit 7 (Pleasant Valley Way), 3.6 mi s, just e on Northfield Ave (CR 508); at South Mountain recreation complex.

PRIMAVERA RISTORANTE
973/731-4779   **42**

Italian. Casual Dining. $11-$28 **AAA Inspector Notes:** Tucked within the gleaming halls of a hotel is this comfortable little place with dark paneled walls and subdued lighting. Hotel guests will find that locals dine here and make up a bulk of the clientele. The food is well prepared and accessible, and includes steaks, pastas and Italian specialties. Service is friendly and accommodating. **Features:** full bar. **Reservations:** suggested. **Address:** 350 Pleasant Valley Way 07052 **Location:** I-280 exit 8B, just n to Eagle Rock Ave, 0.9 mi w, then just n; in The Wilshire Grand Hotel.

WESTWOOD pop. 10,908

IT'S GREEK TO ME
201/722-3511

▼▼▼ Greek. Casual Dining. $10-$35 **AAA Inspector Notes:** This restaurant is a veritable find for those in search of authentic Greek cuisine. Start with the creamy, garlicky and oh-so-good gigantes, giant white beans cooked with tomato and sage. Gyros are, as they should be, good and messy. Servers are happy to bring over extra napkins, or anything else you may need. The dining room is reminiscent of a sunny Greek Island and is bedecked with the country's official blue and white colors. **Features:** patio dining. **Address:** 487 Broadway 07675 **Location:** Jct Westwood Ave and Broadway; center. L D CALL &M

WHIPPANY
- **Restaurants p. 212**
- **Hotels & Restaurants map & index p. 152**

COURTYARD BY MARRIOTT HANOVER WHIPPANY
(973)887-8700 **46**

▼▼▼ Hotel $202-$332

COURTYARD Marriott

AAA Benefit: Members save 5% or more!

Address: 157 SR 10 E 07981 **Location:** I-287 exit 39, 1.5 mi e. **Facility:** 149 units. 3 stories, interior corridors. **Pool(s):** heated indoor. **Activities:** exercise room. **Guest Services:** valet and coin laundry, boarding pass kiosk.

SAVE ⛉ CALL &M BIZ HS 🛜 ✕ 🍴 🖨
/ SOME UNITS 📷

HANOVER MARRIOTT
(973)538-8811 **45**

▼▼▼ Hotel $209-$344 **Address:** 1401 Rt 10 E 07981 **Location:** I-287 exit 39B southbound; exit 39 northbound, 0.5 mi w. Located in a commercial area. **Facility:** 353 units. 8 stories, interior corridors. **Terms:** check-in 4 pm. **Amenities:** safes. **Dining:** 2 restaurants. **Pool(s):** outdoor, heated indoor. **Activities:** exercise room. **Guest Services:** valet and coin laundry, area transportation.

AAA Benefit: Members save 5% or more!

🍴 🍴 ⛉ CALL &M 🏊 BIZ 🛜 ✕ 🖨
/ SOME UNITS 🔒 📷

HYATT HOUSE PARSIPPANY/WHIPPANY
(973)605-1001 **44**

▼▼▼ Extended Stay Hotel $99-$299

H HYATT house™

AAA Benefit: Members save 10%!

Address: 1 Ridgedale Ave N 07981 **Location:** I-287 exit 39, just nw. **Facility:** 135 kitchen units, some two bedrooms. 3 stories, interior corridors. **Terms:** cancellation fee imposed. **Pool(s):** heated outdoor. **Activities:** hot tub, exercise room. **Guest Services:** valet and coin laundry, area transportation. **Featured Amenity:** breakfast buffet. *(See ad this page.)*

SAVE CALL &M 🏊 BIZ 🛜 ✕ 🔒 🖨 🍴
/ SOME UNITS 🔒 HS

Get AAA/CAA travel information in the

digital and printed formats you prefer

(See map & index p. 152.)

WHERE TO EAT

IL CAPRICCIO

973/884-9175 (38)

▼▼▼ ▼▼▼
Italian
Fine Dining
$16-$32

AAA Inspector Notes: Savor sophisticated and classic Italian fare in this bright and formal Tuscan-inspired dining room. The chef/owner has been preparing excellent meals here since 1984. Well-trained servers provide vigilant service and help guests navigate a wine list offering more than 400 selections. **Features:** full bar. **Reservations:** suggested. Semiformal attire. **Address:** 633 SR 10 07981 **Location:** I-287 exit 39, 1 mi e. **Parking:** valet only.

L D CALL ☎ M

NIKKO

973/428-0787 (37)

▼▼▼ Japanese. Casual Dining. $8-$26 **AAA Inspector Notes:** There's more than just good sushi at this cozy restaurant. It offers a varied menu including many teriyaki dishes, udon and soba, donburi and some good vegetarian options. For a full experience you can request a table in the traditional Japanese tatami room. **Features:** full bar, happy hour. **Address:** 881 SR 10 E 07981 **Location:** I-287 exit 39 northbound; exit 39A southbound, 0.3 mi e.

L D

Take Your **Imagination**
to New Destinations

Use AAA Travel Guides online to
explore the possibilities.

Go to AAA.com/travelguide today.

WHITE HOUSE STATION pop. 2,089

HOLLY THORN HOUSE BED & BREAKFAST INN
908/534-1616

▼▼▼▼ Bed & Breakfast. Rates not provided. **Address:** 143 Readington Rd 08889 **Location:** US 202, 4 mi nw on CR 637, just n. **Facility:** Once a cow barn, this comfortable building is filled with collectibles and has rooms of varied themes, all furnished with antiques. There is ample public spaces, including an open living room area. 5 units. 2 stories (no elevator), interior corridors. **Terms:** age restrictions may apply. **Pool(s):** outdoor. **Activities:** game room, massage. 🛍 BIZ 📶 ✕ 🔲

WILDWOOD (H-3) pop. 5,325, elev. 8'
- Hotels p. 217 • Restaurants p. 218
- Hotels & Restaurants map & index p. 215

The four communities that make up this popular shore resort are usually referred to in the plural. Although the Wildwoods—North Wildwood *(see place listing p. 173)*, West Wildwood, Wildwood and Wildwood Crest *(see place listing p. 218)*—are separate municipalities, their boundaries are indistinguishable. Together they occupy the state's southernmost isle, just north of Cape May.

For decades after the mid-18th-century departure of the Ketchemeche Indians, the land's first inhabitants, offshore farmers grazed their livestock. It wasn't until the late 19th century that fishermen and whalers began settling the region.

But it was tourism that quickly became a Wildwoods calling card. First conceived in 1899 as a practical way to keep sand out of visitors' shoes, the boardwalk evolved from a temporary feature to a cherished landmark. The first roller coaster arrived in 1916. Today the boardwalk, nearly 2 miles long, boasts three amusement piers and a variety of shops and eateries.

From Easter weekend through September battery-operated tram cars travel the wooden walkway between Cresse Avenue, at the Wildwood/Wildwood Crest border, and 16th Street in North Wildwood. Passengers can board anywhere along the route; the entire one-way trip takes about 30 minutes. For more information contact Sightseers Tram Car, 5308 Boardwalk; phone (609) 523-8726. The open-air trolleys provided by Five Mile Beach Electric Railway Co. are another fun way to get around the Wildwoods resort area during the summer; phone (800) 487-6559. The Greater Wildwood Chamber of Commerce organizes special events in the spring and fall; for more information phone (609) 729-4000.

The Doo Wop Back to the Fifties Tour is a 90-minute narrated evening bus tour that highlights the Wildwoods' fanciful post-World War II resort architecture. A plethora of plastic palm trees, kidney-shaped swimming pools and candy-colored neon signs accent the space-age designs of motels and restaurants along the tour route. Tours depart Tues. and Thurs. at 8 p.m., mid-June to early September

(See map & index p. 215.)

or by group appointment, from the Doo Wop Experience Museum *(see attraction listing)*; phone (609) 523-1958.

A half-size replica of the Vietnam Veterans Memorial in Washington, D.C., honors those who served in that war. Wildwood's Vietnam Veterans Remembrance Wall, at Burke and Ocean avenues at Fox Park, is a 250-foot-long monument engraved with the names of the more than 58,900 soldiers killed during that conflict.

Because the surf line lies as far as 1,000 feet from shore, the Wildwoods' beaches are among the safest in the state. Towels and umbrellas dot the sand while speedboat enthusiasts race through the water and parasailors glide above it. Surf fishing also is popular. Sterling Harbor Bait & Tackle, 1020 W. Rio Grande Ave., organizes deep-sea fishing excursions as well as boat and kayak rentals; phone (609) 729-1425. Local marinas include the Pier 47 Marina, 3001 Wildwood Blvd., phone (609) 729-4774; and Schooner Island Marina, 5100 Lake Rd., phone (609) 729-8900.

Summer officially begins in Wildwood when a multitude of colorful kites soar above the beach Memorial Day weekend during the 🪁 International Kite Festival. An illuminated night kite fly, music, stunt and indoor kite championships, kite exhibits and kite-making workshops are all part of the fun.

Greater Wildwood Chamber of Commerce: 3306 Pacific Ave., Wildwood, NJ 08260. **Phone:** (609) 729-4000.

Self-guiding tours: A brochure describing a self-guiding walking tour of the area's kitschy landmarks is available at the chamber of commerce. The vivid architectural style is courtesy of the many funky-looking signs, motels and restaurants erected during the 1950s, '60s and '70s.

CAPTAIN SCHUMANN'S WHALE AND DOLPHIN WATCHING is at 4500 Park Blvd. *The Big Blue Sightseer* tours Wildwood Harbor, the inlet and the coast. The captain provides commentary about local ecosystems, the fishing industry and the Wildwoods area and then steers the boat into deeper waters for a chance to spot dolphins, whales and other marine life.

Time: Allow 2 hours, 30 minutes minimum. **Hours:** Cruises depart daily at 10, 1:30 and 6:30, July 4 weekend-Labor Day. **Cost:** Fare for 1:30 p.m. cruise $38; $20 (ages 6-12). Fare for 10 a.m. or 6:30 p.m. cruise $28; $18 (ages 6-12). Prices and schedule may vary; phone ahead. Reservations are recommended. **Phone:** (609) 522-2919 or (800) 246-9425.

DOO WOP EXPERIENCE MUSEUM is at 4500 Ocean Ave. at Burk Ave. and across from the convention center. The Wildwoods, a refurbished Surfside restaurant from the 1960s, is said to contain the country's largest collection of mid-century resort architecture. The museum features 1950s and '60s furniture and household items, a diner interior, jukebox and reference books designed to reflect what it was like during the period when Doo-Wop architecture and motels were in their heyday.

Short videos and a video board display make up the I-Wall, an interactive exhibit about the area and its motels. A neon sign garden showcases restored motel and restaurant signs. An optional 90-minute bus tour carries guests to various Doo-Wop locations nearby. **Time:** Allow 30 minutes minimum. **Hours:** Museum Tues. and Thurs. 3-9, Wed. and Fri. 3-8, Sat.-Sat. 9-9, May-Sept.; by appointment rest of year. Guided 90-minute tours depart Tues. and Thurs. 8 p.m., mid-June to early Sept.; otherwise by group reservation only. Guests should arrive 15 minutes prior to tour departure. Phone ahead to confirm schedule. **Cost:** Free. Guided bus tour $12; $6 (ages 0-12). Cash only. **Phone:** (609) 523-1958. GT T1

GEORGE F. BOYER MUSEUM is at 3907 Pacific Ave. Local antiques, photographs and memorabilia from the late 1800s and early 1900s are displayed. A postcard collection and exhibits about the beach patrol and fire and police departments offer glimpses into this beachside town's past. **Time:** Allow 1 hour minimum. **Hours:** Mon.-Sat. 9-2, mid-June to mid-Sept.; Thurs.-Sat. 9-2, mid-Sept. to early Nov. and mid-Apr. to mid-June. Closed major holidays. Phone ahead to confirm schedule. **Cost:** Donations. **Phone:** (609) 523-0277.

MOREY'S PIERS & BEACHFRONT WATER-PARKS is s. on SR 47, then n. on Atlantic Ave. to Spencer, Schellenger and 25th aves. and the Boardwalk. Overlooking the Jersey Shore, the boardwalk complex features three amusement piers and two beachfront water parks.

The action-packed amusement piers boast games and rides for every age. Surfside Pier creates a high-energy atmosphere with thrilling attractions like "it," The Great Nor'Easter coaster and AtmosFEAR. Mariner's Landing offers an atmosphere of a traditional amusement park with such classic rides as the tea cups, bumper cars and a double-decker carousel. Adventure Pier features a highly interactive amusement environment packed with high thrill rides, art and live entertainment.

Hours: Mon.-Fri. 1 p.m.-midnight, Sat.-Sun. noon-midnight, mid-June through Labor Day; opening and closing times vary, early Apr. to mid-June and day after Labor Day-late Oct. Phone ahead to confirm schedule.

(See map & index p. 215.)

Cost: Ride and waterpark combination pass $75; $57 (under 48 inches tall). Three-pier ride pass $55; $45 (under 48 inches tall). General admission, includes both waterparks $43; $35 (under 48 inches tall). Some activities and rides have individual fees. Rates may vary; phone ahead to confirm. Ticket cards and multiple-day tickets also are available. **Phone:** (609) 522-3900. 🍴

Ocean Oasis Waterpark and Beach Club and Raging Waters Waterpark are s. on SR 47, then n. on Atlantic Ave. to Spencer, Schellenger and 25th aves. and the Boardwalk. At Ocean Oasis Water Park and Beach Club you can race your friends down the newest slide, the six-lane WipeOut and then relax with a drink at Stubborn Brothers Beach Bar + Grill or Water Lilies swim-up bar. Embark on an expedition of wild family fun at Raging Waters Water Park with River Adventure and two adventurous kiddie play areas. Both water parks offer private cabana rentals and their own style of slides, activity pool, food and more.

Locker facilities are available. **Hours:** Daily 9:30-6:30, late June-Aug. 31; schedule varies in May and Sept. Phone ahead to confirm schedule. **Cost:** General admission, includes both waterparks $43; $35 (under 48 inches tall). Cabana rentals are an additional fee. Reduced one-park rates apply before

12:30 and after 3. Rates may vary; phone ahead to confirm. **Phone:** (609) 522-3900. 🍴

SAVE *SILVER BULLET* **SPEEDBOAT** departs from Wildwood Marina at the foot of the bridge at 508 W. Rio Grande Ave. Ninety-minute trips aboard a 70-foot vessel travel the Intracoastal Waterway and the Wildwood coast offering sightings of birds, dolphins and sometimes whales. **Hours:** Trips depart daily at 9:30, noon and 2:30 (also Tues.-Thurs. at 4:30), Memorial Day weekend-late Sept. **Cost:** Fare $30; $17 (ages 2-11). Reservations are recommended. **Phone:** (609) 522-6060.

SPLASH ZONE WATER PARK is at Schellenger Ave. and the Boardwalk. Waterslides and rides range from gentle to thrilling at this water park, which also contains a lazy river, a shaded wading pool, a raft ride and a 1,000-gallon bucket of water that drenches guests. Hurricane Island is an interactive tree house complete with a wide variety of water toys. Frazzled parents can relax in the lounge areas.

Time: Allow 1 hour minimum. **Hours:** Daily 9:30-6:30, late June to mid-Aug.; 10-6, mid- to late June and mid-Aug. through Labor Day; schedule varies, mid-May to mid-June. Phone ahead to confirm opening and closing hours. **Cost:** $35.95; $29.95 (under 48 inches tall); $12.99 (senior citizens). Admission opening-noon or 3 p.m.-closing $25.99; $19.99 (under 48 inches tall). **Phone:** (609) 729-5600. 🍴

© AAA

1677-15

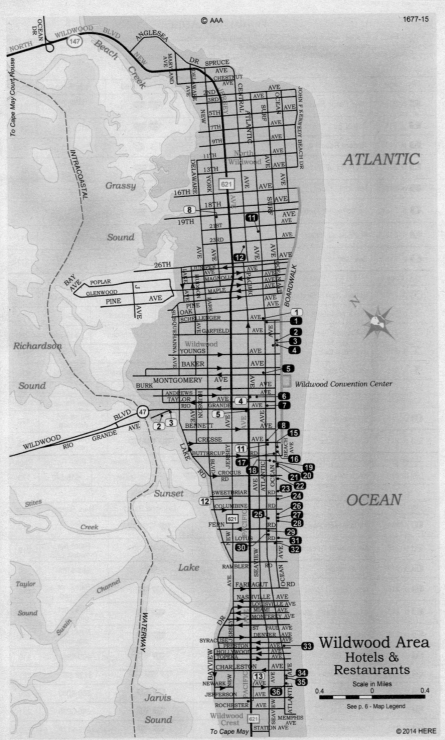

ATLANTIC

North
Wildwood

Grassy

Sound

Richardson

Sound

Wildwood

Wildwood Convention Center

Stites

Creek

Sunset

OCEAN

Taylor

Sound

Lake

Jarvis

Sound

Wildwood
Crest

To Cape May

Wildwood Area
Hotels &
Restaurants

Scale in Miles

0.4   0   0.4

See p. 6 - Map Legend

© 2014 HERE

Wildwood Area

This index helps you "spot" where approved hotels and restaurants are located on the corresponding detailed maps. Hotel daily rate range is for comparison only. Restaurant price range is a combination of lunch and/or dinner. Turn to the listing page for more detailed rate and price information and consult display ads for special promotions.

WILDWOOD

Map Page	Hotels	Diamond Rated	Rate Range	Page
1 p. 215	Blue Palms Resort	◆◆	Rates not provided	217
2 p. 215	Sea-N-Sun Resort Motel	◆◆	$125-$350	217
3 p. 215	**Riviera Resort & Suites**	◆◆	$125-$350 (SAVE)	217
4 p. 215	AA Heart of Wildwood Motel	◆◆	Rates not provided	217
5 p. 215	Mar Lane Motel	◆◆	$85-$175	217
6 p. 215	**Le Voyageur Motel**	◆◆	Rates not provided (SAVE)	217
7 p. 215	The Starlux Hotel	◆◆◆	Rates not provided	217
8 p. 215	Sea Gull Motel	◆◆	Rates not provided	217

Map Page	Restaurants	Diamond Rated	Cuisine	Price Range	Page
① p. 215	**Schellenger's Restaurant**	◆◆	American	$11-$33	218
② p. 215	Urie's Waterfront Restaurant	◆◆	Seafood	$9-$44	218
③ p. 215	Boathouse Restaurant	◆◆	American	$13-$42	218
④ p. 215	Key West Cafe	◆◆	American	$8-$20	218
⑤ p. 215	Marvis Diner	◆◆	American	$6-$22	218

NORTH WILDWOOD

Map Page	Hotels	Diamond Rated	Rate Range	Page
11 p. 215	Summer Nites	◆◆◆	Rates not provided	173
12 p. 215	Candlelight Inn	◆◆◆	Rates not provided	173

Map Page	Restaurant	Diamond Rated	Cuisine	Price Range	Page
⑧ p. 215	Piro's Village Restaurant	◆◆	Italian	$15-$40	173

WILDWOOD CREST

Map Page	Hotels	Diamond Rated	Rate Range	Page
15 p. 215	**Aqua Beach Resort** (See ad p. 219.)	◆◆◆	Rates not provided (SAVE)	219
16 p. 215	**Adventurer Oceanfront Inn**	◆◆◆	Rates not provided (SAVE)	219
17 p. 215	Bel-Air Motel	◆	$68-$168	220
18 p. 215	Aztec Resort Motel	◆◆	Rates not provided	219
19 p. 215	American Safari Motel	◆◆	Rates not provided	219
20 p. 215	Gondolier Motel	◆◆	Rates not provided	221
21 p. 215	Attache Resort Motel	◆◆	$70-$284	219
22 p. 215	Pan American Hotel	◆◆◆	$139-$295	221
23 p. 215	Crusader Resort	◆◆	$80-$280	220
24 p. 215	Nassau Inn	◆◆	$80-$230	221
25 p. 215	Compass Family Resort	◆◆	$65-$178	220

WILDWOOD CREST (cont'd)

Map Page	Hotels (cont'd)	Diamond Rated	Rate Range	Page
26 p. 215	Bristol Plaza Resort	▼▼	$64-$245	220
27 p. 215	**Ocean Holiday Motor Inn**	▼▼	$75-$275 [SAVE]	221
28 p. 215	**Armada By-The-Sea**	▼▼	Rates not provided [SAVE]	219
29 p. 215	Cara Mara Condominium Resort	▼▼	Rates not provided	220
30 p. 215	Jolly Roger Motel	▼▼	Rates not provided	221
31 p. 215	Port Royal Hotel	▼▼▼	$250-$405	221
32 p. 215	**Lotus Inn** (See ad p. 220.)	▼▼	$60-$255 [SAVE]	221
33 p. 215	**El Coronado Resort**	▼▼	$79-$519 [SAVE]	221
34 p. 215	Acacia Beachfront Resort	▼▼	Rates not provided	218
35 p. 215	Beau Rivage Beach Resort	▼▼	$75-$275	219
36 p. 215	**Reges Oceanfront Resort** (See ad p. 220.)	▼▼▼	$152-$365 [SAVE]	221

Map Page	Restaurants	Diamond Rated	Cuisine	Price Range	Page
11 p. 215	Little Italy Family Restaurant	▼▼	Italian	$15-$30	221
12 p. 215	Tony Luke's	▼	Sandwiches	$6-$10	221
13 p. 215	Marie Nicole's	▼▼▼	American	$21-$49	221

AA HEART OF WILDWOOD MOTEL   609/522-4090   **4**
▼▼ **Motel.** Rates not provided. **Address:** 3915 Ocean Ave 08260 **Location:** Oceanfront. Between Spencer and Spicer aves. Adjacent to boardwalk. **Facility:** 74 units, some two bedrooms and efficiencies. 2 stories (no elevator), exterior corridors. **Amenities:** safes. **Pool(s):** heated outdoor. **Guest Services:** coin laundry.

BLUE PALMS RESORT   609/522-0606   **1**
▼▼ **Motel.** Rates not provided. **Address:** 3601 Atlantic Ave 08260 **Location:** Between Lincoln and Schellenger aves. **Facility:** 53 units, some efficiencies. 3 stories (no elevator), exterior corridors. **Amenities:** safes. **Pool(s):** heated outdoor. **Guest Services:** coin laundry.

LE VOYAGEUR MOTEL   609/522-6407   **6**
▼▼
Motel
Rates not provided

Address: 232 E Andrews Ave 08260 **Location:** Between Andrews and Taylor aves. **Facility:** 24 units, some two bedrooms and efficiencies. 3 stories (no elevator), exterior corridors. **Pool(s):** heated outdoor. **Guest Services:** coin laundry.

MAR LANE MOTEL   609/522-7463   **5**
▼▼ **Motel** $85-$175 **Address:** 4310 Atlantic Ave 08260 **Location:** Garden State Pkwy exit 4B, 3 mi se on SR 47, then 0.5 mi n on Atlantic Ave to Montgomery Ave. **Facility:** 25 units, some efficiencies. 2 stories (no elevator), exterior corridors. **Terms:** closed 10/26-5/1, 3 night minimum stay - seasonal and/or weekends, 14 day cancellation notice-fee imposed. **Amenities:** safes. **Pool(s):** heated outdoor.

RIVIERA RESORT & SUITES   609/522-5353   **3**
▼▼
Motel
$125-$350
Address: 325 E Spencer Ave 08260 **Location:** Garden State Pkwy exit 4B, 3 mi se on SR 47, then 0.5 mi n on Ocean Ave. **Facility:** 36 units, some two bedrooms and kitchens. 3 stories (no elevator), exterior corridors. **Terms:** closed 11/1-4/1, 2-4 night minimum stay - seasonal, 14 day cancellation notice-fee imposed. **Amenities:** safes. **Pool(s):** heated outdoor. **Activities:** hot tub.

SEA GULL MOTEL   609/522-3333   **8**
▼▼ **Motel.** Rates not provided. **Address:** 5305 Atlantic Ave 08260 **Location:** Between Cresse and Hildreth aves. **Facility:** 66 units, some efficiencies. 2-3 stories (no elevator), exterior corridors. **Pool(s):** heated outdoor. **Guest Services:** coin laundry.

SEA-N-SUN RESORT MOTEL   609/522-2826   **2**
▼▼ **Motel** $125-$350 **Address:** 3909 Ocean Ave 08260 **Location:** Oceanfront. Between Spencer and Spicer aves. **Facility:** 21 units, some efficiencies. 2 stories (no elevator), interior/exterior corridors. **Terms:** closed 10/1-4/30, 2-4 night minimum stay - seasonal, 14 day cancellation notice-fee imposed. **Amenities:** safes. **Pool(s):** outdoor.

THE STARLUX HOTEL   609/522-7412   **7**
▼▼▼ **Retro Hotel.** Rates not provided. **Address:** 305 E Rio Grande Ave 08260 **Location:** Between Atlantic and Ocean aves. **Facility:** This hotel's retro 1950s décor carries throughout the property, which sits in a prime location across the street from the beach and near the amusement pier and convention center. 36 units, some two bedrooms and efficiencies. 3 stories, interior/exterior corridors. **Amenities:** safes. **Pool(s):** heated outdoor. **Activities:** hot tub, bicycles, game room. **Guest Services:** complimentary laundry.

(See map & index p. 215.)

WHERE TO EAT

BOATHOUSE RESTAURANT 609/729-5301 ③
WW American. Casual Dining. $13-$42 **AAA Inspector Notes:** Overlooking the bay, the dining room and the marina deck of this restaurant afford pretty views. The menu lists steak, veal, chicken and ribs, as well as a good array of seafood, including Cajun mako shark served with rice pilaf and applesauce. Service is prompt and efficient. **Features:** full bar, patio dining, happy hour. **Address:** 506 W Rio Grande Ave 08260 **Location:** Garden State Pkwy exit 4B to southeast side of bridge. D

KEY WEST CAFE 609/522-5006 ④
WW American. Casual Dining. $8-$20 **AAA Inspector Notes:** The warm, friendly staff here serves tasty and affordable American fare in a casual atmosphere. The $2.22 special—two eggs, two pancakes and two slices of bacon—is offered before 10 am Monday through Friday. During the height of the summer season, many guests like to pick up a family-size dinner to go. **Address:** 4701 Pacific Ave 08260 **Location:** Jct Andrews Ave. **Parking:** street only. B L

MARVIS DINER 609/522-0550 ⑤
WW American. Casual Dining. $6-$22 **AAA Inspector Notes:** This nautically themed diner offers an extensive variety of sandwiches, steaks, burgers, salads and breakfast options served all day. Inside, guests will find bright colors, surf boards, fake palm trees and a small outdoor dining area. Prices are very reasonable. **Features:** patio dining. **Address:** 4900 Pacific Ave 08260 **Location:** Jct Pacific and Rio Grande aves. B L D

SCHELLENGER'S RESTAURANT 609/522-0433 ①
WWW WWW
American
Casual Dining
$11-$33
AAA Inspector Notes: This longstanding family-friendly shore restaurant is decorated with a variety of aquatic decorations inside and out. The large menu emphasizes popular seafood dishes such as grilled lobster tail, snow crabs, shrimp cocktail, lobster bisque and pan-seared scallops. A children's menu also is available. **Features:** full bar, early bird specials. **Address:** 3516 Atlantic Ave 08260 **Location:** Between Schellenger and E Cedar aves; downtown. *Menu on AAA.com* D

URIE'S WATERFRONT RESTAURANT 609/522-4189 ②
WW Seafood. Family Dining. $9-$44 **AAA Inspector Notes:** A rustic, nautical theme weaves through the large indoor and covered outdoor dining areas at this casual spot where most seats afford excellent views of the bay. The menu features steak and seafood. For those who are really hungry, try the all-you-can-eat crab. During the first and last two weeks of the season, the restaurant is open only on weekends. **Features:** full bar, patio dining, early bird specials. **Address:** 588 W Rio Grande Ave 08260 **Location:** Garden State Pkwy exit 4B, 2.5 mi se; southeast side of bridge. L D CALL ⛅M

WILDWOOD CREST (H-3) pop. 3,270
• Restaurants p. 221
• Hotels & Restaurants map & index p. 215

Founded in 1905, Wildwood Crest is the Wildwoods' southernmost town. Unlike neighboring beach towns North Wildwood *(see place listing p. 173)* and Wildwood, Wildwood Crest has a historical past: The only Revolutionary War battle fought in Cape May County took place near Sunset Lake. Turtle Gut Park and Memorial, located at New Jersey and Miami avenues, commemorates the site. The lake offers opportunities for fishing, sailboating and water skiing; for information about recreational activities phone (609) 522-0221.

There's no boardwalk in town, although a bicycle trail edges the beach. Two-wheelers can be rented from Bradley's Bikes at Ocean Avenue and Rambler Road, phone (609) 729-1444; and from Crest Bike Rental, 500 E. Heather Rd., phone (609) 522-5763. The offshore waters are home to a large population of bottlenose dolphins; the best way to glimpse them is aboard a sightseeing cruise.

The entire Wildwood resort area is known for its "Doo Wop" architecture, a style popular in the 1950s that is defined by brightly painted, angular buildings, boomerang-shaped roofs, funky neon signs, and futuristic space-age decorative details. A 20-block stretch of Ocean Avenue in Wildwood Crest has a large concentration of Doo Wop-style motels. For information about educational programs and materials contact the Doo Wop Preservation League; phone (609) 729-4000.

STARLIGHT FLEET departs from 6200 Park Blvd. Cruises are narrated by a marine biologist who provides background about the region's marine ecosystem, ocean life and indigenous wildlife. Both the 2-hour weekday morning cruise and 2-hour, 45-minute sunset cruise offer a light meal and the possibility of dolphin sightings. The 3-hour afternoon cruise and 2.5-hour weekend morning cruise offer opportunities to observe dolphins as well as whales. Themed cruises and fishing trips also are available.

Time: Allow 2 hours minimum. **Hours:** Sightseeing cruises depart daily at 10 (Sat.-Sun. at 9:30), 1 and 6, Memorial Day-Labor Day. **Cost:** Morning cruise Mon.-Fri. $30; $20 (ages 7-12), Sat.-Sun. $35; $20 (ages 7-12). Afternoon or sunset cruise $40; $25 (ages 7-12). Phone ahead to confirm schedule and prices. **Phone:** (609) 729-3400 or (609) 729-7776.

Dark Star Pirate Cruises departs from 6200 Park Blvd. Children are asked to help the crew search for treasure, but the whole family can watch a water cannon battle and learn how to speak pirate. **Hours:** Cruises depart daily at 9:30, 11, 12:30, 2, 3:30, 5 and 6:30, Memorial Day-Labor Day. Phone ahead to confirm schedule. **Cost:** $23; free (children under 30 inches tall). Reservations are recommended. **Phone:** (609) 729-3275.

ACACIA BEACHFRONT RESORT 609/729-2233 ㉞
WW Motel. Rates not provided. **Address:** 9101 Atlantic Ave 08260 **Location:** Oceanfront. Between St. Louis and Trenton aves. **Facility:** 51 efficiencies, some two bedrooms. 4 stories, exterior corridors. **Pool(s):** heated outdoor. **Guest Services:** coin laundry.
🛎️ 🏊 📶 ✖️ 🛏️ 🍴 🛄

(See map & index p. 215.)

ADVENTURER OCEANFRONT INN   609/729-1200 🔟6️⃣

Hotel
Rates not provided

Address: 5401 Ocean Ave 08260 **Location:** Oceanfront. Between Cresse Ave and Morning Glory Rd. **Facility:** 113 units, some two bedrooms, three bedrooms and efficiencies. 7 stories, interior corridors. **Amenities:** safes. **Pool(s):** heated outdoor. **Activities:** game room, exercise room. **Guest Services:** coin laundry.

[SAVE] 🍴 🏊 [BIZ] 📶 ✖️ 📱 📺 💻

AMERICAN SAFARI MOTEL   609/522-0157 1️⃣9️⃣

🔱🔱 **Motel.** Rates not provided. **Address:** 5610 Ocean Ave 08260 **Location:** Between Buttercup and Lavender rds. **Facility:** 27 units, some two bedrooms and efficiencies. 3 stories (no elevator), exterior corridors. **Amenities:** *Some:* safes. **Pool(s):** heated outdoor. **Guest Services:** coin laundry.

🏊 📶 ✖️ 📱 📺 / SOME UNITS 💻

AQUA BEACH RESORT   609/522-6507 1️⃣5️⃣

Hotel
Rates not provided

Address: 5501 Ocean Ave 08260 **Location:** Oceanfront. Between Morning Glory and Buttercup rds. **Facility:** 151 units, some two bedrooms, three bedrooms, efficiencies, kitchens and condominiums. 5 stories, interior/exterior corridors. **Pool(s):** heated outdoor. **Activities:** hot tub, game room. **Guest Services:** coin laundry. *(See ad this page.)*

[SAVE] 🍴 🏊 [BIZ] 📶 ✖️ 📱 📺

ARMADA BY-THE-SEA   609/729-3000 2️⃣8️⃣

Motel
Rates not provided

Address: 6503 Ocean Ave 08260 **Location:** Oceanfront. Between Forget Me Not and Rosemary rds. **Facility:** 58 units, some two bedrooms, efficiencies and kitchens. 5 stories, exterior corridors. **Amenities:** safes. **Pool(s):** heated outdoor. **Activities:** game room. **Guest Services:** coin laundry.

[SAVE] 🏊 📶 ✖️ 📱 📺 💻

ATTACHE RESORT MOTEL   609/522-0241 2️⃣1️⃣

🔱🔱 **Motel** $70-$284 **Address:** 5711 Ocean Ave 08260 **Location:** Oceanfront. Between Heather and Lavender rds. **Facility:** 45 units, some efficiencies. 3 stories, exterior corridors. **Terms:** closed 10/14-5/1, 3 night minimum stay - seasonal and/or weekends, 21 day cancellation notice-fee imposed. **Pool(s):** heated outdoor. **Guest Services:** coin laundry.

🍴 🏊 📶 ✖️ 📱 📺 💻

AZTEC RESORT MOTEL   609/522-7000 1️⃣8️⃣

🔱🔱 **Motel.** Rates not provided. **Address:** 411 E Lavender Rd 08260 **Location:** Between Ocean and Atlantic aves. **Facility:** 38 units, some efficiencies. 3 stories (no elevator), exterior corridors. **Amenities:** *Some:* safes. **Pool(s):** heated outdoor. **Guest Services:** coin laundry.

🏊 📶 ✖️ 📱 📺 / SOME UNITS 💻

BEAU RIVAGE BEACH RESORT   (609)729-2121 3️⃣5️⃣

🔱🔱 **Motel** $75-$275 **Address:** 9103 Atlantic Ave 08260 **Location:** Oceanfront. Between St Louis and Trenton aves. **Facility:** 48 units, some two bedrooms and efficiencies. 4 stories, exterior corridors. **Terms:** closed 10/11-5/2, 3 night minimum stay - seasonal and/or weekends, 21 day cancellation notice-fee imposed. **Amenities:** safes. **Pool(s):** heated outdoor. **Activities:** recreation programs in summer. **Guest Services:** coin laundry.

🍴 🏊 📶 ✖️ 📱 📺 💻

▼ *See AAA listing this page* ▼

Use travel time to share driving tips and rules of the road with your teens

(See map & index p. 215.)

BEL-AIR MOTEL   (609)729-4034 **17**
Motel $68-$168 **Address:** 5510 Ocean Ave 08260 **Location:** Oceanfront. Between Morning Glory and Buttercup rds. **Facility:** 27 units, some efficiencies. 2 stories (no elevator), exterior corridors. **Terms:** closed 10/21-4/24, 2-3 night minimum stay - seasonal and/or weekends, 14 day cancellation notice-fee imposed. **Pool(s):** heated outdoor. **Guest Services:** coin laundry.

BRISTOL PLAZA RESORT   (609)729-1234 **26**
Motel $64-$245 **Address:** 6407 Ocean Ave 08260 **Location:** Oceanfront. Between Columbine and Rosemary rds. **Facility:** 55 units, some efficiencies. 5 stories, exterior corridors. **Terms:** closed 10/20-4/24, 2 night minimum stay - seasonal and/or weekends, 14 day cancellation notice-fee imposed. **Pool(s):** heated outdoor. **Activities:** game room. **Guest Services:** coin laundry.

CARA MARA CONDOMINIUM RESORT   609/522-6951 **29**
Condominium. Rates not provided. **Address:** 6701 Atlantic Ave 08260 **Location:** Between Palm and Fern rds. **Facility:** 45 condominiums. 3 stories (no elevator), exterior corridors. **Pool(s):** heated outdoor. **Activities:** playground, game room. **Guest Services:** coin laundry.

COMPASS FAMILY RESORT   609/522-6948 **25**
Motel $65-$178 **Address:** 6501 Atlantic Ave 08260 **Location:** Between Rosemary and Forget Me Not rds. **Facility:** 50 units, some efficiencies. 3 stories, exterior corridors. **Terms:** closed 10/16-5/14, 3 night minimum stay - seasonal and/or weekends, 14 day cancellation notice-fee imposed. **Pool(s):** heated outdoor. **Activities:** miniature golf, game room. **Guest Services:** coin laundry.

CRUSADER RESORT   609/522-6991 **23**
Motel $80-$280 **Address:** 6101 Ocean Ave 08260 **Location:** Oceanfront. Jct Cardinal Rd. **Facility:** 60 units, some efficiencies. 3 stories, exterior corridors. **Terms:** closed 10/7-5/9, 3 night minimum stay - seasonal and/or weekends, 14 day cancellation notice-fee imposed. **Pool(s):** heated outdoor. **Activities:** sauna, game room. **Guest Services:** coin laundry.

Enjoy great member rates
and benefits at AAA/CAA
Preferred Hotels

▼ See AAA listing p. 221 ▼

▼ See AAA listing p. 221 ▼

(See map & index p. 215.)

EL CORONADO RESORT (609)729-1000 [33]

Condominium
$79-$519

Address: 8501 Atlantic Ave 08260 **Location:** Oceanfront. Between Denver and Syracuse aves. **Facility:** 123 condominiums, some two bedrooms, three bedrooms and efficiencies. 6 stories, interior corridors. **Terms:** closed 10/19-4/24, 3 night minimum stay - seasonal, 21 day cancellation notice-fee imposed. **Amenities:** safes. **Pool(s):** heated outdoor. **Activities:** sauna, hot tub, recreation programs in summer, game room, exercise room. **Guest Services:** coin laundry.

SAVE ▮▮ ⊇ BIZ 🛜 ✕ 🛢 📠 🖥

GONDOLIER MOTEL 609/522-6974 [20]

▼▼ Motel. Rates not provided. **Address:** 5701 Ocean Ave 08260 **Location:** Oceanfront. Between Lavender and Heather rds. **Facility:** 43 units, some efficiencies and kitchens. 3 stories, interior/exterior corridors. **Pool(s):** heated outdoor. **Guest Services:** coin laundry. ▮▮ ⊇ 🛜 ✕ 🛢 📠 🖥

JOLLY ROGER MOTEL 609/522-6915 [30]

▼▼ Motel. Rates not provided. **Address:** 6805 Atlantic Ave 08260 **Location:** Between Palm and Lotus rds. **Facility:** 75 units, some two bedrooms and kitchens. 3 stories (no elevator), exterior corridors. **Pool(s):** heated outdoor. **Activities:** tennis. **Guest Services:** coin laundry.

CALL ♿M ⊇ 🛜 ✕ 🛢 /SOME UNITS 📠 🖥

LOTUS INN 609/522-6300 [32]

▼▼▼ Motel
$60-$255

Address: 6900 Ocean Ave 08260 **Location:** At Lotus Rd. **Facility:** 72 units, some two bedrooms, three bedrooms, efficiencies and kitchens. 7 stories, exterior corridors. **Terms:** closed 10/23-4/17, 2-7 night minimum stay - seasonal and/or weekends, 14 day cancellation notice-fee imposed. **Pool(s):** heated outdoor. **Activities:** game room. **Guest Services:** coin laundry. **Featured Amenity:** continental breakfast. (See ad p. 220.)

SAVE ▮▮ ⊇ 🛜 ✕ 🛢 📠 🖥

NASSAU INN 609/729-9077 [24]

▼▼ Motel $80-$230 **Address:** 6201 Ocean Ave 08260 **Location:** Oceanfront. Between Wisteria and Sweetbriar rds. **Facility:** 56 units, some efficiencies. 5 stories, exterior corridors. **Terms:** closed 10/21-4/30, 14 day cancellation notice-fee imposed. **Pool(s):** heated outdoor. **Activities:** game room. **Guest Services:** coin laundry.

▮▮ ⊇ 🛜 ✕ 🛢 📠 🖥

OCEAN HOLIDAY MOTOR INN 609/729-2900 [27]

▼▼▼ Motel
$75-$275

Address: 6501 Ocean Ave 08260 **Location:** Oceanfront. Between Rosemary and Forget Me Not rds. **Facility:** 58 units, some efficiencies and kitchens. 5 stories, exterior corridors. **Terms:** closed 10/20-4/30, 3 night minimum stay - seasonal and/or weekends, 14 day cancellation notice-fee imposed. **Pool(s):** heated outdoor. **Guest Services:** coin laundry.

SAVE ▮▮ ⊇ 🛜 ✕ 🛢 📠 🖥

PAN AMERICAN HOTEL 609/522-6936 [22]

▼▼▼▼ Hotel $139-$295 **Address:** 5901 Ocean Ave 08260 **Location:** Oceanfront. Between Crocus and Aster rds. **Facility:** 78 units, some efficiencies. 4 stories, interior corridors. **Terms:** closed 10/18-5/16, 2 night minimum stay - seasonal and/or weekends, cancellation fee imposed. **Amenities:** safes. **Pool(s):** heated outdoor. **Activities:** recreation programs in season, game room. **Guest Services:** coin laundry.

▮▮ CALL ♿M ⊇ 🛜 ✕ 🛢 /SOME UNITS 🖥

PORT ROYAL HOTEL (609)729-2000 [31]

▼▼▼▼ Hotel $250-$405 **Address:** 6801 Ocean Ave 08260 **Location:** Oceanfront. Jct Palm Rd. **Facility:** 100 units, some efficiencies. 6 stories, interior corridors. **Terms:** closed 10/17-5/6, 2-4 night minimum stay - seasonal and/or weekends, 14 day cancellation notice-fee imposed. **Amenities:** Some: safes. **Pool(s):** heated outdoor. **Activities:** recreation programs in summer, game room. **Guest Services:** coin laundry.

▮▮ ⊇ 🛜 ✕ 🛢 /SOME UNITS 📠 🖥

REGES OCEANFRONT RESORT (609)729-9300 [36]

▼▼▼ Hotel
$152-$365

Address: 9201 Atlantic Ave 08260 **Location:** Oceanfront. Between Trenton and Newark aves. **Facility:** 75 units, some efficiencies. 8 stories, interior/exterior corridors. **Terms:** closed 10/13-5/7, 14 day cancellation notice-fee imposed. **Amenities:** Some: safes. **Pool(s):** heated outdoor. **Activities:** hot tub, recreation programs in summer. **Guest Services:** coin laundry. (See ad p. 220.)

SAVE ▮▮ CALL ♿M ⊇ 🛜 ✕ 🛢 📠 🖥

WHERE TO EAT

LITTLE ITALY FAMILY RESTAURANT 609/523-0999 [11]

▼▼ Italian. Family Dining. $15-$30 **AAA Inspector Notes:** A stunning re-creation of an outdoor Italian market, this casual family dining establishment features a mix of distinctive Northern and Southern Italian cuisine including veal, chops, seafood and pasta. This is a popular family restaurant on this beach resort barrier island. **Features:** early bird specials. **Address:** 5401 Atlantic Ave 08260 **Location:** Garden State Pkwy exit 4B, 3 mi se on SR 47, then 0.5 mi s. D CALL ♿M

MARIE NICOLE'S 609/522-5425 [13]

▼▼▼ American. Casual Dining. $21-$49 **AAA Inspector Notes:** The delightful, elegant restaurant offers friendly, professional service in a relaxed atmosphere. The menu is made up of a variety of delicious fresh seafood and prime meat dishes; save room for dessert. **Features:** full bar, patio dining. **Reservations:** suggested. **Address:** 9510 Pacific Ave 08260 **Location:** 2 mi s of Rio Grande Ave/SR 47; corner of Pacific and E Jefferson aves. D LATE CALL ♿M

TONY LUKE'S 609/770-7033 [12]

▼ Sandwiches. Quick Serve. $6-$10 **AAA Inspector Notes:** This is the beach outpost of the well-known Philly sandwich palace. The traditional cheesesteaks are good, or try the roast pork Italian sandwich with shaved roasted pork, sharp Provolone cheese and broccoli rabe. The window service is simple, yet quick and they have a covered patio with picnic tables for dining. **Address:** 6200 New Jersey Ave 08260 **Location:** Between Sweetbriar and Wisteria rds. B L D CALL ♿M ꗂ

WILLIAMSTOWN pop. 15,567
• Hotels p. 222

BEST WESTERN MONROE INN & SUITES
(856)340-7900

Hotel
$99-$199

AAA Benefit:
Members save up to 20%!

Address: 1151 N Black Horse Pike 08094 **Location:** New Jersey Tpke exit 3, 3.2 mi s on SR 168, then 9 mi s on SR 42; 2 mi s of jct CR 689. **Facility:** 44 units. 2 stories, interior corridors. **Pool(s):** heated indoor. **Activities:** exercise room. **Guest Services:** valet and coin laundry.

SAVE CALL (&M) (≈) (BIZ) (HS) (☎)
(♨) (📶) (💻) / SOME UNITS (🐕)

WOODBINE (G-3) pop. 2,472, elev. 39'

THE SAM AZEEZ MUSEUM OF WOODBINE HERITAGE is between Clay and Franklin sts. at 610 Washington Ave. The 1896 Woodbine Brotherhood Synagogue, one of the state's oldest, houses this museum, which displays more than 2,000 cultural and historical artifacts that help preserve Woodbine's heritage.

Exhibits include a timeline tracing local history back to 1880; the story of Baron Maurice de Hirsch, a philanthropist who facilitated the town's founding by Russian-Jewish immigrants; and documents and historical photographs relating the area's agricultural history and emphasis on diversity, education and tolerance. **Time:** Allow 1 hour minimum. **Hours:** Wed.- Fri. and Sun. 10-4 and by appointment. Closed Jan. 1 and Christmas. **Cost:** Free. **Phone:** (609) 861-5355.

WOODBRIDGE pop. 19,265
• Hotels p. 222 • Restaurants p. 222
• Hotels & Restaurants map & index p. 152

EXTENDED STAY AMERICA WOODBRIDGE-NEWARK
732/442-8333 (116)

(≈≈) Extended Stay Hotel. Rates not provided. **Address:** 1 Hoover Way 07095 **Location:** I-95 (New Jersey Tpke) exit 11, 1.4 mi to US 9 N, then just w on King Georges Post Rd. **Facility:** 140 efficiencies. 3 stories, interior corridors. **Guest Services:** coin laundry.

CALL (&M) (📶) (♨) (💻) (💻) / SOME UNITS (🐕)

HAMPTON INN
(732)855-6900 (115)

(≈≈) Hotel $119-$149 **Address:** 370 US 9 N 07095 **Location:** Garden State Pkwy exit 127 northbound, 1.2 mi n on US 9; exit southbound, just w on SR 501, just w on SR 184, then just n. **Facility:** 154 units. 5 stories, interior corridors. **Terms:** 1-7 night minimum stay, cancellation fee imposed. **Amenities:** Some: safes. **Pool(s):** heated indoor. **Activities:** exercise room. **Guest Services:** valet and coin laundry, rental car service, area transportation.

AAA Benefit:
Members save 5% or more!

(✈) (🍴) (≈) (BIZ) (HS) (📶) (♨) (💻) (💻)

RESIDENCE INN BY MARRIOTT-WOODBRIDGE EDISON/ RARITAN CENTER
(732)510-7100 (114)

(≈≈≈) Extended Stay Hotel
$160-$263 **Address:** 2 Regency Pl 07095 **Location:** I-95 (New Jersey Tpke) exit 11, just e on SR 184 (Pond Rd), then 1.2 mi n on US 9. **Facility:** 107 units, some two bedrooms, efficiencies and kitchens. 3 stories, interior corridors. **Pool(s):** heated indoor. **Activities:** hot tub, exercise room. **Guest Services:** valet and coin laundry.

AAA Benefit:
Members save 5% or more!

CALL (&M) (≈) (BIZ) (HS) (📶) (✖) (♨) (💻) (💻)
/ SOME UNITS (🐕)

WHERE TO EAT

MIE THAI
732/596-9400 (150)

(≈≈) Thai. Casual Dining. $12-$21 **AAA Inspector Notes:** This casual spot has a big reputation and, it seems, an even larger dinner menu. There are plenty of choices of both traditional dishes as well as creative choices. Golden fried crab sausages with sweet and sour plum sauce, boneless crispy duck with tamarind sauce and Thai barbecue are just a snippet of the tantalizing options. Lunch offers a more streamlined menu but the same quick and efficient service. **Address:** 34 Main St (CR 514) 07095 **Location:** 0.9 mi e of US 9.

(L) (D) CALL (&M)

RISTORANTE VENEZIA
732/855-8995 (151)

(≈≈≈) Italian. Casual Dining. $16-$36 **AAA Inspector Notes:** This pretty restaurant, with mottled green walls, blonde wood trim and French doors which open to bustling Main Street, is the perfect setting for an intimate dinner with friends, or a casual dinner with colleagues. Service is efficient, yet unobtrusive, and the food leaves a smile on everyone's face. There is the traditional Italian fare, such as scampi, zuppa and veal, and more inventive dishes, such as roasted salmon with a wine, butter and herb sauce. **Features:** full bar. **Reservations:** suggested, weekends. **Address:** 112 Main St 07095 **Location:** Jct SR 35 (Amboy Ave) and Main St, just e.

(L) (D) CALL (&M)

WOODBURY (E-2) pop. 10,174, elev. 34'
• Restaurants p. 223

Woodbury was occupied by British troops in November 1777. Gen. Charles Cornwallis chose as his headquarters the home of John Cooper, a Continental Congress member denounced for his patriotism by his pacifist Quaker friends. A number of Revolutionary War-era buildings have been preserved.

"Light Horse" Harry Lee, father of Robert E. Lee, made Woodbury his headquarters during military campaigns in South Jersey in 1779. Other local notables include Commodore Stephen Decatur and Capt. James Lawrence, both of whom attended Woodbury Academy. The Hunter-Lawrence-Jessup House, 58 N. Broad St., was the boyhood home of Lawrence, known for his dying command "Don't give up the ship," uttered during the War of 1812. His former home now houses the Gloucester County Historical Society Museum. Exhibits include textiles, samplers, toys, dolls, military artifacts and a Colonial-era kitchen; phone (856) 848-8531.

Greater Woodbury Chamber of Commerce: P.O. Box 363, Woodbury, NJ 08096. **Phone:** (856) 845-4056.

CHARLIE BROWN'S STEAKHOUSE   856/853-8505

▼▼ Steak. Casual Dining. $9-$30 **AAA Inspector Notes:** This budget-friendly steakhouse, famous for its prime rib, offers top quality fare without hurting your pocketbook. The young ones will not be disappointed with the kids' menu, and just might even try something green from the salad bar. Adults will love the quality steaks, chicken and rib dishes. The express lunches are great for those saddled with time constraints. **Features:** full bar, happy hour. **Address:** 111 N Broad St 08096 **Location:** I-295 exit 24 (Gateway Blvd), s to N Broad St, then 1.2 mi s. [L] [D]

WOODCLIFF LAKE pop. 5,730

HILTON WOODCLIFF LAKE   (201)391-3600

▼▼▼ Hotel $159-$289 **Address:** 200 Tice Blvd 07677 **Location:** Garden State Pkwy exit 171 northbound, left on Glen Rd from exit ramp, right on Chestnut Ridge Rd, 0.5 mi to Tice Blvd, then just left. **Facility:** 338 units, some two bedrooms. 4 stories, interior corridors. **Terms:** 1-7 night minimum stay, cancellation fee imposed. **Amenities:** safes. **Pool(s):** outdoor, heated indoor. **Activities:** sauna, hot tub, tennis, playground, spa. **Guest Services:** valet and coin laundry, boarding pass kiosk, area transportation.

AAA Benefit: Members save 5% or more!

[icons]

WOODLAND PARK pop. 11,819

• **Hotels & Restaurants map & index p. 162**

CASTALIA 997 RESTAURANT & LOUNGE   973/785-8880 [40]

▼▼▼ Italian. Casual Dining. $9-$23 **AAA Inspector Notes:** Tucked into a small plaza away from the main highway, this popular and comfortable neighborhood spot serves up excellent Italian dishes. Try one of the great pastas like the tortellini carbonara or bucatini puttanesca, or tender veal Laura (sautéed with white wine, mushrooms and mascarpone cheese.) There is a long list of daily specials and desserts are made in house. **Features:** full bar. **Reservations:** suggested, weekends. **Address:** 997 McBride Ave 07424 **Location:** US 46 exit McBride Ave, 0.6 mi n; in Park West Meadows Shopping Plaza. [L] [D] CALL

WYCKOFF (B-4) pop. 16,696, elev. 355'

JAMES A. MCFAUL ENVIRONMENTAL CENTER OF BERGEN COUNTY is at 150 Crescent Ave. On the grounds of this 81-acre wildlife sanctuary are a nature trail, waterfowl pond and herb and flower gardens. An indoor exhibit hall has natural history displays and live animals. Art exhibits are presented as well. Pets are not permitted,. **Hours:** Grounds open daily 8 a.m.-dusk. Exhibit hall open Mon.-Fri. 8-4:45, Sat.-Sun. 1-4:45. Exhibit hall closed major holidays. Phone ahead to confirm schedule. **Cost:** Free. **Phone:** (201) 891-5571. [icon]

YARDVILLE pop. 7,186

SCOTTO & CRIMANI PIZZERIA   609/585-0071

▼ Pizza. Quick Serve. $6-$20 **AAA Inspector Notes:** The authentic Sicilian deep-dish pizza is the way to go here. This little brick oven pizza shop and Italian dining room is tucked away in a plaza in a residential area and worth the short trip from the New Jersey Turnpike. **Address:** 15 Sunny Brae Blvd 08620 **Location:** New Jersey Tpke exit 7A, 3 mi w on I-195 exit 3A, 2.3 mi s on Yardville-Hamilton Square Rd, then 0.5 mi w on S Broad St; in Dover Park Plaza. [L] [D] CALL

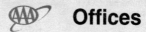 **Offices**

Main office listings are shown in **BOLD TYPE** and toll-free member service numbers appear in *ITALIC TYPE*.
All are closed Saturdays, Sundays and holidays unless otherwise indicated.
The addresses, phone numbers and hours for any AAA/CAA office are subject to change.
The type of service provided is designated below the name of the city where the office is located:

✛ Auto travel services, including books and maps, and on-demand TripTik ® routings.
● Auto travel services, including selected books and maps, and on-demand TripTik ® routings.
■ Books/maps only, no marked maps or on-demand TripTik ® routings.
▲ Travel Agency Services, cruise, tour, air, car and rail reservations; domestic and international hotel reservations; passport photo services; international and domestic travel guides and maps; travel money products; and International Driving Permits. In addition, assistance with travel related insurance products including trip cancellation, travel accident, lost luggage, trip delay and assistance products.
○ Insurance services provided. If only this icon appears, only insurance services are provided at that office.
€ Car Care Plus Facility provides car care services.
▣ Electric vehicle charging station on premises.

AAA NATIONAL OFFICE: 1000 AAA DRIVE, HEATHROW, FLORIDA 32746-5063, (407) 444-7000

DELAWARE

CENTREVILLE—AAA MID-ATLANTIC, 5807 A KENNETT PIKE, 19807. WEEKDAYS (M-F) 8:30-5:00 (SAT BY APPOINTMENT ONLY). (302) 691-5291 ○

DOVER—AAA MID-ATLANTIC, 55 GREENTREE DR RT 8, 19904. WEEKDAYS (M-F) 9:00-5:30, SAT 9:00-3:00. (302) 674-8020 ✛▲○

NEWARK—AAA MID-ATLANTIC, 1201 CHURCHMANS RD, 19713. WEEKDAYS (M-F) 9:00-5:30, THU 9:00-7:00, SAT 9:00-1:00. (302) 292-6360 ✛▲○

WILMINGTON—AAA MID-ATLANTIC, ONE RIVER PL, 19801. WEEKDAYS (M-F) 8:45-5:00. (302) 299-4000 ✛▲○€

WILMINGTON—AAA MID-ATLANTIC, ONE RIVER PL, 19801. WEEKDAYS (M-F) 9:00-5:30, THU 9:00-7:00. (302) 299-4700 ✛▲○

NEW JERSEY

BRICK—AAA MID-ATLANTIC, 521 RT 70, 08723. WEEKDAYS (M-F) 9:00-5:30, SAT 9:00-3:00. (732) 451-0600 ✛▲○

BRIDGEWATER—AAA MID-ATLANTIC, 976 US HIGHWAY 22, 08807. WEEKDAYS (M-F) 9:00-5:30, SAT 9:00-3:00. (908) 722-2202 ✛▲○

EAST BRUNSWICK—AAA MID-ATLANTIC, 260 STATE ROUTE 18, 08816. WEEKDAYS (M-F) 7:00-7:00, SAT 8:00-5:00, SUN 10:00-4:00. (732) 955-9010 ✛▲○€

EATONTOWN—AAA MID-ATLANTIC, 251 STATE RT 35 N, 07724. WEEKDAYS (M-F) 7:00-7:00, SAT 8:00-5:00, SUN 10:00-4:00. (732) 389-5559 ✛▲○€

FAIR LAWN—AAA NORTH JERSEY, 23-16 BROADWAY, 07410. WEEKDAYS (M-F) 8:30-5:00, MON 8:30-8:00 (APR 1-SEP 30), SAT 9:00-3:00. (201) 703-2000 ✛▲○

FLEMINGTON—AAA MID-ATLANTIC, 146 ROUTE 31, 08822. WEEKDAYS (M-F) 9:00-5:30, SAT 9:00-3:00. (908) 483-9440 ✛▲○

FLORHAM PARK—AAA NORTHEAST, 1 HANOVER RD, 07932. WEEKDAYS (M-F) 9:00-5:00, SAT 9:00-2:00. (973) 377-7204 ✛▲○

HAMILTON—AAA MID-ATLANTIC, 2A S GOLD DR, 08691. WEEKDAYS (M-F) 9:00-5:30, SAT 9:00-3:00. (609) 890-2220 ✛▲○

LAWRENCEVILLE—AAA MID-ATLANTIC, 2970 US HIGHWAY 1, 08648. WEEKDAYS (M-F) 7:00-7:00, SAT 8:00-4:00, SUN 10:00-4:00. (732) 244-6800 ✛▲○€

LOGAN TOWNSHIP—AAA SOUTH JERSEY, 525 BECKETT RD, 08085. WEEKDAYS (M-F) 8:45-6:00, SAT 10:00-2:00. (856) 467-6743 ✛▲○

MIDDLETOWN—AAA MID-ATLANTIC, 889 STATE ROAD 35, 07748. WEEKDAYS (M-F) 7:00-7:00, SAT 8:00-5:00, SUN 10:00-4:00. (732) 865-9360 ✛▲○€

MILLVILLE—AAA SOUTH JERSEY, 2190 N 2ND ST, 08332. WEEKDAYS (M-F) 9:45-6:00, SAT 10:00-2:00. (856) 563-0222 ✛▲○

MORGANVILLE—AAA MID-ATLANTIC, 4010 RT 9 S, 07751. WEEKDAYS (M-F) 9:00-5:30, SAT 9:00-3:00. (732) 591-5294 ✛▲○

MOUNT LAUREL—AAA MID-ATLANTIC, 4010 DEARBORN CIR, 08054. WEEKDAYS (M-F) 7:00-7:00, SAT 8:00-5:00, SUN 10:00-4:00. (856) 778-8800 ✛▲○€ ▣

NEWTON—AAA MID-ATLANTIC, 42 HAMPTON HOUSE RD, 07860. WEEKDAYS (M-F) 9:00-5:30, SAT 9:00-3:00. (973) 362-2023 ✛▲○

NORTHFIELD—AAA MID-ATLANTIC, 901 TILTON RD, 08225. WEEKDAYS (M-F) 9:00-5:30, SAT 9:00-3:00. (609) 646-6000 ✛▲○

ORADELL—AAA NORTH JERSEY, 505 KINDERKAMACK RD, 07649. WEEKDAYS (M-F) 8:30-5:00, THU 8:30-8:00 (APR 1-SEP 30), SAT 9:00-3:00. (201) 261-7900 ✛▲○

PHILLIPSBURG—AAA MID-ATLANTIC, 1205 US HWY 22 W, 08865. WEEKDAYS (M-F) 9:00-5:30, SAT 9:00-3:00. (908) 387-0453 ✛▲○

RIO GRANDE—AAA MID-ATLANTIC, 3301 RT 9 S, 08242. WEEKDAYS (M-F) 9:00-5:30, SAT 9:00-3:00. (609) 465-3033 ✛▲○

SECAUCUS—AAA NORTH JERSEY, 700 PLAZA DR, 07094. WEEKDAYS (M-F) 8:30-5:00, WED 8:30-8:00 (APR 1-SEP 30), SAT 9:00-3:00. (201) 902-1393 ✛▲○

SEWELL—AAA SOUTH JERSEY, 380 EGG HARBOR RD C8 & 9, 08080. WEEKDAYS (M-F) 8:45-6:00, SAT 10:00-2:00. (856) 589-6900 ✛▲○

TOMS RIVER—AAA MID-ATLANTIC, 1199 RT 37 E, 08753. WEEKDAYS (M-F) 7:00-7:00, SAT 8:00-5:00, SUN 10:00-4:00. (732) 244-6800 ✛▲○€

UNION—AAA NORTHEAST, 2317 ROUTE 22 WEST, 07083. WEEKDAYS (M-F) 9:00-5:00, SAT 9:00-2:00. (908) 557-5222

VOORHEES—AAA SOUTH JERSEY, 700 LAUREL OAK RD, 08043. WEEKDAYS (M-F) 8:45-6:00, SAT 10:00-2:00. (856) 783-4222

VOORHEES—AAA SOUTH JERSEY, 700 LAUREL OAK RD, 08043. WEEKDAYS (M-F) 8:45-6:00. (856) 783-4222

WAYNE—AAA NORTH JERSEY, 418 HAMBURG TPK, 07470. WEEKDAYS (M-F) 8:30-5:00, TUE 8:30-8:00 (APR 1-SEP 30), SAT 9:00-3:00. (973) 956-2200

WAYNE—AAA NORTH JERSEY, 418 HAMBURG TPK, 07470. WEEKDAYS (M-F) 8:30-5:00, TUE 8:30-8:00 (APR 1-SEP 30), SAT 9:00-3:00. (973) 956-2200

WEST CALDWELL—AAA NORTHEAST, 905 BLOOMFIELD AVE STE B, 07006. WEEKDAYS (M-F) 9:00-5:00, SAT 9:00-2:00. (973) 396-1300

WOODBRIDGE—AAA MID-ATLANTIC, 467 GREEN ST, 07095. WEEKDAYS (M-F) 9:00-5:30, SAT 9:00-3:00. (732) 636-0600

LET'S GET SOCIAL
Stay connected with #AAA

Visit with us on your favorite social media sites for the latest updates on hot discounts, cool destinations and handy automotive know-how.

Talk with us!

- Plus.google.com/+AAAnews
- Twitter.com/AAA_Travel
- YouTube.com/AAA
- Facebook.com/AAAFanPage
- Pinterest.com/AAA

Metric Equivalents Chart

TEMPERATURE

To convert Fahrenheit to Celsius, subtract 32 from the Fahrenheit temperature, multiply by 5 and divide by 9. To convert Celsius to Fahrenheit, multiply by 9, divide by 5 and add 32.

ACRES

1 acre = 0.4 hectare (ha)	1 hectare = 2.47 acres

MILES AND KILOMETERS

Note: A kilometer is approximately 5/8 or 0.6 of a mile. To convert kilometers to miles multiply by 0.6.

Miles/Kilometers		Kilometers/Miles	
15	24.1	30	18.6
20	32.2	35	21.7
25	40.2	40	24.8
30	48.3	45	27.9
35	56.3	50	31.0
40	64.4	55	34.1
45	72.4	60	37.2
50	80.5	65	40.3
55	88.5	70	43.4
60	96.6	75	46.6
65	104.6	80	49.7
70	112.7	85	52.8
75	120.7	90	55.9
80	128.7	95	59.0
85	136.8	100	62.1
90	144.8	105	65.2
95	152.9	110	68.3
100	160.9	115	71.4

Celsius °		Fahrenheit °
100	BOILING	212
37		100
35		95
32		90
29		85
27		80
24		75
21		70
18		65
16		60
13		55
10		50
7		45
4		40
2		35
0	FREEZING	32
-4		25
-7		20
-9		15
-12		10
-15		5
-18		0
-21		-5
-24		-10
-27		-15

LINEAR MEASURE

Customary	Metric
1 inch = 2.54 centimeters	1 centimeter = 0.4 inches
1 foot = 30 centimeters	1 meter = 3.3 feet
1 yard = 0.91 meters	1 meter = 1.09 yards
1 mile = 1.6 kilometers	1 kilometer = .62 miles

LIQUID MEASURE

Customary	Metric
1 fluid ounce = 30 milliliters	1 milliliter = .03 fluid ounces
1 cup = .24 liters	1 liter = 2.1 pints
1 pint = .47 liters	1 liter = 1.06 quarts
1 quart = .95 liters	1 liter = .26 gallons
1 gallon = 3.8 liters	

WEIGHT

If You Know:	Multiply By:	To Find:
Ounces	28	Grams
Pounds	0.45	Kilograms
Grams	0.035	Ounces
Kilograms	2.2	Pounds

PRESSURE

Air pressure in automobile tires is expressed in kilopascals. Multiply pound-force per square inch (psi) by 6.89 to find kilopascals (kPa).

24 psi = 165 kPa	28 psi = 193 kPa
26 psi = 179 kPa	30 psi = 207 kPa

GALLONS AND LITERS

Gallons/Liters				Liters/Gallons			
5	19.0	12	45.6	10	2.6	40	10.4
6	22.8	14	53.2	15	3.9	50	13.0
7	26.6	16	60.8	20	5.2	60	15.6
8	30.4	18	68.4	25	6.5	70	18.2
9	34.2	20	76.0	30	7.8	80	20.8
10	38.0	25	95.0	35	9.1	90	23.4

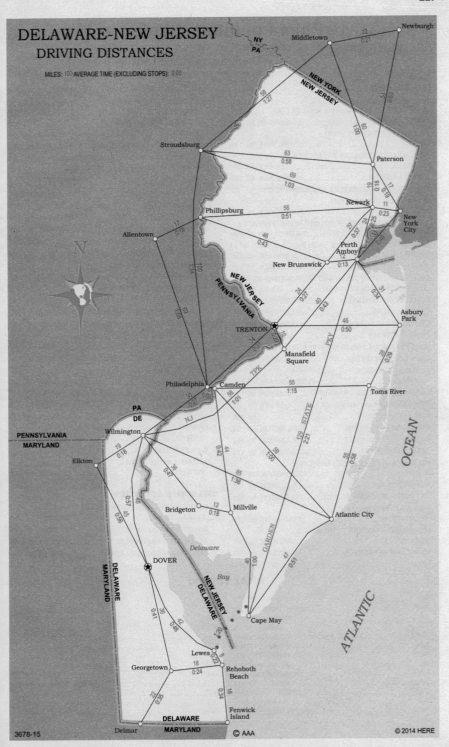

DELAWARE-NEW JERSEY
DRIVING DISTANCES

MILES: 100 AVERAGE TIME (EXCLUDING STOPS): 2:00

NY
PA

Middletown

Newburgh

22
0:21

NEW YORK
NEW JERSEY

58
1:27

51
0:53

Stroudsburg

63
0:58

100
60

Paterson

69
1:03

19
0:18

17
0:19

Phillipsburg

56
0:51

Newark

11
0:23

New York City

Allentown

17
0:18

46
0:43

27
0:37

25

Perth Amboy

New Brunswick

12
0:13

100

24

NEW JERSEY
PENNSYLVANIA

63

24
0:27

40
0:43

31
0:34

Asbury Park

TRENTON

34

10

46
0:50

Mansfield Square

PKY

28
0:29

Philadelphia

TPK

55
1:15

Toms River

30

58
1:01

Camden

STATE

129

221

OCEAN

NJ

PA
DE

Wilmington

PENNSYLVANIA
MARYLAND

19
0:18

44
0:42

59
1:00

53
0:58

Elkton

36
0:47

85
1:36

57
0:36

48
45

Bridgeton

12
0:18

Millville

GARDEN

Atlantic City

Delaware

46
1:00

47
0:51

MARYLAND
DELAWARE

DOVER

Bay

NEW JERSEY
DELAWARE

ATLANTIC

36
0:41

42
0:46

Cape May

1:20

Lewes

8
0:22

Georgetown

18
0:24

Rehoboth Beach

22
0:35

18
0:34

DELAWARE
MARYLAND

Fenwick Island

3678-15

Delmar

© AAA

© 2014 HERE

Points of Interest Index

 Attractions appear at the top of each category
and offer a Great Experience for Members®.

Index Legend

NB. ... national battlefield	NR. ... national river
NBP. ... national battlefield park	NS. ... national seashore
NC. ... national cemetery	NWR. ... national wildlife refuge
NF. ... national forest	PHP. ... provincial historic(al) park
NHM. ... national historic(al) monument	PHS. ... provincial historic(al) site
NHP. ... national historic(al) park	PP. ... provincial park
NHS. ... national historic(al) site	SF. ... state forest
NL. ... national lakeshore	SHM. ... state historic(al) monument
NME. ... national memorial	SHP. ... state historic(al) park
NMO. ... national monument	SHS. ... state historic(al) site
NMP. ... national military park	SME. ... state memorial
NP. ... national park	SP. ... state park
NRA. ... national recreation area	SRA. ... state recreation area

EVENTS & FESTIVALS

HISTORIC SITES & EXHIBITS

SHOPPING & NIGHTLIFE

SPORTS & RECREATION

TOURS & SIGHTSEEING

Photo Credits

Page numbers are in bold type. Picture credit abbreviations are as follows:
▪ (i) numeric sequence from top to bottom, left to right ▪ (AAA) AAA Travel library.

▪ (Cover) Millbrook Village in Delaware Water Gap National Recreational Area, NJ / © Jon Bilous / 123RF.COM

▪ **2** (i) © iStockphoto.com / DenisTangneyJr

▪ **2** (ii) © iStockphoto.com / rKIRKimagery

▪ **2** (iii) © Mira / Alamy

▪ **2** (iv) © Andrew F. Kazmierski / Shutterstock.com

▪ **12** (i) Courtesy of Berry Manor Inn

▪ **12** (ii) © Chris Dew / Killarney Lodge

▪ **12** (iii) Courtesy of Hyatt Hotels

▪ **12** (iv) Courtesy of Montpelier Plantation and Beach

▪ **12** (v) © Elisa Rolle / Wikimedia Commons

▪ **12** (vi) Courtesy of The Shores Resort & Spa

▪ **12** (vii) Courtesy of Alexander Holiday Homes

▪ **12** (viii) Courtesy of Bryce View Lodge

▪ **12** (ix) Courtesy of Vista Verde Guest Ranch

▪ **13** Courtesy of Divi Resorts

▪ **18** (i) © Tom Till / Alamy

▪ **18** (ii) © iStockphoto.com / roc8jas

▪ **19** © National Geographic Image Collection / Alamy

▪ **20** (i) Courtesy of Wikimedia Commons

▪ **20** (ii) Office of the President

▪ **23** (i) © iStockphoto.com / Lanier

▪ **23** (ii) © iStockphoto.com / 1MoreCreative

▪ **23** (iii) © Mira / Alamy

▪ **23** (iv) © iStockphoto.com / DenisTangneyJr

▪ **23** (v) © iStockphoto.com / rKIRKimagery

▪ **24** (i) © Andre Jenny / Alamy

▪ **24** (ii) Courtesy of Hagley Museum and Library

▪ **24** (iii) Courtesy of Nemours Mansion and Gardens

▪ **24** (iv) © Jim, the Photographer / flickr

▪ **54** (i) © Design Pics Inc. / Alamy

▪ **54** (ii) © Ellen McKnight / Alamy

▪ **55** © iStockphoto.com / martateron

▪ **56** (i) Courtesy of Wikimedia Commons

▪ **56** (ii) Courtesy of Wikimedia Commons

▪ **59** (i) © Andrew F. Kazmierski / Shutterstock.com

▪ **59** (ii) © iStockphoto.com / KenKPhoto

▪ **59** (iii) © iStockphoto.com / KenWiedemann

▪ **59** (iv) © John Van Decker / Alamy

▪ **59** (v) © iStockphoto.com / Veni

▪ **60** (i) © Marcio Jose Bastos Silva / Shutterstock.com

▪ **60** (ii) © American Spirit / Shutterstock.com

▪ **60** (iii) © Jeffrey M. Frank / Shutterstock.com

▪ **60** (iv) © American Spirit / Shutterstock.com

▪ **72** © Mira / Alamy

▪ **75** © iStockphoto.com / dolah

▪ **76** © rorem / Shutterstock.com

▪ **77** © Darren Brode / Shutterstock.com

▪ **78** © Anchiy / Shutterstock.com

▪ **79** © iStockphoto.com / Aneese

AAA Reloadable Cards
YOUR EVERYDAY SOLUTION

From country inn

to eating in

With AAA travel money reloadable cards, you can:

- Direct deposit funds
- Load funds from approved paper checks through a mobile app
- Skip the bank - no checking account required
- Keep reloading your card as long as you want

PUT A CARD IN YOUR WALLET

Visit participating AAA offices
or AAA.com/travelmoney

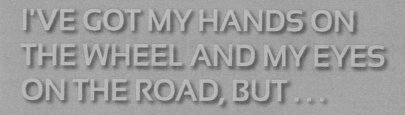